The Migration Conference 2017 Proceedings

The Migration Conference 2017 Proceedings

Compiled by:
Fethiye Tilbe, Elif İskender, Ibrahim Sirkeci

TRANSNATIONAL PRESS LONDON
2017

The Migration Conference 2017 Proceedings

Compiled by Fethiye Tilbe, Elif İskender, Ibrahim Sirkeci

Copyright © 2017 by Transnational Press London

First Published in 2017 by TRANSNATIONAL PRESS LONDON in the United Kingdom, 12 Ridgeway Gardens, London, N6 5XR, UK.

www.tplondon.com

Requests for permission to reproduce material from this work should be sent to: sales@tplondon.com

Paperback

ISBN: 978-1-910781-54-8

Cover Design: Gizem Çakır

Cover Photo: George Adam and Jonathan Liu

www.tplondon.com

Content

iv

About the editors

Fethiye Tilbe works at Department of Labour Economics and Industrial Relations, Namik Kemal University, Tekirdag, Turkey. She was a visiting research fellow at Regent's Centre for Transnational Studies, Regent's University London. Tilbe earned her PhD in Labour Economics from Marmara University, Istanbul. She has carried out field research among immigrant communities in London in 2014 – 2015. Her research on irregular migrant remittances in London was funded by a grant from Turkish Scientific Research Council (TUBITAK). Her recent research focuses on remittances and irregular migration.

Elif İskender is Assistant Professor of Acting at Beykent University, Istanbul, Turkey. She is currently a visiting research fellow at Regent's Centre for Transnational Studies (RCTS), Regent's University London, UK. She obtained her PhD from the Institute of Fine Arts, Department of Stage Arts, Dokuz Eylul University, Izmir, Turkey. Prior to joining Beykent University, she has taught at Dokuz Eylul University for 12 years. At Beykent University Faculty of Fine Arts Department of Acting, she was the Head of Department (2009-2015) and Vice Dean in charge of Erasmus programmes.

Ibrahim Sirkeci is Professor of Transnational Studies and Marketing and Director of Regent's Centre for Transnational Studies at Regent's University London, UK. Prof Sirkeci has been chairing the Migration Conferences since 2012. He is editor of *Migration Letters*, *Remittances Review*, *Göç Dergisi*, three leading specialist journals in the respective subfields of migration studies. Further details can be found at www.sirkeci.co.uk and contacted at @isirkeci.

Acknowledgements

As the conference organisation team, we would like to thank all the contributors to this volume but also thank all participants, reviewers and scientific board members of the 5th Migration Conference (TMC 2017) which was held at Harokopio University, Athens, Greece from 23 to 26 August 2017 (further details can be found at www.migrationcenter.org).

We would also like to thank all supporting organisations and individuals including the following:

- Harokopio University, Athens
- University of California Davis, Gifford Center for Population Studies
- EKKE - The National Center of Social Research
- Hellenic Sociological Society
- Universität Hamburg, Germany
- Albrecht Mendelssohn Bartholdy Graduate School of Law, Germany
- Regent's University Centre for Transnational Studies
- Migration Letters
- Remittances Review
- Göç Dergisi
- Kurdish Studies
- Journal of Gypsy Studies
- Social Cohesion and Development
- The Migration Center
- Institut de Recherche, Formation et Action sur les Migrations, Belgium
- Migration Institute of Finland

Introduction: The Migration Conference 2017

Fethiye Tilbe[1], Elif Iskender[2], Ibrahim Sirkeci[3]

The Migration Conference 2017 was generously hosted by Harokopio University, Athens, Greece, 23-26 August. We are thankful to the Rector of the university and head of the Geography Department as well as so many other colleagues from the host university who made the event a success. We particularly thank Professor Apostolos Papadopoulos, the TMC 2017 co-chair, Professor Ali Tilbe, track chair in literature and migration studies in Turkish, Professor Petra Bendel, track chair in German migration policy, Loukia Maria Fratsea, leader of the host team and volunteers, Tove Lager, Çağla Azizoğlu, Dorina Kalemi, Panagiota Kogiannou, Mehtap Erdoğan, Alexandra Theofili, Athanasios Lakrintis, Monica Dubitsky, George Adam, Jonathan Liu, Gül İnce Beqo, Nirmala Devi Arunasalam, Ülkü Sezgi Sözen, Emilia Lana de Freitas Castro, Serkan Utku, Ahmet Hepgül, the local catering team and the university's campus support teams.

We are also debted to our wonderful keynote speakers who joined us and contributed greatly to the debates and discussions throughout the conference. Oded Stark, Jeffrey H Cohen, Giuseppe Sciortino, Yuksel Pazarkaya, Saskia Sassen, and Neli Esipova have offered rich and strong arguments underlining many key challenges in contemporary migration studies and migration management.

In the TMC 2017 programme, besides a very rich array of academic disciplines represented by participants, also over 60 countries from 7 continents were listed among the places of origin. About 800 paper submissions were reviewed to select around 400 to be presented at the conference. At this point, we should also thank from bottom of our hearts for all colleagues who volunteered to review these submissions. Of course, naturally, the members of the committees put enormous effort into this time-constrained and challenging task.

It is important to acknowledge all the support given to the conference, which has continued to be an independent self-sufficient academic event surviving on participants' contributions and limited funding provided by Transnational Press London. We are pleased and proud to have been able to offer a number

[1] Dr Fethiye Tilbe, Department of Labour Economics and Industrial Relations, Namik Kemal University, Tekirdag, Turkey. E-mail: fthytilbe@gmail.com.

[2] Dr Elif İskender, Visiting Researcher at Regent's University London Centre for Transnational Studies, London, UK and Assistant Professor at Department of Acting, Beykent University, Istanbul, Turkey. E-mail: elifiskender07@hotmail.com.

[3] Ibrahim Sirkeci, Professor and Director at Regent's University London Centre for Transnational Studies, London, UK. E-mail: sirkecii@regents.ac.uk.

of fee waivers and travel bursaries to young researchers who did not have means and otherwise would not be able to join. In future conferences, we will continue offering subsidised registration options for students, unemployed and retired colleagues and constantly seek additional funds for this purpose.

The fields represented at the Conference included anthropology, economics, international relations, law, psychology, sociology, geography, business administration, media and communication, politics, health sciences, literature, linguistics, arts to form nearly 100 parallel sessions accompanied by 4 key note speaker sessions, 2 workshops, 2 exhibitions and 2 film screenings in 4 days. We are very pleased to note that most of the papers presented at the Conference have already been published or under review by peer-reviewed international journals and some been included in edited thematic books.

As a result, only a limited number of papers are included in the volume you are holding and in another volume of proceedings in Turkish language. Readers should also note that these papers have not been edited but this is a simple proceedings compilation of papers submitted and published as is. Although we have made an effort to eliminate some obvious irregularities, all errors and mistakes remaining are of authors. These are made available as eBooks via various platforms and Transnational Press London.

Finally, on behalf of the TMC organisation committee, we would like to invite all interested academics, students, practitiones, policy makers, media and NGO representatives to our next conference. The Migration Conference 2018 will be hosted by the University of Lisbon in Portugal's capital. It is time to pen the date in your diaries: 26-28 June 2018; please check: www.migrationcenter.org for submission deadlines and other details.

Chapter 1. A Psychosocial Perspective of Immigrant Female Killers in TV Series[1]

Anna Zaptsi[2]

Abstract

The aim of this paper is to investigate immigrant female killers on five American television series, from a psychosocial perspective, broadcasted in Spain from 2000 to 2015. On the one hand, in light of exploring the profile of female criminality in order to reveal the bias in fictional female characters, whenever they commit death crimes voluntarily, and, on the other hand, to raise awareness of the most common personality disorders that they tend to have, so as to foster a socially responsible approach of the media production. The selection of the research topic, responds to the striking impacts of the combination of media and psychology in the human kind and in society, and its power in establishing stereotypes of female gender, whenever female protagonists appear on the small screen. Whenever television programs focused on immigrants, a massive employment of negative stereotypes has been observed assigned to the image of the immigrant in all series and also a correlation between reality and fiction.

Keywords: Female criminality, mass media, psychological disorders, psychology, television series.

Introduction

Mass media maintain in their territory the construction of identities and the social thinking of their consumers; that is to say, they act as socializing agents. They influence and configure efficiently conducts, the expression of the emotions and the core values of individuals (García, 2006: 15, 26). Pere Marqués (2001: 10) defines them as:

"means of communication and information which through technological devices, spread information in a simultaneous and indiscriminate way at many recipients, generally unknown to their own editors".

Since the 19th century, there are several types of social media; the radio, cinema and television. According to Yubero (2003), television is the most powerful socialization tool that has ever been found in the whole history of humanity.

It is a compelling tool of communication, which can capture the social behavior and perception of the world that revolves around the empirical reality (Guarinos, 2008: 103).

---

[1] This article forms part of the doctoral thesis that the author is developing in the Interuniversity Doctorate of Communication at the University of Seville. This work is led by Virginia Guarinos and Trinidad Núñez Domínguez, both professors of the University of Seville (Spain).

[2] Anna Zaptsi is a Ph.D. Student in the Interuniversity Doctorate of Communication, Faculty of Communication, University of Seville, Américo Vespucio, 41092, Seville, Spain. E-mail: zaptsi.anna@yahoo.gr.

The small screen is present in millions of households throughout the world, offering ideally entertainment time and information worldwide, for all kinds of people. Its main characteristic is its repetition, and also, its reception in a convenient and cozy environment.

Above all, it proposes and constitutes prejudice that can instantly reach viewers through visual elements (Bonilla, 2005: 40). Incidentally, audiovisual media, and especially television, promote socialization and offer behavior styles, values and attitudes that are imitated and emulated by individuals (Aguaded, 2003: 7). Social Psychology plays a considerable role in the analysis of the formation and transmission of models that television performs. Its input is of interest in raising social awareness, as well as legitimizing ideas or evaluating inequality judgments and even formulating events in their own way (Hogg & Vaughan, 2010: 4).

Skinner (1984: 217-221) through his theory of experimental behavior analysis, explains that the action (watching a favorite show on television) stimulates the individual which in turn provokes a reaction (feelings of joy, pleasure, sadness, perplexity).

More recently, studies that examine and interpret the progress of receiving media messages, or in other words, the impact of the communication and its consumption, led to the birth of a new discipline, the Media Psychology (Igartua & Moral, 2012: 1). Media Psychology, situated between Communication and Psychology, sustains a purpose of revealing the relationship between the audience and the media contents (Beniger & Gusek, 1995; Giles, 2003; Igartua & Humanes, 2004; Moral & Igartua, 2005 [cited by Igartua & Moral, 2012]).

Television messages, evidentially, raise the public opinion and influence the personal perception of the audience about the social image. Thus, they strengthen concrete and strong beliefs, values and stereotypes. From this standpoint, stereotypes, and precisely, gender stereotypes, retain a misbalanced power over the social reality itself that endures in time (Núñez, 2005: 301).

According to Loscertales and Núñez Domínguez:

The discussion about the influence of the current mass media and the effects they actually produce and even the way in which they determine or not, the social interaction, which is a primary goal in our discipline, is already one of the most interesting fields in psychological studies and research (2007: 2-3).

Social stereotypes about women emphasize that they are endowed by nature of different competencies than those of men. Therefore, their role has been predominated by biological and socio-cultural factors that their inclusion in committing crimes is different from that of males (Gila & Guil, 1999: 90).

Female criminality has been practically, invisible in crime studies, primarily because of their limited number of incidents. However, in recent years the crime rate of women has been growing ever since the female population was involved in a great number of murders (López, 2013: 1). The role of women has been overshadowed in many ways, with a traditional image of women plainly as mothers or housewives; however, there is evidence that they are capable of killing known and unknown individuals, or that they can even be serial killers (Arango & Guerrero, 2009: 7).

Television programs could not exclude the matter of immigration on their storylines, especially in this new era of mass immigration. Although they participate as secondary characters or guest stars, they reinforce the notion that immigration leads to increased crime and therefore are associated with negative stereotypes, a trend at an international level. The attribution of immigrants' potential involvement in criminality to situational factors is nested within arguments which in many cases depersonalize and dehumanize immigrants. Immigrants as a group may be more prone (in comparison with the local people) to get involved in illegal acts due to their living conditions in hosting countries (Figgou et al., 2011: 7).

This work aims to contribute to the accuracy of portraying immigrant female killers, due to the fact that women can commit cold-blooded killings in the contrary of their emotional and sensitive figure that is retained in the storyline of violence. Women are almost always depicted with a feminized version of violent behavior that limits their threat and tolerates their crimes, but this study will make an attempt to end sexism by revealing powerful killer women.

Method

The aim of this paper is to investigate female killers on five American television series, from a psychosocial perspective, broadcasted in Spain from 2000 to 2015.

The sample consists of by 20 cases of killer women in five American TV shows, from 2000 to 2015, selected attentively to represent accurately female criminality and the existence of psychological issues.

On the one hand, in light of exploring the profile of female criminality in order to reveal the bias in fictional female characters, whenever they commit death crimes voluntarily, and, on the other hand, to raise awareness of the most common personality disorders that they tend to have, so as to foster a socially responsible approach of the media production.

In order to achieve that, a content analysis coding frame was applied. While as a data collection instrument, four categorical groups of four aspects respectively, have been applied, adjusted to the aims and the interests of this study.

General Aspects: Television Series, Country, Genre, Network, Original Release, Number of Female Killers.

Personal Information: Age, Origin.

Conduct Forms: Modus Operandi, Relation to the victim, Motive, Sentence.

Psychological Aspects: Psychological Disorders according to the Diagnostic and Statistical Manual of Mental Disorders, Fifth Edition (DSMV), Kelleher & Kelleher Typology of Female Serial Killers.

Once the data were obtained, a quantitative analysis of the frequencies for each variable was performed, from which the approach to the psychological profile of the female killers in small screen series was carried out successfully. The selection of the series was executed by consulting the database of television programs on each annual television schedule. Furthermore, the data analysis was achieved with the assistance of the SPSS statistical package, which allows the calculation of frequencies and the outcome percentages and, also, the verification of hypotheses.

Results
General Aspects

Table 1. General aspects of the selected TV Series

Television Series	Country	Original Release	Original Network	Genre	Numbers of IFK
Law & Order: SVU	USA	1999-Present	NBC-TVE1	Police Drama	7
CSI	USA	2000-2015	CBS-Cuatro	Police Crime Drama	2
Monk	USA	2002-2009	USA Network-FDF	Police Comedy Drama	2
NCIS	USA	2003-Present	NBC-TVE1	Police Drama	6
Castle	USA	2009-2016	ABC-Cuatro	Police Comedy Drama	8

Compiled by author

The results of this study (20 cases) were based on five American series on the small screen, broadcasted in Spain from 2000-2015, mainly of police drama genre. However, in recent years they were also found in police comedy dramas (Dramedies).

Personal Information

Table 2. Age of the immigrant female killers in television programs

Age	No.	%
18-24	5	25
25-39	8	40
40-59	4	20
60-80	3	15
Total	20	100

Compiled by author

Fundamentally, the age of the immigrant female killers ranges from 18 (25%) to 60 years old (15%).

Table 3. Origin of the immigrant female killers in television programs

Origin	No.	%
Russia	6	30
Mexico	5	25
Italy	4	20
North Korea	3	15
Iran	2	10
Total	20	100

Compiled by author

Regarding to the variable of origin, the immigrant female killers are mainly coming from Russia (30%) and Mexico (25%).

Conduct Forms

Table 4. Modus operandi of the immigrant female killers in television programs

MO	No.	%
Stabbing	8	40
Firearms	5	25
Strangulation	3	15
Poisoning	2	10
Variety of Methods	2	10
Total	20	100

Compiled by author

Females can commit murders and they achieve it, notably, by stabbing (40%) and by firearms (25%).

Figure 1. Relation to the victims of the immigrant female killers in television programs

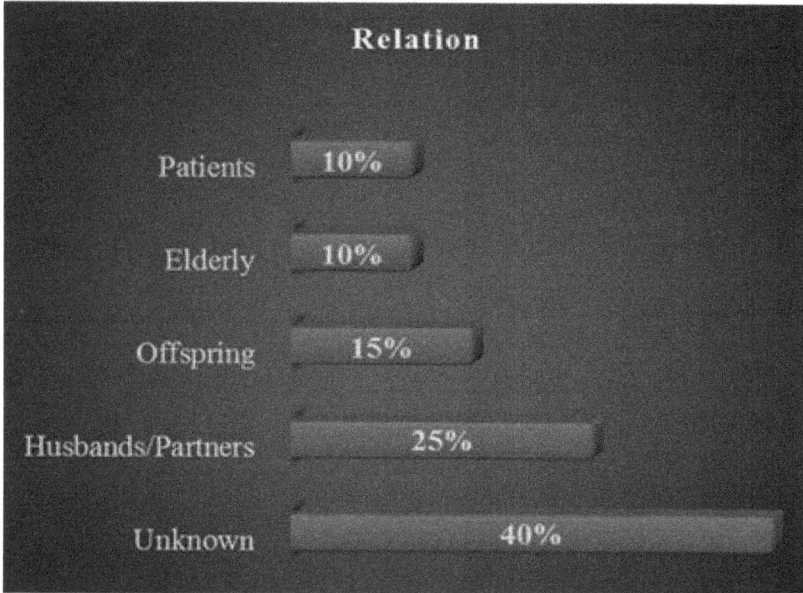

Compiled by author

Figure 1 shows that the most common victims are unknown individuals (40%) to the immigrant female killers and their husbands/ partners (25%), verifying that they are capable of killing both their relatives and unknown people.

Table 5. Motive of the immigrant female killers in television programs

Motive	No.	%
Money	6	30
Anger	5	25
Revenge	4	20
Unknown	3	15
Fear of Abandonment	2	10
Total	20	100

Compiled by author

It has been discovered that money (30%) stimulates assassinations, through fraud or accelerating inheritance with the death of the victim (s).

Table 6. Sentence of the immigrant female killers in television programs

Sentence	No.	%
Incarceration	8	40
Life imprisonment	6	30
Institutionalization	4	20
Murdered by the police	2	10
Total	20	100

Compiled by author

With reference to the sentence process: almost the majority has been incarcerated (40%) or has received life imprisonment (30%). 20% is related to the presence of a psychological disorder.

Psychological Aspects

Table 7. Psychological Disorders according to the Diagnostic and Statistical Manual of Mental Disorders, Fifth Edition (DSMV) of the immigrant female killers in television programs

Psychological Disorder	No.	%
Brief psychotic disorder	7	35
Posttraumatic stress disorder	6	30
Bipolar disorder	4	20
Schizophrenia	2	10
Obsessive- compulsive disorder	1	5
Total	20	100

Compiled by author

Nine immigrant female killers (45%) met the requirements of the Schizophrenia spectrum (Brief psychotic disorder and Schizophrenia), six with Posttraumatic stress disorder (30%) and four with Bipolar disorder (20%), leaving schizophrenia, usually associated with murders, on the last but one place (10%).

Figure 2. Kelleher & Kelleher Typology of Female Serial Killers of the immigrant female killers in television programs

Female Serial Killers

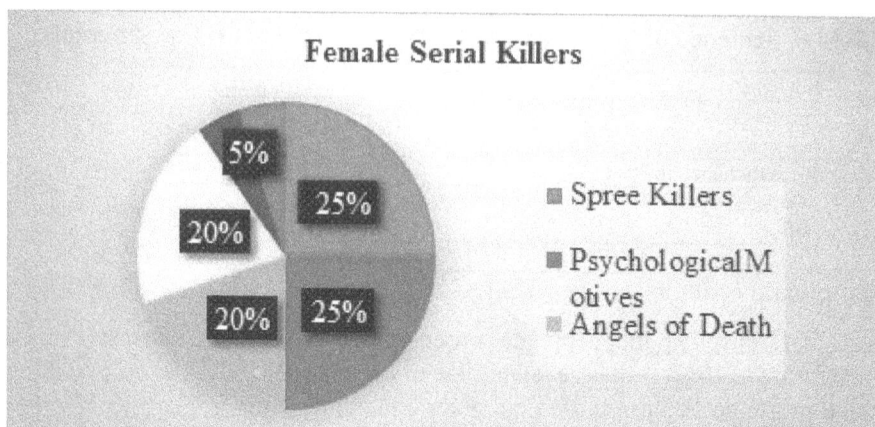

Regarding to the variable of the Kelleher & Kelleher Typology of Female Serial Killers, Spree Killers (25%) with Psychological Motives (25%) proceed to the other categories. Angels of death and black widows (20% respectively) are distinguished from the variable Serial Killers. Interestingly, a link between Spree killers and the Brief psychotic disorder of the previous category is detected.

Discussion

The results of this conducted research upon the immigrant female killers, have allowed us to approach a profile of them in television programs, offering, as well, new findings in this matter, as it has been raised on the purposes of this work.

Women are able to kill both, their relatives and unknown people, are precise and meticulous, and they commit relentless murders using methods such as stabbing and firearms. Surprisingly, a method that used to be linked to the female criminality, namely poisoning, is located on the penultimate position in this study. While prejudice indicates that women murder mainly because of revenge, the results of this investigation determine that they murder in the necessity of money and out of anger.

Risk factors, some of which are, lifestyle instability, poor family environment or lack of education, are considered to be evidence on why they start to kill on such a young age and furthermore why older women decide to kill someone. Sadly, current enemies of the United States (Russia, Mexico, and North Korea) are depicted as atrocious killers, reinforcing an already biased image of criminals based on their nationality. Lastly, the criminal justice system upholds the myth that female murderers were forced to commit murder, although in the end they are incarcerated.

The concept of psychopathy is associated, countless times, with female criminality; it is rather referred to the identification of a number of personality and behavioral characteristics that have become a generally accepted definition of psychopathy. Moreover, the fact that an individual may have a mental illness does not mean that she can also be psychopathic. It is a common but mistaken belief among law enforcement and forensic professionals that people who commit violent, incomprehensible crimes must be crazy or psychotic. Regrettably, this perception is reinforced by the media.

There have not been any representative studies showing any type of psychological disorders, due to a low statistical representation. However, this work aims to clarify the existence of Personality Disorders. Personality disorders can be characterized by a class of personality types which deviate from societal expectations of acceptable behavior. Their behavior is the result of choice, freely exercised, but coupled with a distorted sense of reality.

Although much remains to be investigated, these results add a more positive view of the right path that has to be followed for the future.

Reference

Aguedad Gómez, J. I. (2003). La tele y la escuela: Entre rivalidades y alianzas [Television and School: Between rivalries and alliances] Andalucía Educativa, 40(12), 7-9.

Arango Agualimpia, S., M. and Guerrero Zapata, A. (2009). Aproximación al perfil de la mujer asesina en serie. Ponencia presentada en el V Congreso de Psicología Jurídica y Forense del Caribe. Received from http://psicologiajuridica.org/psj116.html. Accesed: 08.02.2015.

Bonilla Borrego, J. (2005). El cine y los valores educativos. A la búsqueda de una herramienta eficaz de formación [Cinema and educational values. The search for an effective training tool]. Pixel-Bit. Revista de Medios y Educación, 26 (7), 39-54.

Figgou, L., Sapountzis, A., Bozatzis, N., Gardikiotis, A. and Pantazis, P. (2011). Constructing the Stereotype of Immigrants Criminality: Accounts of Fear and Risk in Talk about Immigration to Greece. Journal of Community & Applied Social Psychology, 21, 164–177.

García, A. (2006). Psicología y cine: Vidas cruzadas. Madrid: UNED.

Gila, J. and Guil, A. (1999). La mujer actual en los medios: Estereotipos cinematográficos [The current woman in the media: Cinematographic stereotypes]. Comunicar, VI (12), 89-93.

Guarinos, V. (2008). Mujer y cine. In Loscertales, F. and Núñez, T.(eds.). Los medios de comunicación con mirada de género. Sevilla: Instituto Andaluz de la Mujer. pp. 103-120.

Hogg, M.A. and Vaughan G.M. (2010). Psicología social. Madrid: Editorial Médica Panamericana.

Igartua, J. J. and Moral, F. (2012). Psicología de los medios: panorama y perspectivas [Media Psychology: panorama and perspectives]. Escritos de Psicología, 5(3), 1-3.

López Martín, A. (2013). Las mujeres también matamos [Women can also kill]. Revista Criminología y Justicia, 6(12), 1-7.

Loscertales, F. y Núñez Domínguez T. (2007). La Intervención social. Programa de doctorado. Sevilla: Facultad de Comunicación.

Marqués P. (2001). Aportaciones de los Mass Media en educación. Problemáticas asociadas. Received from http://www.peremarques.net/masme.htm. Accessed: 29.01.2015

Núñez Puente, S. (2005). Género y televisión. Estereotipos y mecanismos de poder en el medio televisivo [Gender and television. Stereotypes and mechanisms of power in the television]. Comunicar, XIII(25), 301.

Skinner, B. F. (1984). The evolution of behavior. Journal of the Experimental Analysis of Behavior, 4 (2), 217-221.

Yubero, S. (2003). Socialización y aprendizaje social. In Páez, D., Fernández, I., Ubillos, S. and Zubieta, E.(eds.) Psicología Social, cultura y educación. Madrid: Pearson. pp. 819-844.

Chapter 2. Establishing Feeling of Security for the People Who Suffer from Conflict

Süleyman Özmen*

Abstract

Life is an illusion that shaped by our perception. This perception can be influenced by different factors and influence our behavior a human being. For example, social media can be used to create the illusion of fear or security in our modern world. Media could lead social developments and also clash similarly as we have seen in the Arap spring. Is security significant for human beings? According to Abraham Maslow's hierarchy of needs theory, security lies at the very basic level. Security is essential for human development. In this article, I will discuss the parameters of risk for security and human perception of security. As a conclusion, many people still suffer and can not fulfill their basic needs in regions of the world. We would constantly on associated with one another and answerable for one another. We need to be concerned and take an action to ensure the security of our world for the dignity of human being. Earth is like a human body. The conflict area is something like a cancerous region of the human body. As cancer spreads to the whole body, conflicts do too. The thing that unites us ought further to bolster a chance to be more excellent over what isolates us.

Key words: Perception, security, conflict, human rights, risks, suffering.

Introduction

Abyssus abyssum invocat (Hell calls hell)

There are many definitions of the concept of security. The simplest definition of security threats refers to the feeling of being away from the concerns and dangers. Security is a mood that a person feels so far away from the damage that one can influence others. Today "security" as a political value, at least in Western mindset, has no independent meaning and is related to the individual or societal value systems. As a social science concept, "security is uncertain and flexible in its meaning" (Brauch, 2008: 61).

In other definition security is, "trust in other people" and repeated psychological need. Besides, we can look to accomplish more excellent control again in our runaway word. We shan't be able to do so if we avoid the challenges, or pretend that all can go on as before. For globalization will be not accidental to our exists today. It may be a movement in our exact an aggregation condition. It is those route that we currently live (Giddens, 2000: 6). Buchan states, "Security is a word with many meanings", and mentions that many authors limit the definition of security as the absence of a military threat or the protection of the nation from an external overthrow or attack cited in Haftendorn (1991: 4).

---

* Assistant Professor, Süleyman Özmen, Istanbul Rumeli University, Head of International Relations Department, Turkey. E-Mail adres : suleyman.ozmen@rumeli.edu.tr

Parameters of risk and security have changed in today's society. Actually, Security is two different things. One is the reality; the second is feelings. How can we separate this? Do you feel secure or not? It depends on your perception. It means your geographical position, your environment, education, economic situation, religion, and culture. The most important thing is that your reality models are imposed by society.

How important is security for human motivation? Abraham Maslow studied on this subject and he proposed the hierarchy of needs theory in psychology field "A Theory of Human Motivation" (Maslow, 2013: 17). Maslow subsequently extended the idea to include his observations of humans' innate curiosity. There are basic needs at the bottom of this pyramid. Basic needs include physiological and safety needs.

Human's physiological needs take the highest priority (Maslow, 2013: 19). As a result of the prepotency of physiological needs, an individual will deprioritize all other desires and capacities. Physiological needs can control thoughts and behaviors, and can cause people to feel sickness, pain, and discomfort.

Changes in security approach and transformation

(The pillar of the world is hope. African Proverb)

From the Roman era to modern day civilians in conflict regions have been unwillingly involved in various ways that were due to the past conflicts. Today's conflicts rarely occur in battlefields that are away from populous areas (UN, Secretary-General's Reports on the Protection of Civilians in Armed Conflict, 25-01-2012 Case Study).

Nature life is not complicated. It is complex that human being puts it in his selfish aspirations and insatiable appetite. We adopt this complexity sometimes; we sometimes hear to illness. In the course of five thousand years of human history, only 292 years have passed without war. Military annals continued throughout human history and is comprised of incidents within the conflict category. These include the regular army that affects the majority of small-scale fighting between the two tribes of the earth's population individuals are listed as the last world war. 20th century bears the distinction of being one of the bloodiest centuries in world history (Levene, 2000: 306).

Millions of people were killed in first and second World Wars, and also more recently over two hundred thousand of civilians died due to atomic bombs in Hiroshima and Nagasaki. Since the finale of the WW II in 1945, there have been some 250 real wars for which 50 million individuals have been slaughtered, tens of millions made homeless, and countless millions injured. Further, the Cold War created the psychological devastation. The Twentieth

Century has been "without the doubt that practically dangerous century for which we need record toward that scale, recurrence furthermore period of the battle which filled it" (Hobsbawm, 1994: 49). In the history of warfare, the twentieth century stands out as the bloodiest and most brutal. Briefly as Rene Dumont said; "I see it only as a century of massacres and wars" (Schmitt, 2007: 404).

Their physical needs relatively satisfied, the individual's safety needs take precedence and dominate behavior (Spraggon, 2015: 2). In the absence of physical security, individuals might (re-)encounter post-traumatic anxiety jumble alternately transgenerational trauma. In the nonattendance of budgetary safety (due with financial emergency what's more absence of fill in opportunities) these well-being necessities indicate themselves to routes for example, such that an inclination for particular occupation security, grievance methods to securing the unique starting with one-sided authority, reserve funds accounts, protection policies, sensible handicap accommodations, and so on. This level may be less averse will a chance to be found for children, as a result they, for the most part, bring a greater need to feel protected (Maslow, 1954: 27).

Dilemma; War and Security

(There are three kinds of people; those that make things happen, those that watch things happen and those who don't know what's happening. American Proverb)

Today security approaches have changed in our complex world. Security is both a feeling and a reality. Cold War as a security dilemma illuminates both history and theoretical concepts. The core argument of the security dilemma is that, in the nonattendance of a supranational power that can enforce binding agreements, a significant number of the steps sought after toward states to bolster their security have the effect of making other States less secure. The anarchic nature of the international system imposes constraints on states' behavior (Jervis, 2001: 38). Accumulation about human security threats, challenges, vulnerabilities, and dangers (Brauch, 2008: 44).

Starting with a philosophical perspective, in the contemporary security examination those "dual minute for counteractive action furthermore recompense from claiming really social also specialized foul uncertainties" gets definitive. That report card puts forward another dream from claiming aggregate security, one that addresses every one of the significant dangers should global peace also security felt around the reality. Our research uncovered that our own may be a time for unparalleled intercontinental around dangers will universal peace what's more security, and common defenselessness the middle of feeble what's more solid.

15

Towards another security consensus, those united countries might have been made clinched alongside 1945, to save succeeding generations from those scourge for war and to guarantee that the horrors of the reality wars were never repeater. Sixty years a considerable length of time after we recognize the sum great that the greatest security dangers we face now, what's more in the decades ahead, try significantly past states waging combative war. They stretch out to that poverty, irresistible sickness also ecological degradation, war and savagery inside states. The threats are from non -state actors as well as states and to human security as well as state security (UN Report, 2004: 11).

That distraction of the united countries organizers might have been for state security. When they spoke of making another framework of aggregate security, they implied it in the conventional military sense: an arrangement to which States join together what's more pledge that hostility against particular case is aggress against all. What's more, submitting themselves in that occasion will respond all things considered. Yet, all they comprehended well is the indivisibility for security, investment advancement what's more human opportunity. In the opening words of the Charter, the United Nations was created "to reaffirm faith in fundamental human rights" and "to promote social progress and better standards of life in larger freedom" (UNFPA, 2004: 17).

Those instances to aggregate security today rest on three fundamental pillars. Today's dangers perceive no national boundaries and must a chance to be tended to. No State, regardless how powerful, might by its identity or endeavors alone settle on itself safe should today's dangers. It can't make it accepted that each state will dependably be able, alternately willing, and should help its obligation with protecting its identity or people groups (UN Report, 2004: 15).

Contrasts of power, riches and geology would determine the thing that we recognize concerning illustration those gravest dangers should our survival and prosperity. Numerous individuals have confidence that the thing that passes for aggregate security today is basically an arrangement to ensuring those rich what's more capable. Such recognitions pose an essential challenge with manufacture aggregate security today. Stated baldly, without mutual recognition of threats there can be no collective security. Self - improvement will rule, the question will predominate also participation for long haul common addition will escape us.

The thing that is necessary today will be nothing short of what another agreement the middle of alliances that need aid frayed, between rich countries and poor. Those pith from claiming that agreement will be simple: we all impart obligation for every other's security. And the test for that agreement will be activity. Aggregate security and the challenge about avoidance at whatever occasion or procedure that prompts extensive scale demise alternately decreased for term possibilities and undermines states as the fundamental unit of the universal framework, which is a risk on global security. Along these lines defined, there need aid six groups from claiming dangers: Financial and social threats, including poverty, irresistible maladies, and ecological corruption. inter-State conflict, interior conflict, including common war, genocide also different extensive -scale atrocities, nuclear, radiological, chemical and biological weapons; terrorism and transnational organized crime

Brauch in an article (2008: 33) discussed the historical development of the concept of security. The theoretical works on security are explained in the context of history, social sciences, philosophy and international law, and the regional security in the United Nations. Then, dialogs identified with security's linkage with peace, improvement and nature's domain need aids analyzed, diverse relations around the individuals four ideas need clarified. Four steps would produce for that stretched security origination. The maintainable advancement and maintainable peace for human-oriented continuation situation through against state-oriented security situation. Toward the conclusion that article emphasizes the vitality about a conceptual chart (Brauch, 2008: 37).

The world's six threats to deal with are risk group. These are terrorism, conflicts between countries, civil war, genocide and other large-scale civil conflict, including violence, nuclear, biological and chemical weapons, order organized crime in excess of hunger, infectious diseases and environmental issues.

"Wanton murdering about honest civilians may be terrorism, not a war against terrorism." This quote from Noam Chomsky emphasizes the urge for measures to protect civilians in conflict regions since it has taken a large negative toll on many people. Currently, there are more than 40 armed conflicts currently in progress around the globe and it is vital that solutions be found to provide humanitarian relief for civilians faced with targeted attacks or trapped in the midst of active fighting.Worldwide constrained uprooting need seen accelerated growth previously in 2014, at the end of the day arriving at phenomenal levels. Those quite a while saw those most astounding uprooting around the record. Toward those end-2014, 59,5 million people have been forcibly displaced as an after effect about persecution, conflict, summed up violence, or mankind's privileges violations. This is 8,3 million persons more than the year before (51,2 million) and the highest annual increase ina single year.

(http://www.unhcr.org/news/latest/2015/6/558193896/worldwide-displacement-hits-all-time-high-war-persecution-increase.html).

Refugees stream starting with Syria and Afghanistan will be expanding in the area. Specifically, those number for refugees from Syria need especially expanded in the previous quite a while. Concerning illustration for 2014 there would an evaluated 13,9 million displaced because of clash or persecution, including 11 million persons recently displaced inside the outskirts of their own nation over. In addition, approximately 42,500 individuals per day are forced to leave their homes due to conflict. Developing regions host about 86% of the world's refugees and Less developed countries provide asylum to 3,6 million refugees.

Unprecedented numbers of migrants and asylum seekers have traveled by sea to European shores in 2015. By mid-November, over 800,000 had reached Italy and Greece, with relatively small numbers arriving in Spain and Malta. According to UNHCR, the UN refugee agency, 84 percent originate from Syria, Afghanistan, Eritrea, Somalia, and Iraq all countries experiencing conflict, widespread violence, and insecurity, or highly repressive governments. Even accounting for misrepresentations of nationality and the presence of migrants seeking to improve their lives, this should be understood broadly as a refugee crisis. More than 800,000 asylum seekers and migrants have arrived in Europe by the sea in 2015, with most traveling onward to northern and western EU countries (https://www.hrw.org/report/2015/11/16/europes-refugee-crisis/agenda-action).

Conclusion

(Laugh and the whole world laughs with you; weep and you weep alone)

Earth is like the human body. The conflict area is something like a cancerous region of a human body. As cancer spreads to the whole body, conflicts do too. What unites us must be greater than what divides us. As United Nations Charter said; "We the Peoples of the United Nations, determined to reaffirm faith in fundamental human rights, in the dignity and worth of the human person, in the equal rights of men and women and of nations large and small...". UN Secretary-General Kofi Annan said: "We will not enjoy security without development, we will not enjoy development without security, and we will not enjoy either without respect for human rights."

UN was absolutely right. We the people of this lonely planet. We are connected to each other. We are responsible for each other. One refugee without hope is too many for humanity. So we need to realize our real responsibilities. We need to wake up, understand what is happening to ourselves. In our planet and even universe have a simple rule that's called butterfly effect.

The first priority must be to ensure that all people are free from such deprivations, and are empowered with the rights and resources needed to provide a social foundation for leading lives of dignity, opportunity, and fulfillment (Raworth, 2012: 7). Humanity's challenge in the 21st century is to eradicate poverty and achieve prosperity for all within the means of the planet's limited natural resources (Raworth, 2012: 1). All problems are our problems and just can be solved in good faith.

References

Books

Barry, Buzan, People, States & Fear: An Agenda for International Security Studies in the Post-Cold War Era, Colchester, UK, 2007.

Brauch, Hans Günter, Úrsula Oswald Spring, Czeslaw Mesjasz, John Grin, Patricia Kameri-Mbote, Bechir Chourou, Pal Dunay and Jörn Birkmann. (Eds.), Coping with Global Environmental Change, Disasters and Security Threats, Challenges, Vulnerabilities and Risks, Springer Books, New York, 2008.

Burgess, J. Peter, The Routledge Handbook of New Security Studies, Published by Routledge, New York, 2010.

Chris T. Hendricson, Environmental Life Cycle Assesment Operational Guide to the ISO Standards, Kluer Academic, Boston, MA, 2002.

Elliot, Gil, Twentieth Century Book of the Dead, Penguin Books, London, 1972.

Forster, Mark Arnold, World at War, Published by Pimlico, London, 2001.

Giddens, Anthony, Runaway, World How Globalization Is Reshaping our Lives, Routladge, New York, 2000.

Hobsbawn, Eric, Age of Extremes The Short Twentieth Century 1914-1991, Abacus Book, London, 1994.

Leech, Joe, Psychology For Designers, Five Simple Steps, United Kingdom, 2013.

Maslow, Abraham H., A Theory of Human Motivation, Martino Fine Books, Eastford, USA, 2013.

Roberts, Adam & Dominik Zaum, Selective Security: War and the United Nations Security Council since 1945, Published by Routledge, London, 2008.

Schmitt, Richard, Research, Measurement, and Evaluation of Human Resources, Nelson Thomson Learning, Toronto, 2007.

Schneier, Bruce, Schneier on Security, Published by John Wiley & Sons, New York, 2008.

Spraggon, Martin and Virginia Bodolica, Mergers and Acquisitions and Executive Compensation, Routladge Taylor & Francis Group, New York, 2015.

Wells, Mike, History for the IB Diploma: Causes, Practices, and Effects of Wars, Cambridge Books, Cambridge, 2013.

Periodical Publications

Haftendorn, Helga, The Security Puzzle: Theory-Building and Discipline-Building in International Security, Author(s): Helga Haftendorn Source: International Studies Quarterly, Published by Blackwell Publishing on behalf of The International Studies Association, Vol. 35, No. 1 (Mar, 1991), pp. 3-17.

Levene, Mark, Why Is the Twentieth Century the Century of Genocide, Source: Journal of World History, Vol. 11, No. 2 (Fall, 2000), pp. 305-336, Published by University of Hawai'i Press.

Schneier, Bruce, Schneier on Security: Privacy and Control, Journal of Privacy and Confidentiality, 2010, 2, Number 1, pp. 3-4.

Jervis, Robert, Cooperation Under the Security Dilemma, World Politics, Volume 30, Issue 2, (January, 1978), pp. 167-214.

Jervis, Robert, Was the Cold War a Security Dilemma?, Journal of Cold War Studies Volume 3, Number 1, Winter 2001, pp. 36-60.

Victor, D. Cha, Globalization and the Study of International Security, Journal of Peace Research, May 2000, vol. 37 no. 3, pp. 391-403.

Internet Resources

Denney, Lisa, Consulting the Evidence: How Conflict and Violence Can Best Be Included in the Post- 2015, Development Agenda, London: ODI, http://www.odi.org.uk/sites/odi.org.uk/files/odi-assets/publications-opinion-files/8486.pdf

Hendrickson, D., State responsiveness to public security needs: The politics of security decisionmaking: Synthesis of findings and implications for UK SSR policy. CSDG Papers No. 12, 2008. London: Conflict, Security and Development Group, King's College London. http://www.securityanddevelopment.org/pdf/Findings.pdf

Jervis, Robert, Cooperation under The Security Dilemma, Published by STOR, http://www.columbia.edu/itc/sipa/S6800/courseworks/cooperation_under_dilemma.pdf

Raworth, Kate, A Safe and Just Space for Humanity, Oxfam Discussion Paper, February 2012, https://www.oxfam.org/sites/www.oxfam.org/files/dp-a-safe-and-just-space-for-humanity-130212-en.pdf

Schneier, Bruce, The Psychology of Security, BT Counterpane, 1600 Memorex Drive, Suite 200, Santa Clara, CA 95050, https://www.schneier.com/cryptography/paperfiles/paper-psychology-of-security.pdf

Spraggon, Martin, Human Behavior & Motivation in Organizations, Ph.D. Associate Professor, Vancouver Island University, https://www.academia.edu/4909759/Human_Behavior_and_Motivation_in_Organizations

Stewart, Frances, Development and Security, Centre for Research on Inequality, Human Security and Ethnicity, CRISE Queen Elizabeth House, University of Oxford, http://www3.qeh.ox.ac.uk/pdf/crisewps/workingpaper3.pdf

Safety Security and Justice Topic Guide, http://www.gsdrc.org/wp-content/uploads/2015/07/GSDRC_SSJ.pdf

http://siteresources.worldbank.org/INTWDRS/Resources/WDR2011_Full_Text.pdf

https://www.academia.edu/4909759/Human_Behavior_and_Motivation_in_Organizations

UN Reports

UN, Secretary-General's Reports on the Protection of Civilians in Armed Conflict, 25-01-2012 Case Study), https://www.icrc.org/casebook/doc/case-study/united-nations-protection-civilians-case-study.htm

UN Report, United Nations A/59/565 General Assembly Distr.: General 2 December 2004 Original: English 04-60231 (E) 301104 *0460231* Fifty-ninth session Agenda item 55, https://www1.umn.edu/humanrts/instree/report.pdf

Noble, Ronald (Interpol Secretary General), The Globalization of Crime a Transnational Organized Crime Threat Assessment, United Nations Office on Drugs and Crime, United Nations publication, Sales No. E.10.IV.6, Vienna, 2010

UNFPA Report, United Nations Population Fund, Quotes on Human Rights, 2004, http://www.unfpa.org/resources/quotes-human-rights

Secretary General's Reports on the Protection of Civilians in Armed Conflict, https://www.icrc.org/casebook/doc/case-study/united-nations-protection-civilians-case-study.htm

A more secure world: Our shared responsibility, Report of the High-level Panel on Threats, Challenges and Change, http://www.un.org/en/peacebuilding/pdf/historical/hlp_more_secure_world.pdf

Great Britain. Foreign and Commonwealth Office, (A more secure world: our shared responsibility), 2005 report of the United Nations, https://www.gov.uk/government/uploads/system/uploads/attachment_data/file/272324/6 892.pdf

UNHCR Global Trends, http://unhcr.org/556725e69.html

http://www.un-documents.net/ocf-11.htm

http://www.unfpa.org/resources/quotes-human-rights#sthash.6cczcqqN.dpuf

http://www.unfpa.org/resources/quotes-culture-and-culturally-sensitive-approaches#sthash.18Ib4UP4.dpuf

Chapter 3. Implications of the European Union-Turkish Migration Agreement for the Slovak Domestic and Foreign Policy[1]

Barbora Olejárová[*]

Abstract

The Slovak Republic is not located on the main migratory routes of people from the third-countries on their way to Western Europe and the state itself has never become final destination for irregular migrants or asylum seekers. Despite this fact, the crisis of migrants coming from the Middle East and sub-Saharan Africa significantly influenced both Slovak domestic and foreign policy and created unprecedented dichotomies between Slovak internal and international stance towards the issue, generating impression that Slovakia is playing both ends. Main aim of the paper is to provide evidence of how intensively can migration waves affect even those countries that are neither source countries nor transit or final destination countries for the migrants. The paper presents position of the Slovak Republic on the ongoing migration crisis and the EU solutions including the deal with Turkey and explains the dichotomy among the opinion of the general public and political leaders on one hand and the official stance country presented as the presiding country of the Council of the EU on the other hand, providing evidence that the argumentation lines of both sites were not as diverse as presented and proved to be right from the long-term perspective.

Keywords: Council Presidency, domestic policy, European Union, migration, the Slovak Republic, Turkey

Introduction

Migration crisis that hit the European Union in 2014 did not influence the Slovak Republic in terms of numbers of irregular migrants and asylum seekers. Yet, it has become one of the central issues of the Slovak domestic and foreign policy following very negative attitude of the Slovak general public and domestic political elites towards acceptance of asylum seekers and third-countries migrants on the state's territory. The definite stance of the country was expressed when the state filled an action for annulment to the Court of Justice of the EU (case C-643/15), challenging legality of the Asylum-Seekers Relocation Decision from 22 September 2015. The basic matter of argument was rejection of obligatory quotas as determined by the Council Decision (EU) 2015/1601. Radical position of the Slovak government was influenced by the upcoming parliamentary election that was supposed to take place on 5 March 2016 and by striving of all political parties to gain public votes by promoting general public will of refusing asylum seekers and settlement of third-countries migrants in the Slovak Republic. However, the domestic opposition towards common European solution to the crisis based on the quota system got into contradiction with the upcoming role of Slovakia as the country presiding over the Council of the European Union in the second half of 2016.

[1] Paper is published as the part of project VEGA no. 1/0783/16.
[*] PhD Candidate at the Department of International Relations and Diplomacy, Faculty of Political Science and International Relations, Matej Bel University, Kuzmanyho 1, 974 01, Banska Bystrica, Slovak Republic, E-mail: barbora.olejarova@umb.sk.

As the presiding country, Slovakia was expected to take over the role of a mediator among the other EU Member States in all areas, including migration. The accrued dichotomy was sharpened by adoption of the EU-Turkey migration deal that assumed allocation of Syrian refugees into the EU Member States based on the free places created according to the aforementioned Council Decision (EU) 2015/1601. Over the course of its Presidency, Slovakia acknowledged effectiveness of the deal with Turkey, but the country was still refusing allocation of refugees to the state's territory. Slovak representatives strived to solve this paradox of supporting the deal with Turkey but refusing obligatory quotas by introducing the concept of effective solidarity in the European Union. The presented paper summarizes Slovak Presidency in the Council of the European Union regarding migration issues and policies; evaluates dichotomy of political statements and adopted measures on the domestic and European level and explains its causes taking into account political development in the country and historical experiences of the Slovak Republic with the third-countries migration. Finally, it points out to the fact, that migration crisis has become one of the central issues of the Slovak domestic and foreign policy although the country was not affected by the crisis directly in terms of increase in detected irregular migrants or asylum seekers. Methodology of the paper is based on the comparison of the Slovak political parties' electoral programs; Eurobarometer statistics; analysis of the Slovak foreign policy documents in the field of migration and the European Commission's progress reports on the EU's emergency relocation and resettlement schemes.

Migration Crisis in Slovakia – Numbers and Policy Reactions

The Slovak Republic is located in the Central Europe surrounded by five other countries – Austria (106,7 km), Czech Republic (251,8 km), Poland (541,1 km), Ukraine (97,8 km) and Hungary (654,8 km). Out of these, only Ukraine is not a member of the European Union and the Schengen area. The geographic location conditions migratory flows passing through the state's territory. Unlike the migratory routes from the countries of origin to the fringes of Europe (Eastern Africa Route, Western and Central Africa Route, Asian Route) and the routes crossing the EU external borders (including the Eastern Mediterranean Route, Central Mediterranean Route, Western Balkan Route, Western Mediterranean Route, Circular Route, Eastern Borders Route, Western Africa Route and the Black Sea Route), the continuation of these routes on the territory of the EU is not particularly classified and named. However, the practical analysis suggests that most migrants continue from the EU borders to the Western and Northern Europe by using routes in the Balkan states and later passing from Hungary to Austria and thus, avoiding the Slovak territory. The only direct route traversing the Slovak Republic is the Eastern Borders Route connecting Belarus, Moldova, Ukraine, the Russian Federation and the eastern EU Member States - Estonia, Finland, Hungary, Latvia, Lithuania, Norway, Poland, Slovakia, Bulgaria and Romania; yet the number of illegal border crossings on this route (1349 in 2016 and 1920 in 2015) is minor compared to the number on the Eastern Mediterranean Route, for example (182,534 in 2015 and 885,386 in 2016). (Frontex, 2017; Kuschminder, de Bresser, Siegel, 2015)

Table 1. Asylum applications, refugees and subsidiary protection in Slovakia

Year	Number of asylum applications	Granted asylum	Refused asylum	Subsidiary protection granted/refused	Suspended procedure
2000	1,556	11	123		1,366
2001	8,151	18	130		6,154
2002	9,743	20	309		8,053
2003	10,358	11	531		10,656
2004	11,395	15	1,592		11,782
2005	3,549	25	827		2,930
2006	2,849	8	861		1,940
2007	2,642	14	1,177	82/646	1,693
2008	909	22	416	66/273	455
2009	822	14	330	98/165	460
2010	541	15	180	57/104	361
2011	491	12	186	91/48	270
2012	732	32	334	104/153	383
2013	441	15	123	34/49	351
2014	331	14	197	99/41	163
2015	330	8	124	41/24	148
2016	146	167	82	12/13	35
2017	59	10	31	11/7	20
Total	58 526	830	8 021	695/1 519	49 493

Source: MVSR (2017).

In regard to geographic location of the country, migration crisis did not hit Slovakia significantly in the sense of numbers. When comparing amount of granted asylums on the Slovak territory (Table 1), we can conclude that the numbers are relatively constant and do not exceed several dozens of granted asylums per year. Quantitative difference is obvious only regarding number of asylum applications. However, the peaks of asylum seekers in Slovakia were not reached over the course of the migration crisis between 2014-2017, as one might assume, but in the period between 2001-2007, i.e. in the years shortly before and after Slovakia joined the EU.

Intrastate Policy Reactions to the Migration Crisis

Despite almost none quantitative impact of migration crisis in the Slovak Republic, migration has become central issue of the Slovak domestic discourse in 2015 - the year preceding the election to the National Council of the Slovak Republic, which was held on 5 March 2016. Resulting from our previous analysis, it is possible to conclude, that the issue of migration has become subject of securitization in the country. (Bolečeková, Olejárová, 2016) General public fears from third-countries migrants showed up in the 2015 November Eurobarometer 84 survey, were over 19 % of population in Slovakia declared that immigration is the biggest threat to our country at the moment, compared to 4% of the people in Eurobarometer 83 from May 2015 (having in mind that the number of foreign population legally present at the Slovak territory at the time was only 1,56 %). (European Commission, 2017a) In an effort to increase the political gain, a rare political unity occurred and all of the political parties generally agreed on the same set of measures aimed to solve the migration crisis. Following the analysis of the parties' pre-election programs, the measures included: protection of the EU external borders; refusing of the EU mandatory quotas on migrants; creation of detention facilities outside of the EU territory which should concentrate migrants heading to the EU in order to review their asylum request; stabilization of situation in the home countries of migrants, especially in Syria, Libya and Iraq; precise selection of asylum seekers and economic migrants, who are not eligible for the refugee status, subsidiary protection, temporary protection or any other form of protection in the EU. Another significant measure adopted by the Slovak government included purchase of a transportable barrier that might be used for redirection of migration flows at the Slovak-Hungarian or Slovak-Austrian border in case the migration flows would have changed their direction to the Slovak territory. Yet, one year after the purchase, this measure turned up to be more a pre-election gesture than a real possibility.

Foreign Policy Responses to the Migration Crisis

Slovak foreign policy responses to the crisis were twofold. On one hand, there was the action for annulment to the Court of Justice (case C-643/15), on the other hand Slovakia applied set of measures on the voluntary basis refuting allegations of lack of solidarity with migrants and the most burdened EU Member States at the external borders, which will be explained in the next chapter. The action for annulment to the Court of Justice (case C-643/15) was targeted against introduction of the quota system for relocation of migrants from Italy and Greece passed by the Council of the European Union on 22 September 2015 - Council Decision (EU) 2015/1601. The scheme proposed relocation of 120,000 people to the EU Member States with Slovakia required taking 802 refugees – 190 from Italy and 612 from Greece. The full text of the Slovak action is not accessible; however, it is based on the legal and political arguments. The first group includes several claims regarding the procedure of adopting the contested legislation. The decision of the Council of European Union (made up of national ministers) was adopted in contradiction to the guidelines set by the European Council (made up of heads of state and government), that stated on 23 April 2015, that there was a need to "consider options for organizing emergency relocation between all Member States on a voluntary basis" and to "set up a first voluntary pilot project on resettlement across the EU." (Vikarská, 2015) – even though conclusions of the European Council are not legally binding (Article 15(1) TEU). The political arguments, on the other hand, refer to the breach of the Principle of proportionality when adopting the contested decision. As stated in the official statement of the Slovak Ministry of Justice, "The contested decision is manifestly incompatible with the principle of proportionality, as it is manifestly neither suitable nor necessary to achieve the desired end." (MSSR, 2015) Moreover, the contested measure is "...not suitable to reach the desired aim (i.e. to relieve the burden borne by the external border states and to show solidarity and fair sharing of responsibility between the Member States as outlined in the decision's preamble), since relocating people is too difficult and their further movement is too unpredictable". (MSSR, 2015)

Migration Crisis and Slovakia – Dichotomy of Attitudes?

Although the migration crisis did not hit the Slovak Republic in terms of enormous increase of people trying to transit the state's territory or settle in the state, the crisis seemingly generated two remarkable dichotomies among the Slovak internal and foreign policy, especially reflecting the Slovak Presidency in the Council of the European Union:

1. Domestic rejection of migrants vs. Slovak Presidency in the Council of the EU

As noted in the previous chapter, Slovak domestic political scene unanimously rejected the mandatory quotas as the solution to the crisis. However, beginning on 1 July 2016, Slovakia took over the Presidency in the Council of the EU with all of the responsibilities connected with this position. The presiding country "... *is responsible for driving forward the Council's work on EU legislation, ensuring the continuity of the EU agenda, orderly legislative processes and cooperation among Member States. To do this, the presidency must act as an honest and neutral broker.*" (Council of the EU, 2017) From this reason, concerns appeared on how will the state that is rejecting common European solutions (based on mandatory quotas) be able to act as a neutral mediator among the other Member States and the EU institutions. Moreover, migration has never been a priority of the Slovak Presidency. In 2012, Slovakia drafted the first conceptual document dealing with the program priorities of the Slovak Presidency called *Preparing the Slovak Presidency of the Council of the EU 2016 – Basic Data and Current Priorities*. The report proposed, that the priorities of the Presidency should reflect the Slovak strategic interests, especially cooperation with the states in the Eastern Europe and in the Balkans; EU enlargement; or the management of water resources of the EU – topics which might have emphasized the particularities of Slovakia as the presiding country. The issue of migration was completely absent in this document, although sustainable migration and asylum policies turned into one of the four main priorities of the Slovak Presidency in 2016, together with economically strong Europe; modern single market; and globally engaged Europe.

2.   Support to the EU-Turkey agreement vs. rejection of mandatory quotas

The second dichotomy is connected to the agreement between the EU and Turkey from 20 March 2016. Despite initial rejection of the EU-Turkey deal by some Slovak political leaders, recent statistics show that the amount of irregular border crossings between BCPs declined from 1 822 177 in 2015 to 511 371 in 2016, which proves effectiveness of the deal that it is generally supported by the Slovak representatives on the EU level. Resettlement from Turkey to the EU Member States is based on the principle 'one-for-one'. "For each Syrian returned from Greece to Turkey, another Syrian will be resettled in an EU Member State. The idea is for a total of 72,000 Syrians to be relocated from Turkey to EU Member States. This number is calculated "within the framework of existing commitments" consisting of 18,000 from the European Resettlement Scheme ... and 54,000 unallocated places under the temporary relocation scheme (places originally allocated for relocation from Hungary but remained unallocated due to Hungary's refusal to participate)." (Provera, 2016, p. 21) However, as noted earlier, Slovakia is refusing mandatory quotas forming basis for resettlement according to the EU-Turkey deal, which creates another important dichotomy in the state's attitude towards migration.

The two aforementioned dichotomies might evoke an impression that the Slovak domestic and foreign policy lines follow different directions, that the state does not act as a reliable member of the EU and that it does not manifest enough solidarity as demanded by the EU treaties. Contrary to these suggestions, following part of the paper presents evidence of how the domestic and foreign policy lines meet at common stands and that the country actually lives up to its obligations as the EU's member state in the field of migration:

1.   Successes of the Slovak Presidency in the Council of the EU in the field of migration despite worries over Slovak neutrality

Few months after the end of the Slovak Presidency in the Council of the EU, it is possible to conclude that the country accomplished its role of the neutral mediator and the intrastate negative opinion on the quota system did not influence the Trio Presidency priorities. Slovakia fulfilled the statement made by the Slovak Prime Minister in July 2016, stating that: *"We are well aware of the presidency country's role, and we want to be an honest broker. It doesn't necessarily mean that we will change our national positions; we will just refrain from putting them on the table."* (Szalai, 2016) Although Slovakia's Presidency did not manage to move the Union closer to a wider agreement on how to handle migration, there are other specific successes such as finalization of the legislative process for the proposals regarding the Smart Borders Package from April 2015; Creation of the European Border and Coast Guard or approval of Regulation changing the *Schengen Border Code in December 2016.*

2.   Shortcomings of the 1:1 resettlement scheme from Turkey based on mandatory quotas

According to the statistical data, the number of irregular border crossings on the Eastern Mediterranean Route declined from 885 386 in 2015 to 182 534 in 2016. This statistical comparison indicates that the migration deal with Turkey works by deterring people from using the route between Turkey and Greece to get irregularly to the European territory. However, the other part of the deal related to the exchange of one irregular asylum seeker from Greece for one Syrian refugee from Turkey and the further relocation of Syrian refugees from Greece to another Member States according to the quotas within the framework of existing commitments consisting of 18,000 places from the European Resettlement Scheme and 54,000 unallocated places under the temporary relocation scheme originally allocated for relocation from Hungary seems to be clumsy. According to the Report of the European Commission on Relocation and Resettlement from April 2017, only 4 618 people were resettled from Turkey to the EU under the 1:1 mechanism. The scheme aims to replace irregular flows of migrants travelling across the Aegean Sea by an orderly legal resettlement process; however, it seems that the relocation based on mandatory quotas is not functioning properly. Thus, despite certain overwhelming caused by the securitization and upcoming parliamentary election, it seems that the Slovak Republic was not completely wrong when claiming (see Ministry of Justice's statement on CJEU stated above) that the system of mandatory relocations will not bring desired outcomes. (European Commission, 2017b)

3.   Mandatory solidarity vs. effective solidarity

Despite refusal of mandatory quotas on migration, it is not possible to claim that Slovakia does not express solidarity in any way. The country decided to help according to its own possibilities – by sending police units to the borders of the most burdened Member States and third countries; by temporary relocating asylum seekers from Austria to the newly re-opened asylum facility in Gabčíkovo; by granting asylum to 149 Assyrian Christians from Iraq; by allocating 500,000 € from the sources of the national lottery company TIPOS for humanitarian projects of non-governmental organizations rendering assistance in the refugee crisis; or by committing to creation of 550 governmental scholarships for refugees until 2021 (Úrad vlády SR, 2015) This concept is called effective solidarity and became one of the most important and debated phenomenon introduced by the Slovak Council Presidency. Moreover, until the final decision of the CJEU will be made, Slovakia adheres to its commitment according to the EU law and takes part in the process of relocation from Italy and Greece despite rejection of the system on the political level. Until 10 April 2017, Slovakia relocated 16 people from Greece, unlike some other EU countries, such as Poland or Hungary, who refuse to participate at the relocation scheme at all. (European Commission, 2017b)

Conclusion

Migration crisis significantly affected the Slovak Republic despite the fact, that the state is not located on the main migratory routes, it is not the final destination or even transit country of migrants from the Middle East and sub-Saharan Africa and the number of refugees and asylum seekers in Slovakia did not exceed several dozens of people pro year since the outbreak of the crisis. Nevertheless, domestic political leaders reacted by securitization of the topic and strictly rejected mandatory quotas on migration, which negatively affected position of the country on the European level and created worries over how will the state fulfil its obligations stemming from its Council Presidency. Despite the general mistrust, we can conclude that the supposed dichotomies among the Slovak domestic and foreign policy did not influence the Trio priorities and the Slovak Presidency in the Council, which brought significant results in the field of sustainable migration and asylum policies. Moreover, although the deal with Turkey seems to be effective in terms of discouraging migrants to use the Eastern Mediterranean Route on their way to Europe, it seems to have certain weaknesses, particularly in the allocation scheme based on the mandatory quotas, exactly in a way as expected by the Slovak representatives – until 10 April 2017, with 72 000 places available, only 4 618 people were resettled from Turkey to the EU under the 1:1 mechanism.

References

Bolečeková, M. and Olejárová, B. (2016). Medzinárodná migrácia: faktor ovplyvňujúci podobu a vnímanie zahraničnej politiky Slovenskej republiky. In: Koziak, T. and Ušiak, J. (eds.) *Zahraničná politika Slovenskej republiky v rámci vybraných oblastí vonkajšej činnosti Európskej únie*. Banská Bystrica: Belianum. pp. 141-175.

Council of the EU. (2017). The Presidency of the Council of the EU. http://www.consilium.europa.eu/en/council-eu/presidency-council-eu/ Received from Accessed: 10.04.2017.

European Commission. (2017a). Public Opinion. Received from http://ec.europa.eu/commfrontoffice/publicopinion/index.cfm/Survey/getSurveyDetail/i nstruments/STANDARD/yearFrom/2012/yearTo/2017/surveyKy/2098 Accessed: 25.03.2017.

European Commission. (2017b). Relocation and Resettlement: Steady Progress Made but More Efforts Needed to Meet Targets. Received from http://europa.eu/rapid/press-release_IP-17-908_en.htm Accessed: 20.03.2017.

Frontex. (2017). Migratory Routes Map. Received from http://frontex.europa.eu/trends-and-routes/migratory-routes-map/ Accessed: 16.04.2017.

Kuschminder, K.; De Bresser, J. and Siegel, M. (2015). Irregular Migration Routes to Europe and Factors Influencing Migrants' Destination Choices. Received from www.merit.unu.edu/publications/uploads/1436958842.pdf Accessed: 15.04.2017.

MSSR. (2015). Summary of the Action. Received from *http://www.justice.gov.sk/Stranky/aktualitadetail.aspx?announcementID=2038* Accessed: 10.02.2017.

MVSR. (2017). Štatistiky. Received from http://www.minv.sk/?statistiky-20 Accessed: 06.04.2017.

Provera, M. (2016). The EU-Turkey Deal. Received from https://jrseurope.org/assets/Publications/File/JRS_Europe_EU_Turkey_Deal_policy_an alysis_2016-04-30.pdf Accessed: 10.04.2017.

Szalai, P. (2016). Can Slovakia Overcome the Paradox of Euro-Sceptic Politics and Euro-Optimist Policies? Received from http://visegradrevue.eu/can-slovakia-overcome-the-paradox-of-euro-sceptic-politics-and-euro-optimist-policies/ Accessed: 05.04.2017.

Úrad vlády SR. (2015). Informácia o možnej podpore aktivít mimovládnych organizácií pri humanitárnej a integračnej podpore utečencom predložených iniciátormi petície „Výzva k ľudskosti". Received from http://www.rokovania.sk/File.aspx/View DocumentHtml/Mater-Dokum-192230?prefixFile=m_ Accessed: 10.04.2017.

Vikarská, Z. (2015). The Slovak Challenge to the Asylum-Seekers' Relocation Decision: A Balancing Act. Received from http://eulawanalysis.blogspot.sk/2015/12/the-slovak-challenge-to-asylum-seekers.html Accessed: 15.04.2017.

Chapter 4. Football player migration in Greece: Wage differences and crowding-out effects

Panagiotis Dimitropoulos[1]

Abstract

Athlete migration has been on the forefront of academic research for more than twenty years since the migration flows of footballers has increased significantly in Europe. Greece is among the top receiving countries of migrant football players in Europe despite the fact that the Greek championship is not highly competitive as other European leagues. The scope of this paper is to provide some initial evidence regarding the flow of foreign football players in the Greek league. The study analyzed a database of all migrant and local athletes that participated in the professional Greek football championship over the period 2001-2013 and performed descriptive analyses. Descriptive evidence suggests that football player migration has increased significantly from 2001 until 2013 yet the relative numbers of foreign athletes are lower than their natives' counterparts. However, foreign athletes are utilized more by their coaches since they have more actual minutes of participation on clubs' official matches and earn higher income than the native football players. These findings provide support to several voices echoing on the crowding out effect of native athletes by migrants.

Keywords: Crowding-out, football players, football league, Greece, migration.

Introduction & Theoretical Background

Athletic migration has been on the forefront of academic research for several decades especially after the Bosman ruling by the Court of Justice of the European Community (EC) which allowed the free movement of athletes within the EC. This decision initiated a new era for professional sports and football particularly (Dubey, 2000; Frick, 2009; McGovern, 2002; Poli, 2010; Poli & Ravenel, 2005). The outcome of this ruling was the increase of player migration flows in the major European championships with the majority of them originating from Eastern Europe and Latin America (Poli, 2010). This flow was the result of club's antagonism to acquire the most competent athletes in order to improve their on-field success.

Of course, the football player migration phenomenon could not leave the Greek football setting unaffected. The international migratory flows of professional players to the Greek professional football clubs is mainly attributed to the fact that clubs in Greece lack the necessary infrastructure for the development of young football players (academies etc.), a fact which leaves a significant gap on the club's roster which has to be covered with foreign players (Anagnostopoulos & Senaux, 2011). However, until now there is no specific research on the literature trying to answer the question of what are the

[1] Panagiotis Dimitropoulos is Teaching Staff of Accounting and Finance, Department of Sport Organization and Management, University of Peloponnese, Valioti Anv. & Plataion str, Sparta, PC. 23100, Greece. E-mail: dimitrop@uop.gr.

synthesis and characteristics of foreign athletes, their utilization and earnings relative to migrants.

The main motivation for this study is the fact that Greece is the seventh highest host country of migrant footballers in Europe based on the data of the Digital Atlas of the CIES Football Observatory. Specifically, foreign athletes in the Greek football clubs comprised 52 per cent of average clubs' roster in 2009 while this number fell to 46.3 per cent in 2015. Almost half of the clubs in the top-division championship have a roster of migrants that count for more than 50 per cent of players. These numbers actually indicate that the Greek clubs are considered as a fruitful destination for several foreign athletes despite the fact that the competitiveness level of the Greek championship is not amongst the most prestigious in Europe relative to England and other significant leagues.

Nevertheless, several voices echoed on the possible crowding out-effect of native athletes due to the increased migration flows. This means that local athletes have fewer opportunities to participate to official matches, improve their skills, abilities and even enhance their valuation on the labor market (Di Maria & Stryszowski, 2009). Kiefer (2014) and Wicker, Prinz, Weimar, Deutscher and Upmann (2013), document that athletes who are more successful on the field enhance their market valuation (and remuneration) since they improve their reputation to the labor market. Moreover, the studies by Bryson, Rossi and Simmons (2014), and Frick (2011) document that players remuneration is a function of their past and current performance and also identify several player characteristics such as player age, games played, international appearances, that contribute on their pay. Also, Bryson et al. (2014) document a wage differential between natives and migrants which is not always justified by individual performance. However, these studies are focused on two prestigious European championships (Italy and Germany) thus literature insofar lacks evidence on the impact of migration within a less prestigious championship.

The scope of this study is to shed further light on the phenomenon of football players' migration in a less developed championship as the Greek league. Moreover, we seek to determine the nationality of migrant athletes, their utilization by their coaches and their remuneration relative to their natives' counterparts. We selected data regarding all football players (natives and foreigners) that were registered on the top-division football clubs over the period 2001 to 2013. Descriptive evidence indicated that football player migration has increased significantly from 2001 until 2013 yet migrant relative numbers are lower than their natives' counterparts. However, foreign athletes are utilized more by their coaches since they have more actual minutes of participation on clubs' official matches and earn higher income than the native football players. These findings provide support to several voices echoing on the crowding out effect of native athletes by migrants. The rest of the paper is organized as follows: The next section provides details on the data selection procedure. The third section provides descriptive results with a relative discussion followed by the final section which concludes the paper.

Data Selection Procedure

The sample includes the population of foreign and native athletes that had been registered in top-division football clubs of the Greek championship during the seasons 2001-02 until 2012-13. A total number of 2361 athlete were extracted and classified on a cross-sectional basis (in the clubs that participated) and on a time-series basis (for every season during the sample period). This procedure produced a total number of 6593 observations for analysis. All data were extracted from Galanis Sport Data, the official statistical service of the Greek championship and also from the Rec.Sport. Soccer Statistics Association. Player data included details regarding their nationality, on-field position, and the minutes of participation in a given season. Players' nationalities were cross-checked using various websites such as inspots.gr, transfermarket.co.gr, and onsports.gr. Also, player's nationalities were grouped based on their geographical and cultural similarities and the level of the sport's infrastructure in each country. For instance, Cypriot footballers were grouped along with the Greek athletes since they compete as native fellows in the Greek championship.

Furthermore, following the "global areas" regional categorization of Magee and Sugden (2002), athletes were grouped according to specific geographical segments such as the Balkan states which includes countries which share their borders with Greece like Albania, FYROM, Bulgaria, and Turkey and of course countries which formed the former republic of Yugoslavia (Serbia, Montenegro, Bosnia, Croatia, and Slovenia) along with Romania. Another, geographical segment is Western Europe and includes countries with significant infrastructure on the sport and highly competitive championship such as England, Germany, France, Spain, Portugal, Italy, and the Netherlands and countries with common boarders from which they attract significant number of athletes (Andorra, Belgium, Switzerland, Ireland, Malta, and Scotland). Furthermore, the segment of Latin American countries (which present increased migration flows of athletes to Europe and Greece), North American countries and Asian-Oceania countries are included where the latter are characterized by insignificant infrastructure on the sport and low migratory mobility towards Greece. Finally, African countries were divided to Central, South, and North African countries and this differentiation was based on their cultural characteristics.

Furthermore, the best way to describe the utilization of foreign athletes on the league was the minutes of participation of each player in every match instead of the number of appearances in the league within a season. This measure describes coaches' trust and persistence on the player and simultaneously the athletic utility of the specific player for the club. Finally, in order to control the wage difference between natives and athletes we managed to extract the actual salaries for four seasons for natives and migrants in one of the most prestigious clubs in the top division championship. Football player salaries are not publicly available in Greece therefore we are bond not to disclose the name of that club and add any further details which may reveal the clubs' identity. In order to enhance our database regarding player remuneration we used football players' market values (as a proxy of players salaries) extracted from the website transfermarkt.de which provides performance statistics and market values of football players. This database has been used extensively by previous research (Wicker et al., 2013; Kiefer, 2014; Frick, 2007) verifying the validity of the database on the estimates of market values it provides.

Evidence and Discussion

Table 1 present descriptive statistics on the percentage of minutes of participation between migrants and native football players and separated by player position. First of all, native athletes are more than migrants in all playing positions. However, migrant athletes participated more on average on the clubs' official matches. Overall, migrant athletes took part on the 37 per cent of clubs' official game minutes of participation while natives participated only on the 28.2 per cent of clubs' total minutes of participation. Differences are evidenced in all playing positions. Findings on Table 1 suggest that football managers in Greece indicate greater reliance to migrant talents since they utilized them in a greater extent than local athletes. This finding corroborates arguments by Frick (2007) where in the German Bundesliga foreign players were utilized more by their coaches and received higher remuneration compared to native athletes.

Moreover, Table 2 complements the findings in Table 1 and provides the average percentage of migrant player minutes of participation based on their geographical area of origin. Once again, migrant players irrespective of their area of origin are utilized more relative to natives. Specifically, players from Latin American countries are overall more utilized relative to the other regions, while forwards and goalkeeper African players seem to be the first priority of coaches on the clubs' rosters. Finally, defenders from central European countries (originating from well developed championships) are on the front line of participation followed by players from Western Europe. These results jointly can be interpreted as a crowding out effect of migrant football players leading to the reduced utilization of native athletes. Practically, football managers in Greece seemed to indicate greater reliance to migrant talents since they utilized them in a greater extent than local athletes.

Table 1. Minutes of participation between migrants and natives based on player position

Player Position	Natives-Migrants	N	Mean	Median	Max	Min	St.Dev.
Goalkeepers	Migrants	229	36.8	28.7	100	0	33.9
	Natives	526	20.2	3.8	100	0	29.1
Defenders	Migrants	608	42.4	42.1	94.8	0	28.8
	Natives	1315	34.6	29.8	100	0	30.5
Midfielders	Migrants	1079	35.2	30.9	95.9	0	27.5
	Natives	1444	26.9	16.05	100	0	28.4
Forwards	Migrants	638	33.7	27.3	100	0	27.7
	Natives	754	25.3	15.1	96.8	0	27.2
Overall	Migrants	2554	36.7	27.3	100	0	28.6
	Natives	4039	28.2	17.7	100	0	29.4

Note: Descriptive statistics refer to the percentage of players' minutes of participation on their teams official matches for every given season of our sample period. The percentage is estimated by dividing each player actual minutes of participation to his clubs overall minutes on the field.

Table 2. Average percentage of minutes of participation based on players' nationality and position on the field.

Player Position	Greek/Cypriots	West Europe	Central Europe	Balkans	Latin America	Africa	Rest of World
Goalkeepers	20.2	35.3	40.9	31.0	41.1	63.9	17.8
Defenders	34.6	43.6	51.5	38.8	42.3	39.4	41.9
Midfielders	26.9	36.6	25.4	31.1	39.4	34.0	34.7
Forwards	25.3	33.1	31.4	29.4	37.1	38.1	23.3
Overall	28.2	37.9	37.1	32.2	39.5	37.6	32.5

Note: the nationality of each athlete codified following the work of Poli (2010) to regions such as Greece-Cyprus (coded 1), West Europe (coded 3), Central Europe (coded 4), Balkans (coded 6), Latin America (coded 8), Africa (coded 13) and the rest of the world (coded 16).

Finally Table 3 Panel B, presents the level and changes of market values extracted from the transfermarkt web site between migrants and natives. As we can see, migrant athletes are characterized by higher market valuations and higher positive annual changes on their market values relative to native athletes. This fact corroborates findings by Bryson et al. (2014) in the Italian championship that foreign players earn a wage premium over natives. This finding can be attributed to the wage penalty that players suffer due to the employer's monopsony power in the wage setting. Also, data from the actual wages of football players over the seasons 2011-12 to 2014-15 of a well esteemed football club presented on Table 3 Panel A, indicate that migrant athletes earn an actual wage premium above the earnings of native athletes ranging from 8.8 million euro in the season 2014-14 to 11.2 million euro during the season 2011-12. Again, wage evidence corroborates arguments about migrants' contributing to a crowding-out effect on local athletes. These findings can be attributed to the fact that as the recruitment of foreign athletes on the detriment of natives' increases, this can create a speculative behavior in the transfer market. This may undermine clubs' future and even the quality of the sport in national level (Poli, Ravenel, & Besson, 2016).

Table 3. Players' salaries and market values between natives and migrants

Panel A: Players actual salaries of a Greek football club and the difference between natives and migrants (amounts in euro).

Seasons	2011 - 2012	2012 - 2013	2013 - 2014	2014 - 2015
Natives	19.950.000,00	19.850.000,00	29.500.000,00	18.075.000,00
Migrants	31.150.000,00	19.650.000,00	47.850.000,00	26.900.000,00
Difference	**-11200000.00**	**200000,00**	**-18.350.000,00**	**-8825000,00**

Conclusion

The scope of this study was to examine the phenomenon of football players' migration in the Greek championship. We selected data regarding all football players (natives and foreigners) that were registered on the top-division football clubs over the period 2001 to 2013. Descriptive evidence indicated that football player migration has increased significantly from 2001 until 2013 yet foreign athletes' relative numbers are lower than their natives' counterparts. However, foreign athletes are utilized more by their coaches since they have more actual minutes of participation on clubs' official matches and earn higher income than the native football players. This study offers useful policy implication for managers in order to consider talent management as a crucial operation that can sustain clubs' future success and viability. According to Dimitropoulos (2010), football clubs in Greece indicated a significant overspending for playing talent. Club managers need to change their position and focus more on training local athletes considering it as a long-term investment. According to Poli et al. (2016), clubs need to be encouraged not to adhere to the recklessly importation of players. Therefore, the abovementioned findings can be used by club officials to consider the appearances of local and migrant athletes on the field by encouraging and supporting academy training and equal opportunities for local talents. Future research can expand the preliminary analysis by examining the association of player values and wages with their athletic performance. Also, it will be interesting to examine how the UEFA's financial fair play regulation has impacted on managers' decision to invest in human resources.

References

Anagnostopoulos, C., & Senaux, B. (2011). Transforming top-tier football in Greece: The case of the Super League. *Soccer and Society*, 12, 722-736.

Bryson, A., Rossi, G., & Simmons, R. (2014). The migrant wage premium in professional football: A superstar effect? Kyklos, *67(1), 12-28.*

Di Maria, C., & Stryszowski, P. (2009). Migration, human capital accumulation and economic development. *Journal of Development Economics*, 90, 306-313.

Dimitropoulos, P. (2010). The financial performance of the Greek football clubs. *Choregia*, 6, 5-27.

Dubey, J. P. (2000). *La libre circulation des sportifs en Europe*. Bern, Switzerland: Stämpfli.

Frick, B. (2007). The football players' labor market: Empirical evidence from the major European leagues. *Scottish Journal of Political Economy*, 54 (3), 422-446.

Frick, B. (2009). Globalization, and factor mobility: The impact of the 'Bosman-ruling' on player migration in professional soccer. *Journal of Sports Economics*, 10, 88-106.

Frick, B. (2011). Performance, salaries and contract length: empirical evidence from German soccer. *International Journal of Sport Finance*, 6, 87–118.

Kiefer, S. (2014). The impact of the Euro 2012 on popularity and market value of football players. *International Journal of Sport Finance*, 9 (2), 95-110.

Magee, J., & Sugden, J. (2002). The world at their feet: Professional football and international labor migration. *Journal of Sport and Social Issues*, 26, 421-437.

McGovern, P. (2002). Globalization or internalization? Foreign footballers in the English League 1946-1995. *Sociology*, 36, 23-42.

Poli, R. (2010). Understanding globalization through football: the new international division of labour, migratory channels and transnational trade circuits. *International Review for the Sociology of Sport*, 45, 491-506.

Poli, R., & Ravenel, L. (2005). Les frontières de la libre circulation dans le football européen: Vers une mondialisation des flux de joueurs? *Espace Population Société, 3*, 293–303.

Poli, R., Ravenel, L., & Besson, R. (2016). Foreign players in football teams. CIES Football Observatory monthly report, No. 12, February 2016.

Wicker, P., Prinz, J., Weimar, D., Deutscher, C., & Upmann, T. (2013). No pain no gain? Effort and productivity in professional soccer. *International Journal of Sport Finance*, 8 (2), 124-139.

Panel B: Player market values between natives and migrants (amounts in million euro)

Variables	Migrants			Natives		
	Mean	St.Dev.	St.Error	Mean	St.Dev.	St.Error
MV	900.2	1291.8	83.21	448.1	749.3	25.36
ΔMV	109.0	535.8	34.51	60.51	250.5	8.479

Note: MV and ΔMV are the level and annual change of players market value for every year as given by the website transfermarkt.de. Panel A presents the salary expense of the club for every season.

Chapter 5. Mobile Application for Asylum Seekers[1]

Antonios Makris[2], Eleni Petraki[3], Xronis Dimitropoulos[4], Styliani Liberopoulou[5], Konstantinos Tserpes[6], Christos Michalakelis[7]

Abstract

The Greek Asylum Service has been operational for four years, in an environment characterized by rapid developments. The movement of refugees and migrants to Europe, was probably the defining development for our continent in the last two years. In 2015, the great unforeseen refugee influx led to the expansion of the Asylum Service. Our country is legally and morally obliged to inform and offer protection to refugees, irrespective of their numbers and whether they have entered Greece in a regular or irregular fashion.

Towards this direction, the Asylum Service, together with the Harokopio University of Athens worked for a jointly funded action of the Asylum, Migration and Integration Fund (AMIF) 2014-2020. The purpose of this action is the design, development and maintenance of a mobile application and the target group would be the asylum seekers who move or are transferred from the country's external borders, and especially the individuals with a refugee profile.

Keywords: Greek Asylum Service, Asylum mobile application, asylum seekers, refugees

Introduction

The Asylum Service ("Asylum Service | Ministry of Migration Policy," n.d.) has been operational for four years, characterised by the movement of refugees and migrants to Europe on a scale unprecedented in recent European history (Eurostat, 2016) ("Asylum in the EU Member States First time asylum applicants registered in the EU Member States," 2016). The great unforeseen refugee influx of 2015 led to the rapid expansion of the Asylum Service

---

[1] This paper and the mobile application was supported by the Greek Asylum Service, Hellenic Ministry of Migration Policy. Special thanks to the Director, Mrs Maria Stavropoulou for her support.
[2] Antonios Makris is PhD Candidate, Department of Informatics and Telematics, Harokopio University of Athens, Omirou 9, 177 78, Tavros, Athens, Greece, E-mail: amakris@hua.gr
[3] Eleni Petraki is Public Relations and Communication Officer, Greek Asylum Service, Leof. Panagioti Kanellopoulou 2 Athens, 115 27, Greece, Email: e.petraki@asylo.gov.gr & press.asylo@asylo.gov.gr
[4] Xronis Dimitropoulos is PhD Candidate, Department of Informatics and Telematics, Harokopio University of Athens, Omirou 9, 177 78, Tavros, Athens, Greece, E-mail: xronis.dm@gmail.com
[5] Styliani Liberopoulou is MSc Student, Department of Informatics and Telematics, Harokopio University of Athens, Omirou 9, 177 78, Tavros, Athens, Greece, E-mail: stelinn@gmail.com
[6] Konstantinos Tserpes is Assistant Professor, Department of Informatics and Telematics, Harokopio University of Athens, Omirou 9, 177 78, Tavros, Athens, Greece, E-mail:tserpes@hua.gr..
[7] Christos Michalakelis is Assistant Professor, Department of Informatics and Telematics, Harokopio University of Athens, Omirou 9, 177 78, Tavros, Athens, Greece, E-mail:michalak@hua.gr

("Asylum Applications -Gender and Age ranges," 2013). The Service's human capital increased significantly, partly thanks to European funds.

The Asylum Service understands fully the importance of the timeliness, authoritativeness and reliability of the information provided to asylum seekers, especially in an environment characterized by rapid developments in asylum law and practice. At the beginning of 2016, the Asylum Service signed with the Harokopio University of Athens, Department of Informatics and Telematics, the agreement for a jointly funded action of the Asylum, Migration and Integration Fund (AMIF) 2014-2020. The purpose of this action is the design, creation and maintenance of a mobile application and the target group would be asylum seekers who are in Greece.

The application draws on already existing material, its updating and its projection in a new user-friendly environment. Additional information on available services has been added. The visitor will be able to see information, activities and procedures concerning the Asylum Service, all analytically displayed so that he/she can be updated on everything he/she needs to know to navigate the asylum procedures in Greece easily. The projected material is multi-lingual. The application is compatible with the most popular mobile operating systems. Into this context, the production of 10 short videos films with instructions and guidance concerning the asylum procedure in Greece have been designed to be uploaded on the mobile application.

The installation and use of the application is free. The downloading of the application and the data updates require an active internet connection, but the application can operate even in an off-line mode. On 9 May 2016, in the course of a one-day conference organized by the Asylum Service, the initiative concerning the mobile application was publicly presented.

Application requirements

According to the requirements of the application the user should have access to information, activities and procedures concerning the Asylum Service, all analytically displayed so that he/she acquires the ability to be updated on everything he/she needs to know in order to "function" as an asylum seeker. The application would ensure easy and quick navigation, as well as the flow of the necessary information so that the user understands the meaning of "asylum" and "international protection". The application should also support multi-lingual material and it should be compatible with the most popular mobile operating systems. Application *downloading,* and data updates require an active internet connection, but the application must operate even in an off-line mode.

In a volatile environment, affected by uncertain factors such as war, foreign policy of many countries and mainly the people, it is obvious that data are very dynamic, changing on a continuous basis and therefore procedures must adapt to each time's conditions. Thus, these data should be offered in a reliable and timely way, since their main purpose concerns refugee survival and their everyday life.

The continuously emerging technology and mobile devices give an excellent opportunity to achieve this objective: users can install the application in any available device and operating system (Android, iOS, Windows) and gain access to information about the procedures and other crucial topics.

The main challenges and problems that had to be overcome during the design of the application can be summarized as follows:

•   Adaptation to user specific features (language, cultural background etc) since it is a multi-ethnic mosaic of people from different cultural, educational, national and social background.

•   Usability (maps, transport, multimedia etc) and what it implies in the light of the above challenge. For example, content direction in the Arabic language follows a "right to left" direction and important issues are expected to be found on the upper right corner of the screen, which is not applicable in the case of the English or French language.

•   Adapting to current conditions and data (operation without Internet access, dynamic content update). The purpose is to keep the functionality transparent to any changes.

•   Improving of service quality driven by the real needs of these people

To meet these challenges the application was suitably designed in order to adapt to the user specific features and provide reliable and on-time information. The application supports multilingualism and the supported languages are English, Greek, French, Arabic, Farsi/Dari, Tigrinya, Amharic and Urdu/Punjabi. All information provided in Arabic, Farsi/Dari, Urdu/Punjabi are provided on a "right to left: direction. An example is shown in Figure 1 as well as the same example in English.

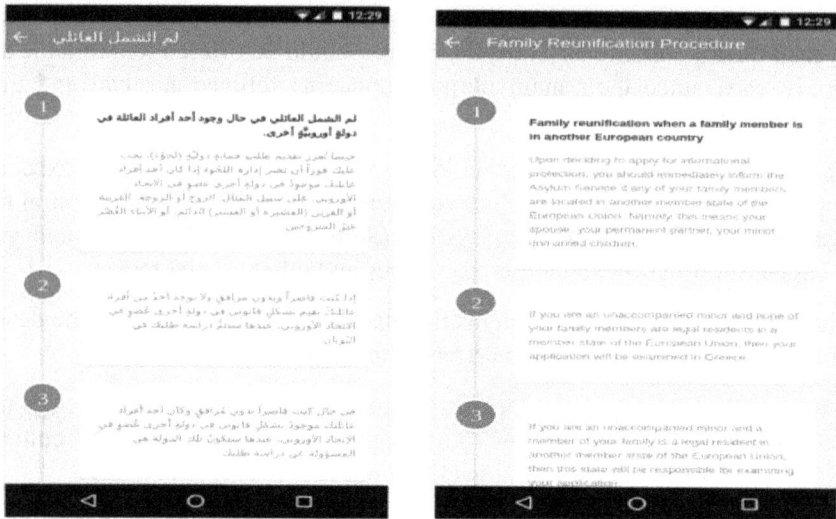

Figure 1. Example of content direction in Arabic and English

The incorporated maps are supplied with points of interest (POIs) and facilities, as well as flow charts about beneficiaries of international protection, links of international organizations and agencies, transport maps and videos with the asylum procedure. In terms of adaptability, the application's design was based on the assumption that users may not have a constant internet access. Additionally, the completion of the asylum process is a moving target because of the ever-changing high level policies the Asylum Agencies are meant to implement. Despite their remarkable effort, the interfacing and interaction with refugees is suffering from constant changes in the political agenda of large number of involved parties, including states, political parties, societies and individuals. The asylum seekers definitely need a smoother and direct way to keep track of the procedure changes and a more familiar interfacing with the Agencies.

The content relies on a dynamic database maintained by a web-based administration system (portal). The information is locally stored into the device, thus minimizing the need for a continuous internet connection. An internet connection is required during the first time the user downloads, installs and launches the application, in order to cache the contents from the database. All information and most of the services are then cached locally into user's device and can be displayed even when the user is offline. Every time the user enters the application the application automatically seeks and downloads all updates. If there no connection the application operates based on the last visited information until the user gains access to the internet and then updated again. This approach ensures the reliability and the on-time provision of the information provided to the end users. The architecture described above is shown in Figure 2.

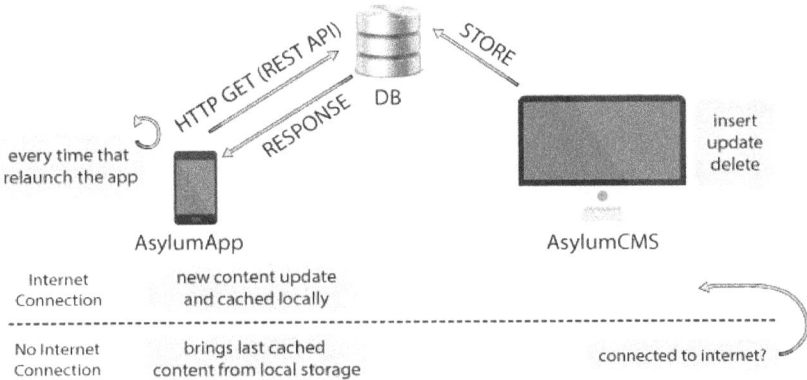

Figure 2. System architecture

It is important to mention that the application does not keep, or otherwise edit sensitive or personal data. The only information that is anonymously stored, only for statistical reasons, is the preferred language and the device last known location.

The application

The application development was based on AngularJS (Google, 2015), AJAX ("jQuery Learning Center," n.d.) and Javascript ("JavaScript," n.d.) using the Ionic framework (Drifty Co., 2016), phpMyAdmin ("phpMyAdmin," 2017) and the CodeIgniter php framework (British Columbia Institute of Technology, 2016).

Information and views of the application

Application users can access information regarding the asylum procedures and especially those related to the necessary steps for asylum registration (international protection), pre-registration, relocation and family reunification. Reliable and timely information is provided to third-country nationals, who are currently in Greece and wish to submit a claim for international protection. Information about the weather conditions, public transportation and general information for Greece are also provided. In addition, there is a short dictionary of Greek words for refugees, aiming at helping them for their interaction with local populations, a translation tool, contact details, useful links and notifications from the Asylum Service. There are also several images that help the user to point about food, facilities, health etc. Subsequently, users are able to see on a map the points of open accommodation facilities (Refugee hosting centre and Hotspots) as well as the points of interest in Greece

(NGO's, medical centers, hospitals, local authorities, asylum units and regional asylum offices).

Finally, the user can be informed about the asylum Skype schedule and make a direct call to the relevant asylum service office. The application allows "dynamic" Skype calls, into the sense that the user is able to contact through Skype if the asylum Skype service is able to serve on this day, for the preferred language and within the servicing hours, according to the timetable, which is also stored into the application. If a Skype call is not available at this time, the application informs the user about the next available time slot.

A representative set of the application's views, regarding the functionality and services that provided to the users, are shown below:

Figure 3 illustrates the main view of the application. The user can access the following information: "Asylum: step by step", "Preregistration", "Relocation" and "Family Reunification". Users are also able to see, on an interactive map, the points of "Open Accommodation Facilities" (Refugee hosting centers and Hotspots) as well as "Points of Interest" in Greece (NGO's, hospitals, local authorities, asylum units, regional asylum offices and the international organization of migration). There is also a short Greek dictionary - "Mini Lexicon", a translation tool - "Translation", information about public transport – "Transport", weather information -*" Weather"* and general info about Greece. Finally, there is a view - "Point it" which helps the users to point at something they need to access, e.g. food, milk, shelter, medical help etc.

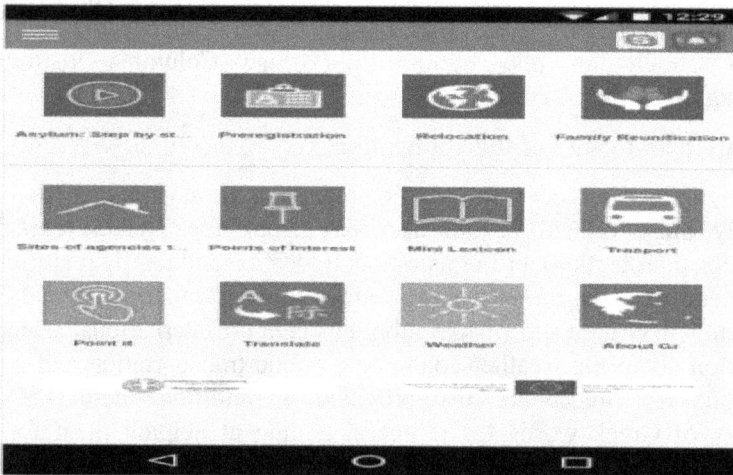

Figure 3. Main view of the application

Figure 4 shows the views about the procedures (a) "Asylum: step by step", (b) "Preregistration" (c) "Mini lexicon, (d) "Point it ", (e) points of open accommodation facilities map and (f) points of interest in Greece, such as

NGO's, hospitals, local authorities, asylum units, regional asylum offices and the international organization of migration.

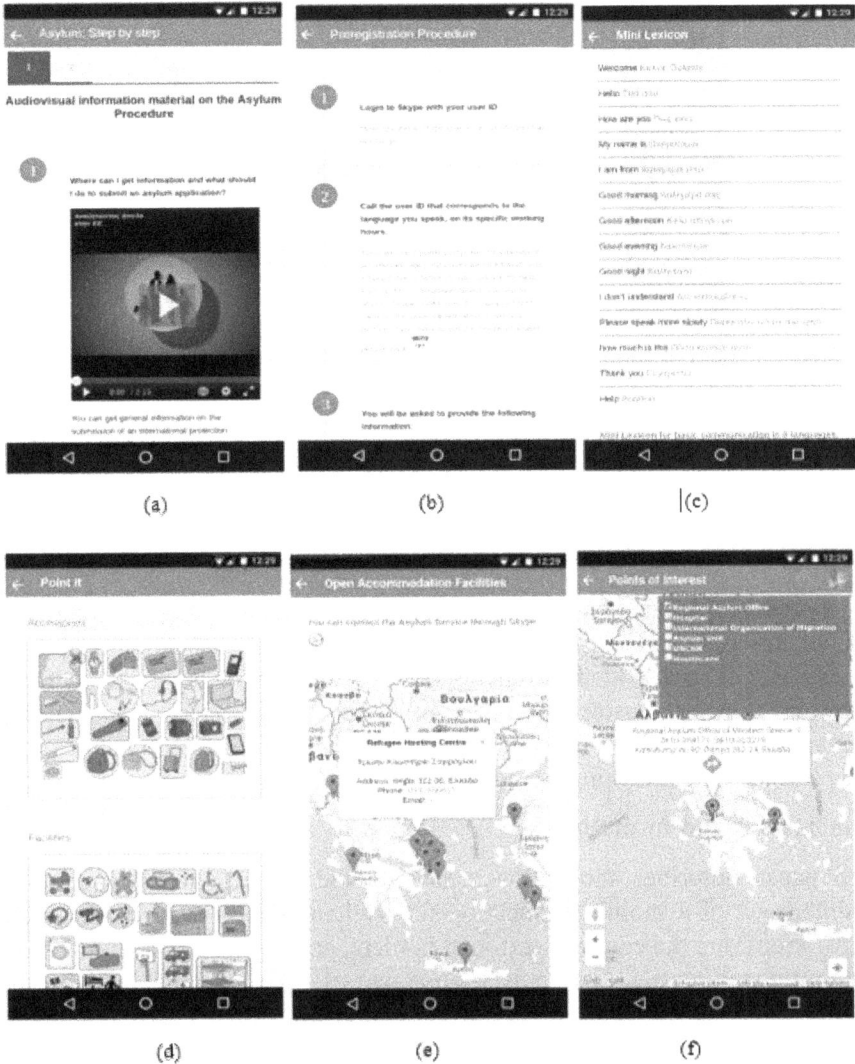

(a) (b) |(c)

(d) (e) (f)

Figure 4. Procedures (a) Asylum: step by step, (b) Preregistration, (c) Mini lexicon, (d) Point it (e) Open accommodation facilities, (f) Points of interest in Greece

Administration system

The administration system "Asylum CMS" was developed seeking to solve two major issues of the mobile application, the support of multilingualism and the need of a daily content updating. Maintenance of the "Asylum" mobile application includes: Charts, Content Items, POIs, Facilities, Notifications, Skype Schedule and Media Manager.

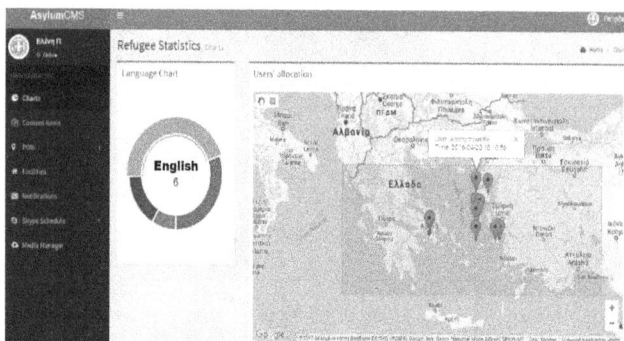

Figure 5. Charts with languages and last known location

As an example, Figure 5 illustrates the refugee statistics of the mobile application users and consists of the language chart diagram.

The dynamic content update is one of the most essential functions and the reason is that gives the ability to manage all the content of the mobile application with simplicity.

As already mentioned, one aim of this project is the development of an application that supports dynamic content management. Skype scheduling is an example of such a kind of functionality, since it has to be updated almost every day. For that reason, administration system provides a simple and quick way to add a new Skype line either at the schedule of relocation either at the Skype schedule of Asylum/Preregistration.

Conclusions and future work

The paper describes the action regarding the design, development and maintenance of a mobile application for asylum seekers who move or are transferred from the country's external borders, and especially the individuals with a refugee profile. The application is part of a joined action between the Asylum Service and the Harokopio University of Athens, Department of Informatics and Telematic and it is funded by the Asylum, Migration and Integration Fund (AMIF) 2014-2020.

The application provides official and up-to-date information regarding the asylum procedures, including pre-registration, relocation and family reunification, as well as useful information such as weather conditions, public transportation, a short dictionary of Greek words, useful links and notifications from the asylum service. There are also several images that help the user to point about food, facilities, health etc. Subsequently, users are able to see on a map the points of open accommodation facilities (Refugee hosting centre and

Hotspots) as well as the points of interest in Greece (NGO's, medical centers, hospitals, local authorities, asylum units and regional asylum offices). Among the important characteristics of the application is that the user can be informed about the asylum Skype schedule and make a direct call to the relevant asylum service office.

Among the directions of the future work is the gathering of usage statistics and their consequent analysis, in order to derive useful information regarding its acceptance and diffusion among the asylum seekers and useful information regarding the asylum seekers themselves. This information can be, among others, a valuable input for the improvement of the offered services and a helpful decision-making tool.

References

Asylum Applications -Gender and Age ranges. (2013). Retrieved from http://asylo.gov.gr/en/wp-content/uploads/2017/03/Greek_Asylum_Service_Statistical_Data_EN.pdf

Asylum in the EU Member States First time asylum applicants registered in the EU Member States. (2016). Retrieved from http://ec.europa.eu/eurostat/documents/2995521/7773598/3-15122016-BP-EN.pdf/30f7b06b-1634-44dd-964c-13a5f9c436eb

Asylum Applications -Gender and Age ranges. (2013). Retrieved from http://asylo.gov.gr/en/wp-content/uploads/2017/03/Greek_Asylum_Service_Statistical_Data_EN.pdf

Asylum in the EU Member States First time asylum applicants registered in the EU Member States. (2016). Retrieved from http://ec.europa.eu/eurostat/documents/2995521/7773598/3-15122016-BP-EN.pdf/30f7b06b-1634-44dd-964c-13a5f9c436eb

Asylum Service | Ministry of Migration Policy. (n.d.). Retrieved from http://asylo.gov.gr/en/

British Columbia Institute of Technology. (2016). CodeIgniter Web Framework. Retrieved from https://codeigniter.com/

Drifty Co. (2016). Build Amazing Native Apps and Progressive Web Apps with Ionic Framework and Angular. Retrieved from https://ionicframework.com/

Eurostat. (2016). *European Union: Asylum in the EU Member States* (Vol. 46). Retrieved from http://ec.europa.eu/eurostat/documents/2995521/7921609/3-16032017-BP-EN.pdf/e5fa98bb-5d9d-4297-9168-d07c67d1c9e1

Google. (2015). AngularJS — Superheroic JavaScript MVW Framework. Retrieved from https://angularjs.org/

JavaScript. (n.d.). Retrieved from https://www.javascript.com/

jQuery Learning Center. (n.d.). Retrieved from https://learn.jquery.com/ajax/

phpMyAdmin. (2017). Retrieved from https://www.phpmyadmin.net/

Chapter 6. Massive Displacement Meets Cyberspace: How Information and Communication Technologies are elping Refugees and Migrants and How We Can Do Better[1]

Joseph G. Bock, Kevin McMahon, Ziaul Haque[*]

Abstract

Since the global response to the earthquake in Haiti in 2010, the use of Information and Communication Technologies (ICTs) for humanitarian assistance has grown dramatically. These technologies include mobile phones, applications ("apps") installed on phones, and computer connectivity or internet-based sites which receive data from or send it to phones. We call these collectively "platforms". Employing them has the potential to improve efforts to assist displaced people, or to liberate them in being more able to help each other, or both. The magnitude and visibility of the current refugee and migrant crisis has yielded a rich harvest of new platforms, a survey of which we cover in this paper. Similar to the acronym ICT4D, commonly used to denote the use of ICTs for development, we refer to the technologies in this paper collectively as ICTs for refugees and migrants, or simply ICT4RM. And while platform development has resulted in a patchwork of initiatives—an electronic version of "letting a thousand flowers bloom"—there are patterns emerging as to which flowers grow and have "staying power" as compared to ones that wilt and die. In hopes of providing guidance to would-be developers, we offer explanations for what leads to a successful ICT4RM initiative.

Keywords: Crowdsourcing, digital apps, machine learning, ICT4D, Information and Communication Technologies, social media.

Introduction

There is a sea change occurring within the humanitarian sector which is reflected in how the world is responding to massive displacement of people. Mobile phones have been around for decades, but their ubiquitous use, including by displaced people themselves, has increased exponentially. So have the capabilities of the phones themselves. We now see less *basic phones* that can only be used for sending text messages and verbal communications. We are seeing more *feature phones* that not only allow for texts and verbal communication, but also have cameras, can record and send pictures and video, and have the capability to browse the internet and access Geographical Information System (GIS) data. And we are seeing ever greater use of *smart phones* which are also capable of downloading and saving various applications ("apps") and have the ability to do more complex functions (like editing a document).

People have to be able to afford a phone, so income level is one factor in their ownership. And owning and using mobile phones tends to increase among

[1] We are grateful to the Fulbright Foundation in Greece and the Bureau of Educational and Cultural Affairs of the U.S. State Department which supported author's work in Greece to assist the Mayor of Athens and his staff in responding to the influx of displaced people during 2015-2016.
[*] Authors are based at School of Conflict Management, Peacebuilding and Development, Kennesaw State University, United States. Contact email: jbock2@kennesaw.edu.

people surrounded by violent conflict. The U.S.'s Central Intelligence Agency estimates that 80 percent of people in Syria, for instance, have mobile phones, as of 2014. Among people in Afghanistan, roughly 60% have a mobile phone, as of 2015 (2017).

The magnitude and visibility of the current refugee and migrant crisis has yielded a rich harvest of new platforms, which involve mobile phones, applications ("apps") installed on phones, and computer connectivity or internet-based sites which receive data from or send it to phones. Similar to the acronym ICT4D, commonly used to denote the use of ICTs for development, we refer to platforms in this paper collectively as ICTs for Refugees and Migrants, or simply ICT4RM. And while platform development has resulted in a patchwork of initiatives—an electronic version of "letting a thousand flowers bloom"—there are patterns emerging as to which flowers grow and have "staying power" as compared to ones that wilt and die. In hopes of providing guidance to would-be developers, we offer explanations for what leads to a successful ICT4RM platform

The use of these platforms is viewed by some humanitarian professionals as a quantum leap in the potential of both humanitarian efficiency and effectiveness, expanding what outsiders can do in global solidarity while also allowing insiders enhanced capacity to help each other. Witness a report by Harvard Humanitarian Initiative entitled *Disaster Relief 2.0*, as if a new generation of humanitarian assistance approaches has been born. Similarly, a new term has been coined that packages this phenomenon well: *liberation technology*, which Diamond has defined as technologies that "empower individuals, facilitate independent communication and mobilization and strengthen an emergent civil society" (2010, p. 71).

Refugees and migrants have described mobile phone capabilities and places to recharge them as "even more important than food" (Benton & Glennie, 2016). In a UN High Commissioner for Refugees (UNHCR) report, written jointly with Accenture, numerous attempts at using mobile phones and internet-based platforms are described. The effectiveness of the ICT4RM deployments have met with varying degrees of success (UNHCR, 2017).

It is important to note that ICTs can, of course, be used for a variety of purposes and can have wide ranging impacts. For many people in the global south, their world has shrunk because of what they have seen and interacted with on the internet and on their phone screens. This has become a driver of emigration. As Collier points out, for a "society that has long been stagnant and impoverished, life, in the sense of opportunity, really is elsewhere, and its young people are fully aware of it…technology and a globalized youth culture expose them to an inviting world just beyond their reach" (2014, p. 222). ICTs are also used for nefarious purposes, such as the coordination of looting by mobs of enraged young people in Manchester, England in 2012 (Collier, 2014).

Methodology

With each platform we report on in this paper, we assess their level of functionality. Some of them function only with one-way communication— typically a traditional website aimed at unidirectional information dissemination. There are others that facilitate two-way communication, such as between tutors and refugees and migrants, or between camp-based health workers and medical experts in other countries. Other ICT4RM initiatives take this two-way communication a step further by producing a collective good (in the sense originally explained by Olson, 1971; and more recently by Martin-Shields, 2016), based on crowdsourced information (with a wide range of people, the "crowd," contributing data), such as a digital map of assets available to, and hazards to be avoided by, displaced people. These involve two-way information-sharing, as well as communication to a group, depicting what that communication has helped to create. Finally, there are ICT4RM deployments that go yet another step further, involving two-way communication, crowdsourcing and machine learning (using artificial intelligence) for a collective good to benefit a group based on communication with that group and mathematically discernable patterns.

Finally, we assess each ICT4RM deployment relative to the degree to which each involved refugees and migrants in the design of the initiative. We then identify whether these displaced people had an ongoing role in making decisions about how the deployment unfolds, is refined, and expands. As explained by Papacoannou (2014), the involvement of "beneficiaries" in the establishment and governance of ICT initiatives is critical to the success of an intervention. In the most ideal circumstance, inclusiveness involves marginalized people having the authority to decide who will be involved in the design, modification and expansion of an ICT4RM deployment, even if they choose to involve non-traditional people who are outside the current power structure (Papacoannou, 2014).

Survey of Ict4rm Deployments

In this paper, our focus is on the benevolent uses of ICT4RM. We concentrate primarily on ICTs that help refugees and migrants navigate their new worlds once they have left their home countries. We have identified nine broad categories of these ICTs, recognizing that there is often overlap between them. The categories are: asylum processing; information gathering and dissemination; family reunification; accessing government services;

education; language training, and skill development; health; cash assistance and livelihoods, and; integration.

Asylum Processing

Refugees who feel they have a legitimate claim for asylum can be aided by ICTs in filing for it. But they also need to know where to do so, and social networking sites like Facebook provide forewarning of restrictions in asylum processes. For instance, in Europe, there is a requirement that people seeking asylum must file a claim where they first arrive. For refugees entering in Greece who aspire to be located in Germany, for instance, social media thus works against the requirement to register where they arrive initially because of fear they will be required to stay in that location.

Tailored ICT platforms have been created to facilitate the filing process. In 2014, the Asylum Service in Attica, Greece started using Skype to set up appointments for registering asylum applications. The aim was to improve access to the registration process while minimizing the time people had to stand in lines. In addition, the Asylum Service began to implement "fast-track" processing of applications of first, though not subsequent, asylum claims. According to the Greek Council for Refugees, asylum claims are registered and processed in one day. But problems were encountered in getting appointments through Skype, resulting in protests by frustrated refugees and migrants.[2]

By June 2015, using Skype to set up an appointment or to make an application for asylum was limited to people literate in English, French, Farsi/Dari, Arabic, Urdu/Punjabi and Bangla. People seeking asylum speaking other languages had to set up appointments by standing in line and meeting in person with the Asylum Service.

On the Turkish side of the Adriatic, Mobile Legal Info Service has been developed. It is a brainchild of Souktel, a Palestinian mobile phone firm specializing in SMS services.[3] In partnership with the American Bar Association, its staff of humanitarian, legal, and technical specialists provide a text message service offering legal advice to Syrians in Turkey.

Information Gathering and Dissemination

A consortium of international humanitarian organizations and Google have developed a website, Refugee.Info, to help refugees and migrants acquire

---

2Asylum Information Database (n.d.). Registration of the asylum application: Greece. Retrieved from http://www.asylumineurope.org/reports/country/GREece/asylum-procedure/procedures/. Accessed: 28.02.2017.

3 See, Souktel. Retrieved from http://www.souktel.org/media/news/syrian-refugees-aba-souktel-launch-mobile-legal-info-servicem. Accessed: 18.05. 2017.

asylum and other legal services, how to get transportation, maps, where to find schools and other educational opportunities, how to stay safe, where to get healthcare, and who to contact in an emergency. It also disseminates important updates.[4] It runs on the Crisis Info Hub, a content management system that uses Google Docs.[5] It provides information in Serbia, Macedonia, and Greece (Athens, Lesvos and Kos). Users can "like" Refugee.Info's Facebook page for updates, and can also send messages to Refugee.Info. It is crowdsourcing information about services, opportunities, challenges, and dangers. The website can be used by refugees and migrants who are literate in English, Arabic and Farsi.

Google has also worked with UNHCR and Mercy Corps to create a digital display for refugees and migrants in Macedonia of frequently asked questions in a mobile application which they call Translation Cards. As explained by UNHCR, "[t]hese simple audio-visual flashcards allow refugees to hear pre-translated answers to their common questions spoken aloud in their own language."[6]

UNHCR has created the Refugee Assistance and Information System (RAIS), a database for refugee assistance. Focusing on assistance in Lebanon, Jordan and Egypt, this system has ten modules that include "a smart search function to find and check refugee profiles; an improved referral system to facilitate communication between partners; an enhanced reports system for keeping track of assistance; mobile data collection so that information gathered during house visits can be uploaded immediately; and a service to manage the appeal for refugee assistance."[7] While there have been complaints that RAIS does not capture other needed information, it has been used extensively and promises to be an integral part of UNHCR's ICT services. According to UNCHR, "RAIS is being used by more than 200 implementing and operational partners in Jordan, Egypt, and Lebanon. Already the system has ... [been used] to help over 1.6 million displaced peoples within the three countries: over 90,000 in Egypt, 815,000 in Jordan, and 600,000 in Lebanon.[8]

---

4 See Refugee.Info. Retrieved from http://www.souktel.org/media/news/syrian-refugees-aba-souktel-launch-mobile-legal-info-servicem. Accessed 28.02. 2017.

5 Crisis Info Hub. Retrieved from https://github.com/google/crisis-info-hub. Accessed February 28, 2017.

6 See UNHCR. Translation Cards. Retrieved from http://www.unhcr.org/innovation/labs_post/translation-cards/. Accessed 24.5.2017.

7 See UNHCR. RAIS: Refugee assistance and information system. Retrieved from http://www.unhcr.org/innovation/labs_post/rais-refugee-assistance-information-system/. Accessed: 26.02. 2017.

8See, UNHCR. RAIS. Retrieved from http://www.unhcr.org/innovation/labs_post/rais-refugee-assistance-information-system/. Accessed 27.05.2017.

A different ICT4RM application was launched by UNHCR in Costa Rica which provides information on services available to refugees and migrants. The website help.unhcr.org was subsequently expanded to include Australia, New Zealand, Niger and Pacific island countries, covering a broad range of services including asylum processing, resettlement, what to do if someone is detained, how to find missing persons, educational programming, legal aid, help for people with disabilities, microcredit, and where to get help finding a job.[9] In addition to disseminating information via websites, this initiative has also communicated via text, using FrontlineCloud, crowdsourcing to assess the needs of displaced people while communicating about services available to meet those needs.[10] One flaw in this platform is that, as it was configured initially, the system did not notify senders of inactive phone numbers. Roughly 40 percent of messages that are sent are not reaching a phone user. In addition, the unknown number of the sender was confusing. To correct these problems, UNHCR advertised the number they were using, and created boxes where people could drop in their numbers to be added to the dissemination list.

In a different use of texting services for refugees, UNHCR's work with Norwegian Refugee Council in the Za'atari camp in Jordan, estimated to be the world's second-largest camp, showed that Facebook postings by refugees that communicated to other refugees is more credible than text messages sent by humanitarian organizations. It was also determined that face-to-face meetings, especially with specific demographic groups (such as women), continue to be valuable for information dissemination and feedback.[11]

UNHCR has also partnered with United Postal Service (UPS) to create a mobile tracking system to work in conjunction with its registration database, recording which people have received what assistance. In their pilot test in Jordan, they found that internet access inconsistency and the volume of data synchronization rendered this system, called UPS ReliefLink, unworkable. In Ethiopia, in contrast, in a subsequent use of this system, it worked well in keeping track of the distribution of blankets and sleeping mats to approximately 700 refugees.[12]

---

9 See UNHCR–Help. Retrieved from http://help.unhcr.org/languages/en/. Accessed: 26.02. 2017.

10 See UNHCR-Innovation (n.d.). Ascend. Retrieved http://www.unhcr.org/innovation/labs_post/ascend/, Accessed: 26.02. 2017.

11 See, UNHCR-Innovation (n.d.). Social media and SMS outreach: Leveraging social media and SMS technology to communicate with refugees in Za'atari camp. Retrieved from http://www.unhcr.org/innovation/labs_post/social-media-and-sms-outreach/. Accessed: 26.02. 2017.

12 See, UPS ReliefLink: Linking refugee registration with distribution data collection. Retrieved from http://www.unhcr.org/innovation/labs_post/ups-relieflink-program/, Accessed: 26.02. 2017.

Similarly, the International Federation of Red Cross and Red Crescent Societies (ICRC), in partnership with Trilogy International Partners, a wireless telecommunications company, has developed Trilogy Emergency Relief Application (TERA). It is an "SMS text system designed for two way communication between disaster affected people and aid agencies."[13] According to ICRC, TERA sends out messages: "To give early warnings of floods, hurricanes and other natural disasters; To provide targeted information on where to find medical help, clean water, food, shelter; To notify victims about vaccination programmes or changes in the aid services being offered; To give detailed advice on a range of issues such as hygiene, avoiding fraud, caring for affected people; [and] To get feedback on the beneficiaries needs and experience of relief services." TERA receives inbound texts that give "feedback to show where aid of various types is most needed… [using] 'fuzzy' keyword recognition to automatically respond to a variety of questions."[14] This latter capability is an example of a platform using machine learning in that it can handle "fuzzy logic," as in when a user enters a word that is different than the one the system was designed with initially, such as in learning that "James" can also be "Jim."

Welcome to Dresden is a smartphone app developed by two IT companies in Dresden, Germany. It provides information to refugees about registration with the local municipality, getting health insurance, and navigating other services.[15]

A Swedish initiative, Setel.in,[16] seeks to bring existing apps and services under one roof. It houses at least twenty platforms which provide customized mobile-based services on information, social, employment, language, education, media and communication, housing, and health.

One of the newer platforms, reflecting how people share what they have by using ICTs (otherwise known as the "sharing economy") is Home4Refugees.[17]

---

13 See, International Federation of Red Cross and Red Crescent (n,d.). TERA (Trilogy Emergency Relief Application) and beneficiary communication. Retrieved from http://www.ifrc.org/en/what-we-do/beneficiary-communications/tera/, Accessed: 26.02. 2017.

14 See, TERA (Trilogy Emergency Relief Application) and beneficiary communication. Retrieved from http://www.ifrc.org/en/what-we-do/beneficiary-communications/tera/, Accessed: 26.02. 2017.

15 See, Smartphone app launched to help asylum seekers in Dresden. Retrieved from https://www.theguardian.com/world/2015/aug/17/smartphone-app-launched-help-asylum-seekers-dresden-germany. Accessed: 18.05. 2017.

16 See, Setelin: Great resources when you settle in Sweden. Retrieved from https://www.setel.in/#/app/categories. Accessed: 19.05.2017.

17 See Home4Refugees. Retrieved from https://www.home4refugees.org/. Accessed: 19.05.2017.

It connects homeowners with spare rooms with refugee applicants. It is similar to AirBnb, but is much narrower and nuanced.

Family Reunification

Trace the Face[18] allows refugees to post photos of themselves and state which family member they are looking for and the circumstances of the disappearance. The platform is run by the ICRC. Another ICT4RM reunification initiative is Refunite. It is a Twitter-based application designed to help reunite friends and families.[19]

Accessing Government Services

One of the more robust ICT4RM areas being developed is focused on helping displaced people navigate government bureaucracies. As Beth Noveck noted in *Smart Citizens, Smarter State* (2015), there is a vast supply of 'technology of expertise' inside the membership of any citizenry that can often be reached by internal crowdsourcing for solutions."

A recently developed comprehensive service is the German app Bureaucrazy.[20] It was developed by Syrian immigrant programmers and has the secondary benefit of assisting German born citizens of all types, providing guidance on how to handle administrative tasks and challenges. Similarly, Mobilearn[21] is a system to help rapid integration and settlement in the UK, while an EU-wide targeted platform in operation now is Ankommen.[22]

Services Advisor[23] is a Canadian platform developed by PeaceGeeks in partnership with UNHCR. It aggregates available services. These include descriptions and locations of where to get food, health services, and shelter. Usable for both Arabic and English readers, it uses a digital mapping tool to depict locations.

---

18 Race the Face. Retrieved from https://familylinks.icrc.org/europe/en/Pages/Home.aspx. Accessed: 19.05.2017.

19 See REFUNITE. Retrieved from https://twitter.com/refunite?lang=en. Accessed: 19.05.2017.

20 Kirchner. S. (2016, August 9). Syrian refugees create app to help navigate German bureaucracy. Washington Post. Retrieved from https://www.washingtonpost.com/news/worldviews/wp/2016/08/09/syrian-refugees-create-app-to-help-navigate-german-bureaucracy/?utm_term=.20cf3c705c13. Accessed: 19.05.2017.

21 See, Mobilearn. Retrieved from https://se.mobilearn.com/en/. Accessed: 19.04.2017.

22 See Ankommen, Retrieved from https://ankommenapp.de/?lang=en. Accessed: 19.04.2017.

23 See, Service Advisor. Retrieved from http://jordan.servicesadvisor.org/#/?language=EN. Accessed: 19.05.2017.

Montreal-based Nonimo Technologies has created Botler, a knowledge-sharing platform for migrants and refugees entering Quebec, Canada. This platform uses artificial intelligence and functions interactively. The technology, otherwise known as a "chatbot" (a robot that responds based on user-provided information) asks questions and users enter answers. The chatbot then informs the user about eligibility, and offers lists of documents needed for registering for a given service (Lohr, 2017).[24]

Education, Language Training, and Skill Development

Educational initiatives can assist refugees and migrants in developing skills, becoming proficient in a language, acquiring cultural awareness, testing for diplomas from primary-through-tertiary degrees and certificates, and in developing marketable skills. Conducting educational programs—even with undocumented, irregular migrants—is much less fraught with legal challenges than when employing people who lack work permits. Thus, education programs provide constructive activities for people looking for something meaningful to do, even if they do not have a job.

It is important to recognize, however, that refugees and migrants are mainly using ICTs for communicating. In a three-country study, Reichel, Siegel, and Andreo found that refugees and migrants were not using ICTs for "looking for a job, getting their qualifications recognized [or] learning the language of the host country...." (2015, p. 6). Couple this with the dearth of training that refugees and migrants reported getting. Within the three countries, 92% had not received generic training for employment, and 84% said they had received no job-related training (2015, p. 111).

The authors of the three-country study conclude that governments have an important role to play in enhancing both employability and integration of refugees and migrants. Specifically, they argue that "governments could provide on-line access to important information and on-line services for migrants through user friendly multi-lingual websites: information on access to rights and services available for migrants, including health and education services, on-line services including on-line language courses, opportunities for jobs and recognition of qualifications" (2015, p. 124).

AMFI International, based in Celano, Italy, is developing on-line educational programs that benefit refugees and migrants.[25] However, their programming

---

24 The chatbot can be found at botler.ai. For more information, see the video on Breakfast Television. Retrieved fromhttp://www.btmontreal.ca/videos/botler-ai-chatbot-answers-quebec-immigration-questions/.Accessed:10.05. 2017.

25 See AMFI International. Retrieved from http://www.amfinternational.org/. Accessed: 22.02. 2017. Regarding a specific course on using ICTs to benefit refugees and migrants, see

thus far has been to educate educators about how to work effectively with refugees and migrants. They are not providing educational services to refugees and migrants directly.

UNHCR, in partnership with BrainPOP, has developed educational programs for refugees in Malaysia using tablets that have preloaded videos and learning apps. Slow internet speeds, however, resulted in student and teacher frustration, and standardized tests showed mixed results. As UNHCR concluded, "Some students improved in their mid-year examination, while others did worse than before. There was no clear evidence on whether the tablets had helped to increase academic performance. And while the two schools spent less on procuring reading materials, overall project costs made up more than those savings."[26]

In 2013, UNHCR, working closely with the Vodafone Foundation, with help from Huawei and Safaricom, launched a pilot project with Lutheran World Federation to provide internet connectivity and tablets to schools in Dabaab, a settlement in Kenya not far from the border with Somalia, where roughly 350,000 people are living who fled poverty, violence, and drought. The project focuses on primary, secondary and vocational education, creating "Instant Network classrooms" that have solar-powered batteries with generator backup, tablets, access to satellite and mobile networks, on-line content, dedicated coaches and technical support staff. One of the major challenges with this initiative has been in overcoming traditional models of teaching which are dominated by lectures. As a result, training programs for teachers in pedagogy and classroom management have been initiated. The program has been expanded to elsewhere in Kenya, Tanzania, South Sudan, and Democratic Republic of Congo.[27]

In Tanzania, UNHCR has collaborated with WorldReader to overcome the chronic lack of textbooks by "going digital." Preliminary evidence indicates that students showed greater enthusiasm by learning digitally than with paper materials, and their tests in reading, writing and English proficiency improved. But students who had not received much or any English instruction did not do well. Two major areas of focus of this project are to solicit user-generated

---

http://www.schooleducationgateway.eu/en/pub/teacher_acadey/catalogue/detail.cfm?id=387 43. Accessed 22.02. 2017.

26See BrainPOP: Increasing refugees' access to learning resources through digital content. Retrieved from http://www.unhcr.org/innovation/labs_post/brainpop/. Accessed 26.02. 2017.

27 See Instant Network Schools. Leveraging mobile technology to improve the quality of education provided for refugees. Retrieved from http://www.unhcr.org/innovation/labs_post/instant-network-schools/. Accessed 26.02. 2017.

content and to establish ways of using solar energy to power the digital readers.[28]

UNHCR has also used ICTs for post-secondary degree and para-professional certification programs. Partners within their educational consortium include the Jesuit Commons Higher Education at the Margins, the African Virtual University, Borderless Higher Education for Refugee Project, the Swiss Humanitarian Organization, InZone, and Australian Catholic University. As with other educational programs that involve students with differing language and cultural backgrounds, establishing admissions requirements has been a challenge. On the one hand, there is a desire for inclusivity. On the other, being overly inclusive can risk the credibility of an educational program (UNHCR, 2017).

Project Virtuous Triangle is a platform being developed by Turkish Red Crescent and Istanbul Sehir University.[29] It links university students and school children with refugees and migrants to foster friendship and provide peer-based support for language training and skill development.

In a study of refugees and migrants in Bulgaria, The Netherlands and Spain, Reichel, Siegel, and Andreo found that "ICTs constitute an important resource for employability and integration of immigrants, who *are in fact using ICT-based resources at similar levels to nationals*" (2015, p. 6, emphasis in original). Generally, they found that older and less educated refugees and migrants were lower in digital literacy and had more limited access to ICTs. They therefore concluded that digital literacy needed to be combined with language learning for refugees and migrants.

Kiron is a provider of online training programs for refugees. Once completed these programs are sometimes used for university credit. Kiron focuses on four countries—Germany, France, Turkey, and Jordan. It has developed partnership with 41 universities. Kiron provides what it calls "tailored academic partnership solutions" for the universities with a view to facilitating sustainable academic prospects for refugee students. Services span from college preparation and overcoming language barriers to assisting with missing legal documents.[30]

---

28 See Worldreader: Using information communication technology to improve refugee children's reading skills. Retrieved from
http://www.unhcr.org/innovation/labs_post/worldreader/. Accessed 26.02. 2017.

29 See http://www.virtuoustriangle.com/. Accessed 12.03.2017.

30 Kiron. Partner with us as an academic institution. Retrieved from
https://kiron.ngo/support-our-mission/as-a-higher-education-institution/. Accessed:
18.05.2017.

A platform focused mainly on skill development is Capital Digital.[31] It is being built in Belgium. It takes a peer-to-peer approach to transfer technical and pedagogical skills to teach coding and computer programming among refugees and migrants. Through audio-visual and gaming functionalities, it transfers basic IT skills.

Health

There have been ICT4RM deployments to improve both mental and physical health. On the mental health side, the Ssyla Digital Therapy Platform, a U.K.-based initiative, connects refugees and migrants with a global network of mental health therapists.[32] It provides real-time therapy sessions for displaced people suffering from trauma and other mental challenges.

Refugee Services Toolkit is a website for psychology professionals seeking guidance in how to address the specific needs of young refugees and migrants. It is being developed by the National Child Traumatic Stress Network.

An ICT4RM initiative for physical health is MedShr. It links doctors across Europe with health professionals working in camp settings.[33] Medical and clinical images are uploaded for analysis by experts. Diagnoses are then sent back to camp-based health workers.

Another platform focuses specifically on maternal-child health. It is called HABABY (a play on the Arabic word Habibi which, roughly translated, means "little dear one").[34]

Cash Assistance and Livelihoods

Cash assistance is sometimes needed, especially in the short-run, to help displaced people through periods of unemployment. But it is important in the long-run that they have a way to make a living, whether by receiving in-kind support or cash for work, or by starting a business of their own. In this section, we cover ICT4RM for cash assistance, job acquisition, and business creation.

Cash Assistance

Given the fluidity of populations of refugees and migrants, a way of keeping track of who is who, and who is eligible to receive what, is a valuable tool. In

---

31 Capital Digital. Retrieved from http://www.unite-it.eu/profiles/blogs/capital-digital-belgium. Accessed: 18.05.2017.

32 See Ssyla Digital Therapy Platform. Retrieved from http://eusic.challengeprizecentre.org/selected/23/ssyla-digital-therapy-platform/.Accssed: 19:05.2017.

33 See MedShr. Share knowledge. Save lives. Retrieved from https://en.medshr.net. Accessed: 19.05.2017.

34 See https://play.google.com/store/apps/details?id=com.phonegap.hababy&hl=en. Accessed 21.05.2017.

Jordan, UNHCR has partnered with Cairo Amman Bank in using an iris scanning system called IrisGuard in conjunction with ATMs to provide millions of dinars to refugees and migrants who are eligible for assistance. UNHCR's assessment is that a full 91 percent of beneficiaries are "satisfied" with this approach to distributing cash. On the other hand, registering recipients consumes valuable time. As UNHCR points out, "Thousands of refugees cannot be sent to register at one bank branch at once....delays in enrollment are problematic." One solution being implemented is to link biometric registration for both intake of refugees and migrants along with the cash assistance registration.[35]

Refugee and immigrant populations have been particularly exposed to scandalous check cashing fees and criminal networks. MONI is a system that facilitates refugees and migrants without formal bank accounts to receive either paychecks or proceeds from government subsidies. Venmo (owned by PayPal) is a platform that allow exchange of cash directly from one person to another.[36] Transferwise is a similar service focusing on person-to-person international cash transactions at current exchange rates.[37]

Job Acquisition

Given the complexities of navigating employment regulations, it is unsurprising that we found only two ICT4RM deployments to help refugees and migrants have or find jobs. Solidarity Salt is one. It is a Greek non-profit which provides employment opportunities to refugee women, who package Greek sea salt to sell in the global market.[38] To make the salt appealing to buyers and to engender solidarity, each bag explains the story behind the salt producer's displacement.

Another is Refugeeswork.au. It is a job finding platform for use by displaced people in Austria.[39] It is supported by sophisticated algorithms. Its mission is to enlighten refugees about all legal, bureaucratic, and regulatory nuances that prevent them from getting a job in the host countries. This e-learning tool

---

35 See Biometric Cash Assistance. Retrieved from
http://www.unhcr.org/innovation/labs_post/cash-assistance/. Accessed: 19.05.2017
36 See https://venmo.com/. Accessed 21.05.2017. Note that the creation and use of biometric data can, of course, enhance the ability of governments and corporations to track people. There are, therefore, ethical considerations related to how the data can potentially be used for discrimination, oppression, or to enhance the accuracy of marketing pitches.
37 See https://transferwise.com/. Accessed 21.05.2017.
38 See, Solidarity Salt. The refugee food company that empowers women to build a new life. Retrieved from https://www.solidaritysalt.com/. Accessed: 17.05. 2017.
39 See Refugee work.at. Online job platform for refugees. Retrieved from https://www.refugeeswork.at/. Accessed: 17.05. 2017.

provides critical information about labor market issues and connects employers to skilled refugee workers.

Given the importance of employment to long-term integration, we are surprised there are not more ICT4RM initiatives like this.[40] Combining guidance on how displaced people can navigate employment regulations, as well as help in finding a job, as has Refugeeswork.au, is a promising combination.

Business Creation

Rafiqi (an Arabic word translated loosely as "companion") is a mentoring website designed to help entrepreneurs develop successful businesses.[41] Going a step further, another initiative, Entrepreneurial Refugees, not only provides mentoring services, but also connects entrepreneurs with local investors.[42]

CUCULA is a German incubatory platform designed to tap refugees' innovative manufacturing and craftsmanship skills through product design.[43] It employs an economic integration model which uses the intercultural expertise of displaced people for innovative design concepts.

Two other business creation platforms are Workeer[44] and Refugeeswork.[45] Both are in use in Germany. Refugeeswork is dedicated solely to employing refugees with programming skills.

For the academic job market and research sector, Chance-for-Success was developed by Carmen Bachmann of Leipzig University. It targets refugees with preexisting academic skills, credentials, and training. It now has over 500 registrations.[46]

---

40 As noted by UNHCR, a job "provides the individual not only with an income but also with independence, social status, and recognition. UNHCR's Executive Committee has recognized that promoting the self-reliance of refugees from the outset will enhance the sustainability of any future durable solution" (2007, 4).

41 See Rafaqi. Connecting the crowd's talent to refugees' needs. Retrieved from http://www.rafiqi.net/, Accessed: 17.05. 2017.

42 See Entrepreneurial Refugees. Retrieved from https://entrepreneurialrefugees.bidx.net/. Accessed: 17.05. 2017.

43 See CUCULA. Refugee company for craft and design. Retrieved from https://www.cucula.org/. Accessed 17.05.2017.

44 See Workeer. A job board for refugees. Retrieved from https://www.edenspiekermann.com/magazine/workeer-a-job-board-for-refugees/. Accessed 20.05.2017.

45 See Refugees Work. Remote IT jobs for refugees. Retrieved from https://www.edenspiekermann.com/magazine/workeer-a-job-board-for-refugees/. Accessed 20.05.2017.

46 While others saw refugees, this German professor saw human potential. Retrieved from http://www.npr.org/sections/goatsandsoda/2017/02/09/513700808/while-others-saw-refugees-this-german-professor-saw-human-potential. Accessed 20.5.2017.

Integration

There are also platforms which address the acculturation dimension of integration. Migrantour[47] is a refugee- and migrant-driven European urban, intercultural walking tour involving 14 cities. It educates displaced people about diversity and community cohesion. It fosters mutual discovery of the cultural identity and customs of both refugees and host societies.

In contrast, an integration platform developed by the German government is Ankommen, which means "arrive."[48] It is being developed as a joint initiative of the Federal Office for Migration and Refugee, Federal Employment Agency, and Goethe-Institute. It focuses on three key areas: social basics about German life; asylum procedures; and cultural practices and norms.

Mobilearn is for new arrivals to the U.K. It provides municipal education and civic orientation to refugees about social integration, employment, housing, language and education.[49] It works on mobile platforms, providing customized translation in five languages (Arabic, Swedish, Somali, Farsi, and English).

Gherbtna (an Arabic word loosely translated as "loneliness in exile…being foreign") is a smartphone-based app that helps Syrians navigate social life in Turkey.[50] It incorporates infographic and animation services to explain Turkish asylum procedures, provides information on jobs and houses, and maintains an interactive help desk through which refugees can seek out information about health, education, and legal services.

Ingredients to Successful Platform Development

There are three main areas that are critical to the success of a given platform. One involves sustainable funding. Another is that functionality should match what users need with a bias towards simplicity rather than complexity. The other is to engage end users at the very beginning and throughout the deployment of a platform.

Sustainable Funding

While volunteer developed and run platforms can arguably maintain viability, it is our assessment that some source of continuous funding is required for a successful deployment. There have been numerous well-designed platforms which have successfully met a niche need only to close due to funding

---

47 See Migrantour. Intercultural urban tour. Retrieved from http://www.mygrantour.org/en/ Accessed 17.05.2017.

48 See Ankomenn. Germany launches smartphone app to help refugees integrate. Retrieved from https://www.theverge.com/2016/1/13/10761150/germany-refugee-smartphone-app-ankommen. Accessed 20.5.2017.

49 See Mobilearn. Retrieved from https://se.mobilearn.com/en/. Accessed 17.05.2017.

50 See Gherbtna. Retrieved from http://8rbtna.com/. Accessed: 18.05. 2017.

challenges. Migreat, for example, is a platform offering legal and process advice for asylum seekers, especially focused on acquiring work visas. It has proven to be popular, with an estimated two million visitors a month. But it has struggled financially. Similarly, The City at a Time of Crisis was a digital mapping effort which recorded and plotted incidents of violence in Athens, Greece against refugees and migrants.[51] The map and listing of events by category are useful for identifying "hot spots" which displaced people should avoid and that police should monitor. Unfortunately, the developers ran out of funding. As David Lepeska noted in *Refugees and the Technology of Exile* (2016), platforms need to be constantly refined and updated to reflect changes on the ground, and sometimes that requires either a way to make a profit or a means by which to get steady donations, so they are financially sustainable.

To prevent such short life-cycles of initiatives, incubators are emerging. Similar to incubators for starting, getting funding, and growing a new business, Techfugees is providing support for developing new platforms for refugees and migrants.[52] In addition to germinating new ideas and helping to secure funding, Techfugees channels global technology talent. Techfugees has chapters in major cities around the world and has sponsored many "hack-a-thons"—sessions in which computer programmers and tech-savvy people share their ideas and work together. Techfugees has focused on reaching the refugees and migrants themselves by supporting Non-Governmental Organizations (NGOs) and governments, both of which can offer more stable revenue streams.

Levels of Functionalities and Involvement

In Table 1, we report our findings of levels of functionality. We refer to these as levels in that there are distinct differences in the kinds of communication undertaken with a specific ICT4RM deployment. The levels move from simple one-way communication to ones that are complex, involving machine learning.

---

51 See http://www.crisis-scape.net/. Accessed 20.05.2017. See also Dalakoglou (2013).
52 See https://techfugees.com/about/ and
https://www.facebook.com/Techfugees/?fref=nf. Accessed 20.05.2017.

Table 1. Levels of functionality and degree of involvement of displaced people

Platform	One-way communication	Two-way communication	Two-way communication and crowdsourcing	Two-way communication, crowdsourcing, and machine learning	Displaced people involved in the design	Displaced people engaged in decisions regarding modifications
Mobile Legal Info Service	X				No	No
Asylum Service in Attica, Greece	X				No	No
Refugee.info		X	X		No	Yes
Crisis Info Hub		X	X	X	No	No
Refugee Assistance and Information System		X	X		No	No
help.unhcr.org		X	X	X	Yes	Yes
UPS ReliefLink		X	X	X	No	Yes
Trilogy Emergency Relief Application (TERA)		X	X	X	No	No
Welcome to Dresden	X				No	Yes
Setel.in	X	X	X	X	Yes	Yes
Home4Refugees			X	X	No	Yes
Trace the Face			X	X	No	Yes
Refunite		X	X	X	Yes	Yes
Bureaucrazy			X		Yes	Yes
Mobilearn		X	X	X	Yes	Yes
Ankommen	X		X		No	Yes
Services Advisor		X	X	X	Yes	Yes
Botler (chatbot)		X	X	X	Yes	Yes
AMFI International	X				No	No
BrainPOP		X	X	X	No	Yes

Instant Network Classrooms		X	X		No	Yes
WorldReader		X	X		No	Yes
Project Virtuous Triangle		X	X	X	No	Yes
Kiron		X	X	X	No	Yes
Capital Digital		X	X		No	Yes
Ssyla Digital Therapy Platform		X	X		No	Yes
Refugee Services Toolkit		X	X		No	Yes
MedShr		X	X		No	Yes
HABABY		X	X	X	No	Yes
IrisGuard	X			X	No	Yes
MONI		X	X	X	No	Yes
Venmo				X	No	Yes
Solidarity Salt	X				No	Yes
Refugeeswork.au		X	X	X	No	Yes
Rafiqi		X	X	X	No	Yes
CUCULA	X				No	Yes
Workeer		X			No	Yes
Refugeeswork		X	X		No	Yes
Chance-for-Success		X	X		No	Yes
Migrantour		X	X		No	Yes
Gherbtna		X	X		Yes	Yes
Migreat		X		X	No	Yes
The City at a Time of Crisis		X	X		No	Yes
Techfugees		X	X	X	No	Yes

Source: Developed by authors.

As shown in Table 1, we found only nine of the 44 deployments, or 20%, involve one-way communication. In contrast, 32, or 73%, provide for two-way communication. But even more deployments also involve crowdsourcing—34 or the 44 platforms, or 77%. Surprisingly, 22, or 50%, use some form of machine learning.

We do not put a value judgment on the level of complexity of an ICT4RM deployment. Just as the renowned economist E.F. Schumacher pointed out in his impactful book *Small is Beautiful* (1973), we wonder if simple is beautiful also. We are not claiming that more complexity is necessarily better, or that technological "bells and whistles" are inherently helpful. We suspect that it is far more important that displaced people be involved in the design and ongoing decision-making regarding an ICT4RM deployment and that it is they who determine level and type of functionality. In fact, we caution that complex technology can be a distraction from the more long-term, harder work on the ground of building human relationships and networks of people dedicated to a common cause.

We found very little evidence of involvement of refugees and migrants in the creation and design of these ICT4RM initiatives. Only 8 of the 44 platforms, or 18%, involved displaced people at the conceptualization and design stage. In contrast, a full 38, or 86%, engaged displaced people in modifying the platform once deployed. We assume there is involvement naturally in the form of feedback about how a given initiative is working. We wonder if greater effectiveness could be obtained with more deliberate efforts to involve the people these initiatives are designed to help at the conceptualization and design stage.

Limitations

We reviewed scholarly literature, "grey literature" (unpublished manuscripts), and websites to identify ICT4RM globally. One limitation of our study is that we reviewed ICT4RM platforms that are explained in English. We did not identify deployments with descriptions unavailable in English.

Second, while we made a good faith attempt to decipher the extent of involvement of refugees and migrants in design and governance of the ICT4RM deployments described herein, we are aware that such involvement is not always obvious. We recognize that a fully accurate assessment of this involvement requires interviews with developers and users.

Finally, this study does not address some of the emerging security risks that ICT4RMs may pose for users. These can involve surveillance, stratification, and data tracking, as recently raised in *Mapping Refugee Media Journeys* (Gillespie et al., 2016).

Recommendations

Given the plethora of ICT4RM initiatives, we recommend that an entity with a steady funding stream take on the challenge of developing a cloud-based computer system with a full suite of capabilities, designed to assist governments and NGOs in multiple ways in managing the influx of displaced people, while also supporting the capacities of these people to help each other. We suspect many of the developers of the various deployments listed in this paper would be keen to contribute (code, ideas, and visions of system architecture, to name a few) to such a collective effort. Governments, NGOs, and displaced people everywhere could use the combined platform as they need it. Think of it as a migration version of the Electoral Risk Management Tool developed by the Institute for Democracy and Electoral Assistance based in Stockholm.[53] This would help alleviate the fragmentation problem depicted by Ben Mason in the *Stanford Social Innovation Review* (2016), in which he warns of duplication and redundancy.

We also recommend an ongoing effort to expand access to the internet. There is cause for optimism here, ranging from nimble initiatives like MeshPoint[54] (a backpack internet provider for over a hundred users, able to withstand extreme conditions) to the large-scale efforts by Google and others to create ubiquitous access. Special provisions for women and the elderly are needed to ensure their access to ICTs. Research by UNHCR suggests that these two groups are less likely than men to have mobile phones and access to the internet (UNHCR, 2016).

Finally, we believe far greater attention should be placed on child and youth migrants. This group is particularly vulnerable to the risks of trafficking, pornographers, zero identity, and the lure of the street. In the 2015 report *Uprooted – The Growing Crisis of Refugee and Migrant Children,* UNICEF estimates that there are approximately eleven million child refugees and migrants (2016). As noted in *Modern Mobility: The role of ICT's in child and youth migration*, this population will be best served by changing the ecosphere from a victim-based to a rights-based operating condition (Raftree, Appel, and Ganness, 2013). A good place to start is in applying the precepts of The Signal Code globally for children. The Code was created in 2017 by Greenwood et al. of the Harvard Humanitarian Initiative. It articulates five information human rights that should be afforded all persons during a time of crisis (2017).

Conclusion

The combination of substantial displacement of people, a rapid growth in the use of mobile phones (many of the "smart" variety), the expansion of and accessibility to the internet, and the compassion people feel for those in need has yielded an impressive array of ICT4RM initiatives. Some are, of course, more useful than others.

As we noted in our introduction, there have been "a thousand flowers blooming." There is impressive innovation, thoughtful design and, in some cases, sophisticated use of mathematics. We feel that success of these platforms will ultimately depend on changing the narrative from one of

---

53 See, International IDEA (n.d.). Tools. Retrieved from http://www.idea.int/data-tools/tools/electoral-risk-management-tool. Accessed: 19.05.2017.

54 See, MesPoint. Retrieved from http://www.meshpoint.me/ Accessed: 19.05.2017.

refugees as burdens to refugees as assets. As noted in *Rebuilding After Crisis: Embedding Refugee Integration in Migration Management Systems*, unlocking the multiplier effects of integration is important not only for this cadre of displaced people but also for future waves (Papademetriou, Benton & Banulesca-Bogdan, 2017).

One of the most impressive dimensions of this new era in addressing how the world responds to a massive displacement of people using liberation technology is that there are contributors to these platforms from all over the globe. People are helping to write code, submit information, categorize events, specify assets and hazards, and analyze data. This is an electronic version of global solidarity. We want to close by saying that we admire this spirit of compassion and willingness to do something to ease the pain and suffering of so many people. And we likewise admire the stamina, determination, and tenacity of displaced people who are trying to keep body and soul together, often reaching out, at the same time, to help other displaced people in need.

References

Banks, K. (Ed., 2013). *The rise of reluctant innovator.* London: London Publishing Partnership.

Benton, M., & Glennie, A. (2016). *Digital humanitarianism: How tech entrepreneurs are supporting refugee integration.* Washington, DC: Migration Policy Institute.

Central Intelligence Agency. (2017). *The World Factbook.* Washington: U.S. Government Printing Office. Found at https://www.cia.gov/library/publications/the-world-factbook/rankorder/2151rank.html. Accessed 21.05.2017.

Collier, P. (2014). *Exodus: How migration is changing our world.* Oxford: Oxford University Press.

Dalakoglou, D. (2013). 'From the Bottom of the Aegean Sea' to Golden Dawn: Security, Xenophobia, and the Politics of Hate in Greece. Studies in Ethnicities and Nationalism, *13*(3), 514–522.

Diamond, L. (2010). Liberation technology. *Journal of Democracy, 21*(3), 69-83.

Gillespie, M., Ampofo, L., Cheesman, M., Faith, B., Iliadou, E., Issa, A., & Skleparis, D. (2016, May 13). *Mapping refugee media journeys: Smartphones and social media networks.* Retrieved from http://www.open.ac.uk/ccig/sites/www.open.ac.uk.ccig/files/Mapping%20Refugee%20Media%20Journeys%2016%20May%20FIN%20MG_0.pdf. Accessed 28.05.2017.

Greenwood, F., Howarth, C., Poole, D. E., Raymond, N. A., & Scarnecchia, D. P. (2017). The signal code: a human rights approach to information during crisis. Cambridge, MA: Harvard Humanitarian Initiative. Retrieved from http://hhi.harvard.edu/sites/default/files/publications/signalcode_final.pdf. Accessed 21.05.2017.

Harvard Humanitarian Initiative. (2011). *Disaster relief 2.0: the future of information sharing in humanitarian emergencies.* Washington, D.C. and Berkshire, UK: UN Foundation & Vodafone Foundation Technology Partnership.

Lapeska D. (2016). Refugees and the technology of exile. *The Wilson Quarterly. 40*(2). Retrieved from https://wilsonquarterly.com/quarterly/looking-back-moving-forward/refugees-and-the-technology-of-exile/. Accessed 28.05.2017.

Lohr, S. (2017, May 10). Canada becomes a magnet for tech talent. *San Francisco Chronicle.* Retrieved from http://www.sfgate.com/business/article/Canada-becomes-a-magnet-for-tech-talent-11137232.php. Accessed 27.05.2017.

Martin-Shields, C. P. (2016). *When information becomes action: How information communication technologies affect collective action during crises* (Doctoral dissertation). Washington, DC: George Mason University.

Mason, B. (2016, March 29). The refugee tech crisis. *Stanford Social and Innovation Review.* Retrieved from https://ssir.org/articles/entry/the_refugee_tech_crisis. Accessed 28.05.2017.

Noveck, B. S. (2015). *Smart citizens, smarter state: The technologies of expertise and the future of governing.* Cambridge: Harvard University Press.

Olson, M. (1971). *The logic of collective action: public goods and the theory of groups.* Cambridge: Harvard University Press.

Papaioannou, T. (2014). How inclusive can innovation and development be in the twenty-first century? *Innovation and Development, 4*(2), 187-202.

Papademetriou, D., Benton, M., & Banelescu-Bogdan, N. (2017). *Rebuilding after Crisis: Embedding Refugee Integration in Migration Management Systems.* Transatlantic Council on Migration: Council Statement.

Raftree, L., Appel, K. & Ganness, A. (2013). *Modern mobility: the role of ICT'S in child and youth migration.* A State of the Practice Report produced by Plan International. Washington, D.C.: Plan International.

Reichel, D., Siegel, M., & Andreo, J. C. (2015). *ICT for the employability and integration of immigrants in the European Union.* Spain: European Commission.

Schumacher, E.F. (1973). *Small is beautiful: Economics as if people mattered.* London: Blond and Briggs.

UNHCR. (2007, May). Note on the Integration of Refugees in the European Union. Retrieved from http://www.unhcr.org/463b462c4.pdf. Accessed 28.05.2017.

UNHCR. (2017). Applying user-centered design and prototyping to humanitarian problem-solving. Retrieved from http://www.unhcr.org/innovation/labs/. Accessed 28.05.2017.

UNICEF. (2016). Uprooted: The growing crisis for refugee and migrant children. New York: UNICEF.

Chapter 7. The Depictions of The Refugee Crisis on the Public Arena: An Analysis of the News Frames Promoted by Spanish Digital Media[1]

Sergio Álvarez[2], Alfredo Arceo[3]

Abstract

Digital media played a prominent role as a source of information about the last refugee crisis. Refugees leave their countries of origin due to threatening events, while migrants are motivated by material conditions. Journalistic framing helps to understand how refugees are depicted in digital press outfits; it consists of selecting and highlighting certain aspects of reality in a text, so that it suggests a definition for the described situation, as well as their possible causes and treatment; frames have been studied from the perspective of news production as well as that of the audiences; they act as abstract structures that organize the elements of a communicative text, but some of them are issue-specific. A content analysis was conducted on news about the refugee crisis published by the top 4 Spanish digital diaries by number of readers, to describe how they framed those contents over a six month period. They were mainly centred around the journeys of refugees, clearly from the perspective of the European receiving countries. Mentions to poverty and physical integrity won over terrorism and crime, generally pointing to the victims' frame over their depiction as intruders. The next challenge is to analyse the effects over the audiences.

Keywords: Content analysis, journalism, media debate, migrants, refugees, sociology of communication.

Introduction

Traditionally, the role of media on portraying an image of refugees has been a wide topic of discussion (Wright, 2002; Pajnik, 2007). This is the first big refugee crisis since new digital media are part of the daily life of many people, particularly the young public. In Spain, this sector of recipients fell foul with printed newspapers a long time ago (Arroyo, 2006), with social media emerging as the preferred alternative to find relevant information (Casero-Ripollés, 2012). All this invites the social scientific community to revise how the news about its shortcomings are presented to the public and discuss about their potential effects.

---

[1] Special thanks to Zamara Suárez, María Bastero and Ayelén Alonso, students from the Advertising and Public Relations degree at Complutense University, who volunteered to participate as codifiers for the conducted content analyses.

[2] Sergio Álvarez is predoctoral research trainee at the Department for Audiovisual Communication and Advertising II, Faculty of Information Sciences, Complutense University from Madrid (UCM), avda. Complutense s/n, Madrid, Spain – 28040. E-mail: sergioalvarezsanchez@ucm.es.

[3] Alfredo Arceo is PhD, tenured professor of the Department for Audiovisual Communication and Advertising II (office 106), Faculty of Information Sciences, Complutense University from Madrid (UCM), avda. Complutense s/n, Madrid, Spain – 28040. E-mail: aarceo@ucm.es.

Literature Review

A Definition for Refugee

Before putting together, a work of such characteristics, it is appropriate to clarify the concepts of refugee and migrant. The most practical decision for the researcher is to endorse the current definition accepted by the United Nations High Commissioner for Refugees (1984), the one adopted at the Cartagena Declaration (1984): refugees are the people in a country different of that of their origin, because of "serious and indiscriminate threats to life, physical integrity or freedom resulting from generalized violence or events seriously disturbing public order".

It is equally important to avoid confusion between the 'refugee' and 'migrant' terms. The latter's movements are motivated by poverty, unemployment and material conditions in general, rather than violence or persecution. Migration is basically a socio-economic phenomenon (Long, 2013). However, as Moldovan (2013) reminds: "[…] it is not possible to eliminate any economic interest for those who seek protection as refugees. For this reason, in some cases, drawing a strict line between the two categories may be a difficult process" (p.682).

Frame Analysis: A Theoretical Background

Framing has become a paradigm for the Theory of Social Communication. It is a concept started by Bateson (1972) in anthropology, and taken by Erving Goffman to interpretative sociology. Goffman (1974) described the frames as: "principals of organization which govern events –at least social ones- and our subjective involvement in them" (pp.10-11). Some sociologists applied frame analysis to the study of Social Movements (Snow & Benford, 1992; Gamson, 1992), as it allowed them to share a definition for the problems they fight against.

Framing in the Theory of Communication

The first developments for frame analysis within the field of Communication were suggested by Gaye Tuchman (1978), in order to understand how journalists frame reality when they compose news pieces. Tuchman described the journalistic frames as institutionalised norms, processes and practices such as how the topics are selected, on which section they are published, etc. In Tuchman's view, information even gets to the point of creating the perceived reality.

Framing in Communication developed into a variety of research perspectives: on the one hand, most Communication scientists specialized delved into the sociological approach to journalistic frames, centred around their construction by media (Gitlin, 1980; Iyengar, 1991), while another group of researchers adopted the Social Psychological approach, focussing on the effects of framing processes on the audiences (Price, Tewksbury & Powers, 1997).

Robert Entman regarded this plethora of approaches as an inconsistent way of contributing to Communication Sciences. Entman (1993) devoted a full definition of framing to get on top of it: "to select some aspects of perceived reality and make them more salient in a communicating text, in such a way as to promote a particular definition of a problem, causal interpretation, moral evaluation, and/or treatment recommendation for the item described" (p.52).

The effects of framing over the audiences were evidenced by a research conducted by Druckman (2001), on which it could be observed how different words or phrases could cause different framing effects, depicting the issue or a potential solution in a positive or negative way, even when those elements are providing the same information. He called this phenomenon the 'equivalency framing effect', but the pioneers in detecting it were Tversky and Kahneman (1981). The second phenomenon described by Druckman (2001) was the 'emphasis framing effect', when a speaker highlights certain considerations about a topic over others, leading their recipients to focus on them. An example related to refugee-depiction could be the emphasis on security issues over humanitarian ones. All frames are abstract and allow a certain degree of generalizability. However, issue-specific frames enable to make interpretations of a particular topic: "Whereas issue-specific frames reveal what aspects of an issue were selected and what were left out, generic frames tell us more about the way the media package any issue" (Kozman, 2016, p. 4).

Issue-specific Frames: Migration and Refugees

Most of the work conducted around the issue of the depictions of refugees, starts from a constructionist approach. Van Gorp (2005, pp.486-487) regards frames as media packages that include, on the one hand, framing devices (certain words, images, graphics, etc); but, inside frame packages, Van Gorp (2007) also recognizes the existence of what he called 'reasoning devices', which are connected to the different elements of Entman's definition: they are "explicit and implicit statements that deal with justifications, causes, and consequences in a temporal order, and which complete the frame package" (p.64). Basing on previous research conducted by Harrell-Bond (1999) and Zetter (1999), Van Gorp defined two opposite frames that Belgian media would use to cover the asylum-seekers problem: refugees as innocent victims in need of help, and refugees as intruders or as a threat to homeland security (2005, p.489). Van Gorp (2007) supports a combined approach to framing, on which frames in production and frames in consumption become two aspects of the same phenomenon, linkable by a shared culture. He considers frames as pure metacommunication with implicit information.

Objectives

The period between September 14th 2015 and March 9th 2016 was full of key events related to the refugee crisis (EU Summits, electoral processes, negotiations with Turkey, etc). The present research looks into the news frames employed by the four most read Spanish digital media outfits (*Larazon.es, Eldiario.es, Publico.es, Elespanol.es*) during the mentioned period, with the purpose of identifying, describing and establishing the frequency of use of the detected frames. In addition, the research attempts to analyse the evolution of the journalistic frames as important events on the refugee crisis were covered by those top digital diaries. Thirdly, it aims to conclude if there is agreement about news frames among the examined media. And finally, this study looks forward to suggest new research lines about framing effects on the audiences, with respect to the depictions of the refugee crisis.

Method

Content analysis was considered as the most appropriate method to deal with published journalistic pieces. Finding an empirical base to study such an abstract object as a news frame is not a new challenge to social scientists from the field of Communication (Tankard, 2001).

Gamson and Modigiani (1989) opted for detecting frames by employing a media package composed of what they called "condensing symbols" (p.3). The methodology applied to the news about the refugee crisis for this study keeps a resemblance with this approach. In first place, it was decided that the headline zone (headline, lead, main image, caption, videos) would provide the key clues about the employed frame in any given news. Secondly, a table was created with 45 items (countries, themes, people, sections, etc) ready to be applied to all news related to refugees or migrants, which were published during the established period. Depending on which of the headline zone elements an item was mentioned, the intensity with which it was present was codified by using a scale from 0 to 8.

Finally, a group of three volunteers contributed to make this research possible by becoming codifiers for the different digital diaries, together with one of the authors of the study. Each codifier was given the task of analysing two out of four sites; that way, all four digital diaries were codified by two different people, allowing us to successfully test the replicability of the proposed content analysis[4]. The corpus describes any news piece found out by entering the keywords 'refugees' or 'migrants', in the Google search engine or in that

---

4 The replicability results showed how the diaries analysed by one of the codifiers got indexes of coincidence of 78 % and 82 %, while the rest of digital outfits included in this study reached well over 90 %. Although an index around 80 % could be acceptable, we opted for rejecting the work of this codifier, as his results were a step behind the rest in trustworthiness.

of each diary; nonetheless, if an entry was not included by one of the codifiers of a certain diary, it was completely eliminated from the analysis.

Results

A list of 45 items provides the researchers with a vast amount of information, but it is more appropriate to focus on the most relevant data for the established objectives of this study.

Table 1. Number of news with a positive, negative or neutral tone in each digital diary

	Público	El Diario	La Razón	El Español
Positive	19	18,5	20	24,5
Negative	58	91,5	244	54
Neutral	130	125	256	108,5

Source: Elaboration of our own (2017). The data for El Diario and El Español is the average between the results provided by their two different codifiers.

The tone suggested by each news piece was conditioned by the vocabulary used in the headline zone (words such as 'tragedy' or 'death' were among the hints) and what appeared in the main image (e.g., disputes, sad or suffering expressions). Most of the news seemed neutral, but articles with a negative tone follow them closely, while the positive tone was the exception (see table 1).

Table 2. Score conceded to the registered concepts by the employed coding method

	Público (207 news)	El Diario (235)	La Razón (398)	El Español (187)
War	70	17	135	70
Journeys	410	978,5	1711	409,5
Terrorism	68	12,5	153	68
Crime	10	30,5	135	10
Xenophobia	59	144	68	59
Poverty	53	98,5	15	53
Physical integrity	161	405	375	161
Riots	23	42	15	23

Source: Elaboration of our own (2017). The data for El Diario and El Español is the average between the results provided by their two different codifiers.

The sections where news appeared published were also considered as a meaningful indication of the hidden frames. The clear dominance of sections that were not considered for being coded is in many cases (particularly at *El*

Diario, and with the sole exception of *Público* –where the International section was the most used one) a result of the opening of special spaces for the refugee crisis on part of the digital diaries; notwithstanding this overall win of the 'other sections' category, the international section is the next one most preferred to inform about refugees, more than Society, Politics or any other place where it could make sense.

Discussion

Overall, there was an immense focus on the journeys of the refugees over any other item, in all four diaries. This fact coincides with the preference for the International section, despite the obvious treatment of the refugees' journeys from the perspective of the countries of reception (coincidence of the category 'journeys' and any mention to European countries were from two to six times more frequent than with the countries of origin, depending on the diary and the period; coincidence between the categories 'journeys' and 'war' were incidental). Physical integrity is another topic frequently aroused, usually related to the risk that the trips impose to the migrants.

Only one of the two frames enunciated by Van Gorp (2005) in his study about migrants in the Belgian press, is identifiable in the Spanish digital media: the depiction of refugees as victims is a constant if we consider the reasoning devices that were codified for this research, while refugees are rarely depicted as threats or as intruders, almost regardless of the diary we might be talking about. Xenophobia, poverty and physical integrity get at least as much attention as terrorism or crime in news related to the refugee crisis, with the sole exception of *La Razón*, where those last two items get the upper hand (if not by a conclusive margin) and invite the reader to think about migrants as a threat.

After splitting the results in five different time periods, the framing tendencies showed that they were basically stable over time during the whole six months. Refugees were mainly framed as people who were coming to Europe because they were in need of help, regardless of how the events of the refugee crisis developed. To name but two remarkable shifts: in the period between La Valeta summit and the beginning of Christmas, *El Español* started to concede more attention to xenophobia than to poverty, physical integrity or disturbances, and *La Razón* did so with terrorism (the Paris attacks had took place on November 13th 2015); xenophobia is generally granted way more attention at *El Diario* and *Público*, than at *El Español* and *La Razón* (over the six month period, terrorism appears at *La Razón* in news related to refugees with twice the intensity of xenophobia, according to our coding method). Otherwise, the same approach towards the topic could be found in October 2015 than in February 2016.

In conclusion, the victims' frame should be the starting point in order to determine the impact of frames sponsored by digital media on the views that the Spanish recipients may have about refugees. In the future, Spanish researchers could conduct polls and focus groups based on the relationships between key concepts that have been detected by carrying out the present study: moderators should arouse topics by couples, such as journeys and European countries, journeys and the risks to their lifes and health, etc. But there are more findings to be discovered in the comparison between the media frames and the frames sponsored by public institutions about refugees. An additional study with public campaign materials, based on the cascade activation model (Entman, 2003) would be worth the effort. We wish to finish this article elevating those research paths to the social scientific community.

References

Arroyo, M. (2006). Los jóvenes y la prensa: hábitos de consumo y renovación de contenidos [Young people and the press: consumption habits and renovation of contents]. *Ámbitos: Revista Internacional de Comunicación, 15*, 271-282 (in Spanish).

Bateson, G. (1972). A Theory of Play and Fantasy. In: Bateson, G. (ed.) *Steps to an Ecology of Mind.* New York: Ballantine Books. pp. 177-193.

Casero-Ripollés, A. (2012). Beyond newspapers: News Consumption among Young People in the Digital Era. *Comunicar, 20*(39), 151-158. Doi: 10.3916/C39-2012-03-05

Druckman, J. N. (2001). The Implications of Framing Effects for Citizen Competence. *Political Behavior, 23*(3), 225-256. Doi: 10.1023/A:1015006907312

Entman, R. (1993). Framing: Toward clarification of a fractured paradigm. *Journal of Communication, 43*(4), 51-58. Doi: 10.1111/j.1460-2466.1993.tb01304.x

Entman, R. (2003). Cascading activation: Contesting the White House's frame after 9/11. *Political Communication, 20*(4), 415-432. Doi: 10.1080/10584600390244176

Gamson, W. A. (1992). *Talking Politics.* New York: Cambridge University.

Gamson, W. A., & Modigliani, A. (1989). Media Discourse and Public Opinion on Nuclear Power: A Constructionist Approach. *American Journal of Sociology, 95*(1): 1-37. Doi: 10.1086/229213

Gitlin, Todd. 1980. *The Whole World Is Watching: Mass Media in the Making and Unmaking of the New Left.* Berkeley: University of California Press.

Goffman, E. (1974). *Frame Analysis: An Essay on Organization of Experience.* New York: Harper & Row.

Harrell-Bond, B. (1999). The experience of refugees as aid recipients. In: Ager. A. (ed.), *Refugees: perspectives on the experience of forced migration.* London and New York: Continuum. pp. 136-68.

Iyengar, Shanto. 1991. *Is Anyone Responsible? How Television Frame Political Issues.* Chicago: University of Chicago Press.

Kozman, C. (2016). Measuring issue-specific and generic frames in the media's coverage of the steroids issue in baseball. Journalism Practice, 1-21. Received from http://www.tandfonline.com/doi/abs/10.1080/17512786.2016.1190660, available on 26.04.2017. Doi: 10.1080/17512786.2016.1190660

Long, K. (2013). When refugees stopped being migrants: Movement, labour and humanitarian protection. *Migration Studies, 1*(1), 4-26. Doi: 10.1093/migration/mns001

Moldovan, C. (2013). The notion of refugee. Definition and distinctions. CES Working Papers, 8(4), 681-688. Received from http://ceswp.uaic.ro/articles/CESWP2016_VIII4_MOL.pdf available on 30.04.2017.

Pajnik, M. (2007). Media images of refugees. *Socialno Delo, 5*(1-2), 1-11.

Price, V., Tewksbury, D. & Powers, E. (1997). Switching Trains of Thought: The Impact of News Frames on Readers' Cognitive Responses. *Communication Research, 24*(5), 481-506. Doi: 10.1177/009365097024005002

Snow, D. A., & Benford, R. D. (1992). Master frames and cycles of protest. In: Morris, A.D., & McLurg Mueller, C. (eds.) *Frontiers in social movement theory.* New Haven: Yale University Press. pp. 133-155.

Tuchman, G. (1978). *Making news: A study in the construction of reality.* New York: Free Press.

Tankard Jr., J. W. (2001). The empirical apprach to the study of media framing. In: Reese, S. D., Gandy Jr., H. O., & Gant, A. E. (eds.). *Framing Public Life: Perspectives on Media and our Understanding of the Social World.* Mahwah, NJ, USA: Lawrence Elbaum Associates. pp. 95-106.

Tversky, A., & Kahneman, D. (1981). The Framing of Decisions and the Psychology of Choice. *Science, 211*(4481), 453-458. Doi: 10.1126/science.7455683

Van Gorp, B. (2005). Where is the Frame? Victims and Intruders in the Belgian Press Coverage of the Asylum Issue. *European Journal of Communication, 20* (4), 484-507. Doi: 10.1111/j.0021-9916.2007.00329.x

Van Gorp, B. (2007). The Constructionist Approach to Framing: Bringing Culture Back In. *Journal of Communication, 57*(1), 60-78. Doi: 10.1111/j.0021-9916.2007.00329.x/full

Wright, T. (2002). Moving images: the media representation of refugees. *Visual Studies, 17*(1), 53-66. Doi: 10.1080/1472586022000005053

United Nations High Commissioner for Refugees (1984). Cartagena Declaration on Refugees. Received from http://www.unhcr.org/about-us/background/ 45dc19084/ cartagena-declaration-refugees-adopted-colloquium-international-protection.html Accessed: 08.04.2017.

Zetter, R. (1999). International Perspectives on Refugee Assistance. In: Ager. A. (ed.), *Refugees: perspectives on the experience of forced migration.* London and New York: Continuum. pp. 136-68.

ANNEX 1. Extract of the codebook for the content analysis conducted on Spanish digital diaries.

1.   Main section of the news
0.   International/World
1.   National/Politics
2.   Culture
3.   Society
4.   Sports
5.   Economy
6.   Others/No section assigned

2.   Definitions for thematic categories
-      **War:** It comprises any reference to past, present of future armed conflicts, between countries or between factions within the same country. It will always be present if the news alludes to invasions, air attacks or civil wars.
-      **Journey:** It comprises every mention to migration and their movements, expulsions, receptions, campsites and the transportation employed in all those events.
-      **Terrorism:** The category would be present when the terms 'terrorism' and 'terrorist' are made evident, or the names of organizations that recur to reach political objectives; and when the news talk about terrorist attacks.
-      **Crime:** any mention to offences (burglaries, assaults, sexual abuses, etc), regardless of them being perpetrated by migrants or, on the contrary, they are the victims.
-      Xenophobia: presence of xenophobic movements in the news, quotes against foreign people or cohabitation problems.
-      **Poverty:** This category comprises every reference to material conditions of life or deficient economic conditions, in the place of origin, in that of arrival, in a campsite or during the route (it excludes the materials and transports already codified in the category 'Journey').
-      **Physical integrity:** employ this code if the news alludes to injured people, dead people or any form of putting on danger the life of a person. This category excludes any reference to hunger as a state that puts a life on risk, because in that case we would be referring to conditions already codified in the category 'Poverty'.
-      **Riots:** This category must be opened when the news report incidents on demonstrations or campsites for refugees, as well as every time that an incident happens between police or Armed Forces, and another person or collective. It excludes everything which was already considered in 'War', 'Terrorism', 'Crime' and 'Xenophobia'.

- **Economy:** This category will appear when the news mentions macroeconomics: costs for the states, public or private investments, economic institutions, financial matters, etc.

3. Coding levels

0. Absence of the category.
1. The category is only present in the lead.
2. The category has a secondary presence in an image (less than a third of the whole picture) or it appears in a video.
3. The category is present in the header or in the caption for the main image.
4. The category is simultaneously present in at least two of the following elements: header, lead and caption.
5. The category is present in the embedded message of a social network.
6. There is a mention to the category in the headline or in the main image.
7. There is a mention to the category in the headline and in the main image.
8. The category is present in all the elements of the headline zone.

Footnote 1: A certain category can only be registered if it objectively appears in the news. We cannot make interpretations; the category has to be objectively present, according to the definitions provided in this guide.

Footnote 2: We also consider the presence of a demonym as a mention to the country or region that it refers to. Equally, the category 'EU Countries' includes any member state bar Spain (which has its own space for codification).

Footnote 3: Multiple categories can be codified within the same news, with the exception of the the cases contemplated in point 2 of this guide.

4. Tone adopted by the diary for the news piece

0. Neutral
1. Positive
2. Negative

Chapter 8. Migration and Refugee Representation in Political Cartoons

Arda Umut Saygın[1]

Abstract

Today, migration, immigrants and refugee issues are closely related to the whole world. The developments about these issues can be followed from the media almost everyday because they have news value. Political cartoons, which are woven with messages based on drawings, are interested in these issues too since they are also media contents. The purpose of this study is to show how the refugee case is handled in political cartoons. In the study, 989 political cartoons which were exhibited between the years of 2013 and 2016 in The Aydın Doğan International Cartoon Competition was selected. Then, both quantitative and qualitative content analysis were applied to them to understand how much place these issues take place and in which context they are discussed. Finally, it is determined that political cartoons about these issues has became even more important year by year.

Key Words: Refugee, Immigration, Political Cartoon, Content analysis

Introduction

Since the cave walls in prehistoric times, humanbeings has always been very curious about drawing about the events happening around them. Likewise, migration is an endless process and people migrate to new places for several reasons. Recent migration flow is caused because of the civil wars or economic and socio-political problems. This huge flow of migration makes millions of people displaced, people become immigrants or refugees and they receive widespread media attention with their poor living conditions and unfortunate destinies. Common images of them in the mainstream media refers to illegal journeys of them, dead bodies of them, threats of them to the public, difficult situations of them and low quality of their lives.

This study focuses on political cartoons which is accepted as a form of communication and type of media content. Therefore, the aim of the study is to show how migration issue and refugees are handled in political cartoons which are full of with messages and criticisms based on drawings.

What is Political Cartoon?

The word "cartoon" is used as a popular synonym for "caricature". Cartoon is a humor and visual communication art, and has the characteristics of identifying a situation by exaggerating it. It exaggerates reality to make people think about it. One type of cartoon is the political cartoons which includes political ironies and aims to make people persuade, politicize and criticize.

An ancient Chinese proverb says that "a picture is worth ten thousand words" (Safire, 1996). Therefore, criticizing intolerance, injustice, political corruption and social evils (Neighbor; Karaca; Lang, 2013: 5) with drawings may be

---

[1] Research Assistant in the Department of Journalism, Gazi University, Emek, Ankara, Turkey. E-mail: ardaumutsaygin@gazi.edu.tr

much more powerful than an article in terms of influencing and persuading people. In fact, political cartoons do this. They are both informative and persuasive and they offer people narratives about social problems and strengthen the taken-for-granted meanings of the world. "By doing so, political cartoons provide metalanguage for discourse about the social order by constructing idealizations of the world, positioning readers within a discursive context of 'meaning making' and offering readers a tool" for discussing about recent events and present conditions (Greenberg, 2002). They generally are thought-provoking about political analysis and they contain clear messages about current political events, politicians, political leaders and developments in the world (Neighbor; Karaca; Lang, 2013: 5)." Political cartoons enable public to actively classify, organize and interpret in meaningful ways what they see or experience about the world at a given moment by catching and strengthening the common sense (Greenberg, 2002). However, interpreting cartoons is a complex process which includes "a broad knowledge of past and current events, a vast repertoire of cultural symbols, and experience of thinking analytically about real-world events and circumstances" (El Refaie, 2009: 181).

Method

This study aims at exploring the representations of refugees and migration issue in the political cartoons. Therefore, refugee and migration related political cartoons were analyzed. Also it is tried to show the amount and ratio of refugee and migration related political cartoons among other political cartoons in various subjects. That's why quantitative and qualitative content analysis were prefered because it allows the researcher to collect and code the information in goal-oriented way.

The research data was collected from one of the glo globally known cartoon competion which is The Aydın Doğan International Cartoon Competition and has been organized since 1993. In Aydın Doğan International Cartoon Competition 989 exhibited cartoons were determined from 2013 to 2016 and quantitative and qualitative content analysis were prefered applied to these 989 cartoons.

At first, quantitative content analysis were applied to 989 cartoons which were exhibited in the years of 2013, 2014, 2015, 2016 in The Aydın Doğan International Cartoon Competition. By doing this, 9 different themes were identified which are Technology, Politics, Militarism, Terrorism, Critique of Ideology (Capitalizm, Religion), Gender (Women's right, feminism, Sexual division of labour), Environment (Ecology, Urbanization, Climate change, Animal rights), Abstract-Individual themes (Loneliness, Elderliness, Love, Alienation, etc..) and Migration-Refugee.

Table 1. Political Cartoon Rates and Frequencies in 2013

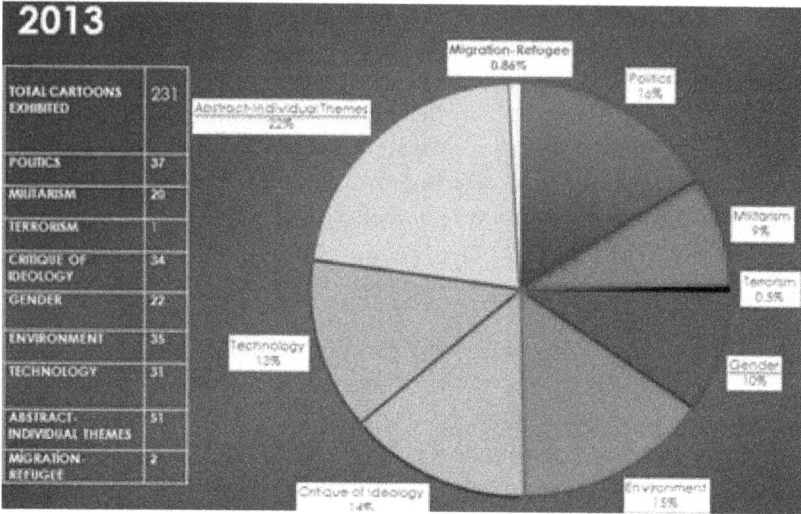

TOTAL CARTOONS EXHIBITED	231
POLITICS	37
MILITARISM	20
TERRORISM	1
CRITIQUE OF IDEOLOGY	34
GENDER	22
ENVIRONMENT	35
TECHNOLOGY	31
ABSTRACT-INDIVIDUAL THEMES	51
MIGRATION-REFUGEE	2

In 2013, 231 political cartoons were exhibited in total and migration-refugee related ones had the lowest rate (0.86) after terrorism (0.5). When we look at the cartoons by themes we see abstract-individual themes took the lead with 51 cartoons. Politics (37), environment (35), and critique of ideology (34) followed it. These statistics will be tmore or less same in 2014.

Table 2. Political Cartoon Rates and Frequencies in 2014

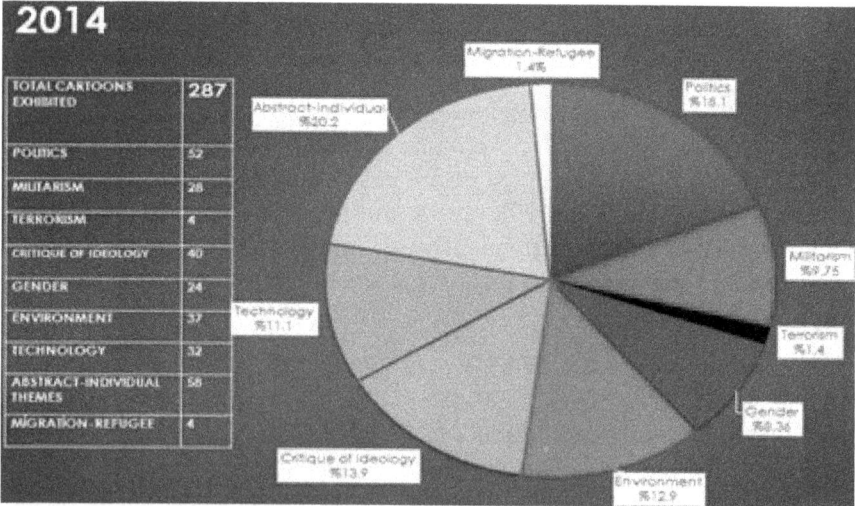

TOTAL CARTOONS EXHIBITED	287
POLITICS	52
MILITARISM	28
TERRORISM	4
CRITIQUE OF IDEOLOGY	40
GENDER	24
ENVIRONMENT	37
TECHNOLOGY	32
ABSTRACT-INDIVIDUAL THEMES	58
MIGRATION-REFUGEE	4

The situation continues in 2014 as well. Among 287 political cartoons, the migration-refugee related ones were in the bottom with only 4 representations and 1.4 ratio.

Table 3. Political Cartoon Rates and Frequencies in 2015

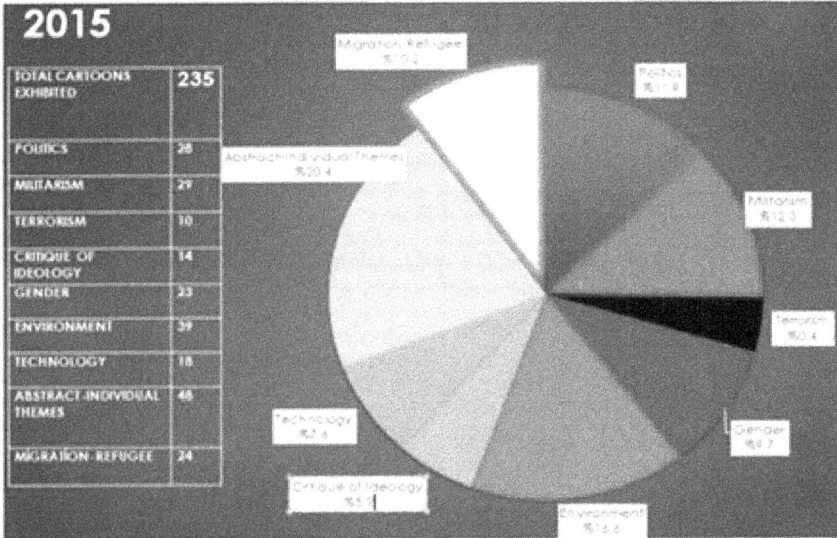

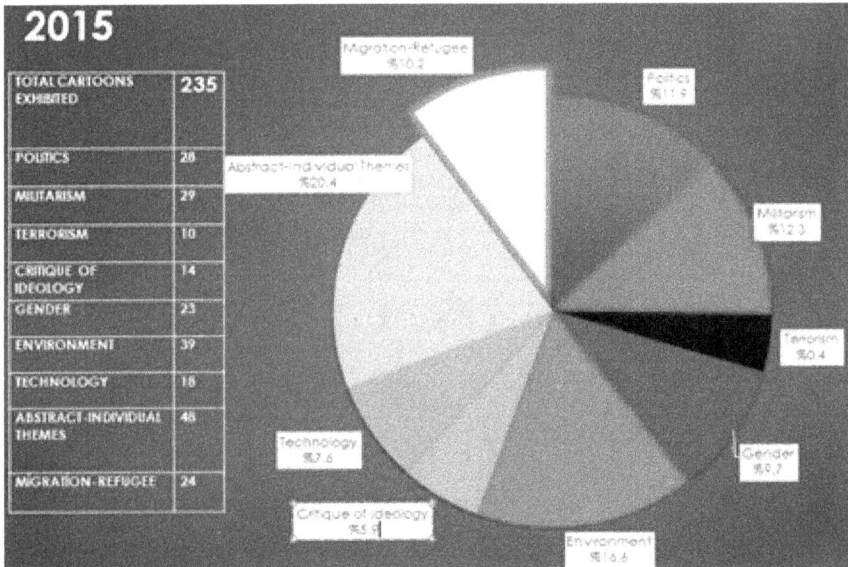

When we come to 2015, in comparison with 2013 and 2014 we see a huge rise in the ratio of migration-refugee related political cartoons with %10.2 percentage and 24 cartoons out of 235.

Table 4. Political Cartoon Rates and Frequencies in 2016

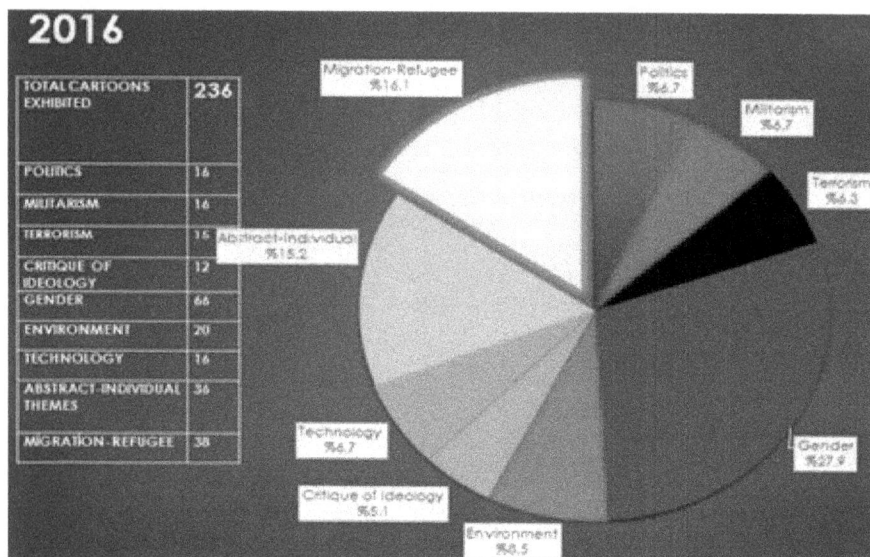

In 2016, migration-refugee related political cartoons takes the second biggest share after gender themes with %16.1 and 38 ratio out of 236. Therefore, after these four years, we see a view like this:

Table 5. Percentage Distribution of Migration-Refugee Related Political Cartoons by Years

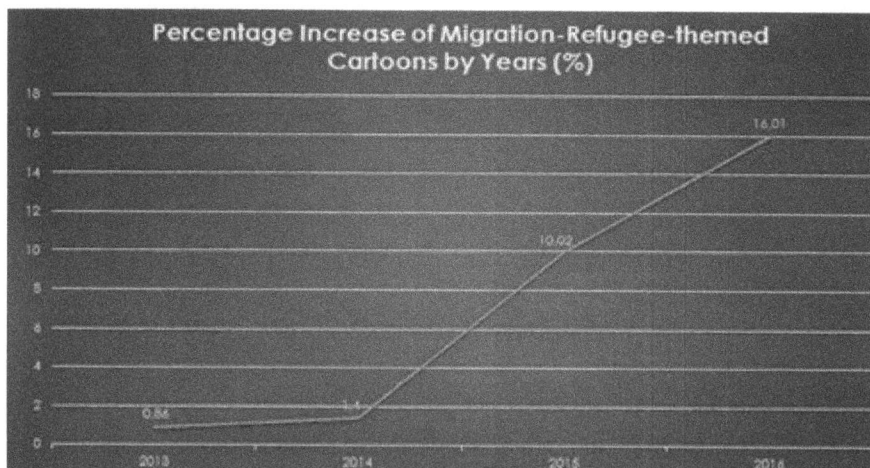

There is a steady increase in migration-refugee related political cartoons in following years from 2013 to 2016. Eventhough it started with 0.86 percentage in 2013, it finished with 16.01 percentage in 2016. After this step, quantitative and qualitative content analysis were applied only to 68 migration-refugee related cartoons and 6 different categories and emphasizing were identified. Two examples of each category is also shown and interpreted on the continuation of the study.

Table 6. Distribution of Political Cartoons by Theme

TOTAL	68
Emphasis on Emphasis on Political Insensitivity	22
Emphasis on Hard Journey Conditions and Death	17
Emphasis on Social Insensitivity	16
Emphasis on Refugees' Europe Expectations	6
Emphasis on Threat Risks	5
Emphasize on the Conditions that Trigger the Migration	2

Emphasize on the Conditions that Trigger the Migration

Agim SULAJ, ALBANIA, 2016   Vladimir KAZANEVSKI, UKRAINE, 2016

There are only two political cartoons that are emphasize on the conditions that trigger the migration. These are doubtlessly war and terrorism. These two situations leave people no choice but migrate.

Emphasis on Refugees' Europe Expectations

Vladimir STANKOVSKI, SERBIA,2016

6 political cartoons out of 68 underlines the Europe expectation of refugees. In the first cartoon, it is seen that people cover themselves with blankets which has printings on cities of Europe. The second cartoon also tells us the expectation of refugees as if European Union is a hero by saving them while they are in the middle of the ocean. Refuugees has Europe dream because of its development level and thats why the migration process ends mostly in Europe or on the way to Europe.

Emphasis on Hard Journey Conditions and Death

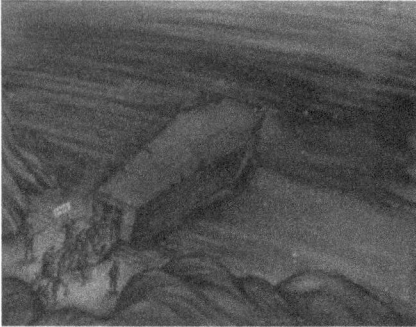

Kürşat Zaman, Turkey, 2016   Musa Gümüş, Turkey, 2015

17 political cartoons emphasis the hard journey conditions of refugees. As I mention above, the migration process can be end on the way to Europe with unfortunate dead. That's why in the first cartoon the ship looks like a coffin. As we see in media contents, traveling through unsafe vehicles causes deads. Therefore, the first cartoon underlines the meaning that boarding the ship is the same as dying. Also, second cartoon shows the ocean as if crime scene. They both refers the inevitable ending while going with ship.

Emphasis on Threat risks

Slobodan Butır, Crotia,2016   Kürşat Zaman, Turkey, 2016

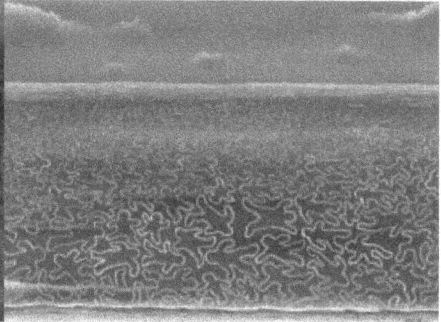

5 political cartoon is about the threats risks coming from refugees. In the first cartoon, a terrorist is hitchhiking a group of people. By doing this, he is able to infiltrated into a country by getting involved into group. In the second

cartoon, at first sight it looks like people are rescued by security forces. However when we look carefully, we see a man wearing a suicide vest. This cartoon also puts emphasis on the idea that refugees may be terrorist and they carry threat risks for societies.

Emphasis on on Political Insensitivity

Vladimir Pavlik, Slovakia, 2016   Mauro Talarico, Italy, 2015

Emphasis on political insensitivity is the category that has the most representations with 22 cartoons. Carttonist were most interested in this issue and the idea that they express in every cartoon is: Eventhough politicians seem like pay attention and try to develop policy about refugees, they do not make any move in real terms, but talking.

Emphasis on Social insensitivity

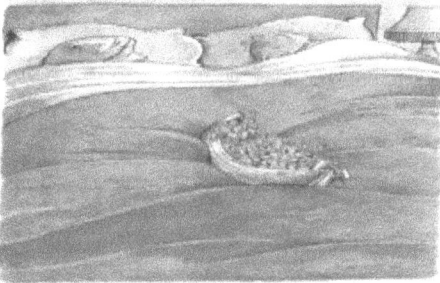

Marco DE ANGELIS, Italy, 2016   Gabriele Corvi, Italy, 2016

Caricaturists are also interested in the topic of social insensitivity with 16 cartoons out of 68. In the first cartoon the quilt that two persons covered while sleeping is like an ocean and people on shipboard is dying on it. The second one also represents the insensitivity of society by veiling.

Conclusion

In the study, it is determined that political cartoons about migration or refugees become even more important year by year. While they took a small space among whole cartoons in 2013 and 2014, we see a radical increase in proportional frequency in 2015 and 2016. It is mostly because of the increase in touching and emotional stories that we see in the media like deaths on a mass scale while migrating or images like three-year-old Aylan draw all attention towards refugee crisis. Apparently, hard journey conditions and deaths of people also came to cartoonists' notice. Also, as we know they also follow the world's agenda and they do not remain indifferent to the developments in the world.

Besides hard conditions and deaths, caroonists also overemphasize the insensitivity of both society and politicians. Idea of showing philosophy of brotherhood by accepting refugees in their country did not touched on by cartoonist. On the contrary, they put emphasis on the insensitivity to the helpless and cureless situation of the refugees. The hope of refugees' fresh start in Europe and reception of immigrants are also workpieces for cartoonists.

References

El Refaie, E. (2009). Multiliteracies: How Readers interpret political cartoons. Visual Communication, 8(2), 181-205.

Greenberg, J. (2002) Framing and temporality in political cartoons: a critical analysis of visual news discourse, *The Canadian Review of Sociology and Anthropology*, May 2002 v39 i2 p181(18). https://faculty.millikin.edu/~moconner/in151h/cartoon2.html, available on: 10.11.2017

Neighbor, T.W.; World, C.K.; Lang, K. (2013). Understanding The World of Political Cartoons, https://www.world-affairs.org/wp-content/uploads/2013/10/2003-Understanding-Political-Cartoons.pdf, available on: 10.14.2017 http://www.nytimes.com/1996/04/07/magazine/on-language-worth-a-thousand-words.html, available on: 10.11.2017

Chapter 9. Forced to Flee: A Case Study Analysis of Sexual Violence During the Syrian Civil War

Emma von der Lieth[1]

Abstract

Since the start of the Syrian Civil War, sexual violence has been rampant, causing most Syrians to cite rape as the primary reason for fleeing their home country. This paper explores the relationship between type of perpetrator and the use of sexual violence during armed conflict in the Syrian Arab Republic. This case study investigates pro-government, opposition, Kurdish, and jihadist groups and analyzes which groups utilize sexual violence and their motivations for doing so. The pro-government group includes the Syrian Arab Armed forces and the shabbiha militia. The jihadist group examined is ISIS, the opposition group is the Free Syrian Army (FSA), and the Kurdish group includes both the People's Protection Units (YPG) and the Women's Protection Units (YPJ). Sources for this research include various reports from non-profit and non-governmental organizations such as the Human Rights Watch, as well as reports from the Syrian Network for Human Rights, United States Department of State, and articles from various news outlets including the BBC. Throughout this case study, various subjects are discussed, including the importance of Syria's history, the use of female combatants, the effects of masculinity and patriarchy on the prevalence of sexual violence, and the use of women as spoils of war. All of these phenomena play an important role in explaining how and why perpetrators use sexual violence. This research shows that sexual violence is used purposefully by jihadist and pro-government groups in Syria, but for differing reasons. Pro-government groups use sexual violence against any whom they perceive to be the enemy, which they believe is any Syrian against the Alawite (Shia) Assad regime. On the other hand, ISIS is more likely than pro-government groups to use women as spoils of war. This is because of the group's emphasis on sexual jihad, and their need to recruit members. With the use of women as spoils of war, ISIS promises members that they can do as they please with these women. The fear of becoming a sex slave for ISIS also helps the group to enforce discipline on the regions they capture. While there is extensive literature regarding the subject of violence against women in conflict, this research is unique in its examination of different types of perpetrators with a narrow focus on Syria. Most importantly, this research provides insight for policy makers around the world regarding the creation of sustainable policy solutions to eliminate sexual violence during conflict.

I. Introduction

As part of a larger project, this research explores the relationship between sexual violence and armed conflict in the Syrian Arab Republic using qualitative methods. The initial research question that this paper seeks to answer is: *Have jihadist, Kurdish, pro-government, and/or opposition groups committed sexual violence in Syria since the start of the Syrian Civil War in 2011?* This question will be examined through case studies represented by pro-government, opposition, Kurdish, and jihadist groups. For the case studies of the groups that have committed sexual violence, this paper will also explore this question: *what is the effect of different armed groups in Syria on the tactics and patterns of sexual violence during the Syrian Civil War?* In essence, of the

---

[1] Department of Public Affairs, Roanoke College, United States.

groups committing sexual violence in Syria, does the type of sexual violence vary by group? How, where, and under what circumstances does each group commit sexual violence? Answering these questions can provide necessary information to prevent one-size-fits all policies and solutions.

The case study analyzes each group (pro-government, opposition, Kurdish, and jihadist) to see if the group has committed sexual violence. Once this answer is determined, the second research question will be examined, if appropriate. Information for the case studies comes primarily from United Nations (UN) reports, US State Department Reports, NGO reports, and news articles. To track the various armed groups and to see if incidences of sexual violence occur in regions where a particular armed group is stationed, a live map of the Syrian Conflict produced by The Carter Center will be used.

Although there have been many studies regarding specific perpetrators of wartime violence[2], there is little documented research that compares and contrasts specific groups of perpetrators in Syria. While most of the major sources explore the motivations behind perpetrators, few delve into the specific patterns and tactics of each group and assess how they compare to one another. This paper seeks to do just that through in-depth case studies.

My previous research regarding perpetrators of sexual violence during armed conflict[3] found that there are particular tactics and patterns that overlap between cases and that differ between cases, however additional comparative cases are needed to definitively provide support for my initial findings. This current research provides those supplementary comparative cases to assess if my previous findings can be supported through further evidence and analysis, specifically in Syria.

The paper is organized in the following manner: Section II provides the literature review, Section III outlines the case study groups, Section IV contains the argument and hypothesis, and Section IV outlines the case studies. Section V discusses the methodology used. Section VI includes the case study. Section VII provides the case study analysis and Section VIII contains the conclusion.

II. A war within a war: Explaining sexual violence during armed conflict

Examining the literature shows a clear consensus amongst the authors that armed conflict and sexual violence have a positive relationship. However, the

---

[2] See, for example, Jeannie Annan et al., "Women and Girls at War: 'Wives', Mothers, Fighters in the Lord's Resistance Army," Unpublished Manuscript, April 2009, 1–40.

[3] Emma von der Lieth, "Bodies as Battlefields: A Mixed Methods Analysis of Sexual Violence During Armed Conflict," Presented at the International Studies Association South Conference, Tampa, FL, 2015, 1–68.

motivations of sexual violence during armed conflict are unclear. Scholars have several explanations for this phenomenon, some of which are conflicting.

The literature utilized focuses on developing countries, which pertains to the Syria case study. The definition of a developing country is contested, as the United Nations does not specifically define the term, and the World Bank has stopped using it altogether.[4] For the purpose of this research, a developing country is one which has a low score compared to other countries on the Human Development Index (HDI) and has low industrialization.[5] The HDI measures: "a long and healthy life, (and) access to knowledge and a decent standard of living."[6] In 2016, Syria received an HDI of 0.536, which positioned the nation at 149 out of 188 countries.[7] Syria's HDI score has been on the decline since the war began in 2011.[8]

Strategy or unfortunate side effect?

It is unclear whether sexual violence during war in developing countries is an intentional act or if it is tolerated. Scholars argue that sexual violence is intentional for several reasons. First, developing countries do not have modern technology that developed countries use in war. Thus, they rely on other methods, such as terrorizing the community and weakening the enemy by preying on women, the weakest in society, to achieve success during combat.[9]

---

[4] "Glossary of Statistsical Terms: Developed, Developing Countries," Organization for Economic Co-Operation and Development, January 4, 2006, https://stats.oecd.org/glossary/detail.asp?ID=6326 ;

Matthew Lynn, "Why the Title of 'Developing Country' No Longer Exists," The Telegraph, May 23, 2016, http://www.telegraph.co.uk/business/2016/05/23/why-the-title-of-developing-country-no-longer-exists/.

[5] "What Is A Developing Country?" World Atlas, March 21, 2017, http://www.worldatlas.com/articles/what-is-a-developing-country.html.

[6] "Human Development for Everyone: Briefing Note for Countries on the 2016 Human Development Report, Syrian Arab Republic" (New York: United Nations Development Program, 2017), 2.

The metric for a long and healthy life is life expectancy at birth. The metric for access to knowledge is the average number of years of schooling received in one's lifetime, for those 25 years of age or older. The metric for standard of living is measured by Gross National Income per capita in international dollars.

[7] "Human Development Reports : Syrian Arab Republic," United Nations Development Program: Human Development Reports, 2016, http://hdr.undp.org/en/countries/profiles/SYR.

[8] Ibid.

[9] Kathryn Farr, "Armed Conflict, War Rape," Pakistan Journal of Women's Studies 16 (1&2): 4, 24; Kathryn Farr, "Extreme War Rape in Today's Civil-War-Torn States: A Contextual and Comparative Analysis," Gender Issues 26, no. 1 (2009b): 6,8,9; Rashida Manjoo and Calleigh McRaith, "Gender-Based Violence and Justice in Conflict and Post-Conflict Areas," Cornell International Law 44, no. 1 (2010): 14; Rehn and Sirleaf, "Women, War, and Peace," 10, 17; Radhika Coomaraswamy, "Report of the Special Rapporteur on Violence against Women, Its Causes and Consequences, Ms. Radhika

In addition, combatants rape enemy women to spread the perpetrators' genes throughout the region, which is a form of ethnic cleansing.[10] Women are also sometimes intentionally given HIV, a deadly disease that can be transmitted to the next generation.[11] In addition, those living in developing countries during armed conflict are at an increased risk when resources are scarce.[12] For example, hospitals and healthcare workers are targeted by combatant groups.[13] This makes it even more difficult for victims to seek help after sexual violence occurs.[14] Thus, combatants commit sexual violence because they know that there is no place for victims to report the act to, nor is there a place for the victim to seek medical care.[15]

However, sexual violence can be tolerated by governmental forces because they do not have the resources to combat it. For instance, perpetrators are usually not punished because of the weak judicial systems in developing countries.[16] Developing countries, especially those experiencing armed conflict, do not have the appropriate political or economic resources to carry out law and order.[17] Developing countries already have poor judicial systems because of poverty, and armed conflict exacerbates these conditions. Thus, sexual violence has become an accepted part of armed conflict in many areas of the world because very few perpetrators have been punished.[18] If there are no consequences for those who commit sexual violence, perpetrators will continue to act with impunity. This phenomenon is hypothesized to be a result of institutionalized power that groups utilize to commit sexual violence, which

---

Coomaraswamy, Submitted in Accordance with Commission on Human Rights Resolution 2001/49: Cultural Practices in the Family That Are Violent towards Women" (United Nations Commission on Human Rights, January 31, 2002), accessed Feb. 28, 2015, http://www.refworld.org/docid/3d6ce3cc0.html, 3-34.

[10] Jennifer Lynn Green, "Collective Rape: A Cross-National Study of the Incidence and Perpetrators of Mass Political Sexual Violence, 1980-2003" (Ph.D. diss., Ohio State University, 2006), 5; Elisabeth Wood, "Variation in Sexual Violence During War," Politics and Society 34, no. 3 (2006): 307-308, 313.

[11] Manjoo and McRaith, "Gender-based Violence," 16; Elisabeth Rehn and Ellen Johnson Sirleaf, 2002, "Women, War, and Peace," New York, NY: United Nations Development Fund for Women, http://www.unwomen.org/~/media/headquarters/media/publications/unifem/210table.pdf, 1, 10.

[12] Rehn and Sirleaf, "Women, War, and Peace," 17.

[13] Ibid, 34.

[14] Farr, "Armed Conflict, War Rape," 10; Rehn and Sirleaf, "Women, War, and Peace," 34.

[15] Jennifer Lynn Green, 2004, "Uncovering Collective Rape," International Journal of Sociology 34 (1): 105; Rehn and Sirleaf, "Women, War, and Peace," 34.

[16] Rehn and Sirleaf, "Women, War, and Peace," 11, 16-17.

[17] Farr, "Armed Conflict, War Rape," 16, 22; Farr, "Extreme War Rape," 9-11 Rehn and Sirleaf, "Women, War, and Peace," 6-7.

[18] Manjoo and McRaith, "Gender-Based Violence," 26-29.

can be seen in cases of rape by UN peacekeepers in the Democratic Republic of the Congo and rape by the Syrian government.[19]

Overall, while there is some ambiguity regarding sexual violence as a strategy or a tolerated practice, looking at the literature as a whole supports the argument that sexual violence during armed conflict is both intentional and tolerated.[20]

Victims

The literature suggests that women are more likely to become victims of sexual violence than men.[21] This results from the low status that women have in society.[22] There are also social stigmas that may arise after a woman has been raped.[23] For example, in some cultures women are deemed unmarriageable or dishonorable to their families if they have been raped.[24] This phenomenon predominantly occurs in Islamic societies and is a reflection of the belief that men must: "guard, supervise, and defend against...his women's virginity."[25] In fact, some women that have been raped are killed by their families to protect their honor.[26] Therefore, the status of women in particular societies hinders them from obtaining the help they need, whether it is medical care or legal protection. This makes them easy targets for armed combatants and also makes the crime less likely to be reported.[27] In addition, some combatants consider women to be "spoils of war,"[28] which not only dehumanizes women but also serves as an insult to the community, especially to the fathers and the husbands of the women.

However, women are not the only victims of sexual violence during armed combat. During the conflict between the Sri Lankan government and the Liberation Tigers of Tamil Eelam (LTTE), men were sexually abused in

---

[19] von der Lieth, "Bodies as Battlefields: A Mixed Methods Analysis of Sexual Violence During Armed Conflict."

[20] Farr, "Armed Conflict, War Rape," 17.

[21] Farr, "Armed Conflict, War Rape," 9-10; Farr, "Extreme War Rape," 19, 21-22; Green, "Collective Rape," 103; Luc Malemo Kalisya et al., "Sexual Violence toward Children and Youth in War-Torn Eastern Democratic Republic of Congo," PLoS ONE 6, no. 1 (2011): 3.

[22] Farr, "Armed Conflict, War Rape," 4, 24; Rehn and Sirleaf, "Women, War, and Peace," 17.

[23] Rehn and Sirleaf, "Women, War, and Peace," 17.

[24] Farr, "Armed Conflict, War Rape," 10-11; Green, "Uncovering Collective Rape," 105; Rehn and Sirleaf, "Women, War, and Peace," 17.

[25] Lama Abu-Odeh, "Crimes of Honor and the Construction of Gender in Arab Societies," in Women and Sexuality in Muslim Societies, ed. Pinar Ilkkaracan (Istanbul: Women for Women's Human Rights, 2000), 372.

[26] Abu-Odeh, "Crimes of Honor," 375.

[27] Rehn and Sirleaf "Women, War, and Peace," 6-7, 17.

[28] Manjoo and McRaith, "Gender-Based Violence," 15.

detention centers by the Sri Lankan armed forces. The Sri Lankan armed forces used sexual violence to obtain confessions and information about the LTTE.[29] A similar pattern can be seen when examining the recent conflict in the Syrian Arab Republic. Although women are at a greater risk of becoming victims of rape in the Syria, there have been reports of men being raped so that the Syrian government can elicit confessions or otherwise embarrass the victims in front of their family members.[30] Previous research has found that, out of four perpetrator groups examined (the Syrian government, UN peacekeepers, the Lord's Resistance Army, and the Group Islamique Armé), the Syrian government was the only group to have committed sexual violence against men and boys.[31]

Perpetrators

There is much variation in the perpetrators of sexual violence. For instance, Cohen et al. state that perpetrators can be state militia, rebel groups, civilians, and/or female.[32] In addition, the authors claim that state militia are "far more likely than rebel groups to be reported as perpetrators of rape and other sexual violence."[33] Cohen et al. suggest that this is the case because state militias often use sexual violence as a form of torture in detention facilities to obtain confessions.[34] However, rebel groups must scrounge for food and supplies, and rely on civilian support for fighters.[35] Therefore, some rebel groups may not want to jeopardize this relationship with the civilian population by committing sexual violence against them.[36] Nevertheless, the authors acknowledge that some rebel groups do perpetrate sexual violence during conflict, but only the most recent studies are exploring why this variation occurs.[37]

---

[29] Charu Lata Hogg, "'We Will Teach You a Lesson:' Sexual Violence against Tamils by Sri Lankan Security Forces" (Human Rights Watch, February 26, 2013), accessed June 5, 2015, https://www.hrw.org/report/2013/02/26/we-will-teach-you-lesson/sexual-violence-against-tamils-sri-lankan-security-forces.

[30] "Syria 2012 Human Rights Report" (Washington D.C.: US Department of State, 2012), 2, 7, 18; "Report of the Independent International Commission of Inquiry on the Syrian Arab Republic" (United Nations, General Assembly, August 16, 2012), 43.

[31] von der Lieth, "Bodies as Battlefields: A Mixed Methods Analysis of Sexual Violence During Armed Conflict."

[32] Dara Kay Cohen et al., "Wartime Sexual Violence: Misconceptions, Implications, and Ways Forward" (Washington D.C.: United States Institute of Peace, February 8, 2013), http://www.usip.org/publications/wartime-sexual-violence-misconceptions-implications-and-ways-forward, 1.

[33] Cohen et al., "Wartime Sexual Violence," 4.

[34] Ibid. See also "Syria: Sexual Assault in Detention" (New York: Human Rights Watch, June 15, 2012), https://www.hrw.org/news/2012/06/15/syria-sexual-assault-detention.

[35] Cohen et al., "Wartime Sexual Violence," 4.

[36] Ibid.

[37] Ibid, 4, 14.

Cohen et al. also state that females are sometimes perpetrators of sexual violence.[38] This phenomenon has occurred in the DRC, Haiti, Rwanda, and Iraq.[39] The authors suggest that women may perpetrate sexual violence along with male combatants in order to fit in or to display their strength and masculinity.[40] The importance of the role of masculinity and sexual violence can be seen from a previous case study of UN peacekeepers in the Democratic Republic of the Congo. In this case, a masculinized culture lead to UN peacekeepers to keep a "mental tally"[41] of the number of women they paid to sleep with to "compete with one another and 'satisfy' their sex drives."[42]

Women may have similar motives as men, such as wanting to humiliate or degrade the enemy.[43] However, it is rare for women to perpetrate sexual violence during war, and this phenomenon may be exaggerated in the media.[44] Other common perpetrators are civilians. One study conducted in 2007 found that women in the DRC reported more rape by intimate partners than by other perpetrators.[45] Another study conducted between 2001-2009 in Columbia during conflict found that approximately 45% of women reported being raped by a family member and about 31% of women reported being raped by an unknown perpetrator.[46] However, Cohen et al. state that it is unclear if rape

---

[38] Ibid, 5.

[39] Ibid. See also Kirsten Johnson, et al., "Association of Sexual Violence and Human Rights Violations with Physical and Mental Health in Territories of the Eastern Democratic Republic of the Congo," Journal of the American Medical Association 304, no. 5 (2010): 553–62; Benedetta Faedi, "From Violence Against Women to Women's Violence in Haiti," PhD dissertation, Stanford University, 2010; Adam Jones, "Gender and Genocide in Rwanda," Journal of Genocide Research 4, no. 1 (March 2002): 65–94; Lisa Sharlach, "Gender and Genocide in Rwanda: Women as Agents and Objects of Genocide," Journal of Genocide Research 1, no. 3 (November 1999): 387–99; Wood, "Armed Groups and Sexual Violence."; African Rights, "Rwanda: Not So Innocent: When Women Become Killers," 1995; Peter Landesman, "A Woman's Work," New York Times Magazine, September 15, 2002. http://www.nytimes.com/2002/09/15/magazine/a-woman-s-work.html (accessed August 11, 2015); Sharlach, "Gender and Genocide in Rwanda: Women as Agents"; Jones, "Gender and Genocide in Rwanda."

[40] Cohen et al, "Wartime Sexual Violence," 5.

[41] Ibid.

[42] Paul Higate, "Peacekeepers, Masculinities, and Sexual Exploitation," Men and Masculinities 10, no. 1 (2007): 106.

[43] Cohen et al, "Wartime Sexual Violence," 5.

[44] Ibid.

[45] Amber Peterman et al., "Estimates and Determinants of Sexual Violence Against Women in the Democratic Republic of Congo," American Journal of Public Health 101, no. 6 (2011): 1065.

[46] Olga Amparo Sanchez et al., "First Survey on the Prevalence of Sexual Violence Against Women in the Context of the Colombian Armed Conflict, 2001–2009: Executive Summary" (Bogatå, Columbia: Casa de la Mujer and Oxfam, 2011), 16.

perpetrated by family members or intimate partners is directly associated with conflict.[47] In addition, rape perpetrated by husbands is often not considered rape in some regions of the world, and therefore is often not reported.[48]

Apart from this project, which encompasses this current paper along with the larger project of *Bodies as Battlefields*,[49] no previous research has conducted a case study that examines each type of perpetrator and analyzes similarities and differences between each group, especially for a specific conflict. This research will do just that through case studies, which will add much needed information to the phenomenon of sexual violence during the Syrian Civil War.

III. Case study groups

Each of the four case studies in this paper examine the use of sexual violence, or lack thereof, by four armed groups during the Syrian Civil War. The armed groups are categorized as follows: pro-government, jihadist groups, opposition groups, and Kurdish groups.

Pro-government groups

Pro-government forces consist of the Syrian Arab Forces and pro-government militias, including the shabbiha (which is the Arabic word for "ghost") and the Jaysh al-Sha'bi (also known as the People's Army).[50] The Syrian government forces include the Syrian Arab Armed Forces, which consists of the Army, Navy, and the Air Force.[51] The President controls elite units such as the 10,000-man Republican Guard, and the President's brother controls the 20,000-man Fourth Division.[52] The Syrian government includes all military and intelligence forces, and those working at checkpoints, detention centers, and prisons.[53] The shabbiha and Jaysh al-Sha'bi militias are local and are an imperative part of Assad's military regime because they "can slaughter under

---

[47] Cohen et al, "Wartime Sexual Violence," 7.

[48] The definition of rape according to Syrian law is: "when a man forces a woman who is not his wife to have intercourse." Further, if the rapist marries the victim, there will be no punishment. See US State Department, "Syria 2012 Human Rights Report," 33.

[49] von der Lieth, "Bodies as Battlefields: A Mixed Methods Analysis of Sexual Violence During Armed Conflict."

[50] von der Lieth, "Bodies as Battlefields: A Mixed Methods Analysis of Sexual Violence During Armed Conflict," 13; Jenkins, "The Dynamics of Syria's Civil War," 6.

[51] "Report of the Independent International Commission of Inquiry on the Syrian Arab Republic" (United Nations, General Assembly, Human Rights Council, November 23, 2011), http://www.ohchr.org/Documents/Countries/SY/A.HRC.S-17.2.Add.1_en.pdf, 6 [referred to as A/HRC/S-17/2/Add.1 in subsequent footnotes].

[52] A/HRC/S-17/2/Add.1, 6.

[53] Detention centers are run by the Air Force, the Political Security Division, the General Security Directorate, and/or the Military Intelligence Directorate; see "Syria 2015 Human Rights Report," 5.

the radar while giving the regime a thin veil of deniability."[54] Shabbiha and the Jaysh al-Sha'bi do not follow any particular rules set up by the Syrian government but do receive support from the Syrian government in the form of airpower and artillery.[55] In fact, most of the shabbiha are made up of Assad's relatives and other Alawites.[56] Further, the shabbiha have been characterized as "hired thugs…ex-convicts released from prison in exchange for loyalty to the Assad regime who are now being used to carry out brutal attacks against opponents of the government."[57] The Jaysh al-Sha'bi mainly defend Alawite, Christian, and Druze regions from opposition groups and the group is armed by Hezbollah and Iran's Islamic Revolutionary Guards.[58] It is important to include these militias in this research because there has already been evidence that shabiha have committed sexual violence.[59] However, previous studies have not examined if the Jaysh al-Sha'bi has committed sexual violence, and if this claim is true, it has large implications for the other groups involved, namely Iran's Islamic Revolutionary Guards and Hezbollah.

Jihadist groups

In this paper, the jihadist group that will be discussed is the Islamic State of Iraq and Syria (ISIS). While Jabhat Fateh Al-Sham (the Front for the Conquest of the Levant, previously known as Jabhat al-Nusra) is also categorized by some as a jihadist group, this paper will not assess sexual violence perpetrated by this group due to lack of information.[60] The goal of ISIS is to establish a Caliphate and an Islamic State.[61] ISIS seeks to establish control over Syria, as the group control schools, courts, and provides social assistance to individuals in regions they have taken over.[62] This shows that "ISIL and al-Nusrah [JFS]

---

[54] Jenkins, "The Dynamics of Syria's Civil War," 6.
[55] Ibid.
[56] Ibid.
[57] Ibid.
[58] Ibid, 7.
[59] von der Lieth, "Bodies as Battlefields: A Mixed Methods Analysis of Sexual Violence During Armed Conflict," 13-20.
[60] Charles Lister, "Dynamic Stalemate: Surveying Syria's Military Landscape," Policy Briefing (Doha, Qatar: Brookings Institution: Brookings Doha Center, May 2014), https://www.brookings.edu/wp-content/uploads/2016/06/Syria-Military-Landscape-English.pdf, 8; Brian Michael Jenkins, "The Dynamics of Syria's Civil War" (Santa Monica: RAND Corporation, 2014), 9; Fred Dews, "A Glossary of Forces in the Syrian Civil War," Brookings Now, May 27, 2014, https://www.brookings.edu/blog/brookings-now/2014/05/27/a-glossary-of-forces-in-the-syrian-civil-war/.
[61] Lister, "Dynamic Stalemate: Surveying Syria's Military Landscape," 3 Beacham Publishing's Terrorism Research & Analysis Consortium (TRAC), "Islamic State (IS) / Islamic State of Iraq and Ash Sham (ISIS) / Islamic State of Iraq (ISIS or ISIL, IS)," Tracking Terrorism, accessed February 21, 2017, https://www.trackingterrorism.org/group/islamic-state-islamic-state-iraq-and-ash-sham-isis-islamic-state-iraq-isis-or-isil.
[62] Jenkins, "The Dynamics of Syria's Civil War," 10.

are more interested in establishing their control over territory in eastern Syria than in overthrowing Assad."[63] This motivation sets ISIS apart from opposition groups, who seek to overthrow Assad and emerged primarily for this reason.[64] For instance, many fighters in the Free Syrian Army (FSA), an opposition group, were "defectors from the Syrian armed forces…who opposed Alawite domination."[65] Kurdish groups have another, separate motivation that will be discussed later in this section of the paper.

Opposition groups

There is a multitude of opposition groups fighting in the Syrian Civil War.[66] This paper examines the Free Syrian Army because it is an umbrella group of armed organizations, which makes data easier to gather and analyze from various groups under this umbrella.[67] The FSA was forged after army defections from the Syrian armed forces, most of whom were Sunni and opposed Assad's regime.[68] There are over a thousand independent groups that have branched off of the FSA, for a total of 50,000 fighters as of 2014.[69] The FSA differs from jihadist groups because the FSA focuses on localized and uncoordinated attacks, rather than a group-wide strategy, to weaken Assad's forces.[70] Further, the FSA and ISIS have fought against each other, notably in September 2013, when the FSA killed an ISIS commander.[71] It is important to note that JFS was at one time a part of the FSA, but that JFS separated itself in September 2013 in order to have a more Islamist group ideology.[72]

Kurdish groups

The People's Protection Units (YPG / *Yekîneyên Parastina Gel*) is the main Kurdish armed group fighting in Syrian Kurdistan, which is located in northern Syria near its border with Turkey.[73] The YPG developed in 2011, when the Syrian Civil War began, and targets the Syrian army and pro-government

---

[63] Ibid.

[64] Ibid, 8; Beacham Publishing's Terrorism Research & Analysis Consortium (TRAC), "Free Syrian Army (FSA)," Tracking Terrorism, accessed November 1, 2016, http://www.trackingterrorism.org/group/free-syrian-army-fsa.

[65] Jenkins, "The Dynamics of Syria's Civil War," 8.

[66] Dews, "A Glossary of Forces in the Syrian Civil War."

[67] Jenkins, "The Dynamics of Syria's Civil War," 8.

[68] Ibid.

[69] Ibid.

[70] Ibid.

[71] Ibid, 9.

[72] Ibid, 8.

[73] Beacham Publishing's Terrorism Research & Analysis Consortium (TRAC), "People's Protection Units (YPG)," Tracking Terrorism, accessed November 8, 2016, http://www.trackingterrorism.org/group/peoples%E2%80%99-protection-units-ypg ; The Carter Center, "Tracking the Front Lines in Syria," Syria Dashboard, accessed February 20, 2017, https://d3svb6mundity5.cloudfront.net/dashboard/index.html.

forces, as well as JFS and ISIS.[74] The YPG is the armed branch of the Democratic Union Party (PYD / *Partiya Yekîtiya Demokrat*).[75] The main goal of Kurdish groups in Syria is to establish a "free, democratic and plural Syria in which all minorities are recognized and respected within the country's political framework."[76] While Kurdish groups target any and all political adversaries, including other Kurdish groups, but they also target pro-government forces.[77]

One of the most important differences between the YPG and other armed groups in Syria is the presence of women fighters.[78] In fact, around 35% of fighters in the YPG in Syria are women, and there is an all-female Women's Protection Unit (YPJ / *Yekîneyên Parastina Jin*) fighting in Syria, which is affiliated with the YPG.[79] Thus, for this research, Kurdish forces will be defined as both the YPG and the YPJ together.

Both groups are at least somewhat associated with the Kurdistan Worker's Party (PKK / *Partiya Karkerên Kurdistanê*), although this claim is controversial.[80] For the purpose of this paper, the YPG / YPJ and the PKK are linked together in some fashion and share similar ideologies but are not considered to be entirely the same group. A justification for this claim is more appropriately discussed in Section VII of this paper. The YPJ has carried out independent operations but has also worked side-by-side with the YPG.[81] The group's motivations for fighting in the Syrian Civil War are unique, as they are not necessarily fighting for statehood, since they believe that states are oppressive, and they are not fighting to secede from Syria, because they do not recognize European borders.[82] The Kurdish groups are fighting against ISIS,

[74] TRAC, "People's Protection Units (YPG)."
[75] Ibid; The PYD is an affiliate of the Kurdistan Workers' Party (PKK) and is Syria's most well-armed and largest armed Kurdish group, see Beacham Publishing's TRAC (Terrorism Research & Analysis Consortium), 2016, "Syrian Kurdish Democratic Union Party (PYD)," Trackingterrorism.org, http://www.trackingterrorism.org/group/syrian-kurdish-democratic-union-party-pyd, (Accessed 8 November 2016).
[76] TRAC, "Syrian Kurdish Democratic Union Party (PYD)."
[77] Ibid.
[78] TRAC, "People's Protection Units (YPG)."
[79] Beacham Publishing's Terrorism Research & Analysis Consortium, "YPJ (Women's Protection Unit," Tracking Terrorism, October 27, 2016, http://www.trackingterrorism.org/group/ypj-womens-protection-unit.
[80] "Women Warriors: A Nightmare for IS," The Sunday Herald, October 19, 2014, NewsBank, EBSCOhost.
[81] Emanuela C. Del Re., "Female Combatants in the Syrian Conflict, in the Fight against or with the IS, and in the Peace Process," in Female Combatants in Conflict and Peace: Challenging Gender in Violence and Post-Conflict Reintegration (Hampshire: Palgrave Macmillan, 2015), 87.
[82] Amy Austin Holmes, "What Are the Kurdish Women's Units Fighting for in Syria?," The Washington Post, December 23, 2015,

and their main targets are Syrian Islamists.[83] There have been many gains and losses of territory in northern Syria by both the Kurdish groups (the YPG/YPJ) and ISIS. As of April 2017, Kurdish groups have most of the territory in Northern Syria and have gained a significant amount of territory since January 2016.[84] In January 2016, ISIS held areas near and in Aleppo, Qarah, and Saluq in the mid-part of Northern Syria.[85] In March 2017, Kurdish groups made considerable gains in these areas, driving out ISIS and taking control of almost the entirety of Northern Syria, with the exception of opposition held-territory just northeast of Aleppo.[86]

IV. Argument and hypothesis

Hypotheses

After examining previous literature regarding sexual violence and armed conflict, the hypotheses for this paper are as follows:

H1: Pro-government forces are more likely to commit sexual violence against civilians across civilians' ethnicity, religion, and/or gender.

H2: Jihadist groups and opposition groups are more likely to use women as spoils of war compared to the other groups examined in this paper.

H3: Kurdish groups are overall significantly less likely to commit sexual violence compared to the other groups examined in this paper.

H3b: *This is because of the influence of females in their government structure as well as on the battlefield.*

The first and second hypotheses are proposed for future research in *Bodies as Battlefields* (2015). The third hypothesis was not suggested in *Bodies as Battlefields* (2015) but is especially important for this specialized research.

Arguments: H1

There is already overwhelming evidence that pro-government forces, such as the Syrian Arab Armed Forces and the pro-government militia, shabbiha have committed sexual violence in Syria.[87] Pro-government forces often commit

---

https://www.washingtonpost.com/news/monkey-cage/wp/2015/12/23/what-are-the-kurdish-womens-units-fighting-for-in-syria/.

[83] Holmes, "What Are the Kurdish Women's Units Fighting for in Syria," ;
TRAC,"People's Protection Units (YPG)" ; "Kurdish People's Protection Unit YPG," GlobalSecurity.org, August 19, 2016,
http://www.globalsecurity.org/military/world/para/ypg.htm.

[84] The Carter Center, "Tracking the Front Lines in Syria."

[85] Ibid.

[86] Ibid.

[87] von der Lieth, "Bodies as Battlefields: A Mixed Methods Analysis of Sexual Violence During Armed Conflict," 13-20.

rape against civilians during incursions, raids, and kidnappings and in government-run prisons, detention facilities, and checkpoints.[88] A majority of the victims are associated with the opposition.[89] In fact, men and boys are more likely to be raped in detention centers than women and girls because they are directly fighting for the opposition, making them easier targets.[90] Further, pro-government forces use sexual violence as a tactic of war to elicit confessions, to gather information about the opposition, to humiliate and degrade the opposition, and to displace citizens.[91] This shows that pro-government forces use sexual violence regardless of ethnicity, religion, or sex.

Arguments: H2

The larger study of *Bodies as Battlefields* (2015) analyzed several different groups, including rebel groups, and hypothesized that rebel groups are likely to use women as spoils of war.[92] For the sake of this project, jihadist, opposition, and Kurdish groups are classified as rebel groups, which are defined as any group fighting against the Syrian government. However, I do not believe that Kurdish groups are likely to use women as spoils of war, which will be discussed in the subsequent hypothesis. Therefore, I hypothesize that jihadist and opposition groups are more likely to use spoils of war.

The most prominent reason why rebel groups are more likely to use spoils of war is because they must recruit soldiers and therefore "rewards" are necessary to fill their ranks. Unlike the pro-government forces, individuals in rebel groups are not being paid to fight, therefore commanders in rebel groups must develop a way to motivate their fighters.[93]

Arguments: H3 and H3b

The Kurdish groups fighting in Syria are inherently different from the pro-government, jihadist, and opposition forces because the group practices a gender-inclusive ideology. According to Asal et al. (2013), groups with gender-inclusive ideology are more likely to use nonviolent strategies, which could potentially result in less instances of sexual violence.[94] Although Asal et al. do not provide an explicit definition of "gender inclusive ideology," it is suggested within their article that this term refers to a "movement...that

---

[88] Ibid, 15.

[89] Ibid.

[90] Ibid, 17.

[91] Ibid, 16-18.

[92] Ibid, 44.

[93] von der Lieth, "Bodies as Battlefields: A Mixed Methods Analysis of Sexual Violence During Armed Conflict," 42.

[94] Victor Asal et al., "Gender Ideologies and Forms of Contentious Mobilization in the Middle East," Journal of Peace Resesarch 50, no. 3 (2013): 308.

actively advocates for their (women's) inclusion."[95] Kurdish forces fit this description for a variety of reasons, such as co-presidency at all political levels within the PKK and having an equal number of men and women within the PKK's ranks.[96] This similar ideology is shown within the YPG / YPJ because women and men fight side by side and have adopted the gender-inclusive ideologies of the PKK.[97] In 2013 in Rojava, "honor killings were criminalized, underage and forced marriages outlawed, and men with more than one wife excluded from all organizations and committees."[98] Women are also encouraged to work in cooperatives such as agriculture, animal husbandry, or sales, and to receive an education.[99] Those who live in the Kurdish Rojava region of northern Syria live in either mixed communes or female-only communes which each contain five committees for education, healthcare, economy, problem-solving, and self-defense (specifically the YPJ).[100] In the women-only communes, women are particularly given the most power and control over their area. All of this shows that the Kurds are a group that "actively advocates"[101] for the inclusion of women.[102]

Asal et al.'s claim may contribute to a lack of sexual violence perpetrated by Kurdish armed forces in Syria. There are a few reasons why a gender-inclusive ideology as well as a female presence in traditionally male armed groups can decrease the likelihood of sexual violence during conflict. First, women in armed groups are extremely important because a culture of masculinity can lead to sexual violence.[103] This can be seen from sexual violence committed by UN Peacekeepers in the Democratic Republic of the Congo (DRC). Initially, the excuse "boys will be boys"[104] was widely used after accusations

[95] Asal et al., "Gender Ideologies and Forms of Contentious Mobilization in the Middle East," 308.

[96] Del Re, "Female Combatants in the Syrian Conflict, in the Fight against or with the IS, and in the Peace Process," 87.

[97] Ibid., 86, 92.

[98] Jesse Claflin, "Kurdish Women's Protection Units (YPJ): The Fight to Protect Democratic Confederalism" (The Gate: University of Chicago's Undergraduate Political Review, February 28, 2017), http://uchicagogate.com/2017/02/28/kurdish-womens-protection-units-ypj-the-fight-to-protect-democratic-confederalism/.

[99] Claflin, "Kurdish Women's Protection Units (YPJ): The Fight to Protect Democratic Confederalism."

[100] Ibid.

[101] Asal et al., "Gender Ideologies and Forms of Contentious Mobilization in the Middle East," 308.

[102] Claflin, "Kurdish Women's Protection Units (YPJ): The Fight to Protect Democratic Confederalism."

[103] Paul Higate, 2007, "Peacekeepers, Masculinities, and Sexual Exploitation," Men and Masculinities 10 (1): 99-119.

[104] Quote by UN mission in Cambodia's Special Representative to the Secretary General, Yasushi Akashi in Sarah Martin, "Must Boys Be Boys? Ending Sexual Exploitation & Abuse in UN Peacekeeping Mission" (Washington, D.C.: Refugees

against UN peacekeeping sexual abuse arose in Cambodia.[105] This argument claims that men who are away from home for long periods of time must satisfy their sex drives. However, this theory is lacking. To combat this argument, Higate states that some believe some peacekeepers to be: "vulnerable to a sex drive that was seen to have a mind of its own."[106]

Further, several authors have suggested adding more female peacekeepers to decrease the prevalence of sexual violence.[107] According to the UN, women made up 17 percent of national peacekeeping operations staff and 29 percent of international peacekeeping operations staff as of 2012.[108] Martin (2005) states that the culture of masculinity has contributed to a tolerance for sexual violence.[109] Traditionally male environments are often characterized by "a bond that protects the members inside from accusations, whether true or not, from the outside."[110] This was seen in the DRC, when civilian staff were not forthcoming with reports of sexual violence.[111] Specifically, Bridges and Horsfall (2009) argue that an increase in female peacekeepers will help to combat sexual violence perpetrated by male peacekeepers.[112] This occurs because female peacekeepers can illustrate the inappropriateness of sexual violence to male peacekeepers.[113] Moreover, female peacekeepers can break the culture of masculinity and report sexual violence cases in a more effective manner.

However, it is important to note that females can and do perpetrate sexual violence in some situations. For instance, female combatants have committed

International, 2005),
http://www.pseataskforce.org/uploads/tools/mustboysbeboysendingseainunpeacekeepingmi ssions_refugeesinternational_english.pdf, 4.

105 Martin, "Must Boys Be Boys," 4.

106 Higate, "Peacekeepers, Masculinities," 106.

107 Martin, "Must Boys Be Boys," 6 ; Susan Notar, 2006, "Peacekeepers as Perpetrators: Sexual Exploitation and Abuse of Women and Children in the Democratic Republic of the Congo," American University Journal of Gender, Social Policy & the Law 14 (2): 422 ; Donna Bridges and Debbie Horsfall, 2009, "Increasing Operational Effectiveness in UN Peacekeeping: Toward a Gender-Balanced Force," Armed Forces & Society 36 (1): 120 ; Natalie Gilliard, 2010, "Peacekeepers or Perpetrators? An Analysis of Sexual Exploitation and Abuse (SEA) by UN Personnel in the Democratic Republic of the Congo," Mapping Politics 3 (29): 30.

108 United Nations Peacekeeping, n.d., "Women in peacekeeping," Un.org, http://www.un.org/en/peacekeeping/issues/women/womeninpk.shtml, (Accessed 17 November 2016).

109 Martin, "Must Boys Be Boys," 6.

110 Ibid.

111 Ibid.

112 Bridges and Horsfall, "Increasing Operational Effectiveness in UN Peacekeeping: Toward a Gender-Balanced Force," 120.

113 Ibid, 122.

sexual violence in the DRC, Haiti, Rwanda, Sierra Leone, and Iraq.[114] In these cases, females were fighting along with male combatants, and most likely committed sexual violence in order to fit in with their male counterparts and display their strength.[115] Although women perpetrating sexual violence does occur, it is a rare phenomenon.[116] In this case, it is necessary to remember that a gender-inclusive ideology goes hand-in-hand with a female presence in armed groups in order to see a decreased likelihood that a group will commit sexual violence. For instance, an increase in women in the political sphere has been shown to decrease violence, and civil wars are more likely in misogynistic societies.[117] This is because gender inclusive norms lead to social norms that reject violence, which is demonstrated by empirical data from Gleditsch et al., (2011) which shows a negative relationship between women's rights and the presence of civil war.[118] Further, one study conducted by Tessler and Warriner (1997) found that attitudes about gender affect attitudes about whether or not to use violence.[119] In fact, "regardless of the sex of the individual, persons who express greater concern for the status and role of women, and particularly for equality between women and men, are more likely than other individuals to believe that the international disputes in which their country is involved should be resolved through diplomacy and compromise."[120] Therefore, the use of violence or nonviolence in a conflict situation is affected by gender ideologies and attitudes.

V. Methodology

There is one case study encompassing all of the three hypotheses previously discussed. Within these hypotheses, each type of group (pro-government, jihadist, opposition, and Kurdish) is examined. For instance, pro-government groups will be discussed, based on *H1: Pro-government forces are more likely to commit sexual violence against civilians across ethnicities, religions, or*

---

114 Cohen et al., "Wartime Sexual Violence: Misconceptions, Implications, and Ways Forward," 5 ; Elisabeth Wood, "Armed Groups and Sexual Violence: When Is Wartime Rape Rare?," Politics and Soceity 37, no. 1 (2009): 131–61, doi:10.1177/0032329208329755, 135.
115 Cohen et al., "Wartime Sexual Violence," 5.
116 Ibid.
117 Erik Melander, "Gender Equality and Intrastate Armed Conflict," International Studies Quarterly 49 (2005): 695–714, doi:10.1111/j.1468-2478.2005.00384.x ; Kristian Skrede Gleditsch et al., "Polygyny or Misogyny? Reexamining the 'First Law of Intergroup Conflict,'" The Journal of Politics 73, no. 1 (2011): 269, doi:10.1017/s0022381610001003.
118 Gleditsch et al., "Polygyny or Misogyny? Reexamining the 'First Law of Intergroup Conflict,'" 268-269.
119 Mark Tessler and Ina Warriner, "Gender, Feminism, and Attitudes Toward International Conflict: Exploring Relationships With Survey Data From The Middle East," World Politics 49, no. 2 (1997): 250–81, EDS consolidation db #1 (coneds1), EBSCOhost.
120 Tessler and Warriner, , "Gender, Feminism, and Attitudes Toward International Conflict: Exploring Relationships With Survey Data From The Middle East."

genders. Jihadist and opposition groups will also be examined, in accordance with *H2: Jihadist groups and opposition groups are more likely to use women as spoils of war than the groups examined in this paper.* Lastly, Kurdish groups will be analyzed, which corresponds to *H3: Kurdish groups are overall significantly less likely to commit sexual violence compared to the other groups examined in this paper.* The subsequent hypothesis provides a tentative explanation for this, H3b.: *Kurdish groups are less likely to commit sexual violence because of the influence of females in their government structure as well as on the battlefield.*

The case study will have a focus on sexual violence. Sexual violence is a complex term that means many different things to many different groups and individuals. One definition that I find to be the most inclusive is by the Integrated Regional Information Network, which characterizes sexual violence as: "any act, attempt, or threat of a sexual nature that result, or is likely to result in, physical, psychological and emotional harm."[121] This definition includes rape/marital rape, forced sodomy, attempted rape or attempted forced sodomy, sexual abuse, sexual exploitation/forced prostitution, sexual harassment, and sexual violence as a weapon of war and torture as acts of sexual violence.[122] However, in order to adequately and accurately analyze sexual violence during conflict, it is necessary to narrow this broad definition. Therefore, for this paper, sexual violence is defined as: *an act of a sexual nature that results in physical, psychological, and emotional harm, such as rape/marital rape, sexual violence as a weapon of war, sexual violence as a tool of torture, forced sodomy, and forced prostitution (including forced sexual slavery).* For the sake of consistency and clarity, only the acts described in the definition above will be considered sexual violence in this research.

Sexual violence is specifically examined because of its broad scope, which allows the findings of this research to be more generalizable. By focusing on sexual violence rather than a specific kind of sexual violence, such as rape, this project can highlight a plethora of abuses being perpetrated by different groups in Syria. However, data regarding sexual violence is underrepresented and difficult to find because of the stigmas that can arise from reporting such cases.[123] Some countries may not have appropriate outlets for victims to report

---

121 Integrated Regional Information Network, 2004, "Definitions of sexual and gender-based violence," Irinnews.org, http://www.irinnews.org/feature/2004/09/01/definitions-sexual-and-gender-based-violence, (Accessed 13 October 2016).
122 Integrated Regional Information Network, "Definitions of sexual and gender-based violence."
123 Farr, "Armed Conflict, War Rape," 10-11; Green, "Uncovering Collective Rape," 105, Rehn and Sirleaf "Women, War, and Peace," 17, 34

sexual abuse, and some victims may be ashamed about the event and do not wish to report it.[124]

VI. Case Study

The following case study specifically analyzes sexual violence, defined as *an act of a sexual nature that results in physical, psychological, and emotional harm, such as rape/marital rape, sexual violence as a weapon of war, sexual violence as a tool of torture, forced sodomy, and forced prostitution (i.e. forced sexual slavery)*. However, the conflicts involved are complex and at times require discussions of other kinds of sexual abuse not present in the definition of sexual violence for this paper.

Background of the Syrian Civil War

The Syrian Civil War began in March 2011 with anti-regime protests in the town of Dara'a.[125] These protests were inspired by similar waves of protests in Tunisia, Egypt, Libya, Bahrain, and Yemen, encompassing a phenomenon called the Arab Spring.[126] Those protesting during the Arab Spring did so for a variety of reasons, but most advocated for human rights, democracy, and increased employment opportunities.[127] Particularly in Syria, protests erupted as a result of long-standing distaste for the authoritarian rule of the pan-Arab Ba'ath government, controlled by the Assad family since 1970.[128] Although the protests were peaceful, the government opened fire on protestors and used bombs and chemical weapons against its citizens.[129] There have been reports by the United Nations that the government has prevented Syrians from receiving adequate food, water, and medical care.[130] In response, the opposition organized and armed themselves against the government. Consequently, the Syrian Civil War broke out as tensions mounted between the Syrian government and different opposition groups.[131]

While there are a variety of opposition groups in Syria, this paper focuses only on the Free Syrian Army, because it is an umbrella group, as previously discussed in Section III. According to author John McHugo, "The Free Syrian Army was established by officers who deserted. Initially it was led by Colonel

---

124 Ibid.

125 "Syria: The Story of the Conflict," March 12, 2015; John McHugo, Syria: A History of the Last Hundred Years (New York: The New Press, 2014), 221.

126 "Syria Profile - Overview," BBC News, September 20, 2016, http://www.bbc.com/news/world-middle-east-14703910 ; McHugo, Syria: A History, 219.

127 McHugo, Syria: A History, 219.

128 "Profile: Syria's Ruling Baath Party," BBC News, July 9, 2012, http://www.bbc.com/news/world-middle-east-18582755.

129 "Syria: The story of the conflict."

130 Ibid.

131 "Syria Profile – Overview."

Riyad al-As'ad."[132] Most opposition groups in Syria are local, which shows that the Syrian regime was beginning to lose control of its own nation and citizens.[133] However, it is rare for a top official in the Syrian government to desert his post.[134] This concept is explored when discussing the importance of being Alawite within the Syrian regime. In addition, this indicates that "the regime would not easily be swept away and the fighting would be bitter and lasting."[135]

This statement would prove to be true when ISIS took the Syrian town of Raqqa in April 2013.[136] As Assad's regime began to lose control over some areas in Syria, especially those east of the Euphrates, ISIS expanded their territory to include parts of Syria in addition to parts of Iraq.[137] The group was able to take over regions of Syria by "uniting disaffected Sunnis in eastern Syria and northwest Iraq. [ISIS] also showed that it possessed military expertise and high-tech public relation skills which would enable it to attract large numbers of foreign fighters."[138] Although the Syrian government and ISIS seem like territorial enemies, there have been speculations that the two groups are closer than they appear.[139] When ISIS first expanded into Syria, the group rarely fought against the Syrian regime. In addition, ISIS is beneficial to the Syrian regime because they could be considered an "opposition" group, thereby including other opposition groups such as the Free Syrian Army in their same terrorist category, simply because both groups are fighting against the Syrian government.[140] Further, opposition groups like the Free Syrian Army now must not only worry about the Syrian Regime, but also ISIS, giving mutual benefits to the Syrian government and ISIS.

There is a key factor at play that provides insight on the current Syrian conflict, and it involves the importance to the Syrian regime of being Alawite. The Ba'ath Party is pan-Arab, however, the Alawite population were not always viewed as Muslims. This ideology stems from one orthodox Islamic scholar in particular, Ibn Taymiyya, who lived during the late 13th and early 14th

---

132 McHugo, Syria: A History, 226.
133 Ibid., 227.
134 Ibid.
135 Ibid.
136 Ibid.
137 Ibid.
138 Ibid.
139 Ibid.
140 Ibid; Some authors have described groups against the government as rebel or opposition groups, but then further break these groups into categories such as "jihadist." According to these authors, ISIS is a "jihadist" group while the FSA is simply an "opposition" or "rebel" group with no further categorization. See Jenkins, "The Dynamics of Syria's Civil War," 8-10 and "Guide to the Syrian Rebels," BBC News, December 13, 2013, http://www.bbc.com/news/world-middle-east-24403003.

centuries.[141] Ibn Taymiyya lived in Syria and felt that Islam had strayed from its initial practice, values, and ideas, and concluded that this was because of what he perceived as the heretical Alawite population, which was a threat to Sunni Islam.[142] *Fatwas*[143] were issued by Ibn Taymiyya regarding the Alawis, which collectively cast the Alawis as non-Muslims and a danger to Islam.[144] Today, jihadists often reference Ibn Taymiyya's *fatwas* to justify their negative thoughts and violent actions towards the Alawite population.[145] In fact, it was not until 1936 that the Alawis were recognized by another *fatwa* as being a part of Shiite Islam, granting Alawis a place in the Muslim community.[146] The Alawis are a minority in Syria, and make up about 15 percent of the population, while Sunnis make up 55 percent of the population.[147] Thus, the fact that Hafez al-Assad, as an Alawite, could take control of Syria and keep the Alawite rule alive with his son, Bashar, is extremely unique. This also explains why many top officials in the Syrian regime, a majority of whom are Alawite, do not desert their posts. Being an Alawite in Syria is something that needs to be protected, not only because the Alawis are a minority group, but because they must defend themselves against those who perceive them to be enemies of Islam.

The tensions between the Alawite Syrian regime and the Syrian Sunni population mounted with attacks by the Muslim Brotherhood and the Fighting Vanguards against the Syrian regime in the late 1970s and early 1980s.[148] These attacks sparked Hafez al-Assad to increase his repression of opposition groups. An example of this is the massacre at Hama in 1982, which was a kind of "last stand," resulting in the deaths of tens of thousands at the hands of the Syrian regime.[149] In addition, there were many other attacks in different Syrian villages, including Jisr Alshaghoor, Sarmada, Kinsafrah, the Al-Raqah school attack, and an attack at Palmyra prison, all perpetrated by the Syrian regime

141 Nibras Kazimi, "A Perfect Enemy," Defining Ideas: A Hoover Institution Journal, August 17, 2011, http://www.hoover.org/research/perfect-enemy.

142 Ibid.

143 A fatwa is a religious or legal order or opinion issued by a mufti, or religious scholar. For a more comprehensive definition, see Yvette Talhamy, "The Fatwas and the Nusaryri/Alawis of Syria," Middle Eastern Studies 46, no. 2 (2010): 177, doi:10.1080/00263200902940251.

144 Kazimi, "A Perfect Enemy."

145 Ibid.

146 Talhamy, "The Fatwas and the Nusaryri/Alawis of Syria," 191; this fatwa was issued by Hajj Amim al-Husayni, who was known for valuing pan-Arab ideology.

147 Kazimi, "A Perfect Enemy."

148 Raphael Lefevre, "No More 'Hama Rules,'" Diwan: Middle East Insights From Carnegie, September 16, 2016, http://carnegie-mec.org/diwan/64609.

149 Ibid.

against its citizens, all of which were terribly brutal and barbaric.[150] The Hama Massacre is important for this research because the kinds of tactics used by the Syrian government echo the attacks by the Syrian Regime in 2011. Syrian authorities took young girls and raped them, mush similar to how females are currently being abused by the regime.[151] Equally as important, there has been little opposition since the Hama Massacre until the recent protest in 2011. The Fighting Vanguard is another interesting aspect because of its use as a recruitment tool by rebel groups today.[152] Rebels in Aleppo named their attempt at breaking the siege "Ibrahim Youssef," who was a member of the Fighting Vanguard.[153] This group fought against the Syrian regime along with the Muslim Brotherhood and led a kind of "Islamic insurrection."[154] Current rebel groups see these attacks on the Syrian government by the Fighting Vanguards as relating to their own opposition against the Syrian regime, and have gained inspiration from the group. Overall, the Hama Massacre represents the religious tensions within Syria and the capability of the Syrian people to organize against themselves against the regime, as well as the regime's ability to brutally repress their perceived enemies.

Pro-government Forces[155]

Rape is so widespread in Syria that most Syrian refugees cite it as their reason for fleeing the state.[156] Since the Syrian Civil War began in 2011, the government's forces have systematically raped the civilian population, across

---

150 The Syrian Human Rights Committee, "Massacre of Hama (February 1982) Genocide and A Crime Against Humanity," SHRC.org, last modified Feb. 14, 2006, https://web.archive.org/web/20130522172157/http://www.shrc.org/data/aspx/d5/2535 .aspx.

151 Ibid.

152 Lefevre, "No More 'Hama Rules.'"

153 Ibid

154 Ibid.

155 The present tense will be used throughout this case study. Although it cannot be definitively said that these particular tactics are still being used at the time this article is being written, or at the time the reader commences this article, it can be logically inferred that the Syrian government's forces are continuing to perpetrate rape through their methods outlined in this paper.

156 Jeanne Sulzer, "Violence Against Women in Syria: Breaking the Silence," Briefing Paper (Paris: International Federation for Human Rights, 2013), https://fidh.org/IMG/pdf/syria_sexual_violence-web.pdf, 13; "Syria 2012 Human Rights Report," n.d. Washington D.C.: US Department of State, 33; Alexandra Bosnan and Melissa Winkler, "Syria: A Regional Crisis" (International Rescue Committee, January 2013), http://www.rescue.org/resource-file/syria-regional-crisis-irc-commission-syrian-refugees-january-2013, 2 [hereinafter IRC]; "Sexual Violence in Conflict, Report of the Secretary-General" (United Nations, General Assembly, Security Council, March 14, 2013), http://reliefweb.int/sites/reliefweb.int/files/resources/N1325944_0.pdf, 18 [hereinafter A/67/792].

all ages and genders.[157] Evidence also shows that the government works alongside pro-government militias, which consist of the Shabbiha and Jaysh al-Sha'bi.[158] For the purpose of clarity within this section, accounts and reports of sexual violence will be separated into two categories: those perpetrated by the Syrian government's forces, and those perpetrated by the shabbiha and Jaysh al-Sha'bi.

Sexual Violence by the Syrian government's forces

The Syrian Network for Human Rights (SNHR) estimates that the Syrian government's forces have committed over 7,500 cases of sexual abuse just during 2011.[159] In 2013, the United Nations provided treatment to 38,000 victims of sexual violence in Syria.[160] The Syrian government's forces systematically use rape as a tactic of war to exert their power over those whom they deem as enemies.[161] The US Department of State reports that the Syrian government's forces commit sexual violence with impunity, "since the government did not attempt to investigate, punish, arrest, or prosecute officials who violated human rights," in addition to protecting abusers within their ranks and even encouraging sexual violence to be used as a tactic to defeat the opposition.[162]

Detention Centers and Checkpoints

Although sexual violence has occurred at the hands of the government in various locations, detention centers is the location where most cases have occurred.[163] Sexual violence is also used to instill psychological trauma in detainees, as they were forced to watch government officials rape other

---

157 "Syria 2012 Human Rights Report," 6-7; A/67/792, 18.

158 "Syria 2012 Human Rights Report," 4; A/67/792, 18; "Violence Against Women, Bleeding Wound in the Syrian Conflict" (Euro-Mediterranean Human Rights Network), accessed June 20, 2015, http://www.wluml.org/sites/wluml.org/files/Euromedrights-VAW-Syria-Nov-2013.pdf, 7 [referred to as Euro-Med in subsequent footnotes]; A/HRC/S-17/2/Add.1, 6.

159 "Syria 2015 Human Rights Report," n.d. Washington D.C.: US Department of State, 9; Syrian Network for Human Rights, 2015, Sexual Abuse: "A Scar of a Lifetime" Rape in Syrian Security Branches: Seven Raped Women in Hama Security Branch, http://sn4hr.org/wp-content/pdf/english/Sustained_shame_en.pdf (accessed 6 February 2017), 4; it is unclear what the SNHR's definition of sexual abuse is, and this definition could vary from the definition used in this paper.

160 Human Rights and Gender Justice Clinic, MADRE, and The Women's International League for Peace and Freedom, "Human Rights Violations Against Women And Girls In Syria" (United Nations Universal Periodic Review of The Syrian Arab Republic, July 25, 2016), https://www.madre.org/press-publications/human-rights-report/human-rights-violations-against-women-and-girls-syria, 2 [hereinafter MADRE Report].

161 "Syria 2015 Human Rights Report," 3; SNHR 9.

162 "Syria 2015 Human Rights Report," 2-3; Stefan Brunner, "Sexual Violence in the Syrian Civil War Is Likely a State Strategy," Campus Press, Yale University, 2014, 2.

163 Ibid., 7.

prisoners.[164] Detainees have been threatened that if they did not cooperate with government officials, their family members would be raped.[165] Other common tactics of rape include gang rapes and forced oral sex.[166] The tactics that the Syrian government forces use are degrading to the victims, for instance women have been raped in front of their husbands, and in front of other detainees.[167] Male adults also experienced grueling forms of sexual violence in detention centers, demonstrated by a case in March 2012, when two male family members were forced by intelligence agents in a Damascus detention center to rape each other.[168]

Children, both female and male, have also been victims of sexual violence in detention centers.[169] However, male children suffered more sexual violence than female children.[170] It is unclear why this is the case; however detention centers in Syria hold a larger number of males than females, thus this could be one explanation for the difference in reported cases of sexual violence between boys and girls.[171] The Syrian government detains and abuses children as a result of their familial connections, or assumed connections, with political dissidents and members of opposition groups, mostly those under the Free Syrian Army.[172] According to the US Department of State, children are detained to "compel parents and other relatives associated with opposition fighters to surrender to authorities."

A majority of those detained did not have a warrant for their arrest, which victims stated was typical behavior for the Syrian regime.[173] The SNHR states that the Syrian government forces does this purposefully, so that they do not have to claim responsibility for their detention center abuses in court.[174] While children are targeted to force relatives to cease their support for opposition groups, those of all ages are detained for this purpose.[175] In addition, arrests can be made for those supporting humanitarian aid groups and for those involved in any kind of anti-regime protests.[176] The Syrian government forces'

---

164 Ibid., 6-7.
165 Ibid.
166 Ibid., 7; MADRE Report, 2.
167 "Syria 2015 Human Rights Report," 7 ; MADRE Report, 8 ; Amnesty International, "I Wanted To Die': Syria's Torture Survivors Speak Out" (London: Amnesty International, 2012), https://www.amnestyusa.org/sites/default/files/mde240162012en.pdf, 5 [hereinafter "Syria's Torture Survivors Speak Out"].
168 A/67/792, 19.
169 "Syria 2015 Human Rights Report," 8.
170 Ibid.
171 Ibid.
172 Ibid; SNHR 2.
173 SNHR, 1.
174 Ibid.
175 SNHR, 1, MADRE Report, 2; A/67/792, 19.
176 SNHR, 1; MADRE Report, 2.

use of sexual violence has been categorized as "torture"[177] because of its use to coerce confessions and obtain information about the opposition.

While most sexual violence occurs in detention centers, checkpoints are another common place of abuse.[178] Syrian government forces commit rape, gang rape, and other forms of sexual violence at checkpoints, mostly against women and girls whom they believe to be affiliated with the opposition.[179] There are various checkpoints located all across Syria, including in Damascus, the Dara'a province, and Aleppo.[180] While Amnesty International has reported cases of sexual violence occurring in Aleppo, it is unclear if the other checkpoints have similar reputations.[181] The United Nations General Assembly Human Rights Council conducted interviews in Syria between February and August 2012 and found that 15 interviewees, "described incidents of sexual violence committed during house searches and at checkpoints during military operations in Homs...and in Al Haffe."[182] At checkpoints, girls have been taken by government soldiers to be raped, and then are released.[183] This is particularly interesting because these rapes are much more private than the rapes in detention centers, or the rapes occurring by government forces and shabbiha detailed in the subsequent paragraphs. However, the implications of these "private" rapes at checkpoints may be symbolic for religious and cultural reasons, which are detailed further when shame and honor are discussed.

Sexual Violence by Shabbiha and Jaysh al-Sha'bi

It is difficult to determine the similarities and differences between shabbiha and Jaysh al-Sha'bi, however both groups are pro-government militias with similar tactics and motivations. In most situations of raids and house searches, shabbiha work alongside Syrian government forces. Jaysh al-Sha'bi have conducted raids alongside the Syrian government forces, particularly in

---

177 MADRE Report, 5; A/67/792, 18; United Nations General Assembly, Human Rights Council, "Report of the Independent International Commission of Inquiry on the Syrian Arab Republic" (Geneva: United Nations, August 16, 2012), 1, 58 [hereinafter A/HRC/21/50].

178 SNHR, 1; Amnesty International, "'Death Everywhere': War Crimes and Human Rights Abuses in Aleppo, Syria" (London: Amnesty International, May 4, 2015), http://www.amnestyusa.org/research/reports/death-everywhere-war-crimes-and-human-rights-abuses-in-aleppo, 40 [hereinafter "Human Rights Abuses in Aleppo"] ; United Nations Security Council, "Conflict-Related Sexual Violence: Report of the Secretary-General" (Geneva: United Nations, March 23, 2015), 18 [hereinafter S/2015/203]; A/67/792, 18.

179 MADRE Report, 2.

180 Alarabi, Aljadid, "The Millions Checkpoints in Syria," Syrian Economic Forum, April 13, 2015, http://www.syrianef.org/En/2015/04/the-millions-checkpoints-in-syria/ ; Amnesty International, 40.

181 "Human Rights Abuses in Aleppo," 40.

182 A/HRC/21/50, 18.

183 Ibid., 92.

Damascus and Aleppo.[184] shabbiha have helped raid various villages in Syria, including Damascus.[185] It is unclear if Jaysh al-Sha'bi, shabbiha, and Syrian government forces have all worked together, and information is lacking in regard to attacks by Jaysh al-Sha'bi. Thus, this section will focus mostly on sexual violence committed by shabbiha.

Raids and Abuse in the Home

The Syrian government forces along with shabbiha use sexual violence as a "weapon of war," according to the UN Independent International Commission of Inquiry on the Syrian Arab Republic.[186] shabbiha raids are "government sponsored" and are tactics used by the Syrian government forces to carry out attacks against their perceived opposition or enemy.[187] The kinds of sexual violence that shabbiha utilize include rape and gang-rape, which often occurred in homes after a village has been raided.[188] Although data is lacking, there were 84 reported cases of "forced vaginal, anal, or oral entry" by shabbiha forces from 2011 to 2016.[189] From February to August 2012, the United Nations General Assembly Human Rights Council interviewed 43 victims of sexual violence, including men, women, and children, five of which had been raped by government forces and shabbiha and seven of which who claimed "rape and sexual assault had been committed by [government] soldiers and the Shabbiha."[190] Some rapes are public, as there have been reports of women being raped in their neighborhood streets after their villages had been raided.[191]

---

184 "Syria - National Defense Forces (NDF)," GlobalSecurity.org, accessed February 26, 2017, http://www.globalsecurity.org/military/world/syria/ndf.htm.

185 Ibid.

186 MADRE Report, 2.

187 "Syria 2015 Human Rights Report," 7 ; Brian Michael Jenkins, "The Dynamics of Syria's Civil War," (Santa Monica: RAND Corporation, 2014), 6.

188 "Syria 2015 Human Rights Report," 7.

189 Women's Media Center, "Documenting Sexualized Violence in Syria," Women Under Siege Syria Crowdmap, February 4, 2016, https://womenundersiegesyria.crowdmap.com/.

190 A/HRC/21/50, 17, the report acknowledges the difficulty of obtaining reports and interviews from victims on the basis of social, religious, and cultural beliefs.

191 Human Rights and Gender Justice Clinic, MADRE, and The Women's International League for Peace and Freedom, "Seeking Accountability and Demanding Change: A Report on Women's Human Rights Violations in Syria Before and During the Conflict, Response to the Second Periodic Report of the Syrian Arab Republic to the UN Committee to End All Forms of Discrimination Against Women" (Geneva: United Nations Committee to End All Forms of Discrimination Against Women, July 2014), 7-8 [hereinafter CEDAW]; Human Rights Watch, "Syria: Sexual Assault in Detention" (New York: Human Rights Watch, June 15, 2012), https://www.hrw.org/news/2012/06/15/syria-sexual-assault-detention ; A/HRC/21/50, 92-93.

The Independent International Commission of Inquiry on the Syrian Arab Republic in two reports noted a pattern that involved sexual violence during house searches and at checkpoints that occurred after Syrian government forces and shabbiha raided villages.[192] The following pattern is corroborated by seven testimonies from the interviews conducted by the United Nations General Assembly Human Rights Council. The raids begin with pro-government forces blockading an area and shelling it. Ground forces, special forces, and shabbiha then begin seeking "defectors, activists, and fighting-age men," most of whom will later be executed.[193] Certain family members of fighters, defectors, or activists are also executed, but this occurrence is much more random.[194] In the home, government forces and shabbiha rape women and girls and force male family members to watch and threaten to shoot men if they do not rape their female family members.[195]

Shame & Honor

There are many different motivations behind the use of sexual violence during conflict. The concept of shame and honor is prevalent in Syrian society and provides one reason why Syrian government forces and militia utilize sexual violence. As discussed in the literature review, victims of rape (mostly female) are subjected to killings to protect their family's honor.[196] In fact, one interviewee from the United Nations General Assembly Human Rights Council's interviews stated that for females in Syrian society, it is worse to be raped than to be killed.[197] In detention centers as well as during raids, rape often occurred in front of women's husbands, fathers, and children to increase shame for the victim and their family, and to make them feel defeated. There have also been instances when government forces return rape victims to their families after abducting them, which not only results in shame for the victim and their family, but also subjects the victims to honor killings.[198] Rape can cause a strain on marriages in Syria, and many female rape victims reported that their husbands left them because of the rape.[199] As a result, the victims

---

192 A/67/792, 18; A/HRC/21/50, 18; 1. United Nations General Assembly, Human Rights Council, "Report of the Independent International Commission of Inquiry on the Syrian Arab Republic" (Geneva: United Nations, February 5, 2013), 17 [hereinafter A/HRC/22/59]; This pattern can be seen in a number of areas, including Tremseh, Al Qubeir, Al-Houla, Kili, Tal Rifat, Taftanaz, Sarmin, Ain Larouz, Atarib, Abdita, Homs, and Al Qusayr, see A/HRC/21/50, 12, 91-92.

193 A/HRC/21/50, 12.

194 Ibid.

195 A/67/792, 18.

196 Farr, "Armed Conflict, War Rape," 10-11; Green "Uncovering Collective Rape," 105; Rehn and Sirleaf, "Women, War, and Peace, 17.

197 A/HRC/22/59, 75.

198 MADRE Report, 2.

199 A/HRC/21/50, 91.

have difficulty surviving, sometimes as single parents, and without the added income provided to them by their husbands.[200]

Sexual Violence Against Ethnic and Religious Groups[201]

According to the Syrian Network for Human Rights, most of those in detention centers are Sunnis.[202] A Syrian artist interviewed by BBC claimed that he "didn't see any Islamists or jihadists or radicals in prison…almost everyone in prison is Sunni."[203] While it is important to note that there are Sunni Islamists and jihadists active in the Syrian civil war, the quotation by the Syrian artist shows that Sunnis not involved in Islamist or jihadist groups are being detained, but rather other Sunnis that by nature are in opposition to the Syrian government.

The shabbiha have perpetrated much brutality against their Sunni opposition during the war, most likely because they not only work with the Syrian government forces, but because most members of shabbiha are Alawites, and some are Assad's extended family members.[204] Since the opposition is mostly Sunni and seeks to overthrow the Assad regime, which provides power to the Alawite population, the shabbiha are loyal to the Alawite cause and thus target Sunnis.[205] As of 2012, 140,000 of the 200,000 soldiers in the Syrian armed forces are Alawite and 80 percent of officers are Alawite. All of those in the military's elite divisions are Alawite.[206] Further, there were 300,000 Sunni conscripts in 2012.[207] However, most of these Sunni conscripts defected after the beginning of the civil war because they were "repelled by the level of

---

200 Ibid.

201 There have been no reported cases of sexual violence by the Syrian government's forces against Kurds, Jews, Christians or Druze.

202 SNHR, 1.

203 Lina, Sinjab, "Drawing the Horror of a Syrian Detention Centre," BBC, December 21, 2015, http://www.bbc.com/news/magazine-35119760.

204 Joseph Holliday, "The Assad Regime: From Counterinsurgency to Civil War" (Washington, D.C.: Institute for the Study of War, March 2013), http://www.understandingwar.org/sites/default/files/TheAssadRegime-web.pdf, 16; A/HRC/22/59, 16.

205 Holliday, "The Assad Regime," 17; There are reports of some Sunnis choosing to fight alongside and support the Syrian government forces, however these peoples are a minority population of Sunnis. See Thanassis Cambanis, "Assad's Sunni Foot Soldiers," Foreign Policy, November 5, 2015, http://foreignpolicy.com/2015/11/05/assads-sunni-foot-soldiers-syria/.

206 Clive Williams, "Syrian Security: Can Bashar Prevail?," ABC News, February 16, 2012, http://www.abc.net.au/news/2012-02-17/williams-syrian-security-e28093-can-bashar-prevail3f/3834550.

207 Ibid.

violence their Alawite officers were willing to inflict on protestors"[208] and instead chose to join opposition organizations, particularly the Free Syrian Army.[209]

There is evidence that government forces have targeted Sunni enclaves near the coast, pushing them to provinces with larger numbers of Sunnis, such as Idlib.[210] One author suggests that radical Alawites living in heavily Alawite areas are attacking predominately Sunni regions in order to "create a rump state that is easy to defend."[211] Two massacres occurred in Houla and Qubeir, which are two Sunni farming settlements near a mostly Alawite-inhabited region.[212] One article claims that the government is specifically targeting Sunnis for punishment and has sent Shabbiha to raid Sunni villages and arrest and torture those living there.[213] Therefore, all of this evidence suggests that the war is becoming increasingly sectarian.

A Deliberate Attack Against the Perceived Enemy

Overall, the Syrian government's forces have attacked the Syrian civilian population, not simply the opposition forces. While the government has stated it aims to attack "terrorists," it is clear that civilians are targeted by the Syrian government's forces because of their focus on "neighbourhoods, towns, and regions with civilian populations."[214] Examples of these attacks include those in residential areas, schools, hospitals, mosques, and shops in a number of governorates including Homs and Latakya.[215] In detention centers, rape has been "perpetrated as a part of a widespread attack against a civilian population"[216] by government forces. When looking at the types of victims of rape by the Syrian government's forces, a deliberate attack to suppress, shame, and instill fear is prevalent. The Syrian government's forces is not committed rape against those in the opposition, they are committing rape against family members of those in the opposition (who themselves are not a part of the opposition), including children of those the government perceives to be their enemies. Sunnis are also targeted, simply because of their religion. This shows

---

208 Zoltan Barany, "Why Most Syrian Officers Remain Loyal to Assad," Arab Center for Research and Policy Studies, June 17, 2013, http://english.dohainstitute.org/release/b8f4f88b-94d3-45a0-b78e-8adad3871daa.
209 Ibid.
210 Holliday, "The Assad Regime," 20.
211 "Syria's Conflict: With Both Barrels," The Economist, June 16, 2012, http://www.economist.com/node/21556952.
212 Ibid.
213 "The Power of Religion," The Economist, July 13, 2013, http://www.economist.com/news/special-report/21580618-islamists-government-proving-harder-opposition-power-religion.
214 A/HRC/21/50, 12-13.
215 Ibid., 79-81.
216 A/HRC/22/59, 78.

that the Syrian government's forces are using rape as a deliberate tactic against anyone they deem to be a threat to their Alawite regime.

Jihadist and Opposition Forces

ISIS was formed in 2013 after it separated from al-Qaeda in Iraq.[217] In 2013 and 2014, ISIS began to take over various regions in Syria, which led to the group's rapid expansion.[218] The Syrian Civil War allowed ISIS to grow because of the conflict between the Alawite (Shia) government and the Sunni majority.[219] As a result, ISIS has attracted militant Sunnis from Syria and beyond to fight for a new Caliphate.[220] Raqqa, city in northern Syria, is known as ISIS's capital, as the group has established judicial, police, and economic institutions here to increase its control over the population.[221]

The FSA formed in 2011 and is an umbrella group.[222] There was a total of 50,000 fighters in 2014.[223] Most fighters are army defections from the Syrian armed forces, most of whom are Sunni and in opposition to the Alawite (Shia) Syrian government.[224] The FSA seeks to weaken the Syrian armed forces, however their attacks are mostly uncoordinated and local.[225] In contrast with jihadist groups, the FSA receives western support and is open to communicating and collaborating with the US and other western nations.[226] The FSA is the group most closely aligned with the ideals and values of the Syrian civilians' original protests in 2011, and had popular support from civilians, at least during the groups' first couple of years.[227] Syrians began to support the group because of extreme regime brutality and retaliation against protesters, such as an armed insurrection and various conventional warfare operations by the Syrian Arab Army in Homs and Syrian forces killing 100

---

217 "Mapping Militant Organizations: The Islamic State" (Stanford University, April 4, 2016), http://web.stanford.edu/group/mappingmilitants/cgi-bin/groups/view/1.

218 Ibid.

219 Zachary Laub, "The Islamic State" (Council on Foreign Relations, August 10, 2016), http://www.cfr.org/iraq/islamic-state/p14811.

220 Ibid.

221 Ibid.

222 Jenkins, "The Dynamics of Syria's Civil War," 8; 1. Charles Lister, "The Free Syrian Army: A Decentralized Insurgent Brand" (The Center for Middle East Policy at Brookings, November 26, 2016), https://www.brookings.edu/wp-content/uploads/2016/11/iwr_20161123_free_syrian_army.pdf, 3.

223 Jenkins, "The Dynamics of Syria's Civil War," 8; Beacham Publishing's TRAC, "Free Syrian Army (FSA)."

224 Jenkins, "The Dynamics of Syria's Civil War," 8.

225 Ibid.

226 TRAC, "Free Syrian Army (FSA)."

227 Lister, "The Free Syrian Army: A Decentralized Insurgent Brand," 3. It is unclear if the popular support the FSA had during its first couple of years is still the same today due to a lack of reliable information.

FSA soldiers in the town of Jisr al-Shughour in 2011.[228] The attack in Jisr al-Shughour was a turning point for Syrians and caused many to join the FSA because they began to realize that "the regime would only go if forced."[229] About 60,000 soldiers from the Syrian forces defected because they did not want to be forced to shoot their own people, and several prominent officers established armed opposition groups, such as Colonel Riyad al-Asad, who formed the FSA in July 2011.[230] Armed opposition groups under the FSA umbrella are mostly made up of defected officers from Syrian forces and Syrian civilian fighters.[231]

Sexual Violence by ISIS

ISIS utilizes sexual violence to exert their supremacy over the Syrian government's forces and over opposition groups in Syria.[232] ISIS commits sexual violence to tighten bonds within their ranks.[233] In addition, sexual violence and the promise of spoils of war help the group recruit more members, fundraise, and enforce discipline and order on the civilian population.[234] The group abducts women and uses them for sexual enslavement, as under Islamic Law, these non-Muslim women are non-believers, and thus are acceptable spoils of jihad.[235] The term "sexual jihad" has also been used to describe the sexual violence committed by ISIS.[236] This term comes from the Nikkah ul Jihad Fatwa in the Tunisian government's effort against Al Qaeda, and became public in 2013.[237] The fatwa states that women should be sexual servants to jihadi fighters so that men do not experience sexual frustration during war.[238] This idea is further supported in

---

228 Ibid., 4.

229 Ibid., 4-5.

230 Ibid., 5; Col. Asad was quoted as stating that: "As of now, the security forces that kill civilians and besiege cities will be treated as legitimate targets," see Ibid., 5.

231 Ibid.

232 Ariel I Ahram, "Sexual Violence and the Making of ISIS," Survival 57, no. 3 (2015): 57–78, doi:10.1080/00396338.2015.1047251, 67.

233 Ibid.

234 James Reinl, "Q&A: Probing Islamic State's Sex Atrocities with the United Nations," Middle East Eye, May 27, 2015, http://www.middleeasteye.net/news/qa-probing-islamic-state-s-sex-atrocities-united-nations-1064004421.

235 Ahram, "Sexual Violence and the Making of ISIS," 67.

236 Reinl, "Q&A: Probing Islamic State's Sex Atrocities with the United Nations" ; 1. Mah-Rukh Alli, "ISIS and Propaganda: How ISIS Exploits Women," Reuters Institute for the Study of Journalism, 2015, 17.

237 The Nikkuh ul Jihad' Fatwa comes from the Tunisian government's effort against terrorism perpetrated by Al Qaeda near the area bordering Algeria and it became public in 2013, see Alli, "ISIS and Propaganda: How ISIS Exploits Women," 17.

238 Ibid.

the Quran, which claims that sex before marriage is forbidden, except in times of jihad, where it can improve men's abilities on the battlefield.[239]

Rules for abducting and keeping sexual slaves are outlined in a pamphlet produced by ISIS in December 2014.[240] Although the pamphlet cannot be independently verified, the Middle East Media Research Institute and the think tank Quilliam believe it can be traced back to ISIS propagandists.[241] The pamphlet states that it is acceptable to take non-Muslims captive, particularly Jews and Christians.[242] The term *al-sabi* is used, which means a woman who has been captured by Muslims during war.[243] It is also permissible to rape a female immediately after she is captured and to have intercourse with female sex slaves even if she has not yet reached puberty.[244] Further, selling, buying, and gifting female sex slaves are also acceptable because "they are merely property."[245] However, an ISIS member may not sell his slave if she becomes pregnant with his child.[246]

According to data collected through interviews by a UN envoy, ISIS has a few patterns of sexual violence. When taking over a territory, ISIS will separate the men and women and execute boys and men over 14 years of age.[247] Mothers and other women, including young girls, are separated.[248] Girls and young women are examined for their physical appearance.[249] The youngest girls and the virgins are sold at higher prices, and most are sold in Raqqa.[250] There is a hierarchy for which ISIS members get to choose their women, sheikhs choose first, followed by emirs and fighters.[251] Each member takes three or four girls for about a month, and then they are resold.[252]

---

239 Ibid.

240 Mah-Rukh, "ISIS and Propaganda: How ISIS Exploits Women," 19; Kecia Ali, "Redeeming Slavery: The 'Islamic State' and the Quest for Islamic Morality," Mizan: Journal for the Study of Muslim Societies and Civilizations 1, no. 1 (2016): 8.

241 Adam Withnall, "Isis Releases 'Abhorrent' Sex Slaves Pamphlet with 27 Tips for Militants on Taking, Punishing and Raping Female Captives," The Independent, 2015, http://www.independent.co.uk/news/world/middle-east/isis-releases-abhorrent-sex-slaves-pamphlet-with-27-tips-for-militants-on-taking-punishing-and-9915913.html.

242 Ibid.

243 Kenneth Roth, "Slavery: The ISIS Rules," The New York Review of Books, September 24, 2015, http://www.nybooks.com/articles/2015/09/24/slavery-isis-rules/.

244 Ibid.

245 Ibid.

246 Ibid.

247 Reinl, "Q&A: Probing Islamic State's Sex Atrocities with the United Nations."

248 Ibid.

249 Ibid.

250 Ibid.

251 Ibid.

252 It is unclear if the women are sold to other ISIS members or to those outside of ISIS.

ISIS Manifesto and al-Khansaa Brigade

There are two women's brigades within ISIS: al-Khansaa and Umm al-Rayan. Al-Khansaa was formed in 2014 and Umm al-Rayan was formed shortly after.[253] Information is lacking in regard to Umm al-Rayan, but there is more information available about al-Khansaa. According to author Del Re (2015), women in both of these brigades are not being used for direct fighting.[254] Most females in the brigades are between 18-25 and receive 25,000 Syrian liras (about 200 US dollars) each month.[255] The female brigades both directly promote ISIS and have created ISIS propaganda videos.[256]

The ISIS manifesto titled: "Women of the Islamic State: Manifesto and Case Study," was drafted by women in the female al-Khansaa Brigade, which is a branch of ISIS and is made up mostly of educated western women.[257] The manifesto was disseminated in late January 2015 by online ISIS supporters, but orginially uploaded by the al-Khansaa Brigade on an ISIS forum.[258] The al-Khansaa Brigade monitors females within the Brigade and punishes those who do not follow strict rules, such as wearing black clothing that covers all parts of the body, which can include wearing black gloves to cover ones' fingers.[259] According to one author, the manifesto states that women are to be hidden and veiled and that men and women are not equal, and thus have different roles in Islam.[260] Specifically, women are to be wives and mothers, and can leave home only to study Islam.[261] The only other situation in which women can leave the home is to wage jihad, but only if all of the men are not available to do so.[262] The manifesto also states that girls can be married as young as age nine, but encourages them to marry at age 16 or 17.[263]

Sexual Violence by the FSA

In 2014, Khalid Saleh, the secretary-general of the Hazam Movement, a brigade of the FSA, signed Geneva Call's *Deeds of Commitment*, which

---

253 Del Re., "Female Combatants in the Syrian Conflict, in the Fight against or with the IS, and in the Peace Process," 87.

254 Ibid.

255 Ibid., 87.

256 Ibid.

257 Mah-Rukh, "ISIS and Propaganda: How ISIS Exploits Women," 13.

258 Quilliam International, "Quilliam Translation and Analysis of Islamic State Manifesto on Jihadist Brides," Quilliam International, February 5, 2017, http://www.quilliaminternational.com/quilliam-translation-and-analysis-of-islamic-state-manifesto-on-jihadist-brides/.

259 Mah-Rukh, "ISIS and Propaganda: How ISIS Exploits Women," 13; 1. Del Re., "Female Combatants in the Syrian Conflict," 87-88.

260 Mah-Rukh, "ISIS and Propaganda: How ISIS Exploits Women," 13.

261 Ibid.

262 Ibid.

263 Ibid., 14.

prohibits sexual violence and is against gender discrimination.[264] The Hazam Movement is made up of defected soldiers from the Syrian government forces in Western Syria.[265] Geneva Call is an NGO which promotes respect for international human rights by non-stated armed actors in armed conflict, and the group aims to protect civilians.[266] The organization was formed in 2000 in Geneva, Switzerland. By signing the *Deeds of Commitment*, the Hazam Movement respects the norms relating to the international standards of prohibition of sexual violence during conflict. For the months after signing, Geneva Call will conduct training for several hundred combatants to teach them the obligations to which they have pledged.[267] The only other group to sign Geneva Call's *Deeds of Commitment* is the YPG/YPJ, who also signed the document in 2014.[268]

As of the writing of this paper, there has only been one reported case of sexual violence perpetrated by the FSA during the Syrian Civil War. The United Nations General Assembly reported that four FSA members admitted to raping a woman and a girl in Aleppo in 2013.[269] When this was discovered, the perpetrators were taken to a Shari'a court in Aleppo.[270] It is unclear if the Shari'a court involved is directly tied to the FSA.

There is no outstanding evidence that the FSA commits sexual violence systematically, strategically, or consistently. The Office of the Special Representative of the Secretary General for Children and Armed Conflict reports that the only groups that use sexual violence against children are pro-government groups and ISIS.[271] In addition, those affiliated with FSA are at risk for being victims of sexual violence at the hands of pro-government forces since they are an opposition group.[272] As previously discussed in the pro-

---

264 "Syria: Major Brigade of the Free Syrian Army Commits against Anti-Personnel Mines and Sexual Violence," Geneva Call, accessed April 6, 2017, http://genevacall.org/syria-major-brigade-free-syrian-army-commits-anti-personnel-mines-sexual-violence/.

265 Ibid.

266 "Mission," Geneva Call, accessed April 6, 2017, http://genevacall.org/who-we-are/.

267 "Syria: Major Brigade of the Free Syrian Army Commits against Anti-Personnel Mines and Sexual Violence."

268 Ibid.

269 A/HRC/22/59, 78.

270 Ibid.

271 United Nations General Assembly Security Council, "Children and Armed Conflict: Report of the Secretary-General" (New York: United Nations, April 20, 2016), http://www.un.org/ga/search/view_doc.asp?symbol=s/2016/360&referer=/english/&Lang=E, 26.

272 Wolfe, Lauren, "Will There Ever Be Justice for Syria's Rape Survivors?," The Nation, May 14, 2014, https://www.thenation.com/article/will-there-ever-be-justice-syrias-rape-survivors/ ; Leila Minano and Cecile Andrzejewski, "How the Assad Regime Used Child Rape As a Weapon of War," Zero Impunity, February 7, 2017,

government section, the Syrian government forces consistently commit sexual violence against those who they perceive to be the enemy. As fighters for a group opposed to the Syrian government, those in the FSA are at risk of sexual violence perpetrated by pro-government groups.

Kurdish Forces

For this research, Kurdish forces will be defined as both the People's Protection Units (YPG) and the Women's Protection Unit (YPJ) together. Only when necessary, the YPG and the YPJ are discussed individually. The YPG was formed in 2011 and has been fighting in the Syrian Civil War in northern Syria near its border with Turkey.[273] The YPG is the main Kurdish group fighting in the war, and the YPJ is the all-female branch of the YPG, which was formed in 2012.[274]

Sexual Violence and Kurdish Forces

There have been no credible reports of sexual violence committed by Kurdish forces in Syria. Along with the FSA, both the YPG and the YPJ have signed Geneva Call's *Deed of Commitment*, which prohibits sexual violence in armed conflict.[275] In addition, women in Syrian Kurdistan are often victims of rape. For instance, there have been reports that al-Qaida affiliate jihadist militias in areas occupied by Kurdish forces had raped women in these areas.[276] There are also reports of criminal groups having kidnapped and raped women in Kurdish-held regions, such as Qamishli.[277] Although the report does not state which al-Qaida affiliated militias are committing these rapes, evidence suggests that the perpetrators those within Jabhat Fatah al-Sham and ISIS.[278]

---

https://zeroimpunity.com/how-the-assad-regime-used-child-rape-as-a-weapon-of-war/?lang=en.

273 TRAC, "People's Protection Units (YPG)."

274 TRAC,"YPJ (Women's Protection Unit" ; Lizzie Dearden, "'Isis Are Afraid of Girls': Kurdish Female Fighters Believe They Have an Unexpected Advantage Fighting in Syria," Independent, December 9, 2015, http://www.independent.co.uk/news/world/middle-east/isis-are-afraid-of-girls-kurdish-female-fighters-believe-they-have-an-unexpected-advantage-fighting-a6766776.html.

275 "Syrian Kurdish Armed Non-State Actor Commits to Ban Anti-Personnel Mines, Sexual Violence and Child Recruitment," Geneva Call, June 16, 2014, http://genevacall.org/syrian-kurdish-armed-non-state-actor-commits-ban-anti-personnel-mines-sexual-violence-child-recruitment/.

276 Jamie Dettmer, "Women in Syria's Kurdistan Region Work to Stop Sexual Violence," Voice of America News, November 27, 2013, http://www.voanews.com/a/women-in-syrias-kurdistan-work-to-stop-sexual-violence/1798818.html.

277 Ibid.

278 Daniel Wagner and Giorgio Cafiero, "In Kurdish Syria, a Different War," Institute for Policy Studies, Foreign Policy in Focus, September 5, 2013, http://fpif.org/kurdish-

In addition, reports of rapes by ISIS have also surfaced, particularly in 2014 in Kobani, near the Syrian border with Turkey.[279] Eyewitness reports have stated that women and children who refused to convert to Sunni Islam were taken by ISIS and put into captivity, where teenage girls and boys were sexually assaulted by ISIS fighters.[280]

A Lion is a Lion, be it Female or Male

In 2014, there were about 7,000 female volunteer soldiers fighting for the YPJ, most of whom were ages 18 to 24.[281] During that same year, there were about 15,000 fighters in the YPG whom were women, which makes up 35% of the organization's soldiers.[282] There are several hundred women's battalions across the Syrian Kurdistan region.[283] The use of women in Kurdish armed groups is not a new phenomenon, as women have used arms for decades in the PKK.[284] Many women in the Pershmerga, the Iraqi Kurdish forces, also fought against Saddam Hussein during the second Kurdish-Iraqi war in the mid-1970s.[285] The PKK and the YPG/YPJ both practice gender-inclusive ideologies, both politically and militarily. The PKK has enforced co-presidency at all levels, which involves one woman and one man sharing the chair position.[286] The same ideologies have been adopted by the YPG/YPJ.[287] About half of the ranks in the PKK include women fighters.[288] The use of women fighters is especially important because the YPG/YPJ use this as a tool

syria-different-war/ ; "Country Reports on Human Rights Practices for 2015" (Washington, D.C.: United States Department of State, April 2016), 21 ; Del Re, "Female Combatants in the Syrian Conflict, in the Fight against or with the IS, and in the Peace Process," 87.

279 Catherine James, "Tales of Torture, Mutilation and Rape as Isis Targets Key Town of Kobani," The Guardian, October 4, 2014, https://www.theguardian.com/world/2014/oct/04/turkey-troops-isis-siege-kobani-refugees-rape-and-murder ; Vanessa Altin, "Inside Kobane: Drug-Crazed ISIS Savages Rape, Slaughter and Behead Children," Mirror, October 11, 2014, http://www.mirror.co.uk/news/world-news/inside-kobane-drug-crazed-isis-savages-4423619.

280 "Women Warriors: A Nightmare for IS."

281 "Women Warriors: A Nightmare for IS."

282 Dilar Dirik, "Western Fascination with 'Badass' Kurdish Women," AlJazeera (Online), October 29, 2014, http://www.aljazeera.com/indepth/opinion/2014/10/western-fascination-with-badas-20141021124105277736.html.

283 Ibid.

284 TRAC, "YPJ (Women's Protection Unit."

285 Del Re, "Female Combatants in the Syrian Conflict, in the Fight against or with the IS, and in the Peace Process," 92.

286 Dirik, "Western Fascination with 'Badass' Kurdish Women."

287 Ibid.

288 Del Re, "Female Combatants in the Syrian Conflict, in the Fight against or with the IS, and in the Peace Process," 87.

to defeat ISIS. ISIS is frightened by the women fighters because they believe if they are killed by a woman, they will not go to heaven.[289]

VII. Case Study Analysis

Findings

Overall, this research concludes that *H1: Pro-government forces are more likely to commit sexual violence against civilians across ethnicities, religions, or genders* is not supported. Pro-government groups do take into account ethnicity and religion, but not gender. The pro-government section of the case study shows that pro-government groups rape women, girls, men, and boys. However, this section also shows that the government utilizes sexual violence against those whom they perceive to be the enemy, which is anyone against the *Alawite (Shia)* government. There is a high importance placed on being Alawite within the Syrian regime, which can be traced back to the history of the Alawites as a people as well as the history of the Assad regime. *H2: Jihadist groups and opposition groups are more likely to use women as spoils of war than the other groups examined,* is partly supported by the case study. Evidence suggests that jihadist groups are more likely to use women as spoils of war, but this statement is inconclusive for opposition groups. Jihadist groups utilize women as spoils of war, particularly in the case of sexual jihad and temporary marriages. There is not enough information to conclude that opposition groups utilize spoils of war, as the FSA has only minimal reports of sexual violence against them. However, a lack of reports does not imply that sexual violence does not occur within the FSA. Unfortunately, the stigma surrounding sexual violence will continue to impede sexual violence research, thus the results for the latter half of H2 are inclusive. *H3: Kurdish groups are overall significantly less likely to commit sexual violence compared to the other groups examined* is supported. There is a correlation between H3 and H3b., which states that *Kurdish groups are less likely to commit sexual violence because of the influence of females in their government structure as well as on the battlefield.* There are no reported cases of sexual violence perpetrated by the YPG or the YPJ. Thus, compared to pro-government and jihadist groups, Kurdish groups are committing fewer acts of sexual violence, and have a higher percentage of women on the battlefield than the other groups.[290] Just as with opposition groups, sexual violence reports are difficult to obtain because they require victims to forward with their traumatic experiences. Kurdish groups and opposition groups are because neither group has the extensive number of reports of sexual violence as the pro-government

---

289 Dearden, "'Isis Are Afraid of Girls': Kurdish Female Fighters Believe They Have an Unexpected Advantage Fighting in Syria" ; Del Re, "Female Combatants in the Syrian Conflict, in the Fight against or with the IS, and in the Peace Process," 93-94.

290 TRAC, "YPJ (Women's Protection Unit."

and jihadist groups. What does this say about the Syrian Civil War and about these groups inherently?

Throughout the case study, several important topics were brought to light, all of which play an important role in the presence of sexual violence during conflict in Syria. These topics will be examined further in order to understand the tactics, patterns, and motivations of the use of sexual violence, or the lack thereof, within each of the four groups.

ISIS and the Syrian Community

As of March 2017, ISIS strongholds include areas in and around Raqqa, Palmyra, Mosul, Deir ez-Zor, and Aleppo.[291] In areas under ISIS control, the group has established courts, welfare institutions, and essential services to civilians in order to gain their support.[292] Some of these essential services include access to public goods such as sanitation and healthcare.[293] Civilians are also forced to pay a tax to ISIS, which funds their jihad.[294] Those who do not pay their taxes are punished, which can range from fines to prison to being killed.[295] International recruitment for ISIS has also been on the decline, at least since 2015,[296] enticing the group to gain support from civilians in the areas they capture by setting up a kind of government that includes taxation and social assistance.[297] ISIS has created this kind of "social contract"[298] in order to win the trust and cooperation of civilians because these civilians are needed to form the Caliphate, which is the goal of the organization. Interestingly, authors Asal et al., (2013) found that groups that provide social services to communities are more likely to adopt strategies of violence.[299] Social services is a way for groups to gain support from the community and decreases the number of fighters who defect "by rendering constituents

---

291 The Carter Center, "Tracking the Front Lines in Syria," The Carter Center, Continuously updated, https://d3svb6mundity5.cloudfront.net/dashboard/index.html.

292 Maya Revkin, "ISIS' Social Contract," Foreign Affairs, January 10, 2016, https://www.foreignaffairs.com/articles/syria/2016-01-10/isis-social-contract.

293 Ibid.

294 Ibid; this tax is called zakat and is traditionally a charitable contribution detailed in the Qu'ran, however Revkin's article suggests that it is being used for the benefit of ISIS.

295 Revkin, "ISIS' Social Contract."

296 Revkin states this in "ISIS' Social Contract," which was published in 2015. In April 2016, FBI Director James Comey stated those attempting to leave the U.S. to join ISIS was on the decline. In January 2016, the U.S. special envoy for the global coalition to counter ISIS stated that ISIS' foreign fighters had decreased from 35,000 to 25,000. See "Flow of Foreign ISIS Recruits Much Slower Now, U.S. Says," CBS News, April 26, 2016, http://www.cbsnews.com/news/less-foreign-isis-recruits/.

297 Ibid.

298 Ibid.

299 Asal et al., "Gender Ideologies and Forms of Contentious Mobilization in the Middle East," 310.

dependent."[300] In the study performed by Asal et al., when groups provided social services, the use of solely violent tactics increased by about 15%.[301] This could perhaps provide some evidence of the use of sexual violence by ISIS compared to opposition and Kurdish groups.

One may think that if ISIS wants to gain support from the community, committing sexual violence will impede their chances of earning popular support. However, the use of spoils of war by ISIS has also been documented, as taxes on slaves are directly transferred to ISIS' public treasury.[302] It is not specified if these slaves include sex slaves, however this shows that ISIS is still willing to perform visible criminal acts that may seem contrary to their "social contract." Further, the offer of sex slaves may indeed be a selling point for membership in ISIS; if civilian men are promised the ability to have multiple women and do with them as they please, they may choose to join the group. However, there is no documented evidence that this has occurred.

Author Maya Revkin reports that in her interviews with Syrians in ISIS-controlled areas, they assert that ISIS has punished its members for crimes including rape because the "legitimacy of the caliphate depends on their ability to police themselves," and "propaganda explicitly advises members to refrain from using violence unless they have a legal basis for doing so."[303] Although Revkin does not go into detail on this matter, this paper concludes that because sexual jihad is outlined in a fatwa, and since the laws that ISIS follows are based on Shari'ah law, sexual jihad has a legal basis and therefore may not be punished.[304] In addition, a pamphlet in which ISIS has outlined the rules for keeping sex slaves has been published, which further supports the idea that rape is legally justified in the eyes of ISIS in particular circumstances.[305] As to which kinds of rapes are punished, or if this punishment of members who have committed rape truly occurs, there is not enough information to come to a conclusion.

The al-Khansaa Brigade versus the YPJ

Both ISIS and the YPG have branches that include all-female brigades. According to a study conducted by Asal et al. (2013), groups with gender-inclusive ideology are more likely to use nonviolent strategies, which could

---

300 Ibid.
301 Ibid.
302 Revkin, "ISIS' Social Contract."
303 Ibid.
304 Alli, "ISIS and Propaganda: How ISIS Exploits Women," 17.
305 Mah-Rukh, "ISIS and Propaganda: How ISIS Exploits Women," 19; 1. Ali, "Redeeming Slavery: The 'Islamic State' and the Quest for Islamic Morality," 8; see also Roth, "Slavery: The ISIS Rules."

potentially result in fewer instances of sexual violence.[306] Both groups are exclusively for females, but there are vast differences in their ideologies, backgrounds, and practices. It is unclear if the YPG and the PKK (Kurdistan Worker's Party / Partiya Karkerên Kurdistanê) are one in the same. The PKK is located in Turkey and has advocated for equal rights and for their own territories since their founding in 1978. The US Department of State recognizes the YPG independently of the PKK, the latter of which they have deemed a terrorist organization.[307] Other reports state that the YPG and the PKK are closely linked and share similar ideologies, but should not be considered the same group.[308] Two separate RAND reports have stated that the YPG and the PKK are allied groups.[309] In a report for The Washington Institute for Near East Policy, Barak Barfi, a research fellow at the New American Foundation, stated that the YPG is the military wing of the PYD and that the PYD (Kurdish Democratic Union Party) is a branch of the PKK.[310] For this report, it will be assumed that the YPG and the PKK share similar ideologies and are linked in some fashion, but are not directly tied to each other. Gender-inclusive ideologies have persisted in the PKK for years, and there is a tradition of equality between male and female fighters in the PKK.[311] For instance, about half of the PKK's ranks are women and the organization requires co-presidency at all levels.[312] Overall, the PKK movement promotes women's emancipation within politics as well as on the battlefield.[313] This relates closely to the behavior of those in the YPG, because the YPG and the

---

306 Asal et al., "Gender Ideologies and Forms of Contentious Mobilization in the Middle East," 308.

307 Mark C. Toner, "Department Press Briefing" (Washington, D.C.: United States Department of State, March 8, 2017), https://www.state.gov/r/pa/prs/dpb/2017/03/268295.htm.

308 Till F Paasche, "Syrian and Iraqi Kurds: Conflict and Cooperation," Middle East Policy Council 22, no. 1 (2015), http://www.mepc.org/journal/middle-east-policy-archives/syrian-and-iraqi-kurds-conflict-and-cooperation?print.

309 Linda Robinson, "Assessment of the Politico-Military Campaign to Counter ISIL and Options for Adaptation" (Santa Monica: RAND Corporation, 2016), http://www.rand.org/content/dam/rand/pubs/research_reports/RR1200/RR1290/RAND_RR 1290.pdf, 20 ; Andrew Parasiliti, Kathleen Reedy,, and Becca Wasser, "Preventing State Collapse in Syria" (Santa Monica: RAND Corporation, 2017), http://www.rand.org/content/dam/rand/pubs/perspectives/PE200/PE219/RAND_PE219.pdf, 3.

310 Barak Barfi, "Ascent of the PYD and the SDF" (Washington, D.C.: The Washington Institute for Near East Policy, April 2016), https://www.washingtoninstitute.org/uploads/Documents/pubs/ResearchNote32-Barfi.pdf, 2.

311 Del Re, "Female Combatants in the Syrian Conflict, in the Fight against or with the IS, and in the Peace Process," 87.

312 Ibid.

313 Ibid.

YPJ fight side by side and are directly affiliated with each other.[314] In addition, Gender-equality policies that are similar to those of the PKK have been adopted by Syrian Kurds in the Rojava region of north-eastern Syria.[315]

Regarding the al-Khansaa Brigade, as of 2015, the women are not being used directly for fighting.[316] There have been no recent credible reports to suggest that women in the al-Khansaa Brigade are mobilized fighters. Females in the brigade are between 18 and 25 and receive 25,000 Syrian liras (200 US Dollars) each month.[317] Although the brigades do not participate in fighting on the front lines, they are known for inspecting women at checkpoints and making sure that women are wearing the niqab and are appropriately diffusing ISIS's ideology.[318] The female brigades also "promote their [ISIS'] work and, even more importantly, their lifestyle and personal choices, on their own media channel with propaganda videos."[319]

Building on Asal et al.'s proposal that groups with gender-inclusive ideology are more likely to use nonviolent strategies, which could potentially result in less instances of sexual violence,[320] it is necessary to discuss the ideology of the YPG and ISIS to assess if the groups in fact utilize a gender-inclusive ideology. In 2015, the al-Khansaa Brigade themselves published a document title: "Women in the Islamic State: Manifesto and Case Study," which was translated by Quilliam, a counter-extremism think tank. Perhaps the most definitive line in the manifesto occurs under the heading, "Proposals for women compelled to serve the community outside the house," in which it is stated that, "women gain nothing from the idea of equality with men apart from thorns."[321] This quotation directly shows that equality between men and women is neither appropriate nor wanted.

---

314 Ibid., 86.

315 Ibid., 92.

316 Ibid., 87 ; Erin Marie Saltman and Melanie Smith, "'Til Martyrdom Do Us Part' Gender and the ISIS Phenomenon" (London: Institute for Strategic Dialogue, 2015), http://www.strategicdialogue.org/wp-content/uploads/2016/02/Till_Martyrdom_Do_Us_Part_Gender_and_the_ISIS_Phenomenon.pdf, 7.

317 Ibid.

318 Ibid., 87-88.

319 Ibid., 87.

320 Asal et al., "Gender Ideologies and Forms of Contentious Mobilization in the Middle East," 308.

321 Charlie Winter, "Women of the Islamic State: A Manifesto on Women by the Al-Khanssaa Brigade" (London: Quilliam Foundation, 2015), https://chainsoff.files.wordpress.com/2015/10/women-of-the-islamic-state31.pdf, 25.

The manifesto continues with the ideas of gender inequality by stating that it is *"sometimes* [author's emphasis] permissible"[322] for women to leave the home under certain circumstances, one of them being if a fatwa rules that women must "engage in jihad because the situation of the *ummah[323]* [author's emphasis] has become desperate, 'as the women of Iraq and Chechnya did, with great sadness'".[324] This quotation shows that women are not to fight alongside men as the women in the YPJ are, and that it is a sad occasion if the day comes where they must engage in jihad. In addition, after the manifesto discusses the circumstances in which women are permitted to take up arms and fight, it states that "it is always preferable for a woman to remain hidden and veiled..."[325] The manifesto claims that the greatest responsibility for a woman is to be a mother and a wife and that the "purpose of her existence" is to bear children.[326]

Since this paper categorizes the PKK and the YPG as being separate entities, albeit linked together through similar ideologies, the YPG follows the ideologies set forth by the PKK. Since the 1990s, women have been present in the fighting forces of the PKK and participated in combat and suicide bombings in Turkey.[327] Initially, women were recruited because numbers for the combat forces were low.[328] However, according to PKK scholar Nihat Ali Özcan, women were used to break down the feudal and tribal family structures to replace them with that of the PKK party organization.[329] The PKK chief at the time, Abdullah Öcalan, established the PKK "as a militant nationalist liberation front with a Marxist-Leninist ideology."[330] This explains why Öcalan sought to empower women, because gender inequality is seen as one of the impetus' of capitalism, and familial structures are also one of the main characteristics of capitalism.[331] After Öcalan was captured, the PKK moved toward a more socialist viewpoint of having no state but instead a direct

---

322 An ummah is a term which means a global community of Muslims, but has been used to mean smaller political communities as well. See Winter, "Women of the Islamic State: A Manifesto on Women by the Al-Khanssaa Brigade," 4.

323 Winter, "Women of the Islamic State: A Manifesto on Women by the Al-Khanssaa Brigade," 8.

324 Ibid.

325 Ibid., 22.

326 Ibid., 17, 18.

327 Dr. Pinar Tank, "Kurdish Female Combatants and the Role of Gender Ideology" (Oslo: University of Oslo, 2016), http://www.hf.uio.no/ikos/english/research/projects/new-middle-east/publications/2015-2016/pt-pb-2016.pdf, 3.

328 Ibid.

329 Ibid.

330 Ibid ; see also Meral Duzgun, "The Kurdish Women's Movement: Challenging Gendered Militarization and the Nation-State," Unpublished Manuscript from University of Westminster, 2015, 26.

331 Ibid.

democracy within the community, which acts as the political unit in place of a state.[332] The main principles on which this community is founded include grassroots participation and decisions being made at lower levels but implemented by higher levels, which leads to liberation, even for women.[333] This organizational method allows women to have greater political participation because it involves "the bottom-up creation of a new vision for society."[334] In the views of the Kurds, patriarchal societies promote gender inequality and make it very difficult for women to achieve emancipation.[335] One author stated that in the YPJ, "there appears to be no requirement to gaining male permission to act in war."[336] Kurdish women are involved not only on the battlefield, but in the political arena as well, for instance women make up 40% of the YPD political party and the use of co-presidencies of one man and one women are not uncommon in the political sphere.[337]

Thus, based on Asal et al.'s assertion that groups with gender-inclusive ideology are more likely to use nonviolent strategies, which could potentially result in fewer instances of sexual violence[338], it can be concluded that the gender ideologies of ISIS and the YPG/YPJ are much different. Clearly, ISIS does not promote any kind of gender-inclusive ideology, while the PKK was precisely founded on an ideology that has promoted gender equality within their community and has spread to various Kurdish regions, including the Kurdish area of Syria. This provides reasoning for the discrepancies between reports of sexual violence by the YPG/YPJ and ISIS.

Masculinity and Patterns of Sexual Violence

A culture of masculinity and patriarchy is present in all groups except the YPG/YPJ, which has a much higher representation of women and was founded on the ideals that a patriarchal society is seen as a main component of capitalism. Author Paul Higate states that: "Masculine identities become hyper masculine due to military interactions influencing how men believe it is appropriate to act...militarization results from group mindsets and the desire to affirm 'manliness' through sexual prowess."[339] In fact, one author describes sexual violence during war as a "masculinized practice" because fighters

332 Ibid, 4.
333 Ibid ; Duzgun, "The Kurdish Women's Movement: Challenging Gendered Militarization and the Nation-State," 24.
334 Ibid.
335 Duzgun, "The Kurdish Women's Movement: Challenging Gendered Militarization and the Nation-State," 25.
336 Ibid., 27.
337 Ibid., 29.
338 Asal et al., "Gender Ideologies and Forms of Contentious Mobilization in the Middle East," 308.
339 Paul Higate, "Peacekeepers, Masculinities, and Sexual Exploitation," Men and Masculinities 10, no. 1 (2007): 101.

during wartime are often characterized as being masculine.[340] Masculinity itself is a term that relates to the essence of manhood, categorized by being masculine and heterosexual, and is also defined by what it is not, which is feminine and homosexual.[341] Sexual violence in war is about masculine domination and can occur against both men and women, just as in the pro-government groups have committed. Sexual violence against men, just as against women, is used to "weaken, demoralize, and destroy collectives of people,"[342] and is used as a tool to empower certain men in certain social arenas, such as the men who fight for pro-government forces in Syria and who are pitted against their perceived enemies, those who do not support the Assad regime. Especially for men, sexual violence is used to feminize them, making them less masculine than their perpetrators.[343] Further, men who experience sexual violence during war feel that they have not properly protected their family members and thus lose another important attribute of being masculine, which is to take care of female family members and be the protector of the household.[344]

Sexual violence against women during war can sometimes be used to recruit members, which may be the case for ISIS, as the group utilizes sexual jihad practices and abducts women to be used as sex slaves.[345] Perpetrating sexual violence as a group can lead to greater cohesion between fighters.[346] This may be one reason why ISIS feels compelled to use sex slaves and to promote the practice of sexual jihad. Since ISIS is not a state-sponsored group, and thereby cannot use forced conscription to obtain new fighters, they must think of other ways in which to recruit members and disseminate their ideological viewpoints. Promising fighters the gift of women and their ability to do as they wish with these women may be one possible way in which ISIS successfully recruits new members.

In addition, sexual violence is used to displace civilians and to empower the masculinized perpetrators. This has occurred during other conflicts, such as those in the Eastern Congo and Rwanda, but also can be seen in the Syrian conflict.[347] Rape is one of the most prevalent reasons why Syrians are fleeing

---

340 Vojdik, "Sexual Violence against Men and Women in War: A Masculinities Approach," 10.
341 Ibid., 3.
342 Ibid.
343 Ibid.
344 Ibid., 13.
345 Mah-Rukh, "ISIS and Propaganda: How ISIS Exploits Women," 19 ; Ali, "Redeeming Slavery: The 'Islamic State' and the Quest for Islamic Morality," 8 ; Alli, "ISIS and Propaganda: How ISIS Exploits Women," 17.
346 Vojdik, "Sexual Violence Against Men and Women in War: A Masculinities Approach," 11.
347 Ibid., 14.

their home country.[348] Both men and women have been targets of public sexual violence, as seen in the types of sexual violence perpetrated by Syrian government forces.[349] Public rapes of men, commonly seen in Syrian government detention centers, are used to signal to the community that: "the enemy has destroyed those who are expected to protect the community, increasing the fear and vulnerability of the community."[350] This allows the perpetrators to assert their masculinity above that of the demasculinized victims.

While opposition groups should, in theory, also follow this masculinized culture, there have been very few reports of sexual violence by opposition groups in Syria. Although this does not mean that opposition groups are not perpetrating sexual violence, it is remarkable the number of sexual violence reports by pro-government and jihadist groups compared to opposition groups. The latter half of H2 (*Jihadist groups and opposition groups are more likely to use women as spoils of war than the other groups examined*) was proven to be inconclusive, thus further research is needed to assess if, in fact, opposition groups are not committing sexual violence. It is interesting that opposition groups do not seem to fit into this mold of masculinity that pro-government and jihadist groups fill so well. Perhaps it is the nature of the Syrian conflict that has bred a new kind of opposition group that is not so much focused on demasculinizing others but more focused on winning a war by using different tactics. However, only more research will provide these answers.

A History of Sexual Violence in Syria

Lastly, it is important to discuss previous sexual violence instances by the Syrian government forces. Sexual violence perpetrated by Syrian government forces is not a new phenomenon, and has occurred in the 1970s during the Syrian government's conflicts with the Syrian Muslim Brotherhood.[351] At that time, Syrian security forces abducted and raped females whom they suspected were associated with the opposition.[352] Further, during interrogations, both men and women experienced sexual abuse.[353] This is very similar to the tactics discussed in the pro-government section of the previous case study.

This episode of sexual violence occurred around the same time that Hafez al-Assad, Bashar al-Assad's father, took power, which symbolized a victory for

---

348 Sulzer, "Violence Against Women in Syria: Breaking the Silence," 13; "Syria 2012 Human Rights Report," 33; IRC, 2 ; A/67/792, 18.

349 "Syria 2012 Human Rights Report," 18 ; "Syria's Torture Survivors Speak Out," 12.

350 Vojdik, "Sexual Violence Against Men and Women in War: A Masculinities Approach," 14.

351 Ahram, "Sexual Violence and the Making of ISIS," 64.

352 Ibid., 64-65.

353 Ibid.

the minority Alawite sect.[354] The Syrian Muslim Brotherhood responded with a military campaign in the mid-1970s that was against the "Alawite infidels."[355] The regime of Hafez al-Assad used violence and rape to respond to the Syrian Muslim Brotherhood, which included the attacks on Hama and Homs in 1982. Sexual violence was used to "reassert regime supremacy."[356]

The kinds of sexual violence described and the situation it stemmed from are eerily similar to today's conflict. The Syrian government felt threatened by the Syrian Muslim Brotherhood in the 1970s, and today they feel threatened by opposition groups, ISIS, and the Kurds. The way in which the Syrian government forces respond have not changed in over 40 years; they choose to humiliate, degrade, and violate their perceived enemy, which is considered to be anyone against the Syrian government. This is not simply an isolated period of time in which the Syrian government forces are committing sexual violence. This is a pattern of sexual violence that is inherent within the Syrian government forces. It is necessary to acknowledge and address this cycle, lest there be another period of systematic sexual violence in the future.

VII. Conclusion

There are many atrocities that have been continuously occurring during the Syrian Civil War. Sexual violence is one of these horrors, and it has greatly contributed to the migration of Syrians to countries around the world. The purpose of this research is to conduct an in-depth analysis of specific armed groups involved in the civil war, and to assess which of these armed groups are committing sexual violence. The findings show that pro-government groups use sexual violence against those who pose a threat to the Alawite (Shia) regime. Jihadist groups utilize sexual violence as well, but in a different fashion, which can be seen from their use of women as spoils of war and their emphasis on sexual jihad. Opposition groups and Kurdish groups have little to no reported cases of perpetrating sexual violence, but for differing reasons. There is a correlation between gender-inclusive ideologies within an armed group and that armed group's likelihood to use less violent strategies during war, including sexual violence, demonstrated by the Kurdish forces. As for opposition forces, their lack of reported sexual violence is rare and provides an interesting case in terms of the literature discussed in Section II. Moreover, it is interesting that in the one reported case of sexual violence perpetrated by FSA members, other members of the FSA were the ones to confront their peers about the situation and send them to Shari'a court. This shows accountability, which is lacking within the pro-government and jihadist groups, in terms of sexual violence. It is unclear why there is only one reported case of sexual

---

354 Ibid., 65.
355 Ibid.
356 Ibid.

violence perpetrated by the FSA, and further research is needed to assess this phenomenon. However, while there are no reports of Kurdish forces committing sexual violence, and there is just one reported case of the FSA committing sexual violence, it is possible that these groups have perpetrated sexual violence and that it was not reported. For the purpose of this research, only reported cases are analyzed, but it is necessary to understand that sexual violence data is difficult to obtain.

Overall, this report can be used by policy-makers to create more sustainable and appropriate solutions. Sexual violence during conflict differs from country to country, as demonstrated in the larger project of *Bodies as Battlefields*. It also varies from armed group to armed group, which is shown within this paper. Together, both projects provide the necessary knowledge for policy-makers to make informed decisions, and ameliorate the growing need for sexual violence research.

Bibliography

Abu-Odeh, Lama, "Crimes of Honor and the Construction of Gender in Arab Societies," in *Women and Sexuality in Muslim Societies*, ed. Pinar Ilkkaracan (Istanbul: Women for Women's Human Rights, 2000), 363–80.

Ahram, Ariel I, "Sexual Violence and the Making of ISIS," *Survival* 57, no. 3 (2015): 57–78, doi:10.1080/00396338.2015.1047251.

Ali, Kecia, "Redeeming Slavery: The 'Islamic State' and the Quest for Islamic Morality," *Mizan: Journal for the Study of Muslim Societies and Civilizations* 1, no. 1 (2016): 1–19.

Ali, Mah-Rukh, "ISIS and Propaganda: How ISIS Exploits Women," *Reuters Institute for the Study of Journalism*, 2015, 1–25.

Aljadid, Alarabi, "The Millions Checkpoints in Syria," *Syrian Economic Forum*, April 13, 2015, http://www.syrianef.org/En/2015/04/the-millions-checkpoints-in-syria/.

Altin, Vanessa, "Inside Kobane: Drug-Crazed ISIS Savages Rape, Slaughter and Behead Children," *Mirror*, October 11, 2014, http://www.mirror.co.uk/news/world-news/inside-kobane-drug-crazed-isis-savages-4423619.

Amnesty International, "I Wanted To Die': Syria's Torture Survivors Speak Out" (London: Amnesty International, 2012), https://www.amnestyusa.org/sites/default/files/mde240162012en.pdf.

Amnesty International, "'Death Everywhere': War Crimes and Human Rights Abuses in Aleppo, Syria" (London: Amnesty International, May 4, 2015), http://www.amnestyusa.org/research/reports/death-everywhere-war-crimes-and-human-rights-abuses-in-aleppo.

Annan, Jeannie et al., "Women and Girls at War: 'Wives', Mothers, Fighters in the Lord's Resistance Army," *Unpublished Manuscript*, 2009.

Asal, Victor et al., "Gender Ideologies and Forms of Contentious Mobilization in the Middle East," *Journal of Peace Resesarch* 50, no. 3 (n.d.): 305–18.

Barany, Zoltan, "Why Most Syrian Officers Remain Loyal to Assad," *Arab Center for Research and Policy Studies*, June 17, 2013, http://english.dohainstitute.org/release/b8f4f88b-94d3-45a0-b78e-8adad3871daa.

Barfi, Barak, "Ascent of the PYD and the SDF" (Washington, D.C.: The Washington Institute for Near East Policy, April 2016), https://www.washingtoninstitute.org/ uploads/ Documents/pubs/ResearchNote32-Barfi.pdf.

Beacham Publishing's Terrorism Research & Analysis Consortium, "YPJ (Women's Protection Unit," *Tracking Terrorism*, October 27, 2016, http://www.trackingterrorism.org/group/ypj-womens-protection-unit.

Beacham Publishing's Terrorism Research & Analysis Consortium, "Free Syrian Army (FSA)," *Tracking Terrorism*, accessed November 1, 2016, http://www.trackingterrorism.org/group/free-syrian-army-fsa.

Beacham Publishing's Terrorism Research & Analysis Consortium, "Islamic State (IS) / Islamic State of Iraq and Ash Sham (ISIS) / Islamic State of Iraq (ISIS or ISIL, IS)," *Tracking Terrorism*, accessed February 21, 2017, https://www.trackingterrorism.org/group/islamic-state-islamic-state-iraq-and-ash-sham-isis-islamic-state-iraq-isis-or-isil.

Beacham Publishing's Terrorism Research & Analysis Consortium, "People's Protection Units (YPG)," *Tracking Terrorism*, accessed November 8, 2016, http://www.trackingterrorism.org/group/peoples%E2%80%99-protection-units-ypg.

Beacham Publishing's Terrorism Research & Analysis Consortium, "Syrian Kurdish Democratic Union Party (PYD)," *Tracking Terrorism*, accessed November 8, 2016, http://www.trackingterrorism.org/group/syrian-kurdish-democratic-union-party-pyd.

Bridges, Donna and Debbie Horsfall, "Increasing Operational Effectiveness in UN Peacekeeping: Toward a Gender-Balanced Force," *Armed Forces & Society* 36, no. 1 (2009): 120–30.

Brunner, Stefan, "Sexual Violence in the Syrian Civil War Is Likely a State Strategy," *Campus Press, Yale University*, 2014, 1–21.

Cagaptay, Soner and Tabler, Andrew J., "The U.S.-PYD-Turkey Puzzle" (Washington, D.C.: Washington Institute for Near East Policy, October 23, 2015), http://www.washingtoninstitute.org/policy-analysis/view/the-u.s.-pyd-turkey-puzzle.

Claflin, Jesse, "Kurdish Women's Protection Units (YPJ): The Fight to Protect Democratic Confederalism" (The Gate: University of Chicago's Undergraduate Political Review, February 28, 2017), http://uchicagogate.com/2017/02/28/kurdish-womens-protection-units-ypj-the-fight-to-protect-democratic-confederalism/.

Cohen, Dara Kay, Amelia Hoover Green, and Elisabeth Jean Wood, "Wartime Sexual Violence: Misconceptions, Implications, and Ways Forward" (Washington, D.C.: United States Institute of Peace, February 8, 2013), http://www.usip.org/publications/wartime-sexual-violence-misconceptions-implications-and-ways-forward.

Coomaraswamy, Radhika, "Report of the Special Rapporteur on Violence against Women, Its Causes and Consequences" (United Nations Commission on Human Rights), accessed February 20, 2017, http://www.refworld.org/docid/3d6ce3cc0.html.

Dearden, Lizzie, "'Isis Are Afraid of Girls': Kurdish Female Fighters Believe They Have an Unexpected Advantage Fighting in Syria," *Independent*, December 9, 2015, http://www.independent.co.uk/news/world/middle-east/isis-are-afraid-of-girls-kurdish-female-fighters-believe-they-have-an-unexpected-advantage-fighting-a6766776.html.

Del Re, Emanuela C., "Female Combatants in the Syrian Conflict, in the Fight against or with the IS, and in the Peace Process," in *Female Combatants in Conflict and Peace: Challenging Gender in Violence and Post-Conflict Reintegration* (Hampshire: Palgrave Macmillan, 2015), 84–99.

Dettmer, Jamie, "Women in Syria's Kurdistan Region Work to Stop Sexual Violence," *Voice of America News*, November 27, 2013, http://www.voanews.com/a/women-in-syrias-kurdistan-work-to-stop-sexual-violence/1798818.html.

Dews, Fred, "A Glossary of Forces in the Syrian Civil War," *Brookings Now*, May 27, 2014, https://www.brookings.edu/blog/brookings-now/2014/05/27/a-glossary-of-forces-in-the-syrian-civil-war/.

Dirik, Dilar, "Western Fascination with 'Badass' Kurdish Women," *AlJazeera (Online)*, October 29, 2014, http://www.aljazeera.com/indepth/opinion/2014/10/western-fascination-with-badas-2014102112410527736.html.

Duzgun, Meral, "The Kurdish Women's Movement: Challenging Gendered Militarization and the Nation-State," *Unpublished Manuscript from University of Westminster*, 2015, 1–44.

Farr, Kathryn, "Armed Conflict, War Rape, and the Commercial Trade in Women and Children's Labour," *Pakistan Journal of Women's Studies* 16, no. 1 & 2 (2009a): 1–31.

Farr, Kathryn, "Extreme War Rape in Today's Civil-War-Torn States: A Contextual and Comparative Analysis," *Gender Issues* 26, no. 1 (2009b): 1–41.

Gilliard, Natalie, "Peacekeepers or Perpetrators? An Analysis of Sexual Exploitation and Abuse (SEA) by UN Personnel in the Democratic Republic of the Congo," *Mapping Politics* 3, no. 29 (2010): 27–35.

Gleditsch, Kristian Skrede et al., "Polygyny or Misogyny? Reexamining the 'First Law of Intergroup Conflict,'" *The Journal of Politics* 73, no. 1 (2011): 265–70, doi:10.1017/s0022381610001003.

Green, Jennifer Lynn, "Uncovering Collective Rape: A Comparative Study of Political Sexual Violence," *International Journal of Sociology* 34, no. 1 (2004): 97–116.

Green, Jennifer Lynn, ""Collective Rape: A Cross-National Study of the Incidence and Perpetrators of Mass Political Sexual Violence, 1980-2003," *PhD. Diss., Ohio State University*, 2006, ii-187.

Higate, Paul, "Peacekeepers, Masculinities, and Sexual Exploitation," *Men and Masculinities* 10, no. 1 (n.d.): 99–119.

Hogg, Charu Lata, "'We Will Teach You a Lesson:' Sexual Violence against Tamils by Sri Lankan Security Forces" (Human Rights Watch, February 26, 2013), https://www.hrw.org/report/2013/02/26/we-will-teach-you-lesson/sexual-violenceagainst-tamils-sri-lankan-security-forces.

Holliday, Joseph, "The Assad Regime: From Counterinsurgency to Civil War" (Washington, D.C.: Institute for the Study of War, March 2013), http://www.understandingwar.org/sites/default/files/TheAssadRegime-web.pdf.

Holmes, Amy Austin, "What Are the Kurdish Women's Units Fighting for in Syria?," *The Washington Post*, December 23, 2015, https://www.washingtonpost.com/news/monkey-cage/wp/2015/12/23/what-are-the-kurdish-womens-units-fighting-for-in-syria/.

Human Rights and Gender Justice Clinic, MADRE, and The Women's International League for Peace and Freedom, "Seeking Accountability and Demanding Change: A Report on Women's Human Rights Violations in Syria Before and During the Conflict, Response to the Second Periodic Report of the Syrian Arab Republic to the UN Committee to End All Forms of Discrimination Against Women" (Geneva: United Nations Committee to End All Forms of Discrimination Against Women, July 2014).

Human Rights and Gender Justice Clinic, MADRE, and The Women's International League for Peace and Freedom, "Human Rights Violations Against Women And Girls In Syria" (United Nations Universal Periodic Review of The Syrian Arab Republic, July 25, 2016), https://www.madre.org/press-publications/human-rights-report/human-rights-violations-against-women-and-girls-syria.

Integrated Regional Information Network, "Definitions of Sexual and Gender-Based Violence," *IRIN News*, September 1, 2004, http://www.irinnews.org/feature/2004/09/01/definitions-sexual-and-gender-based-violence.

James, Catherine, "Tales of Torture, Mutilation and Rape as Isis Targets Key Town of Kobani," *The Guardian*, October 4, 2014, https://www.theguardian.com/world/2014/oct/04/turkey-troops-isis-siege-kobani-refugees-rape-and-murder.

Brian Michael Jenkins, "The Dynamics of Syria's Civil War" (RAND Corporation, 2014), http://www.rand.org/pubs/perspectives/PE115.html.

Jenkins, Brian Michael, "The Dynamics of Syria's Civil War" (Santa Monica: RAND Corporation, 2014).

Kazimi, Nibras, "A Perfect Enemy," *Defining Ideas: A Hoover Institution Journal*, August 17, 2011, http://www.hoover.org/research/perfect-enemy.

Laub, Zachary, "The Islamic State" (Council on Foreign Relations, August 10, 2016), http://www.cfr.org/iraq/islamic-state/p14811.

Lefevre, Raphael, "No More 'Hama Rules,'" *Diwan: Middle East Insights from Carnegie*, September 16, 2016, http://carnegie-mec.org/diwan/64609.

Lister, Charles, "Dynamic Stalemate: Surveying Syria's Military Landscape," Policy Briefing (Doha, Qatar: Brookings Institution: Brookings Doha Center, May 2014), https://www.brookings.edu/wp-content/uploads/2016/06/Syria-Military-Landscape-English.pdf.

Lister, Charles, "The Free Syrian Army: A Decentralized Insurgent Brand" (The Center for Middle East Policy at Brookings, November 26, 2016), https://www.brookings.edu/wp-content/uploads/2016/11/iwr_20161123_free_syrian_army.pdf.

Lynn, Matthew, "Why the Title of 'Developing Country' No Longer Exists," *The Telegraph*, May 23, 2016, http://www.telegraph.co.uk/business/2016/05/23/why-the-title-of-developing-country-no-longer-exists/.

Malemo Kalisya, Luc et al., "Sexual Violence toward Children and Youth in War-Torn Eastern Democratic Republic of Congo," *PLoS ONE* 6, no. 1 (2011): 1–19.

Manjoo, Rashida and Calleigh McRaith, "Gender-Based Violence and Justice in Conflict and Post-Conflict Areas," *Cornell International Law* 44, no. 1 (2010): 1–31.

Martin, Sarah, "Must Boys Be Boys? Ending Sexual Exploitation & Abuse in UN Peacekeeping Mission" (Washington, D.C.: Refugees International, 2005), http://www.pseataskforce.org/uploads/tools/mustboysbeboysendingseainunpeacekeepingmissions_refugeesinternational_english.pdf.

McHugo, John, *Syria: A History of the Last Hundred Years* (New York: The New Press, 2014).

Melander, Erik, "Gender Equality and Intrastate Armed Conflict," *International Studies Quarterly* 49 (2005): 695–714, doi:10.1111/j.1468-2478.2005.00384. x.

Minano, Leila and Andrzejewski, Cecile, "How the Assad Regime Used Child Rape As a Weapon of War," *Zero Impunity*, February 7, 2017, https://zeroimpunity.com/how-the-assad-regime-used-child-rape-as-a-weapon-of-war/?lang=en.

Notar, Susan, "Peacekeepers as Perpetrators: Sexual Exploitation and Abuse of Women and Children in the Democratic Republic of the Congo," *American University Journal of Gender, Social Policy & the Law* 14, no. 2 (2006): 413–29.

Paasche, Till F., "Syrian and Iraqi Kurds: Conflict and Cooperation," *Middle East Policy Council* 22, no. 1 (2015), http://www.mepc.org/journal/middle-east-policy-archives/syrian-and-iraqi-kurds-conflict-and-cooperation?print.

Parasiliti, Andrew, Reedy, Kathleen, and Wasser, Becca, "Preventing State Collapse in Syria" (Santa Monica: RAND Corporation, 2017), http://www.rand.org/content/dam/rand/pubs/perspectives/PE200/PE219/RAND_PE219.pdf.

Peterman, Amber, Palermo, Tia, and Bredenkamp, Caryn, "Estimates and Determinants of Sexual Violence Against Women in the Democratic Republic of Congo," *American Journal of Public Health* 101, no. 6 (2011): 1060–67.

Quilliam International, "Quilliam Translation and Analysis of Islamic State Manifesto on Jihadist Brides," *Quilliam International*, February 5, 2017, http://www.quilliaminternational.com/quilliam-translation-and-analysis-of-islamic-state-manifesto-on-jihadist-brides/.

Rehn, Elisabeth and Ellen Johnson Sirleaf, "Women, War, and Peace: The Independent Experts' Assessment on the Impact of Armed Conflict on Women and Women's Role in Peace-Building" (New York: United Nations Development Fund for Women, 2002),

http://www.unwomen.org/~/media/headquarters/media/publications/unifem/210table.pd
f.

Reinl, James, "Q&A: Probing Islamic State's Sex Atrocities with the United Nations," *Middle East Eye*, May 27, 2015, http://www.middleeasteye.net/news/qa-probing-islamic-state-s-sex-atrocities-united-nations-1064004421.

Revkin, Maya, "ISIS' Social Contract," *Foreign Affairs*, January 10, 2016, https://www.foreignaffairs.com/articles/syria/2016-01-10/isis-social-contract.

Robinson, Linda, "Assessment of the Politico-Military Campaign to Counter ISIL and Options for Adaptation" (Santa Monica: RAND Corporation, 2016), http://www.rand.org/content/dam/rand/pubs/research_reports/RR1200/RR1290/RAND_RR1290.pdf.

Roth, Kenneth, "Slavery: The ISIS Rules," *The New York Review of Books*, September 24, 2015, http://www.nybooks.com/articles/2015/09/24/slavery-isis-rules/.

Saltman, Erin Marie and Smith, Melanie, "'Til Martyrdom Do Us Part' Gender and the ISIS Phenomenon" (London: Institute for Strategic Dialogue, 2015), http://www.strategic dialogue.org/wp-content/uploads/2016/02/Till_Martyrdom_Do_Us_Part_Gender_and_the_ISIS_Phenomenon.pdf.

Sanchez, Olga Amparo et al., "First Survey on the Prevalence of Sexual Violence Against Women in the Context of the Colombian Armed Conflict, 2001–2009: Executive Summary" (Bogatâ, Columbia: Casa de la Mujer and Oxfam, 2011).

Sinjab, Lina, "Drawing the Horror of a Syrian Detention Centre," December 21, 2015, http://www.bbc.com/news/magazine-35119760.

Sulzer, Jeanne, "Violence Against Women in Syria: Breaking the Silence," Briefing Paper (Paris: International Federation for Human Rights, 2013), https://fidh.org/IMG/pdf/syria_sexual_violence-web.pdf.

Talhamy, Yvette, "The Fatwas and the Nusaryri/Alawis of Syria," *Middle Eastern Studies* 46, no. 2 (2010): 175–94, doi:10.1080/00263200902940251.

Tank, Pinar Dr., "Kurdish Female Combatants and the Role of Gender Ideology" (Oslo: University of Oslo, 2016), http://www.hf.uio.no/ikos/english/research/projects/new-middle-east/publications/2015-2016/pt-pb-2016.pdf.

Tessler, Mark and Warriner, Ina, "Gender, Feminism, and Attitudes Toward International Conflict: Exploring Relationships With Survey Data From The Middle East," *World Politics* 49, no. 2 (1997): 250–81, doi:EDS consolidation db #1 (coneds1).

The Carter Center, "Tracking the Front Lines in Syria," *Syria Dashboard*, accessed February 20, 2017, https://d3svb6mundity5.cloudfront.net/dashboard/index.html.

The Syrian Human Rights Committee, "Massacre of Hama (February 1982) Genocide and A Crime Against Humanity," *The Syrian Human Rights Commitee*, February 14, 2006, https://web.archive.org/web/20130522172157/http://www.shrc.org/data/aspx/d5/2535.a spx.

Toner, Mark C., "Department Press Briefing" (Washington, D.C.: United States Department of State, March 8, 2017), https://www.state.gov/r/pa/prs/dpb/2017/03/268295.htm.

United Nations, "Women in Peacekeeping," *United Nations Peacekeeping*, accessed February 20, 2017, http://www.un.org/en/peacekeeping/issues/women/womeninpk.shtml.

United Nations General Assembly, Human Rights Council, "Report of the Independent International Commission of Inquiry on the Syrian Arab Republic" (New York: United Nations, August 16, 2012).

United Nations General Assembly, Human Rights Council, "Report of the Independent International Commission of Inquiry on the Syrian Arab Republic" (New York: United Nations, February 5, 2015), http://www.ohchr.org/Documents/Countries/SY/A.HRC.S-17.2.Add.1_en.pdf.

United Nations General Assembly Security Council, "Children and Armed Conflict: Report of the Secretary-General" (New York: United Nations, April 20, 2016), http://www.un.org/ga/search/view_doc.asp?symbol=s/2016/360&referer=/english/&Lang=E.

United Nations Security Council, "Conflict-Related Sexual Violence: Report of the Secretary-General" (New York: United Nations, March 23, 2015).

Vojdik, Valorie K., "Sexual Violence Against Men and Women in War: A Masculinities Approach," *Nevada Law Journal* 14, no. 3 (2014): 1–40.

von der Lieth, Emma, "Bodies as Battlefields: A Mixed Methods Analysis of Sexual Violence During Armed Conflict," *Presented at the International Studies Association South Conference, Tampa, FL*, 2015, 1–68.

Wagner, Daniel and Giorgio Cafiero, "In Kurdish Syria, a Different War," *Institute for Policy Studies*, Foreign Policy in Focus, September 5, 2013, http://fpif.org/kurdish-syria-different-war/.

Williams, Clive, "Syrian Security: Can Bashar Prevail?" *ABC News*, February 16, 2012, http://www.abc.net.au/news/2012-02-17/williams-syrian-security-e28093-can-bashar-prevail3f/3834550.

Winter, Charlie, "Women of the Islamic State: A Manifesto on Women by the Al-Khanssaa Brigade" (London: Quilliam Foundation, 2015), https://chainsoff.files.wordpress.com/2015/10/women-of-the-islamic-state31.pdf.

Withnall, Adam, "Isis Releases 'Abhorrent' Sex Slaves Pamphlet with 27 Tips for Militants on Taking, Punishing and Raping Female Captives," *The Independent*, 2015, http://www.independent.co.uk/news/world/middle-east/isis-releases-abhorrent-sex-slaves-pamphlet-with-27-tips-for-militants-on-taking-punishing-and-9915913.html.

Wolfe, Lauren, "Will There Ever Be Justice for Syria's Rape Survivors?" *The Nation*, May 14, 2014, https://www.thenation.com/article/will-there-ever-be-justice-syrias-rape-survivors/.

Women's Media Center, "Documenting Sexualized Violence in Syria," *Women Under Siege Syria Crowdmap*, February 4, 2016, https://womenundersiegesyria.crowdmap.com/.

Wood, Elisabeth, "Variation in Sexual Violence During War," *Politics and Soceity* 34, no. 3 (2006): 307–42.

Wood, Elisabeth, "Armed Groups and Sexual Violence: When Is Wartime Rape Rare?" *Politics and Soceity* 37, no. 1 (2009): 131–61, doi:10.1177/0032329208329755.

"Glossary of Statistsical Terms: Developed, Developing Countries," *Organization for Economic Co-Operation and Development*, January 4, 2006, https://stats.oecd.org/glossary/detail.asp?ID=6326.

"Syria 2012 Human Rights Report" (Washington, D.C.: United States Department of State, 2012), https://www.state.gov/documents/organization/204595.pdf.

"Syria: Sexual Assault in Detention" (New York: Human Rights Watch, June 15, 2012), https://www.hrw.org/news/2012/06/15/syria-sexual-assault-detention.

"Syria's Conflict: With Both Barrels," *The Economist*, June 16, 2012, http://www.economist.com/node/21556952.

"Profile: Syria's Ruling Baath Party," *BBC News*, July 9, 2012, http://www.bbc.com/news/world-middle-east-18582755.

"The Power of Religion," *The Economist*, July 13, 2013, http://www.economist.com/news/special-report/21580618-islamists-government-proving-harder-opposition-power-religion.

"Guide to the Syrian Rebels," *BBC News*, December 13, 2013, http://www.bbc.com/news/world-middle-east-24403003.

"Syrian Kurdish Armed Non-State Actor Commits to Ban Anti-Personnel Mines, Sexual Violence and Child Recruitment," *Geneva Call*, June 16, 2014, http://genevacall.org/syrian-kurdish-armed-non-state-actor-commits-ban-anti-personnel-mines-sexual-violence-child-recruitment/.

"Women Warriors: A Nightmare for IS," *The Sunday Herald*, October 19, 2014, NewsBank EBSCOhost.

"Report of the Independent International Commission of Inquiry on the Syrian Arab Republic" (United Nations, General Assembly, Human Rights Council, February 5, 2015), http://www.ohchr.org/Documents/Countries/SY/A.HRC.S-17.2.Add.1_en.pdf.

"Human Development Reports: Syrian Arab Republic," *United Nations Development Program: Human Development Reports*, 2016, http://hdr.undp.org/en/countries/profiles/SYR.

"Syria: The Story of the Conflict," *BBC News*, March 11, 2016, http://www.bbc.com/news/world-middle-east-26116868.

"Country Reports on Human Rights Practices for 2015" (Washington, D.C.: United States Department of State, April 2016), https://www.state.gov/documents/organization/253159.pdf.

"Mapping Militant Organizations: The Islamic State" (Stanford University, April 4, 2016), http://web.stanford.edu/group/mappingmilitants/cgi-bin/groups/view/1.

"Flow of Foreign ISIS Recruits Much Slower Now, U.S. Says," *CBS News*, April 26, 2016, http://www.cbsnews.com/news/less-foreign-isis-recruits/.

"Kurdish People's Protection Unit YPG," *GlobalSecurity.org*, August 19, 2016, http://www.globalsecurity.org/military/world/para/ypg.htm.

"Syria Profile - Overview," *BBC News*, September 20, 2016, http://www.bbc.com/news/world-middle-east-14703910.

"Human Development for Everyone: Briefing Note for Countries on the 2016 Human Development Report, Syrian Arab Republic" (New York: United Nations Development Program, 2017).

"What Is A Developing Country?" *World Atlas*, March 21, 2017, http://www.worldatlas.com/articles/what-is-a-developing-country.html.

"Mission," *Geneva Call*, accessed April 6, 2017, http://genevacall.org/who-we-are/.

"Syria: Major Brigade of the Free Syrian Army Commits against Anti-Personnel Mines and Sexual Violence," *Geneva Call*, accessed April 6, 2017, http://genevacall.org/syria-major-brigade-free-syrian-army-commits-anti-personnel-mines-sexual-violence/.

"Syria - National Defense Forces (NDF)," *GlobalSecurity.org*, accessed February 26, 2017, http://www.globalsecurity.org/military/world/syria/ndf.htm.

Chapter 10. The Points of Continuity: Muslim Migration from Monarchist and Socialist Yugoslavia to Turkey

Vladan Jovanović[1]

Abstract

My paper points out some (unexpected) similarities in migration of Yugoslav Muslims to Turkey during the two ideologically opposed regimes: the monarchist (1918-1941) and the early-socialist Yugoslavia (1945-1955). In both cases the migration was a state-facilitated process, as Yugoslav primary sources have shown. Despite a kind of international benevolence towards the de-Ottomanization of the Balkans, the Yugoslav Kingdom attempts in demographic engineering sharpened its ethnic and religious boundaries, compromising its own minority policy at the same time. Although the uncontrolled emigration was legalized after the Yugoslav-Turkish Convention was signed in 1938, many manipulative factors have survived. Treating Kosovo Albanians as 'people of Turkish culture and language' enabled their legal expatriation and relocation to Asia Minor during the both interwar and postwar years. Furthermore, the expected improvement of their social status was why many ethnic Albanians declared their nationality or even mother tongue differently, depending on current propositions for emigration. This circumstance was systematically abused by both Yugoslav states in a very similar manner which I intend to show. Owing to restriction of their civil and religious rights, cultural and educational marginalization, the growing waves of Turkish and Albanian migrants continued to move towards Turkey within the two decades after the Second World War.

Keywords: expatriation, migration, Muslims, Turkey, Yugoslavia

Motivational capacity of social segregation

If we ignore the Milošević short-lived simulation from the early 1990s - a hasty federation created in the midst of a struggle for Yugoslav legacy - there were actually two Yugoslav states: the interwar monarchy and the socialist republic established after the Second world war. Unlike the interwar kingdom, the socialist Yugoslavia was mostly represented in historiography as a more humane society with a more equitable minority policy, which is generally not hard to prove. However, while doing my research on emigration of Yugoslav Muslims to Turkey, I have noticed several points of continuity that could challenge the notion of impeccable socialist Yugoslavia.

The political and social situation of Muslim population in Macedonia and Kosovo after the fall of the Ottoman Empire was unfavorable for several reasons. The aagrarian reform and colonization processes after both world wars were similar in their nature and the extent. Due to a disintegration of feudalism, former Muslim landowners remained without sources of income, so most of them had to start trading in order to secure their existence. The fourth of all the estates provided for the colonization of Christian settlers were properties abandoned by Muslims after 1912. In both cases the so-called

---

[1] Dr Vladan Jovanović is a Research Fellow at the Institute for the Recent History of Serbia, Trg Nikole Pašića 11, 11000 Belgrade, Serbia. E-mail: vladanjovanovicc@gmail.com.

'abandoned plots' were used as a prize for Serbian and Montenegrin war volunteers (Jovanović, 2015, pp. 87-103).

Among prevailing reasons for migration there was a fear of retaliation for the crimes against Christians committed during the wars of 1912-1918, political repression over Yugoslav Muslims, their social extrusion and cultural neglecting. On the other hand, Turkish propaganda began to encourage Muslims to emigrate by emphasizing that, since the Ottoman Empire collapsed, the Turks in newly established Balkan countries should not suffer of contempt and slavery.

Certain forms of educational and cultural discrimination were obvious in both Yugoslavias. The establishment of Turkish schools within the Albanian communities, the lowest rate of Muslims employed in civil service, but also the banning of their political parties and political instrumentalisation of religious jurisdictions - are some of the possible sources of dissatisfaction and overwhelming sense of injustice (Jovanović, 2007).

Despite the constitutional obligation to finance the Muslim religious infrastructure in Macedonia and Kosovo (along with the Islamic Religious Community), Yugoslav administration demonstrated the lack of tolerance through politicization of Muslim priests and schools, and especially in terms of aubusing Muslim property. Many mosques and graveyards were turned into army warehouses, gardens and homesteads. Yugoslav Department of Religions interdicted such usurpation, but their colleagues from the Ministry of agriculture usually evinced dissent (Osmanović, 1922).

Political activity of "southern Muslims" in the interwar period was carried out through the organization *Cemiyet* that gathered both feudal and religious circles of the Turkish-Albanian communities from 1919 to 1925. Its leadership was well-connected to the ruling Serbian Radical Party, betraying the hopes of Muslim population. In fact, the ruling radicals used this coalition rather to inhibit Serbian opposition, than to solve the most vital issues of Muslims, such as educational, religious and agrarian. However, the success of Cemiyet in parliamentary elections in 1923 triggered a series of repressive measures taken by the government: forced migration to Asia Minor, night raids, blockade of Turkish merchants, electoral manipulation, but also physical elimination. Turks had their own newspaper *Hak* which was banned by the Skopje County soon in 1924. Simultaneously with the banning of Cemiyet party in the next year its leader Ferhat Draga was arrested and consequently, emigration increased. District officials started to fill passports for whole days and nights in order to speed up the expatriation process (Jovanović, 2007, pp. 96-99).

Reserved, or even hostile attitude of Muslims towards Serbian or Yugoslav state during the both world wars made authorities suspicious about them in

Sandžak and Kosovo, whether it was a royal or socialist Yugoslavia. In other words, their modest participation in the anti-fascist movement turned them into "undesirable" minority even in Tito's Yugoslavia. For this reason, already in 1945 Sandžak lost its territorial autonomy which was projected only two years earlier, nothwithstanding the war crimes that *Chetniks* commited to Kosovo and Sandžak Muslims, have also reinforced the sense of collective fear and existential threat. In this way, the people of Sandžak were "punished" for not being revolutionary enough, which turned them into an "unreliable element", which quite affected their social status. The ban of wearing the veil and the abolition of Muslim religious schools encouraged further emigration (Bandžović, 2006, p. 668).

The postwar emigration was encouraged through rigid social measures by which the socialist government fought the "religious narrow-mindedness" (Bandžović, 2006, pp. 478-479). The persistent atheistic propaganda seemed to be too radical for a conservative and patriarchal Muslim society. Having lost their class position in the era of nationalization and expropriation, the richer Muslims began to leave Yugoslavia along with traders and artisans: "They were afraid of losing the religious liberty they had enjoyed during the Kingdom of Yugoslavia and strongly believed that `religion without a king` was something impossible" (Karadžoski, 2009, p. 122). The scenes of lawyers riding mules in Muslim villages in order to promote emigration to Asia Minor were typical for the late-1940s, especially after the Cominform resolution of 1948, when many Albanians were accused of espionage in favor of Enver Hoxha's Albania (Bandžović, 2006, pp. 510-513).

Even after 1945 the measures of collectivization, expropriation and land holding limitations directly affected Turkish landowners. The Law on nationalization of rental buildings and building lots (1958) decreased the migration intensity, because it prevented the owners of selling their own land (Karadžoski, 2009, pp. 123-124). The most notable interest in emigration was among the peasants and former landlords whose property was nationalized by the new state. Besides, the socialist regime treated the peasants as a symbol of backwardness, trying to organize them according to the Soviet model of cooperative farming. There was a general agreement that this "non-revolutionary" area should not be developed economically but displaced, as the "Muslim fatalism hampered the initiative and desire for progress", thus preventing the formation of the industrial working class. One of the most influential Serbian politicians, Jovan Veselinov, had a very interesting recommendation for local authorities in Sandžak: "Finish your schools, serve in the army, and move out from here. We cannot raise factories everywhere" (Bandžović, 1991, p. 103).

The problem of national identity of Muslims and its legal dimensions were particularly demoralizing for potential emmigrants because they had to declare differently on national censuses: "Muslim-neutral" (1948), "Yugoslav-neutral" (1953), "Muslim in ethnic sense" (1961), or "Muslim by nationality" (1971, 1981). Furthermore, during the census of 1953 Kosovo Albanians had to declare themselves as Turks and move to Macedonia for a while, if they ever intended to leave the country. For such interest in emigration the socialist government has blamed the "religious fanaticism" of Muslims and their sympathy for Turkish capitalism (Jovanović, 2013, pp. 208-209). The majority of Albanian nationalist intellectuals have persistently spread the anti-migration propaganda, because they considered the migration an insurmountable obstacle for the eventual unification of Kosovo and western parts of Macedonia with Albania (Ilijevski, 2007, pp. 167-182).

State-facilitated migration patterns

In both monarchist and socialist regime, the methodology of expatriation was similar, ranging from withdrawal from Yugoslav citizenship to a simplified emigration procedure and administrative complication for returnees as well. The emigration of Muslims from Yugoslavia to Turkey was officially sanctioned in 1928 by the Law of Citizenship. If the "non-Slavic" citizens renounced their Yugoslav citizenship within five years, they would be removed from military and county registers. In the late-1920s Turkish passports were exposed to a restricted visa-system, while the outgoings were encouraged by many bureaucratic benefits. In the mid 1930s the Yugoslav consulate in Istanbul refused to meet the needs of those who wanted to go back to Yugoslavia because their return would affect municipal budgets. Confusing definition of potential immigrants - the "people of Turkish Culture" (1938) or "of Turkish ethnicity" (1953) - was used by Turkish authorities periodically to suspend immigration of Albanian immigrants.

Considering the methodology and patterns of state-facilitated emigration, we cannot avoid series of (in)direct measures, by which the Yugoslav governments incited Muslims to migrate, using the state institutions. The so-called Inteministerial Conference dealt with emigration problems in September 1935. It decided to encourage bilateral arrangements with Albania and Turkey, suggesting at the same time the measures to be taken in order to speed the non-Slavic migration towards Turkey (shortcuts in passport procedure, frequently call for Muslim conscripts, economical pressure in tobacco production, depose of potential emigrants from public service, nationalization of family names, etc.). Moreover, the measures contained a strong propagandistic mission aimed at attracting Albanians into Turkey, by putting about good life in Asia Minor (Jovanović, 2006, pp. 105-124).

The primary idea about expulsion of disloyal Albanians by removing 200.000 Muslims to Turkey culminated with the official Yugoslav-Turkish Convention, signed in July 1938. On the Turkish side, this project was seen as an "evacuation of the lost territories", and therefore similar arrangements with Romania and Bulgaria were concluded as well. The main Turkish interest in these immigrants was to populate desolated territories in eastern Turkey, as well as to use Yugoslav Muslims in the fight against Kurds (Avdić, 1991, pp. 112-117). Yet, the Convention was not ratified for several reasons: in addition to financial disagreements and Ataturk's death, a possible obstacle to ratification was the fear of Yugoslav Prime Minister Milan Stojadinović that he will lose Muslim votes in the upcoming elections (Jovanović, 2013, pp. 209-210).

Just like in the prewar period, Muslims used to travel by train and after a stopover in Salonika, they would continue by boat towards Istanbul. After they sold their property for a pittance, the emigrants were given disposable passports labeled as "stateless". They could visit Yugoslavia only after five years spent in Turkey (Bandžović, 2006, p. 539). Though, the procedure of emigration after 1945 created a less administrative problems than in the interwar period. After the intervention of Macedonian leadership, Yugoslav authorities decided to facilitate the release of citizenship. They allowed to potential emigrants to sell their property before they receive formal renunciation of citizenship in order to avoid the application of the Law on nationalization. In addition, passport fees were waived, while poor families were exempt from all transportation fees. Interestingly, emigrants from socialist Yugoslavia were allowed to carry home furnishings, a horse cart and two head of cattle, just like the Convention of 1938 had required. According to the pre-emption rights, Muslim emmigrants were required to offer their farms to „national authorities" within 45 days. It seems that the indemnification of immigrants` property was the hardest issue to be solved. Problems arose in January 1950 when the Ankara Protocol on Compensation of Turkish property in Yugoslavia was signed. It provided that Turkish property owners should be exempt from all liability including taxes, mortgages and other debts incurred before the nationalization (Jovanović, 2013, p. 210).

Already in 1951 the idea about expulsion of Albanians has been revived and all the Muslims began to declare themselves as Turks, in order to be considered for emigration, according to the procedure. Therefore, between the two national censuses in Kosovo (1948-1953) the number of people who identified themselves as Turks increased as much as 26 times! This declaration had to preserve both Yugoslavia and Turkey from unpleasant international reaction regarding the expatriation of the Albanians.

In October 1951 Turkish government demanded from their Yugoslav partners to ratify and implement the Convention of 1938, particularly its financial terms. For that reason Yugoslav President Tito invited Turkish Foreign Minister Fuad Köprülü to visit Yugoslavia. During a diner in Split in the late-January 1953 they reached a verbal agreement on emigration process. Nothing was signed on this occasion, so the entire event became known as the Gentleman's Agreement that was supposed to revive the Yugoslav-Turkish Convention of 1938 (Pezo, 2013). In addition, this agreement was formally aimed at "humanitarian family reunification", while the Turkish side treated kinship relations so broadly that they could apply to anyone. Furthermore, the notion of "Turkish nationality" was too expansive, very suitable for abuse (Pačariz, 2016, pp. 153-154). Consequently, the Turkish government started to complain about the large number of ethnic Albanians who had arrived as "Turks from Yugoslavia" (Bandžović, 2006, pp. 533-534).

As for the Albanians, there was a kind of alternating interest, or occasional sympathy among Turkish authorities for the Albanian immigrants, manifested through temporary suspension of their immigration. Since the licenses were massively issued to Macedonian Albanians, Turkish Consul in Skopje started to reject Albanian applications for a while. At the same time, his colleague from the Turkish Embassy in Belgrade said that Turkey is "willing to accept Albanians tacitly" (Jovanović, 2013, pp. 211-212).

As noted before, in both periods the initiative came from the Turkish officials (H. Saka, R. Aras, F. Koprulu, Turkish Embassy in Belgrade), while Macedonia was a transit area for expatriates. The similarity was evident in simplified procedure of citizenship withdrawal, and therefore it was easy to obtain the documents that prove "Turkish origin". At the same time, it was almost impossible to return to the land of eviction. Furthermore, the emigration mechanism in both periods was entrusted to Yugoslav ministries of agriculture and agrarian reform, in which there was obvious personal continuity (Sreten Vukosavljević was the state secretary of agricultural reform in 1920s, but also the Minister of Agriculture and Colonization in the first socialist government in 1945). Strikingly similar were disarmament actions among Kosovo Albanians that usually preceded major migration tides in early 1920s and the mid-1950s. In 1955/56 the State Security carried out a weapon collection campaign among the Albanians, just like the one from the early-1920s. As a consequence, there were 22.000 new personal files created, 'allowing' the Albanians to retain their inconvenient status of the 'most distrustful element'.

Similarities in the extent of migration and international context

Between the two world wars the Yugoslav authorities used to register only regular cases of emigration, losing the sight of illegal immigration and the real extent of this phenomenon. Therefore, the official statistics are incomplete, underestimating the actual number of emigrants. According to the Yugoslav Statistical Yearbook for the period 1930-1939 only 13,678 people emigrated to Turkey. On the other hand, the political abuse of other sources has led to the almost fantastic exaggeration, especially in the Albanian historiography. In both cases, there were fake numbers of displaced Albanians, although their emigration in the first decade after the Second World War outreached the entire interwar period. The Yugoslav official sources present figures of 450,000 Yugoslav Muslims who emigrated to Turkey during the period 1918-1949 (Jovanović, 2013, p. 213).

The post-war immigration to Turkey culminated in the mid-1950s, when the most wealthy Muslims were moving out, capable to start business in Turkey. Poorer population emigrated before 1966 when the immigration wave has fallen sharply. Many historians tend to connect it with the political decline of Serbian naionalist politician Aleksandar Ranković[2], but there is no solid documentation that would confirm this. Even in the mid-1950s, Kosovo Albanians considered Macedonia a transit point on their way to Turkey in spite their religious leaders and intelligence urged them to stay in Yugoslavia in order to avoid further false ethnic identification - as Turks (Crvenkovski, 1957, pp. 6-13).

The Yugoslav official statistics from 1952 to 1965 show that 390,000 Turks and Albanians received release from Yugoslav citizenship which corresponds with Yugoslav diplomatic sources from 1970 that registered nearly 300,000 Turkish citizens who came from socialist Yugoslavia. Interestingly, during the 1960s more than three-quarters of emmigrants were actually Turks. An English historian Hugh Poulton tried to comprehend those shifts in number of Turks in Macedonia, scoring with a conclusion that Albanians began to identify themselves as Turks *en masse*, while the ethnic Turks declared as "Muslims" (Poulton, 2003, pp. 83-84). The fact that the post-war migration was almost twice as large as the one between the two world wars might seem surprising for those who use to idealize the minority policy of the socialist regime.

In addition to these similarities in motivation and mechanism of migration, there were some parallels in the international context as well. In 1938, when the Yugoslav-Turkish convention was signed, Yugoslav Prime Minister Milan Stojadinović was openly flirting with fascism, while the Balkan pact of 1953 (following the Gentlemen Agreement) was an expression of a strong anti-Soviet orientation of socialist Yugoslavia. Both Yugoslav-Turkish

---

2 Ranković was the most powerful Yugoslav communist of Serbian ethnic origin of that time. During the 1950s he advocated a „hardline approach" against Kosovo Albanians, as a head of military intelligence and secret police. He fell from power in 1966 when he was expelled from the Yugoslav Communist Party.

demographic arrangements (1938, 1953) have been achieved in the shadow of the two Balkan Pacts. The first one was signed in 1934 between Romania, Greece, Turkey and Yugoslavia while the other was signed in February 1953 between Yugoslavia, Greece and Turkey, growing into a military alliance the very next year. Moreover, in both cases Yugoslavia was approaching the leading military alliances. At the end of 1930s, the Kingdom of Yugoslavia was turning towards Germany, while in 1953 it approached NATO, seeking for a protection from the possible Soviet attack.

However, Yugoslavia was not the only country having such a "double" experience with Muslim migration. Moreover, both methodology and patterns of Muslim migration from Bulgaria were similar to the last detail (Vasileva, 1992, pp. 346-352). In the mid-1930s Turkish government negotiated with Bulgaria about displacement of 789.000 Bulgarian Muslims to Turkey. After the Second world war, due to a bad religious and cultural position, the Bulgarian Turks have decided to move to Turkey again (more in: Şimşir, 1985). Although the number of potential emigrants increased significantly after 1947, Bulgarian authorities started to obstruct the procedure of issuing passports. However, the first great postwar migration started in August 1950 when Bulgarian government was ready to send off 250.000 Bulgarian Turks towards Turkey, though „only" 150.000 managed to emigrate (Vasileva, 1992, pp. 346-352).

Concluding notes

Since the ethnic and religious minorities were seen as a "necessary evil" in the interwar Yugoslavia, one could expect completely the opposite when the communist regime proclaimed an absolute discontinuity with their predecessors in 1945. However, whether it was a monarchy or socialist community, Yugoslavia appeared a land where Muslims were easily identified with the rulers from the Ottoman era (regardless of their ethnic or social origin), which created an atmosphere for radical solutions, such as expatriation or even forced migration. Behind these two migration projects there was a strong intention for homogenization: in 1930s its core should be the ethnicity and religion, while in 1950s the ideology should be the main factor of cohesion. It was almost the same process in two completely different situations under two ideologically opposed political systems.

During the first decade of the socialist regime the Yugoslav authorities failed to achieve comprehensive integration of national minorities primarily due to a lack of economic and cultural development of areas with a Muslim majority. Under such circumstances, Muslim emigration from Yugoslavia to Turkey became a state-facilitated process, as a part of a broad Balkan "demographic de-Ottomanization" trend. At the same time, the interweaving of identity boundaries indicated a sort of pragmatism, demystifying stereotypes on 'ethnicity obsession' in the name of which the Muslims would sacrifice their own prosperity.

In spite of prevailing stereotypes about Serbian hegemonism and 'affinity' towards the ethnic engineering, one could conclude that the whole idea was constantly being thrown in Yugoslavia from the Turkish side, during the both 1930s and 1950s. Regardless of its political or ideological structure, Yugoslavia was nothing but a 'partner in crime' who gladly accepted the idea of emigration for further implementation. In times when Yugoslavia was economically even more stable than Turkey, there was undue emphasis on economic motives of Muslim migration while historians usually neglected or overstated their political motivation. Besides the objective difficulties, the causes were also inconsistent enforcement of authorities in providing minority rights (such as bilingual education and administration). The insufficient economic development of Muslim communities in Yugoslavia has further hindered the integration of minorities, while the benefits of land reform were partly reversed by establishing peasant cooperatives. Most of these issues were not resolved until the end of the Yugoslav state; all the more, these unresolved issues have indirectly led to the disintegration of the entire state.

Although the Muslim migration to Turkey was a broad Balkan process (Romania, Bulgaria, Greece), the Yugoslav case was somewhat different. By using the Yugoslav-Turkish agreements Yugoslavia tried to expel Albanians as "people of Turkish culture". It seems that this was precisely the main motivation/incentive in both migration periods. Disloyalty of an 'undesirable nationality' was seen as a propensity to irredentism during the interwar period, but also as a product of a blind devotion to both Soviet and Albanian leaderships, the most dangerous ideological enemies of the Yugoslav socialist regime in the early-1950s.

References

Avdić, A. (1991). Jugoslovensko-turski pregovori o iseljavanju muslimanskog stanovništva u periodu izmedju dva svetska rata. [Yugoslav-Turkish negotiations about the interwar Muslim migration]. *Novopazarski zbornik*, 15, 112-125 (in Serbian).
Bandžović, S. (2006). *Iseljavanje Bošnjaka u Tursku.* [Emigration of Bosniaks to Turkey] Sarajevo: Institut za istraživanje zločina protiv čovječnosti i međunarodnog prava (in Bosnian).
Bandžović, S. (1991). *Iseljavanje muslimana iz Sandžaka.* [The migration of Muslims from Sandzak]. Sarajevo: Bublioteka Ključanin (in Bosnian).
Crvenkovski, K. (1957). The problems created by the emigration of Turkish minority from NR Macedonia. in: Archive of Yugoslavia, collection: Savez komunista Jugoslavije (XVIII), folder 4, archival units 7-12, no. 6.
Ilijevski, B. (2007). The Ethno-Demographic Changes in the 1950s in the People's Republic of Macedonia: The Emigration Process of the Turkish and Muslim Population, *Istorija*, XLIII/1-2, 167-182
Imamović, M. (2003). Bošnjački etos: identitet i ime [Bosniak ethos: the identity and name], *Prilozi*, 32, 315-329 (in Bosnian).

Jovanović, V. (2015). Land reform and Serbian colonization. Belgrade`s problems in interwar Kosovo and Macedonia, *East Central Europe*, 42 (1), 87-103;

Jovanović, V. (2007). Iseljavanje muslimana iz Vardarske banovine: između stihije i državne akcije. [Muslim migration from Vardar Banovina: between the spontaneity and state action]. In: Mile Bjelajac (Ed.), *Pisati istoriju Jugoslavije: viđenje srpskog faktora.* Beograd: INIS, 79-99 (in Serbian).

Jovanović, V. (2013). Jugoslovensko-turski demografski aranžmani do sredine pedesetih godina 20. veka. [Yugoslav-Turkish demographic arrangements by the mid-1950s] In: Đurković M., Raković, A. (eds.). *Turska - regionalna sila?* [Turkey - a regional power?] Beograd: Institut za evropske studije, 205-215 (in Serbian);

Jovanović, V. (2006). Interministerijalna konferencija Kraljevine Jugoslavije o iseljenju `neslovenskog elementa` u Tursku (1935). [Interministriel conference of Kingdom of Yugoslavia about emigration of "non-Slavic element" into Turkey] *Prilozi*, 35, 105-124 (in Serbian).

Karadžoski, V. (2009). Socio-Political, Religious, and Economic Reasons for Macedonians` Movement to Turkey, in: Roth, K., Hayden, R. (eds.), Migration in, from, and to Southeastern Europe, Part 1, *Ethnologia Balkanica. Journal for Southeast European Anthropology*, 13 (Special issue), 121-127.

Osmanović, R. parliamentary discussion in: *Stenografske beleške Narodne skupštine Kraljevine SHS*, CVI session, 25 July 1922. (in Serbian)

Pačariz, S. (2016) *The migrations of Bosniaks to Turkey from 1945 to 1974. The case of Sandžak.* Sarajevo: Center for Advanced Studies.

Pezo, E. (2013). Komparativna analiza Jugoslovensko-turske konvencije iz 1938. i "Džentlmenskog sporazuma" iz 1953. Pregovori oko iseljavanja muslimana iz Jugoslavije u Tursku, [Comparative analysis of the Yugoslav-Turkish Convention of 1938 and the "gentlemen's agreement" in 1953. Negotiations on emigration from Yugoslavia to Turkey] *Tokovi istorije*, 2, 97-120 (in Serbian)

Poulton, H. (2002). *Balkan. Manjine i države u sukobu.* [The Balkans. Minorities and Conflicting States] Subotica: Čikoš Holding (in Serbian).

Şimşir, B. N. (1985). *Türk Basınında Bulgaristan Türkleri: Zorla Ad Değiştirme Sorunu. Başbakanlık Basın-Yayın ve Enfermasyon Genel Müdürlüğü*, Ankara.

Vasileva, D. (1992). Bulgarian Türkish Emigration and Return, *International Migration Rewiew*, 26 (98), 342-352.

Chapter 11. Cinema and Migration: The Representation of Illegal Immigration of First and Third Generation[1] Turkish Worker to European Countries in Turkish Cinema: A Comperative Analysis of the Films *"The Bus"* (1977) and *"The Island of Hope"* (2007)

Levent Yaylagül[2], Nilüfer Korkmaz-Yaylagül[3]

Abstract

Labour migration from Turkey to European Countries has started with bilateral international agreements signed between Turkey and European Countries around the 1960's. The oil crisis at 1973 decreased the demand for migrant worker resulting with an illegal migration wave to European countries. Those emergent social developments have influenced the Turkish cinema and some films about illegal immigration were shooted at that period. The film "the Bus" directed by Tunç Okan is one of the first examples of this category about first generation illegal immigrants. Another film "the Island of Hope", shooted after 30 years, at 2007 by Mustafa Kara subjected about illegal immigration concerning third generation illegal immigrants. Those two films were evaluated using qualitative content analysis technic in the context of the question of how first and third generation illegal immigrants are represented in Turkish cinema. Graphic image and dialogs were used as analysis unit. The contents of the two films were analysed within the framework of questions such; personal details, expectations, the country of immigration, the ways of immigration, the problems faced by immigrants, the realisation of the expectations, and the final status. First generation immigrants represented in the film "the Bus" are male with rural backgrounds, muslims with sunni sect, unskilled agricultural worker and their immigration incentive is economic. At the film "the Island of Hope" not only men, instead women, couples and even pregnant women were among the illegal immigrants. The main incentive of immigration is also economic, but the immigrants are not only the illiterate and the unskilled worker. For the first-generation immigrants, the image of Europe is expressed negatively such as; death, unemployment, deportation, being victims of sexual abuse, nostalgia and fear. For the third-generation immigrants however, even they experience similar problems and disappointment, Europe is represented such a home for the survivors, who could find a job and could realize their dreams. In both films, the loser was facing endings such death, alcohol, drug addiction and prostitution. To be deported to Turkey was one of the most prevalent options for the illegal immigrants.

Keywords: illegal immigration, Turkish cinema, content analysis.

Introduction

The 1950's in Turkey were periods of a social change rising from not just the government change, also from politico-economic changes. One of the most

---

[1] The terms first and third generation illegal immigrants have been used in order to cathegorize the time periods of immigrants. "First generation" is used for illegal immigrants around the 1970's, "second generation" is used for political immigrants around the 1980's and 1990's and "third generation" is used for illegal immigrants around the 2000's who have immigrated for any reason.

[2] Associate Professor, Akdeniz University, Communication Faculty, Radio, Television and Cinema Department, Antalya, Turkey.

[3] Assistant Professor, Akdeniz University, Faculty of Literature, Gerontology Department, Antalya, Turkey.

important results of these transformations are migration and related urbanisation (Kongar, 1979). The migration wave from Turkey to Europe has started after the agreement signed between Germany and Turkey at 30 October 1961, followed by others (Holland, Austria, Belgium 1964, France 1965, Sweden 1967, Switzerland 1971 and Denmark 1973) more than a half million people have immigrated to Europe in ten years (Abadan-Unat, 2006). The demand for foreign workforce decreased due to economic crisis at 1973 and the European Countries brought the foreign migration to an end. However, migration has never stopped and was turned to illegal immigration mainly through political asylum and family reuniation. Those social developments have affected the film industry as a social institution and films concerning migration to Europe were shooted. Since the 1970's dramas of Turkish immigrants to Europe took place in Turkish cinema (Makal, 1987).

Cinema is one of the main channels where social problems come to order. Cinema is considered as a seventh branch of art where stories of dramas are manifested by visual displays and dialogs on the light of historical and sociological conditions. Cinema is nourished by stories based on the dream world of the screen writer and directors or on true stories and it is a form of art whereby social realities emerged by historical and sociological conditions affected by artistic and social counsciousness are conveyed to society by the agency of artists. The issue of illegal immigration is presented dramatically as a historical problem experienced by individuals coming from certain social classes. In this context cinema films cannot be interpreted only through counsciousness of their developer, also through their shaped counsciousness framed by the historical and social context (Tolan, 1975:155-162).

The examination of the fact how immigration and illegal immigration is presented to the society through cinema is important in order to understand social developments. From this perspective, cinema is a channel where developments in social structure are reflected directly or indirectly. Cinema is affected by historical and social conditions and can shape the culture of the society with its contents presented. Turkish cinema has dealt with the issue of immigration as a social agenda around the 1950's and the issue of illegal immigration around the 1970's and gave a social message to potential immigrants and other members of the society. Opponent ideas were directed towards social problems with the expansion of freedoms of expression, thought and organisation around the 1960's (especially 27 May and 1961 Constitutions), and this has resulted in social realistic filmshooting (Dorsay, 1989; Refiğ, 1971).

Within this framework, the aim of this analysis is to reveal how worker candidates travelling illegally to European Countries after legal immigration was stopped at 1973, are presented in Turkish cinema. The film "the Bus" directed by Tunç Okan shooted at 1977 and the film "the Island of Hope", shooted at 2007 by Mustafa Kara were selected to reveal the presentation of illegal immigrants in a 30-year period considered as first and third generation immigrants in Turkish cinema.

Among limited films with the subject of international migration and focused on illegal immigration, two films shooted at 1970's and 2000's were examined using purposive sampling method in order to evaluate the changes in economical, cultural conditions and expectations of illegal immigrant worker to European countries. The reason why those two films were selected is that in both films the main subjects were the dramas of illegal immigrants, the problems faced by illegal immigrants, the directors being Turkish and that they were shooted between the period of 1970 and 2000 and that both films were showing the main features of the periods they were shooted.[4]

Methods

This investigation paper has adopted a historical/ qualitative approach in the context of cinema/society, in accordance with the problematic of the representation of first and third generation illegal Turkish immigrant worker in Turkish cinema. The films "the Bus" and " the Island of Hope" have been examined using qualitative content analysis method. The aim in using this technic is to expose the ideas and opinions of films in accordance with the opinion that films mirror the views of their developers explicitly or implicitly (Berger, 1998; Berelson, 1952; Krippendorf, 1980; Cavanagh, 1997).

Hereby, contents containing informations have been analysed in the texts of two films about illegal immigration. Contents of the films have been systematically analysed using standart questions. Results of the questions have been taken out of the text analysed qualitatively using text reading. The aim was to interpret the film contents. Film contents were analysed thematically within the framework of illegal immigration discourse problematic. The technic and aesthetic dimentions of films (factors such as the language of the film, style, camera, light and montage) were therefore disregarded.

As the aim of this research is to evaluate what was said by the Turkish cinema about illegal immigration, the question how it was said has been disregarded. Mainly dialogs and visual images displaying the themes were investigated.

---

[4] Another example of this kind of films is the film "Journey to Hope" directed by Xavier Koller, the scripwriter is Feride Çiçekoğlu shooted at 1989, the subject of the film is the drama of a family from Maraş trying to immigrate to Switzerland illegally. This film won the best foreign film Oscar at 1989 on behalf of Switzerland. Therefore the film "Journey to Hope" has been left out of scope.

Answers for questions such; the personal details, expectations, the countries of immigration, the problems experienced by immmigrants, the fulfillment of the expectations and the final situations of first and third generation illegal immigrant worker have been sought.

Categories have been identified according to the researchers aims. Images and visual materials (dialogs) have been examined. Words, sentences, phrases and the full text have been examined. As the theme of the films is illegal immigration, all discourses about illegal immigration have been researched. Films were accepted as texts and qualitative codes related to the content of the films were excluded during the reading period. All elements of the content have been evaluated in the frame of the research questions. Informations related to a specific group have been gathered together. Film contents have been analysed and the answer of the question how Turkish cinema is reflecting the illegal immigrant worker problem has been sought in the view that film contents are reflecting the social changes. It was aimed to trace the socioeconomic and cultural changes in Turkey related to illegal immigration via two films shooted in 30 years timeframe.

Findings

Who immigrates where and how?

In the film "the Bus", first period of illegal immigrants is represented, characters consist of men between the age of 30 and 40, with rural backgrounds, unskilled agricultural worker travelling to Stokholm, Sweden by bus through a human trafficker, a Turkish member of a German gang. Some the offical customs officer were paid to help the gang. Characters are speaking Turkish using local rural dialect. They all are muslims with sunni sect, some of the worker pray namaz during the stopover. No emphasis is given to individual ethnic and religious identities among the first-generation immigrants. All men are heterosexual. The main incentive of immigration is economic.

In the film "the Island of Hope", third generation immigrants are represented. There is a great variation among the immigrants' characteristics. Individuals from rural areas as well from urban cities such Istanbul, between the age of 20 and 30, skilled and unskilled are migrating. They consist of women, men, single, married, pregnants from several education levels ranging from primary schools to university graduates. Several professions such as bodyguards, writer, jongleur is migrating for several reasons in a Turkish cargo liner illegally to London. Characters in this film are speaking Turkish using a local rural dialect and Istanbul Turkish. They are muslims with sunni sect and heterosexuals. Yusuf from Maraş praying at his father's grave before heading to Istanbul on his way to London and some of the passengers praying namaz in the boat give clues about their sunni islam believe. Only an alevi saying is playing at Cevdet Ede's restaurant in London, while Yusuf was visiting. Except of this scene there are no other signs of Alevi sect in the film.

Illegal Immigration Incentives and Expectations from Immigration

The economic development wasn't realized even after 50 years of the constitution of the Turkish Republic. The young republic couldn't feed its citizens and therefore send them to several European Countries as a cheap workforce. After the economic crisis at 1973 the legal immigration ways were closed and citizens who lost their hope from their countries tried illegal immigration risking their lives. The dream for a better life which couldnt be reached in their home countries was considered such a good reason for migration.

The incentive of immigration for the first-generation immigrants is economic. Nine unskilled agricultural workers immigrate due to unemployement. The main aim is to approach work and money. Money for them means welfare, peace and happiness. The driver of the old, wornout bus, Ahmet says to immigrants " this is civilisation here, you are rescued, money, money", hereby he is resuming the expectations of the immigrants. The aim is to have a proper job, to gain more money than in Turkey, to live a comfortable life, and future. This is shortly said among immigrants as "to escape to" European countries.

The main incentive of third generation immigrants in the film "the Island of Hope" is economic as well. This is mentioned such as " I work since years for others but dont have anything" and the 8-month pregnant women saying " we have limited resources, we want to go to London for a better future for our child".

Other incentives for immigration are; escaping from prison due to a murder, improving skills, learning a foreign language and adventure are among other reasons for illegal immigration to London. The jongleur Umut is aiming for a job, profession and money, he is mentioning his situation such as "I have searched, the opportunities there are great, you play in 2-3 serials and just after 6 months you play a key role". The novel writer Tuğra has taken the boat standing for his servant in order to search for an adventure and is mentioning this such as " I feel sometimes drained, I have to do something!". Asil wants to escape as he is afraid to be charged with a murder while working as a bodyguard in a bar. Sibel on the other hand is trying to escape from prostitution gang.

The main reason for illegal immigration are financial difficulties, unemployement and a hope for a better future. Expectations for a better life, not just reduced to job and income, education and a skilled job expectation are among factors for illegal immigration to European Countries. As also mentioned by Bourdieu (1984) the final aim of the cultural capital which was aimed by third generation illegal immigrants is to transform it by time into economic capital, so that the main aim of migration is financial. While pushing factors such poverty, unemployement and shortage of land are factors for first generation immigrants, work, life conditions, pulling factors such education, factors such wealth and freedom were important for third generation immigrants (Lee, 1966).

The Image of Europe from the View of the Illegal Immigrants

Stokholm, the host city of immigration at the film "the Bus" was represented as a civilized city with its bright lighted, clean streets, public transportation, metro, cars, schools, nurseries and care centers. With its package stores, shops, restaurants, travel agencies, as a paradise of wealth and consumption. One of the illegal immigrant in the bus is reading a journal title "Teknikboken" from the window of a bookstore which could be considered as a sign of the superiority of technic. On the other hand, that the immigrants were having difficulties in using the moving staircase puts an emphasis on the Turkish society being backward than the European technic. The western capitalism relies upon a pragmatist phylosophy whereby the wealth and richness is growing via technic and the produced material needs to be consumed in order to reach financial saturation. This is the result of capitalist economical structure founded upon maximising the profit (Cem, 1977).

The host city London at the film " the Island of Hope" on the other hand is presented as organized, with planned streets, steady stream of traffic, luxurious cars, high-speed trains, red London busses, statues, squares, historical or modern buildings, big shopping centers, bridges, playgrounds, amusement parks. Those presentations are controversial to steppe fields of Anatolia, village of Maraş city which Yusuf was watching from the car window on the way to Europe. The home environment was represented comfortable and peaceful and people are happy with their personal care and consumables.

The European image for Turkish people has been coded as civilisation, meaning richness, consumption and happiness since the Ottoman reformation period and followed by the Turkish Republic. Turkish citizens tried to bear a resemblance to Europe from the economical and cultural perspective and to copy the western institutions and values. They were not interested about after which historical, social/ class struggle the Westeuropean "civilisation" was realized, instead identified themselves with financial wealth and freedom creating a imaginary European image (Berkes, 2006:381).

Problems Faced by Illegal Immigrants

Migration has traumatic effects on migrants who migrate from traditional societies to industrial societies. The migrants face problems such as culture shock, east-west conflict, identity problems. Most of those problems are arised due to cultural differences. Coming from an agricultural background and being tranditional and muslims, the migrants have different attitudes, values and practices than the christian, capitalist, individualistic western society.

Problems arised due to cultural differences

Through immigration to European countries, illegal immigrants become a part of the capitalist individualistic western culture with their rural rooted traditional cultures. The conflicts of these two structures are experienced by illegal immigrants deeply. Their inclusion into a different sociocultural setting requires adaptation and has caused often traumatical effects.

Illegal Turkish immigrants were aware of the historical, social and cultural differences of the host countries. They intend to adapt in order to exist in such a different environment. At the film "the Bus", the immigrant worker, shave, groom and brush their teeth at the refleshing place before they enter the Stockholm city. A worker from the same group adjusts his hat such as Humpery Bogard's he has seen in a shopwindow. These all show how predisposed to integration the illegal immigrants were in material issues.

Westernisation efforts were concentrated since the last century, until the creation of the Turkish Republic; the Parliament and Political Parties have been established, a switch to western type of democracy has occured and a transition towards the west in the areas of law, ownership, lifestyle and clothing has started. The political and social structure since the start of the 19th century has started to resemble the western societies. Individualism and financial wellfare ideas are lying at the root of the western culture. While the west was considered on one hand as a civilisation with high technology and economic wellfare, on the other hand a reaction to westernisation became evident and the western culture has been seen as an alienation from religion/culture and spirituality and the western culture was identified with Christianity (Berkes, 1975).

Ziya Gökalp (1963) has discussed the westernisation problem defining "moral values and civilisation" and proposed to adapt the dimentions of finance, technic and science under the concept of civilisation and the moral and intellectual dimentions under the concept of moral values and proposed the protection of moral culture based on Islam and considered the Turkish moral values to be superior than the western culture. The question of how the western culture defined by Ziya Gökalp as civilisation and the Turkish intellectual cultural structure defined as moral values can collocate or whether they actually can collocate is not answered. The westernisation culture in Turkey is coded either as a "she remained single monster" or as the "imperialist west" (Ilhan, 1982). As a result of this, westernisation has been simply adressed as adopting the material side of the western civilisation and refusing its spiritual side. Whilst the material and moral aspects of the western culture and civilisation are complementary (Berkes, 2006).

Efforts towards westernisation in material areas such military, industrial, education, clothing and measurement units were made during the Ottoman Turkish modernisation period but it wasn't comprehended that the social mentality in the west shaped by Renaissance, Reform and Enlightenment periods needs to be enlighted (modernised) as well (Aktar, 1993). But the western and eastern culture and financial structures have been allways different either from material or mental, ideological, social and moral dimentions of life (Tanpınar, 1996). The ideology of institutions and rules of the Turkish society is eastern. Since the foundation of the Turkish Republic the Turkish society aimed to industrialize and to become a nation but it couldn't industrialize and make a financial progress and create a national culture. The eastern culture in Turkey has allways defined itself in an opposition to the western culture. The eastern/muslim and western/christianity are both sides on this controversity (Safa, 2016). This has came out as a cultural shock of illegal worker who experienced the migration process. The worker answered the driver of the bus to Stokholm saying " you will start work tomorrow, soon you will be like a pig" as " God, forgive me" and similariy at the film "the Island of Hope" Yusuf has a salami in his hand and says his friend Asil that nothing tastes the same. Asil anwers by saying " that might be pig", he leaves the salami on the desk and says "God, forgive me". To eat pig is forbidden in islamic belief and is identified with christianity.

First generation illegal immigrants have difficulties to understand the problems in Sweden arising from cultural differences. Especially about sexuality. Characters of the film "the Bus" were surprised on their way to the metro toilet as they were seeing a couple having sex in the telephone kiosk. Naked lay figures, pornographic journals, and advertisements including sexuality were some of the other things surprising them. But in the western culture, sexuality is experienced freely. Swedish women can participate the social life with clothes they like, they can drink alcohol at any hour even on the street and dance with men. At the sex bar where Mehmet went with the homosexual guy he met at the toilet men and women were watching pornographic films together, the playboy of the year is elected by women and that playboy has sex with the women who has elected for him in front of everybody. Mehmet is watching the scene confused and concerned. That the

Swedish at the bar eat, drink, have fun and have homo/heterosexual sex and this all is perceived naturally and not wasn't found to be odd by Swedish individuals.

At the film "the Island of Hope", even though the third-generation immigrants live in London, they exist in their own culture. At the retaurant Öz Sofra of Cevdet Ede, where Yusuf is taking shelter in, the Turkish culinary culture can be seen from the menu such as; soup, meetballs, karnıyarık and kadayıf. Similarly, the Turkish cafehouse of Hamdi is not any different than a traditional cafehouse in Turkey. They are watching Turkish TV channels, play backgammon and cardgames same such as in Turkey. When Yusuf sees all the signboards in Turkish, he tells Asil " were we escaping from Turkey for this?" in a humorous manner. By escaping from their place, they cannot escape from the culture and history.

The immigrants can not experience a full transformation and integration neither can they keep the culture and ideological integrity they had in Turkey. As a result of this they acquire a hybrid culture, a mix of rural, islamic culture from Turkey and a urban culture typical for European Countries. The reason for the hybridisation is the hegomanic effect of the western culture on other cultures (Crehan, 2002), seen as the main reason for the trauma of the immigrants. The emptyness arising from the release from the own culture cannot be fulled with the new western culture. The immigrants don't have the intellecutal infrastructure of the western culture. While they can easier adapt in clothing, consuming, it is not that easy to adapt in their cultural beliefs and world views. They are stuck between the tradition and innovation and cannot adapt to the new rules of the new culture. This attitude is mainly based on the Turkish-Islamic codes they grew up with, of topics such sexuality which are resistant to innovations and considered as a tabu.

At the film "the Island of Hope" Yusuf is working in the Turkish restaurant but eating fish and chips while they are out with Asil. Yusuf meets a British women and falls in love with her. This is his first sexual experience. He starts to use cocain with her, cannot concentrate while working. Cevat Ede is warning him "Something is happened to you, you are allways distracted and are late for work. What is the reason? Tell me if you have a problem and are in trouble. (Yusuf stares and pulls his head down) Is it a women issue? I was also once falling in love with a foreign women in the past. I have left my family. I would lose everything if I wouldn't understand on time that I made a mistake. I understart, you are young, but don't do something wrong. You are here to start a new life, it is up to you to use the opportunities. I am like your father. Let me give you an advise. Don't lose your essence wherever you are." But Yusuf can't keep his essence unless he loses his essence. He became a cocain addict and lost his job.

Racism

Racism is the darkest side of the western capitalism, racists act humiliating and exlusive to all others different than themselves. The native population is prejudiced, cautious and distrustful towards the immigrants. At the film "the bus", the police checked the legal pass of the bus driver Ahmet on his journey from Stokholm to Hamburg, while the European citizens were passing the control easily. He was send to digital rectal examination with the suspicion of being a drug trafficker. The driver of the taxi he takes in Hamburg doesnt even take his salutation in German. He is afraid when he sees the security personnel in front of the restaurant he came to meet the gang leader. While the immigrants in Stokholm run away from the police, one of them loses his way and asks a Swedish man taking his dog out in Turkish "did you see the bus, friend?". The man is afraid from the immigrant, takes his dog and runs away. The same worker cannot find the bus, crouchs down by a river, hits against a passenger, falls into water and freezes to death under a bridge. The man who is the reason of his fall turns back and says "looser!". The immigrants are usually identified with criminal aktivities. A Swedish says the immigrants in metro station "do you have hash? I can pay a lot".

At the film "the Island of Hope", the British holligans who came into a Turkish cafe to watch a football game ask Asil whether he is Afghan and make fun of him by saying "Turkey, gulu gulu" and show his back when he was saying that he was from Turkey. The British holigans are blaming the immigrants instead of capitalism for their current social conditions and show a nationalist perspective. They identify themselves with an industrial football team, become a new identity in that way and reproduce the capitalist system by attributing themselves a superiority from the successes of their team. Racism is not only a problem for football fans, also for middle class, educated British citizens. Vildan is working as an au-pair and refuses to eat breakfast with the family. When she shouts to the kids for littering up the table, her employer says " you might treat the children that way in your country, but not here, don't shout the kids again, people are accusing you for being bearish, they are right". This is a good example of a racist attitude towards individuals with different backgrounds. A negative value is attributed to the foreigner and their clothing, physical appearance, behaviours and ethnic identities are reasons for otherisation.

The liberal multicultural society mentality around the 1980's was unsuccessful in practice and neo-liberal economy politics, the right-wing, conservative policies forced the immigrants to turn back to their own cultural, ethnic and religious identities and resulted with not being integrated into the western society. This increaed their exlusion from the society. Through the high technology and economy, the western world exploits the cheap labour but doesn't share its wealth and rights.

Solidarity and Exclusionary Networks

Around the 1960's the unskilled Turkish worker migrated to European countries in order to supply shortage of labor. Unsuccessful sociocultural integration efforts directed individuals to live in their own communities. The Turkish population in Europe came together with individuals with similar backgrounds to forget their loneliness. Factors such as Islamic religion and ethnic similarities were bases of solidarity. People share here their culture and values and transform them into informal solidarity networks. Migrants live in the towns or cities through their associations such as in a community. Despite the tension arising from the closeness and competitions, they feel tied to the community as they share the difficulties to live in a foreign land. There is a stratified structure in those communities according to the economic wellbeing and leadership abilities (such as Cevdet from the Restaurant and Hamdi at the cafe at the film "the Island of Hope"). Those networks provide shelter and work for illegal immigrants. While those networks exist for third generation immigrants, there were not availabe for first generation. The 8 month pregnant women says pointing at her husband "his brother has a restaurant in Manchester, he will work there". So there is not an uncertain adventure instead a planned future. The earlier immigrants are motivating for the new ones. Their success gives the new ones the hope to succeed. Yusuf tells Cevdet Ede during his holiday from London his desire to immigrate to London. Cevdet first tells about the difficulties to live there and than gives him his business card saying " Call me in case you can come to London, I can't assure you anything, will just try my best to help you". When Yusuf comes to London, Cevdet gives him a bed in the restaurant and a job. He takes Asil to his friend Hamdi. Tells him " Here is a guest from Turkey, his name is Asil, he just came from Turkey, do you have any job for him?". Hamdi answers " Sure I can, there is also a bed to sleep behind". Similarly when the au-pair Vildan got abused by her lesbian boss, she takes shelter in her hairdresser friend from Istanbul. Her friend finds her a dishwasher job in a restaurant. The support system is nourished to provide shadow employement and cheap workforce in Turkish workplaces. But in case of any disagreement or conflicts, this solidarity turns into exclusion and punishment. Asil is fired from the cafe for the reason he has chucked the hooligans out from the cafe, Yusuf is fired for the reason being a drug addict and not being able to work effectively. Yusuf had to turn back to Turkey. Vildan is also send out from the friends home for the reason of being a sexworker. Unwritten rules of those communities is lay down the exclusion in case of breaking the rules (Schmalenbach, 1961).

Immigrants who live in same areas share similar desires, values and are close together. The members know each other. Ethnic similarities such the Turkish background or being muslim create a social network. Being a member of this community gives security and strenght.

The End Awaiting the Illegal Immigrants

In the film "the Bus" the illegal immigrants are cheated by the smugglers, besides the money they got frauded, the smuggler took their last money saying that he will pay the police for the application. They are being flat broke in Stockholm. Two of the worker died. Their money was stolen, they lost their hope for the future, and they had to face similar conditions as in Turkey. The reason why they stared the policeman while breaking the door of the bus is their defeat and despair to the future. The hope for the first generation immigrants resulted with total despair. The repeadetly squash of the bus, representing the immigrants, at the final scene of the film "the bus", is a cinematographic expression of the drama arising from the lost hopes of the illegal immigrants to Europe.

At the film "the Island of Hope" the jongleur Umut's fall into water while transferring from the ship to the lifeboat and his death between the screw of the ship gives a clue about the real end of the illegal immigrants. The drug addict Yusuf turns back to his village Maraş with the balls of Umut in his hands. Vildan's father came from Istanbul to London to take her back to Turkey. The writer Tuğra turns back to Turkey and writes his memories in his new book titled "the Island of Hope". Asil, who was afraid of found to be quilty from a crime he was thinking he did, was informed by his girlfriend that he wasn't taken quilty. Even so, he decided not to turn back to Turkey, and tears his ticket to Istanbul into peaces and throws it into the Thames river. He decided for his future in London instead to go to Istanbul for emotional reasons.

Conclusion

This research investigated how the first and third generation illegal immigrants to Europe are represented in Turkish cinema. The first-generation migrants migrated for financial reasons, they couldn't succeed, were unemployed, cheated, exluded from the society as they didn't know the Swedish language, could not communicate and integrate in the western culture, were sexually abused and experienced racism. As a result, they either died or were deported back to Turkey. A negative image of Europe was represented.

At the film "the Island of Hope" third generation immigrants were not composed of man only, women, couples and even pregnant women were among the immigrants. Even though in this film, the main incentive of migration was financial as the film "the bus", individual and cultural features of the migrants were differentiated. The third-generation immigrants were not coming only from rural areas, they were not unskilled and illiterate, some of the immigrants were coming from metropols such Istanbul, were educated and migrated to learn a language, improve their abilities or just for adventure. The main advantage for them was the solidarity network of the previous Turkish immigrants. The self employers let the newcomers work under the counter in their workplaces as a cheap manpower. The supporting solidarity networks can turn into exclusion and punishment networks in case of negative cultural, traditional and legal attitudes of the immigrants. For the ones who can find a job, Europe can be a place to live and they prefer to stay in European countries despite the maldupays and nostalgia.

In films where illegal immigration, the process of travel and travellers struggles and dramas were told, the western image is given as negative, exclusionary and racist. Both films resemble each other in themes such drug addiction, sexuality, sexual abuse, alcohol, racism, exploitation, cultural differences language and communication difficulties, adaptation problems, identity and nostalgia. Even though having a 30-year difference, they have a similar approach in theme, language, actors, story, location and conflict. The European civilisation myth is broken in both films, Europe is represented from the eyes of the illegal immigrants' experience as exclusion, exploitation, othering and racism.

References

Abadan-Unat, N. (2006). Bitmeyen Göç-Konuk İşçilikten Uluslararası Yurttaşlığa. İstanbul: Bilgi Üniversitesi Yayınları.

Aktar, Cengiz (1993). Türkiye'nin Batılılaştırılması. İstanbul: Ayrıntı.

Bauman, Zygmunt (1997). Modernite ve Holokost. Çeviren: Süha Sertabiboğlu. İstanbul: Sarmal Yayınevi.

Berger, Arthur Asa (1998). Media Research Techniques. 2nd Edition. London: Sage.

Berelson, Bernard (1952). Content Analysis in Communication Research. Glencoe: Free Press.

Berkes, Niyazi (2006). Türkiye'de Çağdaşlaşma. Editör: Ahmet Kuyaş. 9. Baskı. İstanbul: Yapı Kredi Yayınları.

Berkes, Niyazi (1975). Türk Düşününde Batı Sorunu. İstanbul: Bilgi.

Bourdieu, Pierre (1984). Distinction: A Critique of the Judgement of Taste. London: Routledge and Paul Kegan.

Cavanagh, S. (1997). "Content Analysis: Concepts, Methods and Applications". Nurse Researchers. April (1). 4(3). p.:5-13.

Cem, İsmail (1977). Türkiye'de Geri Kalmışlığın Tarihi. 6nd Edition. İstanbul: Cem Yayınevi.

Crehan, Kate (2002). Gramsci, Culture and Anthropology. London: Pluto Press.

Dorsay, Atilla (1989). Sinemamızın Umut Yılları. İstanbul: İnkılap Kitabevi.

Göklap, Ziya (1963). Türkleşmek, İslamlaşmak, Muasırlaşmak. 2. Baskı. Ankara: Serdengeçti.

İlhan, Atilla (1982). Hangi Batı. İstanbul: Bilgi.

Kongar, Emre (1979). Türkiye'nin Toplumsal Yapısı. 3. Basım. İstanbul: Bilgi.

Krippendorf, Klaus (1980). Content Analysis: An Introduction to Its Methodology. Newbury Park: Sage Publications.

Lee, E.S. (1966). "A Theory of Migration". Demograpy. 3 (1): 47-57.

Makal, Oğuz (1987). Sinemada Yedinci Adam. İzmir: Ege Yayıncılık.

Refiğ, Halit (1971). Ulusal Sinema Kavgası. İstanbul: Hareket Yayınları.

Safa, Peyami (2016). 20. Asır Avrupa ve Biz. 6. Basım. İstanbul: Ötüken Yayınları.

Schmalenbach, Herman (1961). The Sociological Category of Communion. (in) Theories of Society. Eds.: Talcot Parsons et all. New York: Free Press. Pp.: 331-347.

Tanpınar, Ahmet Hamdi (1996). Yaşadığım Gibi. İstanbul: Dergah.

Tolan, Barlas (1975). Toplum Bilimlerine Giriş. Ankara: Kalite Matbaası.

Chapter 12. Legal and Circular Migration in the European Union Mobility Partnerships

Katarzyna A. Morawska[1]

Abstract

In the light of current migration crisis, the biggest emphasis is presently put on the asylum policy. The hostile attitude or even reluctance of the European societies towards immigrants make the debate on immigration policy even more complex and though. In this context, it is not easy to convince the Europeans of the advantages coming from legal migration. Nevertheless, from over two decades the EU institutions, especially the European Commission, have been supporting the need for effective cooperation with third countries in the field of migration. That is why the concept of Mobility Partnerships has been introduced within the EU immigration policy. The aim of this article is to present and evaluate the impact of existing declarations signed between certain Member States and third countries on legal migration and analyse their influence on the inflow of foreigners to the EU.

Key words: *European Union, EU immigration policy, legal migration, Mobility Partnerships, circular migration*

Introduction

The events of the year 2015 related to the unprecedented influx of migrants into the European Union (the EU) brought about increased interest in the immigration policy. The European Commission recalls, promoted since 2000, stand emphasizing the need for effective cooperation with third countries in the field of migration in order to efficiently prevent illegal immigration to the EU.[2]

The purpose of this article is to elucidate the Mobility Partnerships under the European immigration policy as well as the analysis of their assumptions contained in the documents of the EU institutions. The partnerships are non-binding agreements concluded between the Member States of the European Union and third countries, the purpose of which is broadly understood cooperation in the field of migration management. The article is particularly concerned with mobility, that is supporting the legal migration, including circular migration of third-country nationals to the EU.

The conducted research is predominantly of theoretical and qualitative nature. The first part of the paper presents the characteristics of Mobility Partnerships. The theoretical assumptions of Mobility Partnerships have been subjected to a legal and comparative analysis, which is followed by their confrontation with the actual provisions of the signed declarations. In the sections devoted to the analysis of official documents of the European Union the dogmatic method has been applied. The analysis of Eurostat and OECD statistics provides a source of information on the initial changes in the number of third-country nationals flowing to particular Member States from the countries which were the first to sign the Mobility Partnerships. The conducted

---

[1] Research officer, Emigration Museum in Gdynia, ul. Swietojanska 45/31, 81-368 Gdynia, Poland. E-mail: k.morawska@muzeumemigracji.pl, kata.morawska@wp.pl,
[2] European Commission, (2001). A common policy on legal illegal migration, Brussels, COM (2001) 672.

research and the critical evaluation of the source materials, mainly the literature on the subject, made it possible to evaluate the adopted Mobility Partnerships.

Mobility Partnerships

In December 2005, the European Council adopted the so-called global approach to migration, which assumes broad cooperation between the EU Member States and countries from which arrive the highest numbers of immigrants.[3] The global approach aims to combine all political migration strategies in a more coherent way. Mobility Partnerships established between the EU and third countries are a key instrument supposed to foster implementation of the global approach to migration.[4]

According to the communication published in 2007, Mobility Partnerships are supposed to foster effective management of migration flows.[5] The EU aims to create in this way a framework for dialogue and cooperation with countries in its immediate neighbourhood and with countries whose citizens have been entering the EU for a long time (i.e. Morocco, Tunisia, Egypt). In practice it is supposed to be *an offer of several Member States regarding easier access to their labour markets for citizens of particular third countries. (...) The individual offers would be grouped into one package and presented to a third country as a broad-based EU offer.*[6]

The accession of Member States to partnerships with individual third countries is not mandatory and their content is not legally binding. Partnerships are an instrument of a complex legal nature owing to the fact that their provisions do not always fall within the scope of the EU powers. Although in accordance with the provisions of the Treaty of Amsterdam plenty of the issues related to asylum and migration were "communized", the decision on admission of migrant workers in the territory of the Member States remains a national competence (Art. 79 TFEU).

The cited Communication of the Commission contains, however, a number of elements that can be included in the content of the Mobility Partnerships. These are both obligations of third countries as well as of Member States. Among the postulates to be fulfilled by third countries one can find, among others, effective readmission of own citizens and cooperation in determining their identity and, under certain circumstances, readmission of third-country nationals and stateless persons who entered the EU through the territory of a given Member State. In addition, third countries should undertake initiatives to reduce the scale of illegal immigration, streamline border controls and prevent forging travel documents. Combat against smuggling and human trafficking is of equal importance. In order to eliminate illegal immigration, the EU partners may be also required to undertake to improve their economic and social situation. Implementation of the partnerships assumes full respect

---

[2] European Council, (2005). Presidency Conclusions, 15-16 December 2005, European Council Summit in Hampton Court, p. 2.

[3] European Commission, (2006). Global Approach to Migration a Year Later: Towards a Comprehensive European Migration Policy, Brussels, COM (2006) 735.

[4] European Commission, (2007). Communication on Circular Migration and Mobility Partnerships between the European Union and Third Countries, Brussels, COM (2007) 248, p. 9-10.

[6] Ibidem.

for fundamental rights of individuals and provides financial and technical assistance to third countries.[7] On the other hand, Member States commit themselves to introduce *mechanisms facilitating labour migration, which should correspond to the labour market needs of the concerned Member States, in line with their assessment, with full respect of the principle of the Community preference for EU citizens.*[8] Properly formulated provisions can prevent the phenomenon of brain drain, i.e. the outflow of educated citizens. The Member States should also take actions to streamline the procedure for issuing short-stay visas to third-country nationals, which should contribute to an increased interest in legal forms of migration.

Mobility Partnerships in practice

The first Mobility Partnerships were signed in 2008 with Moldova and the Republic of Cape Verde.[9] Both documents, deemed as a model for other agreements, provide for the promotion of solutions supporting legal migration accompanied by reduction of illegal migration flows. It is worth emphasizing, however, that the latest partnerships (with Jordan, Tunisia and Belarus) no longer contain annexes detailing specific initiatives proposed by individual states or the European Commission.

The partnerships begin with a very similar preamble referring to the existing forms of cooperation between Member States and partner countries and to the key EU documents on migration (i.e. to European Commission communications and Council conclusions). In the introduction the parties undertake to facilitate population flows and better manage migration movements, including combat against illegal immigration. The provisions of the first partnerships focus on three main themes: mobility, legal migration and integration; migration and development; border management, travel documents and fight against illegal migration and human trafficking. Partnership with Armenia has initiated cooperation in the issues of international protection and asylum.[10] Each category contains some more detailed assumptions of the contracting parties.

The declarations contain also provisions on the practical implementation of the Mobility Partnerships. These agreements are considered as a long-term form of cooperation based on a political dialogue that will evolve over time. There are scheduled regular meetings (twice a year) at an appropriate level in order to review priorities of the partnerships and to evaluate them. The partnership promises the implementation of initiatives aimed at maximizing the positive impact of migration on the development of third countries through, among other things, encouraging financial transfers made by migrants and promoting circulation and returns of foreign workers to their home countries. Another significant element is also the promise of a mechanism monitoring the movement of people and assessing the impact of migration

---

[6] Ibidem, p. 4-5.

[7] Ibidem, p. 5.

[8] Council of the European Union, (2008). Joint Declaration on a Mobility Partnership between the European Union and the Republic of Moldova, 9460/08 ADD 1, Brussels 2008, Council of the European Union, Joint Declaration on a Mobility Partnership between the European Union and the Republic of Cape Verde, 9460/08 ADD 1, Brussels 2008.

[9] Council of the European Union, (2011). Joint Declaration on a Mobility Partnership between the European Union and Armenia, 14963/11 ADD 1, Brussels 2011.

on the domestic labour market. The last part of the partnerships is an annex which contains proposals for concrete measures aimed at realization of the assumptions contained therein. Individual projects are an initiative of the parties - the Member States, the partner country, the European Commission or several specified partners.

Regarding the provisions supporting legal migration to the Member States all agreements contain provisions on the need to effectively inform potential migrants on employment opportunities and living conditions in the EU countries as well as on risks of illegal migration. For this purpose, there is proposed, among others, cooperation with the European employment portal, seminars and exchanges of information between institutions and bodies responsible for managing the population flows, and even preparation of a manual containing relevant information on residence and employment in EU countries for potential migrants. In addition, the provisions stipulate support of the Member States for all institutions and their staff, including employment agencies and state bodies involved in migration management. The Partnerships include also proposals to introduce measures that will facilitate obtaining visas for migrant workers, temporary work and migrants' circulation programmes as well as recognition of professional and academic qualifications of partner countries citizens. Particular attention has been paid to students and young professionals who have been offered various forms of mobility to the EU. Collaboration of academic centres in order to enable the exchange of students and researchers is also incorporated. In many partnerships, there is a promise of special courses on entry procedures and integration measures in host countries for future migrants in order to prepare them for their stay and work in the EU to be taken even before leaving a home country.

Analysing the partnerships as a whole, it is clearly observed that the signed declarations focus mainly on two aspects – the enhanced border control and the fight against illegal immigration. What stems from the provisions of the partnerships is the observation that the Member States are more interested in the tightened control or even reduction in the flow of population, rather than in the increased legal mobility of third-country nationals.[11] Economic migration, migrants' rights or mutual recognition of workers' qualifications have been marginalized, and issues related to family reunification or migrant integration in the Member States have been almost completely ignored. The resignation from provisions on labour migration was probably the result of the EU's lack of competence in certain areas - the Member States did not agree to delegate to the organization the competences related to economic migration, which remains a sphere of competence attributable to the Member States. This explains why the Mobility Partnerships, on the one hand, are not focused on the regulation of labour migration and, on the other one, are not binding.

Evaluation of Mobility Partnership

The European Commission is convinced of the effectiveness of the Mobility Partnerships and points out that the lack of binding force of the declarations makes it

---

[10] Parkes, R. (2009). Mobility Partnerships: valuable addition to the ENP repertoire? A checklist for revitalising ENP, German Institute for International and Security Affairs, Working Paper FG 1, No. 03/2009, SWP Berlin.

less time-consuming to adopt them in comparison with legal acts with binding force.[12] In the communication, which evaluates the first Mobility Partnerships signed with Moldova and the Republic of Cape Verde, the institution emphasizes their flexibility - they can be quickly adapted to the current needs of the partners.[13] At the same time, as documents of political nature, they do not require ratification and implementation in partner countries, which significantly shortens the entry into force of the agreements. At any moment, the project may be joined by interested countries, which was the case with the Netherlands, which joined the partnership several months after signing the declaration with the Cape Verde.

According to the Commission, the signed agreements are the most innovative and highly developed instrument for implementation of the global approach to migration. It is estimated that the partnerships meet the assumptions and priorities of both the EU and partner countries. The only risk involved in this form of cooperation is the collection of actions taken individually by the Member States in the framework of their existing cooperation and their replication in the partnership. This argument is quite often quoted in the literature, as Member States are reluctant to duplicate their actions, especially when the existing forms of cooperation function well.[14] In its evaluation of Mobility Partnerships, the Commission emphasizes the fact that this mechanism is versatile and comprehensively reflects all elements of the global approach to migration, whereas the instruments used so far have focused only on its selected aspects.[15]

The advantage of the partnerships is their complementarity with other Community policies, instruments and the EU measures in the areas of migration and their positive impact on strengthening ties with partner countries. The EU joint activities in the sphere of migration strengthens the national migration policy whose implementation only at the national level is increasingly difficult.[16] The evaluation of the agreements given by the Commission is, therefore, definitely positive, and the institution seems to be full of optimism when it comes to the future of the partnerships.

The European Commission focuses mainly on the positive aspects of the Mobility Partnerships; however, the objective assessment of the agreements is not clear. Above all, the question arises as to the actual promotion of legal migration to the EU. It is

---

[11] European Policy Center, (2014). Mobility partnerships - An effective tool for EU external migration policy?, retrived from:
http://www.epc.eu/events_rep_details.php?cat_id=6&pub_id=2696 (accessed: 25 January 2014).
    [12] European Commission, (2009). Commission Staff Working Document Mobility partnerships as a tool of the Global Approach to Migration, Brussels, SEC (2009) 1240, p. 4.
    [13] Reslow, N. (2010). The new politics of EU migration policy: analysing the decision – making process of the Mobility Partnerships, Maastricht University, Netherlands 2010, p. 17.
    [14] European Commission, (2009). Commission Staff Working Document Mobility partnerships as a tool of the Global Approach to Migration, op. cit., p. 6.
    [15] Reslow, N. (2010). Explaining the development of EU migration policy: the case of Mobility Partnerships, Paper prepared for the fifth Pan-European Conference on EU Politics, Porto, Portugal, 23 - 26 June 2010, p. 4.

quite difficult to conclusively assess the impact of the legal migration initiatives on the actual increase in labour migration from the partner countries to the EU. Currently, statistical data is the only way to evaluate the effectiveness of the partnerships. This method is imperfect as it does not indicate the extent to which the signed agreements have contributed to changes in the flow of the partner countries nationals to the Member States. In addition, most of the statistical data does not cover temporary migrants. Despite these difficulties, it is worth having a look at statistics reflecting the number of migrants in particular countries. The analysis of Eurostat statistical data conducted by N. Reslow points to the lack of impact of the partnerships signed with Moldova, Armenia, Georgia and the Republic of Cape Verde on the number of short-stay visas issued to nationals of these countries or residence permits in the Member States.[17]

The statistical data presented by the OECD gives similar conclusions as to the changes in the number of immigrants from Moldova, the Republic of Cape Verde, Georgia and Armenia, which occurred since the conclusion of the individual partnerships until 2014.[18] As in the case of the Eurostat data, it is difficult to identify a clear impact on the scale of migration to the Member States that are parties to the partnerships. In the case of Moldova only in Germany there was noted an increase in the number of immigrants in 2008-2013 (699 people in 2008, 1039 in 2013). Other EU countries noted in that time significant declines in the influx of citizens of Moldova (for example in Italy the decline from 22 000 in 2008 to 3 700 in 2014). A similar situation concerns citizen of the Republic of Cape Verde - the increased inflow was noted in France, the decline in Spain and Portugal. Growth trends are more pronounced in the case of Georgia, as in most of the partner countries the number of immigrants from this country increased (particularly in Germany and Italy). Mixed trends are also visible in statistics for Armenia. In several Member States, including Belgium, France and in particular Germany, the number of immigrants from Armenia has increased since the Mobility Partnership was signed. There are also countries such as the Czech Republic and Poland, where these numbers fell, as well as those where major changes in the number of citizens from Armenia were not observed (Italy).

Hence, it is difficult to talk about the real impact of the partnerships on mobility. However, it should be stressed that these statistics may change in the long term. What is more, the mobility of migrants is affected by various factors not related to the signed declarations, for example the economic and political situation, social moods and many others. Reliable sources showing a direct impact of the signed declarations on the increase in immigration to the Member States do not exist, which unfortunately hiders research in this area.

Too much focus on the obligation to readmit its citizens and better border controls, imposed on third countries by Member States, is a strong objection to Mobility Partnerships. One may get the impression that readmission and fight against illegal immigration, and not legal immigration or mobility, are the core of these agreements.

---

[16] Reslow, N. (2015) EU "Mobility" Partnerships: An initial assessment of implementation dynamics, Politics and Governance, Vol. 3, No. 2/2015, p. 119-120.

[18] Organisation for Economic Cooperation and Development, retrieved from: https://stats.oecd.org/Index.aspx? DataSetCode= MIG, accessed: October 6, 2016).

Such an approach stems from the fact that only in such a way, i.e. offering to partner countries certain facilitations and aid in the management of migration and the obscure promise of legal migration, the EU is able to gain consent to the readmission of citizens of these countries.[19] Third countries have a negative attitude to the condition of readmission, in which they can see benefits only for the EU.[20] This reluctance stems from costs and financial burden associated with the implementation of the readmission agreements. This procedure is not in the interest of third countries whose economies benefit from money transfers sent by migrants, regardless of whether their stay is legal or not. A. Triandafyllidou rightly notices that it is hard to believe that the partner countries are able to meet the demanding expectations of the EU.[21] A long list of requirements that third countries must fulfil to win "the prize" in the form of a Mobility Partnership may make their provisions not viable.

Mobility Partnerships, despite a positive implication of their name, are not entirely based on cooperation between equal partners sharing the same objectives.[22] A negotiating position of European countries is certainly stronger, especially if the declaration is to be signed by a few or a dozen EU countries. The real contribution of third countries in the creation of the projects is then thought-provoking. For example, Georgia or Morocco did not propose any initiatives contained in the agreement on their own. J.P. Cassarino drew attention to double selectivity of the partnerships.[23] On the one hand, they are signed by countries which undertake to implement conditions set by the EU (concerning readmission, border protection, etc.). On the other one, they apply only to certain categories of immigrants, who have the possibility to take advantage of the proposed forms of arrival to the EU Member States. Moreover, provisions of the partnerships bind only the Member States which signed them, while the readmission agreements apply to the whole territory of the EU.

The fact that the partnerships are a very flexible instrument, and participation in them depends solely on the will of the Member States, on the one hand, can be an advantage, and, on the other one, may adversely affect the integrity and legitimacy of the EU policy.[24] It suffices to look at the number of the EU countries which joined the partnerships. Many countries signed the declaration with Georgia (16) and Moldova

---

[19] Carrera, S., Hernandez, Sagrera, R. (2009). The Externalisation of the EU's Labour Immigration Policy. Towards Mobility or Insecurity Partnerships?, Centre for European Policy Studies, Working Document No. 321/2009, p. 19.

[19] Cassarino, J.P. (2008). Patterns of Circular Migration in the Euro-Mediterranean Area: Implications for Policy – Making, CARIM 2008/29, p. 8.

[20] Triandafyllidou, A. (2014). Attempting the Impossible? The Prospects and Limits of Mobility Partnerships and Circular Migration, retrieved from: http://www.eliamep.gr/wp-content/uploads/en/2009/02/eliamep-thesis-1-2009triandafylli dou.pdf (accessed: 27 January 2014).

[22] Kunz, R., Maisenbacher, J. (2013). Beyond conditionality versus cooperation: Power and resistance in the case of EU mobility partnerships and Swiss migration partnerships, Migration Studies, Vol. 1, No. 2/2013, p. 201

[22] Cassarino, J.P. (2009) EU Mobility Partnerships: Expression of a New Compromise, retrieved from: http://www.mi grationinformation.org/Feature/display.cfm?ID=741 (accessed: 27 January 2014).

[24] Carrera, S., Hernandez, Sagrera, R. (2009). The Externalisation of the EU's Labour Immigration Policy. Towards Mobility or Insecurity Partnerships? op. cit., p. 36.

(15), while only five are parties to the agreement with the Republic of Cape Verde.[25] There are countries that are involved in several partnerships (France, Poland, Belgium) and those that do not participate in any project (Austria, Finland, Malta). Countries decide to sign a declaration when cooperation with the given country is in their national interest and is consistent with their policy.[26] Hence, we can see the clear division: states from the southern regions of Europe are interested in cooperation with the Mediterranean countries and Africa while other Member States prefer cooperation with the region of Eastern Europe.[27]

It seems that voluntary participation in the partnerships is after all a good idea. In this case, they are joined by states which really seek cooperation, which greatly increases the likelihood of compliance with the commitments. The aspect which has already been raised is the actual added value of Mobility Partnerships. In the case of the declaration with the Republic of Cape Verde, whose signatories are Portugal, Spain, France and Luxembourg, most of the initiatives contained in the document are proposals made by one of the EU countries. It should be noted that these initiatives had been expressed before in bilateral agreements concluded between the Member States and the Republic of Cape Verde.[28] Therefore, the question arises, to what extent it is a new form of multilateral cooperation, and to what it is simply gathering together projects that had existed before. It is also wondering why proposals for specific measures to be undertaken by individual Member States were skipped in the recent declarations.

Conclusion

Cooperation in the field of legal migration may lead to better coordination and coherence of activities, but looking at the signed declarations certainly we cannot talk about revolutionary changes. Due to not very advanced stage of implementation of the agreements and the lack of their thorough evaluation by the EU, it is difficult to clearly indicate positive effects noted by the participating states. However, we should hope that in the face of the current immigration crisis, the European Union will finally take concrete actions in terms of effective migration management at European level. The analysis of the Mobility Partnerships carried out in this article points to the untapped potential of this instrument, which despite its weaknesses, may positively affect the European immigration policy.

---

[25] The Netherlands joined the partnership a few months after it was signed.

[26] Reslow, N. (2010). The new politics of EU migration policy: analysing the decision – making process of the Mobility Partnerships, op. cit., p. 23.

[27] Ibidem, p. 22.

[28] Chou, M.H., Gibert, M. (2010). From Cotonou to Circular Migration: the EU, Senegal, and the "Agreement Duplicity", Paper for "Migration: A world in Motion", Maastricht, the Netherlands, 18-20 February 2010, p. 10.

Chapter 13. Some Results of Irregular Migration in Turkey

Melek Zubaroğlu Yanardağ[1], Umut Yanardağ[2]

Abstract

The issue of irregular migration in Turkey is gaining an increasingly important dimension. In the context of irregular migration, it is known that many foreigners use Turkey as a target or transit country for economic and political reasons. Only in 2016, 174,466 irregular migrants were apprehended in various regions of Turkey. This number has been increasing, especially in recent years. The current irregular migration movements in Turkey affect not only Turkey but also the European countries around it. In 2014, 280 thousand people illegally reached Europe by sea and land. In 2015, this number increased to 1,046,600. It is known that irregular migration concentrates on the Aegean, Mediterranean, and Marmara coasts. According to the Turkish Coast Guard Command, a total of 490 irregular migrants lost their lives while illegally trying to cross into European countries in 2015, 2016, and the first months of 2017. This picture makes it necessary to address the human dimension of irregular migration from a broader perspective. While coping with irregular migration, policies should be developed by keeping the human dimension of the subject in mind through investigating the causes that drive migrants to irregular migration. In parallel with this, fighting against human smugglers is indispensable. At this point, social work profession, which has to take an active role in the field of migration, must be maintained by improving its practices on the basis of human rights. While working with irregular migrants, social workers must stay away from stigmatizing and judicial attitudes and advocate for the protection of the human rights of these migrants.

Keywords: Irregular Migration, Irregular Migrants, Social Work Profession, Advocacy.

Introduction

Irregular migration refers to a person's entering a country illegally, staying in a country illegally, or not leaving a country within legal time allowed though entering it legally. Turkish Red Crescent Association Immigration and Refugee Services Directorate defines an irregular migrant as follows: "A person who tries to reach a country other than the country s/he is a citizen of due to financial impossibility or criminal record, has no legal right to stay in the country s/he migrates to, and enters such country by violating its laws" (Turkish Red Crescent Association Immigration and Refugee Services Directorate, 2017).

Regular migration refers to migration waves that take place in accordance with specific plans and legal permissions. It is known that the number of professionals, businessmen, and students migrating to Turkey has increased especially in the last two decades. The official data of the early 2000s show

---

[1] Melek Zubaroğlu Yanardağ, Assistant Professor of Social Work in Faculty of Economics and Administrative Sciences of Mehmet Akif Ersoy University, Burdur-Turkey. Istiklal Campus, 15030 Burdur, Turkey. E-mail: mzyanardag@mehmetakif.edu.tr, ezgimlk@gmail.com
[2] Umut Yanardağ, PhD, Social Worker in Burdur Public Hospital, Eski Antalya cd. 15030 Burdur, Turkey. E-mail: umutyanardag@gmail.com

that approximately 160,000 foreign nationals live in Turkey with a residence permit (İçduygu, Sert & Karaçay, 2009).

According to the most recent accessible data of the General Directorate of Migration Management, there were 174,466 irregular migrants in Turkey in 2016 (http://www.goc.gov.tr/icerik3/irregular-migration_915_1024_4746). Before a detailed coverage of the issue of irregular migration, it will be beneficial to provide some information about the foreigners in Turkey in general.

Foreigners/ Migrants in Turkey

Considering the history of movements of migration to Turkey, the first serious flow of migration took place after 1979 as a result of the Iranian Revolution. This was followed by the migrants fleeing from Iraq and Bulgaria and taking refuge in Turkey and those coming from the Soviet countries to Turkey for economic reasons such as finding a job in the late 80s and early 90s. In the subsequent period, an intensive migration occurred especially from the Middle East and Africa countries (e.g. Iran, Iraq, Afghanistan, Syria, Somali). Majority of them were transit migrants, whereas those taking refuge in Turkey as a result of the recent Syrian war are migrants under temporary protection.

The data of the General Directorate of Migration Management compiled in 2016 indicate that over 3 million foreign nationals enjoy international and temporary protection in Turkey. Majority of them (80%) include 2,758,409 Syrians that are under temporary protection. According to UNHCR, another large group demanding human and legal protection in Turkey contains 285,025 refugees coming from Iraq, Afghanistan, Iran, Somali, and some other countries (8%). In addition, 422,895 foreign nationals have a residence permit including human residence (12%). Of all the migrants, 8% (254,260) are Syrians living in camps, whereas 72% (2,504,149) are Syrians living outside camps (International Refugee Rights Association, 2016). The rate of migrants other than those with a residence permit is a result of irregular migration, but they are included in the system as they are included in the registries of official authorities.

Estimations regarding the numbers of migrants show that there are four main flows of foreigners to Turkey: (1) irregular migrants for work-related purposes; (2) transit migrants; (3) asylum seekers and refugees, (4) regular migrants (İçduygu and Kirişci, 2009).

However, some shifts are possible between these categories. For example, a regular migrant may become an irregular migrant by not leaving the country within legal time allowed. Or, a migrant waiting in Turkey to go to a third country as a refugee may become an irregular migrant in a European country by entering it through illegal ways.

Recent, more detailed information about irregular migration in Turkey will be presented in the following section.

Some Results of Irregular Migration in Turkey: Present Data

İçduygu and Aksel (2012) take the concept of irregular migration to refer to the migrants that are legally not allowed to stay in a country. They define an irregular migrant in Turkey as a person who uses Turkey while passing to a third country or staying or working in the country without required documents. Accordingly, there are two simultaneous models for irregular migration in Turkey: a) transit migration and b) circular (or cyclical) and labor migration. Refugees' and asylum seekers' movements mostly involve irregular crossing of borders.

Irregular migration also involves a group of migrants that enter Turkey from time to time, leave the country after a while, and then enter it again, who are included in the category of circular migration or labor migration. This type of migration to Turkey mostly occurs from the former Soviet Union countries. Among these migrants are servants, building workers, agricultural laborers, and sex workers (Erder and Kaşka, 2003).

Turkey pays attention to signing readmission agreements with transit and target countries within the scope of fight against irregular migration. Within the framework of works to this end, Turkey has signed readmission agreements with Syria, Greece, Kyrgyzstan, Romania, Ukraine, Russia, Moldova, Belarus, and the European Union since 2001. Readmission Agreement and the Roadmap Towards the Visa-Free Regime were concurrently signed with the European Union in Ankara on 16 December 2013 and ratified by the Grand National Assembly of Turkey on 25 June 2014 (Turkish General Directorate of Migration Management, 2017). However, visa exemption that will allow Turkish citizens to travel to Europe as required by the readmission process, which is a recent topic on the agenda, has not been introduced yet. This has opened the sustainability of the agreement up for discussion.

The number of irregular migrants apprehended in Turkey only in 2015 was 146,485. Half of them (around 70 thousand) were Syrian-origin. This number rose to 174,466 in 2016 (See Figure 1). In 2016, Syrians (around 70 thousand) were followed by Afghans (31,360), Iraqis (30,947), Pakistanis (19,317), and other nationals (approximately 25 thousand) as irregular migrants (Turkish General Directorate of Migration Management, 2017).

Figure 1. Apprehended Migrants

NUMBER OF IRREGULAR MIGRANTS APPREHENDED IN TURKEY PER YEAR

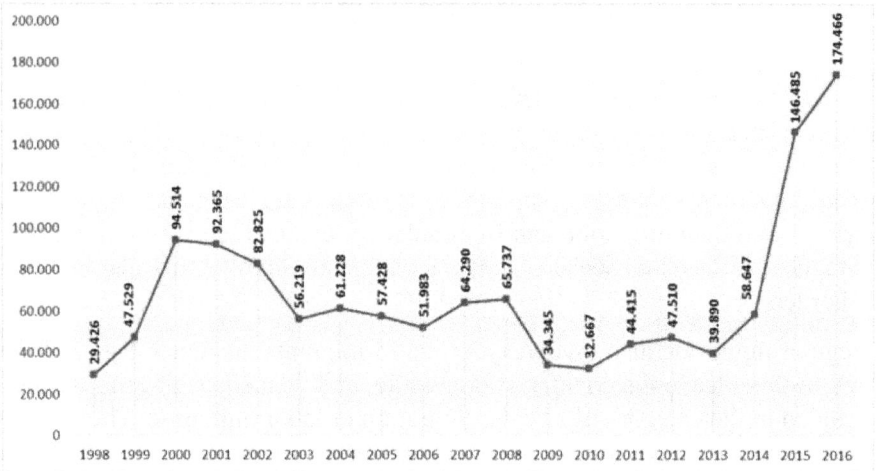

(Turkish General Directorate of Migration Management, 2017)

Figure 2. The Number of Human Smuggling Victims Detected in Turkey by Year

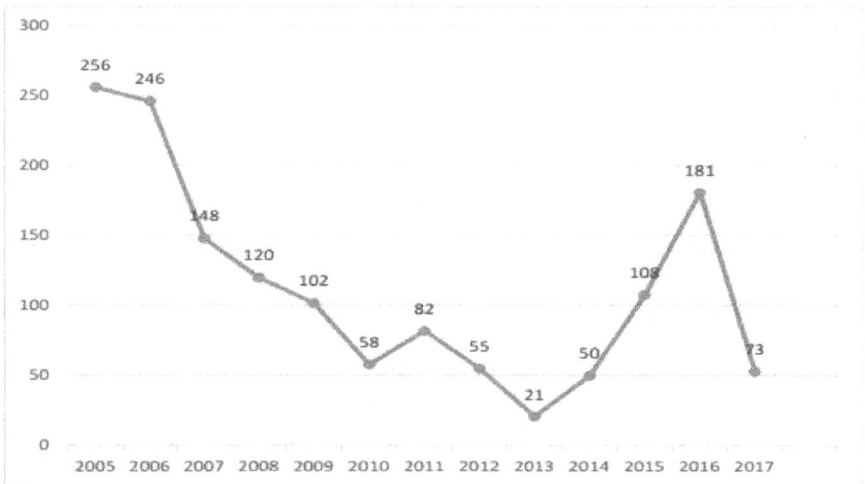

(Turkish Red Crescent Association Immigration and Refugee Services Directorate, 2017)

93,916 irregular migrants were apprehended in the first four months of 2017. As to the provinces in which migrants were apprehended in 2016, the biggest number of irregular migrants were apprehended in the provinces located in the Aegean, Mediterranean, and Marmara regions, in Şırnak, Hakkari, and Ağrı provinces of the eastern Turkey, and in Artvin province of the Black Sea Region (Turkish General Directorate of Migration Management, 2017). The ranking of the irregular migrants apprehended in 2016 by nationality has Syrians, Afghans, and Iraqis respectively (Turkish Red Crescent Association Immigration and Refugee Services Directorate, 2017).

Though the number of human smuggling victims seems to have decreased compared to the years 2005 and 2006, it started to rise again as of 2015. The number of human smuggling victims detected in the first months of 2017 is 73 (See Figure 2).

Figure 3. Migrant Smugglers in Turkey

NUMBER OF MIGRANT SMUGGLERS DETECTED PER YEAR

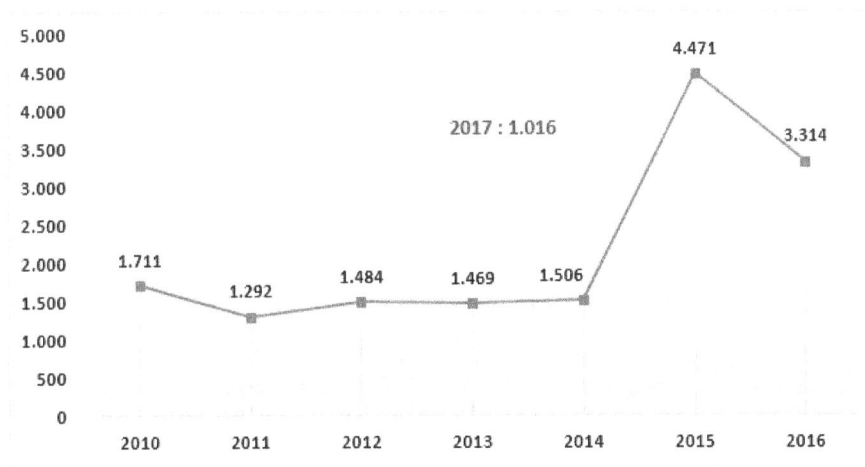

(Turkish General Directorate of Migration Management, 2017)

Particularly as of the 1990s, land and sea borders between Greece and Turkey have become one of the most active migration corridors in Europe gradually. The data provided by Turkish General Staff for the period of September 2006 to December 2011 show that more than one-third of irregular crossing of borders (approximately 40%) occurred nearby Greek-Turkish land and sea borders during migrants' attempts to pass to Greece (İçduygu & Aksel, 2012).

Surely, migrants are not alone while making plans for irregular migration to overseas countries. Many human smugglers undertake the organization of such illegal migration by exploiting migrants economically. As is clear in Figure 3, the number of migrants apprehended has increased a lot in recent years. This number only stands for those apprehended. 4,471 migrants were apprehended in 2015; 3,314 in 2016; and 1,016 in the first a couple of months of 2017. The increase in the rate of human smugglers in recent years may be about the big rise in the number of migrants (especially Syrian migrants) in Turkey and extension of the supply of these kinds of organizations.

According to the data provided by Turkish Coast Guard Command, 490 migrants have lost their lives on all coasts of Turkey in the last three years (2015, 2016, and the first months of 2017). On these coasts, 133,298 people and 343 human smugglers have been apprehended (See Table 1).

Table 1. Statistics of Irregular Migration on the Coasts of Turkey in Recent Years

Years	The Number of Irregular Migration Incidents	The Number of Irregular Migrants	The Number of Irregular Migrants with a Loss of Life	The Number of Apprehended Organizers
2015	2,430	91,611	279	190
2016	833	37,130	192	118
2017 (1st to 5th months)	105	4,557	19	35
Total	3,368	133,298	490	343

(Turkish Coast Guard Command, 2017)

Data about irregular crossing of borders to the EU by sea and land indicate that it increased 2.5 times from 2014 to 2015. 280 thousand people illegally reached Europe by sea and land in 2014. It had risen to 1,046,600 in 2015. The first stop of 862,138 of them was Greece, while that of 153,422 was Spain. According to UNHCR, 1,008,616 out of 1,046,600 used the seaway in 2015. Out of 862,138 people passing to Greece, 857 thousand used Turkey as a transit country through seaway. In addition, it is reported that despite the harsher conditions in winter months, 110,257 of 118,249 refugees arriving in Greece, Italy, Malta, and Spain in the first 2 months passed through Turkey (UNHCR; Çarmıklı & Kader, 2016). In 2016, 123,246 migrants illegally passed to Greece through seaway (Turkish Red Crescent Association Immigration and Refugee Services Directorate, 2017).

The irregular migrants apprehended are kept in return centers from the time they are apprehended to the time they leave Turkey or are deported from the country in accordance with the administrative decision taken by the Ministry of Interior. In Turkey, there are 19 return centers operated by the Ministry of Interior General Directorate of Migration Management. Criminal actions are taken against migrant smugglers pursuant to the law effective in Turkey. According to the effective law, refugees trying to flee from the country are accepted as victims falling into the hands of criminal gangs, and victims are not considered criminal. 8- to 12-year sentence and pecuniary penalty are imposed on human smugglers committing the crime. Such sentence and penalty get severe if the victims have died during the act (Turkish Red Crescent Association Immigration and Refugee Services Directorate, 2017).

A Discussion on Irregular Migration with Social Work Perspective

It is a known fact that one of the most important working areas of social work profession is migration. When working with migrants, social workers make objective evaluations in accordance with human rights and the ethical principles of their profession. In this regard, social work practices are concerned with the high benefit of vulnerable groups.

The most recent definition of social work profession made in 2014 (IFSW & IASSW, 2014) is as follows:

"Social work is a practice-based profession and an academic discipline that promotes social change and development, social cohesion, and the empowerment and liberation of people. Principles of social justice, human rights, collective responsibility and respect for diversities are central to social work. Underpinned by theories of social work, social sciences, humanities and indigenous knowledge, social work engages people and structures to address life challenges and enhance well-being."

Though social work addresses all people, professional practices mostly deal with vulnerable risk groups. One of these risk groups involves migrants and thus irregular migrants. Protection and improvement of the psychosocial well-being of these groups is essential for social work profession. Social workers must stay away from stigmatizing and judicial attitudes and advocate for the protection of the human rights of these migrants. Apart from that, national and global organization of protective and preventive works is quite important. As we all know, illegal migration is a global issue. When fighting against irregular migration, perhaps all the social service networks, civil society networks, and human rights protection organizations around the world have to work collectively. In this sense, it is essential to improve the conditions that cause individuals, families, groups, and communities to be irregular migrants in the places where they live. The above-mentioned networks must focus on these matters.

In general, no individual wants to leave the land s/he lives on or the social environment s/he exists in unless it is compulsory or his/her personal choice. Irregular migrants, who we can call as the victims of the economic or political policies existing in the countries, prefer this way because they have to do so. As noted by Kofi Annan, the former Secretary-General of the United Nations, in a conference of the International Labour Organization (ILO) about 13 years ago, those people who have entered or are working in the country they are now without a legal permit are stigmatized as illegal, disguised, undocumented, or irregular. The expression 'illegal migrants' has some connotations referring to the committal of a crime. What this definition refers to is again irregular migrants (ILO, 2004). What is intended to be indicated here is that stigmatizing irregular migrants as offenders will not contribute to the solution of the problem.

The findings presented under the title of Some Results of Irregular Migration in Turkey show that problems and illegal processes concerning irregular migration have been increasing both in Turkey and in Europe, and particular attention should be paid to the human dimension of the problem. In this regard, social workers and other professionals working in the field of migration as well as security forces and military staff dealing with migration and migrants should be trained. Moreover, as stated before, the advocating functions of professional networks and civil society networks should be made effective on a country basis.

References

Çarmıklı, E. Ö. & Kader, M. U. (2016). Türkiye'de Göçmen Kaçakçılığı: Mülteci Krizinin Öteki Yüzü [Migrant Smuggling in Turkey: The Other Side of Refugee Crisis]. USAK Raporları [International Strategical Research Organisation Reports], No: 45. (in Turkish).

Erder, S. and S. Kaşka 2003 Irregular Migration and Trafficking in Women: The Case of Turkey, International Organization for Migration, Geneva.

ILO (2004). *Towards a Fair Deal for Migrant Workers in the Global Economy.International Labour Conference,* 92nd Session. Link: http://www.ilo.org/public/english/standards/relm/ilc/ilc92/pdf/rep-vi.pdf Date: 06.03. 2017.

İçduygu, A. and Aksel D. B. (2012, September). *Irregular Migration in Turkey,* Published by IOM, Ankara.

İçduygu A. and Kirişci K. (2009). *Land of Diverse Migrations: Challenges of Emigration and Immigration in Turkey,* Istanbul Bilgi University Press, Istanbul.

Uluslararası Mülteci Hakları Derneği [International Refugee Rights Association] (2016). Türkiye'deki Göçmenlerin Genel Durumu [General Situation of Migrants in Turkey]. Link: http://www.umhd.org.tr/?s=155 Date: 03.03.2017 (in Turkish)

Turkish Coast Guard Command (2017). Statistics on Irregular Migration. Link: http://www.sahilguvenlik.gov.tr/baskanliklar/harekat/faaliyet_istatistikleri/duzensiz_go c_istatistikleri.html Date: 08.03.2017

Turkish Redcrescent Association Immigration and Refugee Services Directorate (2017, March). *Report on Migration Statistics.* Link: https://www.kizilay.org.tr/Upload/Dokuman/Dosya/89056060_goc-istatistik-raporu-mart-2017.pdf Date: 09.03.2017.

http://www.goc.gov.tr/icerik6/duzensiz-goc_363_378_4710_icerik Date: 23.03.2017

https://mirekoc.ku.edu.tr/sites/mirekoc.ku.edu.tr/files/Policy%20Brief%201%20TR.pdf Date: 02.01.2017

http://www.goc.gov.tr/icerik6/turkiyenin-duzensiz-gocle-mucadelesi_409_422_424_icerik Date: 03.03.2017

http://www.goc.gov.tr/icerik3/irregular-migration_915_1024_4746 Date: 03.03.2017

Chapter 14. Credit Constraints and Rural Migration: Evidence from Six Villages in Uttar Pradesh

Ruchi Singh[1]

Abstract

Rural economies in developing countries are often characterized by credit constraints. Various studies confirm that rural labor migration in developing countries is an outcome of capital market imperfections. Lack of easy accessibility to credit followed by exorbitant rate of interest charged by informal sources of credit worsens the condition of poor households. Uttar Pradesh is among few most backward states of India and exhibits highest rate of male out-migration among all states (NSSO).[2] Although few attempt have been made to understand trends and patterns of male out-migration from Uttar Pradesh (UP)[3], there is dearth of literature on linkage between credit accessibility and male migration in rural Uttar Pradesh. The current study tries to fill this void. Objective of the study is to assess the role of credit accessibility in determining rural male migration. To meet the objective and to have better understanding of the role played by credit constraints in migration decisions, the study undertake primary survey of 370 households in six villages of Jaunpur district in UP. Simple statistical tools and binary logistic regression model have been used. The result of empirical analysis shows that accessibility and various sources of credit play very important role in male migration in rural UP. Study also found that relationship between credit constraints and migration varies across various social groups in UP. Thus more financial inclusion shall be encouraged in rural Uttar Pradesh and an attempt shall be made to ensure easy access of credit to rural households. Various ongoing schemes on financial inclusion shall be more properly implemented and encouraged among rural households to prevent them from various kinds of exploitation by local moneylender.

Keywords: Credit constraints, Out-Migration, Male, Rural, Households, Poor, Informal

I. Introduction

Financial constraints are one of the major characteristics of developing economies (Mahendra, 2014; Berg 2013). Suboptimal choices made by households are often an outcome of credit constraints (Rossi and Seren 2014). While there have been some studies on credit constraint in developing countries, the role of credit constraints in determining migration decisions is negligible in rural Uttar Pradesh. Thus, the major objective of the paper is to analyze the role of credit accessibility in migration decisions. Migration is most often adopted strategy to cope with risks and uncertainties in developing countries (Stark and Bloom, 1985; Taylor, 1999; de Haas, 2010). Literature also shows that non-farm activities such as migration is a coping strategy rather income maximization (Kerr 2005; Bryceson 2006; Orr et al. 2009; Michaelowa et al. 2010; Cole and Hoon 2013). There is simple underlying logic behind that farmer in developing and poor countries have very small land holdings, have very less liquid assets and don't have easy accessibility of

---

[1] Doctoral Scholar, School of Economics, Central University of Hyderabad Telangana, India, Email: eco.ruchisingh@gmail.com
[2] National Sample Survey Organisation
[3] Uttar Pradesh

credit. These financial constraints restrict the migration from very poor households. Lack of collateral, weak credit contract enforcement and underdevelopment of insurance services discourage formal sources to serve this market segment (Ghosh, Mookherjee, & Ray, 2000).

Migration is not new a phenomenon in rural Uttar Pradesh rather is an age-old phenomenon. Poor infrastructure, stagnant agriculture economy, fragmentation of land due to huge population pressure, lack of credit sources, poverty, lack of non-farm opportunities etc. are inherent characteristics of the state. Huge share of population resides in rural area with agriculture as primary occupation. Few studies have been done to analyze characteristics, patterns and determinants of male out-migration from Uttar Pradesh (Khan, 1986; Singh et.al, 1980; Singh, 2014), but there is dearth of literature on migration and credit constraints in context of UP. Paper makes an attempt to fill this void and try to throw light on role played by credit constraints in male out-migration from rural UP. The study will comparatively analyze sources and accessibility of credit for both migrant and non-migrant households[4]. The paper is divided in four parts. Part one will be dealing with introduction, objectives and data and methodology adopted, justification and limitation of the study. Part two will disentangle exhaustive literature on credit constraints and migration. Part three will confer results and discussions with the help of case study of six sample villages in Jaunpur district. Part four will be concluding remarks and policy suggestions.

I.II. Objectives

i) To comparatively analyze accessibility and sources of credit of migrant and non-migrants households.

ii) To assess the role of credit accessibility in determining rural male migration.

I.III Data and Methodology

To disentangle existing work done on migration and credit accessibility, paper has undertaken extensive literature review. To meet the objective and to support theoretical findings and to understand role of credit accessibility in migration decisions, the study undertakes primary survey of 370 households in six villages of Jaunpur district, namely Chitkon, Jarasi, Rampur Soiri, Asbaranpur, Manecha and Yonouspur in three blocks i.e. Dhobi, Jalalpur and Shahganj. Simple random sampling technique has been used for selection of sample villages and households. Fifteen percent of total number of households has been selected for the survey in each village. An attempt has been made to

---

[4] Migrant household refer to household with at-least one male out-migrant; Non-Migrant household is the household with no male out-migrant.

include households from all caste to have better understanding of credit accessibility and migration as villages are divided in caste based segments in UP. Structured questionnaire along with focused group discussion, in depth interviews, key informant method were used for data collection seeking information regarding credit accessibility and migration. The collected data were tabulated and analyzed with the simple statistical techniques. Wealth scores for households have been calculated on 20 items/assets using principal component analysis. Logistic regression model have been used to analyze credit constraints as determinants of migration.

I.IV Justification of the Study

UP is leading state in male out-migration in all states in India (NSSO). Jaunpur have been selected for current study as it has second highest number of male out-migrants in all 75 districts of UP after Azamgarh (NSSO). Although few attempts have been made to analyze trends and determinants of male out-migration from UP, studies on credit constraints and migration is negligible. As discussed above few studies have been done on determinants, characteristics and pattern of male out-migration from rural UP, but literature on credit constraints and its linkage with male out-migration in rural UP has attracted little attention.

I.V Limitations and future direction

The study focuses only on linkages between credit constraints and migration from rural Uttar Pradesh thus the paper has regional limitations. Moreover the study takes into account only male migration as female often migrates as a result of marriage. Study only focuses on credit constraints as determining factor of migration decisions, however by taking into account impact of migration via remittances on credit accessibility of households as well more interesting study and more wide analysis can be derived.

II. Review of Literature

Current section will disentangle existing studies on role of credit constraints and accessibility in migration decisions. Fink et. al (2014), found that off farm labour is not the result of optimal labour allocation, but instead is household inability to cover short-term needs with savings or credit. Rossi and Serena (2014), in their study found that a credit constraint facilitates women participation in labour, whereas there is no significant effect of credit constraints on labour supply of men. Tran et.al (2014), found that credit constraints have negative impact on household's consumption per capita and informal credit can act as a substitute to mitigate the negative influence of formal credit constraints. Kumar et.al (2013) in their study found that binding credit constraints adversely affect production and livelihood choices and is significant barrier in preventing escape from poverty. Abramitzky et.al (2012), found that wealth discourages migration. Angelucci (2012), found that credit constraints often restrict migration even in the absence of positive net benefit of migration. Delpierre (2012) shows that migration is indeed an investment subject to cash constraints. Dormel et .al (2009) found that credit market imperfections do increase the persistence of unemployment. Stampini and Davis (2009) found that nonagricultural labor income relaxes credit constraints to farming. Credit constraints play very crucial role in self-selection in migration (Chiquiar and Hanson, 2005; Borjas, 1987). Temporary migration and other income smoothening is strategy adopted as a means of alleviating credit market imperfections by rural households in poor developing countries (Mesnard, 2004; 2009; Rapoprt ,2002 ;Stark & Levhari ,1982; Morduch,1995 ;Besley, 1995).Many studies found that credit constraints may generate an inverse U-shaped relationship between income and migration (Faini and Venturini 1993;1994 ; Massey,1988 ;Hatton and Williamson,1998; 2002). Halliday (2006) mentions migration as ex-post strategy and found that wealthier households have less credit constraints thus, are better able to finance migration.

III Results and Discussions: Findings from Field

Current section will deal with analysis and discussion of findings from field. Part III.I will comparatively analyze accessibility and sources of credit between migrant and non-migrant households. Part III.II will empirically analyze the same.

III.I Credit Constraints and Rural Male Migration: Comparative analysis of migrants and non-migrants households

This section will deal with comparative analysis of credit sources and accessibility in sample villages of Jaunpur district as per their migration status. Comparative analysis of migrant and non-migrant households will give insights on role-played by credit constraints in migration decisions. It can be seen that 72.4 percent of sample households in rural UP reported that their household income is insufficient. In non-migrant households number of households reporting insufficient income is high in comparison to migrants groups. Migration via remittances diversifies resources and can be one of the reasons for comparatively low households reporting insufficient income in sample villages. Moreover the tabulation is done on post migration scenario, income sufficiency situation for migrant households might be different prior to migration. A percentage of households not having easy access to credit is high in non-migrant households. Intra group comparison of migrant and non-migrant households shows that share of households not having easy access to credit is higher.

Table 1. Source and Access to Credit of Sample Households according to their Migration Status

Variable	Migrants	Non-Migrants	Total
HH Income sufficient			
Yes	83(33.6)	19(15.5)	102(27.6)
No	164(66.4)	104(84.6)	268(72.4)
Easy access to credit			
Yes	121(48.9)	42(34.2)	163(44.1)
No	126(51.1)	81(65.8)	207(55.9)
Prefer formal or informal			
Formal	105(42.5)	23(18.7)	128(34.6)
Informal	142(57.5)	100(81.3)	242(65.4)
Usually get credit from			
Formal	100(40.5)	23(18.7)	123(33.2)
Informal	147(59.5)	100(81.3)	247(66.8)
Types of credit agencies			
Formal			
Cooperative societies	0(0.00)	0(0.00)	0(0.00)
Commercial banks	99(40.1)	23(18.7)	122(33.0)
Others	0(0.00)	0(0.00)	0(0.00)
Informal			
Landlord	0(0.00)	0(0.00)	0(0.00)
Agricultural money lender	67(27.1)	60(48.8)	127(34.3)
Professional money lenders	1(1.0)	1(0.8)	2(1.0)
Traders	0(0.0)	0(0.0)	119(32.2)
Relatives/friends	80(32.4)	39(31.7)	117(35.1)
Do you have Crop insurance?			
Yes	19(7.7)	6(6.2)	25(6.8)
No	208(84.2)	91(93.8)	299(80.8)
No Land	20(8.1)	26(21.1)	46(12.4)
Total	247	123	370

Source: Field Survey 2016.

Figures in parenthesis represent percent to total

It can be seen that for both migrants and non-migrants households major source of credit is informal and majority of households don't have easy assess to credit.

Table 2 shows differences in accessibility of credit across various social groups. Social group upward caste have easy accessibility of credit and also get credit from formal sources, whereas in SC and OBC group majority of households don't have easy access to credit and major source of credit is informal sources.

It can be seen that for both migrants and non-migrants households major source of credit is informal source of credit. Major problem faced by sample households in accessing formal credit is documentation and time consuming and in accessing informal source of credit are exorbitant and high rate of interest charged by moneylenders. Moreover sometimes accessibility of credit in hour of need is not easy because of non-repayment of previous credits. Moreover another major problem associated with informal source of credit is that on non-repayment of credit by poor households, household members have to work in farm of moneylenders during peak season as a labour and they don't receive any wages for that.

Table 2. Source and Access to Credit of Sample Households according to their Migration Status

Variable	SC		OBC		Upward Caste	
	Migrants	Non-Migrants	Migrants	Non-Migrants	Migrants	Non-Migrants
HH Income sufficient						
Yes	3(6.5)	4(7.1)	17(16.5)	0(0.0)	63(64.3)	15(42.9)
No	43(93.5)	52(92.9)	86(83.5)	32(100.0)	35(35.7)	20(57.1)
Easy access to credit						
Yes	4(8.7)	12(21.4)	30(29.1)	6(18.8)	87(88.8)	24(68.6)
No	42(91.3)	44(78.6)	73(70.9)	26(81.3)	11(11.2)	11(31.4)
Usually get credit from						
Formal	4(8.7)	6(10.7)	17(16.5)	0(0.00)	79(80.6)	17(48.6)
Informal	42(91.3)	50(89.3)	86(83.5)	32(100.0)	19(19.4)	18(51.4)
Total	46	56	103	32	98	35

Source: Field Survey 2016.

Figures in parenthesis represent percent to total

III.II Empirical Analysis: Logistic Regression

This section will empirically analyze the role of credit constraints in determining migration decisions.

$P(Y=1) = \beta_0 + \beta_1$ (Primary source of income) $+ \beta_2$ (Wealth score) $+ \beta_3$(Social group) $+\beta_4$ (Income sufficiency) $+ \beta_5$ (Crop insurance) $+ \beta_6$ (Source of credit) $+ \beta_7$ (Easy access to credit) $+ \beta_8$(Total monthly household income with remittances) $+ u_i$... *Equation –1*

$P(Y=1) = \beta_0 + \beta_1$ (Primary source of income) $+ \beta_2$ (Wealth score) $+ \beta_3$(Social group) $+ \beta_4$ (Income sufficiency) $+ \beta_5$ (Crop insurance) $+ \beta_6$ (Source of credit) $+ \beta_7$ (Easy access to credit) $+ \beta_8$ (Total monthly household income without remittances) $+ u_i$... *Equation –II*

Where Y is dependent variable and is decision to out-migrate or not by rural male in Jaunpur district. It has binary values, whether male out-migration takes place i.e. to out-migrate=1 and no male out-migration i.e. not to out-migrate=0.Set of independent or explanatory variables are primary source of income, wealth score, social group, income sufficiency, crop insurance, source of credit, easy access to credit, total monthly household income with and without remittances and u_i random or stochastic error term.

Table: Logistic Regression Model: Migration as risk and income diversification strategy

Logistic Regression Model: Credit Constraints and Migration		
Dependent Variable: Male Out-Migration=1, No Male Out-Migration=0		
Statistical Method: Logit		
Model	I	II
No. of Observations	370	370
Log Likelihood	-158.00111	-197.3610
Prob (Chi²)	0.0000	0.0000
Pseudo R²	0.3285	0.1612
Explanatory Variables	Coefficients (p value)	Coefficients (p value)
Primary source of income		
Others®		
Cultivation	-.6496(0.090)*	-.4421(0.178)
Wealth score⁵	-.1466(0.201)	.2437(0.007)***
Social Group		
SC®		
OBC	.8950(0.008)***	1.3845(0.000)***
Upward caste	.9716(0.037)**	.3543(0.376)
Income sufficient		
No®		
Yes	-.8845(0.144)	-.1949(0.683)
Crop Insurance		
No®		
Yes	0.8910(0.311)	.0616(0.912)
Source of credit		
Formal®		
Informal	0.6705(0.199)	-.5121(0.212)
Easy access to credit		
No®		
Yes	-2.5388(0.000) ***	-1.0803(0.006)***
Total monthly income (With-Without	0.00018(0.000)***	.0000(0.002)***
® Reference category, ***p<0.01, **p<0.05, *p<0.1 level of significance		

Source: Field Survey.2016

The findings of the logistic regression model show that covariates such as social group OBC, easy accessibility of credit and total monthly income with and without remittances is highly significant in both models. Social group

---

⁵ Wealth Score have been computed using 20 Households Assets/Items using principal component analysis.

upward caste and cultivation as primary source of income is significant in model I and wealth score is significant in model II. Logit results show that households, which have easy access to credit, have less chances of male out-migration in comparison to households, which don't have easy access to credit. Social group OBC is highly significant in both models. Total monthly income with and without remittances is highly significant. Source of credit is not significant. Model II shows that as wealth increases migration increases as well and there is positive relationship between migration and wealth score.

IV. Concluding remarks and Suggestions

Results and analysis show that accessibility of credit is a significant factor in migration decisions. Despite the fact that there are huge wage differences associated with migration credit constraints restrict the poorest especially SC households to reap the benefits of migration. The poorest households don't have collateral nor they have savings to finance out-migrations and for same reason they are often denied from formal sources of credit. Comparatively better off households such as OBC households in our study opt for migration as a strategy to diversify income and risks associated with agriculture and imperfections in credit markets. Richer sections of society have easy accessibility of credit and also opt for formal sources therefore migration decisions are unaffected from credit accessibility. Although informal sources of credit are comparatively easily accessible than formal source for poor households but because of exorbitant rate of interest charged by money lenders poor often adopt migration as risk and income diversification strategy. Although there are various ongoing schemes on financial inclusion for rural households but they lack proper implementation, awareness and is often out of the reach of the needy households. As a result poor households opt for informal source and become vulnerable to various kinds of exploitation by local moneylenders. Thus more financial inclusion shall be encouraged and facilitated in rural households and an attempt shall be made to ensure easy access of credit to rural households in hour of need.

References

Abramitzky, R., Boustan, L. P., & Eriksson, K. (2013). Have the poor always been less likely to migrate? Evidence from inheritance practices during the Age of Mass Migration. Journal of Development Economics, 102, 2-14.

Angelucci, M. (2012). Conditional cash transfer programs, credit constraints, and migration. Labour, 26(1), 124-136.

Berg, E. (2013). Are poor people credit-constrained or myopic? Evidence from a South African panel. Journal of Development Economics, 101, 195-205.

Besley, T. (1995). Savings, credit and insurance. *Handbook of development economics, 3*, 2123-2207.

Borjas, G. (1987) 'Self-selection and the earnings of immigrants', American Economic Review, 77(4), 531-53.

Carroll, Christopher D. 2001. A Theory of the consumption function, with and without the liquidity constraints. Journal of Economic Perspectives, Vol. 15(3), pp.23-45.

Cole, Steven M and Parakh N Hoon, Piecework (Ganyu) as an Indicator of household vulnerability in rural Zambia,Ecology of food and nutrition, 2013, 52 (5), 407–426.

Chiquiar, D. and Hanson, G. (2005) International Migration, Self-Selection, and the distribution of wages: Evidence from Mexico and the United States, Journal of Political Economy 113(2): 239-281.

Delpierre, M. (2012). The impact of liquidity constraints and imperfect commitment on migration decisions of offspring of rural households. Review of Economics of the Household, 10(1), 153-170.

De Haas, Hein.2010. "Migration and Development: A Theoretical Perspective". *International Migration Review, 44*(1):227-264.

Dromel, N. L., Kolakez, E., & Lehmann, E. (2010). Credit constraints and the persistence of unemployment. Labour Economics, 17(5), 823-834.

Duca, John V. and Stuart S. Rosenthal. 1993. Borrowing constraints, household debt, and racial discrimination in loan markets. Journal of Financial Intermediation, Vol. 3(1), pp.77-103.

Faini, R. and Venturini, A. (1993) 'Trade, aid and migrations. Some basic policy issues', European Economic Review, 37, 435-442.

Faini, R. and Venturini, A. (1994) Migration and growth: the experience of Southern Europe, CEPR Discussion Paper 964.

Fink, G., Jack, B. K., & Masiye, F. (2014). Seasonal credit constraints and agricultural labor supply: evidence from Zambia (No. w20218). National Bureau of Economic Research.

Ghosh, P., Mookherjee, D., & Ray, D. (2000). Credit rationing in developing countries: an overview of the theory. Readings in the Theory of Economic Development, 383-401.

Halliday, T. (2006). Migration, risk, and liquidity constraints in El Salvador. Economic development and cultural change, 54(4), 893-925.

Hatton, T. J. and Williamson, J. G. (1998), The Age of Mass Migration: Causes and Economic Impact (New York: Oxford University Press).

Hatton, T. J. and Williamson, J. G. (2002) 'What fundamentals drive world migration?', NBER Working Paper 9159.

Jappelli, Tullio. 1990. "Who is Credit Constrained in the U.S. Economy?". Quarterly Journal of Economics, Vol. 105(1), pp.219-234.

Kerr, R. B. (2005). Informal labor and social relations in northern Malawi: The theoretical challenges and implications of ganyu labor for food security. *Rural sociology, 70*(2), 167-187.

La Cava, Gianni and John Simon. (2005). "Household Debt and Financial Constraints in Australia". Australian Economic Review, Vol. 38(1), pp.40-60

Mahendra, Edo. (2014). Financial constraints, social policy and migration evidence from Indonesia, DEMIG project paper 25, International Migration Institute (IMI), Oxford Department of International Development.

Massey, D. S. (1988). Economic development and International migration in comparative perspective, Population and Development Review 14(3), 383-413.

Michaelowa, Katharina, Ralitza Dimova, and Anke Weber, "Ganyu labour in Malawi: Understanding rural household's labour supply strategies," Mimeo, 2010.

Orr, Alastair, Blessings Mwale, and Donata Saiti-Chitsonga, "Exploring seasonal poverty traps: the 'six-week window' in southern Malawi," The Journal of Development Studies, 2009, 45 (2), 227–255.

Rossi, M., & Trucchi, S. (2012). Liquidity constraints and labor supply. Center for Research on Pension and Welfare Policies Working Paper, 127, 12.

Mesnard, A. (2004). Temporary migration and capital market imperfections. Oxford economic papers, 56(2), 242-262.

Mesnard A. (1999): ìMigration internationale, accumulation díÈpargne et re- tour des travailleursî PhD. dissertation, Ecole des Hautes Etudes en Sciences Sociales, Paris, 380p.

Morduch, Jonathan, "Income smoothing and consumption smoothing," Journal of Economic Perspectives, 1995, 9, 103–103

Rapoport, H. (2002). Migration, credit constraints and self-employment: A simple model of occupational choice, inequality and growth. Economics Bulletin, 15(7), 1-5. Singh, R. (2014). The Role of Social Networks in Migration: A case study of out-migration from Uttar Pradesh to Mumbai. *Journal of Studies in Dynamics and Change (JSDC)-ISSN: 2348-7038, 1*(3), 137-144.

Stampini, M., & Davis, B. (2009). Does nonagricultural labor relax farmers' credit constraints? Evidence from longitudinal data for Vietnam. Agricultural economics, 40(2), 177-188.

Stark, Oded, and Davi E.Bloom.1985."The new economics of labor migration". *American Economic Review*, 75(2):173–78.

Taylor, J, Edward.(1999).The new economics of labour migration and The role of remittances in migration process. *International Migration 37:63-88.*

Appendix Table: Definition and Descriptive statistics of used Variables

Variable name & definition	No of observations	Mean	Std dev.	Min	Max
d_outmigrate: dummy (if outmigrated=1,if not outmigrated =0)	370	.6676	.4717	0	1
Primary source of income					
Others®					
Cultivation	370	.2702	.4447	0	1
Wealth score	370	-0.0000	2.6302	-3.583601	5.208136
Social Group					
SC®					
OBC	370	.3648	.4820	0	1
Upward caste	370	.3594	.4804	0	1
Income sufficiency					
No®					
Yes	370	.2757	.4475	0	1
Crop Insurance					
No®					
Yes	370	.0676	.2513	0	1
Source of credit					
Formal®					
Informal	370	.6676	.4717	0	1
Easy access to credit					
No®					
Yes	370	.4405	.4971		
Total monthly household income with remittances	370	28537.84	29148.88	1000	100000
Total monthly household income without remittances	370	22215.27	25578	0	100000
d_Dummy Variables and ® Reference Category Notes:for dummy variable the means give the number of positive values Std dev, Standard deviation					

Chapter 15. The Effect of Migration upon Lexical Aspects of the Movers' Mother Tongues: The Example of Pomak in Turkey

Hasan Boynukara[1], Uğur Altıntaş[2]

Introduction

After their migration throughout the decade of 1920s, Pomak people underwent numerous cultural changes, especially in their languages. Being an endangered minority language, Pomak is a Slavic language which demonstrates a reciprocal effect with Turkish language in western parts of Turkey. Upon considering the current danger that Pomak is facing extinction, it would be beneficial to analyze the lexical and morphological differences in the Pomak language amongst the areas where Pomak minorities live. So as to gain necessary data three villages –Tayfur, Çanakkale; Toybelen, Balıkesir; Armağan, Kırklareli- in the Northwestern part of Turkey have been visited and Pomak people are firstly asked to translate fifty basic sentences, and later they are interviewed about the current status of Pomak in the area. Obtained translations have been recorded, and their morphological and vocal similarities and differences have been identified and analyzed. Collecting the data, the effect of Turkish on Pomak is analyzed from a perspective of language ecology. This study is intended to supply linguistic information on Pomak and to help create ways to avoid an undesired extinction of such a colorful language.

Pomak is the name given to a Balkan community that dwell mainly in five countries Bulgaria, Macedonia, Turkey, Albania and Greece (Neuburger, 2000). This community differs mainly with their religion –namely Islam- , and other distinctive cultural element such as ceremonies and language (Koyuncu, 2013). They are believed to have been made to convert to Islam under the rule of Ottoman Empire (Balikci, 2007), therefore they are given many other names than Pomak in the states they reside(Neuburger, 2000). They were generally peasants who were dealing with sheep keeping and other rural activities. Today the estimated number of Pomaks in the mentioned countries is between three million and six million. Most probable reason why Pomaks could not go further than being a religious minority is that almost all the authorities, from the 16th century on, under whose power Pomaks have been living, have asserted some pressures especially in terms of religion. Experiencing Russian pressure during Communism era, Pomaks turned their inclination to being Turkish (Balikci, 2007; Brooks, 2002; Eminov, 1993). That is clearly manifested in their migration patterns

---

[1] Prof. Dr., Namık Kemal University, Tekirdag, Turkey.
E-mail: boynukarahasan@yahoo.com
[2] Instructor, Kırklareli University, Turkey. E-mail: uguraltintas@klu.edu.tr

especially in 1924 and post-1989 period. They were scattered around Turkey, range of which varies from Kırklareli (Lozengrad) to Kayseri. Even though they extend to a large area of land, there is no reported case of organized Pomak nationalist or racist activity. From a very broad point of view, they are content with their current status.

When Pomaks accomplished their migration to Turkey, the first difference – and possibly the primary source of the problems on integration- was the language. Pomaks speak a language that is very similar to Bulgarian, however, some Pomaks claim that their language is close to Turkish even though there is much limited overlap between the two. Pomak is, like Bulgarian and Russian, a Slavic language which is now under the threat of dying. In many locations, new generations choose not to learn it, and already the parents are unwilling to transfer this language to their children. The generation up to 20 years of age has been observed to be unable to understand or produce in the language, while the generation between 20 and 40 is able to understand but unable to produce. Amongst the places observed, it has been seen that the more a community has to come into contact with the surrounding community, the more their language is under the effect of exchange.

Pomaks have been distributed such a large area in Turkey that the preservation of their language, as well as development a different nationalist –or a racist- behavior have been made all but impossible. Surely, this is not a situation specific to Turkey; in many other Balkan countries as well, Pomaks dwell mainly in rural areas which possess a very limited language use opportunities. Also, with the effect of industrialization and global economy, many new-generation Pomaks opt not to reside in villages, but to move to big cities, which, as a whole, poses a great threat to already suffering Pomak language just like many other minority languages. Due to the vast wideness of the area that Pomaks live in, Pomak language is expected to remain local –spoken by one thousand maximum in a particular area-, and immense structural and pragmatic differences in Pomak language is also anticipated.

In many cases, surrounding language is seen to affect –and again in many cases tend to kill- the minority language through dominating the current sociological, technological and other cultural vocabulary; especially newly-emerging lexical items are generally borrowed from the surrounding language. The effect of Turkish upon Pomak is both obvious and mutual (Adamou, 2010). Since Pomak language takes some of its roots from Turkish language, it has already got some lexical items with the same phonological and semantic traits. Furthermore, because Pomaks are distributed around Turkey in a vast area and with population of less than 3,000 for each village or town, their language is more prone to be eroded and altered with Turkish lexicon. The aim of this study is to show the current level of changes experienced by Pomak language, and help to assist those who study upon the death of Pomak language in Turkey. A more comprehensive study would be beneficial in the area, and also an inter-country studies –such as Turkey-Greece, or Greece-Bulgaria- would show exactly how much pressure that comes from surrounding languages the Pomak language is currently undergoing.

Methodology

Three villages in the northwestern part of Turkey –namely Armağan, Kırklareli; Tayfur, Çanakkale; and Toybelen, Balıkesir- have been chosen for this study since they are known to have received immigrants mainly from Drama (Selonika, Greece) between the years 1924 and beginnings of 1930s. All these three villages have been visited, and publicly, Pomak people have been informed about the content and the aims of the study, and later they have been asked to translate 50 random sentences. Amongst these 50 sentences; 32 were about everyday speech, while 7 were professional life, 8 cultural events and lastly 3 were about food. Later on, a short chat with the attendees has been conducted and their opinions about the current status and future of Pomak language have been discussed.

These collected sentences have been analyzed if there is any specific difference in terms of lexical choices. If there is any difference in this aspect, then these sentences have been put under an analysis. It has been observed that since the attendees are natural bilinguals, their translations have been situational rather than verbatim translation.

Findings and Discussion

The first question that has been asked to translate is the very common greeting sentence of "How are you?". The translations from all the attendees were more or less the same. However, even though the verbatim translation is "*Kako-si*"[3] or "*Kaksi?*", all agreed that "*Kinaprayşt?*"(=What are you doing?) is also a valid translation. This may be due to the fact that Turkish sentence "*Ne yapıyorsun?*" which is commonly used with a similar meaning to "How are you?" has been translated into Pomak and fossilized to an idiomatic expression. The answer for this question showed a difference between Toybelen dwellers and Armağan dwellers, in that both Toybelen and Armağan Pomaks use the expression "*Hubosam*", which means "nice" or "beautiful" in Bulgarian language, while Armağan Pomaks choose to say "*Zdravosam*" but Toybelen people do not. One of the Toybelen attendees

---

[3] For the translations, sentences were introduced in Turkish. Also, since there is not a Pomak alphabet, Turkish inscription has been used.

stated that he could understand what the interlocutor meant, but still it is not a common word in their village.

So many common words such as "tea", "today", "book", "quite" have been directly transferred from Turkish. When asked about the meaning of "book", one of the Armağan attendees stated that previous generations used to know all these statements. Simply, today's Pomaks in all three areas have a very limited vocabulary which is eroding over time. One of the biggest lexical entity that is directly affected from this erosion is numbers. Toybelen attendees could count up to five; all could do so, but none could go further. On the other hand, Armağan attendees differed in their counting; only one could go up to ten, but the others remained at six. However, the one who could count to ten was unsure about the correctness of it since there was nobody to control. This may have stemmed from the level of illiteracy of the first Pomak immigrants; or over time, the numbers have been replaced with Turkish equivalents. Since numbers are directly related to positive thinking at schools which provide education in Turkish language, the latter overweighs the former. Also, Armağan attendees claimed that old generations were able to count up to a hundred, which supports the latter, too.

Armağan attendees translated the word "toilet" as in Turkish, however Toybelen attendees chose "*Muşraka*". When asked, Armağan attendees stated that they had never heard of such a word. In addition, for the translation of "Good night", Armağan attendees replied as "*Dobroveçe*", but Toybelen attendees left it completely blank. Even if they know the meaning of the word "*mesto*" (=farm), Armağan attendees chose to use "*tarla*" which is the Turkish equivalent of the word. In both places, the word "father-in-law" and the expression "my condolences" have been left blank. Again, they stated that they must have lost the meaning of these words and expressions over time. Moreover, these examples clearly show that even in very simple everyday usages Pomak language is under a great effect of erosion in both places.

During the early phases of settlement after a migratory movement, people are expected to switch to their mother tongue when they need to produce a structure that is hard to do so in terms of lexical and structural aspects. When two complex sentences one of which was structurally hard reported speech, while the other was complex in terminology, they chose to use Turkish language rather than Pomak. The question "what time" includes a lexical item related to a technologically advanced entity, therefore they are unable to produce a verbatim translation. Also, they tend to choose Turkish language when they need to use a Turkish vocabulary in the sentence. Even though the word "vine leaf" exists in Pomak language as "*loznik*", they showed a clear sign of reluctance when they were asked to translate a sentence that contained the word "*sarma*" which is the name of a meal made of "vine leaf". These examples may lead to two possible deductions, first of which is the fact that the very language which a minority has, tend to be close to a further development. Newly emerging words are not produced, but are generally preferred to be adopted from the surrounding language. Another example is that when a Pomak –both in Armağan and Toybelen- is asked where his son is, he may reply "*atide askeriye*", however for Tayfur attendees, it has been stated that adding a morphological element is skipped. In Turkish language, "serving for army" is "*askere gitmek*"(= going to the soldier/army). Most probably, Pomaks have chosen to adopt the word "*asker*" and adapt the word "*gitmek*". For Toybelen and Armağan Pomaks, this adoption is limited to lexical level because in morphological level a clear adaptation can be seen with the suffix added to the word "*asker*". Also, when asked to translate the sentence "turn off the radio", dwellers of both Armağan and Toybelen chose the words "*zat* vari" which is also used with doors and windows with the meanin of "close". Turkish word "*kapatmak*"(=closing) is used both for doors or windows and for electronic devices. Pomaks might have simply translated the word "*kapatmak*" from Turkish, and adopted the word "radio". With the word "radio", necessary morphological additions are done, and also Toybelen attendees make sound alteration by pronouncing the word as "*radye*". Second conclusion that can be drawn is that after a period of time, and under the effect of being obsolete in a limited area and usage, mother tongue of the immigrants is replaced by the surrounding language. In early periods, immigrants think in their mother tongues, and make mistakes in the surrounding language; and with generations, they start to think and make mistakes vice versa. Therefore, it would be safe to claim that current Pomaks' mother tongue is surely Pomak; but their primary language is Turkish, which, as a whole, is a very common situation with immigrants' languages in many areas.

Apart from the effects of surrounding Turkish language, Pomak has also followed the common path of minority languages, which is the modifications and alterations in the phonological system. In Pomak language, this process of change has been observed particularly in the sounds "*a*" and "*o*". Toybelen and Tayfur attendees produced the exclamation "*Shut up*" as "*Malçi*", while Armağan Pomaks pronounced it as "*Molçi*". Similarly, Toybelen and Tayfur Pomaks use the word "*Boli*" as the equivalent of "pain", but Armağan Pomaks produce it as "*Bali*". In both cases, no meaning interference has been observed. Nonetheless, it is believed that Pomak language has been experiencing emergence of new accents all over Turkey, and other countries.

Tayfur Pomaks, just like their geographical location, stands between Toybelen Pomaks and Armağan Pomaks, in that there is all but no difference with other two usages. The most obvious effect of Turkish language upon Tayfur Pomak is related to the technological tools. Firstly, they translated the phrase "make a phone call" with the words "*telefon*" and "*taeg*" latter of which means "to pull". In rural Turkish, "make a phone call" is used as "*telefon çekmek*". In this phrase, "*çekmek*" means "to pull". Pomaks are considered to translate this usage from Turkish. In addition, old Tayfur Pomaks have been reported to have used the word "*tekerlek*", which stands for "tire, wheel" in both Turkish and Pomak, with the meaning of "clock" most probably because of its round shape. However, contemporary Pomaks of Tayfur do not make use of "*tekerlek*" with this meaning, and in all three villages, there is no exact question for "what time".

Even though no translation for "My condolences" has been offered by Toybelen and Armağan Pomaks, one Tayfur attendee used the sentence "*Glavata datie civo*" which is the direct verbatim translation of "*Başın sağolsun*" which is the Turkish equivalent of the phrase. Interestingly, Toybelen Pomaks stated that they could understand this phrase but it was definitely not Pomak. This could lead to the conclusion that productive and generative aspects of Pomak is under the control of Turkish in all three locations.

Pomaks' Views on Their Language

After compiling the sentences translated, Pomaks were asked to make comments about the history, current status and future of their language. In all three places, Pomaks were observed to be pessimistic about the survival of their language. All stated that new generations do not –and are not keen to- learn Pomak language. They all believe that the point of no return has been passed already about the future of Pomak language.

One Toybelen attendee contended that they were forced to speak Turkish; using Pomak at school was strictly prohibited. When asked if that was a hostile attitude towards the language, he replied "… no, it was not a hostile attitude toward our language per se. It was a necessary step at that time (1950s). It was a newly-founded state, and there were many other *muhacir* (a group of Balkan immigrants that came before Pomaks to the same village) students as well. What was going to happen, if we had started to speak among ourselves without them not understanding what we were talking about. They would definitely start to think that we were talking about them, even swearing at them." Pomaks did not act so radically with their languages in Turkey, and they chose to learn and actively use Turkish language.

Some Pomaks are already known to be Turkish nationalists in other European countries as well. However, some new generation Pomaks act so offensively to Pomak language. Both in Toybelen and Armağan, Pomak is reported to have been called as *"gavurca   "* that means "foreign language" in a very hostile and exclusionary manner. One Armağan attendee told the anecdote that once his nephew exclaimed him to stop using that despicable *"gavurca"*, but after a time, when he went to Bulgaria, he experienced the importance of Pomak at firsthand.

The most optimistic about the future of Pomak language was Tayfur Pomaks. They are striving to teach Pomak language to their young; however, they still complain that new generation does not want to learn Pomak, and thus not engage in any activity to learn this precious language. All the attendees from the three locations agree that Pomak is a valuable language. One of the attendees even has a sideline as a "guide" for Bulgarian tourists in Gallipoli.

Conclusion

As a conclusion to this study, it has been observed that Pomak language is under a big threat of lexical erosion and extinction. In all three areas which have been studied, Pomak is seen as a value for their communities, transferring this so-called value to younger generations is a problematic aspect of Pomak. This is partly because Pomak has no academic or literary value, and also there is no standard inscription of it in Turkey. With very few who can make verbal production, it would be safe to claim that Pomak is also suffering from being forgotten due to current industrial lifestyle; however, even in the past, vast geography that Pomaks were scattered throughout Turkey also caused it to be of limited use and little –or no- production. From a sociological perspective, Pomaks simply ignored their Pomakness and language. Still, this situation is understandable considering the turmoil they were through in all countries in Europe.

Contrary to the expectation, the level of interference from Turkish language and the lexical erosion has been found very similar despite the immensely different geographical, cultural and social structures of the three villages studied. Therefore, one possible conclusion to draw is that the cause of threat Pomak is facing is similar in these villages; lack of academic and literary use, lexical deficiency, and loss of popularity among young generations. It is another righteous cause that Pomak has a very limited professional use, which is already dominated by Turkish. This study also showed that Turkish has become the primary language of the Pomaks, who choose to think in Turkish first and translate into Pomak. Many colloquial sentences or utterances take their roots from Turkish equivalents. In some cases, sad to say, they just speak Turkish sentences in Pomak lexicon.

The extent of erosion and threat which Pomak is currently undergoing cannot be understood without handling it more comprehensively in international level. Current status of Pomak language in other European countries should be analyzed in a similar scientific manner. Increasing the amount of academic record of Pomak language, in this respect, can be an initial step to preserve it. As Shariatmadari (2010) contends, *"endangered languages aren't the same as endangered species; their greatest value isn't scientific, but cultural."* However, to protect this cultural treasure, scientific methodology is the very first tool to deploy.

References

Adamou, E. (2010). Bilingual speech and language ecology in Greek Thrace: Romani and Pomak in contact with Turkish. Language in Society, 39(2), 147. https://doi.org/10.1017/S0047404510000035

Balikci, A. (2007). Visual Ethnography Among the Balkan Pomak. Visual Anthropology Review, 23(1), 92–96. https://doi.org/var.2007.23.1.92

Brooks, R. S. (2002). Step-Mother Tongue: Language and Ethnicity among Bulgarian Pomaks. Berkeley Journal of Sociology, 46, 27–45. Retrieved from http://www.jstor.org/stable/41035567

Eminov, A. (1993). Turks and Other Muslim Minorities of Bulgaria. In Copyrighted Material (pp. 1–29).

Koyuncu, A. (2013). Balkan Savaşları Sırasında Pomakların Zorla Tanassur Edilmesi (1912-1913). Otam, (33), 139–196.

Neuburger, M. (2000). Pomak Borderlands: Muslims on the edge of nations. Nationalities Papers, 28(1), 181–198. https://doi.org/10.1080/00905990050002506

Shariatmadari, D. (2010). The death of a language. The Guardian, February 5, 5–9. Retrieved from https://www.theguardian.com/commentisfree/2010/feb/05/bo-language-extinct-linguistics

Chapter 16. Diversity and creativity in the center of Athens: Co-existence or implicit conflicts?

Aggeliki Demertzi, Eva Papatzani*

Introduction

As Greece is plagued by the multidimensional crisis combined with the recent refugee flows, the center of Athens becomes once more the focus of public discourse's attention. A range of European and Greek policies on migration have been launched during the last decades regarding not only the macro-scale of the migrants' legal status but also their (permanent and/or temporary) settlement in central Athens. In parallel, many policies and practices -both by public and private initiatives- are being emerged regarding the creative activities, creative groups, cultural policies etc. In general, a turn to the importance of culture and creativity and its socio-economic impact is being observed. Inevitably, these trends form some of the aspects of the urban policy making.

At the same time, during the last few decades Greece constitutes one of the main gateways of migration flows into Europe, and particularly Athens is the main city of reception of new populations. Despite the fact that social networks and informal activities of everyday life have spread immigrants' settlement across Attica region, the historical center of Athens remains the fundamental pole of attraction for diverse ethnic groups, either as a transit place or as a place of permanent settlement. The socio-economic and spatial transformations of the center in the last decades have allowed the development of a variety of small businesses, hangouts and immigrant communities which until now are benchmarks for a wide range of migrant groups affecting their everyday life, creating also a vital laboratory of the everyday negotiation of diversity and difference (Papatzani, 2015). Even before the outburst of the crisis, the center of Athens was placed at the core of the so-called "crisis of Athens' center", a narrative portraying central Athens' diversity as the cause of social contradictions (Maloutas et al., 2013; Koutrolikou and Siatitsa, 2011). Both the official policy institutions and the predominant discourse have convicted Athens' center as a ghetto, have lunched repressive policies in order to eliminate immigrants' presence and have proposed measures in order to facilitate native residents' return to the area.

Creative and Cultural Industries (CCI) increasingly accumulate the interest in many socio-economic and spatial levels of policies or everyday practices. This emerging trend tends to create new balances and transformations in the

---

* Authors are based at the National Technical University of Athens, Greece.
E-mail. evaliapap@yahoo.gr.

spatial and socio-economic level becoming more and more influential factor of policies and practices both in public and private degree. According to many recent studies, the historic center of Athens constitutes the main place of accumulation of CCIs based on a series of historical, social and spatial reasons. After a decade of different approaches regarding the center of Athens, it seems that new types of policies are being emerged by the part of the municipality of Athens, putting the CCIs as well as the cultural and creative activities at the epicenter of the urban policies planned. The current policies range from a new upgrading program of the historical center of Athens to the formation of an initiative including "active citizens" and various "creative" practices.

This paper aims to unfold the ongoing discussion on the creative activities, as a part of the proposed socio-spatial policies as well as their impact on the everyday diversity at the center of Athens. It explores the historically formatted multiethnic and multicultural everyday reality, the boundaries and opportunities of CCIs and their historicity in Athens, as well as the ways that public policies and practices could promote the co-existence, or the observable results are overlapping. It focuses on the historical center of Athens, which has always been a fundamental pole of attraction for immigrant population. At the same time, the center has a long tradition in creativity (mostly in arts and crafts) which has been transforming during the last years incorporating the tradition roots. Through the ongoing research attention is drawn on the simultaneous historical reproduction of the two phenomena (migrants' and Creative & Cultural Industries' settlement) as a significant part of the total historical socio-economic reproduction of the urban space of the center of Athens. The paper finally aims to explore the ways that these policies and practices coexist or conflict with the diverse everyday reality of the residents and users of the center of Athens.

The methodology of research combines the theoretical part of literature review, the research on the current policies and fieldwork based on open discussions with residents/professionals/users of the center of Athens, using semi-structured questionnaires. It combines our research fields regarding on one hand the diversity and the migrants' settlement patterns in Athens during the crisis and on the other the creative industries and the symbolic economy in Athens.

Creativity and Creative Industries today, during the crisis and in the past

It is widely known that Culture, through the notions of "Creativity", "Creative Industries" or "Creative Sectors", their characteristics and their impact on space, has gained an upgraded role during the recent decades in strategic socio-economic development as well as in spatial transformations and policies. This discussion is becoming wider given the fact that new social and economic transformations are leading globally. The outset of focusing on creative industries was when new scientific studies were launched in early '00s about "Creative Cities" (Landry, 2000), "Creative Class" (Florida, 2002) and cultural policy and cultural products (Garnham, 2005). Indicatively, it includes a wide range of activities such as arts, crafts, design, architecture, audiovisual arts, ICT etc. At the same time, UK Government began to investigate both the role and the policy instruments that could enhance "Creative Industries'" added value as well as their appropriate definition and categorization (DCMS and Creative Industries Programme, 2001; DCMS and Creative Industries Task Force, 1998).

Before the main definitions presented a short retrospection is needed. Thus, within the scope of the 1960's and 1970's transition of production from compact Fordish model to new productive procedures, more flexible, technological and innovation oriented, new business models arose, and productive processes have separated both structurally and spatially and a new flexible division of labor came into forefront. The so-called "new economy" (Scott, 2006) concentrates new dynamic economic sectors such as new technologies, new-industrial production, financial services, culture production etc. replace the traditional sectors of massive production models. The main characteristics of these sectors could be referred to:

- Production is not realized at a unique (vertical) enterprise but is conducted under an enterprise network often made up of big collaborative schemes or with the co-existence of smaller and smart specialized enterprises.

- Job market in these sectors is characterized by extreme flexibility and competitiveness, including individual contracts and many times the most creative parts of employees are collaborating within temporary project-oriented teams

- Final products are mainly competitive over their quality and not their cost

- New economy's activity is located at specific and particular places – clusters (i.e. Silicon Valley, Third Italy etc.)

Beyond the "new economy's" orientation the so-called "cultural turn" (Bianchini and Parkinson, 1993) has emerged to give prominence to the rising role of culture and to describe the necessity of studying the cultural parameters within the context of production, distribution and consuming of cultural products that could not be interpreted by the known political economy rules and tools any more. Creative Industries are "those industries which have their origin in individual creativity, skill and talent and which have a potential for wealth and job creation through the generation and exploitation of intellectual property" (DCMS and Creative Industries Programme, 2001). As of 2015 the DCMS (DCMS, 2015) definition recognizes nine creative sectors, namely (Bianchini and Parkinson, 1993): Advertising and marketing, Architecture, Crafts, Design: product, graphic and fashion design, film, TV, video, radio and photography, IT, software and computer services, Publishing, Museums, galleries and libraries, Music, performing and visual arts. There are also some other classifications such as "symbol creators" (Hesmondhalgh, 2002), intellectual property model (World Intellectual Property Organizations (WIPO), 2003), the European Union classification (KEA European Affairs et al., 2006) the UNESCO classification (Creative industries and development, 2004) etc.

Like across all Mediterranean, many techniques and local know-how have been developed historically and traditionally in Greece and Athens. During the 20th century, within the historic urban setting of Athens there did exist plenty of small artisanal industries mainly of low technology, specialized in activities with artistic quality such as goldsmithery, printing, tanning, ceramics etc. Simultaneously, Athens has always been the epicenter of performing arts. It is calculated that the total product of CCIs is approx. 3% of Greek GDP presenting an impressive growth (~70%) during the last years. At the same time, it should be mentioned that, during the deep economic crisis, as shops and ateliers close or shrink, the creative arts professions in central Athens, although have been significantly affected by the new situation, it seems to have a unique resistance.

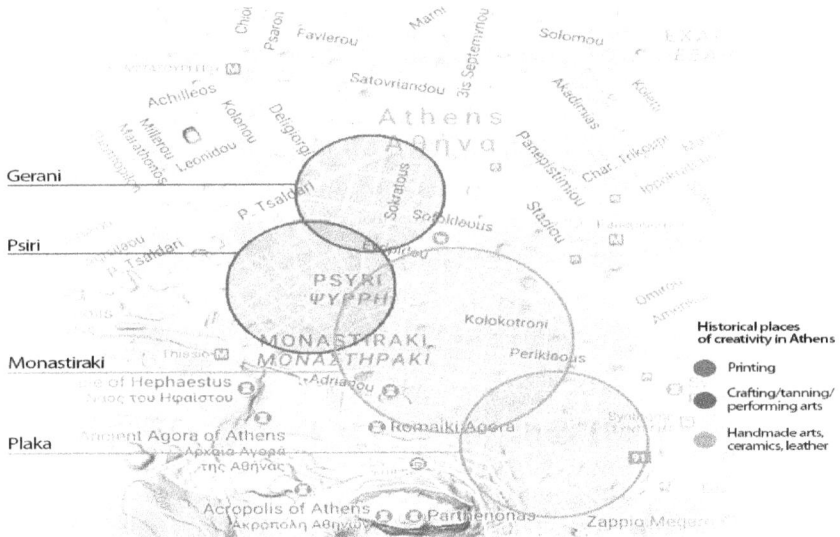

Map 1: Historical places of creativity in central Athens. Source: Authors' observation, editing.

Immigrants' settlement patterns in central Athens

In the last few decades Athens is the main city of reception of new populations, either for permanent settlement or as a transit place. Especially, during the last two years under the continuing refugee flows, Athens' character as a transit place emerged crucially.

The urban development of the Greek capital historically along with the dynamics of migrants' settlement has created settlement patterns which largely differ from those of the countries of the European or American North (enclosed communities or ghettos) and are more similar to the south-European settlement patterns characterized by social mix at the same place and vertical social stratification (Arapoglou and Sayas, 2008; Leontidou, 1990; Maloutas and Karadimitriou, 2001; Vaiou et al., 2007). The factors that differentiate the patterns of migrants' settlement in the Greek case are the differentiated forms of urban development, the different production processes, the reduced influence – existence of central urban planning, the morphology – typology of the urban space and also the issue of the "informal" which characterizes a variety of aspects of urban everyday life (Leontidou, 1990; Vaiou et al., 2007). The removal of local people from the center to the suburbs since the 70's left behind empty apartments and working places and aging population (Maloutas, 2013). It also produced central areas which include old housing stock, poor social equipment and lack of infrastructure.

Research on Athens, has demonstrated the two major settlement patterns for immigrants: the settlement in the very center of the municipality of Athens, and the one in neighborhoods of residence near the center or in other municipalities of Attica (Vaiou et al., 2007). It was in the 90's when the center attracted the first migrants from the Balkans and the former Soviet Union (Vaiou et al., 2007). Especially during the decade 1991-2001 the migrant population increased in a way it was reflected at the official population census, when Greece was transformed in a destination country for migrants from the aforementioned countries. The places and the forms of settlement depended on different factors like the capability of housing and labor finding, the purpose of continuing the migration route or not, the social networks developed, the differentiations regarding the country of origin, the gender etc (Emke-Poulopoulou, 2007). Additionally, the many transportation stations located in the center of Athens (both for intercity and urban transportations), the location of cheap hotels and the large public spaces and squares functioning as places of encounters along with the cheaper rentals contributed to migrants' settlement choices in the specific area (Vaiou et al., 2007).

These aforementioned procedures of a "prosthetic urban development" without central planning along with the dynamics of migrants' settlement patterns in Athens have contributed to the smoother and informal integration of the new populations (Arapoglou and Sayas, 2008; Vaiou et al., 2007). As previous researches have shown, the dynamics of migrants' settlement produced low levels of racial discrimination and segregation (Arapoglou et al., 2009), strong social networks and places of co-habitation between them and the locals in many areas of the city. Despite the fact that the integration's bet has to do firstly with the immigrants' legitimacy regime, the urban space's habitation itself could consist an informal mean of integration at the host society (Vaiou et al., 2007). This is usually realized through the migrants' everyday activities, either regarding the labor, the habitation, or even their leisure time. It should be mentioned though that the diversity or "hyper-diversity" that characterizes the city of Athens (Maloutas et al., 2014) does not exclude cases of smaller concentrations based on social and ethnic networks (Emke-Poulopoulou, 2007) or even some crucial inequalities - usually inside the same neighborhoods- that are hardening especially during the crisis (Arapoglou et al., 2009).

Urban crises and urban policies in Athens

Even before the outburst of the crisis, the center of Athens was placed at the core of the so-called "crisis of Athens' center", a narrative portraying central Athens' diversity as the cause of social contradictions (Maloutas et al., 2013). Although at the early 90's the mainstream discourse focused on the general denunciation of the migrants' "invasion", today is clearly characterized by anti-immigrant and racist elements (Kalantzopoulou et al., 2011). Both the institutional policy and the predominant discourse have convicted Athens' center as a ghetto of lawlessness, insecurity and crime (Maloutas et al., 2013). The aforementioned transformation of the discourse about the center of Athens, has already been investigated from scholars in Greece, interrelated at the same time with a broader discussion regarding the urban crises' governmentality. Koutrolikou identifies three "critical moments" regarding the -so called- "crisis of the center of Athens": The Crisis of the centre of Athens I: "Ungovernable country at the mercy of hood-wearers" during the period 2008-2009, The Crisis of the centre of Athens II: The "Centre of terror and fear" during the period 2007-2012 and the Crisis of the centre of Athens III: "humanitarian crisis" and "assistance" programs during the period 2010-2014 (Koutrolikou, 2016). As Arapoglou also notes "fear and omnipotence, war and fleeing, deregulation and reform are linked and are components of neo-liberal politics" (Arapoglou, 2013).

Relying on these narratives and along with the hardening of national and European politics on migration, a significant number of policies has been launched during the last decades regarding the center of Athens. These range from repressive practices in order to eliminate immigrants' presence in the center of Athens, to regenerative urban plans that impose some Creative & Cultural Industries as the solution for "cleaning" the center. Four inter-related tactics regarding the governmentality of urban crises have been identified: The emergency and its permanence, the politics and geographies of fear, the Public and its "enemies" and the (il)legalities defined (Koutrolikou, 2016). Politics of immigrants' persecution from the city center emergerd as dominant through official operations such as Operation "Xenios Zeus" with the declared aim of combating "illegal migration and crime" (Papakonstantis, 2012). The name of the operation refers to the ancient Greek god Zeus' patronage of hospitality and guests but in fact, operation "Xenios Zeus" is anything but hospitable towards foreign migrants and asylum seekers in the Greek capital. A key tactic of the operation was the use of police powers to conduct identity checks to verify the legal status of individuals presumed to be irregular migrants (Human Rights Watch, 2012).

Plus, based on the constructed reality mentioned above, the politics of planning of the recent years regarding the center of Athens were developed and constructed on the arguments about the uninhabited and inapproachable city center, aiming to the return of the "desirable" users and uses. Along with the persecution of the undesirables, the main characteristic of these policies was the proposed measures in order to facilitate "native" residents' return to the area. There are many examples such as the recent program for the "Regeneration of the Commercial Triangle of Athens", the "Return to Athens" program, the "Cooperate in the historical center" program, the "Action Plan for the center of Athens" and the "Integrated Urban Intervention Project".

Our analysis shows that the aforementioned policies and practices are launched both by public and private initiatives and are either formal or informal. Although they proclaim that they involve (or intend to involve) a wide range of actors from the official authorities to "creative groups" of "active" citizens, they are mainly addressed to groups of people that do not live, work or spend their leisure time in the center. They focus on the "return" of the "native" residents in the center through practices that involve only the "desirable" users and uses. They are usually relying on an analysis for the center that considers it as an "empty vessel" or a "non-space", forgetting that its real residents and users are currently residing there. At the same time these policies focus on proposals including CCIs, as a new rapidly growing sector which could promote social and economic development and cohesion, ignoring though that CCIs have already a long tradition in Athens anyway.

Case study: The center of Athens

Despite the fact that social networks and informal activities of everyday life have spread immigrants' settlement across Attica region, the historical center of Athens and especially the area west of Omonia square remains the fundamental pole of attraction for diverse ethnic groups, either as a transit place or as a place of permanent settlement. Although the eastern part of Omonia known as the "Commercial Triangle" historically functioned as a pole of attraction for the Athenians, the west part always attracted the poorest population and the cheaper commercial shops. We focused on "Gerani" area in the west part of Omonia square, which in past was mostly known about the printing services, and during the recent decades as one of the main immigrants' settlements as place of residence, work, ethnic entrepreneurship and leisure time.

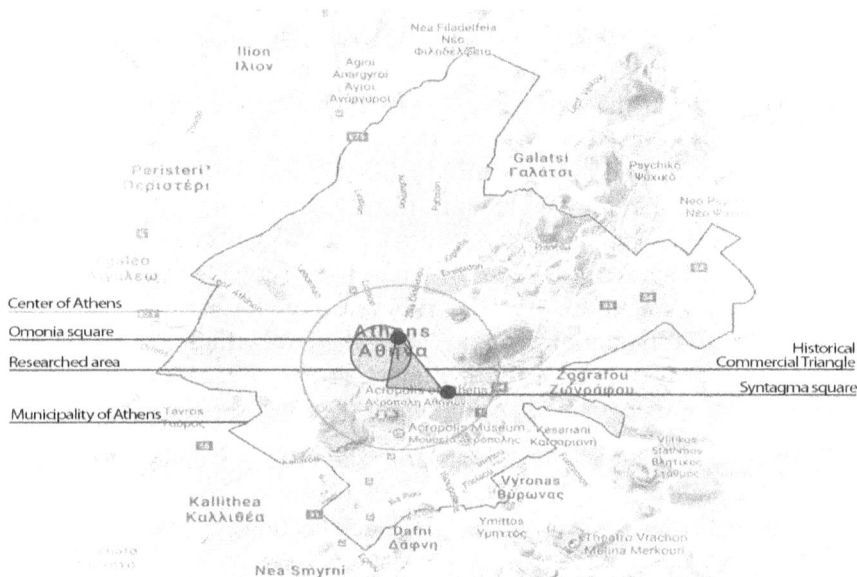

Map 2: The center of Athens and the researched area. Source: Google maps, Authors' editing.

The area around Omonia square was always a place of commerce, services and offices. At the same time, from the decade of nineties until today, it holds the first position -maybe in national level- of ethnic entrepreneurship's concentration, an issue that has already **touched off a large discussion among the academic community (Tsiganou, 2013).** Previous research had identified specific commercial enclaves from the Balkans and the former Soviet Union, while the first Pakistani and Bangladeshi enterprises were also established there, after the first law for migrants' "legalization" at the late 90's (Psimenos, 2004). According to data drawn from the Athens Chamber of Commerce and Industry, in the area are concentrated till now a large number of ethnic businesses from different countries of origin and differentiated products and services. Most of these enterprises, due to the offering services – like call centers or money transfer – are addressed mostly to immigrants. Others, like the food markets or the commercial shops, usually attract Greek clients equally with immigrants, mostly because the local people who frequent this area are of low income (Papatzani, 2015). Qualitative research in the area has highlighted the importance of the specific place for the development of the ethnic entrepreneurship, in a way that dialogues with the theory of mixed embeddedness (Kloosterman and Rath, 2001).

As far as the residence is concerned, the existing reserve is mostly old constructions with significant lack of functioning equipment. According to the informers the area continues attracting immigrant residents, not only due to the low rents, but due to the sense of "security" that anonymity offers along with the opportunity for "useful" encounters regarding basic aspects of everyday life in the new city, especially for those without documents (Papatzani, 2015). The center is also a pole of leisure for immigrants, both for the newcomers and for those residing in Athens for decades. The socio-economic and spatial transformations of the center in the last decades have allowed the development of a variety of hangouts and immigrant communities which until now are benchmarks for a wide range of migrant groups affecting migrants' everyday life, creating also a vital laboratory of the everyday negotiation of diversity. It is where they find opportunities for (usually an informal) job, or for apartments to reside until they are able to continue their journey or find a solution for their legal status in Greece.

Recently, one of the most prestigious print shops of 60's and 70's in Athens has been reopened after 2.5 decades of dereliction. Now, the premises of "Romanzo" are operating as a "Creative Hub", hosting creative professionals or teams as well as a café-bar and an event and exhibition hall. The founder of "Romanzo" has stated several times his vision of "transforming the whole neighborhood beginning with this hub towards the regeneration of the dead zone of Athens, the revival of neighborhoods, the change of city image through the healthy entrepreneurship" or that "we have gave life to a place of Athens that had been written off". The decision of establishing at that certain place, was based on studies that characterized the area as ghetto, or non-place etc.

The qualitative fieldwork conducted for the needs of the current research included in-situ observation, notes, mapping and basically qualitative interviews with local store employees and professionals in the area. The interviewees were Greek owners of commercial stores (e.g. clothing, optical

Figures: Aspects of the urban space and the ethnic entrepreneurship in the area. Source: Street view.

stores etc) and immigrants from Pakistan and Bangladesh employees (in commercial stores with mobile phones, computers and clothes). The conversations developed around 3 major issues: their opinion about the operation of the aforementioned Creative Hub, the transformation of Gerani during the past years and the everyday co-habitation between locals and immigrants in the area.

There were differentiated answers regarding the ethnicity of the interviewees, as well as the years residing in Athens (as regards the immigrants interviewees). The Greeks responded that the previous years with the police intervention as well as the "Romanzo" opening, the tranquility has reappeared: "I wish there were more initiatives like this one" said one of them assuming that it is a way for the limitation of migrants' presence in the area.

On the other hand, immigrants, scared of police and racist attacks, believe that the main factors influenced the neighborhood are the great leaving of their compatriots to other countries of Europe and their initiatives of self-organization against cases of criminality. Despite "Romanzo" seems aware of immigrants' daily life proclaiming that it aims at their integration with many initiatives, the immigrants seem to know about "Romanzo" activities superficially. Some of them consider it as a dance school or a café-bar, however its activities have never caused implications and they are neutral or positive disposed. At the same time, the majority of the migrants interviewees (but some locals too) remarked that their (commercial) activities take place during the day and in early afternoon they return home being afraid of police or racist attacks and as a result they are not coincide with "Romanzo" activities which are mainly taking place after evening.

Discussion, Conclusions

Trying to explore the ways that the recently established Creative Hubs affected the everyday reality in the area, we should firstly mention that the majority of these changing factors (increased police controls, racist practices, economic crisis, applied urban policies etc) began before the opening of "Romanzo" and its impact on immigrants' everyday life at this point is debatable. At the same time "Romanzo" itself attracts a public different that the existing one in the area, functioning as a pole for the broader city of Athens, usually ignoring the established local everyday relations and bonds existing in Gerani.

The simultaneous "resistance" against the pressure of the economic crisis, not only of the creative activities in Greece but also of the ethnic entrepreneurship in the area should be also mentioned. As the conducted interviews have shown, "Migrants' shops in Omonia can withstand the pressure of the crisis because here is our city center" (Migrant from Egypt). It seems that the settlement of both ethnic entrepreneurship and CCI's in the area is a phenomenon historically reproduced that constitutes a significant part of the total historical socio-economic reproduction of the urban space of the center of Athens.

Regarding the policies that are being suggested or applied as a whole, they are usually relying on the "empty vessel" or "non-space" admissions for the city center. Despite the transitional character of the specific place until nowadays, the new subjects "in transition" are not included in an "empty vessel", as the place has been formed by the populations which have already settled for years and have created places of reception, social networks and communities. Besides, these policies go after the "return" of the "desirable" users and uses, a fact that arose from our small research in Gerani. "Romanzo" has already a vision for the regeneration of the whole neighborhood but the main users of the space, the immigrants, have actually no really bonds with what is being drawing for their place of living and working. Both sides seem to follow two parallel ways, but the one part has a plan, an organization and full access to the information for achieving its target, when the other is trying to adapt in a very complicated and continuously transforming environment.

Regarding the above, we argue that till today, the aforementioned policies and practices tend to exist in a parallel way to the everyday reality of the center of Athens, without clear intersecting. At the same time, we assume that they will certainly do have a social, economic and urban impact that is a subject of constant negotiation and conflict. Though, creative professions and ethnic diversity are not by fault contradictory notions. In a progressive direction the existing users (locals and immigrants), uses and activities should be included in the planned policies. Also, creativity and creative professions would add new cultural elements to the historical and traditional Athenian mosaic. The combined historicity and potentials in creativity and ethnic diversity in the center of Athens could be a very ambitious opportunity aiming at multidimensional objectives if driven from the perspective of the "right to the city".

References:

Arapoglou, V., Sayas, J. (2008). Urban development processes and spatial patterns of immigrants' segregation in the wider area of Athens. Geographies, 14, 24-45 (in Greek).

Arapoglou, V., Kavoulakos, K.I., Kandylis, G., Maloutas, T. (2009). The new social geography of Athens: migration, diversity and conflict. Contemporary Issues (Synchrona Themata), 107, 57-66 (in Greek).

Arapoglou, V. (2013). Crisis in the center of Athens: Welfare policies in the neoliberal era. In T. Maloutas, et al. (Eds.), The center of Athens as a political stake (pp. 283-303). Athens: National Centre for Social Research/ Harokopio University (in Greek).

Avdikos, V. (2014). The cultural and creative Industries in Greece. Thessaloniki: Epikentro (in Greek).

Bianchini, F., Parkinson, M. (1993). Cultural policy and urban regeneration: The West European, experience. New York: Manchester University Press.

Creative industries and development: UNCTAD XI High-level Panel on Creative Industries and Development, 13 June 2004, Geneva.

Department for Culture, Media & Sport (DCMS) Creative Industries Economic Estimates January 2015", Retrieved from: https://www.gov.uk/government/uploads/system/uploads/attachment_data/file/394668/ Creative_Industries_Economic_Estimates_-_January_2015.pdf (PDF). Retrieved from:

DCMS, Creative Industries Programme, 2001. Creative industries mapping document, 2001. Dept. for Culture, Media and Sport, London.

DCMS, Creative Industries Task Force, 1998. Creative industries: mapping document, 1998. Creative Industries, Dept. for Culture, Media and Sport, London.

Demertzi, A., Avgerinou-Kolonias, S., Klabatsea, E. (2015). Traditional Creative Professions and Local Know-How as a Regeneration factor of the Historic Centre of Athens, Changing Cities Conference: Spatial, Design, Landscape, 2nd International Conference, Porto Heli, Peloponnese, Greece, Department of Planning and Regional Development, University of Thessaly

Emke-Poulopoulou, I. (2007). The challenge of migration. Athens: Papazisis (in Greek).

Florida, R. (2002). The rise of the creative class. New York: Basic Books.

Garnham, N. (2005). From cultural to creative industries. Int. J. Cult. Policy, 11, 15–29.

Hesmondhalgh, D. (2002). The cultural industries. London: SAGE.

Human Rights Watch. (2012). Hate on the streets. Xenophobic violence in Greece. Retrieved from: https://www.hrw.org/sites/default/files/reports/greece0712gr_ForUpload_1.pdf

Kalantzopoulou, M., Koutrolikou, P., Polihroniadi, K. (2011). The dominant discourse about the city-centre of Athens. Retrieved from: https://encounterathens.files.wordpress.com/2011/05/encounter-logos-15052011.pdf (in Greek).

KEA European Affairs, European Commission, Directorate-General for Education and Culture, Turun Kauppakorkeakoulu, MKW Wirtschaftsforschungsgesellschaft (München). (2006). The economy of culture in Europe: a study prepared for the European Commission (Directorate-General for Education and Culture), Brussels: EC: KEA European Affairs.

Kloosterman, R., Van der Leun, J. and Rath, J. (1999). Mixed Embeddedness: (In)formal Economic Activities and Immigrant Business in the Netherlands. International Journal of Urban and Regional Research, 23(2), 253–267.

Koutrolikou, P., and Siatitsa, D. (2011). The Construction of a 'Public' Discourse for Athens Centre: Media, Migrants and Inner-city Regeneration. In International RC21 Conference. Amsterdam.

Koutrolikou, P. (2016). Governmentalities of Urban Crises in Inner-city Athens, Greece. Antipode, 48(1), 172–192.

Landry, C. (2000). The creative city: a toolkit for urban innovators. London: Earthscan Publications.

Lefevre, H. (1968). Le Droit à la ville. Paris: Anthropos.

Leontidou, L. (1990). The Mediterranean city in transition: social change and urban development. Cambridge: Cambridge University Press.

Maloutas, T., Karadimitriou N. (2001). Vertical social differentiation in Athens: Alternative or complement to community segregation?. International Journal of Urban and Regional Research, 25, 699-716.

Maloutas, T. (2013). The degradation of the center of Athens and the choices of residential area from the high and middle strata. In T. Maloutas, et al. (Eds.), The center of Athens as a political stake (pp. 29-51). Athens: National Centre for Social Research/ Harokopio University (in Greek).

Maloutas, T., Kandylis, G., Petrou, M., Souliotis, N. (2013). Introduction: Resetting the issue of central Athens on the daily agenda. In T. Maloutas, et al. (Eds.), The center of Athens as a political stake (pp. 11-25). Athens: National Centre for Social Research/ Harokopio University (in Greek).

Maloutas, T., Souliotis, n., Alexandri, g., Kandylis, G., Petrou, M. (2014). Urban policies on Diversity in Athens (Work package 4: Assessment of Urban Policies, Divercities: Governing Urban Diversity). Retrieved from Divercities website: https://www.urbandivercities.eu/wp-content/uploads/2013/05/Urban-policies-on-Diversity-in-Athens.pdf

Papakonstantis, M. (2012). Operation Xenios Zeus and illegal immigrants. Immigration's Topics EMMEDIA, 2(4), 3-4 (in Greek).

Papatzani, E. (2015). Negotiations of boundaries and cohabitation terms in the center of Athens, Geographies, 25, 136-140 (in Greek).

Psimmenos, I. (2004). Migration from the Balkans. Social exclusion in Athens, Athens: Papazisis (in Greek).

Scott, A. (2006). Creative cities: Conceptual issues and policy questions. Journal of Urban Affairs, 28(1), 1-17.

Souliotis, N. (2013). Cultural economy, sovereign debt crisis and the importance of local contexts: The case of Athens. Cities, 33, 61 – 68.

Tsiganou, I. (2013). Entrepreneurship, "dangers" and competition in the historic center of Athens: the construction of a research object. In T. Maloutas, et al. (Eds.), The center of Athens as a political stake (pp. 145-167). Athens: National Centre for Social Research/ Harokopio University (in Greek).

Vaiou, D. ed. (2007). Intersecting Patterns of Everyday Life and Socio-spatial Transformations in the City. Migrant and Local Women in the Neighborhoods of Athens. Athens: L-Press/ NTUA (National Technical University of Athens) (in Greek).

World Intellectual Property Organizations (WIPO) (2003). Guide on surveying the economic contribution of the copyrights based industries. Geneva: WIPO

Chapter 17. The Role of Religious Groups on the Daily Religious Lives of European Turks

Yakup Çoştu*, Feyza Ceyhan Çoştu

Introduction

European Turks have experienced a tough adaptation process in their host countries because of the coming back to their homeland possibility has considerably decreased. Although acquiring citizenship in the host countries has several achievements legally, they came across problems such as a crisis of religious and national identity, conflicts of generations and cultures, and alienation. Turkish immigrants have established a number of community organizations and solidarity networks within the framework of the legal rights granted to them by the host country, primarily to provide services in various areas. One of the organizations that has been founded by European Turks are mostly mosque based organizations.[1] The most important part of these organizations founded especially by Turkish immigrants who are close or sympathisers to religious groups and movements in Turkey or connected with them. These organizations were very similar to religious groups and movement in Turkey and in time they have become institutive for fulfilling differentiated demands of immigrant communities. Because of their active role in the everyday religious life of European Turks analysing those civil religious organizations and the religious and cultural life around it is so valuable.

In this paper, from the beginning of the migration until today, Turkey-connected religious groups and communities' influence on immigrants' daily religious life will be discussed with a macro-sociological point of view. Besides, the influences and reflections of their religious discourse and practice in their daily religious life will also be analysed.

Turkish Immigrants in Europe and its Religious Structure

Western European countries, soon after the Second World War focused on underdeveloped countries for supplying their lack of labour force in a development process. They have tried to supply their needs signing bilateral agreements. Within this frame, those countries focused on Turkey, and in 1961 starting with Germany bilateral labour work agreement series moved

---

* Dr. Yakup Çoştu is Associate Professor in Sociology of Religion Department, Faculty of Divinity Hitit University, Çorum, Turkey. E-mail: yakupcostu@hitit.edu.tr
[1] See further informations: for Germany see. Perşembe, 2005; Altıntaş, 2008; Yurdakul, 2009; Yükleyen & Yurdakul, 2011; Adıgüzel, 2011. For Austria see. Kroissenbrunner, 2003. For France see. Arabacı, 1997. For Belgium see. Yanaşmayan 2010. For Netherland see. Hatunoğlu 2002; Hıdır, 2012. For Denmark see. Jorgensen 2010; Özmen, 2012, For Sweden see. Korkmaz, 2011; For Norway see. Rogstad, 2009; For Britain see. Çoştu, 2013.

on to Austria, Belgium, Holland in 1964, France in 1965, Sweden in 1967, Switzerland in 1969 and Denmark in 1970. (Abadan-Unat, 2006). The migration process has started from Turkey to Europe with these bilateral agreements under the name of "temporary workers". The purpose of the process of migration was coming back to their homeland at first, however in time it has become permanent due to various reasons such as waves of chain migration (family unification, marriage, etc.), educational and economic opportunities, refuge, the formation of the second and third generations, acquiring citizenship, burying their dead in a cemetery assigned for them in the host countries.

At the present time, Turkish immigrants have become a kind of a demographic power that cannot be ignored in the economic, social, cultural and political life of the European countries. According to the statement of the Turkish Ministry of Foreign Affairs, about 5.5 million Turkish people live abroad and 4.6 million have chosen to settle in Western European countries and the rest of them have settled in North America, Asia, the Middle East and Australia.[2] By means of the ongoing migration process and rising generations in immigrant countries, that number has been growing day by day.

Referring the Turks that migrated to European countries as "temporary workers" in 1960, it is obvious that neither the Turks nor the receiving countries had any policy about migration with the thought that they would "go back to their homeland". Since the late 1970s, the receiving countries' point of view has changed in the way that Turks wouldn't be temporary but permanent. So they developed some strategies and policies such as social security laws, repentance laws for illegal or tourist-worker, family reunification laws, foreigner laws etc. The purpose of these new laws was to take the migration wave under control and supporting immigrant integration in Europe. Turkey as an emigration country, during those days, started to take some serious steps about preventing its own citizens from assimilation and helping them to integrate successfully. Among those in the late 1970s Ramadan and Eid Al-adha celebrations, The Presidency of Religious Affairs' practises such as sending "seasonal religious official" to the countries mostly populated by Turkish temporary workers could be counted (DIB, General Directorate of External Relations, 2012).

The Presidency of Religious Affairs (DIB) is an official institution providing public service on religious affairs in Turkey. As an official and constitutional institution, DIB tries to meet societal needs and requirements through internal and external networks providing services. The external remit of DIB

---

[2] See. http://www.mfa.gov.tr/yurtdisinda-yasayan-turkler_.tr.mfa (Accessed date: 30.03.2017).

is organized in countries where Turkish citizens live, and are served by the Counsellors of Religious Services connected to the Turkish Embassies. There are also semi-official religious foundations in relation to these Offices under the name of "Turkish Religious Foundations". In the early 1980s, DIB had started the practice of sending religious officials (i.e. Imams) whose salaries are paid by the Turkish government, abroad to serve at mosques and masjids. Added to this, in the present period and in some Western European countries, such as Germany, Austria, Belgium, Denmark, France, Netherlands, England, Sweden, Switzerland, there are Turkish Religious Foundations and about 1500 mosque unions related to them (see. Çoştu & Ceyhan Çoştu, 2015).

Turkish immigrants' first attempts to be organized in Europe came about in the middle of the 1960s and the very beginning of the 1970s, during those years, the religious life of Turkish immigrants had no sign of well-structured organization but some personal efforts (Abadan-Unat ,2006). The religious life of the first generations was limited just practising some basic rituals. For that purpose, small flats were rent or purchased. When there was no possibility of returning to their homelands, more than that the second and the third generation raised there over time so those small places because insufficient. Besides, expectations increased and became different so they opened a way for more organized and institutional structure (Küçükcan 1999).

During the migration process, from the early 1960s to the middle of the 1980s, there were no official religious services for Turkish immigrants living in Europe. For 20 years or there about, those people had been destined to be on their own for that period of time. Within that period also religious services had been carried out mostly with the hand of some religious groups and communities in Turkey. Those activities, on one hand, had an important mission with respect to protecting and carrying out immigrant Turks' religious and cultural existence, however, on the other hand, the religious groups and communities' different religious discourses, ideological and politic activities made it so difficult to live in unity but rather deepened the competition and disintegration.

After the last 20 years, from the middle of the 1980s, the Presidency of Religious Affairs became organized in European countries, embraced immigrant citizens of Turkey and carried out religious services via the government. That also means that fulfilling unity, eliminating differences and disagreements in the religious field (see. Çoştu, 2013).

Since the middle of 1970, the first religious organizations started to be founded, and their numbers have been increasing day by day. The community expanded the religious services changing the places they have hired or purchased into mosques or masjids. Those places were not there just for religious practises but also for the educational, social and cultural activities and they have been made into more institutionalized foundation and organizations in time. At the present day, most of the religious-based foundations and organizations founded by Turks somehow are connected with a specific mosque.

The Role of Religious Groups in the Lives of European Turks

When Turkish immigrants living in various European countries started to lose hope on returning to their mainland and realised that they were there to stay, the necessity of building their own identity and belonging became obvious. The civic organisations they built differentiates in accordance with the ethnic, cultural, ideological and political discourse of each subgroup which constitutes the society. Although there is no certain information on the number of civic organisations which belong to Turkish communities living in Europe, it can be observed that these organisations are mainly in the areas/cities heavily populated by immigrant groups.

During the formation process of religious organizations, or in other words religious support networks; immigration reasons, settlement patterns and identity focuses of subgroups, and political, ideological and religious situation of Turkey had a defining role (Küçükcan, 1999; Perşembe, 2005; Abadan-Unat, 2006; Sirkeci et all., 2016). Social priority differences of immigrants and their religious identity focuses influenced the formation of the mentioned organisations. Furthermore, the fact that there is no one type of culture, political focus, and religious practice in Turkey had also played a significant role in their formation.

Most of the organisations and foundations that have religious services for Turks living in Europe reminds disunity and local discourses of religious groups, communities, and movements in Turkey. Discourses and political standpoints of these organisations mainly follow the agenda determined in Turkey, and shape their envisagement for the future as well as their envisions of the past according to these ideals (Küçükcan, 2004: Çelik, 2008).

Using a macro approach, discourses of religious organisations built by Turkish immigrants living in Europe can be categorised under four main titles:

1. Organisations affiliated with Sufi movements in Turkey and Northern Cypriot: Organisations or associations founded by followers or admirers of Mahmut Ustaosmanoglu/Ismail Ağa Movement, Muhammed Reşit Erol/Menzil, Sheikh Nazım Kibrisi are in this category.

2. Organisations affiliated with religious movements in Turkey: Organisations and associations in this category were built by immigrants who were sympathisers of religious groups such as Suleyman Hilmi Tunahan/Suleymancı, Nur Movement and their subgroups. The ones founded by immigrants who had Alevite discourse are also in this category.

3. Organisations affiliated with religious-political movements in Turkey: Organisations founded by immigrants who are members or sympathisers of Milli Görüş, Alperen Ocakları and Nationalist/Idealist movement, which have both religious and political discourses, are in this category.

4. Semi-official religious organisations affiliated with official religious discourse in Turkey: Turkish Religious Foundations *(Diyanet)* which carry out their activities in conjunction with Religious Services Consultancy under The Embassy of the Turkish Republic in European Countries are in this category.

While this variation in religious lives of European Turks can be considered an affluence, at the same time it can cause serious problems due to the discriminative feature of the differences between religious groups.

Religious places structured under various associations and foundations that belong to Turks in Europe perform many religious and social functions. Service areas of these structures vary due to some religious and social factors. The main reasons of these variations can be explained as below:

It was mentioned that these associations or foundations built by followers or sympathisers of religious groups, community and movements exist in Turkey, due to the differentiation in religious, political and ideological discourses of these groups, which aim to protect their specific community structure, the groups can have rivalry and sometimes even tension among each other. Intellectual, social and economic-based these tensions can cause disintegration among immigrant communities, as well as can have a role in damaging the group unity and socio-cultural integrity.

Each passing day the number of mosque/masjid/ dervish lodge/djemevi centered organisations that belong to Turks in Europe is increasing. This increase brings a rivalry on religious services. This rivalry can result in a race towards domination on religion. In order to attract immigrants, the religious structures; first, diversify their service areas, and thus aim to increase the number of their members, and second, make significant efforts to open new religious places, and thus aim to strengthen the institutional structure.

The religiosity understanding of these organisations can sometimes cause problems, which under normal circumstances could be seen as ordinary issues in daily life, but for the citizens living overseas, they can be a significant issue. For example, this situation can be observed in calculations of the daily prayer schedules and the times of pre-dawn and fast-breaking meals during Ramadan (see. Perşembe, 2005). Some organisations serving Turkish immigrants follow different time schedules for daily prayers, pre-dawn and fast-breaking meal times. It is known that there are significant differences between the times set by these schedules (see. Çoştu, 2013). These types of differences in religious practices among immigrant communities from time to time can have an impairing role on protection and maintenance of religious and social harmony, and unity.

Another reason for differentiation in the service areas of religious associations and foundations is related to their different understanding of 'religious identity'. For example, the way that they describe religious identity based on some approaches such as conservatism, nationalism, modernity, ethnic differences and political opinion gives these religious support networks a heterogeneous structure. Every group shapes their religious attitude and approach in accordance with the criteria they base their religious identity, hence gravitates towards different practice areas, and provides their services accordingly.

Additionally, the service areas of religious groups and movements founded in places heavily populated by Turkish immigrants, and the ones founded in places that Turkish population are scarce can also vary. Religious organisations from places heavily populated by Turkish, as a result of the supply and demand factor, and in order to strengthen their institutional structure, provide services in various areas. Besides the differentiation within the context of population density, in the places which have a considerable Turkish population a different level of segregation can be observed. Various religious groups can build separate mosques in very close distances and head towards new service areas in order to attract Turkish and Muslim populations living around the mosque.

Another reason for service area differentiation of these organisations is related to the professional competency, education status, age, and language proficiency of the people who provide religious and cultural services. As a matter of fact, services provided by a religious official who has a high education degree have a professional competency, loves his/her profession and has a good grasp of the language, and by someone who does not have these qualities cannot be the same.

Conclusion

In European countries, there are many organisations which provide religious and cultural services, aimed at their own immigrant communities as well as other Muslim communities, through religious places (mosque, masjid, derwish lodge, djemev etc.) established by Turkish immigrants living there. These organisations, considering the expectations of their audiences, incline towards different service areas in the establishments they have built in accordance with their identity, ideological standpoint, and religious understanding. As a result, religious places of European Turks, connected with other organisations, differ from their roles given in the mainland and turn into places that have social, cultural and educational activities alongside religious ones. In these places knowledge is being shared, social networks are being established, and immigrants find a shelter for themselves.

Most of the associations and foundations which predominantly provide religious services to Turks in Europe operate in correlation with religious groups and communities in Turkey. The places these civic structures provide religious services in, and the religious experiences developed within have a heterogeneous nature. This situation, on one hand, can have a negative effect on the adaptation period and can result in conflicts and rivalry in between groups. On the other hand, they act as social solidarity networks and should be seen as institutionalised products of a struggle to protect and to maintain religious and national identities in a strange land.

Every religious organisation that belongs to the Turks is structured around some religious place/s (mosque, derwish lodge, djemevi) and have a distinctive community formation. Each one has a specific religious appearance from the content of their religious discourse to their activities. Within the legal borders of the host countries they conduct religious, cultural and educational activities in order to maintain their integrity and to protect from cultural disintegration.

The activities carried out and aimed for immigrants make a significant contribution to the protection of their religious and national identities, increasing their solidarity and helping them to integrate the countries they reside. Besides, these places have activities to minimise the possible effects of open or hidden assimilation which second and third generations encounter, therefore seen as natural and matchless shelters by sensitive families.

It is observed that the immigrants who stay close or participate in activities of these religious organisations maintain their cultural and religious identities. The ones who have no relations with these places or prefer a secular lifestyle seem to lose their religious identities and become assimilated linguistically and culturally.

References

ABADAN-UNAT, Nermin. (2006). Bitmeyen Göç Konuk İşçilikten Ulus-Ötesi Yurttaşlığa, [From Guest Worker to Transnational Citizen]. İstanbul: İstanbul Bilgi Üniversitesi Yayınları. (Turkish).

ADIGÜZEL, Yusuf. (2011). Yeni Vatanda Dini İdeolojik Yapılanma Almanya'daki Türk Kuruluşları, [Religious and Ideological Situations in the New Homeland; Turkish Organizations in Germany]. İstanbul: Şehir Yayınları. (Turkish).

ALTINTAŞ, İsmail. (2008). Dış-Göç ve Din; Almanya'daki Türklerin Dini Hayatına İlişkin Sosyolojik Bir Çözümleme, [External-Migration and Religion; A Sociological Analysis on the Religious Life of Turks in Germany]. İstanbul: Dem Yayınları. (Turkish).

ARABACI, Fazlı. (1997). "Fransa'da Müslüman Toplumun Örgütlenmesi ve Türk İslam Kimliğini Korumada Cami ve derneklerin Fonksiyonu" [The Organization of Muslim Society in France and the Function of Mosques in the Protection of Turkish Islamic Identity]. Diyanet İlmi Dergi, Cilt: 33, Sayı: 3, ss. 87-106. (Turkish).

ÇELİK, Celaleddin. (2008). "Almanya'da Türkler: Sürekli Yabancılık, Kültürel Çatışma ve Din", [Turks in Germany: Continuous Foreignness, Cultural Conflict and Religious]. Milel ve Nihal, cilt: 5, sayı: 3, ss. 105-142. (Turkish).

ÇOŞTU, Yakup. (2013). İngiltere'deki Tük-Müslüman Göçmenler; Dini Organizasyonlar, [Turkish Muslim Immigrants in the UK; Religious Organizations]. Çorum: Lider Matbaası. (in Turkish).

ÇOŞTU, Yakup & Feyza CEYHAN ÇOŞTU, An Investigation on the Turkish Religious Foundation of the UK (Diyanet)", *Turkish Migration, Identity and Integration*, Ed. İ. Sirkeci, B. D. Şeker, and A. Çağlar, Transnational Press London, London, 2015. pp. 149-157.

DIB, General Directorate of External Relations, 2012

HATUNOĞLU, Bedri Yavuz. (2002). Hollanda'da Türk Sivil Örgütlenmesi ve Türkevi Örneği, [Turkish Non-Governmental Organizations in the Netherlands and the Case of Turkish House]. (Doktora Tezi), Sakarya: Sosyal Bililer Enstitüsü, Sosyoloji anabilim Dalı, Sakarya Üniversitesi. (Turkish).

HIDIR, Özcan. (2012). Hollanda'daki Türkler; Kurumlar, Başarılar, Sorunlar ve Geleceğe Yönelik Perspektifler, [Turks in Holland; Institutions, Achievements, Problems and Future Perspectives]. Rotterdam: IUR Press. (Turkish).

JORGENSEN, Martin Bak. (2010). "Turks in Denmark: Patterns of Incorporation and Collective Organizing Processes", Insight Turkey, Vol. 12, No. 1, ss. 163-183.

KORKMAZ, Arif. (2011). Göç ve Din; İsveç'teki Kululular Örneği, [Migration and Religion; The Case of Kulu in Sweden]. Konya: Çizgi Kitabevi. (Turkish).

KROISSENBRUNNER, Sabine. (2003). "Islam and Muslim Immigrants in Austria: socio-Political Networks and Muslim Leadership of Turkish Immigrants", Immigrants & Minorities, Vol. 22, No: 2&3, ss. 188-207.

KÜÇÜKCAN, Talip. (1999). Politics of Ethnicity, Identity and Religion Turkish Muslims in Britain, Aldershot: Ashgate.

KÜÇÜKCAN, Talip. (2004). "The Making of Turkish-Muslim Diaspora in Britain: Religious Collective Identity in a Multicultural Public Sphere", Journal of Muslim Minority Affairs, Vol. 24, No. 2, ss. 243-258.

ÖZMEN, Nebile (2012). Çokkültürlü Toplumda Sosyal Entegrasyon ve Din, [Social Integration and Religion in Multicultural Society]. İstanbul: Çamlıca Yayınları. (Turkish).

PERŞEMBE, Erkan. (2005). Almanya'da Türk Kimliği Din ve Entegrasyon, [Turkish Identity in Germany; Religion and Integration], Ankara: Araştırma Yayınları. (Turkish).

ROGSTAD, Jon. (2009). "Towards a Success Story? Turkish Immigrant Organizations in Norway", Turkish Studies, Vol. 10, No. 2, ss. 277-294.

SİRKECİ, İbrahim, Tuncay BİLECEN, Yakup ÇOŞTU, et al, *Little Turkey in Great Britain,* Transnational Press London, London, 2016.

TRIANDAFYLLIDOU, Anna. (2010). "Muslims in 21 st Century Europe", Muslims in 21 st Century Europe Structural and Cultural Perspectives, Ed. A. Triandafyllidou, New York: Routledge, ss. 1-26.

YANAŞMAYAN, Zeynep. (2010). "Role of Turkish Islamic Organizations in Belgium: The Strategies of Diyanet and Milli Görüş", Insight Turkey, Vol. 12, No. 1, ss. 139-161

YURDAKUL, Gökçe. (2009). From Guest Workers into Muslims: the Transformation of Turkish Immigrant Associations in Germany, Newcastle upon Tyne: Cambridge Scholars Publishing.

YÜKLEYEN, Ahmet & Gökçe YURDAKUL. (2011). "Islamic Activism and Immigrant integration: Turkish Organizations in Germany", Immigrants 6 Minorities, Vol. 29, No. 1, ss. 64-85.

http://www.mfa.gov.tr/yurtdisinda-yasayan-turkler_.tr.mfa (Accessed date: 30.03.2017)

Chapter 18. The Role of Loneliness in the Process of Addiction Development among FSU Immigrant Drug Users in Israel

Liat Yakhnich[1]

Abstract

This paper aims to illustrate the trajectories of development of drug addiction among FSU immigrants, and to stress immigrant users' sense of loneliness as the core issue that characterizes these trajectories. The paper is based on a qualitative phenomenological study that explored the characteristics of drug abuse among FSU immigrant drug addicts in Israel. The information was gathered by interviewing 19 Russian-speaking recovering addict counselors employed in Israeli addiction treatment centers. The interview analysis yielded two main trajectories of addiction development among FSU immigrants. The most common one is characteristic of older users who immigrate with already-existing drug problems which almost always become aggravated after immigration. The second trajectory is typical of younger users who immigrate in late childhood and early adolescence, and start using drugs after immigration (and usually in proximity to it). The core issue that characterizes both trajectories is the immigrant users' sense of loneliness. Implications for prevention and treatment based on the interviewees' reflections, as well as on extant literature, are discussed.

Keywords: Immigration, drug abuse, immigrant youth

Background

Immigrants from the former Soviet Union (FSU) account for approximately 13% of the Israeli population and comparatively high rate of drug abuse, with about 25-50% of the Israeli treatment services' patients having FSU origins. This high incidence of drug dependence may be mainly attributed to high rates of substance abuse in immigrants' countries of origin and to the stress associated with immigration.

Immigration is a potentially stressful and challenging experience that involves coping with multiple sources of distress, e.g. language and cultural barriers; family stress; social exclusion and marginalization. Separated from their families and friends, some immigrants cope with these hardships by turning to alcohol and drugs. Social exclusion, loss of social relations and acculturation-related challenges may enhance immigrants' sense of loneliness, that is often closely related to emotional problems and drug abuse.

The study

The information for this study was gathered by interviewing 19 male Russian-speaking recovering addict counselors employed in Israeli addiction treatment centers. Their ages ranged from 29-52 years, with the majority aged 33–45. All had immigrated from the FSU (8 from Ukraine, 5 from Russia, 3 from Caucasus, and 3 from Belarus, Kazahstan and Moldova, respectively) during 1991–2001. Their ages at immigration ranged from 8–37 years. The duration

---

[1] PhD, Beit Berl College, Israel. Email: liatyakhnich@gmail.com

of their substance abuse ranged from 4 to 27 years. All but 6 had used drugs prior to immigration, their abstinence period ranged from 4 to 16 years. All had been working in treatment facilities for 2–13 years. The participants were recruited at their work places.

During the data analysis "significant statements" were identified, using a "horizontalization" process (Moustakas, 1994). These statements were grouped into clusters of meaning, that were reorganized in the process of identifying the central themes that emerged from the interviews (Creswell, 2007). After completing the data analysis, eight of the participants were contacted and asked to review the results, a process referred to by Lincoln and Guba (1985) as "member checks."

Findings

The interview analysis yielded two main trajectories of addiction development among FSU immigrants. The most common one is characteristic of older users who immigrate with already- existing drug problems which almost always become aggravated after immigration (13 participants). The second trajectory is typical of younger users who immigrate in late childhood and early adolescence, and start using drugs after immigration (and usually in proximity to it) (6 participants). The core issue that characterizes both trajectories is the immigrant users' sense of loneliness. Older and younger immigrant drug users' experiences of loneliness have certain common features as well as substantial differences.

Older Users

Nine participants used to consume "hard" drugs in the FSU and came to Israel already addicted. Their age at immigration ranged between 18 and 37, with the majority immigrating in their early twenties. Four participants in this group didn't use "hard" drugs prior to immigration, but had an experience with "soft" drugs, alcohol, or mild criminal behavior. After their immigration, their drug abuse deteriorated rapidly and severely. It appears that older users often perceive immigration as a chance to change their lives. Sometimes the user's family initiates the immigration in a desperate attempt to save their child: "I was sure that if I leave to another country this will stop. It was a solution" (Roman); "My parents believed that if I stayed there (in the FSU) I would die. They tried to save me" (Pavel).

However, very soon after their arrival, they sink back into abuse and find solace in the immigrant users' social network: "The salvation doesn't come just because you move" (Pavel); "The day we arrived my cousin introduced me to Russian guys that smoked and cooked (prepared drugs)" (Sasha); "It was easy. You feel it, you see it in people's eyes, you pick it up like a radar…in a few days I had drugs" (Evgeny).

Not only is the drug problem unsolved with immigration, it usually deteriorates rapidly due to high accessibility and great variety of drugs in Israel, as well as to less strict law enforcement. Moreover, other immigration-related variables are reported as closely connected to this process.

Immigration stress

Stress associated with immigration is perceived as a crucial factor that aggravates the addiction. Immigration exposes the user to new, unfamiliar challenges. "There, many users had some degree of control over the abuse. Here it's different – there is a lot of stress in immigration – money, work, relationships. Some manage to cope with it, but others don't. This stress intensifies the deterioration" (Vladimir). The pattern of self-medicating that had already been established before immigration is brought into play and is perceived by the user as an escape route from the difficulties of the new life: "Immigration brought new things with it. I had to rent an apartment, to find work, to study. And I struggled with the addiction. These difficulties crushed me. I had no coping habits, no mechanisms of managing myself, no decision-making abilities, nothing. The only thing that was clear and stable in my life was the drugs".

Lack of familial support

Family members are usually stressed and don't support the user the way they did before immigration, and in some cases, are even pushed away and alienated by drug use: "Your parents are trying to cope with immigration, it's hard for them to get along, and they work hard for peanuts. So when they find out you're stealing from them they say 'goodbye'. In Russia they wouldn't do it, but here they understand there is no choice" (Dima).

Loneliness and isolation

A crucial factor in the fall-off process is the immigrant user's sense of loneliness: "When you are absolutely alone, don't understand people and they don't understand you, you realize you are just a little bolt. When I realized that, I wanted to commit suicide, but I couldn't do it. So I kept using more and more, I just sank deeper and deeper and it didn't matter anymore" (Dima).

The peer group of other immigrant users actually alleviates this sense of loneliness: "The loneliness was awful. There was a terrible lack of human relationships. I was looking for belonging – for acceptance, human warmth, and intimacy. I was looking for it in this terrible place – I was surrounded by junkies, but it gave me some momentary illusion of belonging" (Semyon).

Many immigrant users feel isolated and alienated in the new Israeli milieu and at the same time they don't really try to integrate in it: "I didn't want to come here in the first place. I didn't connect to the Israelis, didn't speak Hebrew. I didn't even accept the weather – it was too hot. I was negative about everything" (Nikolay). Lack of familial support and social isolation increase users' distress and the sense of loneliness, thus leading them toward relapse and aggravated drug abuse.

Younger Users

The trajectory of loneliness and drug-taking develops somewhat differently among younger users. 6 participants immigrated to Israel during childhood and early adolescence (8-15) with no prior experience of substance use or criminal behavior. They started using drugs within two years on average after immigration. All attribute the onset of abuse at least partially to immigration: "My addiction has its roots in my childhood; I would probably have ended like this anyway. But immigration definitely contributed its share and accelerated the process" (Igor).

Peer rejection

The onset of drug abuse in this population is mainly attributed to the social exclusion, lack of belonging and a sense of inferiority: "It was a very difficult phase in my life. I was the only immigrant in my class. They had their language, their humor. They were laughing at me. I felt different and deficient" (Igor). Some immigrant youngsters experience overt hostility that results in their sense of disappointment and alienation: "'Smelly Russian'… I don't want to be smelly, I'm not smelly. I came to my homeland as I was promised, as I fantasized… and they call me "smelly." It was very hard for me, with all my expectations of this country" (Mark).

The young immigrants' feelings of inferiority and alienation often result in violent behavior that serves to restore their social status: "I got into fights. This was my way to prove myself, to show them they shouldn't mess with me" (Igor). Grouping with other immigrant youth and taking part in group violence also provide immigrant teens with a sense of control and power: "When more Russian children came to the school there was an immediate click. Suddenly we became a force; we had the power, like some mini-mafia. This brought us respect" (Garik). Beyond violence, some immigrant groups promote other antisocial behaviors, such as shoplifting, drinking, drug use.

Ineffective adult figures

Often the adults do not provide the needed assistance and support. The participants report their teachers and other educational staff being highly ineffective in dealing with their stress. In some cases the system totally ignores the immigrant students' needs, thus making them feel transparent: "I hardly attended school for 4 years. There was a period I didn't come to school for 4 months! No one asked why! They just didn't want to deal with me. And when

I was finally caught for stealing, they just expelled me… I just needed someone to see me, just to be there for me" (Tolik). Some teachers fail to realize the stress of the immigrant students and adopt a negative attitude toward them: "In the beginning the teachers tried to be patient, but soon I became the 'problematic Russian.' They didn't try to find out what was really happening, so I always was the guilty one. I became the scapegoat and soon I felt comfortable in this role" (Grigori).

Insufficient parental involvement

Many immigrant parents are not available and fail to provide their children with the support they need. Garik describes the situation in which he was physically assaulted at school: "They (the parents) asked me how was it at school. I said: 'OK. My nose is broken'. They didn't know what to do, they didn't try to defend me." Immigrant parents have to contend with the challenges of immigration and invest most of their time and energy in work which don't leave them enough space for being available to their children: "My parents were busy with surviving. In Russia they protected me; here I was alone trying to find my way outside where I was exposed to all kind of things, and my instincts took over… These kids don't intentionally search for drugs; they search for attention. Some, like me, find drugs" (Grigori).

Low parental involvement deepens the sense of loneliness of some immigrant children who in any case feel rejected and unwanted by their peers and teachers: "I had parents but they were not there. I woke up in the morning, went to school, came back, and ate – all alone. They came in the evening, tired; I had no one to talk to" (Mark).

Drug abuse as a way of dealing with loneliness

Social rejection, parental unavailability and ineffective school staff involvement leave some immigrant children alone in coping with the hardships of immigration and adolescence. These children manage by seeking inclusion and attachment to youngsters in a similar situation: "These kids feel alone and connect to others who share this loneliness. The abuse has a social nature – they drink *together*, use drugs *together*, and they believe it strengthens their bonds" (Roman). Thus, immigrant peer groups serve as a solution to loneliness and social exclusion. In many cases these groups turn to antisocial activities that provide their members with a sense of superiority and power, along with substance abuse that serves as a bonding facilitator and a way of fleeing difficult emotional states: "They can't talk about what they feel, so they need a substitute, and alcohol and drugs do the work" (Roman).

Conclusions

Apparently, the first trajectory of addiction development among FSU immigrants has its roots in earlier, pre-immigration stages of users' lives. It is largely shaped by such experiences as transition to other society characterized by distinct drug-related reality and policy, coping with adaptation difficulties, loss of familial and social support networks and sense of loneliness and isolation. The second trajectory is set in motion after the immigration by immigrant youth's experience of peer rejection, inability of educational staff and parents to meet their needs, and, like in the first trajectory, sense of loneliness.

It appears that sense of loneliness and drug abuse create a snowball effect in both younger and older immigrant user populations. The initial sense of loneliness that originates in the immigration experience, whether due to unfulfilled expectations, immigration stress, and low family support among older addicts, or peer rejection and adult figures' inadequacy among younger users prompts drug-taking as a way of self-medicating and enhancing a sense of belonging. However, this same behavior further magnifies the sense of loneliness by undermining the user's hope for recovery, heightening social withdrawal, and escalating coercive social interactions. Notably, the highly negative experiences described by the participants in the study may be largely characteristic of immigrant youth already at risk for delinquency and drug abuse. Other immigrant youngsters, who also have to contend with multiple difficulties during their adaptation may experience them at a more moderate level due to a broader base of social support or personal factors that promote their resiliency.

The study has a number of implications. In particular, the findings emphasize the importance of loneliness and marginalization in the deterioration of young immigrants. Preventive practices should involve alleviating the sense of loneliness by education toward greater multicultural awareness and acceptance at school could help immigrant adolescents feel a greater sense of belonging, promoting positive social interactions between young immigrants and their local peers, encouraging social bonding among the young immigrants through positive and constructive activities (e.g. youth movements, volunteering, evening schools), and promoting access to such protective factors as familial and community support. Empowering immigrant families appears as a crucial issue in preventing the initiation of abuse and its exacerbation among young immigrants, along with promoting the availability and sensitivity of the school staff toward immigrant adolescents who suffer from social rejection. Special effort should be made in locating youngsters already involved in moderate anti-social activities or showing a predisposition for violent behavior. Special emphasis should be placed on assisting young adults, who, in contrast to adolescents, are not present in educational settings, and whose difficulties may remain unnoticed. Reaching this population requires promoting greater awareness of drug abuse issue among physicians, teachers at Hebrew classes ("Ulpans"), social workers and other professionals who are involved in immigrants' absorption.

References

Creswell, J. W. (2007). Qualitative inquiry and research design: Choosing among five traditions (2nd ed.). Thousand Oaks, CA: Sage.

Lincoln, Y. S., & Guba, E. G. (1985). Naturalistic inquiry. Newbury Park, CA: Sage.

Moustakas, C. (1994). Phenomenological research methods. Thousand Oaks, CA: Sage.

Chapter 19. Intergenerational Voices on Identity in Migration: Greek Islanders Speak[1]

Melissa Afentoulis[2]

Abstract

Limnos,[3] like many parts of Greece, experienced successive and long periods of foreign domination, traumas of war and economic devastation. During the decades of 1950's - 1970's, compounded by social and economic instability, many Limnian islanders arrived as young immigrants to Australia looking to build a 'normal' life. In this paper, through oral history case studies, I examine how the first and subsequent generations of migrants engage with concepts of home and belonging and the role of ethno-regionalism in the reconstruction and redefinition of identity in the diaspora. Ethno-regional identity, of interest in this research, remains both durable and significant as it reforms on foreign soil though it has received comparatively little academic attention. Identity formation and reformation and the role of 'return' visits to the ancestral home emerge as transnational patterns that lead to a rediscovered identity shaping the next generation. This 'history from below' is not only about the potential loss of Australian migration historiography, but also the legacy of the oral narrative that links the past with the lives and memories of the present and future descendants galvanising this community's continuity.

Keywords: Belonging, identity, migration, oral history, transnationalism.

Introduction

In September 2013, I conducted an interview with John[4], a thirty-nine-year-old, second-generation[5] migrant descendant, who asserted to me emphatically that:

I feel I belong in Australia but personally I consider myself to be Greek...We are a hybrid...being Greek is very important...My ancestors are from there ...the sense of connection is strong!

John was born in Melbourne in the mid-1970s; his mother was born in Limnos, Greece. This astounding proclamation gave me an opening to explore identity construction among Limnians and its reformation in the context of the Australian contemporary diaspora.

---

[1] Sincere thanks to The Migration Conference 2017 organising committee for accepting this paper for presentation at the conference held at the Harokopio University Athens, Greece.

[2] Melissa Afentoulis is a PhD scholar at the School of Historical and Philosophical Studies, Faculty of Arts, University of Melbourne, Parkville 3010 Victoria, Australia. E-mail: m.afentoulis@student.unimelb.edu.au.

[3] This island is generally known as Lemnos in the English-speaking world.

[4] Extensive oral interviews with narrators cited in this paper are in possession of the author.

[5] Scholars have identified definitional problems with the use of this term. See Yiu. 2009. My definition of 'Second-Generation' includes children born in Australia to 'First-Generation' migrants and immigrant children under 12 who accompanied their migrant parents.

This paper draws from my PhD oral history project and inter-generational case study of mass migration from the Aegean island of Limnos, to Australia. Three narrator cohorts were interviewed in this study, using an oral history framework: the first-generation, descendant second-generation and those who never left the island, to provide a unique historical perspective on migration, departure and return. Whilst there are several aspects that I would wish to focus on today, such as the role of *ethno-regional identity* (Chryssanthopoulou, 2009; 2006; 2003) that emerged as a key factor in the settlement of Limnians and its impact on the next generation, due to limited time available I will concentrate on how 'return' visits to the ancestral home affect identity formation and consolidation and have influenced second-generation, life trajectories.

The Limnian Diaspora in Australia

In the post-war years, like many other Greeks (Tamis, 2005; Appleyard, 1991; Dimitreas, 1998), many people left the island because the circumstances for survival and betterment were difficult. Limnos was a predominantly rural, pastoral island. Crop-sharing was a common practice where farmers worked the land and land owners received half of the produce at the end of the season. Land ownership was confined to the few. Most people did not have the means to own farming and pastoral land, except what was inherited over generations and acquired through a woman's dowry. An inequitable economic and social structure, combined with inefficient farming methods meant that large families lived a rural subsistence, founded on traditional and ethno-regional values and practices. Upward mobility was very difficult. Migration was considered the way to achieve 'a better future'.

Concepts of Home and Belonging – Changing Viewpoints

Baldassar uses the concept of 'migrancy', a term she applies in her research with Italian migrants to Australia, from the north-east region of Veneto (Baldassar 2001: 10). It provided me with a useful lens from which to interpret issues of belonging and meanings of home, particularly in generational terms including the intersection with those who had remained on the island and those who left. The term migrancy is defined as:

'...a set of processes that extend beyond settlement to incorporate the continuing connections between home and host countries over time, including those of the subsequent generations' (Baldassar 2007, 294).*

Such a conceptualisation solidifies a growing body of work, to illuminate migration as an on-going experience that impacts lives across generations and requires the use of a framework that includes the homeland as Bottomley, an Australian anthropologist, contends (1992, 14).

The term 'home' has been a constant reference throughout my study. But the narrative is invested with different meanings for each generation. Whilst the concept is central in diasporic identity, the meanings and values that have emerged in the narrative of each generation is located within the realm of their different experiences of migration, time and place. The first-generation respondents have used the term *patrida*[6] to fiercely denote, the localised birthplace as their belonging. In the context of place, physical and imaginary, home is connected to their memories of a place as it was lived and experienced by them. It provides historical legitimacy that enables them to feel, as Burrell says, 'a powerful sense of rightful attachment to the land itself, ensuring that the homeland becomes almost overburdened with the emotional imagery of belonging.' (Burrell, 2006: 102). For these immigrants, home epitomises, 'that complex mix of the physical and tangible and the emotional and imagined.' (103). The emerging narrative in this research from first-generation immigrants, however, also reveals tensions and ambiguities (Baldassar, 2008), that develop over time about the transformative aspects of diasporic identity and meanings of home (Baldassar,1998), because of the experiences in migration.

Due to time limitations, I will skip the section that uses oral testimony to more effectively demonstrate this point. Suffice to say that, the nostalgia and yearning about the homeland reflected in the first-generation narrative (Katerina and Haralambos interviews, May 2014; Maria, interview June 2013; Jim, interview June 2013 and others), can be characterised as misunderstood and 'unrequited' for them, in the return. Several narrators articulate the experience of perceived rejection and personal invalidation from their compatriots (Katerina 2014; Toula and Sophia, interviews May 2014; Kostas, interview March 2014), which they expected to be, otherwise. This of course was contradicted in the interviews with 'those that never left' (Ekaterini interview, August 2014; Eleni interview, June 2014). The chasm and perceived lack of understanding and sensitivity, between those who left and those who stayed is significant and reflects rejection rather than affirmation, recognition and perceived, rightful status, at least on behalf of visiting emigrants. Significantly, and not withstanding some of these ambiguities, all informants have persisted in returning to the ancestral home, as often as possible. They undertook improvements to their ancestral houses, making them comfortable and liveable as a gesture of defiance perhaps, or as an act of re-claiming their heritage and sense of place in the ancestral island, homeland and asserting their migration success. They take pride in seeing their adult children and grand-children travelling back to the ancestral home, enabling

---

[6] A term used by narrators to refer to homeland (fatherland) in Greek. Often localised meanings, such as, To nisi mou (my island), To horio mou (my village) and To spiti mou (my home) are used to signify homeland.

their 'return' and facilitating the cultural bridge (Skrbis, 2008; Skrbis, Baldassar and Poynting, 2007) that links the identity of migrant generations on a transnational continuum.

Narratives of Visits Home and Identity Reconstruction

The focus in this case study is about the changing, evolving and transformatory aspects of diasporic identity across generations (Giorgas, 2008; Lee, 2008, 2004; Levitt, 2009; Levitt and Walters, 2002; 2001; Levitt De Wind & Vertovec, 2003). The return trajectory of second-generation interviewees is diverse and significantly different to the previous generation, both in motivation, dynamics and specificity. For the second-generation, the idea of home is frequently negotiated at each stage of their lives and experiences. Through their 'return'[7] visits they can re-imagine the significance, without the burden of history, unlike their parents. They construct their own identity canvas and discover new meanings of home with each return visit, as free agents, choosing to take ownership and consolidate, or not, one or multiple homes as part of their identification. Unlike their parents, the second-generation returned to the ancestral home as autonomous adults with their own history, largely unburdened by a prior history with this land. For many, the return was a revelation and a 'rite of passage', a term used by Baldassar, (1998: 156), that applies especially to young men. In most cases, there was little nostalgia or emotional 'baggage' attached to the ancestral home, prior to their first trip, especially for those born in Australia. The significance of returning to the ancestral homeland for the second-generation has been consistently expressed as a discovery, a re-awakening and in some cases a challenging and ambiguous experience that had led to a re-defined identity. The narrative of Australian-born, Andrew (Interview, March 2014) illuminates this theme, well. Having moved from an inclusive, extended family network in inner Sydney, a migrant area in the 1960s, his family relocated for work reasons, to a more homogeneous outer Sydney suburb. Andrew refers to a 'shocking' experience of change from the inner Sydney suburb of Tempe to Riverwood and a 'middle class' high school chosen by his parents. His 'enlightenment' came when he first visited Greece as a young adult and suddenly realised that he had a Greek identity. For Andrew, the impact of having lived in a social 'bubble' that essentially placed him in a situation of denial, about who he was, is considerable. His trajectory illustrates how, his social reality crystallised in the telling of his story. The astounding finding of an 'inner self' instigated a process of positive affirmation of his heritage and belonging that resulted in a

---

7 Those born in Australia are essentially not returning, as they had never left, but the return characterises a sense of re-connecting with the ancestral homeland, even though it's a different experience to their parents.

more complex, nuanced and holistic sense of a cultural identity, that helped him to begin to re-define himself.

Despina, in her mid-fifties was born in Melbourne. She is a successful academic and confident woman, married to a non-Greek, with two adult children. She grew up in a migrant populated area, surrounded by manufacturing industries from the 1950s to the 1970s. She went to the local state schools. As she reflects on the question of identity, she says:

For a while I thought I was more Australian than Greek, until we decided to fix our house there! (Despina interview, August 2013)

Despina and her family now return to the homeland on a regular basis. This is becoming a common trend in the last 10 – 15 years, among Limnians of this generation. The ancestral home acts as an anchor for belonging to more than one place. For some, the first return visit was a turning point in resolving identity ambiguities. This is what Baldassar refers to as, a 'transformatory rite-of-passage brought by the ties to one's ancestral past' (1998: 156). For many respondents, the ancestral background had never been fully integrated or consciously understood as part of their actual identification and connection to home as they were growing up in Australia. They were keen to belong and to be 'Australians'. Until their first adult trip to the ancestral place, home for them was unambiguously identified as Australia. The 'return' visits, for some, have been a way of connecting and linking family stories to a newly found reality. For others, the experience of return was, more challenging. Whilst affirming their ancestral connection to the parental home, it also had the effect of magnifying the conundrum of an experience of being *xenos* (a stranger) in place. This diasporic phenomenon is similarly characterised by other migration literature. For example, Kindinger highlights the negotiation of identity and place of Greek women of American backgrounds who returned. Rather than being a passive condition, she describes it as, 'a dynamic practice that reflects, but also shapes people's dispersion(s) across the world' (Kindinger 2011: 390-91).

Discussion and Reflections

For some respondents, the experience of return, initially, had indeed been a destabilising rupture (Spiros interview, May 2014; Sonia interview, March 2014; Elizabeth interview, October 2014). However, most narrators experienced a pattern of numerous return visits, the construction of on-going relationships, connections and re-connections with relatives, making firm friends during their island visits. They gained an increased knowledge and understanding of the island and its recent history, unknown to them before.

This paper seeks to contribute to emerging research on identity transformation and reconnection to the homeland, through second-generation 'return' visits.

While the participants in this research have not returned permanently, their experiences of 'return' highlight an identity transformation in the second-generation that re-ignites a connection to the ancestral home, shared by the first-generation. Identity formation and reformation and the role of 'return' visits to the ancestral home emerge as transnational patterns that lead to a rediscovered identity that shapes the next generation in meaningful and unprecedented ways.

References

Appleyard, R. (1991). The Greeks in Australia: A new diasporic hellenism. In: Vryonis. S. Jr., (Ed.). *Greece on the road to democracy: from Junta to PASOK, 1974-1986.* New York: Orpheus Publishing Inc.

Baldassar, L. (2008). Missing kin and longing to be together: emotions and the construction of co-presence in transnational relationships. *Journal of Intercultural Studies* 29 (3), 247-266.

Baldasar, L. (2007). Transnational families and aged care: the mobility of care and the migrancy of ageing. *Journal of Ethnic and Migration Studies* 33 (2), 275-297.

Baldassar. L. (2001). *Visits Home: Migration experiences between Italy and Australia.* Melbourne, Victoria: Melbourne University Press.

Baldassar, L. (1998). The Return visit as pilgrimage: Secular redemption and cultural renewal in the migration process. In: *The Australian Immigrant in the 20th Century – Searching for neglected sources, Visible Immigrants, Five,* edited by Eric Richards and Jacqueline Templeton, 127-156. Canberra: Australian National University Press.

Bottomley, G. (1992). *From Another Place: Migration and the politics of culture.* Cambridge, England, Melbourne: Cambridge University Press.

Burrell, K. (2006). *Moving Lives: Narratives of Nation and Migration amongst Europeans in Post-War Britain.* Hampshire, England & Burlington, VT, USA: Ashgate Publishing.

Chryssanthopoulou, V. (2009). Gender and Ethno-Regional Identity among Greek Australians: Intersections. In Tastsoglou E. (ed) *Women, Gender and Diasporic Lives: Labor, Community and Identity in Greek Migrations.* Langham, MD: Lexington Books.

Chryssanthopoulou, V. (2006). The Kytherian Diaspora: Its Role in the Formation of the Kytherian Community and Identity within the Context of Globalisation. *International Panionian Conference Papers.* Kythera, Greece: Society of Kytherian Studies.

Chryssanthopoulou, V. (2003). Gender, Work and Ethnic Ideology: Castellorizian Greeks in Perth Australia. *Greek Review of Social Research* 110, Special Issue (2003): 107-40.

Dimitreas, Y. (1998). *Transplanting the Agora: Hellenic Settlement in Australia.* Australia, NSW: Allen and Unwin.

Giorgas, D. (2008). Transnationalism and Identity Among Second Generation Greek-Australians. In: *Ties to the Homeland.* Lee, H. (Ed.). Newcastle, UK: Cambridge Scholars Publishing. pp. 53-72.

Kindinger, E. (2011). Of *Dópia* and *Xéni:* Strategies of belonging in Greek-American Return Narratives. *Journal of Mediterranean Studies,* 20(2), 389-415.

Lee, H. (Ed.). (2008). *Ties to the Homeland: Second Generation Transnationalism.* Newcastle, UK: Cambridge Scholars Publishing.

Lee, H. (2004). 'Second generation' Tongan transnationalism: hope for the future? *Asia Pacific Viewpoint,* 45 (2), 235-254.

Levitt, P. (2009). Routes and Roots: Understanding the Lives of the Second Generation Transnationally. *Journal of Ethnic and Migration Studies* 35(7), 1225-1242.

Levitt, P. (2001). *The Transnational Villagers.* Vol. 46. Berkeley: University of California Press.

Levitt, P. and Waters, M. (Eds.). (2002) *The Changing face of home: the transnational lives of the second generation.* New York: Russell Sage Foundation.

Levitt, P., De Wind, J., and Vertovec, S. (2003). International perspectives on transnational migration: an introduction. *International Migration Review,* 37(3), 565-575.

Skrbis, Z. (2008). Transnational families: theorising migration, emotions and belonging. *Journal of Intercultural Studies.* 28(3), 231-246.

Skrbis, Z., Baldassar, L., and Poynting, S. (2007). Introduction – Negotiating Belonging: Migration and Generations. *Journal of Intercultural Studies* 28(3), 261-269.

Tamis, A.M. (2005). *The Greeks in Australia.* Melbourne, Australia: Cambridge University Press.

Yiu, J. (2009). Theorising second-generation transnationalism: Practice versus process. Paper presented at the 104th Annual Meeting of the American Sociological Association in San Francisco, California, held on 7-11 August 2009.

Chapter 20. Refuge for the Rohingya in Southeast Asia?

Jera Lego[1]

Abstract

The plight of the Rohingya has increasingly come under the international spotlight since 2015 when hundreds of them were stranded for days on boats in the Andaman Sea and denied entry by neighboring countries. The "crisis" had eventually come to an end when fishermen from the island of Aceh in Indonesia rescued many of them, and nearby Southeast Asian countries— Thailand, Malaysia, and Indonesia, through the Association of Southeast Asian Nations (ASEAN)—eventually agreed to provide temporary shelter and aid. As a result, some observers argue that significant policy change is forthcoming. This paper (i) evaluates Southeast Asian responses to the plight of the Rohingya, particularly during the "boat people crisis," (ii) assesses the prospects for refuge and protection of the Rohingya in the region, such as whether policy-focused change has been happening, and (iii) outlines the nature of refuge that the Rohingya are likely to receive in the region. The paper concludes that significant change is unlikely, and that the possibilities for protection and assistance remain limited.

Keywords: ASEAN, Indonesia, Malaysia, refugees, Rohingya, Thailand

Introduction

The plight of the Rohingya has increasingly come under the international spotlight since 2015 when hundreds of them were stranded for days on boats in the Andaman Sea and denied entry by neighboring countries. The "crisis" had eventually come to an end when fishermen from the island of Aceh in Indonesia rescued many of them, and nearby Southeast Asian countries— Thailand, Malaysia, and Indonesia, through the Association of Southeast Asian Nations (ASEAN)—eventually agreed to provide temporary shelter and aid. ASEAN continues to be criticized for its insufficient response but the fact that temporary shelter and assistance were provided, and statements by some ASEAN leaders since then, have lead some commentators to believe that "policy-focused change, while incremental, may be happening" (Orchard, 2016), or at least feel encouraged that some ASEAN member states have "breached the diplomatic impunity and organizational cover which Myanmar has been using to oppress the Rohingya and systematically engage in gross human rights violations" (Jones, 2017). Others regard the summits held in response to the Rohingya boat crisis as "a significant step towards the institutionalisation of mechanisms" to deal with current and future crises (Wolf, 2015).

This paper (i) evaluates Southeast Asian responses to the plight of the Rohingya, particularly during the "boat people crisis," (ii) assesses the prospects for refuge and protection of the Rohingya in the region, such as whether policy-focused change has been happening, and (iii) outlines the

---

[1] Jera Lego is a research associate at an international economics research institute in Tokyo, Japan. She is working independently on her research on refugee issues. Email: jera.beah@gmail.com

nature of refuge that the Rohingya are likely to receive in the region. The paper will build on previous research examining government and nongovernment responses emerging from Thailand, Malaysia, and Indonesia, as well as more recent reports and other secondary sources by various nongovernment organizations (NGOs). The paper will begin with a background on the situation of the Rohingya and earlier efforts to seek refuge in Southeast Asia, followed by a narration of the so-called "boat people crisis" in 2015 and the various country and regional responses. The paper then considers whether Southeast Asian countries' policies toward the Rohingya and other refugees are likely to change significantly and argues that possibilities for protection and assistance remain highly limited, emanating mostly through interventions made by the Office of the UN High Commissioner for Refugees (UNHCR), local NGOs, and networks of NGOs, working closely with local communities, operating, ironically, with the acquiescence of and in opposition to the state.

Myanmar's "Perpetual Other"

The Rohingya are an ethnic Muslim minority living in northern part of Rakhine State (formerly known as Arakan) in Myanmar, whose historical roots are highly contested. Imtiaz Ahmed writes of two opposing views (2004, 2010). On one hand, some believe they are descendants of Arab and Persian traders and soldiers who arrived and settled in Arakan as early as the ninth century, to which Muslims from Afghanistan, Persia, Turkey, north India and the Arabian Peninsula have since been added, resulting in a dialect that is a mix of Persian, Urdu, Pushtu, Arakanese, and Bengali. Another view, one that is supported by the government of Myanmar, is that the Rohingyas are descendants of Bengalis from the Chittagong area of Bangladesh, who initially migrated only in the 15th or 16th centuries, and were later brought back in larger numbers by the British as a deliberate policy to repopulate Arakan state with Bengalis (Rosenblat, 2015). For those who subscribe to the former view, those Muslims in Arakan/ Rakhine had been fleeing to the Bengal region to escape from the Burman Army's invasions but voluntarily returned to Arakan/ Rakhine state after British annexation of Burma in 1824. Either way, their arrival alongside the British in 1824, and continued support for the British during the Second World War, served to instill the perception of Arakanese Muslims' loyalty to British colonial masters. In the end, the Arakanese Muslims' affinity with the British worked against them and encouraged them to construct a new identity, 'Rohingya,' which distanced them from the majority Buddhist Arakanese (Ahmed, 2010: 58). For the same reasons, the Government of Myanmar prohibits the use of the term 'Rohingya' arguing that it is the creation of 'Bengali intruders' whose claims to earlier historical ties to Burma are insupportable (Chan, 2005).

Under Burmese military rule during the postwar period, the Rohingya continued to be excluded and oppressed, forcing them to flee time and again. In 1978, a wide-scale census known as *Nagamin* (Dragon King) supposedly intended to clear out illegal immigrants turned into a brutal operation with reports of destruction of mosques, brutality, rape, and murder, forcing more than 200,000 Rohingyas from northern Arakan to flee into the area between Teknaf and Cox's Bazaar in Bangladesh (Grundy-Warr, & Wong, 1997; Matthieson, 1995). The following year, most of these Rohingyas returned to Myanmar under an agreement between the two countries (Ahmed, 2010: 16). In 1982, a new Citizenship Law effectively rendered the Rohingya stateless (along with people of Indian and Chinese descent). Between 1991 and 1992, some 250,000 Rohingyas were once again driven to Bangladesh. Over the next few years, many Rohingyas returned to Myanmar in accordance with a 1992 Memorandum of Understanding (MOU) signed between the Bangladesh and Myanmar but whether their return was truly voluntary remains contested (Lewa, 2009; Grundy-Warr & Ong, 1995; Ahmed, 2010). In 1993, the UNHCR signed an MOU with Myanmar to allow access to the Rohingyas, promote repatriation, and monitor reintegration. Myanmar, however, at times withdrew from or halted the repatriation process while the Rohingyas opposed repatriation for fear of persecution.

In 2012, violence once again erupted, following reports of the rape of a Buddhist Rakhine woman by three Muslim men. Killings, arson, and destruction of property were perpetrated by both Arakanese Buddhists and Muslims, but rights groups report that the situation soon escalated into sustained and targeted attacks by Rakhine civilians and security forces against Muslims, predominantly Rohingyas. Human Rights Now has documented excessive use of force, mass arrests, and killings perpetrated by military forces in collusion with Arakanese (HRW, 2012). Some argue that this was the result of simmering communal hostilities between Rakhine Buddhists and Muslims (Kipgen, 2015). Others maintain that Myanmar's military government is behind propaganda to stir up anger against the Rohingya and that they are responsible for Islamophobic pamphlets that have been circulating in Western Myanmar (McDonald, 2012). At least 200,000 Rohingya in the Rakhine State have fled their homes since June 2012 (Fortify Rights, 2014). The UN Office for the Coordination of Humanitarian Affairs reports that more than 143,500 remain internally displaced in Rakhine as of August 2015 (UNOCHA, 2015). Meanwhile, in 2014, Myanmar's Ministry of Information instructed all Rohingya to register as Bengalis, effectively excluding them from the national census. In February 2015, President Thein Sein announced the revocation of all Temporary Registration Certificates thereby denying the vast majority of Rohingya any form of identity documents and preventing them from being able to vote in the upcoming November 2015 elections.

In October 2016, several hundred members of a Rohingya militant group Harakah al-Yaqin allegedly raided border guard posts, killing nine police officers (Robinson, 2017). Myanmar's security forces immediately responded with "area clearance operations" that caused some 65,000 Rohingya to flee within a span of three months. In February 2017, the Office of the UN High Commissioner for Human Rights (UNOCHR) released a report documenting an unprecedented level of violence against the Rohingya including "the killing of babies, toddlers, children, women and elderly; opening fire at people fleeing; burning of entire villages; massive detention; massive and systematic rape and sexual violence; deliberate destruction of food and sources of food sources" perpetrated by "either Myanmar security forces or Rakhine villagers." The report found "total disdain for the right to life of the Rohingyas," "acts that amount to persecution against a particular religious and ethnic group," and "very likely commission of crimes against humanity" (UNOHCHR, 2017). Renewed violence in 25 August 2017 has forced another 429,000 Rohingya to flee to Bangladesh, according to UNHCR estimates as of 22 September 2017, adding to over 33,000 Rohingya refugees already residing in camps in the Cox's Bazaar region of Bangladesh.

Seeking Refuge in Southeast Asia

While hundreds of thousands of Rohingya have found refuge in Bangladesh, the situation there is far from ideal. There the Rohingya face many difficulties; they are stigmatized, resented by the local population, restricted in their movement, deprived of the most basic of needs such as sufficient food, proper shelter, sanitation, and clothing. They are prohibited from seeking employment and are vulnerable to various forms of violence inflicted by security officials, locals, and other refugees as well (Ahmed, 2010: 27-35). Not surprisingly, those who could manage have sought refuge elsewhere.

Malaysia

The Rohingya had been arriving in Malaysia since the 1980s. Some 15,000 who arrived in early 1990s received some assistance from the Malaysian Red Crescent Society and some limited documentation from the UNHCR (Cheung, 2011: 53). By 1993, the UNHCR had registered and issued certificates to some 5,100 of them but Malaysian authorities often did not honor these certificates. As such, the Rohingya were subjected to arrest, detention, and punishment much like other undocumented migrants, and often, deportation to the Thai-Malaysia border. In October 2004, the

Malaysian government announced that they would regularize the residency of the Rohingya. Starting on 1 August 2006, the government started the process of registration of approximately 12,000 Rohingya refugees with a view to granting them IMM13 permits. Throughout this process, immigration authorities apparently did not rely or engage with the UNHCR; they relied instead on a few Rohingya community representatives to perform the registration. Amid allegations of corruption and fraud, the registration exercise was suspended (Equal Rights Trust, 2010). Since then, the Malaysian government has occasionally expressed interest in regularizing the status of Rohingya in Malaysia but registration, protection, and assistance have mainly been possible only through the UNHCR's activities. Moreover, the number of Rohingya has grown steadily—some 61,000 as of August 2017.

Thailand

Some Rohingya have found refuge on the border between Myanmar and Thailand, along with tens of thousands of other ethnic minorities in several camps there. Still, many others have tried to make it further to Australia or at least Malaysia via the Andaman sea with nearby Thailand as a transit point. Rohingya have been landing on Thai shores as early as 2003 and the Thai military had apparently been planning on setting up detention centers off the Andaman coast to prevent the Rohingyas from landing on Thai soil since 2008 (Phuketwan, 2008). Around the end of 2008 and early 2009, international outcry erupted when Thai authorities were found to be pushing-back a number of these boats. The *South China Morning Post* (SCMP) reports that since December 2008, there have been at least two incidents of expulsion of Rohingya refugees done by the Thai military. The first expulsion allegedly occurred on December 11 when 580 Rohingya were detained for two days, divided into three or four unpowered boats and then cast adrift. Of these 580 Rohingya, 192 were rescued by the Indonesian navy when their boat ran aground in Aceh on 7 January, 150 were found by the Indian navy shipwrecked on Tilangchang Island in the Andamans on the 10 January, while the other 238 are feared dead or missing. The second expulsion is believed to have occurred on 17-18 December when 412 Rohingya were again towed out to sea in unpowered boats by the Thai military. The boat had drifted for a week until the refugees saw light on an island. 300 of the refugees jumped overboard and swam to the shore. Only 11 survived and were picked up from a nearby island on December 28. Another two were found alive floating in the sea on 30 December. The 103 who remained onboard were the ones rescued by the Indian coastguard on December 27 (South China Morning Post, 2009). Responding to this international outcry, Thailand then changed to a so-called "help on" policy, whereby officials were ordered to refuse disembarkation but were to re-provision boats with humanitarian supplies and then direct them south towards Malaysia (HRW, 2015). This account of earlier encounters between Rohingya asylum seekers and Thai authorities only shows that rejection of refugees at sea is by no means new to Southeast Asia.

The "Boat People Crisis" of 2015

The so-called "boat people crisis" of 2015 was triggered in May when Thai police discovered more than 175 graves of suspected migrants at dozens of vacated trafficking camps along the border between Thailand and Malaysia. The discovery prompted a crackdown leading traffickers to abandon their human cargoes at sea instead of bringing them ashore where police may be waiting for them (Lefevre & Marshall, 2015). Over the next few weeks, boats carrying hundreds of people would arrive on Thai, Indonesian, and Malaysian shores, momentarily capturing the world's attention and eliciting responses from the highest levels of government. A total of some 8,000 people were believed to have been stranded at sea in May 2015 (IOM, 2015). The UNHCR estimates that many of these Rohingya, and also Bangladeshis, spent an average of 76 days on board these boats and rights groups such as Amnesty International have documented grave abuses inflicted during these journeys including extortion, beatings, being thrown overboard, and killings (Amnesty International, 2015).

Rejection and Rescue

The first boat to run aground was on May 10th in North Aceh in Indonesia from which 578 people disembarked either by swimming to shore or by floating in large cooking pots guided by others. Of these were 100 Bangladeshis who were deported in August while the rest remain in temporary shelters in Lhokseumawe in Indonesia. On 11 May, another boat carrying 1,107 passengers arrived in Langkawi in Malaysia. On the same day, passengers and media report that a gray smugglers' boat carrying between 800-900 passengers was provided with food and water and then towed by Indonesian authorities towards Malaysia (ChannelNewsAsia, 2015). The same gray vessel was believed to be turned away by Malaysian authorities two days later, on 13 May, along with yet another vessel, this time a green one, carrying about 400 passengers (Ng & Doksone, 2015). On the same day, the UNHCR issued a press release expressing alarm at reports of push-backs by Southeast Asian countries (UNHCR, 2015). On 14 May, journalists and Thai naval authorities found the second green vessel floating of the coast of Thailand while the other gray vessel sank off the coast of Aceh in Indonesia. On 15 May, 820 passengers from the sunken gray vessel were rescued by fishermen off the coast of Aceh. Of these were 500 Bangladeshis who were later repatriated while the rest were transferred to temporary shelters in Langsa and Medan in Indonesia. Meanwhile, the green vessel was once again escorted out to sea by Thai authorities on 15 May and again by Malaysian authorities on 16 May. By 19 May, the UNHCR along with the Office of the High Commissioner for Human Rights (OHCHR), the International Organization for Migration (IOM), and the Special Representative of the UN Secretary General (SRSG) for International Migration and Development issued a joint statement urging countries in the region to search for and rescue refugees and migrants at sea, allow them to disembark, and protect their human rights. The following day, on 20 May, the Foreign Affairs Ministers of Indonesia, Malaysia, and Thailand met in Kuala Lumpur to discuss their common problem and subsequently issued a Joint Statement setting out agreed upon "interim measures" for dealing with the crisis. On the same day, 20 May, 409 passengers of the green vessel were rescued by fishermen from Aceh. Over 300 of them were sent to a temporary shelter in Langsa, Indonesia. Hundreds of other passengers were found stranded on islands in various locations along the coast of Myanmar. The UNHCR estimates as of the end of June 2015 that more than 5,000 refugees and migrants in at least 8 vessels had been abandoned by human smugglers in the Bay of Bengal and the Andaman Sea. Of these, at least 70 died while on board due to exhaustion, dehydration, or disease and at least 1,000 remain unaccounted for (UNHCR, 2015).

Regional Response

The Joint Statement issued by Indonesia, Malaysia and Thailand on 20 May was seen as some measure of success. Among other things, Indonesia and Malaysia indicated that they would provide "temporary shelter" to the estimated 7,000 people stranded at sea, but they made it clear that they expected the "international community [to] take responsibility for the repatriation of the irregular migrants to their countries of origin or resettlement to third countries within a period of one year" (Joint Statement, 2015). Another condition was that the international community must take on all financial responsibility. Turkey pledged $1 million to IOM and Qatar $50 million to Indonesia (Missbach, 2015). Perhaps more impressive, on 29 May, the Thai government convened another meeting with representatives from UNHCR, the IOM, the United Nations Office on Drugs and Crime, and senior officials from 17 countries in the region. The meeting resulted in a list of 17 proposals concerning immediate responses, the prevention of irregular migration, and addressing root causes. Observers point out that this second meeting was significant for having raised substantial pledges by donor countries ($3 million by the US in response to an IOM appeal for $26 million and $4.6 million by Australia for assistance in Rakhine State), for getting Thailand to allow the US to fly over its airspace in search for other migrants still believed to be lost at sea, and for the meeting to have taken place at all with the inclusion of Myanmar (Ganjanakhundee, 2015). At the same time, the meeting is seen as insufficient for not having tackled persecution and abuse faced by the Rohingya. Observers also note that the statements released from the meeting did not even mention the word refugee or Rohingya (an acknowledgement of Myanmar's refusal to use this term) and instead referred to them as either migrants, irregular migrants, or vulnerable migrants (Foster & Gecker, 2015). Yet another meeting was held by the members of the Association of Southeast Asian Nations (ASEAN) on July 2nd entitled "Emergency ASEAN Ministerial Meeting on Transnational Crime Concerning Irregular Movement of Persons in Southeast Asian Region" at the Grand Hyatt Hotel in Kuala Lumpur. Among the possibilities mentioned were the creation of a Task Force to respond to similar situations in the future and the establishment of a trust fund for humanitarian and relief efforts related to the irregular movement of people in Asia (ASEAN, 2015).

Overall, the response by regional governments was seen by many NGOs as lackluster. The Asia-Pacific Refugee Rights Network (APRRN), an umbrella organization of more than 200 organizations concerned with protecting and assisting refugees issued a statement welcoming recognition by governments of the need (1) to intensify search and rescue operations, (2) to ensure the safety of migrants and refugees at sea, (3) to explore disembarkation options and reception arrangements. At the same time, the organization expressed concern that (1) the pledges made on 29 May were one-time offers rather than longstanding commitments, (2) refugees including women and children are still being detained in Malaysia and Thailand in woefully overcrowded and inhumane conditions, (3) the taskforce promised on the 2 July meeting had yet to be created, and (4) ongoing persecution, sectarian violence, and root causes of discrimination faced by the Rohingya have yet to be addressed (APRRN, 2015).

Acehnese Hospitality

Among the three countries that the Rohingya reached, Indonesia can be said to have provided the warmest welcome. Rights groups such as Amnesty International have commended the response by local people and officials in Indonesia, particularly in Aceh. As earlier mentioned, although the Indonesian central government only permitted disembarkation on 20 May, local officials in Aceh with the assistance of local residents allowed some 578 people to disembark on 10 May, while Acehnese fishermen had rescued 820 passengers and 490 passengers on 15 and 20 May, respectively. Amnesty International also found that local officials in Lhokseumawe donated land to house hundreds of arrivals in an integrated community shelter for Rohingya, and numerous civil society organizations are working to meet the Rohingyas' basic needs such as housing, food, water, medical care, and education (Amnesty International, 2015). Antje Missbach, in a forthcoming paper, documents her observations of the practices and outcomes of assistance provided to the Rohingya, framing these in the context of hospitality. Despite evidence of good relationships that developed between the Rohingya 'guests' and Acehnese hosts, many problems also occurred. Faced with uncertainties, many of the Rohingya began to abscond, quite likely return to Malaysia. Of 1,807 that were initially rescued, only 119 remained as of November 2016. Missbach concludes that while the Acehnese response was indeed more forthcoming than that of other Southeast Asian countries, it does not represent a sustainable solution for the stateless Rohingya who have nowhere to run (Missbach, forthcoming). Nevertheless, the Indonesia government has continued to show support for the Rohingya. On 13 September 2017, 34 tons of aid for Rohingya refugees were flown to Bangladesh. Indonesian president Joko Widodo had reportedly called for an immediate end to violence in the Rakhine and promised significant humanitarian aid (Sunstar, 2017).

Signs of Change?

Despite all the international criticism, the Rohingya crisis did not make its way to the 30th ASEAN Summit's official agenda in April 2017. The 25-page Chairman's Statement on the summit mentions four issues under the heading "Regional Issues and Developments," namely, South China Sea, Maritime Security and Cooperation, the Korean Peninsula, and Terrorism and Extremism. The statement did welcome the entry into force of the ASEAN Convention Against Trafficking in Persons, Especially Women and Children (ACTIP), acknowledge contributions to the Trust Fund to Support Emergency Humanitarian Relief Efforts in the Event of Irregular Movement of Persons in Southeast Asia, reaffirm "commitment to addressing the irregular movement of persons in the region," reiterate the need to explore establishing a Task Force to respond to "crisis and emergency situations rising from irregular movement of persons in Southeast Asia," and mention efforts to improve border management. The statement also "noted with satisfaction the ASEAN Intergovernmental Commission on Human Rights' progress on the promotion of human rights," and reaffirmed the vision of a "people-oriented and people-centered ASEAN," all without any mention of the abuses against the Rohingya. Moreover, ASEAN Chairman and Philippine Foreign Secretary Alan Peter Cayetano on 24 September 2017 released a statement condemning attacks against Myanmar security forces, expressing support for the Myanmar government's "effort to bring peace, stability, and the rule of law," all without referring the situation of the Rohingya (Cabico, 2017). This omission of the very word "Rohingya" and their situation is not surprising given that ASEAN countries continue to observe noninterference as a guiding principle in intra-ASEAN relations.

Observance of this rule, however, has not been absolute. ASEAN countries have, on occasion, openly criticized other ASEAN countries.

On 4 December 2016, Malaysian Prime Minister Najib Razak led a rally protesting what he called Myanmar's genocide of the Rohingya. In a meeting of ASEAN foreign ministers on 19 December 2016, Malaysian Foreign Minister Anifah Aman said that the situation of Rohingya Muslims was now "of a regional concern and should be resolved together." More recently, on the sidelines of the recently concluded summit, Indonesian President Joko Widodo discussed the Rohingya crisis with Myanmar State Counsellor Aung San Suu Kyi. Widodo was said to have told Suu Kyi that stability in Myanmar was important not only for the country but also the region. Regardless of Najib's or other leaders' motivations in voicing their criticism, these instances reveal that there is significant concern for the plight of the Rohingya, at least in Muslim-majority Malaysia and Indonesia. Concerning the recent statement by Philippine Foreign Affairs Secretary, Malaysia's Anifah Aman was quick to disassociate Malaysia, saying the statement was "not based on consensus," that it was a "misrepresentation of the reality situation," and furthermore calling on the government of Myanmar to end the violence, and "resolve the Rohingya refugee problem" (Walden, 2017). Moreover, Malaysian authorities seem to have at least come to terms that Rohingya will continue seek refuge there. On 11 September, Immigration Department director-general Datuk Seri Mustafar Ali said, "The influx will happen, and Malaysia is one of the refugees' destinations. I want to emphasise that we will follow whatever policy decisions made by the Home Ministry, including letting the Rohingya refugees in to prevent them from being killed," (Tan, 2017). Do all of these suggest significant change in ASEAN's reception of refugees, particularly the Rohingya?

Refuge in Southeast Asia?

Despite more open criticism of the government of Myanmar, the fact remains that neither Thailand, Malaysia, nor Indonesia have acceded to the UN refugee conventions. Nor do any of these first asylum countries have any formal national asylum frameworks. As such, any protection and assistance offered to the Rohingya remain ad hoc and unsustainable for a longer period of time. The Rohingya and other refugees and asylum seekers, for that matter, are subject to arbitrary arrest, detention, and punishment like any undocumented migrant. Morover, the discourse regarding any refugee or asylum seeker remains one of humanitarianism rather than one of human rights. This distinction is important because only the latter suggests a responsibility by receiving countries to provide protection and assistance. Even with pronouncements in the media that the Rohingya could be welcome in Malaysia, or that the UNHCR and NGOs are allowed to operate on Thai or Malaysian soil, they are still treated as illegal immigrants rather than asylum seekers in need of protection.

What these recent statements by Malaysia and Indonesia suggest are that majority-Muslim countries in the region are willing to publicly advocate for oppressed Muslim minorities, especially if their situation directly affects recipient countries. However, there is little evidence to suggest that formal asylum frameworks are forthcoming. Refuge for the Rohingya remains a humanitarian concern rather than a matter of rights and responsibility to provide protection. Finally, there does not appear to be any concern to acknowledge the Rohingya's grievances, historical claims, their right to maintain their identity, nor perhaps even their right to exist as a people. Instead, Myanmar's neighbors are concerned with likely influx and the possibility of another regional crisis. Without concern or will to address the root of the problem, nor any determined effort to establish frameworks for receiving asylum seekers, refuge for the Rohingya can only be partial and fleeting.

References

Ahmed, I., ed. (2010) The Plight of the Stateless Rohingyas. Dhaka: The University Press Ltd.

_____ (2004). Globalization, Low-Intensity Conflict & Protracted Statelessness & Refugeehood: The Plight of the Rohingyas. GSC Quarterly 13 (Summer/ Fall)

Amnesty International. (2015). Deadly Journeys: The Refugee and Trafficking Crisis in Southeast Asia. https://www.amnesty.org/en/documents/ASA21/2574/2015/en/.

Asia Pacific Refugee Rights Network (APRRN) (2015, October 12) "APRRN Statements on Maritime Movements in the Indian Ocean." Available at http://www.aprrn.info/1/index.php/resources/publications-and-materials/aprrn-statements/323-aprrn-statement-on-protection-at-sea

Association of Southeast Asian Nations (ASEAN) (2015, July 2) Chairman's Statement. Emergency ASEAN Ministerial Meeting on Transnational Crime Concerning Irregular Movement of Persons in Southeast Asia (EAMMTC). Kuala Lumpur, Malaysia. http://www.asean.org/images/2015/July/chairman_statement/ADOPTED%20Chairmans%20Statement%20of%20EAMMTC%20Concerning%20Irregular%20Movement%20of%20Persons%20in%20the%20Southeast%20Asia%20Region%20as%20of%202%20July%202015.pdf

Cabico, G. K. (2017). Malaysia calls Cayetano statement on Rohingya crisis a 'misrepresentation of reality.' The Philippine Star. 25 September. http://www.philstar.com/headlines/2017/09/25/1742499/malaysia-calls-cayetanos-statement-rohingya-crisis-misrepresentation (accessed 25 September 2017).

ChannelNewsAsia (2015). Indonesia navy tows migrant boat out of Indonesian waters: Spokesman. 12 May. http://www.channelnewsasia.com/news/asiapacific/indonesia-navy-tows/1840976.html

Cheung, S. (2011) "Migration Control in South and Southeast Asia." Journal of Refugee Studies 25, No. 1: 50-70.

Fortify Rights. (2014). Policies of Persecution: Ending Abusive State Policies Against Rohingya Muslims in Myanmar. February. http://www.fortifyrights.org/downloads/Policies_of_Persecution_Feb_25_Fortify_Rights.pdf

Foster, M.J. & Gecker, J. (2015). Myanmar Shows Up, Donors Give Money, but no 'Miracle' Solution at Asian Migrant Crisis Talks. The Star Tribune. 29 May. http://www.startribune.com/no-miracle-solution-at-asian-migrant-crisis-meeting/305495101/

Ganjanakhundee, S. (2015). US Patrol Flights Get Nod. The Nation. 30 May. http://www.nationmultimedia.com/national/US-search-flights-get-nod-30261287.html

Grundy-Warr, C. & Wong, E. (1997). Sanctuary Under a Plastic Sheet: The Unresolved Problem of Rohingya Refugees. IBRU Boundary and Security Bulletin (Autumn): 79-91.

Human Rights Watch (HRW). (2015). Southeast Asia: Accounts from Rohingya Boat People. 27 May. https://www.hrw.org/news/2015/05/27/southeast-asia-accounts-rohingya-boat-people.

_____. (2013) All You Can do is Pray: Crimes Against Humanity and Ethnic Cleansing of Rohingya Muslims in Burma's Arakan State. https://www.hrw.org/sites/default/files/reports/burma0413webwcover_0.pdf

_____. (2012) The Government Could Have Stopped This: Sectarian Violence and Ensuing Abuses in Burma's Arakan State. https://www.hrw.org/sites/default/files/reports/burma0812webwcover_0.pdf

_____. (1996) Burma: The Rohingya Muslims: Ending a Cycle of Exodus? http://www.hrw.org/reports/pdfs/b/burma/burma969.pdf

International Organization for Migration. (2015). IOM Appeals for USD 26 Million for Migrants in SE Asian Boat Crisis. Press Release. http://www.iom.int/news/iom-appeals-usd-26-million-migrants-se-asian-boat-crisis

Joint Statement: Ministerial Meeting on Irregular Movement of People in Southeast Asia. (2015). Putrajaya. http://reliefweb.int/report/myanmar/joint-statement-ministerial-meeting-irregular-movement-people-southeast-asia

Jones, W. J. (2017). Myanmar's Rohingya: Human Rights Abuses and Systemic Violence.

Kipgen, N.(2014). Addressing the Rohingya Problem. Journal of Asian and African Studies 49, No. 2: 234-247.

Lefevre, A. S. & Marshall, A.R.C. (2015). Special Report: Inside Thailand's Trafficking Crackdown. Reuters. 9 July. http://www.reuters.com/article/2015/07/09/uk-thailand-trafficking-specialreport-idUKKCN0PJ13V20150709?ref=browsi

Lewa, C. (2009). Northern Arakan: An Open Prison for the Rohingya in Burma. Forced Migration Review 32: 11-13.

Lewa, C. (2008). Asia's new boat people. Forced Migration Review, 30, 40-42.

Matthieson, D.S. (1995). Plight of the Damned: Burma's Rohingya. Global Asia 4, No. 1: 86-91.

Missbach, A. (forthcoming). Facets of hospitality: The temporary stay of Rohingya refugees in Aceh.

Missbach, A. (2015). Towards a Real Solution to Southeast Asia's Refugee Crisis. The Diplomat. 19 August. http://thediplomat.com/2015/08/towards-a-real-solution-to-southeast-asias-refugee-crisis/

Ng, E. & Doksone, T. (2015). Malaysia Turns Away 800 Boat People; Thailand Spots 3rd Boat. Associated Press. 14 May. http://news.yahoo.com/worries-grow-rohingya-bangladeshi-migrants-boats-070751524.html

Orchard, P. (2016). Regionalizing Protection: AU and ASEAN Responses to Mass Atrocity Crimes against Internally Displaced Persons. Global Responsibility to Protect 8(2-3): 295-326.

PhuketWan. (2008). Deathship' Burmese Muslims Forced Back to Border. 28 March. http://phuketwan.com/tourism/deathship-burmese-muslims-forced-back-to-border/

Rosenblat, M. O. (2015). A Rational Approach to the Rohingya Crisis. The Diplomat. 8 July. http://thediplomat.com/2015/07/a-rational-approach-to-the-rohingya-crisis/

South China Morning Post. (2008). Trail of Misery. 29 April.

South China Morning Post. (2009). A Timeline of Events in the Andaman Sea. 18 January.

Sunstar. (2017). "Indonesia sends 34 tons of aid for Rohingya." 13 September. http://www.sunstar.com.ph/network/news/2017/09/13/indonesia-sends-34-tons-aid-rohingya-563884 (accessed 25 September 2017).

Tan, V. (2017). Immigration: Rohingya refugees allowed entry into Malaysia. The Star Online. (11 September) http://www.thestar.com.my/news/nation/2017/09/11/immigration-rohingya-refugees-allowed-entry-into-malaysia/ (accessed 26 September 2017).

United Nations High Commissioner for Refugees (UNHCR) (2015). Southeast Asia: Mixed Maritime Movements. April-June. http://www.unhcr.org/554c6a746.html

_____. (2015). UNHCR alarmed at reports of boat pushbacks in South-east Asia. Press Release. 13 May. http://www.unhcr.org/555345959.html.

_____. (2014). Bangladesh Fact Sheet. Available from http://www.unhcr.org/50001ae09.pdf

United Nations Office for the Coordination of Humanitarian Affairs (UNOCHA) (2015) Myanmar: Internal Displacement in Rakhine State. August. http://reliefweb.int/sites/reliefweb.int/files/resources/Affected_Map_IDP_Sites_Rakhin e_OCHA_Aug2015_A4.pdf

UNOHCHR. (2017). Report of OHCHR mission to Bangladesh: Interviews with Rohingyas fleeing from Myanmar since 9 October 2016 Flash Report. http://www.ohchr.org/Documents/Countries/MM/FlashReport3Feb2017.pdf (accessed 25 September 2017).

Walden, M. (2017). Malaysia rejects ASEAN declaration on Rohingya as 'misrepresentation' of reality.' Asian Correspondent. 25 September. https://asiancorrespondent.com/2017/09/malaysia-rejects-asean-declaration-rohingya-not-line-reality/#xDp4xXBGIJd3X9ZO.97 (accessed 25 September 2017).

Wolf, S.O. (2015). Rohingya Crisis and the 'Boat People' Conference: Towards a Regional Solution? 18 June. http://www.e-ir.info/2015/06/18/rohingya-crisis-and-the-boat-people-conference-towards-a-regional-solution/ (accessed 26 September 2017).

Chapter 21. Immigration Theme in Elif Shafak's Novels

Reyhana Jafarova[1]

Abstract

Immigration factor played a certain role in the formation of the world public social idea. At all times, societies had to leave places they lived for other places. Immigration can be designated as people's leaving their places for other areas or countries, temporarily or permanently on social, political and economic reasons. Therefore, immigration influenced social factors such as policy, economy, geography and culture. This manifested itself particularly, in the literature which is an integral part of the culture. Immigration literature is a distinct example of this effect. Contemporary American immigration literature is the result of people's mass flow to the United States of America. This literature is comprised by the works of immigrant writers representing different ethnic groups. The purpose of this paper is to examine immigration theme based on the novels by Elif Shafak. She is one of the authors who played a great role in the formation and development of Turkish American literature, which is a comparatively young branch of American immigration literature. The cases in her novels are based on different nationalities, cultures and countries. Belonging to a certain nation is of less importance in her novels. She tries to reveal her heroes' identity from multicultural perspective.

Keywords: immigration, immigration literature, Turkish American literature, Elif Shafak

Introduction

Two world wars, ethnic conflicts, revolutions, political and economic crises of the XX century led to especially large-scale immigration compared to previous centuries. Consequently, the role of immigration significantly increased, and in some cases, it became a decisive factor in the world social and political processes, in the history of different nations and states.

The development of industry created a great demand for working class after World War II and the developed countries hosted citizens of other countries in their own country. During this period, the United States was among the countries that received the largest number of immigrants. People who represented various national, racial and religious groups began to flow to the United States. America was a land of new opportunities for them. İmmigration to the United States was realized with several immigration waves. The first wave of people who came to the United States, left their country mostly, because of economic and political reasons. High education was a main reason for a new wave of immigrants to come to the new world in the next stages.

A brief summary of Immigration literature

It is impossible to think of immigration, as a social fact, without having its own place in the literature. In this context, from the first oral literature samples until today, "migration" has been reflected in the literary production. In the

---

[1] Reyhana Jafarova is a PhD student in the Department of World Literature, Philology Faculty, Baku State University, Zeynal Khalilov str,23 ,Baku , Azerbaijan.
E-mail: reyhane@mail.ru

past, immigration literature was intended to be a section, particularly covering topics related to the immigration life. Writers touched immigration theme in their works, describing immigrants' life, difficulties the immigrants came across during the adaptation process in the host country. Nowadays widening its scopes, contemporary immigration literature covers the themes such as multiethnicity, multiculturalism, multilingualism, humanity and so on. It includes immigration fictions which narrate the story reflecting the social life of all nations. This literature with its translated works appeals to the audience of different nationalities. So bilateral relations between literature and migration has become more obvious. In this regard, it is important to identify aspects of the relations between literature and immigration.

As Pourjafari and Vahidpour state, *that even though "the description of the migration experience and the difficulties of adaptation play a primary role in this literature, actually, migrant literature can be very diverse, either thematically or structurally"*(Pourjafari & Vahidpour 2014, p 680)

A cursory glance at the scientific discourse on migration literature in Europe of the last two decades also shows that it is increasingly heralded as a 'new world literature'. The main argument of this claim is that immigration literature transcribes the experience of everyday life in a globalized world and reflects on the challenges of existence in multicultural and multilingual contexts.

Previously, the transmission of national traditions was the major theme of world literature, nowadays transnational histories of immigrants are of great importance.

Immigrant literature also explores the idea of "self and other". New approach in the contemporary immigration literature is the definition of new immigrants' "self" and " other" which helps to shape the immigrant's new identity. It reflects the ambiguities of the immigrant experience.

A brief summary of immigrant literature in the United States of America

As prominent Russian scientist, professor Y.B. Boriev states "*There is a trend of bilingualism and hybridity in the immigration literature. It enriches one language with the other one, as well as, native (national) culture with the culture of the host country. This literature builts a bridge between countries, peoples and cultures".* (Борев Ю.Б 2001) In this regard, the role of immigrant literature in the USA literature is undeniable. When we speak about immigration literature in the United States, we mean works combining the lives of communities living in immigration, their adaptation to a new country, their wishes and desires. Therefore, USA Immigration Literature can be divided into the following branches: Scandinavian-American literature,

Jewish American literature, Asian American literature (Chinese, Japanese, Korean, Iranian and Turkish) and etc. (Glenda R. Carpio, 2012)

Turks' immigration to the United States of America

Migration from Turkey to the United States draw attentions with three different migration waves. The reason of the first wave immigration was the economic collapse factor of the Ottoman Empire and conflict between nations at the beginning of the twentieth century. The second wave occurred in the 1950s and 1960s. The main reasons for this wave were conditions for higher education in the United States. A large number of people of the science and art emigrated from Turkey to the United States on the second wave. With the third and final wave, turks representing different social groups went to the United States at the end of 1980. (Faiza Meberbeche Senouci,2016)

The interaction between American culture and the Turkish minority in the United States, along with Turkish-American ties in Turkey and Turkish culture, shapes Turkish identities. Although Turkish identities are shaped in the context of American cultural environment and global trends, some Turks in the U.S. still manage to live, socialize and communicate in the ways they were used to back home in Turkey.

Social structure of Turkish immigration in the Unite States is constantly changing, renewed and being reformed and different level classes and various interests are mixed in this community.

Turkish Immigraton Literature in the United States of America

The formation of Turkish immigration literature in the United States refers to the last period of Turks' immigration to the United States. Mustafa Ziyalan, Faruk Ulay, Guneli Gun and Elif Shafak are writers who played important roles in the formation Turkish immigration literature in the United States. Each of them contributed to the creation and formation of this literature.

Immigration literature created by the writers of Turkish origin in the US is a rich source of investigation. This literature is characterized by two languages and two cultures. The writers, who represents this literature, have works in both languages.It reflects the cultural environment referred to common process and context. The literature with these characteristics has a place in both literatures.

In the article, an internationally famed writer, Elif Shafak's novels related to immigration will be analyzed.

Elif Shafak has published 15 books,10 of which are novels. All her works reflect postmodern novel conception.

She writes fiction both in Turkish and English. Her writing draws on diverse cultures and literary traditions, reflecting interests in history, philosophy, Sufism, oral culture, and cultural politics. She was awarded the title of Chevalier de l'Ordre des Arts et des Lettres in 2010.

Elif Shafak mostly focuses on issues like east-west, tradition-modernity, love-mysticism, women's identities and immigration in her novels. (Yusuf Aydoğdu, 2014) Her works have been translated into 30 languages.

Originally, some of her works were written in English, which later were translated into Turkish. In this article, we will study three of her novels, the main theme of which is immigration: The Saint of Incipient Insanities (Araf), Honour (Iskender), Bastard of Istanbul (Baba ve Piç). All three novels describe heroes' immigration life.But the reasons for living their countries are different: high education, better life, people's mass displacement. Although the main heroes of the novels are of different nations, all of them left Turkey.

"The Saint of Incipient Insanities"

"The Saint of Incipient Insanities" was published in America by Farrar, Straus and Gioux Publishing House in 2004 and translated into Turkish by Aslı Bichen. The translated version of the novel, "Araf" was published by Metis Publishing House the same year.

The names chosen for the novel in both languages are not without purpose. If "The Saint of Incipient Insanities" emphasizes the madness, "Araf" means "threshold". On the one hand, the author tries to reveal characters' mental state, on the other hand, aims to clarify their feelings and emotions they feel in threshold.

"The Saint of Incipient Insanities" takes place in multicultural Boston, and revolves around the social, cultural and emotional experiences of a group of graduate students from Turkey, Morocco and Spain, especially their interactions with both native and marginal Americans.

A novel starts with the conversation between Omar Ozsipahioglu and his Moroccan roommate, Abedin in one of Boston bars in the morning. Omar feels deep pain with losing the dots of his twenty-year-old's name. He has lost not only his name's dots. In fact, this sense of loss is not related to his culture, homeland, and his family. He feels emptiness with the loss of his dots. This feeling has never left him. He thinks that the best way to look better from others' perspective is moving away from himself as much as possible. "*To be included to the American environment, Omar left his names' dots and entered as Omar Ozsıpahıoglu. The first necessity of living in a foreign country is alienation to the man's name, to what he is closely connected*" (Elif Shafak, 2004).

When you leave your homeland behind, they say, you have to renounce at least one part of you. If that was the case, Omer knew exactly what he had left behind: his dots! Back in Turkey, he used to be ÖMER ÖZSİPAHİLİOĞLU. Here in America, he had become OMAR OZSIPAHILIOGLU. His dots were excluded for him to be better included. After all, Americans, just like everyone else, relished familiarity—in names they could pronounce, sounds they could resonate, even if they didn't make much sense one way or the other. Yes, few nations could perhaps be as self-assured as an American in reprocessing the names and the surnames of foreigners. (Elif Shafak 2004) .

At the beginning of the novel Omar searches for an apartment to stay in the new country and decides to stay with Moroccan Abed and Spanish Piyu. On the third day of his arrival in the United States, he feels "backlash", which he describes as freedom (Shafak, 2011). But on the other hand, Omar seems get to use to American culture. Though it was his first visit to Boston, he got accustomed to American cinema, music and food.

All characters, described in this novel brought with them their traditions, religions and customs. The author confronts her characters with the problems related to name, language, religion, time, loneliness and strangeness.

One of the main characters of the novel is Gail. She is Omer's wife. Gail is an American of Jewish origin. She has a panic attack and social phobia. Gail, who does not like to be together with humans, has tried to be away from their conversations, jokes and attitudes since she has known herself. She is described as "pessimistic anxious, antisocial" character in the novel. Although Gail is an American, she is the one, who feels strangeness most of all. Her alienation is shown with her name. She is against the name "Zarpandit ", given to her from her birth. She got used to the people's confusion when they first hear her name. Zarpandit is unusual name for them. So, she is a stranger.

Abed is always honest and righteous. Opposite to Omer, he introduces himself as a "whole Muslim". Religion for Omar who drinks a large part of the time and eats pork, is only word written in his identity card. Omer's other roommate, Piyu is a catholic Spaniard. He is obsessed with cleanliness. Piyu likes cleanliness and order not only in the kitchen, but in every aspect of his life and tries to control everything. Another character is Piyu's girlfriend, Catholic and Mexican immigrant Alegre, who is introduced as a fine girl. Bu she has also psychological problems. Having been continuously criticized by her mother for her overweight in childhood, Alegre counts each calorie in everything, she eats and drinks.

Despite belonging to different nationalities and communities, these young people living in the same place, are trying to live appropriately to the American lifestyle. The writer describes multiculturalism,fragmentation, non-belonging and alienation within crossing lives of the young people in Boston who belong to different countries, religions and cultures.

At the end end of novel,with the Gail's suicide , the author appeals to the readers: *Who is real stranger; the one who lives in one country, and knows his belonging to another place or the one who lives as a stranger in his own country and does not have any place to belong to?* (Elif Shafak 2004)

The Bastard of Istanbul

The Bastard of Istanbul was published in 2006. Here immigration is described as mass displacement of Armenians from Turkey to the different parts of the world, especially to the USA. The Bastard of Istanbul is a novel, the main core of which is devoted to the conflict between two nations: Turks and Armenians. The history of this conflict goes back to the beginning of the XX century.

The Turkish-Armenian relations are described from both sides in the novel. The viewpoints of the Armenian diaspora in the United States and the Turks in Turkey are explained by a meeting between Kazanchi and Chakmachian families. In addition, the book examines the Turkish-Armenian social life and discusses common feelings and thoughts among Turkish and Armenian societies.

The story centers around Asya Kazanchi and Armanoush Chakhmakhchian. At age nineteen, Armanoush travels secretly to Istanbul to search for her Armenian roots. The author tries to give viewpoints of two nations on 1915 events through these girls' speech. Armanush finds it difficult to find her own values and personality. *'At first I was not able to be an Armenian. I need to find my identity. If I can make a trip to the past of my parents.''* (Elif Shafak 2007) She goes to Istanbul with a sudden decision to objectively evaluate the Armenian roots in Turkey, next to his step-father's family. Armanush was brought up in the family where each family member is fanatical Turkish enemy. Even though many Armenians like Chakhmakhchian family left Turkey at the beginning of XX century, they transmit their feelings from generation to generation. According to them, Armenians are still suffering. When Armanush introduces Asya to her virtual Armenian friends, their first question was about Asya's attitude to 1915 events.

The author describes the situations where both nations suffered.

During her short visit to Istanbul, Armanush brought the relocation of the Armenians in a very dramatic way and at every opportunity. She was waiting for apology from Turks. But even Armenian Aram, who has lived all his life in peace in Turkey, does not agree with Armanush:*"You, Armenians in the Diaspora do not have any Turkish friends. The only thing you are familiar with is your stories from your grandparents. Those stories are extremely sad. But believe me as in every country, there are good people and bad people in Turkey. I have Turkish friends who are closer to me than my own brother* "(Elif Shafak,2007 p 279)

Elif Shafak says that the purpose of writing this book is not to humiliate Turkishness, but rather to contribute to the creation of a humane and peaceful environment between Turks and Armenians, and that the novel is a fictional and imaginary product in the nature of a literary work. (https://tr.wikipedia.org/wiki/Baba_ve_Pi%C3%A7)

Honour

"Honour" is another novel about immigration written by Elif Shafak. It was published in 2011. The novel was written in English and aferwards it was translated into Turkish. The name of the Turkish version is " Iskender".It is the protagonist's name.

The relationship between Iskender and his mother, Pembe and honour killing are the basic fictions of the novel. All other events are related to this mother-son relationship. The novel was narrated by Iskender and his sister Esma. It lets the readers to see the events from different points of view.

Iskender is a multi-faceted, nervous, rebellious young man, living identity crisis. He is sensitive to the problems immigrants experience in London. He thinks that it will be solved with power, so that he is interested in boxing.

After moving to London to work, a family of Turkish-Kurdish origin lives a family tragedy on the grounds of crime they faced to. Besides the problems the family comes across in the immigration life, there is violence, east-west confrontation, identity problems which are highlighted in the novel.

Everyday problems of the family living in the London's migration district and struggle of each family member to survive in the foreign country, internal and external factors caused collapse of the family are described in the novel.

In London, they have a choice: stay loyal to the old traditions or try their best to fit in. After Adem, a father of the family abondons his family, Iskender, the eldest son, must step in and become the one who will not let any shame come to the family name. And when Pempe begins a chaste affair with a man named Elias, Iskender will discover that you could love someone with all your heart and yet be ready to hurt them. The most beloved person becomes the most hated. (Yusuf Aydoğdu 2014)

The author's aim is not to narrate a classical honour murder. She deals with the heroes' lives and changes in their characters, their characteristic features which they can never change in the modern world.   On the other hand, a person has all the feelings that one can have. Depending on the situation, they emerge from man's inner world. It looks like a little detail in the novel but it's a very important scene. Because there are two sides in Iskender. He has a potential to hurt a bird. But at the same time he will take him, protect him, show him compassion; He has a side to love.It is clearly shown in the part, where Iskender is in prison. He regrets for what he has done. Having been rebellious and aggressive, living the east-west conflict, Iskender reaches maturity in prison.

Although this novel simply takes a tragic story between a mother and son or the honor killing at the center of the novel, the writer basically tries to question many different subjects such as the social status and position of women, conflicts imposed by the east-west tradition, patriarchal tradition, immigration life and so on by linking them with main subject. (Yusuf Aydoğdu 2014)

Conclusion

Immigration played a tremendous role in the people and nations' social life. it influenced all fields of society. Immigration life was reflected in the works of immigrant writers belonging to different national minorities. Previously, immigration fiction was connected with adaptation process and difficulties the immigrants came across with.

Nowadays a text, for being accepted as an immigration literature should concern not only immigration life, at the same time lives and cultures of the nations and peoples from different backgrounds. The theme and narrative perspective play an important role in the classification of the text. Biography of the immigrant author does not indicate the text as immigration literature.

Contemporary immigration literature describes identity shifting, multiculturalism, humanism.

Comparatively new branch of American immigration literature, Turkish American literature was established with Turks' last immigration wave to Turkey. Elif Shafak is among those who played an active role in the development of the Turkish American literature.

The analysis of Elif Shafak's novels deals with all the themes essential to works of immigrant fiction. As the reasons for immigration is different, the novels mentioned in this article were investigated from different angles.

Though the analyzed novels are closely connected to immigration life, multiethnicity is the main factor highlighted in these novels. Here clash of cultures occur. People who represent different religions, languages and nationalities try to know themselves and understand others.They realize that there is not much difference between them and others. The writer recommends a distinctive choice to the people who can not belong to any place: to be many and majority. It is also one of the key features of contemporary migration literature.

References

1. Elif Shafak (2004) *"The Saint of Incipient Insanities"* Farrar, Straus and Giroux in New York .
2. Elif Shafak (2007) *The Bastard of Istanbul*, Penguin Books, London
3. Elif Shafak (2012) Honour, Penguin Books, London
4. Elif Şafak (2010) *Araf,* Doğan kitab, İstanbul
5. Elif Şafak (2010) *Baba ve Piç,* Doğan kitab, İstanbul
6. Elif Şafak (2011) *İskender,* Doğan kitab, İstanbul
7. Fatemeh Pourjafari, Abdolali Vahidpour (2014) *Migration Literature: A Theoretical Perspective,* The Dawn Journal Vol. 3, No. 1 , 679 -692 Received from http://thedawnjournal.in/wp-content/uploads/2013/12/2-Fatemeh-Pourjafari.pdf
8. Faiza Meberbeche Senouci (2016) *The Turkish Diaspora In The United States: Immigration And Identity Formation* International Journal of Academic Research and Reflection, Vol. 4, No. 2, 32 -39 Received from http://www.idpublications.org/wp-content/uploads/2016/02/Full-Paper
9. Glenda R. Carpio (2012) *Contemporary American Immigrant Literature,* RSA Journal 23/ 54-72 Received from http://www.aisna.net/sites/default/files/rsa/rsa23/23_carpio.pdf
10. Mustafa Aydemir (2013) *Arada Kalanlarin Romani: Araf,* Avrasya Uluslararası Araştırmalar Dergisi,Cilt:1 •Sayı:2, 27-43, Received from http://www.avrasyad.com/Makaleler/
11. Yusuf Aydoğdu (2014) *Elif Şafak'in İskender Romaninda, Kurgunun Ele Aliniş Biçimi, Çatişma Unsurlari Ve Karakterler,* Bingöl Üniversitesi Sosyal Bilimler Enstitüsü Dergisi Cilt: 4/ Sayı:8/ , 155-166 , Received from https://www.academia.edu
12. https://tr.wikipedia.org/wiki/Baba_ve_Pi%C3%A7
13. http://www.elifsafak.com.tr
14. Борев Ю.Б (2001) *Теория литературы,* Литературный Процесс,Москва Том IV, 624

Chapter 22. The Ionians in Anatolia and the Mother Goddess Cybele Cult

Seher Selin Özmen*

Abstract

"Migration" has been an important concept for explaining social and cultural change throughout the history of archaeology. Religion, on the other hand, as an important medium for the interaction of different societies and cultures, has been one of the main results of migrations. In antiquity cults spread through different geographical areas by trade, wars and migration. The immigrants brought their beliefs to the new lands and also, they adopted the local cults. During the 12th and 11th century B.C., a large-scale immigration called "Aegean Migrations" occured from Eastern Europe and Balkans to Anatolia. While the first wave of the Aegean Migrations was a movement of discovery the second peak period caused radical changes with the Ionian, Aeolian and Phrygian settlement in Anatolia. The Phrygians who came from the Balkans to Anatolia destroyed the Hittite State and settled in the Kızılırmak River basin. While The Aeol tribes settled between today's Çanakkale-İzmir shores, the Ionians established a union of twelve city-states between 900-700 BC. These cities were Miletos, Myus, Priene, Ephesos, Kolophon, Lebedos, Teos, Klazomenae, Phocaea, Samos, Khios, and Erythrai. An Aiol city, Smyrna, later joined the union. Ionia had the most glorious period between 650 and 494 BC. Ionian Golden Age came to an end when Miletos, the leader of the union, was occupied by the Persians in 494 BC. However, it is proven in the inscriptions that the union continiued its life till the 1st century B.C. When the Ionians came to Anatolia they met the Mother Goddess Cult who had been prayed for thousands of years. The Goddess was given the title of "Matar / Mother" and her characteristic features were created in Phrygia. The recognition of the Mother Goddess Cult in Ionia can be explained by the relations with Phrygia. The purpose of this presentation is to reveal with the archaeological finds that the Ionians, who came to Anatolia with the Aegean Migrations adopted the Mother Goddess Cult Cybele and they added their own cultural characteristics to her.

Key words: Aegean Migrations, Ionia, Mother Goddess, Cybele, cult.

Introduction

Neolithic period had marked a decisive turning point with agriculture and settlement which had brought social order to human life. In cultural sense social order means a society that develops common behavior in ethical values, customs and beliefs. Cultural and social changes that have taken place throughout history have always arisen as the consequences of major events like wars, natural disasters and migration. All the migrations in world history have created cultural interactions. People who move to a foreign place they come with their culture: their language, their customs and their religion.

There are three main categories of resource materials traditionally used to reconstruct information from ancient societies: archeology, ancient literary sources and epigraphy. Archaeology as an applied science researches, finds, collects, classifies, and interprets the material cultural remains of mankind.

* Dr. Seher Selin Özmen, Namık Kemal University, Faculty of Science & Literature, Department of Archeology, Tekirdag, Turkey. E Mail: sozmen@nku.edu.tr

Migration has become one of the main topics (Dommelen, 2014: 477) and a central concept in archaeological thought because it can clarify the questions of the material culture finds (Hakenbeck, 2008: 9). Religious sites have a particular importance in archaeology for understanding interaction of ancient cultures.

Bronze Age and Iron Age migrations are important for the crosscultural issues. The newcomers and the settlers intermingled with each other. It is not surprising that the oldest evidence of European language and culture is in Anatolia. During the 12th and 11th century B.C., a large-scale immigration called "Aegean Migrations" occurred from Eastern Europe and Balkans to Anatolia. The Hittite Kingdom was destroyed by these immigrations. This was a very important turning point from which Aeolies, Ions and Dors from continental Greece passing over the Aegean islands began to settle down to the Western Coast of Anatolia where there was not a central authority. Aeolies extended south from the throat to Smyrna and included the island of Lesbos; Ionia, included the coastal settlements from Phokaia to Miletos and the islands of Samos and Chios; and, in the very southwest corner of Anatolia, the Dorian Hexapolis included Knidos, Rhodes, and Kos (Greaves, 2011: 505). The ancient writers Herodotus, Strabo and Pausanias dedicate a detailed narrative to the legendary corpus concerning Ionian migration. Today the Aegean migrations are commonly called the Aeolian, Ionian and Dorian migrations which are, in reality, a set of migratory movements composed of populations of different geographical origins from almost all regions of mainland Greece (Vanschoonwinkel, 2006: 115, 136).

The first excavations in Ionia were held by Ekrem Akurgal who is one of the second generation archaeologists educated in Germany during the early period of the Turkish Republic. The main important written works about the Anatolian Mother Goddess are of Cevat Şakir, Sabahattin Eyüboğlu and Azra Erhat who concentrated on the cultural inheritace of Anatolia.

The Ionians established a union of twelve city-states between 900-700 BC. These cities were Miletos (Milet), Myus (Avşar Kalesi), Priene (Güllübahçe), Ephesos (Efes), Kolophon (Değirmendere), Lebedos (Gümüldür), Teos (Sığacık), Klazomenae (Kalabak-Urla iskelesi), Phocaea (Foça), Samos (Sisam adası), Khios (Sakız Adası), and Erythrai (Çeşme). An Aiol city, Smyrna (İzmir), later joined the union.

The interaction between the immigrants and the local populations in the region can be thought not as a conflict between two different cultural and ethnic groups but as a complex, centuries-long process of adaptation (Greaves, 2011: 509). Herodotus tells a lot of stories about the Anatolian peoples with whom the Ionians encountered. Among these the earliest was the Phrygian people. The recognition of the Mother Goddess Cult in the

Ionian cities can be explained by the relations with Phrygia and then Lydia. But before the Phrygians, the same female divine with different names, had been prayed for thousands of years in Anatolia. According to a famous historian of religion Mircea Eliade, the relationship between the Goddess with leopard in Çatalhöyük, the Goddess Hepat of the Hittites and Cybele of the Phrygians indicates a religious continuity in Anatolia (Eliade, 2003: 176). The Ionians by adding the characteristics of their Goddesses continued to worship the Mother Goddess that existed Anatolia when they entered there.

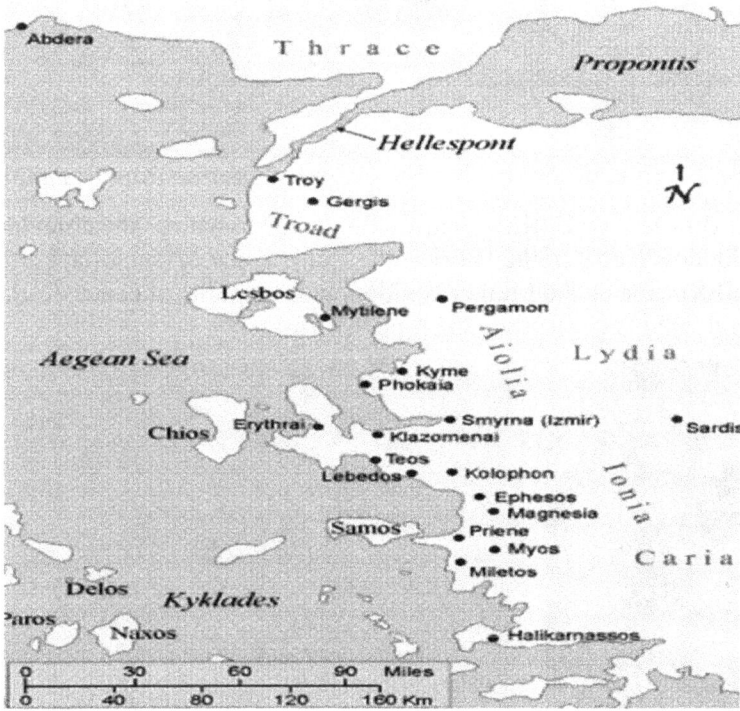

Figure 1: Ionian settlement

This paper presents, by using archaeological data, what are the Greek features added to the Anatolian Mother Goddess who had a hybrid character after the Ionian migration.

Anatolian Mother Goddess

The Neolithic Age finds in Central Anatolia at Çatalhöyük and Hacılar excavations show that during the Neolithic in Anatolia respect to fertility for agricultural production was symbolized by the figurines of female body. Besides the female figurines, symbols of bulls and wall paintings in Çatalhöyük indicate praying to the Mother Goddess. Figurines are sometimes in the shape of a young woman, a pregnant woman or an old woman. The seated Goddess is the famous image on a throne flanked by lions found in Çatalhöyük.

Figure 2: Terracotta Seated Mother Goddess Figurine from Çatalhöyük

In the Bronze Age Hittites identified Arinna, the wife of the chief God, with the Goddess Hepat of the Hurries, the local people of Anatolia. Late Hittites prayed Kubaba as the Mother Goddess in their political center Karkamis by the mid 2000 B.C. (Roller, 2013, pp. 69-70).

Figure 3: Kubaba Relief from Karkamis, 9th century B.C.

Phrygians emerged as a political power in Anatolia after 750 B.C. During the period of King Midas, they became a dominant kingdom in all Central and Southeastern Anatolia. Although the Mother Goddess Cult had showed similar symbols with the Late Hittites, it had found its characteristic features in Phrygia. The most important information obtained from the inscriptions is that the name of the Goddess is used together with "Matar", that is, "Mother". The main source of information about the Mother Goddess Cult is the rich archeological material that has spread throughout the Phrygian cultural domain. Step monuments, facades and niches are the typical Phrygian cult features. Several monuments are close to natural, sheer rocks. Niches and smaller facades are sometimes situated at sheer lone rocks at a location high above the ground. Larger step monuments usually have a large open area around them while smaller ones can be found on difficult rocks. They are usually located at the peak of a ridge or rocky outcrop. In some cases the whole rock was turned into a monument. Generally different monumental forms are not close together. There are only a few sacred sites, both a step monument and a facade, rarely idols or niches can be found together. Instead of different forms, it is possible to find the grouped step monuments more commonly. The rock-cut imitations of a copmplete building in which Matar standing must be an essential part of Phrygian religious iconography later spreading to Ionia and beyond (Ersöz, 2006: 177-205).

Among the descriptions of the Mother Goddess in Central and Eastern Phrygia the largest and well-preserved five impressive figures were found in Gordion, Bahçelievler, Etlik, Ayaş and Boğazköy. In almost all examples, the Goddess' appearance is identical. In a frontal pose she is standing with the arms on her chest as a mature woman in a garment which is covering her body without showing any lines.

Figure 4: Cybele Statue from Boğazköy, mid 6th century B.C. and Cybele Relief from Bahçelievler, 6th century B.C.

In West Phrygia, the most important Mother Goddess depiction is the Aslankaya monument. Here inside the triangular pedestal there are two sphinxes and in the lower niche, the Goddess stands as a high relief with a garment completely covering her body. There are two lions on the two sides of the Goddess. An interesting detail is the lion cub whose legs holding by the Goddess and hanging upside down. There are also two lions standing on either side of the rock monument. This is the motif of the Potnia Theron, or Mistress of Animals consists of a standing female figure (the Potnia Theron) ranked by a pair of wild animals.

Despite her name Mother, there is little that relates Matar to fertility in Phrygia. Instead, she seems to have been first and foremost a Goddess of power, a city protector, and the most eminent official goddess, the mother and protector of the king and the state (Roller 1999:111–115).

Figure 5: The Aslankaya Monument

Anatolian Mother Goddess After the Ionian Migration: Changing Image of Cybele

Ionia as a region hosting some of the finest, the most famous and well preserved sites in the world has an extraordinary potential for archaeological research. But there are very limited historical sources available for the study of Archaic Ionia. These are the myths of the so-called "Ionian Migration" and references from later historians. The prime source is "Histories" of Herodotos. The fame and importance of the works of the Ionian philosophers have also been more important over the interpretation of Ionian history. On the other hand in Ionia the surviving inscriptions are mostly in Greek which was used largely to cult purposes. In Ionia, the archaeological evidence from the Archaic period provides information coming from a few key sites by the old excavations and the publication of detailed modern excavations (Greaves, 2010: 2-26).

In Ionia, there are various examples of temples on acropolis locations for reasons of both natural and political geography. Despite being generally unhealthy environments for humans, swamps also appear to have been a favored location, one of them is the Temple of Artemis at Ephesus. Although this location was evidently prone to flooding, leading to the destruction of the first temple building, it was felt to be sufficiently sacred to rebuild the temple on the same spot. At the Temple of Artemis at Ephesos, the use of amber demonstrates cult continuity from the Bronze Age (Greaves, 2010: 173-174).

In Ephesus, there are remains that are so perfect as to be able to imagine something like walking in the ancient city and walking on those streets. Pompeii, Herculaneum and Akrotiri, the most famous archaeological sites in the world, were preserved because they were buried by volcanic ash in a sudden catastrophic event. In Ionia Ephesus, situated between the Mount of Panayir in the north and the Mount of Bulbul in the south, is one such site where there is a remarkable preservation. Exposed to a catastrophic flood as a result of a landslide in the 8th century B.C. buried and covered including the Ephesos Temple of Artemis and a number of amber beads, the ruins of the Library of Celsus and the Street of the Curetes in a great depth of soil (Greaves, 2010: 3-4).

After the Ionians settled in Ephesus, they joined the Greek Goddess Artemis and local Goddess Cybele in some common qualities. They substituted their Artemis' role, despite of her virgin status, for the local Anatolian Mother Goddess Cybele. Artemis of Ephesus was not a hunter, unlike Greek Artemis but she was Potnia Theron, or Mistress of Animals like Cybele.

There are many similarities between Artemis and the Phrygian Goddess Cybele. Indeed, among all the Greek Goddesses, mostly Artemis shares the qualities of the Anatolian Mother Goddess. According to Erhat, this is especially important to show a splendid continuation of Mother Goddess Cybele in Ionia (Erhat, 2008, p. 59). Artemis is depicted with a cylindrical crown, as worn by the Phygian Mother Goddess, with a conical posture with two animals on both sides. More importantly the grape-like bumps believed that represented the breasts in the past, but today they are more likely to be sacrificed bull testers. During the Hellenistic period, however, Artemis Ephesia had some Greek characteristics and she was seen as the daughter of Zeus and Leto and the twin brother of Apollo, like Artemis of Greece. She became Artemis of Ephesus, a mix of Asian and Hellenic Goddesses.

Figure 6: Artemis Ephesia

Figure 7: The Port Sanctuary made for Cybele in Phokaia, 6th century B.C.

Harbors are seemed to had been other favored locations for sanctuaries. There are two sanctuaries on the harbor at Phokaia: the Temple of Athena and immediately below it, the well known sanctuary of Cybele (Greaves, 2010: 172-174). Among the Ionian cities, Phokaia is of great importance. At Phokaia there are strong evidences indicate that the Mother Goddess Cybele Cult continued as the Cult of Athena, the original Greek Goddess. The Port Sanctuary is directly beneath the temple of Athena which overlooked the city's harbor (Özyiğit, 2003: 105). The earliest phases of the sanctuary are probably to be dated to the late 6th or the 5th century B.C. During the 4th century B.C. and later, such rock-cut niches were to become a feature of

Matar sanctuaries in other Ionian cities but the Phokaian niches seem to have been among the earliest in the Greek world.

The archaeological finds in the Ionian cities has pointed to the visual changes and the Greek additions of the Anatolian Mother Goddess from the Archaic to the Roman period. Samples are less specific from the Archaic Period when there was a preexisting, and predominant Anatolian culture being in the region than the later times. There are marble reliefs depicted Mother Goddess Cybele standing in front of an architectural structure called naiskos which is similar to the facade ornamentation on the Phrygian rock monuments. And also number of major polis / city cults appear to have developed out of Anatolian origins. It has long been recognized that the very non-Greek cult images of Artemis at Ephesos must have had an Anatolian origin. New researchs of the evidence show that there were also many other cult sites in Ionia that showed affinity with the traditions of Anatolia (Greaves, 2010: 196-197).

According to Roller, there is a difference between the Phrygian and Greek Mother Goddesss cults of the is noteworthy: while the cult monuments of Phrygian Matar seem to represent both elite and popular religious expression; the Greek votives were located well away from urban settlements such as the sancuary at Phokaia (Roller, 1999: 140). Greaves points out that the Sacred Ways in Ionia connecting the cult activities of several key sites can be seen as a mixture of Anatolian and Greek traditions in terms of combining nature and urban life (Greaves, 2010: 184).

While there were numerous small votive naiskoi of standing Cybele in Ionia during the early period of contact with Phrygia and Lydia; the Mother Goddess was begun to depict as a seated figure during the mid 6th century B.C. Why the Goddess's standing visual form changed to a seated image is possibly can be explained by Greek tradition of seated statues at Ionian sanctuaries. This type spread to the Aegean islands and was carried by migration to the western Mediterranean. In the late sixth century B.C., the Goddess acquired a new attribute, the tympanum, which had no antecedent in Anatolia, yet was to become a crucial symbol of her character in the Greek world (Roller, 1999: 139). In Classical and Hellenistic Period the Mother Goddess underwent some other changes also in costume and attributes.

Figure 8: Statuette seated Cybele from 5th century B.C., National Archaeological Museum of Athens

Figure 9: Naiskoi with seated Cybele in from late 4th century B.C., National Archaeological Museum of Athens

Figure 10: Seated Cybele in Naiskos from National Archaeological Museum of Athens

Figure 11: Statuette of seated Cybele from late 4th century B.C., National Archaeological Museum of Athens

Figure 12: Votive relief of Cybele from late 4th century B.C., National Archaeological Museum of Athens

Figure 13: Votive Relief of Matar with older and younger God, Ephesus, 3rd-2nd century B.C. from Archaeological Museum of İzmir

Ephesus furnishes an example of a mountain sanctuary of Meter-like the samples in Phrygia-located at the base of the Mount of Panayir. The sanctuary consists of niches some of which still containing images of the Goddess. There were also a series of small votive reliefs in Ephesian sanctuary depicting the goddess standing, accompanied by one or two lions by her side. In several examples, a young male stands at her right, and in a few cases, she has both a young man at her right and an older man on her left (Roller, 1999: 200)

Figure 14: Seated Cybele from Priene 2nd century B.C.

Terracotta statue of Cybele from Priene shows the Goddess sitting on a throne wearing the Greek costume of chiton and himation. She holds in her right hand a patera with knob and on her left hand a large tympanum. The Goddess has a lion on her lap (Vermaseren, 1987: 206).

Conclusion

Cultural interaction is one of the inevitable consequences of immigration. As a part of the cultural structure of a society, religion played an important role for interaction by the migrations, especially in polytheistic antiquity. Religious sites are important for archaeology to solve the problem about the different cultural finds on the same stratigraphy at the same sanctuary.

From the earliest times to the present day, mankind has believed in a divine power that would meet the needs, protect and provide continuity. This belief reinforced through various rituals, has been humanized sometimes in the form of male or female figurines or idols. In the Palaeolithic Age when man struggles to survive the challenges of nature, hunting based on male power was important, and therefore the belief was expressed by the symbols of male. In the Neolithic period, with the agricultural revolution and settlement, fertility gained importance and female body was identified with the soil. Thus in Anatolia the Mother Goddess belief emerged. Indeed this was a process in which the Goddess gained importance as the "Mother who gave birth to male".

During the Bronze Age, the identification of Arinna, the wife of the Chief God in the Hittites, with the Goddess Hepat of the Hurries, the local people of Anatolia, is an important ring in the continuity of the Anatolian Mother Goddess belief. In the Iron Age, after the destruction of the Hittites, the immigrant Phrygians, emerged as the most important political power in Central Anatolia. They adopted the Anatolian Mother Goddess belief adding some new features from their own cultural background. There were similarities between Late-Hittites' "Kubaba" and the Phrygians' "Cybele" both in visual image and pronounciation of the names. The Goddess was given the title of "Matar / Mother" in Phrygia and her original attributes produced by the crosscultural relationship of the Phrygians and the local people. Matar was a noble, always depicted as a standing Goddess in the Phrygian period.

The Phrygian Mother Goddess came to the Greek world from Anatolia during the early 6th century B.C. and from the Greek cities in Western Anatolia her worship spread to the Greek mainland and further west. The Greek Mother Goddess is very much a composite figure, that was neither totally Greek nor totally Phrygian including both Anatolian and Hellenic elements. Roller's opinion about the difference between the Anatolian and the Greek cult monuments can be explained by the Matar's priority in Phrygia and her secondary position in the Greek Pantheon. On the other hand Greaves' view on the subject matter that it is not a difference but a hybridization between two cultures.

When the Ionians came to Anatolia the naiskoi from the Ionian Greek cities show the visual form of the Mother Goddess developed first as a standing with the attribute of the lion; the concept of a seated Cybele developed in the Greek cities of Ionia during the mid 6th century B.C. Her visual form with a different costume in traditional Greek style can be explained by the newcomers' additions to the cult from their cultural background like the Phrygians did. Changes in costume, pose, and attributes mean the interaction between the Greek cults and the pre-existing "Phrygian" style. After the destruction of the Phrygians and the Lydians, it is so normal that influence of the Greek elements are felt more. Beyond that it must be remembered that the oldest samples of the Mother Goddess in Anatolia were a seated figure with lions.

References

Dommelen, P. (2014: 477). World Archaeology. Moving On: Archaeological Perspectives on Mobility and Migration http://www.tandfonline.com/doi/pdf/ 10.1080/00438243.2014.933359

Eliade, M. (2003). Dinsel İnançlar ve Düşünceler Tarihi - Taş Devrinden Eleusis Mysterialarına. (Çev. Ali Berktay). İstanbul: Kabalcı Yayınevi.

Erhat, A. (2008). Kybele. Mitoloji Sözlüğü. İstanbul: Remzi Kitabevi

Ersoz Berndt, S. (2006). Phrygian Rock-cut Shrines Structure, Function, and Cult Practice. Culture and History of the Ancient Near East Volume 25, Brill: Boston

Greaves, A. (2010) The Land of Ionia Society and Economy in the Archaic Period. Chichester/Malden, MA: Wiley-Blackwell

Greaves, A. (2011). The Greeks In Western Anatolia. The Oxford Handbook of Ancient Anatolia10,000–323 B.C.E. 500-514 (Ed: Sharon R. Steadman and Gregory Mcmahon) Oxford University Press.

Hakenbeck, S. (2008) Migration in Archaeology: Are We Nearly There Yet? https://www.academia.edu/293108/Migration_In_Archaeology_Are_We_Nearly_There _Yet

Özyiğit, Ö. (2003). Anadolu / Anatolia 25. http://dergiler.ankara.edu.tr/dergiler/ 14/715/9072.pdf 105

Roller, L. (1999). In Search of God the Mother: The Cult of Anatolian Cybele. London: University of California Press, p.139

Vanschoonwinkel, J. (2006) Greek Migrations to Aegean Anatolia in the Early Dark Age. 115-168 Greek Colonisation, Volume 1: An Account of Greek Colonies and Other Settlements Overseas by Gocha R. Tsetskhladze (Ed.). Brill: Boston

Vermaseren, M. J. (1987). Corpus Cultus Cybelae Attidisque (CCCA) I Asia Minor. Brill: p. 206.

Figures

Figure 1: Gorman, V.B. (2001). Miletos, the Ornament of Ionia-A History of the City to 400 B.C.E. The University of Michigan Press: USA, p. 281

Figure 2, 3, 4, 14: Kulaçoğlu, B. (1992). Anadolu Medeniyetleri Müzesi-Tanrı ve Tanrıçalar. Kültür ve Turizm Bakanlığı Yayını: 1992. pp. 29-41, 131, 139-140, 148.

Figure 5: Claerhout, I. and Devreker J. (2008). Pessinus Ana Tanrıça'nın Kutsal Kenti. İstanbul: Homer Kitabevi, p. 191

Figure 6: Artemis Ephesia's head of the sculpture. Seipel, W. (2008) Efes Artemisionu Bir Tanrıçanın Kutsal Mekanı. Ege Yayınları. p. 161.

Artemis Ephesia sculpture (https://www.google.com.tr/search?q=Artemis+Ephesia&dcr=0&tbm)

Figure 7: Photos from Phokaia by Selçuk Tümöz.

Figure 8, 9, 10, 11, 12: Photos from National Archaeological Museum of Athens by S. Selin Özmen.

Figure 13: http://www.soniahalliday.com/category-view3.php?pri=TR39-8-08.jpg

Chapter 23. The Alevi Youth in the German Diaspora

Deniz Cosan- Eke[1]

Introduction

The migrant's identity construction is a salient theme in the public and political integration debate in Germany as well as in other European countries. The Alevi community faces a variety of specific challenges in transnational space, such as the protection of its identity and the recognition of its cultural and religious differences. For Alevis, the prospect of being recognized both as a religious and cultural group and an immigrant group in Germany has created a growing social and political movement and a diaspora to Germany. Consequently, after more than 50 years, the children of Alevi migrants to Germany, especially of third generation, are starting to grow up in a transnational context within a diasporic consciousness.

Today I will talk about the data on the construction of Alevi youth identity that is examined by the literature on diaspora and identity. In my presentation I will focus on the perception of Alevi youth in Germany in terms of state of belonging and integration, in order to evaluate their interpretation of Alevism and to show their expectations from the Alevi movement in diaspora. This discussion may provide meaningful and practical contributions to the literature on Alevi studies and can be used in the area of migration and diaspora studies.

1. Empirical Data and Methods

Today I will introduce a part of a much larger comparative study that deals with the Alevi movement in Germany and Turkey. The aim of this research is to fill the gap in the literature by analyzing how the Alevi youth organizations in Germany play a role in "reshaping" Alevi identity. For this purpose, the main research question looks at how Alevi youth in the German diaspora have constructed their identity. To answer this question, the current research gives voice to the claims and ideas of Alevi youth among the members of the BDAJ, the Federation of Alevi Youth in Germany (*Almanya Alevi Gençler Birliği-Bund der Alevitischen Jugendlichen in Deutschland*), the largest Alevi youth organization. This research is important both because it deals with the first comprehensive discussion about the perspectives of Alevi youth on the Alevi movement and because it supposes that the viewpoint of Alevi young people can offer hints to identify the direction of the Alevi movement in diaspora and in its homeland.

On the basis of a literature review on these issues, the empirical data were collected in various cities in Germany during different periods over the course

---

[1] Ludwig-Maximillans University, Social and Cultural Anthropology, Munich, Germany.

of three years. Before beginning the interviews, an impression of the inter-generational relations and transnational practices among Alevis was gained through informal conversations with the members of different Alevi organizations and ethnographic experience as a participant observer of Alevi religious and cultural events in Germany. The fieldwork was completed in four months, from August to November 2014, but the ethnographic experience has been ongoing since September 2011. Furthermore, interviews were made in Munich, Hamburg, Neufahren, Ulm, Dortmund, Köln, Stuttgart, Lünen, Augsburg, Ingolstadt, Freising and Duisburg. To examine how the youth in Alevi communities define and interpret themselves, the participants of the interviews were selected among young people between the age of 17 and 31 who self-identify as Alevis. Overall, 54 participants were interviewed for this research, 29 women and 25 men. The people in the sample group were born and raised in Germany and have always lived there, except for one participant, who arrived in Germany when she was a child. The participants' level of education ranged from graduate studies to primary school education. 3 people only graduated from elementary school; 8 young people are high-school students, and 13 participants are either continuing with or have graduated from vocational training. One of the important details is that the interviews were made with 34 university students and 6 master students, all of which are women. Only one male participant has enrolled for a master program at university.

The questionnaire was prepared mainly as a methodological tool. 56 questions were asked, all of them open-ended, to allow participants to express new ideas and describe their story, their perceptions and experiences about their personal, inter-generational and transnational world. In the questionnaire, in addition to personal questions, such as age and education, the questions included the migration experiences of the participants and their family, and their ideas and expectations about the Alevi movement, especially about the BDAJ (Federation of the Alevi Youth in Germany).

Data collection was done in several ways: by phone, by post, through face to face conversation and computer-mediated communication (CMC) such as e-mail and chat boxes (MSN messenger, Facebook). E-mail interview using the aforementioned interview techniques was the main form used in this research because the questionnaire was first sent to a small group of close friends, and later, using the snowball technique, it was supplied to a larger number of Alevi young people all over Germany. Also, interviewing by e-mail provides cost-effective, extended access to a larger numbers of participants when compared to face-to-face interviews. In addition to face-to-face contact, phone and CMC interviews, different cultural activities and religious rituals were attended to gather general observations.

Reviewing the literature on transnational migration, identity, and diaspora, and more specifically on Alevi immigrants and their children in Germany, this research focuses on the process of migrating to Germany, on the connections to the country of origin and on how they strengthened their relationships with the country of settlement in order to understand the effects of the transnational practices and inter-generational relationships on the identity construction in diaspora.

2. The Construction of Alevi Youth Organization

The BDAJ-Federation of Alevi Youth in Germany (Almanya Alevi Gençler Birliği- Bund der Alevitischen Jugendlichen in Deutschland) was established as a part of the AABF in 1994 and it became an officially registered association in 1999, when it started to make autonomous decisions. The organizational structure of the BDAJ still has connections with the AABF, because the National Chairman of the BDAJ is co-opted by the board members of the adult community of the AABF. When a person between the age of 16 and 27 becomes a member of an Alevi association in Germany, s/he becomes concurrently a member of the BDAJ.

The BDAJ was chosen for the fieldwork of this article not only because it is the self-governed Alevi youth organization from the AABF, but also because it is the largest immigrant youth organization in Germany that represents the interests of over 33,000 children, adolescents and young adults below the age of 27. The BDAJ is divided into 140 member-associations and is distributed throughout 5 states in Germany (Bremen, Hamburg, Berlin, Schl.Holstein, Lower Saxony), Hessen (incl. 2 local Young organizations from Rheinland-Pfalz), Baden-Württemberg (incl. Saarland), Nordrhein-Westfalen and Bavaria). Since 2011, the association has been a member of the German Federal Youth Council (Deutscher Bundesjugendring- DBJR),[2] which is an umbrella organization of the Youth in Germany and thus provides valuable pioneering work about the intercultural opening of the Youth League scene. In the same year, the BDAJ started a high school group initiative in order to develop a student network, to increase the degree of organization among students, and to encourage the establishment of university groups. In 2013, more than 25 Alevi university groups came together, and the governing body Federation of Alevi students in Germany (Almanya Federal Alevi Öğrenciler Birligi- Bund der Alevitischen Studierenden in Deutschland- BDAS) was launched. Alevi Youth Group at the University currently exist in the following cities: Berlin, Bochum, Dortmund, Duisburg-Essen, Erlangen / Nuremberg, Frankfurt, Freiburg, Giessen, Hamburg, Heidelberg, Kiel, Kassel, Cologne,

---

[2] For more information, look at the link : <http://www.dbjr.de/service/english.html > (retrieved on 12.11.2014)

Konstanz, Mannheim, Marburg, Münster, Siegen, Stuttgart, Trier, Ulm, Worms and Wuppertal.

The main objectives of the BDAJ can be summarized in their function to transfer Alevi faith and philosophy to the next generations, to support the integration of Alevi youth in Germany, to develop projects for human rights, gender equality, freedom of all faiths, rights of oppressed minorities and environmental issues, and also to connect with political parties and all democratic organizations to support social development[3].

3. Results of the Fieldwork

3.1 Connections to the country of origin

Even though many Alevi immigrants have settled down permanently in Germany and 67% of the Alevis in Germany are now German citizens[4], they have maintained their connections and close relationships to their country of origin. The majority of participants in the research are third-generation Alevis in Germany and their migration stories are connected to the Bilateral Recruitment Agreement of 1961, which was signed between Turkey and West Germany and invited Turkish immigrant groups to come to West Germany as foreign/migrant workers. Therefore, it is not surprising that, when asked when and why they came to Germany, all of the young people responded using their family migration stories as focal markers of their identities.

To illustrate this point, Mazlum Dogan, one of the ex-presidents of the BDAJ, claims that one of the aims of the BDAJ is not only to accompany the integration process of the Alevi youth in Germany, but also to create an alternative in Turkish politics through their organizations. Therefore, he emphasizes: "We have attempted to contribute to the success of the democratizing process in Turkey by means of organizing demonstrations and marches in Berlin and Cologne with thousands of people"[5]. Hence, it is possible to underline that the Alevi youth immigrants use the country of origin as a reference to define their identity. When I asked the participants of the research about the most important problem(s) of Alevis, the majority of the answers focused on the same issues as those illustrated in the following statement:

"The most important problem of Alevis at this time is the assimilation politics such as the compulsory religious classes in Turkey, which prevent the Alevi youth and children from learning Alevism correctly in Turkey".

---

[3] For more Information, look at this link: <http://bdaj.de/images/stories/PDF/2011-11%20infobroschre.pdf > (retrived on 12.01.2017)

[4] Bundesamt für Migration und Flüchtlinge. 2009

[5] <http://rudaw.net/english/world/24112013> (Retrived on 12.03.2017)

In addition, the participants stated that the biggest current problem of Alevism is that it has been exposed to assimilation, discrimination, and non-recognition. The interesting point to emphasize here is that the perceived problems are experienced in Turkey rather than within the Alevi community in Germany. Only one participant argued that the biggest current problem of Alevism is a "degeneration of Alevism that emerges in moral and religious contexts because Alevis could not correctly transfer the knowledge about their faith and tradition to the next generations in Germany". Even though this research indicates that Alevi youths maintain contacts with their country of origin[6] through kinship, culture, politics, and other identity markers, 51 participants stated that they did not want to return to Turkey to live; three participants mentioned the possibility of living in Turkey for a short time because they have many relatives and friends there. However, nobody showed a determination to live in Turkey their whole life or the will to return to Turkey even if the Alevi community were recognized as a cultural and religious community and they obtained their rights as equal citizens in Turkey. Actually, Clifford (1994:309)[7] states that the return to the country of origin may not be idealized by all diasporic groups and so the process of identity formation may create a tension in the conceptualization of the citizenship as a form of social and political belonging. When the desire to return to Turkey was not realized by their family, younger Alevis have developed an awareness of national belonging that includes a common ethic/religious or cultural background. The national consciousness or awareness is mostly ʹimaginedʹ as Benedict Anderson has remarked, and can be transformed throughout time because Alevis have described themselves mostly in ideal terms. However, it should not be eluded that the Alevi youth have started to lose all sense of belonging to Turkey. The following quote illustrates the main reason for the increasing sense of belonging to the country of settlement:

"We visit our relatives almost every year in the summer but I was born in Germany and I donʹt want to return to Turkey because I have accepted that Germany is my homeland and so I would like to live here. Also, the political arrangements are not enough to protect freedom of expression in Turkey and Alevis are suppressed by the Turkish government because of their faiths and culture. Therefore, it is so repellent for me to return and live in Turkey".

The complexity of the identity construction of Alevi youth has become even more multifaceted. In my research, Alevi youth have sometimes transferred remittances as donations to the Alevi community in Turkey, which were used to construct a *cem* house in Kahramanmaras. They also provided social and

---

[6] "Country of origin" is used purposely to define the youth or the third generations in Germany, because they are not accepted the „homeland „concept when we talk about Turkey in a few infomal conversational interviews.

[7] Clifford, James.1994. "Diasporas". Cultural Anthropology 9. pp: 302-338.

financial assistance to Alevis after the 2011 Earthquake in Van. In addition to fundraising campaigns for the remittance transfer, the members of the BDAJ participated in organizing tours that took place on the anniversary of the Alevi massacres in different cities in Turkey in order to display protests and demonstrations against these massacres.

The data on the places to visit and the number of participants to the tours for Sivas or Corum massacres is variable. What is certain, however, is that the members of the BDAJ have participated regularly each year on July 2nd in Sivas and on July 3rd in Corum to the commemorative demonstration. According to the report from the Europe Alevi Youth Union, the AAGB (*Avrupa Alevi Gençler Birliği*), about the Sivas-Corum Tour in 2015, neither the AABF (*Almanya Alevi Birlikleri Federasyonu)* nor the BDAJ (Almanya Alevi Gençler Birliği) have organized or financed it. The AAGB organized the tour and coordinated Alevi youth. The tours were financed by the participants of the tours and the union treasury of the AAGB. Also, the AAGB, which has 160 youth organizations in Europe, assumed responsibilty in case of accidents. When the BDAJ organized these tours before 2015, 30-40 young people had joined them. In order to increase the number of the participants, the AAGB organized these tours in 2015 and 80 young people from 9 different countries in Europe participated. According to Nadir Bal, the president of the AAGB, these tours have contributed to empower the Alevi identity of the youth:

"These commemoration tours have aimed to raise the awareness of the youth towards Alevi history and their identification by means of getting to know Alevi places (*türbe* or *tekke*) and their living conditions in Turkey; to get in touch with other Alevi young people and also to promote a cooperation among Alevi youth who live in different countries".

To summarize, remittance transfers and participation to the cultural, religious and political activities in Germany and Turkey aim not only to improve the transnational practices of the Alevi movement but also for Alevis to identify themselves with their religious values instead of their nationality in diaspora. Moreover, the massacre anniversary is also salient to refresh the collective memory and to strengthen the collective consciousness of a group.

3.2 Strengthening Relations with the Host Country: Integration and Recognition

It is important to look at how Alevis gained awareness of their culture and identity in diaspora. Ma Mung (2005: 35) states that "ethnic identity is past-oriented, towards the preservation of a memory of origins and the building-up of a history of these origins". In this respect, Alevis emphasize suppression, mistreatment and discrimination throughout their history. Indeed, there are many bitter events in Alevi history, such as the episodes of Maraş, Çorum,

Sivas and Gazi quarter, and these memories are also a way to maintain their collective identity.

Even though Alevis tend to define their identity based on the history of repression and the continuous suppression they have endured, the identity construction of Alevi youth in diaspora differs from these perceptions and views in two main points. The first concerns Alevi youth´s negative emotional reactions against their country of origin, which include experiences of discrimination and a tendency to compare the description of their identity with that of the Alevis living in Turkey. The second point focuses on the relationship with the country where they have settled, which encompasses their recognition process and their efforts to integrate in Germany such as learning the language and engaging in educational and job activities.

In order to focus on one vision for its activities and its support to integration in Germany, every year the BDAJ (Federation of Alevi Youth in Germany) chooses a motto that appears in their Journal of Plural[8] and in other places, such as their internet site or their workshops. In 2011, their motto was -*Unser Deutschland-Ein Wir-Land* (Our Germany-A We-County) - in order to emphasize Alevi youth's belonging to and integration in Germany. One of the ex-presidents of the BDAJ, Mazlum Dogan, explained why the federation of Alevi youth locates itself within the German society:

"The Alevi Youth Union is now one of the biggest youth groups in Germany and the government recognizes it officially. We aren't different from other German organizations. Most of the projects of this union are funded by the German government because of their contribution to the interreligious and intercultural dialogue among the different religious groups in Germany"

Serdar Akin, the national chairman of the BDAJ and the new director of the European Alevi Youth Union, highlights the main aims of the BDAJ. In his words:

"The BDAJ aims to form young people who have Turkish background and later became citizens of Germany. In recent years, we have attempted to surpass the 'integration' debates and to endorse the policies of 'social inclusion', because in this way we want to become a part of the German society, while maintaining the characteristics that Alevis have. We think that multiculturalism is an important resource for Germany. Our main suggestions can be summarized as follows: the BDAJ has coordinated different projects with various religious or cultural institutions or associations. For example, we made one important project which name was "Together against Prejudice" with Judith Synagogue from 2011 to 2014. The main aim of the project was to

---

[8] Plural. "Unsere Deutschland-Ein Wir Land".2012. The Journal of BDAJ. Ausgabe: 1-2. 12/2011-2012.

increase the dialogue between young people who have immigrant backgrounds and diverse beliefs. We organized different activities together, such as workshops, sport and artistic activities in order to struggle against prejudices and to understand each other"[9].

As it was advertised on the internet site of the BDAJ, the German Catholic Rural Youth Movement (KLJB) and the BDAJ have started the cooperative project – Bird-Bridge of interreligious dialogue, which was supported by the Federal Ministry for Family Affairs, Senior Citizens, Women and Youth (BMFSFJ) from 2012 to 2015. As Serdar Akin points out:

"We want to build bridges between the Catholic and Alevi youth. It is one important object of our movement to strengthen the intercultural and interreligious dialogue. It is not enough to talk about integration, I think that we implemented it- this was the object of our project."[10]

As can be seen in detail in its internet site, the BDAJ is a cooperation partner with 14 different religious, cultural and political groups, such as the Evangelist youth, the Christian youth, a multicultural forum, a group that provides information about anti-racism, the youth groups of SPD and Green Party, etc.[11] However, an interesting point is that they do not have any contact with Sunni organizations or other Turkish organizations as cooperation partners. The reason is that Sunni youth organizations or The Youth in DITIB are not seen as an independent organization from the perspectives of the Turkish state against the Alevis and even the thought of these Sunni organizations have acted in virtue of the Director of Religious Affairs (Diyanet Isleri) in Turkey and they would like to keep their distance from them.

To summarize, the BDAJ has made several efforts to explain Alevism and Alevis to the German society through their activities and projects, which have included different religious and cultural groups in Germany. In this way, they have tried to accelerate successful integration, to decrease prejudices against the Alevi community in Germany, and to contribute to struggle for their rights.

Furthermore, many members of BDAJ take into account that a higher education would be a good chance to engender wider acceptance from the German society. While they have organized many political, social and cultural activities in order to support the integration of the Alevi youth in Germany, the BDAJ has also proposed some suggestions and critiques for the German integration policies, especially concerning the education system in Germany. With Serdar Akin´s words,

---

[9] For more information, look at this link: http://www.multikulti-forum.de/en/commitment/together-against-prejudice/

[10] http://www.mijarc.org/fr/node/356 < retrived on 12.09.2016>

[11] http://bdaj.de/kurzportrait/ < retrived in 10.09.2015>

"In Germany, we have criticized the state´s school system because 9-year-old children are required to choose one type of school among Gymnasium, Realschule and Hauptschule in order to continue their education. But, as an Alevi Youth Union, we have suggested that students should be separated from each other in school as late as possible, since they can get more tolerance if they study with diverse cultural, ethnic or religious groups. Also, some people still have bias against immigrants, but many members of our Union (BDAJ) define themselves as Germans with Turkish or Kurdish origin, even though many of them are German citizens. We believe that we are the part of German society, so we support the policies and actions of social inclusion in Germany that enable the participation of Alevi youth in the decision-making processes that affect their lives".

Consequently, my research indicates that Alevi youth try to integrate in the cultural and social life in Germany, although most of them argue that it is not easy to pass through the psychological or social barriers in German society. In fact, their education level and their language skills help them to reach a good place in Germany society. The vast majority of young Alevi people in my research will probably be able to work in qualified positions in Germany, since 34 participants are currently studying in or have graduated from university, while 8 participants have studied at high-school level and 13 participants are continuing their vocational training.

The major prerequisite for having a good education and also better integration is the knowledge of the German language. A higher education level also affects the participation processes to the labor force and may allow to reach a higher life standard, both economically and socially. The language knowledge helps youth Alevis to participate in a larger social environment than their own and also encourages them to participate politically by means of the feeling of belonging to the settled country. My research shows that the Alevi youth in the BDAJ is a good example of how to facilitate the conditions for political and social integration in the settled country.

4. Conclusion

The recognition of Alevis as a religious and cultural community in Germany has created a growing social and political movement and a diaspora in Germany. In this research I have explored how Alevi migrants' children in Germany, especially those in the third generation, are growing up in transnational connections with the diasporic consciousness.

The first point is that the Alevi youth in the German diaspora can be essentially characterized as a social organization that assures a social entity beyond the collective misfortune in the history of Alevis. Third-generation Alevis have tried to form a notion of belongingness to Germany rather than Turkey, even though most of them claim that, because of their migration background, it is difficult to be accepted in Germany, even if they have German citizenship and can speak German perfectly. To overcome these barriers, they maintain that they should protect their values and beliefs and spread Alevi organizations in order to teach their identity, values and faiths to the next generations.

The second point is that most of the participants did not consider Alevism as a religion, although religion is also a significant component to identify themselves with both the feelings of belonging to the Alevi community and also the question of integration of the third-generation Alevis in Germany. The main reason is that the Alevi youth in diaspora intersect various subcategories with different interests as a result of the closed contact with German culture and most of them stated that they do not have enough information about Alevism, even though they say freely "I am Alevi" in their everyday life. They criticized primarily *dedes*, the religious leaders, and their family, because they did not teach them about Alevism. It is also important to point out that most *dedes* could not speak good German, which made the contacts difficult. Therefore, to be a member of the BDAJ is very important for the Alevi youth in order to feel a sense of belonging to one community and to protect their continued solidarity. Actually, most of the young people described Alevism as a kind of lifestyle for political struggles rather than a religion. Despite the fact that the Alevi community has been accepted as a religious community and has gained many rights concerning its religious status in Germany, the recognition process of Alevis in Germany was primarily achieved by legitimizing their demands in the political field and recognizing their political struggle.

To summarize, the BDAJ has worked both an autonomous structure from the AABF (German Alevi Federation), and also as a Young Union of the AABF because a member of the youth group of one Alevi organization is simultaneously also a member of BDAJ. Therefore, both BDAJ and AABF have similar approaches to the struggle for recognition in Germany. For instance, both of them have hold off some debatable issues which deal with nationality, ethnicity and differences in the rituals, in order to increase the number of the memberships and to be able to strengthen their organizational structure.

The young Alevis in Germany have diverse political, social, economic and educational conditions and so their struggles and opportunities as immigrants differ from the first-generation immigrants that came from Turkey after the 1960s, at least compared with that of the parents of the young Alevi. The young Alevi immigrants increasingly regard Germany as their country and they feel more integrated into the society than their family since they have been raised in Germany, have studied in Germany and can speak the German language very well. According to Karakaşoğlu. "As recently as the 1990s, two-thirds of Turks wanted to return at some point. But this attitude has changed: more and more Turks really want to stay here forever." The case, of the Alevi youth reinforces the same tendency, since all of the participants stated that they would not like to return to and live in Turkey. In the present research, the third-generation Alevis in Germany define themselves as a part of German society.

Finally, the identity of the Alevi youth in the German diaspora have been affected by both the homeland and the settled country because the construction of identity is an active and interactive process through which the individuals build new ways of interpreting themselves. The identity of the Alevi youth in Germany is formed not only by the historical, personal, and collective memories, but it is also the product of the ongoing socio-political struggles.

Chapter 24. Language and Identity Problems

Neriman Hocaoğlu Bahadır[1]

Abstract

Migration, language and identity are three interrelated concepts. These concepts have important effects on the lives of moving families, as their lives are social realities. In this research, it is aimed to focus on the 1989 migration from Bulgaria to Turkey in order to determine the problems especially language related problems, which people who immigrated in 1989 and afterwards to Turkey came across and their effects on their identities. To be able to find proper results qualitative method was used in this study. In-depth interviews were conducted to understand the difficulties in relation to language inabilities, adaptation problems, perceptions, acceptance or exclusion. So the research questions are: What were the problems of immigrants who moved from Bulgaria to Turkey? and How did these problems affect their identities? The novelty of this research is that it is focused on not only to people who emigrated but also their children who were born either in Bulgaria or in Turkey. So, it is possible to make comparison among the people who lived the act of moving and their children whom may also have lived or just felt it in their lives. This also makes it possible to determine changes in time.

Keywords: acceptance, identity, language, migration.

Introduction

Migration is an important social reality and it has effects on moving people's identity construction. Both migration and identity are intensively explored concepts. These concepts have been the subject of many researches from various disciplines.

The migration of Turkish people from Bulgaria to Turkey in 1989 is one of important turning points of these people's life. The country they live in, their houses, neighbours, habits, languages and identities have changed noticeably with this migration. In this paper, it is focused on three concepts which are closely interrelated; migration, identity and language. It is aimed to find out the effects of language in constructing identity in the case of 1989 migration. There may be many factors, which affect the identity construction of these people, but here it will be focused on the migration as the general factor and language as the more specific factor in this construction process.

In this research, first it is aimed to give brief information about the concept of identity. Then it is focused on the 1989 migration and its effects on identities and then the language factor on the construction identity is examined.

It is preferred to use mainly qualitative method in this study so; in-depth interviews and literature review are used as research methods. The reasons for choosing these methods are to see the construction process of identities

---

[1] Neriman Hocaoğlu Bahadır is an Assistant Professor in Department of Interntional Relations and a Coordinator of International Relations Office of Kırklareli University, Kayalı Campus, Kırklareli, Turkey. E-mail: nerimanhocaogl@gmail.com

of people who immigrated in 1989 by observing their perceptions. The in-depth interviews were carried out in June and July 2017. There were 20 interviewees and 14 of them were women and 6 of them were men. 9 of the interviewees immigrated to Turkey under the age of 12 and 11 of them over the age of 27. The interviews took place in the houses of the interviewees or at cafes. Tape-recorder was used with the permission of the interviewees during the interviews. Mostly the same open-ended questions were asked to the interviewees in order to maintain similarities and differences of their thoughts. All the interviews were transcribed and translated in order to analyse the data. Lastly, it should be noted that the names of the interviewees are not announced to eliminate the problems of ethics.

Identity

Identity is a concept, which is described and explained many times according to different disciplines. Even though defining the concept of identity is not the aim of this research, some of these definitions are noted in order to examine the subject in general.

Identity as an answer to the question of who we are is described by Richard Jenkins. According to him identity is a human capacity and it includes "...who we are, knowing who others are, them knowing who we are, us knowing who they think we are, and so on.." (Jenkins, 2008:5). Starting from this point, it is crucial to note that identity is closely related with perceptions. By means of perception human beings place and describe themselves, they also place and describe others, the others knowing and placing themselves and then they describe who the others think they are and where they place them. Therefore, the central question is who we are and it is asked to the interviewees how they perceive themselves and who they are within the context of migration. Most of them noted that they are immigrants one of them said " I define myself as Turk. Turkish people living in Turkey define me as Turk, as well. I don't tell that I am an immigrant ..." (E., 30, dietician). This statement is important because the interviewee prefers to hide the reality that he is an immigrant. He explained the reason for hiding this reality as: "... in primary school, when the teachers learnt that I was an immigrant they were humiliating me and my friends who were also immigrants. Because of such situations I started to hide that I was an immigrant" (E., 30, dietician). From this statement, it can be seen that how the people's perceptions can affect a person's life.

Brubaker and Cooper (2000: 14-21) prefers to explain the term of identity with group of idioms instead of giving a full thick definition. They explain the term by using three groups of idioms; identification and categorization, self-understanding and location and commonality, connectness, and groupness. Here, identification and categorization and self-understanding and location can be evaluated as close to the Jenkins definition. As it is also related with the question of who we are. However, Brubaker and Cooper (200:15) note the importance of modern state as an important agent of identification and categorization besides selves and the others. This point should be emphasised within the context of this research, because the Bulgarian state was an important agent in constructing the Turkish people's identity in Bulgaria and the regime also played an important role in this construction process. The third group of idioms are also significant in this research because some of Turkish people from Bulgaria have more strict connectness and groupness with the people who feel the same thing while others do not have so.

Another point, which should be noted, is that identities are constantly constructed. Richard Jenkins (2008:5) states this reality, as identity "is a process -identification– not a 'thing' It is not something that one can have, or not; it is something that one does." Stuart Hall (1991:19) also notes that identity is a process and he adds "Identity is always an open, complex and unfinished game - always 'under construction'." The changing nature of identity is essential within the context of this research because the identities of the immigrants have changing points in their life cycle. The place they lived, the social, political and economic environment they were in and the languages they spoke to communicate all changed. So, their identities have changed, as well. Identities are alive and active instead of being static, fixed or inactive. Construction of identities is a process as it is stated above; it is never completed but always under construction.

The Identity of Turkish Minority in Bulgaria

Turkish minorities were the second largest group living in Bulgaria. However, they were not always accepted throughout history. Türkkaya Ataöv (1989:135-140) gives examples of accepting them as Turks as well as seeing them as Turkified Bulgarians throughout history. She also explains the history of Turkish entity in the Balkan Peninsula, including Bulgaria. She gives the detail of how, from where and when they came to Balkans and Bulgaria. Even though this settlement and their ethnic origin are contested in a period in Bulgaria there are many academic researches portraying "their physical traits, ways of life, language and religion." (Ataöv, 1989:139) In this research, it is not aimed to trace back the Turkish entity in the Balkan Peninsula or to prove or disprove these claims but accepting their existence or claiming that there were no Turks in Bulgaria affected the lives of these people, their acts and their existence in the social life. This situation also affected their identity construction process.

Policy changes in Bulgaria had effects on the identities of Turkish people living in Bulgaria. These changes can be seen as fractions in their identity construction process. Before 1945, there were different policies related to the minorities but after this date it changed. They got some rights. Their existence was constitutionally recognized (Eminov, 1997:5). However this period did not last for a long time and after 1956, there were a policy change and the minorities of Bulgaria started to be identified as Bulgarians and they were started to be forced to change their names with Bulgarian ones (Eminov, 1997:6). The process started at the end of 1950s came to its culmination stage between December 1984 and March 1985 when all the Turkish people living in Bulgaria were forced to assume Bulgarian names and the message that "There are no Turks in Bulgaria" was announced again and again in the districts such as Sliven, Haskovo, Veliko Turnovo, Blagoevgrad, Silistra and Ruse (Eminov, 1997:8-13). They were found guilty for speaking Turkish, wearing traditional clothes such as shalvar, practicing their age-old customs (Ataöv,1989;146). Most of the interviewees have bad memories about the period after the name changing campaign. One of the interviewees noted that she did notcome across with any problems related to be Turk in Bulgaria until the change of their names. She added that after that process the department she was working in the hospital was changed and her sister who was also working in the same department as a doctor was dismissed (G., 60, nurse). Another interviewee who was a teacher in Bulgaria during that period said that wearing shalvar was prohibited and they were tasked with going from house to house and controlling if shalvars were cut or not (E, 57, teacher).

It is clear that Turkish minorities in Bulgaria experienced changing policies; firstly, they were suppressed and then they were recognized and lastly their Turkish identity was ignored for a period. All these affected the lives of families in many ways; economically, socially and psychologically. Migration can be seen as the outcome of these effects. Since the end of 19th century, there were migration flows from Bulgaria to Turkey and the last one started in 1989. More than 300.000 people immigrated from Bulgaria to Turkey after 1989 (Zhelyazkova, 1998). This immigration lasted for a long time. After a while it became illegal, but it did not stop. Turkish people living in Bulgaria moved from a country where they were seen as minority for a while and as Bulgarian for some time to a country where they thought they would become part of majority.

Turkish immigrants from Bulgaria became majority in some ways. For instance, they became a part of majority in terms of their ethnic origin, religion, language and culture. However, they were still minority in the country they immigrated to be majority because of the same criteria, which made them majority. They were different because of their accent, culture and life style. They were speaking Turkish but the Turkish they were speaking was different because they were using Bulgarian sentence structures with

Turkish words and this sounded strange. There were some other differences in vocabulary and intonation. They were the others of Bulgarian in Bulgaria and they became the others of Turkish people living in Turkey. Some of the reasons that caused them to leave the country they were born were that their identity was not accepted in Bulgaria, they were called and assumed Bulgarian and they were forced to assume Bulgarian names. However, the situation did not change for some of them in Turkey as they were called Bulgarian in Turkey, as well. One of the interviewees stated that in the first years, she changed many jobs and her bosses called her Bulgarian and asked her "Why did you come? Go back." She also noted "They were catching us from the vocabulary we were using then. The words we were using were different. They were catching us from our clothes." (M, 50, teacher). They had a dilemma. Even though there were differences in meaning, they were called Bulgarian both in Bulgaria and in Turkey. This caused effects on their identity construction process. They had to struggle in order to be accepted in both countries. Their identity changed in the receiving country, as it is fluid, flexible and changeable.

These people left their lives, their houses, neighbors, relatives, jobs, social status and wealth in Bulgaria with the aim of finding better economic, living and working conditions. They wanted to be accepted by the majority. But it is difficult to note that all of them attained their objectives. One of the interviewees noted that she came to Turkey with the dream of becoming teacher in Turkey as she was educated to be a teacher. But she could not be a full- time paid teacher in Turkey. She could not be teacher in Bulgaria, either (M., 50, teacher). Another interviewee also stated that she thought that she would have been engineer in Turkey as she was an engineer in Bulgaria (N., 56, engineer). Both of them had a desire to be able to do the job they were educated for but they could not find a proper position.

After a while they became **in between**; "not yet belonging "here" but no longer there" (La Barbera, 2015:3). One of the interviewees indicated, "Our neighbors who are living in Bulgaria externalize us…" (M., 50, teacher). Another interviewee stated "We were Turks in Bulgaria and we were different than the Bulgarian people but nearly all the Turks were same in our region but now we, the Turkish minority who were immigrated to Turkey, are different than the Turks living in our region in Bulgaria. We are different here in Turkey, as well. But the level of difference has changed since the day we immigrated." (E, 58, teacher). It is clear that they are different than the Turkish people living in Bulgaria now and they are also slightly different than the Turkish people living in Turkey.

The Effects of Language in Constructing Identity

The identity construction process of the Turkish people who migrated from Bulgaria was affected by many things such as the policy changes in Bulgaria, the oppression, the immigration process, economic problems, social problems and the adaptation to the new conditions in Turkey. In the adaptation process, the language they use has importance in constructing their identity.

Before focusing on the effects of language in constructing the identities of Turkish immigrants from Bulgaria, it would be appropriate to point that what language means and what the relation between language and identity is. Edward Sapir defines language as "a purely human and noninstinctive method of communicating ideas, emotions, and desires by means of a system of voluntarily produced symbol" (2004:5) and he adds that it is a tool of significant expression (2004:17). Sapir also notes that:

Language is a guide to 'social reality.' ... Human beings do not live in the objective world alone, nor alone in the world of social activity as ordinarily understood, but very much at the mercy of the particular language which has become the medium of expression for their society. It is quite an illusion to imagine that one adjusts to reality essentially without the use of language and that language is merely an incidental means of solving problems of communication or reflection. The fact of the matter is that the 'real world' is to a large extent unconsciously built up on the language habits of the group. (1949:68)

This expression is really critical to show the importance of language and here language is defined as a social reality and a medium of expression for the society. But it is not just a tool for expression or communication as David Kilgour (1999) notes by citing Sapir: "Language is not only a vehicle for the expression of thoughts, perceptions, sentiments, and values characteristic of a community; it also represents a fundamental expression of social identity."

According to Bonny Norton, "language constructs our sense of self" (Darvin and Norton, 2015:36) in other words identity is constructed by language (Norton, 2006:3). She also cites Weedon to clarify language and identity relation and according to this citation, Weedon notes that "Language is the place where actual and possible forms of social organization and their likely social and political consequences are defined and contested. Yet it is also the place where our sense of ourselves, our subjectivity, is constructed." (Norton, 2006:5). It is clear that language is seen as the place the construction of an identity occurs. So, the effect of language use in identity construction process should not be underestimated.

Here, "symbolic power" and "symbolic capital" notions of Bourdieu should also be indicated as Bourdieu defines symbolic power as a "a credit; it is the power granted to those who have obtained sufficient recognition to be in a position to impose recognition" and he adds that symbolic power is "the power to make things with word" (1989:23). He also explains the relation between symbolic power and symbolic capital and notes that symbolic power depends to the symbolic capital and it has to be based on it (1989:23). Starting from this point of view, Schjerve and Vet evaluate language as a symbolic power, which determines the positioning of the individuals in social markets (2012:135). So, it can be expressed that having language power has effects in positioning the individuals in social community and their interactions in this community with the language power they have affect in constructing their identities. The existence of language power and resources will maintain interaction, mobility and employability of the individuals but inexistence of this power may cause inabilities in interaction and finding proper jobs. For instance, one of the interviewees stated "Language problems made me introverted, I could not improve my social standing and I could not go places that I aimed or dream because of these problems…" (I.,49, veterinary). It is clear that language as a symbolic power has impact on identity construction and this impact can be either positive or negative depending the resources and power the individuals have. In the case of this interviewee, it has negative effect, as he could not reach to the position he aimed.

Language Problems and their effects in constructing identity

As it is stated in the previous part, there are many things such as; immigration eeconomic, social, adaptation and language problems that may have effects on identity construction process of the Turkish immigrants from Bulgaria. In this research, it is focused on language related problems and in order to reveal the effect of language related problems some questions were asked to the interviewees.

According to the answers of the interviewees, it can be indicated that there are three types of problems the immigrants came across because of language related inefficiencies or differences. First of them is "othering". The questions related to the perceptions of the immigrants about themselves and the perceptions of others about their identity shows that the Turkish immigrants from Bulgaria find themselves different than the rest of the community in Turkey because of the differences in language use, their ways of living, and their view of life. Even though language is not the only factor of othering but it is still one of the factors, which causes the perception of othering. The second problem, the immigrants noted, is humiliating attitudes. Most of the interviewees experienced a humiliating attitude because of the language they use, their accent and the words they choose. For example, one of the interviewees said "Some of them were clowning on me. We learnt Bulgarian. That was the language in Bulgaria. For that reason, there were people who found it odd but I didn't take offence. I am not speaking wrongly. We have a strong accent but we can not change it" (N, 56, engineer). The third problem is that they were called Bulgarian. This is one of the most annoying things they experienced. They strongly emphasises that they are not Bulgarian but they just came from Bulgaria. Most of them noted that they feel themselves oblige to explain that they are not Bulgarian. One of them indicated that

"It is strange to be called Bulgarian in Turkey because we left our lives in Bulgaria in order not to be seen as Bulgarian or assimilated. However, in Turkey our parents were called Bulgarian, as well. Nobody called me Bulgarian because I have been educated in Turkey and nobody can understand that I am from Bulgaria as long as I express it. But I really get annoyed when I see someone who called the immigrants from Bulgaria Bulgarian. Even the politicians, who should know the situation better than the society, call Bulgarian to the Turkish immigrants from Bulgaria. This is really ironic as it is what our families and we escaped from but it finds us here in Turkey. It is our fate." (N., 35, teacher)

Another interviewee expressed that she read a lot of history books in order to be able to explain their situation and she also noted that she especially emphasises that she is a Turk who was born in Bulgaria (H., 33, teacher).

These were the general grouping of the language related problems they came across and they affected the identities of the immigrants especially the older generation because the younger generation, who educated in Turkey, did not feel the language related effects as much as their parents. According to the questions about how language related inefficiencies affected their lives, most of them noted that they became more silent, more introverted and they were not be able to achieve their goals or increase their social status. For instance, one of the interviewees said "You want to talk but you cannot… You cannot join in a conversation … short sentences. … When I went to congress, in such platforms, it was more difficult." (H., 66, doctor). People experienced these problems and they affected their identities but there was one more striking example about the effect of language problems as one of the interviewees told that she could not continue her education because of language problems. She expressed that "We were misusing some of the words. We were speaking Bulgarian Turkish. They did not understand us. We did not understand them. For that reason I could not start my education." (Z., 32, worker). She immigrated to Turkey when she was 11 and she was not as lucky as other immigrants who moved to Turkey at the same age with her. Language related problems affected her directly. The outcome of this effect is clearer and more tangible. These problems also affected their better and quicker adaptation to the society.

Conclusion

Turkish people experienced different policies related to their ethnic origin in Bulgaria. They were minority in Bulgaria even though all of them did not feel the same way. After the immigration, they became the part of majority in Turkey but some of them feel as minority in Turkey because of different reasons.

The immigrants came across many different problems such as economic, social, adaptation and language problems. Some of them could not find a job for what they were educated and some of them could not reach to the point they aimed. There were negative and positive outcomes of their problems especially language related problems. For example, language inefficiencies hindered their social integration partly because they refused to take part in dialogues if it is not compulsory and they prefer to be more silent and use short answers and sentences. They became more introverted. They were not able to achieve their goals related to their profession. However, there were positive effects, as well. As they noted, they read more and improved themselves. So, the negative effects they were experienced can also be seen as a pushing factor. This pushing factor affected the younger generation more positively as they did not experienced many of the problems their families experienced and they benefited from their experinces.

Finally, it can be noted that they became in between. Their identity has changed and shaped according to their experiences both in Bulgaria and Turkey. For that reason, they are like neither the Turkish people in Bulgaria nor the Turkish people in Turkey. They have the properties of both communities. This can be evaluated as richness but these people feel the effects of being different, as well.

References

Ataöv, T. (1989). The Turks of Bulgaria. pp. 135-152. Received from http://www.politics.ankara.edu.tr/dergi/pdf/44/1/theturksofbulgaria.pdf available on: 25.06.2017

Bourdieu, Pierre. (1989). Social Space and Symbolic Power. Sociological Theory, Vol.7, No.1. pp. 14-25.

Brubaker, R. and Cooper, F. (2000). Beyond "Identity". pp. 1-47. Received from http://www.sscnet.ucla.edu/soc/faculty/brubaker/Publications/18_Beyond_Identity.pdf available on: 11.05.2017

Darvin, R. and Norton, B. (2015). "Identity and a Model of Investment in Applied Linguistic. Annual Review of Applied Linguistics, Vol.35.

Eminov, A. (1997). Turkish and Other Muslim Minorities in Bulgaria, New York:Routledge.

Hall, S. (August 1991). Globalisation Europe's Other Self, Marxism Today. pp. 18-19. Received from http://www.unz.org/Pub/MarxismToday-1991aug-00018 available on: 20.05.2017

Jenkins, R. (2008). Social Identity, 3rd Edition, Abingdon: Routledge.

Kilgour, D. (1999) The Importance of Language. Retrieved from http://www.david-kilgour.com/mp/sahla.htm available on 13.09.2017

La Barbera, M. (2015). Identity and Migration: An Introduction. In Identity and Migration in Europe: Multidisciplinary Perspectives. MariaCaterina La Barbera, ed. Switzerland:Springer. pp. 1-13.

Norton, B. (2006). Identity as a sociocultural construct in second language education. In TESOL in Context (Special Issue). K. Cadman and K. O'Regan, eds. Received from http://faculty.educ.ubc.ca/norton/Norton%202006%20in%20Australia%20TESOL.pdf available on: 13.09.2017

Sapir, E. (1949). The Status of Linguistics as a Science. In Culture, Language and Personality: Selected Essays. David G. Mandelbaum, ed. Berkeley: University of California Press. pp.65-77.

Sapir, E. (2004) Language: An Introduction to the Study of Speech, New York: Dover Publications Inc.

Schjerve, R. R. and Vetter, E. (2012) European Multilingualism: Current Perspectives and Challenges, Bristol: Multilingual Matters.

Zhelyazkova, a. (1998). The Social and Cultural Adaptation of Bulgarian Immigrants in Turkey. In Between Adaptation and Nostalgia: The Bulgarian Turks in Turkey. Antonina Zhelyazkova, ed. Received from http://www.omda.bg/public/imir/studies/nostalgia_1.html available on: 02.09.2017

Chapter 25. The Certainty of Uncertainty; The Critical Tool of Certainty in a Migrant's Journey to Effectively Control Issues in Human Security, Fraud and Integration for the Benefit of the Migrant and the Receiving Country

Sherene Ozyurek[1]

Abstract

From an Australian perspective, which can be extended to other countries' migration frameworks, this study raises the notion that "uncertainty" negatively modulates systemic issues in recurring themes of human security violations, fraud and non-integration. Such understanding could lead to insights into migrants' decision-making processes resulting in the subsequent use of unintended pathways. Literature and case study reviews were undertaken, coupled with a quantitative approach analysing retrospective data from the Department of Immigration and Border Protection and the Australian Federal Police to determine the ineffectiveness of current legislative tools that do not take certainty into account and to determine the impact of uncertainty on migrants in Australia's migration program as a receiving country. Practical recommendations are presented for consideration by policy-makers to ensure certainty for the migrant, including; to combat human security violations via the provision of visa pathways for applicants to remain after lodging a complaint, ensuring that both employment and human securities can co-exist; to effectively control fraud via the removal of discretion, ensuring certainty in pathways of decision-making processes to combat unintended pathways; and finally, the permeation of certainty throughout the migration program, ensuring that steps to attain citizenship are not out of necessity but instead a step towards successful integration.

Keywords: citizenship, fraud, human security, integration

Background:

This inquiry provides an insight into the link between *uncertainty* in legislative tools and three important systemic factors of a migration program, namely; human insecurity, fraud and non-integration, which can all have a negative impact on the receiving country. It is raised that understanding how *uncertainty* negatively modulates these factors, both independently and collectively, can lead to insights into the understanding of the decision-making processes migrants face in their journey to migrate (see Diagram 1). Robertson (2008)

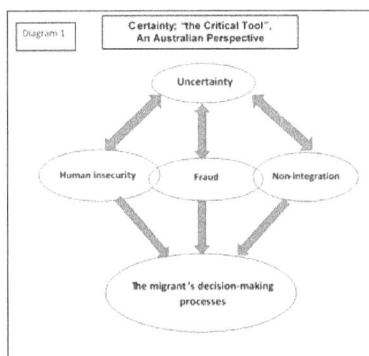

stated that the motivations behind citizenship choices were multifaceted. This paper acknowledges the complex nature of the matter, however, seeks to provide insights into the decision-making patterns of migrants caused by legislative and policy changes which results in *uncertainty* for the migrant, not only in their migration journey but in some cases until they reach their goal of citizenship.

---

[1] Senior Lawyer, FCG legal Pty Ltd, Melbourne, Australia; Accredited Immigration Law Specialist, Law Institute of Victoria, Australia; Lecturer, Postgraduate Immigration Law Program, Victoria University, Australia; PhD Candidate, Victoria University, Australia; sherene@fcglegal.com.

Methodology:

In this study, a sociological and empirical approach was undertaken in relation to the importance of *certainty* in a migrant's journey. The impact on Australia's migration program, visa holders and the receiving country was analysed via literature and case study reviews coupled with a quantitative approach to analyse retrospective data (2011-2015) produced by the Migration Review Tribunal–Refugee Review Tribunal ("MRT-RRT"), caseload statistics data produced by the Australian Government over a four year period (one year prior to the introduction of the Fraud Principal and four years afterwards) (Australian Government Migration Review Tribunal-Refugee Review Tribunal (AGMRT-RRT), 2010-2014 & AGMRT-RRT, 2015) as well as data produced by the Australian Federal Police (Australian Federal Police Annual Reports (AFPAR), 2010-2014) pertaining to labour exploitation and data from the available aggregate statistics from Australian Government agencies over the past four to five years.

Results and discussion:

In this study, the negative modulatory impact of *uncertainty* in the legislative framework on issues pertaining to the themes of human insecurity, fraud and non-integration and its subsequent impact on migrants' decision-making processes have been investigated. This inquiry raises the notion that ensuring *certainty* for the migrant in the development of policies and the legislative framework is a practical tool that could positively impact on the above mentioned themes and could provide a further substantive effect of removing unintended pathways in the migrants' decision-making processes in their journey and consequently any non-beneficial effect on the receiving country's migration program.

Uncertainty, a cause of human insecurity and its impact on migrants' decision-making processes and consequential effects on the receiving country

This study highlights that despite an increase in visas granted in the employer linked visa streams over the years (see Fig 1), obtaining accurate data about the extent of labour exploitation in Australia is extremely complex (Boese, Campbell, Roberts, & Tham, 2013). This supports the notion that the lack of *certainty* the migrant faces acts as a deterrent for reporting a breach of human security. This paper raises the notion that the co-existence of providing migrants a pathway to preserve their visa after complaint and hence providing *certainty* for the applicant is a critical tool in combatting human security violations.

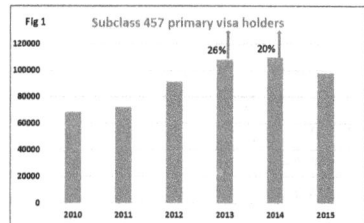

Fig 1   Subclass 457 primary visa holders

A reason for such low reporting was highlighted by Boese, et al., 2013, stating, *"temporary migrant workers are sometimes seen as particularly precarious because their ability to remain in the host country is often dependent on maintaining the goodwill of an employer and staying in a job."* The author further presented two interviews with 457 visa (employer linked visa stream) holders that highlighted that exact point. One visa holder stated: *"the thing is, if you're on a 457 visa, you're scared of saying things, because you're worried that they might say: Unfortunately we're terminating your contract'. That means that you kind of keep so many stuff to yourself ... You're still worried that if I lose this job I'm only given a month to get another job or else I'll pack my stuff and leave,"* and the other visa holder stated *"It is just a cloud that hangs over anyone on a 457 visa ... You always think that if my job come to an end within 28 days ... I'm very, very conscious of that, and that preoccupies me subconsciously at work ... Personally I won't complain. I won't do anything that I feel would jeopardize my visa. So I might end up having to put up with things which I feel are not really things I should be tolerating, because I sort of feel: okay, if this relationship breaks down at any time I'm in trouble"* (Boese et al., 2013).

Changes to the employer linked visa stream were introduced in July 2013[2] to strengthen the Department of Immigration and Border Protection's (the Department) capacity to identify and prevent illegal employer practices and breaches of human security in maintaining the integrity through the implementation of sponsorship obligations for the employers (Australia's Migration Trends (AMT), 2012–13).

However, these amendments were inconsistent with the existing legislative framework as what remained was a condition that visa holders were to work only for his or her sponsoring employer.[3] If a migrant breaches this condition, they are subject to cancellation of their visa and, serious consequences follow from a breach of this visa condition.

This was also followed by the introduction of legislation in 2016 (AG-FRL-2016), which provided for civil penalties for receiving a benefit from a migrant for sponsorship purposes. However, the functionality of this is yet to be determined and in our view, not effective as it imposes penalties on both the employer and migrant therefore providing a disincentive for either party to complain.

Fig 2 Cases of labour exploitation investigated by Australian Federal Police

These amendments were not effective in providing migrants more confidence to report more cases of labour exploitation. The investigated cases since the implementation of employer sanctions in 2013 were reduced by 9% (from 23 to 21 cases), reflecting the ineffectiveness of those changes in ensuring human security (see Fig 2). This is further concerning given the fact that the number of employer linked primary visa holders during 2014 increased by approximately 3% compared to their number in 2013 (as shown in Fig 1). This is an extremely low reporting considering that the number of employer linked temporary visas granted over that period was 746,869 visas (Phillips & Spinks, 2012).

The proposition of *certainty* for the migrant via a pathway to preserve their visa after lodging a complaint is a critical step to ensure that human security in employer linked visas is not compromised (see Diagram 2). The anticipated success of this proposition can be demonstrated in the Partner visa stream which provides a victim of violence,

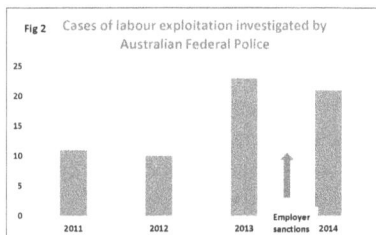

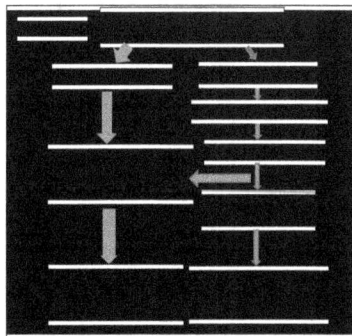

---

[2] *Migration Amendment (Reform of Employer Sanctions) Act 2013 (Cth)* No. 10, 2013
[3] *Migration Regulations 1994* (Cth) Schedule 8, Condition 8107

either physical and/or mental harm, to proceed to permanent residency despite no longer having a sponsor.[4] Both situations provide the applicant encouragement to bring to light any breach of their human security due to the *certainty* and the availability of a pathway for the migrant (Richards & Lyneham, 2014). Furthermore, as the pathway of complaint is not a viable option, the migrant instead uses an alternative unintended pathway, which at times is achieved by the use fraud as a necessity to allow them to be eligible to apply for another visa and to "self-remove" themselves from the circumstances.

Therefore, the first recommendation of this study pertaining to the factor of human security is the use of *certainty* as a critical tool via a provision of a visa pathway. This will ensure that both employment and human securities can co-exist for the migrant and the benefit of the receiving country.

Uncertainty; a cause for the use of fraud as a motivating factor in the migrant's decision-making processes and its effects on the receiving country

This notion is demonstrated by review of Public Interest Criteria 4020 ("PIC 4020"), otherwise known as "the Fraud Principal", which was introduced in April 2011 into the Australian Migration program.[5] The policy surrounding PIC 4020 was to significantly increase the level of integrity in visa applications by providing a strong disincentive to those providing a bogus document or information that is false or misleading by way of a three year ban on applying for other visas.[6] However, reviews of the migration program since the implementation of this principle has shown an increase of migrants using unintended pathways, resulting in subsequent systemic issues in the migration program (Azarias, Lambert, McDonald, & Malyon, 2014, and AGDIBP, 2014b).

This is demonstrated by examining the General Skilled Migration ("GSM") program which is the intended pathway for an economic migrant. The pathway for GSM, particularly for students at the time the PIC 4020 was introduced, required a skills assessment, which required a component of practical work experience.

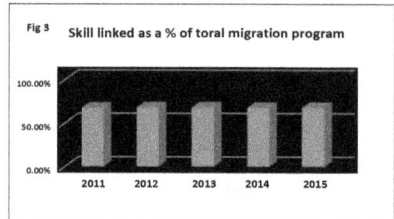

Fig 3 Skill linked as a % of toral migration program

This work experience was difficult to obtain by recent graduates during their studies as they had yet to attain their qualification. This difficulty led to the facilitation of false documents in relation to work experience. The ineffectiveness of PIC 4020 was highlighted in a case study of two registered Australian migration agents who sold a "three-year working visa", which in reality, were only encouraging onshore international graduate students with no alternative pathways to lodge applications onshore for GSM which would ultimately be refused due to the lack of work experience (McKenzie & Baker, 2014). The reason they were three-year visas is that the time to process the application through the Department and to then seek merits review equated to an average of three years, noting the ban period began at time of Departmental decision. In addition during processing students were able to obtain the relevant work experience and then reapply offshore. The fishing for alternative

---

[4] *Migration Regulations 1994 (Cth)*, Schedule 2, subclass 820/801
[5] *Migration Regulations 1994* (Cth), Schedule 4, PIC 4020
[6] *Migration Regulations 1994 (Cth)*, Schedule 4, item 4020(2).

pathways for an economic migrant is not uncommon. This case study supports the notion that PIC 4020 clearly did not provide a disincentive to apply and the ability for the migrant to remain during review to gain experience was viewed as a way to achieve *certainty* in their journey.

Data analysis showed that while the migration planning numbers for this stream over the period from 2011 to 2015 were consistent (see Fig 3), with the introduction of PIC 4020, there was a substantial increase of reviews at the MRT with an increase of 580% of applications lodged at the MRT for GSM in 2012 and a further 120% increase over 2013 (see Fig 4) (a total increase of 700% compared to 2011) (AGMRT-RRT, 2010-2014). It is interesting to note that while all these changes took place in GSM, another stream, namely, the Partner visa stream, where the PIC 4020 principal came into effect in 2013, showed an increase of 160% rate of refusal (see Fig 5) (AGMRT-RRT, 2010-2014). That was the biggest increase in the last five years and happened at the same time GSM stream was stagnated, regardless of whether the PIC 4020 was introduced as a disincentive in the stream or not (AGMRT-RRT, 2010-2014). It

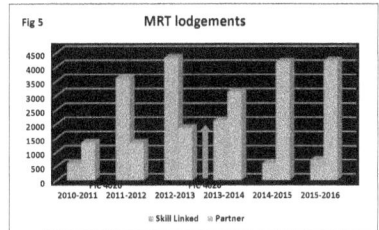

Fig 5   MRT lodgements

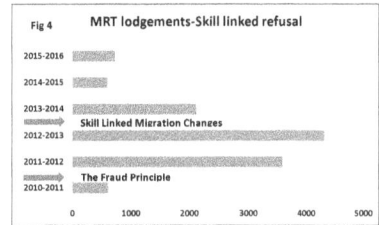

Fig 4   MRT lodgements-Skill linked refusal

is worth noting that the migration planning numbers were also consistent during these years in this stream (AGDIBP, Migration Programme Statistics, 2010- 2015). This supports the hypothesis that PIC 4020 implemented in isolation did not provide a deterrent for economic migrants from seeking alternative pathways. It relates back to the case study that unintended economic migrants are looking at pathways regardless of the ultimate consequence and Partner visas have one of the highest processing times second to GSM to enable the applicant to work while their visa was getting processed and during review (AGDIBP, 2015a).

To strengthen the importance of the notion of the necessity of *certainty* in combatting fraud "by the removal of discretion", and for the purposes of a comparative, this paper demonstrates the effectiveness of the expansion of PIC 4020 in 2014 to include an increased ten-year ban based on identity fraud.[7] It is worth noting that concurrent with the introduction of the *new identity* requirement, *PIC 4020* has been re-badged as the 'integrity' PIC (AGDIBP, 2014a).[8] This increased ban,

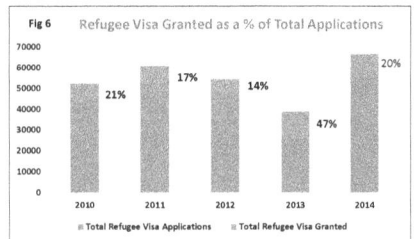

Fig 6   Refugee Visa Granted as a % of Total Applications

---

[7] *Migration Amendment (2014 Measures No. 1)* Regulation 2014 (Cth), Select Legislative Instrument No. 32, 2014

[8] *Ibid*

specifically in relation to identity fraud, was introduced across the majority of the migration program including skilled and Partner streams (AGDIBP, 2014a).

Therefore, the second recommendation of this study pertaining to combatting fraud is the use of *certainty*, as a critical tool, by removing discretion. This will ensure unintended pathways are not utilised for a short-term gain by an unintended economic migrant and this consequently benefitting the receiving country in seeking skilled migration. Hence, the removal of discretion from this tool (a source of uncertainty), allows for *certainty*, a critical tool that is required for the policy measure to be effective. This inquiry further recommends that the approach to combat fraud needs to be implemented in alignment with all policies of the migration program and not only "in isolation," as this contributes to ineffectiveness of the Australian model.

Uncertainty; a cause in the migrant decision-making process to seek citizenship out of necessity resulting in unsuccessful integration for the migrant and consequential effects on the receiving country

Australia is one of the world's most diverse multicultural immigrant societies. Like many other countries, Australia faces issues in successfully implementing policies that effectively encourage the engagement and integration of the migrant into the receiving country, while carefully balancing their emotive belonging to the sending country. In this inquiry, two case studies are highlighted:

Case Study One: (Identity vs. Necessity):
Refugees granted asylum in Australia are subject to a condition on their permanent visa that they cannot return home unless the Immigration Minister approves a request. (AGDIBP, 2015b).[9] This is understandable, as the basis of seeking protection is from circumstances in the sending country. However, this case scenario represents an enforced misconception that a refugee wants to give up their identity and never return to the sending country (see diagram 3). This highlights the disassociation between the Government obligations/legislations to protect refugees and their hopes and emotive feelings towards their home country.

A snapshot of the involvement of Australia as a receiving country can be shown from the data presented in Fig 6, showing the percentage of refugee visas that have been granted over the years (Australia's Offshore Humanitarian Programme: 2013–14) & Phillips, 2015). Although a small % of refugee visas have been granted, Australia continues to face issues pertaining to the unsuccessful integration of many Refugees, as shown by the first case study discussed above and as documented by (Karlsen, 2015). Furthermore, Sheridan (2011), revealed that those issues of unsuccessful integration do extend also to other migrants streams.

Case Study Two (Uncertainty vs. Necessity):
This case study reflects the fact that the phenomenon of attainment of citizenship for reasons of *certainty* does not only occur in the Protection visa stream. Migrants in

---

[9]*Migration Amendment (Permanent Protection Visas) Regulation 2013 (Cth)* Select Legislative Instrument No. 106 of 2013)

streams, where applicants find themselves in uncertain circumstances, such as by use of unintended pathways or in circumstances where there are breaches of their human security as discussed in this paper, seek to remove themselves from their *uncertainty* through the attainment of citizenship. By doing so, the migrant attains *certainty* by removing these circumstances required for grant or possible cancellation of their visa, which cannot be determined unfavourably against the migrant once citizenship is attained (see Diagram 4). However, in doing so, many migrants end up making a decision to relinquish their native citizenship, the sending country, as it does not allow dual citizenship. Subsequently, this can cause issues in resistance by the migrant in the receiving country to ensure they preserve their identity in other ways. Banulescu-Bogdan, 2012, also stated that "*there is little evidence that trying to ensure country loyalty by restricting dual citizenship have any benefit towards improving labour market outcomes or integration*". Indeed Australia allows its citizens to hold dual nationality (AGDIBP, 2015c) while other countries may not. However, this step by countries, such as Australia and its intended benefits by doing so, does not come into fruition if it is not reciprocated in the sending country.

It is raised that in cases where dual citizenship is not available by either the receiving or sending country, that citizenship can be attained as an immediate necessity rather than the motivation to "belong" and its conflict in some cases, with the migrants' hopes of return. Therefore, migrants attaining citizenship out of motivations of necessity does not equate to the fostering of successful integration. The consequence of that to the receiving country is in the well discussed themes of lack of social integration and again, despite the *certainty* of citizenship, their journey to attain *certainty* may make the migrants continue to view the receiving country as a short-term gain. Furthermore, migrants, despite being granted permanent residency are subject to constant and inconsistent changes to the law. Migrants only hold travel rights for five years after grant of permanent residency, after which time they must satisfy residency requirements or demonstrate sufficient ties to Australia.

Therefore, the third recommendation of this study pertaining to the factor of *certainty* in fostering successful integration policies for the benefit of the migrant and the receiving country is to ensure that the *uncertainty* in the migration programs, does not consequentially become the primary motivation by the migrant to attain citizenship. Future amendments in the migration and citizenship programs must be considered not in isolation of one another and should recognise the importance of multiple belongings and recognise the fact that forced patriotism based on the attainment of citizenship as a certain necessity rather than a choice does not foster successful integration and needs to be considered throughout the migrant's decision. Both the migration and citizenship programs must be considered as linked programs rather than separate programs and policies. The consideration of *certainty* as a tool to control the factors mentioned in this paper, could therefore help to overcome migrants' *uncertainty* and consequential unintended motivations in attaining citizenship to foster more successful integration in the receiving country.

Conclusion

This inquiry raises the notion that *"measures to control human security, fraud and integration will be more effective for both the migrant and the receiving country if certainty is considered as a critical tool when implementing these legislative policies"*. By examining the link between *uncertainty* and the abovementioned factors, independently and collectively, evidence was provided that such factors in the presence of *uncertainty*, negatively impacted on migrants' decision-making processes with a consequential negative impact on the receiving country. *Certainty* is therefore an integral tool in implementing successful legislative policies to ensure cohesion in the migration program.

The author argues that policy-makers need to consider that for issues pertaining to human security, the provision of a visa pathway for the applicant to remain after lodging a complaint will ensure that both employment and human securities can co-exist. Secondly, the approach to effectively control fraud needs to consider the removal of discretion to ensure certainty in pathways of decision-making by the migrant. Further, this control measure must align with all policies of the migration program and not be "in isolation". This will overcome the reported ineffectiveness in combatting unintended migrants in the receiving country. Lastly, for both the benefit of the migrant and the receiving country, the permeation of certainty throughout the migration program is required to ensure that steps to attain citizenship is for the right purpose, instead of a necessity which causes issues resulting in unsuccessful integration.

In summary, this paper provides an Australian perspective and a platform to analyse other countries' migration programs, in understanding three important and interlinked factors that impact on migrants' decision-making process either negatively or positively depending on the existence of *uncertainty* or *certainty, respectively,* in the legislative tools. *Certainty* is a tool that needs to be infused into different legislative policies because of its positive impact on the migrants' decision-making processes and their consequential impact on the receiving country's migration program. The recommendations provided are attempts to offer practical solutions that can be applicable to other countries' migration frameworks.

References

Australian Federal Police annual Reports (2010-2014). Retrieved from http://www.afp.gov.au/~/media/afp/pdf/a/afp-annual-report-2011-2012.pdf

Australian Government, Department of Immigration and Border Protection (AGDIBP). *Migration Programme Statistics* (2010-1015), Retrieved from https://www.immi.gov.au/ media/statistics/statistical-info/visa-grants/migrant.htm

Australian Government, Department of Immigration and Border Protection. (2014a). *Migration Amendment (2014 Measures No. 1) Regulation 2014, Explanatory Statement, Select Legislative Instrument 2011 No.32, 2014;* Issued by the Minister for Immigration and Border Protection on Mar 22, 2014. Retrieved from https://www.immi.gov.au/Live/Pages/document-fraud.aspx

Australian Government, Department of Immigration and Border Protection, Discussion Paper (2014b). *Reviewing the Skilled Migration and 400 Series Visa Programmes,* September 2014, 1-21. Retrieved from http://www.immi.gov.au/pub-res/documents/reviews/skilled-migration-400-series.pdf

Australian Government, Department of Immigration and Border Protection, *Family Visa processing times statistics* (2015a). Retrieved from https://www.immi.gov.au/about/charters/client-services-charter/visas/5.0.htm

Australian Government, Department of Immigration and Border Protection. (2015b). *How can a protection visa holder request permission to travel to their home country?* Retrieved from https://www.immi.gov.au/faqs/Pages/How-can-a-protection-visa-holder-request-permission-to-travel-to-their-home-country.aspx

Australian Government, Department of Immigration and Border Protection. *Dual citizenship*. (2015c). Retrieved from www.citizenship.gov.au/current/dual_citizenship/

Australian Government- Federal Register of Legislation (AG-FRL) (2016). *Migration Amendment (Temporary Activity Visas) Regulation 2016*. Retrieved from https://www.legislation.gov.au/Details/ F2016L01743/Explanatory %20Statement/Text

Australian Government Migration Review Tribunal-Refugee Review Tribunal (2010-2014). *MRT-RRT caseload statistics (2010–2014)*. Retrieved from http://www.mrt-rrt.gov.au/Forms-and-publications/Statistics.aspx

Australian Government Migration Review Tribunal-Refugee Review Tribunal (Financial Year till 31 May 2015). *MRT-RRT caseload statistics (31 May 2015)*. Retrieved from www.mrt-rrt.gov.au/Forms-and-publications/Statistics.aspx

Australia's Migration Trends, 2012–13, prepared by: *Economic Analysis Unit Strategic Policy Evaluation and Research Branch Department of Immigration and Border Protection*. Retrieved from http://www.immi.gov.au/pub-res/Documents/statistics/ migration-trends-2012-13.pdf

Australia's Offshore Humanitarian Programme: 2013–14 *prepared by the Programme Management and Integrity Section of the Department of Immigration and Border Protection (DIBP) in Australia*. Retrieved from http://www.immi.gov.au/pub-res/Documents/statistics/australia-offshore-humanitarian-program-2013-14.pdf

Azarias, J., Lambert, J, McDonald, P & Malyon, K. (2014). Robust New Foundations, A Streamlined, Transparent and Responsive System for the 457 Programme, An Independent Review into Integrity in the Subclass 457 Programme Published September 2014, *Australian Government, Department of Immigration and Border Protection*. https://www.immi.gov.au/pub-res/Documents/reviews/streamlined-responsive-457-programme.pdf

Banulescu-Bogdan, N. (2012). Shaping Citizenship Policies to Strengthen Immigrant Integration. *Migration Policy Institute, August 2, 2012*. Retrieved from http://www.migrationpolicy.org/article/shaping-citizenship-policies-strengthen-immigrant-integration

Boese, M., Campbell, I., Roberts, W. & Tham, J-C. (2013). Temporary Migrant Nurses in Australia: Times and Sources of precariousness. *Economic and Labour Relations Review, 24*(3), 316-339.

Karlsen, E. (2015). Refugee resettlement to Australia: what are the facts? Parliament of Australia, Department of Parliamentary Services, Law and Bills Digest Section. Updated 3 February 2015. Retrieved from http://www.aph.gov.au/About_Parliament/ Parliamentary_Departments/Parliamentary_Library/pubs/rp/rp1415/RefugeeResettlement

McKenzie, N. & Baker, R. (2014). Visa fraud suspects fled after wiring $1m overseas. *The Sydney Morning Herald,* (8 August 2014). Retrieved from http://www.smh.com.au/federal-politics/political-news/visa-fraud-suspects-fled-after- wiring-1m-overseas-20140807-3dbmu.html

Phillips, J. & Spinks, H. (2012). Skilled migration: temporary and permanent flows to Australia. *Social Policy Section, Department of Parliamentary Services, Parliament of Australia*, Updated 6 December 2012. Retrieved from http://parlinfo.aph.gov.au/parlInfo/ download/library/prspub/1601351/upload_binary/1601351.pdf;fileType=application%2Fpdf

Phillips, J. & Spinks, H. (2013). Immigration detention in Australia. *Social Policy Section, Department of Parliamentary Services, Parliament of Australia*, Updated 20 March 2013. Retrieved from http://parlinfo.aph.gov.au/parlInfo/download/library/prspub/1311498/ upload_binary/1311498.pdf;fileType=application/pdf

Phillips, J. (2015). Asylum seekers and refugees: what are the facts? *Parliament of Australia, RESEARCH PAPER SERIES, 2014–15, Updated 2 March 2015*. Retrieved from http://www.aph.gov.au/About_Parliament/Parliamentary_Departments/Parliamentary_Library/pubs/rp/rp1415/A sylumFacts

Richards, K & Lyncham, S. (2014). Help-seeking strategies of victim/ survivors of human trafficking involving partner migration. *Trends & issues in crime and criminal justice, 468, February 2014, Australian Government, Australian Institute of Criminology*. Retrieved from http://www.aic.gov.au/media_library/publications/ tandi_pdf/ tandi468.pdf

Robertson, S.K. (2008). Residency, Citizenship and Belonging: Choice and Uncertainty for students-Turned –Migrants in Australia. *International Journal of Asia Pacific Studies, IJAPS, 4*(1), 1-23.

Sheridan, G. (2011). How I lost faith in multiculturalism? *The Australian*, April 02, 2011. Retrieved from http://www.theaustralian.com.au/national-affairs/how-i-lost-faith-in-multiculturalism/story-fn59niix-1226031793805

Chapter 26. On Immigrant Radicalism and Immigrant Nihilism - Thoughts on Migrations from the Middle East to Turkey-

Mehmet Evkuran*

i.

No matter the reason, recent immigration from the Middle East to Turkey is not just a 'displacement'. It will have a deep and lasting impact on people. Migrant individuals and groups are forced to rethink their perspectives on the world and their personal values deradicalizing themselves as a consequence. This radical position is usually a result of the strife affecting their peace and comfort at home. Migration, if it is caused by civil war, or other traumatic events, may lead to the reversal of values or increased radical returns to their cultural and ethical values and beliefs. An immigrant who is deliberating between nihilism and radicalism has to try various ways to solve this dilemma.

Whether an immigrant is running away from something or running towards something determines their behavior in the country of residence. The first scenario causes an immigrant to take a conservative stance on protecting their identity and values; the second one causes signifies that the spirit of the immigrants is forced to change. So the migratory mind begins to see and define itself in the new social mirror. Immigrant radicalism and immigrant nihilism are expressions of these two different positions.

In voluntary migrations, the prevailing instinct is to meet new and different individualities try to understand it, and even integrate it. This integration can vary depending on the individula's level of education, cultural flexibility, and location of networks of solidarity. In massive and painful compulsory migrations, the immigrant's world of emotion and thought sharpens. In cases in which the families are scattered and fragmented, an eternal traumatic interaction takes place that affects future generations.

The Arab Spring turned into a very different picture in Syria. Contrary to expectations, the regime has not collapsed; rather it has survived with the support of its international allies and has fought against its people. This had theo-political consequences, and the sleepy sectarian fault lines soon took action. The Shiite-Nusayri elites, who held power, gathered around its sectarian social base (Korkmaz; 2015, 25). This situation transformed the political clash into a Shia-Sunni conflict. The meaning of this development for the Middle East is the dissemination of sectarian conflict. The sectarian identities in the Middle East are very strong and the borders are unreal and

* Mehmet Evkuran is Pfofessor of Islamic Theology in Hitit University, Çorum/Turkey, E-mail: mehmetevkuran@hotmail.com

304

durable, on the contrary they are coercive and mannered. For this reason, it is inevitable that any problem in any Middle Eastern country will affect the region. It is necessary to add to this discussion long-term chaos in Iraq.

The reflection of these problems as they affect Turkey can be categorized under two headings. The first problem is refugees as a result of mass migration, and the second is the rising sectarian tension. Today Turkey has more than 4 million immigrants, most of whom are Syrians. In addition to Syrian refugees there are also refugees from Afghanistan and Iraq. In this case, Turkey has become the country with the highest number of refugees in the world. This is an intolerable amount for most European countries. Turkey sacrifices much for immigrants as both a state and a society. However, it is also true that there are some challenges.

The war in Iraq and Syria is widespread and the negative, destructive effects of chaos has spread across the Middle East. The strengthening of Salafism in the Sunni world is one of its signs. The radical Salafi movement which is based on the enmity of Shiism, is attempting to spread in Turkey but has not been very successful.

Empathizing with the emigrant is not to submit to his theological conflicts. Helping one to immigrate does not call for looking at the spread of internal tension and anger around him. Turkey has its own democratic experience and understanding of religion, offering it a different and unique position as compared to other predominately Islamic countries. Therefore, when Turkey resolves its immigration problems, it has to protect and strengthen its social order.

In this study, the phenomenon of migration and refugees will be dealt with in the context of the problem of redefinition of religion and values. It will be argued how immigrants can prevent their tensions from being carried to Turkey, while their humanitarian problems are simultaneously resolved.

ii.

Anatolia has traditional and cultural bases of migration. For example, internal migrations are generally not considered migrations. In fact, changing places is a natural lifestyle for Turkish people as they have came from a nomadic culture. Our cultural and political origins are mostly in the East, or because it was open to the East, those coming from the East or South would not be seen as immigrants. The ones that fit the definition of immigrants are mostly from the West. Salonica immigrants who came to the country after 'Mübadele (exchange)' and; Bulgarian immigrants from Bulgaria in the 1990s are the main examples. There are also Caucasian immigrants who have more roots than their roots.

During the Republican period, a large number of people migrated from Turkey to European countries as workers. The history of academic studies on identity and belonging problems of Turkish immigrants living in Europe is new (Çoştu; 2016, 209).

I can say that our cultural sense is a selecteivity for immigration. Those who are forced to leave the country due to a tragedy (war, genocide, exile, etc.) literally migrate the word. They are also called 'Muhajir' in an older expression.

Historically, the Anatolian lands are extremely familiar to human mobility and migration. Surveys reveal that about 6 million people have came to our country as immigrants during the last 200 years of Anatolian history (Şen; Özkorul, 90).

It is not a matter of debate but it is necessary to draw attention to the difference between the concepts. In legal texts there are differences between immigrants, asylum seekers and refugees. Sometimes the differences become very important and change our perspective. The term 'asylum seeker' is used to describe people who temporarily go to a country other than their home country and whose status is unclear. The concept of immigrants generally has positive associations. For this reason, it has become widespread in the academic circles to deal with the concepts of immigration and migration. In this study, the difference between the concepts was ignored and the concept of migration was used.

Folkloric and cultural readings on the image of 'immigrants' in our culture reveal that uninvited guests suddenly come to our home as 'God's guest', perhaps 'Hızır/Godsend'. In addition, according to our Islamic values, the concept of the refugee refers to the case of Hijrah of Prophet/migration. This double affinity and affirmation provides immigration protection, immunity and cooperation.

Turkish society, bearing traces of a nomadic past, is not forced to empathize with immigrant identity. We have common grounds in terms of religion and faith with immigrants. For this reason, the 'ansar-muhajer brotherhood' emphasized by the government authorities, has a warm provision in society.

But the rules and behavior of real life are different. It is a common situation that beliefs and values are sometimes overcome in the face of the enforcement of the truths. This example is about the Syrian immigrants in our country. Nearly all of those who migrated from Syria are people who flee the regime's attacks. The situation of Syrian immigrants who take refuge in Turkey with their families is more tragic. Studies on the integration of immigrants in different cities of Turkey are being carried out. Public and civil society initiatives aim to alleviate the problems of immigrants. Many families send their children to schools so that only immigrants; classes have been created in schools.

Besides these positive developments, some problems also arise. Some political circles criticize the Government's immigration policy and speak an anti-immigrant rhetoric. These circles argue that the foreign policy that has been followed has dragged the country into a dangerous adventure that immigrants harm the country's economy and social structure, and that terrorist organizations have entered the country on the immigrant wing. Even the president of the main opposition party said in election campaigns that, he will say to immigrants 'now you should go back to your own countries'.

We set aside the political debates; it is a fact that Turkey has experienced an unprecedented number of immigrants in recent years, and that Turkey is shouldering almost all of the social-economic burden of this phenomenon. It does not seem 'smart' to allow this burden when one considers national resources and socio-political problems. The Turkish authorities say that protecting migrants is a historical, religious and humanitarian duty and they express the sentiments of the general public. In these words, there is also a clear reproach in Western countries where they avoid taking responsibility.

Indeed, the politics of immigrants in Western countries are such a problem that it will open up a new file of human rights violations. There are newly added to the images of violence, harassment, and discrimination applied to immigrants at borders. In addition, it is embarrassing for the shake of humanity that immigrants who want to pass through Europe by sea are prevented from approaching their coasts and even their boats are sunk. The images of Aylan, its dead bodies found in our coasts in 2016, and Ümran, who looks around with his toy under the regime's bombs in Syria, have increased the interest and affection for the immigrants in our country.

As Iraq and the war in Syria are prolonged, Turkey has more negative effects on it. The striking result of the war in the Middle East is the strengthening of Salafism in the region. It has a devastating effect and profoundly shakes the political and social structure of the region. Criticism about the salafism of the Sunni world is rising (Korkmaz; 2014, 449). But the salafism can find a place of life and chance of activity among the community segments.

There is an image struggle in social media about immigrants. There are occasional negative opinions and views about Syrians in social media. The basic message of such publications is "'While our children are martyred in Syria, the Syrians live a sweet life in Turkey." These campaigns, which present an exaggerated language to the events of the Syrians, try to show the immigrants like persona non grata. Whereas it seems that the defender sharings of immigrants is much greater in number and effect. The main motto of these shares supported by the tragic images is as follows: "You say the Syrians should come! Here are those who can not come!" By comparison, it can be said that the immigration phenomenon is now part of Turkey's social life. It is seen that the crisis has been managed successfully so far and has not turned into a bigger problems with the influence of the political thoughts as well as being very welcoming, helpful and sharing the Turkish people as compared to the West.

Nevertheless, it is not right to ignore the problems of immigration with regard to social structure. Sharing the same religion does not remove the cultural differences between them. Sharing a belief brings people a certain horizon and common concerns. But culture, a product of concrete life, continues to preserve its originality. How will faith be experienced and; family relationships, female imagination, political behavior, and so on be shaped by culture? Cultural differences are alleviated for a period of time with an emphasis on common immanence, but the flow of life continues to emphasize differences.

According to official data, the origin countries of majority of immigrants to Turkey are as follows: Iraq, Iran, Egypt, Syria, Azerbaijan, Afghanistan, the Balkan countries, Uzbekistan and Kyrgyzstan. Some immigrants come with student status and have the opportunity to stay in the country for many years (2016 Göç Raporu, 44). For example, immigrants from Kazakhstan, Turkmenistan and Libya. Immigrants' profiles reveal a concentrated summary of the Middle East, Balkans and Central Asia geography. Different cultures meet and interact.

In order to meet the needs of immigrants, a wide range of studies are being undertaken and projects are passed on. Important studies are continuing in education, health, housing, language, and working subjects (Göç Projeleri, http://www.goc.gov.tr/icerik/goc-projeleri_409_570).

The necessity of the steps to be taken in terms of cultural interaction is understood more and more with every passing day. In particular, Syrian migrants who reside in certain densely populated areas of a large number of people, especially the politics of the minds of immigrants should be produced. The most important problem preventing cohabitation is cultural ghettoization. This situation, also called 'parallel lives', creates risky potentials in terms of social peace. Clear and unbiased cultural communication is essential for solving this problem. The host is more responsible for communicating and maintaining. Having a tradition of immigration and empathy is our greatest advantage. Islam, a common belief, contains 'other elements' that are necessary for communication and empathy.

It is necessary to accept this interaction, which will happen mostly in the moderation of the landlord. The communication discourse should reflect the sensitivities of the landlord as well as the tragedy of the immigrant. Otherwise, it is undoubtedly that the works that are not touched by the facts will cause much harm from the wounds.

One of the most important points to be considered in this framework is that the civil war in Syria has triggered sectarian conflicts. The presence of DAEŞ in Syria has become a clear threat to us from the potential. As a matter of fact, the country that gave the most open and sincere struggle with the DAEŞ terrorist organization is Turkey. As a result of the measures taken by Turkey, significant gains have been achieved in the fight against DAEŞ.

In addition to the security measures taken at the border, the action capacities of DAEŞ, or other terrorist organizations are very limited thanks to the studies carried out in the cities. However, there is another deeper problem in terms of culture: DAEŞ ideology (Evkuran; 6-7).

For Turkey, it is very important to combat the ideology rather than the military and organizational threats of DAEŞ. On July 15, 2016, Turkey, which had overcome a treacherous and bloody coup attempt, is implementing OHAL and is concerned with many national and global issues.

The acceptance of immigrants in our country does not require the adoption of their cultures and ideologies as well. Particularly, it is necessary to be careful about the widespread beliefs and thoughts that will lead to religious radicalization. The radicalization of immigrants is natural who came from a conflict and tragedy tends to convey sharp thoughts alongside his own story. It is not natural to radicalize the people of the country, and it is necessary to take steps to prevent this kind of skidding.

Local and universal tendencies coexist in the identity of immigrants. War, exile, genocide-driven migrations force migrants to think and act mordantly. He is forced to represent his identity more radically. He tends to exhibit radical attitudes in the country he is going to. This leads to political and cultural problems. These problems can be overcome with well-planned strategies. In particular, common values can be created by emphasizing and providing improvements in lifestyle.

In the training and seminars to be given to immigrant families, our values should be explained with flexible methods. In particular, an education method should be followed that emphasizes pluralism in religious understanding and immigrats teach to think flexibly. The historical, cultural, and political authenticity of Turkey has important values will go to the Middle East and even to the world. But in order to be able to do that, we need to avoid taking steps that would put our own originality at risk.

References

Evkuran Mehmet (2015), "Salafism as a Crisis Theology and Social Movement -An Analysis on Salafi Ideology and Its Impacts on Muslim World", ("Bir Kriz Teolojisi ve Toplumsal Hareket Olarak Selefilik-Selefi İdeoloji ve İslam Dünyasındaki Etkileri Üzerine Bir Analiz "), İlahiyat Akademi Dergisi-Gaziantep Üniversitesi İlahiyat Fakültesi Dergisi, v. I, nu. 1-2, pp. 71-90

Cengiz, S (2010). "Göç, Kimlik ve Edebiyat", Journal of World of Turks: v. II, nu. 3, pp.185-193.

Çoştu, Yakup; Çoştu Ceyhan, Feyza; (2016), "An Essay of Meta-Analysis on Seeking Identity of Euro-Turks", Turkish Migration 2016-Selected Papers, London, pp. 209-215.

Korkmaz, Sıddık (2014), "Selefiliğe Karşı Reddiyeler", Tarihte ve Günümüzde Selefilik, Ensar Neşriyat, İstanbul.

Korkmaz, Sıddık (2015), Şîa'nın Oluşumu Hz. Ali'nin Vasîliği Düşüncesi, İz Yayıncılık, İstanbul.

Şen, Yusuf Furkan, Gözde Özkorul (2015), "Türkiye – Avrupa Birliği İlişkilerinde Yeni Bir Eşik: Sığınmacı Krizi Bağlamında Bir Değerlendirme" Göç Araştırmaları Dergisi, Temmuz-Aralık.

2016 Türkiye Göç Raporu, T. C. İç İşleri Bakanlığı Göç İdaresi Genel Müdürlüğü, 2017 http://www.goc.gov.tr/icerik/goc-projeleri_409_570 (erişim tarihi 15.08.2017, 12.45)

Chapter 27. Brain Migration: Factors and Models

Andrej Privara[1], O. Tolstoguzo[2], Maria Pitukhina[3], Magdalena Privarova[4]

Abstract

State development in terms of innovative economy is of a great challenge. At the same time, innovative economy development is possible only with both human resources development and human capital quality upgrading. It is important both to develop and improve human capital assets in order to achieve necessary results. Not only human capital assets advancing relate to skills enhancing, but also brain migration policy regulating, scientific schools' development as well as state policies aimed at market participants' discrimination elimination. There are listed a number of factors affecting brain migration and innovative development which are closely interconnected. As a result, a gravity model of contemporary brain migration is developed.

Key-words – brain migration, factors, gravity model, innovative economy, R&D.

Literature review

In 2010 A. Breinbauer from the Institute of Danube and Central European Studies defined several brain migration models[5] (Fig. 1). According to A. Breinbauer during 1960-2000 brain migration has been mainly characterized with "brain-drain" from the EU in the USA. The next stage of brain migration known as brain overproduction in donor-states is called "brain overflow". This "braincirculation" between donor- states and recipient-states started in the 1990s is famous for the Cold War end and Iron Curtain demolishing. After that period a new stage of re-immigration or homeland return happened - "brain regain". "Brain circulation" is mainly characterized with brain migration mobility which is determined by global trend of increased migration in the world. "Transnational mobility" is the newest and latest stage in brain migration policy, when living both in donor-state and recipient-state becomes equally comfortable.

Australian researcher R. Appleyard[6] points out the brain migration paradigm change. According to his theory these changes are connected not only with geographical, professional and time issues but mainly depend on state brain

---

[1] PhD., assistant professor of the Faculty of National Economy, University of Economics in Bratislava, Slovakia.

[2] Doctor of Economics, Russian Science Academy, Institute of Economics, Russia.

[3] PhD., senior researcher of Budget monitoring center, Petrozavodsk State University, Russia.

[4] PhD., professor of the Faculty of National Economy, University of Economics in Bratislava, Slovakia.

[5] Breinbauer A. Brains on the move / A.Breinbauer / Migrations from and to southeastern Europe «Longo editore» [Edited by A.Krasteva, A.Kasabova, D.Karabinova].- Ravena, 2010.

[6] Appleyard R. Skilled Migration in the Globalized World /R. Appleyard/The world in the mirror of international migration. "MaxPress". – Moscow, 2002. – Issue 10. – P.7-17

migration policy. I. Ushkalova and I. Malakhov from Moscow State University offer the following models of brain migration regulation by a state[7]:

- *active regulation concept* (state controls brain migration with different instruments, namely legal, administrative and economic). Also, it includes migrants' returning programs popular in the EU countries, such as Bluecard system, Marie Curie Foundation scholarships, Erasmus Mundus programmes, the EU road map based on qualifications and mobility, different PhD scholarships, etc.;

- *non-interference concept* (the state can't influence brain migration);

- *future commitment concept* (brain migration problems might be resolved only at international level and within a period of time).

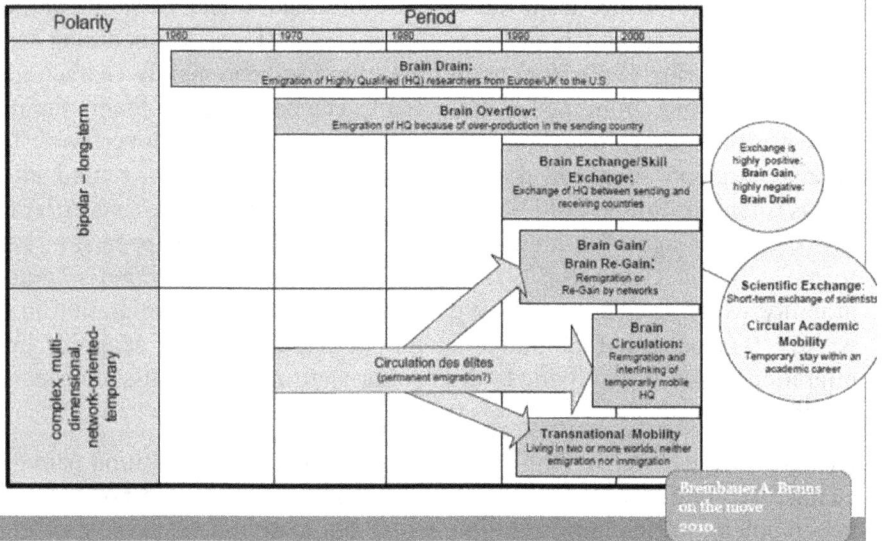

Fig.1. Brain migration models (Breinbauer), 2010

The issue of brain migration in Russia for example doesn't receive proper attention, unlike educational migration. Thus, Russia has recently begun to support educational migration within the state program "Global Education"[7]. This program finances Russian citizens enrolled to one of the leading international universities. The "Global Education" programme is pursuing the following goals:

---

[7] Ushkalov I., Malaha I. Utechka umov kak global'nyj fenomen i ego osobennosti v Rossii //Socis. – 2000.- №3. - C.110-117.

- to educate not less than 1500 of Russian citizens in leading international educational organizations in accordance with priorities of Russian economy;
- to employ not less than 1500 of Program participants who have graduated from leading foreign institutions[9].

The state program "Global education" is targeting educational migration, but there are no similar instruments to support brain migration into Russia. The Strategic Initiatives Agency has launched "Global education" program recently and is planning to return 15 000 Russian and Soviet scientists. The Russian Federation government is currently supporting the Russian Science Academy program aimed at attracting 100 famous Russian scientists.

Thus, it is quite evident that a state shall develop brain migration policy related to innovative development. In order to determine this policy outlines, let's consider some factors affecting brain migration and innovative development of a country that are closely interconnected.

Main factors characterizing brain migration

Since 2000 the global trend has been fixed, namely, migration increasing. For the last 15 years migration steams has grown by 32%, and nowadays there are about 232 million of migrants all over the world[11]. Professor A. Krasteva from New Bulgaria University points out brain migration rapid increase. She states that brain migration amounts to 1/3 of global migration, and produces more influence on a society rather than labour migration[8].

The following factors could be pointed out, that might define scientists' high mobility in the world:

- standard of living, institutional and social standards that affect living conditions in a donor-state and recipient-state (traditional migration factor);
- state policy aimed at new technological development that leads to a growth of investments in science and technologies;
- transboundary knowledge streams establishing (researchers' mobility, scientific co-authorship, right for the co-ownership on inventions), science is getting more international and global;
- brain de-qualification, scientific fraud (affecting the staff quality).

According to "UNESCO Science Report: towards 2030 – Executive Summary 2015[9] (further UNESCO report) there are the following trends to be observed

---

[8] Krasteva, A. Immigration and integration: European experiences / A.Krasteva. - Bulgaria. Sofia: Manfred Worner Foundation, 2008.

[9] Privarova M., Privara A. Circular migration and its impacts in the current stage of globalization// nternational Journal of Environmental and Science Education. - Volume 11, Issue 18, 2016, Article number ijese.2016.960, Pages 12909-12917.

in the world: investments growth in science and technology; increased number of huge international scientific projects as well as scientific publications and patents; scientists' high mobility. That is why a stable tendency for a sharp increase in the quantity of researchers is well-observed. There are 7.8 million researchers, and this number has raised by 21% since 2007. Most of them are located in the EU, China and the USA. In 2013 there were 440,6 thousand scientists in Russia, their share from 7,3% to 5,7%. The share of scientific publications in the world has grown by 28% compared to 2008. In 2014 1.27 million of articles were published (leaders: the USA and the EU). Fig. 2 portrays changes in the quantity of researchers in different countries for the period 2007 to 2013.

Figure (Fig.) 2. Change in the quantity of researchers in different countries

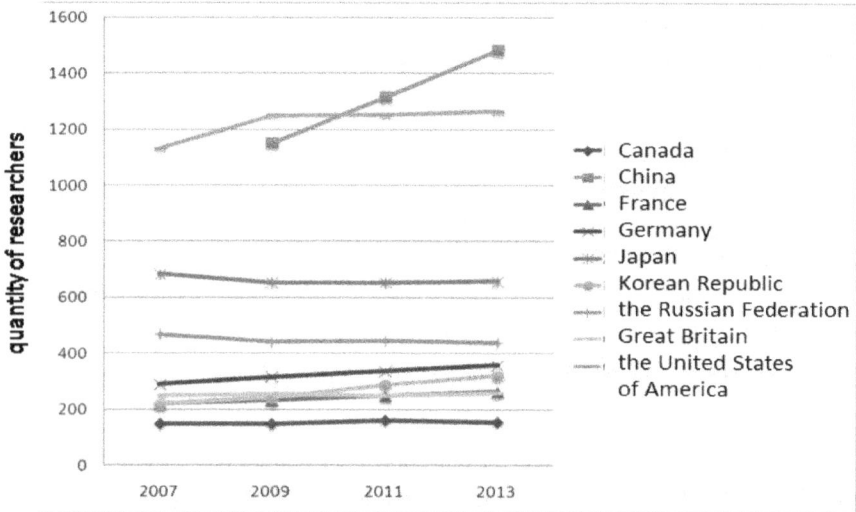

Information source: UNESCO report: towards 2030 – Executive Summary: https://en.unesco.org/unesco_science_report. The date for the period 2007-2013 is used (UNESCO Science Report is published once every 5 years).

Let's compare most innovative countries' R&D expenses with the level of economic development (Table 1).

R&D expenses per-capita allow us to see the positions of various actors involved in international innovation dimension. Thus, the Table 1 shows that most expenses on R&D (in percentage of GDP) are carried on by Japan, France and Sweden.

Interconnection between investment in global GDP and R&D surely stimulates the growing export at the expense of high technology and scientific industries development (Fig.3). Group-countries by their shares in a world GDP correlate with group-countries by their shares in global R&D share.

Table 1. GDP per-capita and R&D expenses, 2013

Country	GDP per-capita (2013)[10]	R&D expenses against GDP, % (2013)[11]
Norway	**64 406**	2,85%
The USA	**53 042**	2,81%
Sweden	**44 658**	**3,30%**
Germany	43 884	2,25%
Denmark	43 782	3,06%
Finland	39 740	**3,32%**
Japan	36 223	**3,47%**
Italy	35 281	1,25%
The EU	33 052	2,3%
Russia	25 248	1,12%
Iran	15 590	0,31%
Georgia	7 160	0,13%

According to UNESCO Science Report the growth of R&D investments was 31% between 2007 and 2013 (which is higher than 20% growth of global GDP). Leading countries are the USA (28% growth), China (20% growth) and Japan (10% growth). The rest of the countries share 23% growth (among them Russia has only 1,7% growth).

Insignificant contribution (into the innovation development of global economics – Fig.3) of low income countries in comparison with high income countries and countries with the income higher than average, is explained by the fact that the main capital substitution in weak countries is very slow. So, the capital surplus (investments) is transferred to some other countries (that have more favorable conditions for the capital).

The EU, the USA and China, which are the leading actors in global economics and politics, have recently stated the priority of new type of economy creating.

Fig. 4 represents the change in R&D expenses per one researcher, which

---

[10] UNESCOScienceReport.Towards 2030
http://www.unesco.org/new/fileadmin/MULTIMEDIA/HQ/SC/pdf/USR_final_interacti ve.pdf
[11] Ibidem

obviously underlines the appropriate quality of working place and intellectual work conditions.

Fig. 3. Group-countries by their shares in a world GDP correlating with group-countries by their shares in global R&D share

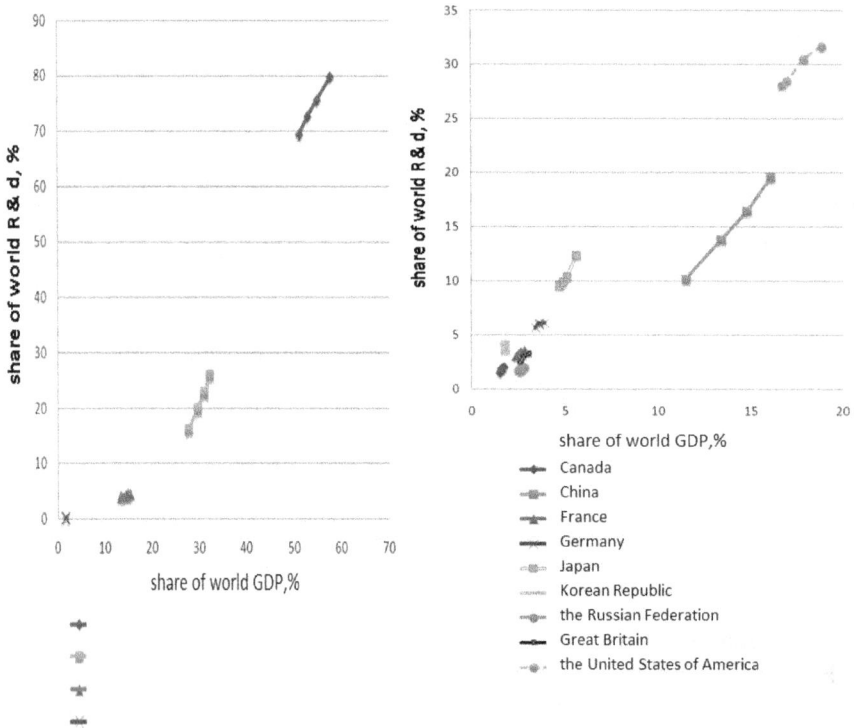

Information source -UNESCO report, 2015.

It is not a secret that research skills seriously depend on innovation economy creating. The most important feature of this economyy is that the human intellect replaces manual labour. The focus is shifting to a mental activity, where data processing, analyzing and interpreting is becoming the key point.

According to N. Fowler from Mississippi University, huge brain migration streams to the USA depend on the USA migration policy in different periods of time, because migrants are generally treated in in the USA a more tolerant way[12]. His statement is supported by the Table 2 data showing scientists quantity as well as their citation indices in different countries including the OECD member-states such as Russia, Georgia, and Iran. The USA is a leader

---

[12] Opinion: Encouraging Brain Migration (the Scientist) URL: http://www.the-scientist.com/?articles.view/articleNo/32480/title/Opinion--Encouraging-Brain-Migration-/

in terms of brain migration and citation index (they belong to the top three countries along with Sweden and Denmark). It is important to point out that citation index of Georgia is higher than that of Finland, Germany, and Italy.

Fig. 4 R&D expense change per one researcher in a number of countries.

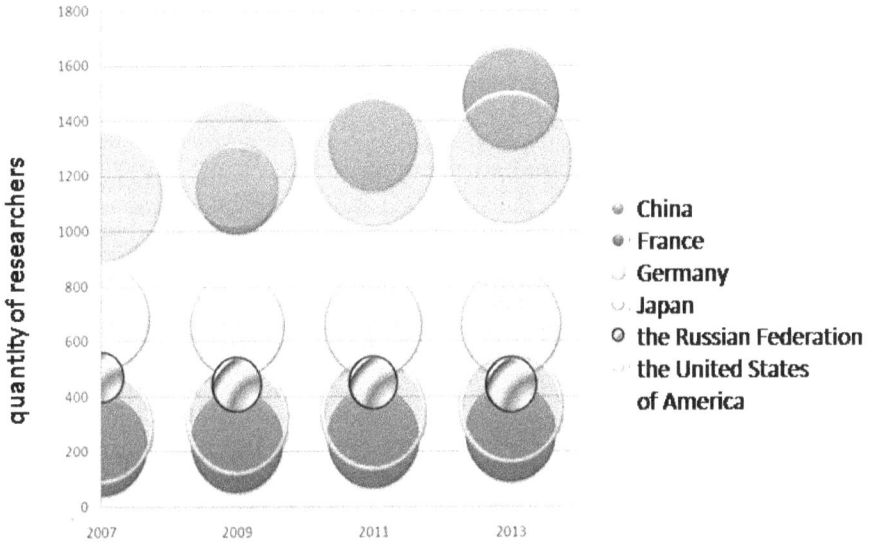

UNESCO Science Report: towards 2030 – Executive Summary: https://en.unesco.org/unesco_science_report

Table 2. Researchers' citation index by a country, 2013

Country	Citation index (2013)[16]	Amount of TSQ staff[17]
Norway	1,27	28 343
The USA	**1,32**	**1 265 064**
Sweden	**1,34**	62 294
Germany	1,24	360 310
Denmark	**1,50**	40 858
Finland	1,27	39 196
Japan	0,88	**660 489**
Italy	1,17	117 973
the EU	-	-
Russia	0,52	**440 581**
Iran	0,81	54 813
Georgia	1,29	-

Information source: UNESCO Science Report. Towards 2030 [Electron resource] /UNESCO. – Electron article – [France], 2015. – URL: http://www.unesco.org/new/fileadmin/MULTIMEDIA/HQ/SC/pdf/USR_fina

l_interactive.pdf, (15.11.2015). The data used for the period 2007-2013. (UNESCO Science Report is issued once every 5 years).

Georgia is a very interesting case, since Georgian citation index is higher than that of scientists from Finland, Germany, and Italy. Iran has similar quantity of publications indexed in international data base SCOPUS/WebofScience which is similar to the quantity of Russian publications[13].

Let's compare some cross-country strategies. As an example, we are using data on different countries from the UNESCO Scientific Report.

The below-listed countries are implementing new economy strategies: China, France, Germany, Korean Republic, USA, Japan (Fig.5). On the top of that, Japan and the USA which increased their patent work comparing to publications (Fig.6). Strategic zones maintaining in economy management is performed in Russia, Great Britain, and Canada. Countries that manage to attract some brains and finances will definitely be the winners.

Fig 5. R&D dynamics in % of GDP.

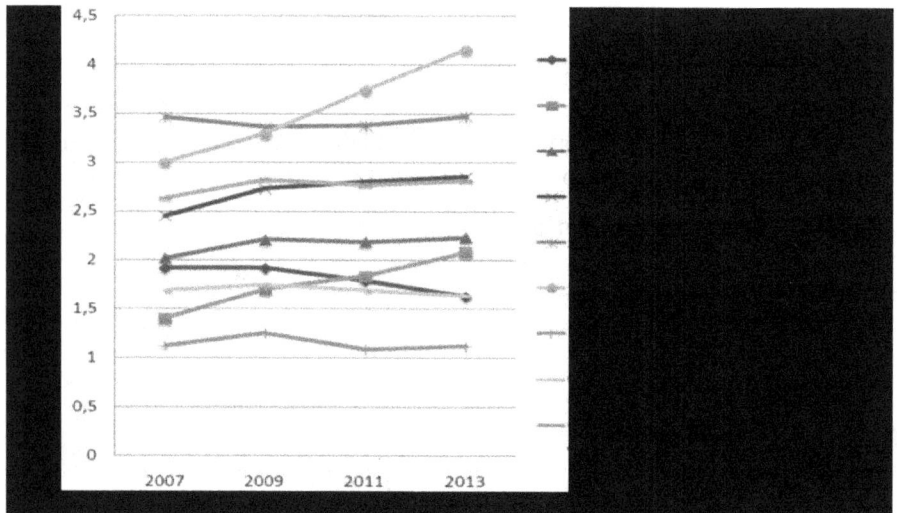

UNESCO Science Report: towards 2030 – Executive Summary: https://en.unesco.org/unesco_science_report

---

[13] UNESCO Science Report. Towards 2030
http://www.unesco.org/new/fileadmin/MULTIMEDIA/HQ/SC/pdf/USR_final_interactive.pdf

Fig. 6. Number of patents and publications (by citation index Thomson Reuters Web of Science Citation Index Expanded/)

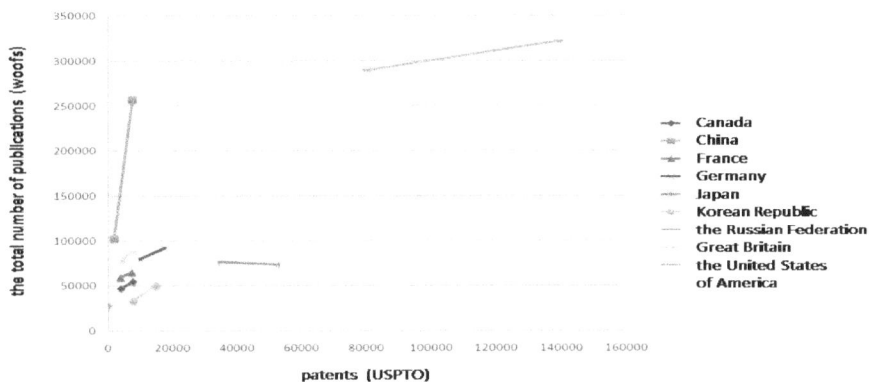

Источник информации – Доклад ЮНЕСКО, 2015.

UNESCO Science Report: towards 2030 – Executive Summary: https://en.unesco.org/unesco_science_report

Undoubtedly, science internalization does affect brain migration. Universities are becoming international institutions; student mobility and international cooperation are scaling up tremendously.

Modern communication technologies implementation as well as information increase certainly affect people's movement, researchers' mental models are connected online more often. At the same time this trend is not yet significant. The UNESCO data shows that despite Internet and online platforms brain migration is still a global trend. After obtaining doctor degree, scientists feel the need to change their location[14].

Recently there has been some change not only in the amount, but also in the quality of brain migration policy. At the same time it is impossible to neglect a serious problem of researchers' downshifting and de-qualification.

According to the research done by N. Shmatko from the National Research University - Higher School of Economics, the researchers' supply in the USA is significantly higher than its demand. Thus, there are about 36 000 applicants each year for 3000 free working places in academic market. To sum it up, 12 people per 1 working place leads to high competition in this industry in the

---

[14] UNESCO Science Report. Towards 2030.http://www.unesco.org/new/fileadmin/MULTIMEDIA/HQ/SC/pdf/USR_final_interactive.pdf

USA [15]. 73,6% of scientists who gained PhD in the USA would like to stay in the country with the exception of nationals from Germany, France, and Scandinavia. Among those who would like to stay are Chinese (90%), Indians (86%), Central Eastern Europeans (83%).

The OECD data shows that biggest employment challenges are experienced by migrants in Israel, Belgium, and Luxemburg.

A. Krasteva points out that researchers who migrated to the EU are often employed in libraries, information centers and might hold a "postdoc" position (temporary position with lower salary), before they get a position of professor at university[16].

We believe that de-qualification happens everywhere because of the post modernistic crisis and a global mindset structure, characterized by total imitation of true knowledge, creating pseudo modern and pseudo industrial surrogates and empty brands, which are pushed to the front line of scientific thought and innovative scientific and technologic progress with no reason[17].

Gravity model for a brain migration

Gravity model for brain migration will be developed based on a data presented in the UNESCO Science Report 2030. The defined model is a so called logical-semantic model which is the description of an object corresponding to all known and logically coherent statements and facts.

The gravity model of brain migration is a particular case of S.Stouffer's model[18] where a number of migrants moving for a certain distance is directly-related to a number of opening opportunities and inversely-related to a number of intervening opportunities. Not only the intensity of brain migration depends on a traditional migration factor, but also a systemic impact of other factors implementing in a given model. Unlike low-qualified employees, researchers understand better opening opportunities connected with strategic consequences of systemic global redrawing.

Therefore, the traditional trend (presented in Figure 7 in variables "RD expenditure" and "GDP per capita") of brain migration includes new

[15] Shmatko N., Suslov A., Kirchik O. Mobil'nost' nauchnyh kadrov na nacional'nom i mezhdunarodnom rynkah truda http://econorus.org/onim/upload/knbc.pdf

[16] Krasteva, A. Immigration and integration: European experiences / A.Krasteva. - Bulgaria. Sofia: Manfred Worner Foundation, 2008.

[17] Pitukhina, M. Migracionnye processy v sovremennom mire. Petrozavodsk State University, Petrozavodsk, 2015.

[18] Stouffer's gravity model means that "the migration stream is assumed to be directly related to the number of opening opportunities and inversely related to the number of the intervening opportunities". S. Stouffe takes intervening opportunities as everything that prevents this migration stream (transport expenses, local laws preventing migration, migrant's information unawareness, negative attitude of the local population, etc.).

phenomena, namely, the geographical brain reorientation. Scientists seem to prefer BRICS countries more frequently.

It has become quite evident for such countries as the USA and Europe, Russia and China that the key problem of transferring to a new technological structure cannot be solved only by efforts focusing on attracting intellectual workers from donor-states to recipient-states.

Figure 7. Gravity model for brain migration, 2013

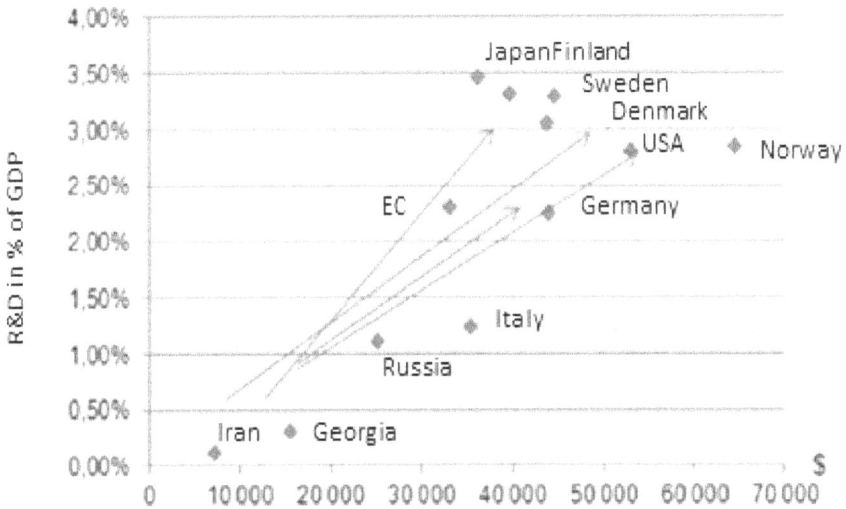

Information resource – gravity model is performed by authors

Geography of transboundary knowledge and brain migration

Transboundary knowledge streams (brain migration, scientific co-authorship and right for the joint ownership of inventions) strongly depend on factors which have nothing to do with science, but they can be easily explained in terms of new geography and neo-institutional theory.

Low income countries and countries with the income lower than average will be known as peripheral countries or periphery, whereas high income countries and countries with income higher than average will be central or center. The suggested model reveals increased concentration of economic indices and brain migration in the centre and lack of stimuli for developing innovations in the periphery. Figure 8 represents this picture. The article states that the reason is the information and digital discrimination set by market institutions, which is directed from large conglomerations (centre) to the periphery[19].

Figure 8. Group-country shares' changing in the world GDP (%) and patents, 2008 and 2013. The bubble size is the quantity of patents.

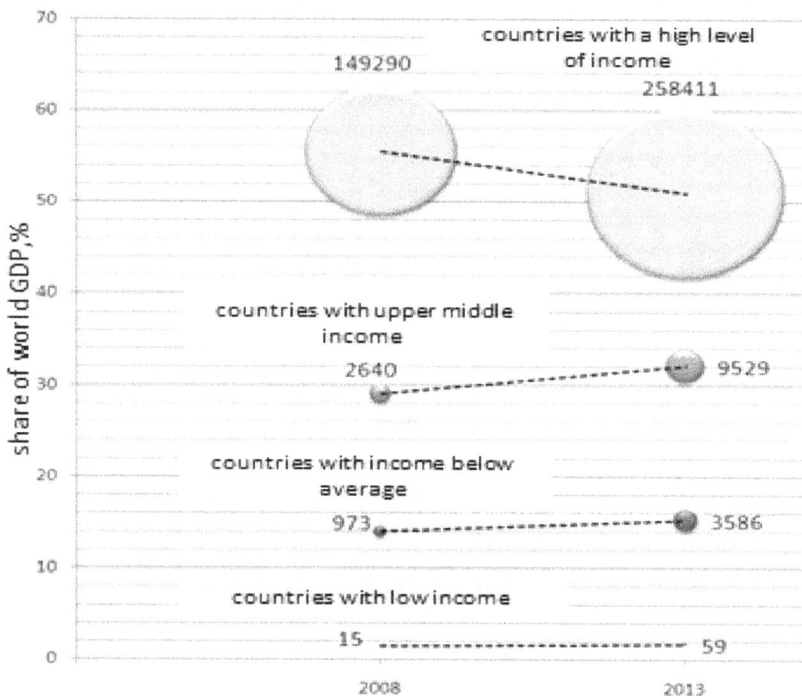

Information resource - UNESCO report, 2015.

The agglomeration trend is observed not only in separate countries, but also inside the countries. Thus, comparative analysis of "innovative activities of organisations" index from 2010 to 2013 showed the definite trend for increasing "innovativeness" of St. Petersburg agglomeration which is the industrial and innovative centre of the Russian North-West to the disadvantage of the periphery innovativeness[20]. The ratio between the quantity of patents for inventions/ useful models and the quantity of researchers supports the concentration of innovative activities mainly in the centre (Table 3).

---

[19] Tolstoguzov O.V. Innovacionnaja aktivnost' v regionah Severo-Zapada Rossii v uslovijah krizisa // Innovacii. – 2016. – №1 (207). – P.85-92.
[20] Ibidem

Table 3. Population quantity, the quantity of researchers and patents granted in the Russian North-West (2013)

	Population,	Researchers,	Patents for
St. Petersburg	5132	78773	11330
The rest regions of	8625	16901	2894

Information resource: Federal State Statistics Service (Rosstat)

Nowadays, economic processes are determined by subjects' economic coordination as well as technological, social, historic or any other factors. The main issue is to understand reasons for economy development, which occur firstly due to increased profits in industry markets, and their spatial distribution. The first part of the problem is explained by organization models as well as by structure of international and interregional industry markets which resulted from social division of labour and traditional distribution of productive forces.

The second part is focused on the factors influencing innovations development and the distribution of growing profits caused by these innovations and spatial effect of their implementation. By applying innovations (which have appeared both due to the diffusion – flow of knowledge and technologies from the outer area and generation – creation of their own inventions or any other objects of intellectual property) a country or region can get a serious source of the economic rent, with its economics efficiency being determined not only by its size, but also by its distribution regulated by existing formal and informal institutions. Innovations are source of artificial competitive advantage and the rent, accordingly. They appear due to the knowledge commercialization and realization of the process "from knowledge to practice".

At the same time, according to neo-institutional theory (see, for example, the articles by J. Hodgson, O. Williamson, E. Furubotn and R. Richter) various forms of agents' interactions appear during the process as well as due to the influence of definite institutional factors, which set the rules. In order to change economic reality, it is necessary to change institutional structures. The latter, in their turn, influence communication means and information exchange, as a result, economic exchanges as agents' actions and economic results are synchronized by the correct stimulus system.

Innovation activity geography has the following structure: developed innovation centre and backward (in economic and innovative aspects) periphery. Let's take the unchanged property structure and spatial innovation system distribution (it can change only due to the evolution) as a geographical invariant. Geographical invariant genesis of country/region's innovative activities should be searched as follows: who, where and how innovative activities are implemented.

Next, some main properties should be marked, which this geographical invariant of innovative activities relate to (within the new geography and neo-institutional approach limits):

Firstly, UNESCO report states that developed countries have shifted their focus in the field of scientific discoveries to performing problem-oriented investigations to financing applied sciences. At the same time the high innovation efficiency reflects the greatest competence in innovative activities and making a portfolio for the production cost. Unfortunately, due to resource insufficiency and qualification the periphery can't provide the informational and legal support along the whole chain "from knowledge to practice" and create a "turnkey" portfolio of rights for an innovative product.

Graphs comparing (Fig. 9 and 10) reveal a different role in this chain.

Fig. 9. Group-countries' innovation policy efficiency is measured by publications quantity (according to Thomson Reuters Web of Science Citation Index Expanded), it is given per a researcher and one dollar of R&D.

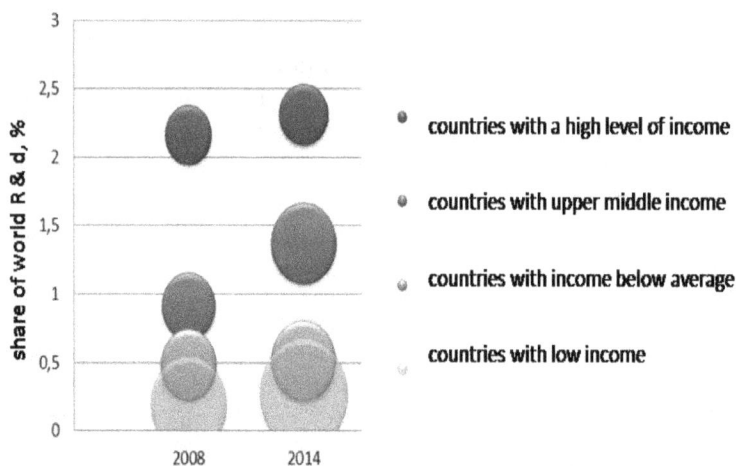

Information source: UNESCO report, 2015.

The periphery (countries with low income and income lower than average) create more publications (according to Thomson Reuters Web of Science Citation Index Expanded) per a researcher and one dollar of R&D, but they create much fewer patents (represented by UNESCO) per one researcher and one dollar of R&D.

Fig.10. Group-countries' innovation policy efficiency measured in the quantity of patents (represented by NESCO) per one researcher and one dollar of R&D.

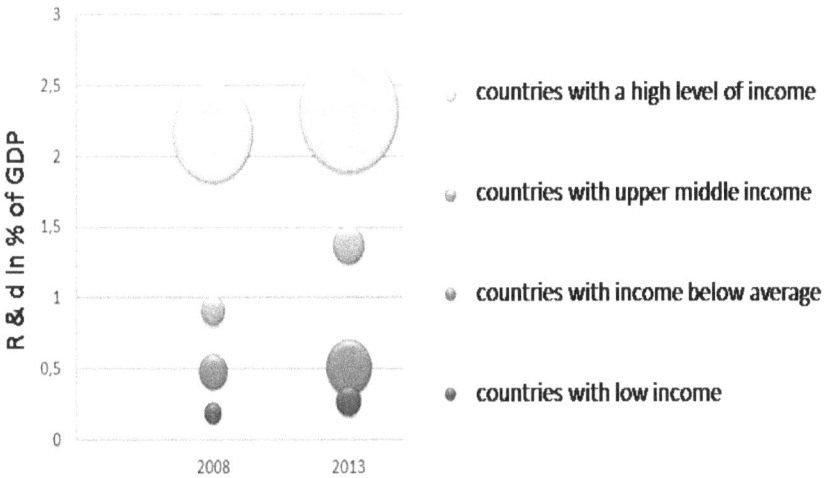

Enformation source: UNESCO report, 2015

The relative non-optimality in the chain "from knowledge to practice" and among its subjects (author, employer, owner-licensee, licensor, investor, etc.) is mainly caused by settled economic order, when economic and institutional conditions in the centre and periphery differ greatly. Large companies with great market power (transnational corporations) happened to be in big agglomerations and innovatively developed countries, if to consider that industry markets are imperfectly competitive (chamberlain type), economic agents' behavior is greatly determined by cooperative and non-cooperative strategies of biggest companies, cartel agreements and so on. The issue of taking advantages of new knowledge lies in the dominance of the innovative centre over the periphery. Due to concentration of market power resources the centre controls the innovative process.

Secondly, the migration and concentration of intellectual workers depend on the conditions enumerated above. The innovative activity is more intensive when this concentration is higher. As they try to get into fast developing companies and industries. If an industry is steadily developing or declining, intellectual workers do not go there. Since the fixed capital is substituted very slowly in the periphery (countries with the low income and income lower than average), its surplus (the investment part) transfers into other countries (where the capital conditions are more attractive). The intellectual workers follow it.

Groups of countries show this in Figure 11.

Fig. 11. The share of researchers from the world index, %.

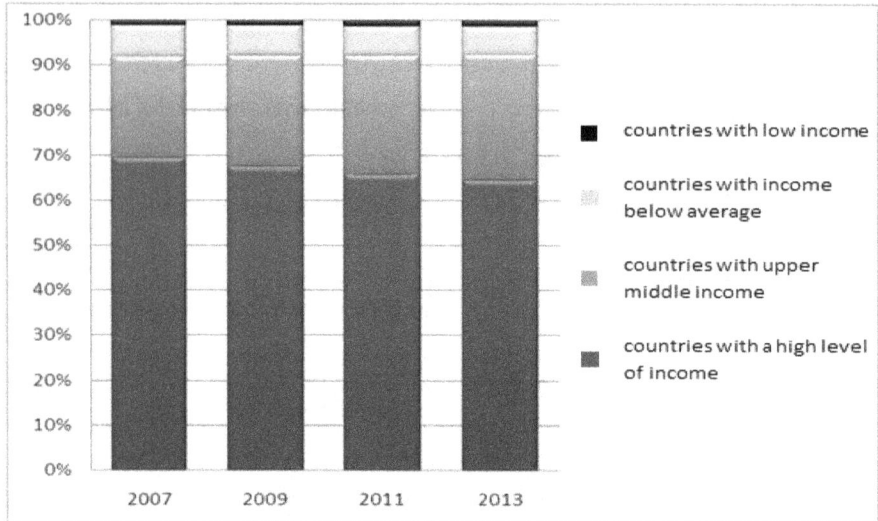

To create innovations, it is necessary to concentrate research and development work (R&D) as well as increase the share of those involved into R&D.

Thus, the centre and periphery have various quality innovation institutions which help researchers perform their creative work and enable those involved to concentrate their different successful effort on supporting legal, organizational and instrumental environment providing the protection of innovation process participants' interests. The opportunity to attract intellectual workers of the appropriate qualification, to raise education level and innovative mentality in the country or a region depend on the environment friendliness and perceptivity.

Thirdly, the institutional maturity, in particular, that of intellectual property and appropriate contract system. The critical reason for breaking innovation optimality relates to the opportunistic behavior of economic agents. This opportunism consists of deviating from the standard model, these deviations in periphery are mainly caused by market power concentration influence (compared with the centre) resulting in different activities of informal institutions. This opportunism may be forced, it can be determined by external forces as well, and it can contradict the joint interests of the local community, that is, an agent submits the iron hand of the market power. The agreement can't be broken and the agent must follow discriminating market relations.

Conclusion

Undoubtedly, brain migration skills influence innovative economy development. It is innovations that lead to artificial competitive advantage and economic rent development, thus, natural resources' presence or absence is of much less importance. Brain migration together with a wide use of information-communication technologies and innovative process's infrastructural support (promoting the elimination of digital discrimination and development of the unified information space) as well as institutional support of the formula "from knowledge into practice" are the most important constituents of innovative and economic development of all countries without any exceptions.

While creating the state policy oriented at innovative society development, it is necessary to perform systemic work aimed at providing efficient decisions and coordinating all agents involved into the process within concrete economic space and time.

The essence of innovation activities results from the state of national economics and local innovative system, existing institutions and external influence rate determined by market relations and power settled in a world industry markets.

Activity of world trade institutions that settle definite economic and trade order as well as require high skills within limits of the world arbitrage practice. High skills allow national legacy priority establishing over the international one in a country which also includes intellectual property sphere and helps discriminate non-residents. Unfortunately, periphery due to resource insufficiency and qualification can't provide informational and legal support along the whole chain "from knowledge into practice" and create a "turnkey" portfolio of rights for an innovative product.

Alongside the positive influence of brain migration based on the analysis mentioned above, there is a negative effect. Brain migration goes hand in hand with destructive globalism influence characterized by total imitation of true knowledge in the form of pseudo-industrial surrogates and empty brands.

Strategically, brain migration is not the factor determining innovative policy success in this or that country. The more important factor is scientific schools' presence. Such knowledge reproduction is much more vital than brain import from other countries. It is the scientific schools that prepare the country transfer to a new technological structure and can filter surrogates hindering the real knowledge economy.

The innovative process is a very unsatisfactory in countries with poorly developed economics and innovations. The inner demand for innovations can be the source for the development in large agglomerations and innovative centres. However, the periphery needs an increased role of a state as innovations' main customer and warrantor. Therefore, countries with insufficient innovative level have to use administrative resources to accelerate their innovative development, but they should be very careful not to break any WTO regulations. The latter contain certain recommendations and procedures of supporting industries by a state.

Thus, considering all the terms mentioned above, periphery states can achieve the goal of creating innovative competitive products and developing fair exchanges in a world trade, only through economy mobilization and scientific schools' total control, eliminating digital discrimination institutions and the contract system improving within the contract law limits (claims according to international arbitrage practice) as well as settling the compulsory coherence of trading rights and terms both for the centre and periphery. It is also necessary to regulate brain migration through various state programmes creating aimed at brain migration development, for example, such programmes as "Global education" in Russia.

Acknowledgment

The paper is prepared under the Russian Humanitarian Science Foundation Grant 15-02-00231/14

Bibliography

Appleyard R. Skilled Migration in the Globalized World /R. Appleyard/The world in the mirror of international migration. "MaxPress". – Moscow, 2002. – Issue 10. – P.7-17

Breinbauer A. Brains on the move / A. Breinbauer / Migrations from and to southeastern Europe «Longo editore» [Edited by A.Krasteva, A.Kasabova, D.Karabinova].-Ravena, 2010.

Krasteva, A. Immigration and integration: European experiences / A. Krasteva. - Bulgaria. Sofia: Manfred Worner Foundation, 2008.

Opinion: Encouraging Brain Migration (the Scientist) URL: http://www.the-scientist.com/?articles.view/articleNo/32480/title/Opinion--Encouraging-Brain-Migration-/

Pitukhina, M. Migracionnye processy v sovremennom mire. Petrozavodsk State University, Petrozavodsk, 2015.

Privarova M., Privara A. Circular migration and its impacts in the current stage of globalization// nternational Journal of Environmental and Science Education. - Volume 11, Issue 18, 2016, Article number ijese.2016.960, Pages 12909-12917.

Shmatko N., Suslov A., Kirchik O. Mobil'nost' nauchnyh kadrov na nacional'nom i mezhdunarodnom rynkah truda http://econorus.org/onim/upload/knbc.pdf

Tolstoguzov O.V. Innovacionnaja aktivnost' v regionah Severo-Zapada Rossii v uslovijah krizisa // Innovacii. – 2016. – №1 (207). – P.85-92.

UNESCO Science Report. Towards 2030 http://www.unesco.org/new/fileadmin/ MULTIMEDIA/HQ/SC/pdf/USR_final_interactive.pdf

Ushkalov I., Malaha I. Utechka umov kak global'nyj fenomen i ego osobennosti v Rossii //Socis. – 2000.- №3. - C.110-117.

Chapter 28. Put the Burden on Whom? Transit or Destination Countries: The Cases of Greece and Croatia

Rukiye Deniz[*+]

Abstract

Europe has been experiencing an influx of migrants since mid-2015. Several people try to reach Europe in search of a better life away from their war-devastated homelands. Their first entry into Europe is mainly the countries close to their homelands. Greece, therefore, has been the focus of the international community due to vast numbers of persons reaching its shores every single day, especially since the escalation of the Syrian civil war. Selected as a hotspot, it received assistance from the European Union. On the other hand, Croatia has been unexpectedly subjected to thousands of migrants within a short period of time. Eventually, it was awarded financial support from the Union. Upon migrant crisis, the EU introduced new mechanisms to support the states facing migrant influx. In this article, measures and attempts by the European Union to support Greece and Croatia in handling the migrant crisis are reviewed. The article tries to answer to what extent such attempts have been successful in assisting Greece and Croatia.

Keywords: Croatia, EU, Greece, hotspot, migrants, migration policy

Introduction

Commenced with the Barcelona Process in 1995, the European Union ("EU") migration policies were shaped through 5-year programmes, namely Tampere, The Hague, and Stockholm. The EU acknowledged the fact that its security is directly proportionate to stability and security in source countries. Therefore, the 5-year programmes and other tools such as the European Neighbourhood Policy focused on supporting those countries and enhancing the cooperation with them to ensure security as well as developing a common European migration policy. Through these programmes, the EU created a set of rules and systems needing the cooperation of all stakeholders for a full implementation. In mid-2015, the EU adopted "A European Agenda on Migration" (Commission, 2015). Different from the previous programmes, the 2015 document came as an emergency response to the migrant[1] crisis in the Mediterranean. It sets out priority areas to tackle the migrant crisis and emphasises that all actions require the close cooperation of all Member States ("MSs") besides other parties such as civil society or international organisations. It also acknowledges the challenge faced by the frontline countries like Italy, Hungary, and Greece, and underlines the concept of "shared responsibility" several times. In addition to the existing European tools for managing migration, the 2015 document lays the basis for analysis within the scope of this article.

[*+] Istanbul Medeniyet University, Department ofÂ International Relations, Istanbul, Turkey. Email: rukiyedeniz@ymail.com
[1] The term migrant is used as a generic term which includes refugees, immigrants, and asylum seekers.

There are several studies on how the EU has responded to the migrant crisis escalating in mid-2015. Researchers question the efficiency of the European tools developed to manage migration by giving examples from the two transit countries: Italy and Greece. As these two are the most preferred transit countries and are selected as "hotspots", researchers analyse Italy and Greece with regard to EU common migration policy. The current literature mainly focuses on the policies and their application. There is limited literature focusing on Croatia in addressing the refugee crisis. Therefore, the purpose of this article is to examine the roles of Greece and Croatia as transit countries in the implementation of the European Union's common migration policy between 2015 and 2016. By analysing the two cases individually, the article aims to form a basis for a comparison and to make policy recommendations based on the analysis of the current situation.

Method

This study employs both a qualitative and quantitative approach to the problem. News articles and official documents of the EU such as agreements, directives, and reports are analysed for the purpose of the study. Secondary data analysis was conducted using official statistics by the EU agencies and international organisations. The news articles utilised in this study are selected based on their credibility, and the information provided is confirmed from different sources.

European Tools for Managing Migration

Europe has been a destination for migrants, especially since the 1950s. At first, the European states developed individual policies, but after the 1980s, there emerged a need to adopt and implement a common policy for migration started to be linked with public order, domestic stability, terrorism, and transnational crime (Huysmans, 2000). Primary components of the common European migration policy are summarised to present an overview.

Common European Asylum System (CEAS)

Common European Asylum System (CEAS) has a set of standards to be followed by the MSs in receiving and evaluating asylum application, providing housing and food to asylum seekers, and determining which state is responsible for evaluating the application. The standards include Asylum Procedures Directive, Reception Conditions Directive, Qualification Directive, Dublin Regulation, EURODAC Regulation. Qualification Directive lays the basis for granting of refugee status while EURODAC Regulation sets the rules for fingerprinting.

European Asylum Support Office (EASO)

Active since 2011, European Asylum Support Office (EASO) provides expertise in asylum procedures. It ensures the fulfilment of obligations of the MSs under the EU *acquis* and international law. EASO aims to collect data on the implementation of CEAS in order to improve current practices. EASO also supports the MSs for the relocation of asylum seekers.

Dublin System

Dublin system refers to the principles establishing the Member State responsible for the examining of an asylum application. The first Member State in which a person applies for asylum is determined as the responsible state. A person should apply for asylum in the first EU country s/he reached. If s/he travels to another country, s/he can be deported back to the first entry country. It should be noted that Germany made an exception to this rule for Syrians during the 2015 crisis.

Frontex

European Border and Coast Guard Agency ("Frontex") is an EU agency responsible for European border management. Among its other responsibilities, it monitors migratory flows, conducts joint operations, assists search and rescue operations. Between 2014 and 2016, Frontex organised joint operations called "Poseidon" (host country: Greece) and "Triton" (host country: Italy) to save lives at sea and to support these two important transit countries. Frontex has a pool of equipment, border guards and other staff, and whenever there is an urgent need for assistance to a MS, it deploys equipment, border guards, and other staff from the pool. The MSs contribute to the pool.

Hotspot Approach

Hotspot approach was adopted by the EU in May 2015. As explained by the European Commission in the document titled "A European Agenda on Migration",

"...the Commission will set up a new 'Hotspot' approach, where the European Asylum Support Office, Frontex and Europol will work on the ground with frontline Member States to swiftly identify, register and fingerprint incoming migrants. The work of the agencies will be complementary to one another. Those claiming asylum will be immediately channelled into an asylum procedure where EASO support teams will help to process asylum cases as quickly as possible," (Commission, 2015, p. 6).

Currently, Italy has four hotspots (Pozzallo, Lampedusa, Trapani and Taranto) while Greece has five (Lesvos, Kos, Chios, Samos, Leros). EASO provides experts to hotspots upon demand, and Frontex sends officers assisting hotspot personnel with fingerprinting and registering migrants as well as taking part in border surveillance activities.

Relocation and Resettlement

Relocation is the transfer of asylum seekers who need international protection from one Member State to another. The asylum application is examined in the country of relocation (EASO, Relocation of applicants for international protection).

Resettlement, on the other hand, refers to the procedure through which refugees from outside the EU are granted the right to reside in an EU country.

Cases of Greece and Croatia

Case of Greece: A Hotspot

Greece faces an enormous number of irregular migrants pouring into the country through the Eastern Mediterranean migration route. By February 7, there are 62,600 migrants in Greece (Commission, 2017). Nonetheless, the UNHCR data estimates that Greece has the capacity to accommodate 35,000 people (Frontex, 2017). Considering the high number of migrants and the gap between the number of people and real capacity as well as the economic crisis experienced in the country, it comes as no surprise that Greece had several difficulties along the way in handling the migrant influx. Acknowledging the hardships encountered by Greece, the European Commission supported it in different ways and called for solidarity and burden-sharing among the MSs.

When the official EU documents are examined, it is observed that MSs support Greece financially. For example, over €352 has been awarded to Greece in emergency assistance since 2015. "The emergency funding comes on top of the €509 million already allocated to Greece under the national programmes for 2014-2020," (Commission, 2016, p.10). Greece is supported by EASO and Frontex in fingerprinting adults at five hotspots, providing them guidance on asylum procedures. According to EASO's Annual General Report 2015, "In 2015, EASO developed further its activities to support Member States under particular pressure in their asylum and reception system, particularly by providing support to Greece and Italy and by strengthening EASO's capacity to respond in a timely and effective manner to emergency situations," (EASO, 2016, p. 19). The Justice and Home Affairs Council foresaw in September 2015 to relocate 63,302 asylum seekers from Greece. However, 12,707 people have been relocated as of May 2017. Also seen in the graphic below, the situation has improved, but the MSs are still far from reaching the target anytime soon.

Conditions at the reception centres should be considered as well. There are several concerns relating to security, hygiene, food, heating. In addition to these data, it is worth noting that recent news articles report poor conditions for migrants stuck in Greece in winter in 2017. The international community asks for housing "in dignified living conditions" (Medecins Sans Frontieres, 2017).

Relocations from Italy and Greece (October 2015 - April 2017)

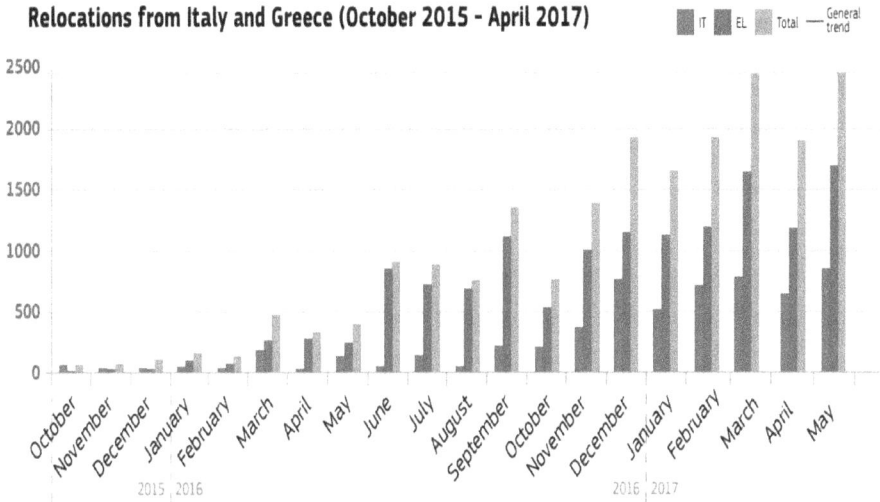

Source: European Commission

Relocation and Resettlement – State of Play (16 May 2017)

Case of Croatia: Caught Unprepared

Being in the Western Balkan migration route, Croatia was not so much preferred by migrants. However, it became subject to a sudden influx in September 2015 after Hungary built a 500-km razor-wire fence on its border with Serbia ("Hungary to build second border fence to stop refugees", 2016). The Croatian government set up a temporary reception centre having the capacity to accommodate 5000 people. The situation continued in 2016 as well with the Hungary-Serbia border still closed. Upon arrival of thousands of migrants, Zoran Milanović, the then-prime minister of Croatia, expressed that Croatia will do its best to provide the migrants with food; however, they will need to move on to their final destinations. He insisted "Croatia will not become a migrant hotspot," ("Croatia 'will not become a migrant hotspot'", 2015).

In the Croatian example, it is possible to follow the events chronologically through the documents in the Commission's database as well as news stories. On October 6, 2015, Commissioner for Migration, Home Affairs and Citizenship, Mr Dimitris Avramopoulos paid a visit to the Croatian government. In his speech, he reminded that Croatia could use Civil Protection

Mechanism (humanitarian aid instrument of the EU) and Frontex to handle the migrant influx more efficiently. He also declared that "The Commission stands ready to deploy migration management support teams in hotspot areas to identify, register and fingerprint all new arrivals effectively. But it is up to Croatia to decide if they need help," (Commission, 2015). On 25 October 2015, Commission President Jean-Claude Juncker held a meeting with leaders of Western Balkan route in Brussels. After the meeting, the leaders assigned focal points who will facilitate the communication between countries in the Western Balkan route so as to deal with the migrant influx immediately and more efficiently. The leaders agreed on a statement which includes 17 points on different issues related to migrant management (Commission, 2015). Below are the related points to the scope of this article:

• Limiting the secondary movement of migrants: The states will not allow migrants to move to the border of another country without informing it.

• Supporting refugees and providing shelter and rest: The states will provide fundamental needs of migrants such as food, shelter, sanitary material. If they do not have the sufficient resources, they will call for support from Civil Protection Mechanism.

• Managing the migration flows together: The states will guarantee registration of migrants. They will share information regarding the number of migrants and possible special needs with other states. They will cooperate with EU agencies such as Frontex and EASO.

• Border management: The states commit to effective management and control of borders. They re-emphasised that if a migrant does not apply for international protection of their country, they may refuse their entry into the country.

Having agreed on this statement, Croatia decided to benefit from the Civil Protection Mechanism to provide beds, blankets, tents, etc. to the migrants (Progress following Western Balkans Route Leaders' Meeting, 2015) and to demand assistance from Frontex within the scope of the statement (Contact Points Video Conference, 2015). Several other reports (Thirteenth Contact Points Video Conference, 2016; Fourteenth Contact Points Video Conference, 2016; Commission reports on progress in Greece, Italy and the Western Balkans, 2016) show that there is a progress in the reception conditions in those countries; however, it is constantly emphasised that "all Member States must commit to end the 'wave-through' and must insist on the application of EU rules on asylum and border management," (Commission reports on progress in Greece, Italy and the Western Balkans, 2016). This statement clearly shows that the countries in the Western Balkans route still act individually rather than following the EU standards.

As summarised in this section, Croatia is also affected by the migration influx. Contrary to the statement of Zoran Milanović, Croatia has been more or less a hotspot. However, it can be said that it is not a destination for migrants; thus, there is still no debate on how to integrate them into the society (Tatalović & Jakešević, 2016).

Discussion

Greece and Croatia have experienced the migrant crisis at different scales. Greece needed not only financial support but also had to convince the MSs to relocate migrants. It received financial support, but relocation mechanism failed to some extent. Croatia, on the other hand, took a firm stand on the migrant issue, and did wave through and sent the incoming migrants to its neighbours. It did, also, provide urgent humanitarian support.

The EU's tools for tackling migration seem to be well-structured enough although there is still room for improvement. Having different mechanisms to answer humanitarian needs (Civil Protection Mechanism), to manage borders (Frontex), and to facilitate asylum procedure (EASO), the EU is not always able to ensure the cooperation of all MSs. For well-structured mechanisms to be efficient and beneficial, they must be used by all MSs. In the cases of Greece and Croatia, it is seen that the MSs do not do very well with supporting these two countries in dealing with the migrant influx since 2015.

A vast majority of the MSs do not refrain from contributing to the financial assistance systems of the EU and giving in-kind aid to those in need. However, when it comes to relocation and resettlement programs, it is observed that they are rather slow in answering the calls from Greece or Croatia. For example, at a meeting of interior ministers, leaders could not agree on the obligatory relocation scheme, and instead, opposing ministers suggested to provide more resources to secure the external borders of the EU ("No compromise in sight", 2016). Authors argue that the MSs do not abide by their obligations clearly stated in the Article 80 of the Treaty on the Functioning of the European Union. The MSs might consider the relocation of migrants to their countries as a matter of national policy; at this point, the MSs may reconsider their goals and limits and decide if they aim to form a centralised migration policy.

It can be inferred from the abovementioned facts that although the scale of the "crisis" is different in Greece and Croatia (since Greece is more reachable, therefore much preferred by the migrants), when compared, it is seen that they more or less experience the same problem: not enough support from the MSs.

As Carrera, S. & den Hertog, L. (2016) explain the hotspots carry the heavy burden of refugees on their shoulders.

Conclusion

It can be said that especially Greece handled the situation well to some extent, considering the economic crisis. Nonetheless, the current systems of the EU need further collaboration and cooperation among the MSs in order to secure the well-functioning of common migration policy. New initiatives to encourage the MSs to take on more responsibilities are necessary. As suggested by Carrera (2016) Dublin system together with the new relocation scheme should be renounced. More effective and humane asylum systems which at least give options to the migrants about the country they want to live in should be introduced. Burden-sharing and solidarity among the MSs should be adopted as the principles of any new system.

Additionally, the EU should quit using "illegal" as a definition of persons leaving their countries behind in search of a haven, and rather employ "irregular" to define them. Thus, it may lead to a more positive understanding of the migrants among society.

It should be noted that, ultimately, migrants will continue their efforts to reach Europe in the hope of a better future ("We will find a way", 2016). Policies should give a chance for a better future for people born in less fortunate areas of the world.

References

Abdul-Ahat, G., Graham Harrison, E. & Kingsley, P. (2016, March 8). 'We will find a way': Syrian refugees react to planned EU-Turkey deal. *Guardian.* Retrieved November 8, 2016, from https://www.theguardian.com/world/2016/mar/08/we-will-find-a-way-syrian-refugees-react-to-planned-eu-turkey-deal

Al Jazeera. (2016, August 26) Hungary to build second border fence to stop refugees. *Al Jazeera.* Retrieved January 09, 2017, from http://www.aljazeera.com/news/2016/08/hungary-build-border-fence-stop-refugees-160826084509375.html

Baczynska, G. (2016, November 18). No compromise in sight, EU ministers at odds over immigration. Retrieved November 11, 2016, from http://www.reuters.com/article/us-europe-migrants-eu-idUSKBN13D1AF

Carrera, S. & den Hertog, L. (2016). A European border and coast guard: what's in a name? *CEPS Article in Liberty and Security in Europe, No: 88.*

European Asylum Support Office. (2016). *EASO Annual General Report 2015.* Luxembourg: European Asylum Support Office.

European Asylum Support Office. Relocation of applicants for international protection. Retrieved from https://www.easo.europa.eu/sites/default/files/public/BZ0116194ENN_0.pdf

European Commission. (2015). *A European Agenda on Migration.* Brussels. Retrieved from https://ec.europa.eu/home-affairs/sites/homeaffairs/files/what-we-do/policies/european-agenda-migration/background-information/docs/communication_on_the_european_agenda_on_migration_en.pdf

European Commission. (2015, October 6). Remarks of Commissioner Avramopoulos, Retrieved from http://europa.eu/rapid/press-release_SPEECH-15-5786_en.htm

European Commission. (2015). Leaders' Statement. Retrieved from http://ec.europa.eu/news/2015/docs/leader_statement_final.pdf

European Commission. (2015). Progress following Western Balkans Route Leaders' Meeting. Retrieved from http://europa.eu/rapid/press-release_IP-15-5924_en.htm

European Commission. (2015). Contact Points Video Conference. Retrieved from http://europa.eu/rapid/press-release_IP-15-5952_en.htm

European Commission. (2016). Thirteenth Contact Points Video Conference. Retrieved from http://europa.eu/rapid/press-release_IP-16-148_en.htm

European Commission. (2016). Fourteenth Contact Points Video Conference. Retrieved from http://europa.eu/rapid/press-release_IP-16-189_en.htm

European Commission. (2016). Commission reports on progress in Greece, Italy and the Western Balkans. Retrieved from http://europa.eu/rapid/press-release_IP-16-269_en.htm

European Commission. (2016). Commission Recommendation on the resumption of transfers to Greece under Regulation (EU) No. 604/2013. Brussels.

European Commission. (2016). Eighth report on relocation and resettlement. Brussels.

European Commission. (2017). Ninth report on relocation and resettlement. Brussels.

Frontex. (2017). Annual Risk Analysis 2017.

Huysmans, J. (2002). The European Union and the Securitization of Migration. Journal of Common Market Studies, 38(5), 751-777. Retrieved May 24, 2017 from http://onlinelibrary.wiley.com/doi/10.1111/1468-5965.00263/pdf

Medecins Sans Frontieres. (2017, January 9). Thousands trapped in freezing temperatures in Greece and the Balkans. Retrieved from http://www.msf.org/en/article/migration-thousands-trapped-freezing-temperatures-greece-and-balkans

Tatalović, S. & Jakešević, R. (2016). Newly Arriving Migrants and National Minorities in Croatia.

Weaver, M. (2015, September 18). Croatia 'will not become a migrant hotspot' says prime minister. *Guardian.* Retrieved November 21, 2016 from https://www.theguardian.com/world/2015/sep/18/croatia-refugees-zoran-milanovic-migrant-hotspot

Chapter 29. Support or Obstacle? Effects of Immigrants on Domestic Labor Force in Turkey

Atakan Durmaz[1], Özge Korkmaz[2]

Abstract

The phenomenon of migration, as old as human history, is one of the most interested subjects of countries in the 21st century, especially in the last 10 years. Undoubtedly, one of the important reasons for this is the fact that migration has significant influences on from economic to social life almost every subject in terms of both emigrating countries and receiving countries. The fact that economic factors and security problems are the main causes of migration movements also laid the groundwork for the work done in the field of economy to concentrate on this subject. At this point, there are also studies of the impact of receiving countries on labor market, although the impact of migrant movements on emigrating countries' economy is largely a matter of focus. However, there is no consensus on the work done in this regard. As a matter of fact, some studies have found that immigrants have a negative effect on the labor market because they are willing to work at lower wages, while in some studies they have found that immigrants have a positive influence on the labor market by increasing labor supply in areas where the local labor does not want to work. At this point, Turkey has taken its place in studies in the literature as a country that both emigrating (especially from the early 1960s to the 1990s) and receiving country (especially in the last 10 years because of events happening in neighboring countries). Although the vast majorities are refugee status, a growing number of immigrants are involved in the labor market and this affects the position of the local labor force on the labor market. From this point of view, the effect of immigrants on the labor force participation rate of the local labor force has been examined by means of regression analysis, using immigrant data from 26 provinces in Turkey between 2011 and 2015. According to the study results; Migrants allowed to work in Turkey have a positive effect on the participation rate even if just a bit. From a gender perspective, it has been found that immigrants have positive effects on women's labor force participation rates. But, there has been no significant impact on the male labor force participation rate of migrants. In the study, there has been also found that the increase in the level of education of men has a positive effect on the labor force participation rate, while in women, it has been found to be a negative effect of the higher education graduation although the primary and high school graduation has a positive effect on the labor force participation rates.

Keywords: Migration, migrants, labor market, labor force, participation rate

Introduction

Immigration has become one of the most important topics of popular debate in the social science literature (especially economics). One of the most important questions about immigration concerns is the beneficial and harmful effects of immigrants on the immigration country economies. At this point, immigration is thought to have negative effects on the labor market at least in the short term. Unfavorable effects of migration on domestic workers' employment opportunities and wages are one of the main concerns in the

---

[1] Assist. Prof. Dr., Bayburt University, Department of Economics, Turkey.
E-mail: adurmaz@bayburt.edu.tr
[2] Assist. Prof. Dr., Bayburt University, Department of Economics, Turkey.
E-mail: ozgekorkmaz@gmail.com

debate about migration. However, there are also studies that show that this is not true and that immigrants have many positive effects on the local labor market.

Some of the earliest studies on this subject assume that this migrant population is a different production factor. In other words, the labor factor is composed of immigrants and domestic people, and immigrants and domestic people are thought to be irreplaceable (Grossman 1982). However, such a distinction is difficult to make. As a matter of fact, subsequent studies have focused on a skillful distinction between different groups of labor inputs. Altonji and Card (1991); Dustmann et. al. (2005) how the skills are described in detail depends on the work, but the typical dimensions are education attainment, Card (2001) occupation, or Borjas (2003) experience and education. More recently, some articles (Ottaviano and Peri 2006; Manacorda, Manning and Wadsworth 2006) have taken further steps and relied on the excellent substitutability assumption of immigrants and domestic peoples in the predefined skill categories using nested production technologies.

The theory of economy is very suitable for helping to understand the possible consequences of migration for receiving countries, and the theoretical aspects of the possible effects on the labor market of the receiving countries are well understood. However, it is not wrong to say that the theorem's estimates are clearly cut off. It is in line with the economic models that some domestic workers who change the size or composition of the workforce resulting from migration can harm the labor market; However, similar to the theory, the shift in skills of the workforce is also compatible with the fact that migration does not have any effect on the wages and employment of local workers, at least in the long run. Economic models foresee that the effects of immigration on the labor market depend on the nature of the receiving country's economy and on the skill mix of immigrants compared to the local labor force (Dustmann et. al., 2008).

This statement shows that the various possible outputs comply with economic theory. Migration can reduce wages and employment of indigenous people. Nevertheless, it is not at all consistent with economic theory to think that long-run responses to migration have no effect or that immigration increases the wages of migrant labor supplement workers. In the case of long-term effects, however, it is important that the economy is open to trades and the flexibility of harmonizing the economy with the output mix produced outside of wages.

The impact of migration on the labor market is not limited to wages alone. At the same time, new job opportunities created in the labor market are another factor to be addressed at this point. Although immigrants have a good reason to enter the labor market and rival the local workforce for their current job opportunities, in some cases they have shown new opportunities for the local workforce by creating new employment opportunities.

Method and Dataset

The study aimed to investigate the effect of immigrants on the labor force participation rate of the local labor force has been examined by means of regression analysis, using data of immigrant with permission to work from 26 provinces in Turkey between 2011 and 2015. From this point of view, factors affecting the labor market were considered separately as male and female labor force in this study and factors affecting the local labor market in study are covered in the following variables. Table 1 shows dependent and independent variables used in the study.

Table 1. Descriptions of Variables

	Name of Variables	Description
Independed Variables	OKULBITIRMEYEN	The ratio of analphabet to total labor force
	YOGR	The ratio of Higher education graduate to total labor force
	TOPLAMGOCMENSAYISI	Number of migrants allowed to work
	LISEALTI	The ratio of under high school graduate to total labor force
	LISEMYO	The ratio of high school graduate to total labor force
Depended Variables	ISGUCU_ERKEK	Working participations ratio of male labor force
	ISGUCU_KADIN	Working Participations ratio of female labor force

The models examined are as follow:

Model1: $ISGUCU\_ERKEK_{it} = \alpha 0 + \alpha 1 OKULBITIRMEYEN_{it} + \alpha 2 YOGR_{it} + \alpha 3 TOPLAMGOCMENSAYISI_{it} + \alpha 4 LISEALTI_{it} + \alpha 5 LISEMYO_{it} + \varepsilon_{it}$

Model2: $ISGUCU\_KADIN_{it} = \alpha 0 + \alpha 1 OKULBITIRMEYEN_{it} + \alpha 2 YOGR_{it} + \alpha 3 TOPLAMGOCMENSAYISI_{it} + \alpha 4 LISEALTI_{it} + \alpha 5 LISEMYO_{it} + \varepsilon_{it}$

When determining the variables used in the models, Forward Stepwise-Wald method, which is a variable elimination method has been used.

As in time series, the variables' being stable in panel data analysis is quite important to avoid spurious regression problems. The levels or differences at which each series is stable must be determined so that the models mentioned above can give accurate and reliable results. This is possible with unit root analysis. In order to determine the Unit Root test to be used in a study, first of all, it must be researched that whether there is a correlation between the units or not. Since panel regression models depend on cross-sectional independence hypotheses between units.

Cross-sectional independence tests are used in order to determine whether the models dealt include unit and time effects. The Frees and Fisherman's tests are used to research the existence of cross-sectional independence between units. In the case that there is not a cross-sectional independence between the models, the First Generation unit root tests are used for the stability analyses of the series. The Fisher Phillips Perron unit root test is a First Generation unit root test (Choi, 2001). In the wake of determining the stability, the specifications of the models that will be estimated in panel data analysis must be determined. The Breusch-Pagan Lagrange Multipliers (LM) Test is used to decide whether the models to be estimated include unit and time effects. Breusch-Pagan LM test Statistics is as follows (Breusch-Pagan, 1980):

$$LM = \frac{NT}{2(T-1)} \left[\frac{\sum_{i=1}^{n}(\sum_{t=1}^{T} u_{it})^2}{\sum_{i=1}^{n}\sum_{t=1}^{T} u_{it}^2} - 1 \right]^2$$

Another test used to research the specifications of the models to be estimated is the F test. It is used in order to determine whether there is a unit effect.

Results

In the panel data analysis, firstly, whether there is cross-section dependency between the units should be investigated. For this purpose, Friedman and Frees' cross-section dependency tests were used in the study and the findings are presented in Table 2.

When the table is examined, it can be seen that there is no cross-section dependency in the models. In this direction, the 1st Generation Unit Root Tests and the Fisher Phillips Perron Unit Root Test were used to determine the levels / differences that the variables were stationary in the study. The analysis results are presented in Table 3.

Table 2. Results of Frees and Friedman's Cross-sectional Dependency

MODEL 1 (Dependent Variable: ISGUCU_ERKEK)
Frees' test of cross sectional independence = 1.548
Critical values from Frees' Q distribution
alpha = 0.10 : 0.4892
alpha = 0.05 : 0.6860
alpha = 0.01 : 1.1046
Friedman's test of cross sectional independence = 6.338, Pr = 0.9999

MODEL 2 (Dependent Variable: ISGUCU_KADIN)
Frees' test of cross sectional independence =2.477
Critical values from Frees' Q distribution
alpha = 0.10 : 0.4892
alpha = 0.05 : 0.6860
alpha = 0.01 : 1.1046
Friedman's test of cross sectional independence = 12.154, Pr = 0.9853

Table 3. Fisher Phillips Perron Unit Root Test

Variables	Statistics	Prob.
OKULBITIRMEYEN	129.491	0.000[***]
YOGR	126.505	0.000[***]
TOPLAMGOCMENSAYISI	101.029	0.000[***]
LISEALTI	117.527	0.000[***]
LISEMYO	151.053	0.000[***]
ISGUCU_ERKEK	123.067	0.000[***]
ISGUCU_KADIN	130.380	0.000[***]

[*], [**] and [***], respectively, 0.10, 0.05 and 0.01 indicates the level of statistical significance.

After determining the levels / differences that the series are stationary in the study, the LM test was performed to determine the estimation methods. The Hausman test was applied in case of unit effect in the models and the findings are presented in Table 4.

Table 4. LM ve Hausman Test

MODEL 1			
Test	Statistics	Prob.	Decision
LM	133.92	0.000***	Unit effect. The classic model is not suitable.
Test	Statistics	Prob.	Decision
HAUSMAN	11.71	0.038**	The difference between the parameters is systematic. The fixed effect model is suitable.
MODEL 2			
Test	Statistics	Prob.	Decision
LM	74.88	0.000***	Unit effect. The classic model is not suitable.
Test	Statistics	Prob.	Decision
HAUSMAN	32.11	0.000***	The difference between the parameters is systematic. The fixed effect model is suitable.

*, ** and ***, respectively, 0.10, 0.05 and 0.01 indicates the level of statistical significance.

Table 5. Diagnostics Tests

MODEL 1				
Autocorrelation Test	Statistics	Heterockedasticity Test	χ^2 Statistics	Prob.
BHARGAVA,FRANZINI & NARENDRANATHAN'S DURBIN WATSON TEST	1.3173	WALD	1006.36	0.0000***
MODEL 2				
Autocorrelation Test	Statistics	Heterockedasticity Test	χ^2 Statistics	Prob.
BHARGAVA,FRANZINI & NARENDRANATHAN'S DURBIN WATSON TEST	1.7409	WALD	366.90	0.0000***

*, ** And ***, respectively, 0.10, 0.05 and 0.01 indicates the level of statistical significance. In BHARGAVA,FRANZINI & NARENDRANATHAN'IN DURBIN WATSON test, if the test value is smaller than two, it is determined that the model is an autocorrelation problem.

From Table 4, it can be said that the fixed effect model is suitable for all models. At this stage of the study, all models were estimated and then the results of the diagnostic tests related to the model were to be included. Related findings are reported in Table 5.

As shown in Table 5, there are different variance and autocorrelation problems in Model 1 and Model 2. For this reason, it was thought that robust estimators should be used in predicting models and model predictions were presented by means of resistant standard predictors at this stage of study.

According to Table 6 where the results for Model 1 and Model 2 are included, migrants allowed to work in Turkey have a positive effect on the participation rate even if just a bit. From a gender perspective, it has been found that immigrants have positive effects on women's labor force participation rates. But, there has been no significant impact on the male labor force participation rate of migrants. In the study, there has been also found that the increase in the level of education of men has a positive effect on the labor force participation rate, while in women, it has been found to be a negative effect of the higher education graduation although the primary and high school graduation has a positive effect on the labor force participation rates.

Discussion

The technological developments and the results of these developments have allowed the production factors to move without limit. This situation reveals both the favorable and the unfavorable results of the countries. As a matter of fact, the labor is moving the sedan to get to the frontier. The resulting situations are a good example of this. Immigrants, while being dependent on the social and economic structure of the receiving countries, sometimes have a positive effect on the labor market of the receiving countries, but sometimes this is the opposite. In this sense, Turkey has emerged as a country which has a lot of immigrants especially in the last period in parallel with the developments in its surroundings. And as a consequence of this situation, the influences of immigrants on the domestic labor market are an important debate in both academic and political circles. In this respect, the study results show that while immigrants who are allowed to work have no influence on male domestic labor force, immigrants who are allowed to work have positive effect on female domestic labor force working participation.

According to these results, migrants allowed to work in Turkey have a positive effect on the participation rate even if just a bit. From a gender perspective, it has been found that immigrants have positive effects on women's labor force participation rates. But, there has been no significant impact on the male labor force participation rate of migrants. So that, it can be said that immigrants who are allowed to work in Turkey have created new job opportunities in the sectors which increase women's participation on the working. In the study, there has been also found that the increase in the level of education of men has a positive effect on the labor force participation rate, while in women, it has been found to be a negative effect of the higher education graduation although the primary and high school graduation has a positive effect on the labor force participation rates.

Table 6. Results of Model 1 and Model 2

Dependent Variable: ISGUCU_ERKEK (Model 1)				
Variables	**Coefficient**	**Robust Error**	**Std.**	**Prob.**
Constant	13.9161	4.1425		0.003***
LISEALTI	0.5241	0.1146		0.000***
LISEMYO	0.2646	0.0727		0.001***
OKULBITIRMEYEN	-0.0153	0.0467		0.745
YOGR	0.1366	0.0429		0.004***
TOPLAMGOCMENSAYISI	-2.75E-06	0.00005		0.958
R^2= 0. 8100	Wald $_{statisctics}$ =42.80 (0.000)***			
Dependent Variable: ISGUCU_KADIN (Model 2)				
Variables	**Coefficient**	**Robust Error**	**Std.**	**Prob.**
Constant	-10.4013	6.5632		0.126
LISEALTI	0.7351	0.1412		0.000***
LISEMYO	0.2631	0.0827		0.004***
OKULBITIRMEYEN	0.0892	0.0659		0.188
YOGR	-0.1682	0.0715		0.027**
TOPLAMGOCMENSAYISI	0.0003	0.00001		0.000***
R^2= 0. 7397	Wald $_{statisctics}$ = 64.76 (0.000)***			

*, ** And ***, respectively, 0.10, 0.05 and 0.01 indicates the level of statistical significance.

References

Altonji, J. G. and D. Card (1991). The Effects of Immigration on the Labor Market Outcomes of Less-skilled Natives. In J. M. Abowd and R. B. Freeman (Eds.), Immigration, Trade, and the Labor Market, Chapter 7, pp. 201-234. Chicago: University of Chicago Press.
Baltagi, B. H. (2005). *Econometric Analysis of Panel Data*. John Wiley Sons.

Borjas, G. J. (2003). The Labor Demand Curve is Downward Sloping: Reexamining the Impact of Immigration on the Labor Market. Quarterly Journal of Economics 118 (4), 1335-1374.

Borjas, G.J (1999). "The economic analysis of immigration", Chapter 28, Handbook of Labor Economics, vol. 3, pp. 1697–760, place: publisher.

Breusch T. and Pagan A. 1980. "The Lagrange Multiplier Test and Its Applications to Model Specification in Econometrics". *The Review of Economic Studies*, 47, pp. 1287-1294.

Card, D. (2001). Immigrant Inflows, Native Outflows, and the Local Labor Market Impacts of Higher Immigration. Journal of Labor Economics 19 (1), 22-64.

Chiswick, B.R. (1993). "Review Of İmmigration And And The Work Force: Economic Consequences For The United States And Source Areas, Journal Of Economic Literature, vol. 31, pp. 910–1.

Christian Dustmann, Albrecht Glitz, Tommaso Frattini (2008). "The Labour Market Impact of Immigration", *Oxf Rev Econ Policy*, 24 (3): 477-494. doi: 10.1093/oxrep/grn024.

Choi, In (2001), "Unit Roots Tests for Panel Data." Journal of International Money and Finance, 20: 229- 272.

Dustmann, C., F. Fabbri, and I. Preston (2005). The Impact of Immigration on the British Labour Market. Economic Journal 115 (507), F324-F341.

Eckstein, Z. and Y. Weiss (2004). On the Wage Growth of Immigrants: Israel, 1990-2000. Journal of the European Economic Association 2 (4), 665-695.

Edin, P.-A., P. Fredriksson, and O. Aslund (2003). Ethnic Enclaves and the Economic Success of Immigrants- Evidence from a Natural Experiment. Quarterly Journal of Economics 118 (1), 329-357.

Ethier, W. J. (1984). Protection and Real Incomes Once Again. Quarterly Journal of Economics 99 (1), 193-200.

Filer, R. K. (1992). The Effect of Immigrant Arrivals on Migratory Patterns of Native Workers. In G. J. Borjas and R. B. Freeman (Eds.), Immigration and the Work Force: Economic Consequences for the United States and Source Areas, Chapter 8, pp. 245-269. Chicago: University of Chicago Press.

Friedberg, R.M. and Hunt, J. (1995). "The Impact of Immigration on Host Country Wages, Employment And Growth, Journal of Economic Perspectives, vol. 9, pp. 23–44.

Frees, E.W. (1995), "Assessing Cross-Sectional Correlation in Panel Data", Journal of Econometrics 69:393, 414-496.

Frees, E.W. (2004), Longitudinal and Panel Data: Analysis and Applications in the Social Sciences, Cambridge: Cambridge University Press.

Friedman, M. (1937), "The use of ranks to avoid the assumption of normality implicit in the analysis of variance", Journal of the American Statistical Association, 32: 675–701.

Grossman, J. B. (1982). The Substitutability of Natives and Immigrants in Production. Review of Economics and Statistics 64 (4), 596-603.

Hoyos, R. E. D. and Sarafidis, V. (2006). *'Testing for Cross-Sectional Dependence in Panel Data Models'.* The Stata Journal, 6(4), pp. 482-496.

Manacorda, M., A. Manning, and J. Wadsworth (2006). The Impact of Immigration on the Structure of Male Wages: Theory and Evidence from Britain. CReAM Discussion Paper No.08/06.

Ottaviano, G. I. P. and G. Peri (2006). Rethinking the Effects of Immigration on Wages. NBER Working Paper No. 12497.

Chapter 30. Human Trafficking: Is the Law of the Western Societies Effective or Not?

Alexia Kapsampeli[*]

Abstract

The human trafficking is widely thought to be the modern form of slavery. It started before many years and still exists. Nowadays a great number of people, especially women and children, are trafficked, mainly from poor to developed states, in order to be exploited either for sex or for labor. The Western societies, including the international organizations and institutions, have taken measures, as they have tried to eliminate it. The most characteristic attempt is the Palermo Protocol. However, the legislation has been proved ineffective, therefore the states in collaboration with the organizations should realize the basic dimensions of this phenomenon and legislate based on them.

Introduction

Human trafficking is one of the most serious global issues nowadays. It is a multi-billion-dollar criminal industry that denies freedom to 20.9 people around the world. It is said to be the third most profitable business for organized crime after drugs and armed trade, as traffickers are estimated to earn approximately $9.5 billion annually. There are six key conceptual approaches commonly used for human trafficking: 1) as a modern form of slavery, 2) as an exemplary of the globalization of crime, 3) as a problem of transnational organized crime, 4) as synonymous with prostitution, 5) as migration issue and 6) as a human rights challenge.

The rapid growth in trafficking of human beings and its transnational nature has prompted the international community to take measures. It is said that there were over 30 intergovernmental bodies in Europe only focusing on human trafficking and smuggling by the late 1990s. Human trafficking has become the subject of much empirical research, academic debate, and advocacy in diverse fields such as criminology, politics, law, human rights, and sociologies of migration, gender and public health. It has become from 'a poorly funded, NGO women's issue in the early 1980's into the global agenda of high politics of the United States Congress, the European Union and the United Nations'. However, there remain considerable gaps and limitations in our knowledge and understanding of human trafficking.

The aim of this assignment is to critically evaluate whether the Western societies' legislation for human trafficking is effective and adequate.

Methodology

In this paper, a legal, as well as critical approach, are proposed to develop the main issue. The legislation- in particular the United Nations Protocol to

---

[*] E-mail: alexiakapsabeli@hotmail.com.

Prevent, Suppress and Punish Trafficking in Persons, Especially Women and Children (also known as the Palermo Protocol), the United Nations Convention against Transnational Organized Crime, the United Nations Universal Declaration of Human Rights 1948, the European Convention on Human Rights and Fundamental Freedoms 1950, the European Commission Communication of 20 November 1996 on Trafficking in Women for the Purpose of Sexual Exploitation, the United Nations Convention on the Rights of the Child (UNCRC) (1989), the Optional Protocol on the Sale of Children, Child Prostitution and Child Pornography (2000), the International Labor Organization Convention No. 182 Concerning the Prohibition and Immediate Action for the Elimination of the Worst Forms of Child Labor (1999) and the Optional Protocol to the Convention on the Rights of the Child on the Involvement of Children in Armed Conflicts (2000)- was studied thoroughly. The data collected by the author comes from literature and other sources, especially academic texts journals, newspaper articles and electronic resources. In particular, the data obtained from the Internet may not have been monitored.

Main Body

The origins of trafficking can be traced back to the ancient practices of slavery and the slave trade. Slaves were generally treated as commodities of the owners. They did not have personal rights and freedoms. Slavery and trade in human beings have been evolving into new and more complex forms of abuses in modern labour systems. The most commonly identified and most discussed form of human trafficking is sexual exploitation. It is defined by the Coalition against Trafficking in Women as: 'all prostitution exploits women, regardless of women's consent.' In other words, the women are forced to work as prostitutes trapped by threats of violence and by demands that debts incurred in the course of migration be repaid.

The second form of human trafficking is trafficking for labour exploitation. Labor traffickers such as recruiters, contractors, employers and others often make false promises of a high-paying job or exciting education or travel opportunities to lure people into horrendous working conditions. The employers exert such physical or psychological control - including physical abuse, debt bondage, confiscation of passports or money – that the victims believe they have no other choice but to continue working for them. Globally, the International Labour Organization estimates that there are 14.2 million people trapped in forced labour. Another important form is the trafficking of children that is about taking children out of their protective environment and preying on their vulnerability for the purpose of exploitation. Criminal networks and individuals exploit children in prostitution, street, hawking, car window cleaning and other street-based activities, because they are easily replaced by another child, if they are arrested. In some parts of the world, there is a connection between the trafficking of children and the drug trade. Last but not least, child labourers work for the multinational companies that dominate world trade in cocoa link farms in West Africa. Human trafficking constitutes first and foremost a violation of human rights and an offence to the dignity and the integrity of the human being, in accordance with the European Union, the Council of Europe Framework Decision on Combating Trafficking in Human Beings 2002 and the Council of Europe Convention on Action against Trafficking in Human Beings 2005. In addition, fundamental human rights protected under the UN Universal Declaration of Human Rights 1948 and the European Convention on Human Rights and Fundamental Freedoms 1950 are violated because of human trafficking. These are the right to life and security of person, the right to be free from slavery or servitude, the right to freedom of movement, the right to be free of torture or cruel, inhuman and degrading treatment, the right to health and right to free choice of employment. As for children, their rights to be protected from exploitation, to remain with their family, to be protected from sexual violence, to have time to play, to go to school and so lose the opportunity to improve their lives in the future are violated. Under these circumstances, the United Nations Convention for the Suppression of the Traffic in Persons and of the Exploitation of the Prostitution of Others was adopted in 1949. It was a legal turning point, because it was the first legally binding instrument. However, it has been criticized for confining trafficking exclusively to the cross-border movement of persons into prostitution and ignoring other forms of labour trafficking. Consequently, vast numbers of women and men have been excluded from the assistance and protection they require. As of today, only 66 countries have ratified this Convention. One of the reasons for the low ratification rate is several countries did not want to criminalize prostitution as required in the Convention. After 50 years, the United Nations Protocol to Prevent, Suppress and Punish Trafficking in Persons, Especially Women and Children, also known as the Palermo Protocol, was adopted by General Assembly resolution 55/35 in Palermo, Italy. This and other two Protocols -the Protocol against the Smuggling of Migrants by Land, Sea and Air and the Protocol against the Illicit Manufacturing of and Trafficking in Firearms, their Parts and Components and Ammunition- have supplemented the United Nations Convention against Transnational Organized Crime.

According to the Protocol, the three main elements of 'trafficking in persons' are: "a) the recruitment, transportation, transfer, harboring or receipt of persons, b) by means of the threat or use of force or other forms of coercion, of abduction, of fraud, of deception, of the abuse of power of a position of vulnerability or of the giving or receiving of payments or benefits to achieve the consent of a person having control over another person, c) for the purpose of exploitation". The Protocol recognized that it is not necessary for a victim to cross a border, so trafficking within countries or specific regions, such as the European Union, can be prosecuted.

In 2007 The United Nations launched a Global Initiative to Fight Human Trafficking to promote 'a global multi-stakeholder strategy' to tackle 'a crime that shames the humanity. The initiative boasted a lot of collaborative partners from government and non-governmental organizations, transnational corporations, to celebrity-led networks of goodwill ambassadors. As for Europe, the first European Commission Communication of 20 November 1996 on Trafficking in Women for the Purpose of Sexual Exploitation already recognized that it cannot be tackled effectively without a multi-disciplinary and coordinated approach which involves all concerned players- NGOs and social authorities, judicial, law enforcement and migration authorities- and which involves both national and international cooperation. In the United States, the Congress passed the Trafficking Victims Protection Act of 2000 (TVPA). The TVPA is updated every two years and applies only to federal cases. In 2010 the former President declared January to be Human Trafficking Awareness month and 11th January was named National Human Trafficking Awareness Day. In the last year, Barack Obama signed a bill to punish people involved in human trafficking and provide resources to victims. For the first time, the federal legislation specifically addressed domestic human trafficking and prioritized the need to confront the demand for child sex, according to Yasmin Vafa, an official with the Human Rights Project 4 Girls.

Evaluation Section

Under these circumstances, it can be said the Western societies have attempted to take measures against human trafficking through the legislation. However, the goal has not been achieved, as they are widely thought to have failed to take a holistic approach to the issue. Notably, critics have noted the tendency of states to place immigration controls and national security concerns before human rights protection of trafficking victims. States have been criticized for conflating anti-trafficking with immigration and asylum controls instead of protecting victims and preventing a range of trafficking harms. This opinion is adopted by many researchers, such as Penny Green and Mike Grewcock in their work "The War against Illegal Immigration State Crime and the Construction of a European Identity" as well as the Professor Sharon Pickering in "Border Terror: policing, forced migration and terrorism". Ratification is another crucial factor. Many states have not ratified the conventions, due to the fact that prostitution is not illegal, both for sellers and buyers. It is not really considered work or violence against women, but mainly immoral and a public nuisance. Consequently, sexual exploitation cannot be punished. Others think trafficking in women for sexual exploitation is mainly a sub-category of irregular/illegal immigration; as a result, they have not taken measures in the correct direction. As for trafficking in children, states have not protected them adequately. In many countries, the compulsory education age is inconsistent with the minimum employment age. Others have failed to stipulate 'hazardous industries' or allow children to carry out work in these industries. A human rights framework to deal with trafficking could help supplement global action against the practice. It should articulate legal obligations imposed upon states, such as obligations to prohibit trafficking, prosecute traffickers, protect victims, and address the causes and consequences.

Conclusion

Nowadays one of the most serious crimes across the world is human trafficking. Millions of people, especially women as well as children, are victims of traffickers who earn billions of dollars. Human trafficking is as old as trade. In the past slaves who were the owners' properties did not have freedoms and rights, as the victims of trafficking. Today the most common forms of trafficking are sexual exploitation, labor trafficking and trafficking of children. The victims can be protected by many conventions of International Organizations such as the United Nations Protocol to Prevent, Suppress and Punish Trafficking in Persons known as Palermo Protocol. Even the European Union and the United States have taken measures for this purpose. However, Western societies' legislation has been proved ineffective, as human trafficking has not been eliminated and the victims have not been protected adequately. For this reason, it is widely thought that both the states and the international organizations should cooperate more intensively, in order to create a more effective legal framework against human trafficking.

References

UNICEF, Understanding child trafficking: Training manual to fight trafficking in children for labor, sexual and other forms of exploitation, 2009 last accessed on 15th January 2017 http://www.unicef.org/protection/Textbook_1.pdf,

Maggy Lee, Trafficking and Globe Crime Control, SAGE Publications, 2011

Wong Diana, The rumor of trafficking: border controls, illegal migration and the sovereignty of the nation-state, in William van Schendel and Itty Abraham "Illicit Flows and Criminal Things: States, Borders and the Other Side of Globalization", 2005, Bloomington:Indiana University Press, pp. 69-100

Unknown author, http://f3magazine.unicri.it/?p=281, last accessed on 18th January 2017

Unknown author, http://www.eden.rutgers.edu/~yongpatr/425/final/timeline.htm, last accessed on 19th January 2017

Unknown author, https://www.unodc.org/documents/human-trafficking/2008/BP023TheEffectivenessofLegalFrameworks.pdf , last accessed on 8th February 2017

Unknown author, https://www.unodc.org/unodc/en/human-trafficking/what-is-human-trafficking.html?ref=menuside last accessed on 12th March 2017

Christina Seideman, The Palermo Protocol: Why it has been ineffective in reducing human sex   trafficking, http://digitalcommons.pepperdine.edu/cgi/viewcontent.cgi?article=1152&context=globa ltides, last accessed on 25th January 2017

United Nations Office on Drugs and Crime, The Global Initiative to Fight Human Trafficking, https://www.unodc.org/pdf/gift%20brochure.pdf last accessed on 15th February 2017

Unknown author, http://eur-lex.europa.eu/legal-content/EN/TXT/?uri=uriserv%3Al33095, last accessed on 20th February 2017

Penny Green and Mike Grewcock, The War Against Illegal Immigration State Crime and the Construction of a European Identity, http://www.austlii.edu.au/au/journals/CICrimJust/ 2002/16.html, 2002, last accessed on 21st February 2017

Sharon Pickering, Border Terror: policing, forced migration and terrorism, Global Change, Peace and Security: formerly Pacific Review, Volume 16, Issue 3, 2004

The Council of Europe Framework Decision on Combating Trafficking in Human Beings 2002, http://eur-lex.europa.eu/legal-content/EN/TXT/?uri=URISERV%3Al33137 last accessed on 19th February 2017

Tom Obokata, Trafficking of Human Beings from a Human Rights Perspective Towards a More Holistic Approach, Martinus Nijhoff Publishers, 2006

Heli Askola, Legal Responses to Trafficking in Women for Sexual Exploitation in the European Union, Hart Publishing, 2007

Cheryl Wetzstein, http://www.washingtontimes.com/news/2015/jun/1/obama-signs-human-trafficking-law/, last accessed on 22th February 2017

Unknown author, https://polarisproject.org/labor-trafficking, last accessed on 30th January 2017

Unknown author, http://migrationeducation.de/44.1.html?&rid=216&cHash= 7808e911ca5245e39aba175a9fbab022, last accessed on 10th March 2017

Unknown author, http://www.ilo.org/ipec/areas/Traffickingofchildren/lang--en/index.htm, last accessed on 11 March 2017.

Compiled by F. Tilbe, E. Iskender, I. Sirkeci

Chapter 31. Diaspora Bonds as a New Foreign Capital Tools: A Research on the Countries Applying and Potential of the Turkish Diaspora[††††††††††††]

Atakan Durmaz[‡‡‡‡‡‡‡‡‡‡‡‡], Adem Kalça[§§§§§§§§§§§§§]

Abstract

Developing countries that want to sustain their economic development and close the economic gap between developed countries need foreign capital, especially because of insufficient domestic savings. In this context, there are many ways in which countries resort to attracting foreign capital. However, since the early 1990s, some countries have seen diaspora as a source of foreign capital they need and have developed methods for this source. One of these methods is the diaspora bond, which emerges as a new generation financial borrowing instrument and which has different advantages in terms of both the issuing country and the buyer compared to other financial instruments and is generally presented only to diaspora members. From this point of view, the aim of this study is to present the effectiveness of these diaspora bonds used as a new generation borrowing instrument and to provide an alternative source of foreign capital that Turkey needs in line with its economic objectives. It is also to raise awareness of this issue.

Keywords: diaspora, diaspora bonds, foreign capital, growth

Introduction

Mobilization of the capital is in the process of integration, which begins with the mobilization of goods and services, starting with mobilizing of goods and services today, when the walls have been destroyed, the borders have gradually come to a halt, customs walls have left their protection free to trade, and the world has become a global village. Now, states and private sector members who are not satisfied with the markets within their borders have turned their eyes to world markets. While exporting goods and services in the 19th and 20th centuries was the main objective of foreign trade, nowadays it is added to import foreign capital next to this target. However, it is not so easy to import foreign capital nowadays when it is difficult to trust even the nearest ones of human beings. In such an environment, one of the alternatives of the states is the investors of their own race who live outside their homeland.

The nationalist movement of 1789 French Revolution has been used for various purposes as diverse as nationalism many times. The purpose of using the 21st century is the same for many countries; To provide foreign finance to the development of the country. How is it? With this question, the concept of diaspora is introduced. Diaspora; Ancient Greek: διασπορά - "scattering" refers to the scattering of seeds (Bergsten and Choin, 2003) In political

---

[††††††††††††] This work is an improved and audited version of the report "II. International Symposium on Sustainable Development, June 8-9 2010, Sarajevo / Bosnia Herzegovina".
[‡‡‡‡‡‡‡‡‡‡‡‡] Assist. Prof. Dr. Bayburt University, Department of Economics, E-mail: adurmaz@bayburt.edu.tr
[§§§§§§§§§§§§§] Prof. Dr., Karadeniz Technical University, Department of Economics, E-mail: akalca@ktu.edu.tr

literature, it is the name given to the disintegration of a nation or nation from its motherland to other countries. Countries with diasporas with high economic strength are taking a step forward in the days that they are riding.Diaspora; Ancient Grek: διασπορά – that means "scattering, broadcasting, scattering particles (Bergsten, Choin, 2003). In the political literature: it is the name which is given to the spread of a folk or a nation from their homelands to other countries. The purpose of this article is; Given the contributions of the Israeli and Indian diaspora to these countries, it considers the economic power of the Turkish diaspora in Europe and the contribution it can make to the Turkish economy.

Diaspora Bonds, Israel and India Case

A Diaspora bond is a debt note issued by a country, a sub-sovereign person or a private company to increase financing from abroad diasporas (Ketkar and Ratha, 2007). If foreign exchange demands are a way of keeping the diasporic income stream on a regular basis, issuing bonds on a solid currency (foreign exchange) to the diaspora is a way of attracting foreign capital from abroad. Diaspora estimates are not yet widely used as a financial development tool. As mentioned above, Israel has been applying for this source since 1951, while India has been attaching great importance to boosting solid foreign exchange financing from its own diaspora since 1991. Israel, which has been launched by the Development Corporation for Israel (DCI) in 1951, has made a total of over $ 25 billion in foreign capital inflows. In India, the amount of debts issued by the Government-Owned State Bank of India (SBI) has increased by more than $ 11 billion day-to-day.

Diaspora bonds are different from foreign currency deposits (FCDs) that many developing countries use to provide foreign exchange flows. Diaspora bonds are typically long-term securities that are repaid only on maturity (precious papers). FCDs, on the other hand, can be withdrawn at any time. This is undoubtedly true for demand deposits and savings deposits. At the same time, however, deposits can be withdrawn at any time by giving up some of the accrued interest. In addition, FCDs tend to be more volatile, requiring banks to hold larger reserves against FCD commitments (debts). Thus, FCDs can be a fund investment (convertibility to investment) decreases. On the contrary, diasporic bonds are a long-term source of foreign financing. For this reason, the income of these accounts can be used to finance the investment (Ketkar and Ratha, 2007).

The Jewish Diaspora in the United States has contributed to the economic development of Israel by purchasing the proceeds from Development Corporation for Israel (DCI). DCI was founded in 1951 with the explicit purpose of increasing the foreign exchange inflows to Israel from the Jewish diaspora abroad by exporting irrevocable treasuries. Israel sees this financial instrument as an important source of continued ties with the Jewish Diaspora, as well as a constant source of foreign capital from offshore countries. The diaspora can also be regarded as a credit source at the same time, especially when the country is experiencing borrowing problems from other external sources. In DCI's diasporic debates, the maturity and quantity flexibility is the issue. DCI is being reimbursed at the time of the treasuries and there appears to be no claim before the date. In addition, 200 million dollars of surrendered treasures were never demanded.

In 1951, Israel issued a law known as the "Israel Independent Exporter Law" that allowed the country to export its first diasporic bond. Since the beginning of the program, the volume of export of these estates has reached 25 billion dollars. In May 1951, David Ben-Gurion formally launched the sale of the first president of Israel, diaspora treasures, at a meeting in New York in the USA, and then went on tour of many countries where the Jewish Diaspora lived to provide support for the sale of these estates. This first venture has been quite successful and sales have reached $ 52.6 million. When it arrived in September 2005, the DCI estimates were roughly 32% of Israel's external debt of $ 31.4 billion (Romano, 1998).

Table 1. Diaspora bonds issued by India

Bond Type	Amount	Year	Maturity	Minimum	Coupon
India Development Bond USD GBP	$1.6 bn	1991	5 years	Not available	9.50% 13.25%
Resurgent India Bond USD GBP DM	$4.2 bn	1998	5 years	2,000* 1,000** 3,000*	7.75% 8.00% 8.25%
India Millennium Deposits USD GBP EUR	$5.5 bn	2000	5 years	2,000* 2,000* 2,000*	8.50% 7.85% 6.85%

Source: Ketkar and Ratha (2007).

To get a long-term debt assurance, India run debt from its non-residence of diaspora of India as a result of *Development Bonds (IDBs)*($1.6 billion dollar) following the 1991 balance of payments crisis,*Resurgent India Bonds* (4.2 billion dollar) with the burden of the sanctions in 1998 Nuclear explosion and India Millennium Deposits (IMDs) in 2000 ($5.5 billion). It was mediated by a state bank, the State Bank of India (SBI). In the years when the IDBs were experiencing a balance-of-payments crisis, the IDBs went to provide funding for Indians (NRIs) who live outside India instead of the foreign currency they invested abroad. The earnings of the IDB, RIB and IMD for investors are higher than the gains they have made from a similar financial instrument in the country of their residence. India is also profitable because diaspora investors are willing to pay an interest under the rates they demand from the market (Murray, 2006).

The IDB, RIB and IMD are five-year maturities. Borrowings can be in various currencies. Unlike the Jewish Diaspora, the Indian Diaspora did not reduce patriotism in the RIBs except for a very small discount on IMDs. The profit of the corporate estates (BB term) was 7.2%. For this reason, there was no discount in the RIBs. India Diaspora Debtors provided little discounts compared to Israeli DCI estimates (Zakaria, 2006).

Table 2. Comparison of diaspora bonds issued by Israel and Indi

India	Israel
Annual issuance since 1951	Opportunistic issuance in 1991, 1998 and 2000
Development oriented borrowings	Balance of payments support
Large though declining patriotic discount	Small patriotic discount, if any
Fixed, floating rate bonds and notes	Fixed rate bonds
Maturities from 1 to 20 years with bullet repayment	SBI distribution in conjunction with int'l banks
Targeted towards but not limited to diaspora	Limited to diaspora
SEC registered	No SEC registration
Non-negotiable	Non-negotiable

Source: Zakaria (2006).

Structure of the Turkish Diaspora

It is not possible to say that Turkey has a politically defined diaspora in its full sense. However, it is possible to put the Turks who live outside of the motherland into the diaspora, considering the wide-view definition. Although Turks living abroad and accepting the citizenship of many countries have gathered under the roof of various associations and foundations in their countries, they could not transform these associations into the economic diaspora in a way that would be within the business association with the motherland. The capital flow, which first started in the form of foreign labor savings, emerged as a result of the labor migration movement from Turkey to Western European Countries starting in 1961 and provided significant contributions to the Turkish economy for many years. The economic, demographic and socioeconomic conditions of Turkey and the Western European countries have been influential in this decision of the Turks going to Turkey from Turkey (Artukoğlu, 2005).

The foreign currencies to which the workers working abroad can be regarded as capital flows cannot be ignored. However, when considering the savings of entrepreneurs of Turkish origin who are living abroad and especially in the European Union countries, many of them are citizens of the country they live in and are dealing with the trade there is the question which is how these savings can be drawn to the motherland. The first thing that could come to mind is the creation of an economic diaspora power that is closely related to Turkey, ie Turkey. To show how important this matter is, the structure, economic and social status of the Turkish population living in Europe will be tried to be considered numerically.

Turkish Population in EU Countries

According to the research made by TAVAK, by the end of 2015, numbers of the Turkish immigrants living in European Union countries has reached 5.4 million and Turkish immigrants are close to 1.6% of the EU population. In this way the population of Turkish origin reaches a higher level than the 8 EU countries and brings to the 19th Great national community of the European Union. Just as in Germany, Turks living in EU countries also constitute a young population. In this context, it can be said that the target countries are a dynamic group in the era of business formation, which wants to create a perspective to them. Their newly established ties have citizenship.

Table 3. The Turkish Population in EU Countries (2015)

Country	Total Turkish People	Number of Turkish Citizens
Turkish Immigrants in EU-28 Countries		
Belgium	135.000	39.532
Denmark	59.920	28.934
Germany	3.090.000	1.678.166
France	434.540	323.421
Netherland	478.330	142.698
Austria	247.500	106.000
Sweden	40.766	10.840
UK	180.000	90.000
Other 19 EU Countries	130.000	--
Total (1)	**4.796.056**	**2.419.491**
Turkish Minorities		
Greece	150.000	-
Bulgaria	500.000	-
Romania	20.000	-
Total (2)	**670.000**	-
Turkish immigrants and minorities in the EU		
EU-28 Total. (1+2)	**5.466.056**	**2.419.491**

Source: TAVAK (2015).

Economic Contribution of Turks working in Europe Countries

The population of 4.2 million people living in Europe constitutes approximately 1.372 million working populations. The unemployment rate among the Turks is higher than the unemployment rate in that country. This is because the average age of the Turkish population is smaller and the proportion of working women is lower than the total population in the EU countries.

A total of 1.372 million employees in the European Union countries with a total working population of 0.69 contributed approximately € 80.7 billion to the Gross Domestic Product (GDP) of the Turkish EU at current prices in 2015 (TAVAK, 2015). The EU contribution of 80.7 million Euros, which 4.1 million Turks living in the former 15 member European Union countries have made in the EU GDP in 2015, exceeds the GDP of EU-25 member 8 countries.

Table 4. Turks working in the EU Contribution to Gross Domestic Product(2015/current prices)

Country	Total GDP (Billion Euro)	Contribution of the Turks (Billion Euro)	Distribution(%)
Belgium	313,0	2,2	2,7
Denmark	221,4	1,6	2,0
Germany	2.307,9	53,4	66,2
France	1.781,1	7,5	9,3
Netherlands	528,0	8,1	10,0
Austria	256,4	4,6	5,7
Sweden	305,2	1,0	1,2
United Kingdom	1.892,7	1,8	2,2
Other EU Countries	3.767,9	0,5	0,6
GDP EU-15	10.769,8	80,7	100
EU-25	11.373,6	80,7	100

Source: TAVAK (2015).

Table 5. Turks living in EU and EU countries in per capita Gross Domestic Product

Country	Total	Turks
EU-15(Million Euro)	19.769,8	80,7
EU-25(Million Euro)	11.373,6	80,7
EU-15(Million Population)	389,4	4.1
EU-25(Million Population)	463,5	4.1
EU-15 per capital GDP(Euro)	27.600	19.700
EU-25 per capital GDP(Euro)	24.500	19.700

Source: TAM (2007).

The Turkish population in the former 15 EU countries received a 0.75 percent share of the GDP in 2015. The proportion of European Turks is at the level of 1 percent. The fact that their unemployment is more than double the unemployed in the country they live in is the main reason why the economic contribution of the Turks is lower than the share of the population. Compared to 25 EU member countries, European Turks outperform 12 member countries in GDP per capita.

Compared to the per capita GDP figures, Turkish employees reach 71 per cent of the total EU-15 members (27,600 euros) with an annual rate of 19,700 euros.

Turks have also begun to become an important factor in the economic life of their countries. The number of Turkish entrepreneurs who have lived independently in the EU-15 countries has reached 82,400. The new members of the EU, Poland, Czech Republic and Hungary, have a significant number of Turkish businesses. Almost all of the Turks living in these countries earn their lives through independent study. Considering the Turkish population in Bulgaria and Romania, which joined the EU in early 2007, there are also 26,000 entrepreneurs of Turkish origin.

Table 6. Turkish Entrepreneur Development in EU Countries (EU-15)

Indicator	1997	2002	2007	2008	2015
Number of Entrepreneurs	62.000	82.300	102.000	108.000	146.000
Average Investment per Business (€)	97.000	112.000	107.000	107.000	115.000
Total Investment amount (€ billion)	6	9,2	10,9	11,6	22
Average Turnover per Business (€)	415.000	425.000	445.000	458.000	460.900
Annual Total Revenue (€ billion)	25,7	35	45,4	32,9	46,1
Number of employees per business	4,1	5	4,6	4,6	4,8
Total employment	254.000	411.000	469.000	662.400	700.800

Source: TAVAK (2015).

Result

It has now been understood that it is not enough for the development of the country to endure only with domestic resources and to realize exports with exports of goods excelling only at cost. Countries are as much dependent on foreign capital as they are before they realize their development. Even the most powerful economies in the world are unable to deter themselves from being caught up in foreign capital. In order to be able to rise to a level that can compete with strong economies in Turkey, it needs foreign capital. However, for the sake of achieving these extremely timid investments, countries with very sensitive balances, such as Turkey, have to pay more attention to those with high risk premiums.

While it is in such a situation and has a population that is spread to the whole of the world and cannot be underestimated, it seems quite wise for Turkey to turn to this source. It is known by everyone that interest payments made by a significant portion of Turkey's budget, such as 60%, are due to borrowing at high interest rates. It is possible that the Turks living outside the motherland can be formed like a diaspora by alleviating this burden and helping the economic development of Turkey and providing internal support during the European Union process. When we look at economic data in Europe, it is understood that the investment potential of Turks living outside the country is about 40 billion TL. When Turkey's budget deficit is thought to be TL 52 billion, the extent to which this investment potential is transferred to Turkey is likely to make a great contribution to the country's economy. However, the most important point that should not be forgotten is that such a formation should be led by the state itself and not by the private sector, but by an active role. Even if this process is left to the institutions outside the state, at least they must closely monitor every phase of state formation and should intervene when they see it. Such an approach will both increase the citizens' confidence in the system and prevent repetition of frauds that have been carried out in the past and for personal benefit.

References

C. Fred Bergsten and Inbom Choi," The Korean Diaspora in The World Economy",Washington,D.C,January 2003.

Chander, Anupam. 2001. "Diaspora Bonds," 76 *New York University Law Review 1005, October.*

Chander, Anupam. *2005.* "Diaspora Bonds and US Securities Regulation: An Jnterview", Business *Law Review,* University of California, Davis, School of Law, May 1, 2005.

El Qorchi, Mohammed. 1005. "lslamic Finance gears Up," *Finance and Development, Volume* 42, Number 4, international Monetary Fund, December.

Fred W. Riggs," Diasporas and Ethnic Nations causes and consequences of Giobalization", www2.hawaii.edulftedr/diaglo.htm, 15 Nisan 2001.

Gabi SHEFFER, "Middle Eastern Diasporas: Introduction and Readings", wwwc.cc.columbia.edulsec/dlc/ciao/olj/merialmeria797sheffer.htm, 17 Nisan 2001.

Gallya Lahav and Asher Arian," Jsraelias in ajewish Diaspora: The Multiple Dilemmas of a Giobalized Group", www2.hawaii.edulfredr/lahav.htm, 19 Nisan 2001.

Oğuzhan Sokmen Artukoğlu, Yurtdışı İşçi Tasarruflarının Türkiye Cumhuriyet Merkez Bankası, Banka Sistemi Ve Türkiye Ekonomisi Üzerine Etkileri, Uzmanlık Yeterlilik Tezi, Ankara, 2005 Kasım.

Rehavi, Yehiel and Asher Weingarten. 2004. "Fifty Years of External Finance via State of lsrael Non-negotiable Bonds," Foreign Exchange Activity Department, Assets and Liabilities Unit, Bank of Israel, September 6.

Romano Roberta. 1998. "Empowering investors: A Market Approach to Securities regulation," *107 Yale Law Journal 2359, 2424.*

Compiled by F. Tilbe, E. Iskender, I. Sirkeci

Suhas L. Ketkar And Dilip Ratha, Development Finance Via Diaspora Bonds Track Record and Potential, Paper Presented At The Migration And Development Conference At The World Bank, Washington DC. May 23, 2007.

Turkish European Foundation for Education and Scientific Studies (TAVAK). (2015), "Avrupa Birliği ve Almanya'da Türk Girişimcilerin Ekonomik Gücü ve Türkiye'nin Ticaret Hacmindeki Konumu", TAVAK: İstanbul.

Türkiye Araştırmaları Merkezi Vakfı (TAM), Hollanda ve Avrupa Birliği'ndeki Türk Nüfusu, Hane verilen ve girişimcilerin ekonomik gücü, Nisan 2007, Essen

World Bank. 2005. Global Economic Prospects 2006: Economic Impiications of Remittances and Migration, Washington, D.C.

Zakaria, Fareed. 2006. "How Long Wiil America Lead the World," *Newsweek,* June 12.

BORDER CROSSING

ISSN:2046-4436
e-ISSN: 2046-4444

Volume 7
Issue 2
July - December 2017

TRANSNATIONAL PRESS LONDON

Chapter 32. Of Crocodiles, Magumaguma, Hyenas, and Malayitsha: Zimbabweans Crossing the Limpopo in Search of a Better Life in South Africa

Chipo Hungwe[*]

Abstract

Many stories have been told of how 'hyenas' facilitate undocumented migration and in the process negotiate and protect migrants from the much feared magumaguma who prey on the 'innocent lives' of would-be migrants desiring a better life in South Africa. The paper relies on first hand accounts of individuals who have crossed the Limpopo River and Zimbabwe-South Africa border as undocumented migrants. It utilises qualitative in-depth interviews of Zimbabwean migrants in Johannesburg. These individuals have had to deal with some, if not all, of the following: 'hyenas', crocodiles, magumaguma and the malayitsha. This paper demonstrates the central role of human smugglers such as the malayitsha and hyenas/impisi and the precarious nature of undocumented Zimbabwean migration showing the sheer will to survive against all odds; migrating to a perceived better life. Death will not deter migration or the aspiration to change one's life by migrating. The paper creates a good case for the need for further research targeting the magumaguma and the malayitsha so that a critical mass of literature can be created on these human smugglers. This paper is important as it comes up with a conceptual framework on understanding undocumented Zimbabwean migration to South Africa.

Keywords: Agents, *dabulapu*[1], migration, malayitsha, survival, undocumented.

Introduction

Zimbabwean migrants must be seen as people moving away from insecurity to what is perceived as a better place, which, however, turns out to be also very insecure, especially the journey to South Africa, which is the focus of this research. The trip to South Africa facilitated by human smugglers is fraught with all kinds of dangers – from the crocodiles in the Limpopo river to the magumaguma in the forests, the South African National Defence Forces, police and home affairs officials at road blocks and sometimes the malayitsha himself turning against the migrants such that some aspiring migrants never make it to their destination while others arrive wounded emotionally and physically and with horrific stories that they have to live with for the rest of their lives. And yet, some, arrive safely to their relatives and go on to encourage others to use the same means to join them in Johannesburg – a social and economic space evaluated as much better than home where people can at least 'survive'. What is clear is that undocumented migration from Zimbabwe has continued even in the era of the US dollar because of continued economic and political challenges bedevilling the country. This paper discusses the role of human smugglers in the Zimbabwe-South Africa migration chain and the function of the family network in sustaining migration. The new economics of

---

[*] Midlands State University, Zimbabwe. Email: hungwec@msu.ac.zw
[1] Dabulapu is an informal Zulu term which means to cut short. Zimbabweans use it to refer to illegal/undocumented migration

labour theory and the displacement economies approach helps explain the reasons for migration based on the survival of the family which deploys members as and when necessary. The paper ends with a diagrammatic conceptualisation of undocumented Zimbabwean migration to South Africa and its consequences.

Literature Review

International migration is on the rise facilitated by processes of globalisation and transnationalism. While South-West migration has traditionally dominated, there is an increase in South-South migration (Castles 2002; Castles and Miller 2009; Migration and remittances Fact Book 2016, UNDESA 2016). The number of international migrants reached 244 million in 2015, an increase of 71 million 71 million or 41% compared to 2000 (UNDESA 2016). The majority of migrants (72%) were between 20-64 years reflecting a close connection between migration and labour activity (ibid). Officially recorded remittances to developing countries amounted to $431.6 billion. Globally there has been an increase in perilous trips of migrants resulting in robbery, rape, violence and deaths of many at sea, crossing flooded rivers, traversing deserts etc. The picture is that of increased precariousness of migration (Standing 2011). Death as a common feature of migration has increased but that has not weakened the determination of the migrants.

The reasons for Zimbabwean migration are a combination of economic and political factors, (Crush and Tevera 2010; Tevera and Zinyama 2002). Bolt (2015:20) says "they have come to South Africa...at different times, responding to different interrelated pressures, both economic and political". Insecurities at home are a major motivation for migration. Zimbabwean migration will be understood within the displacement economies approach. The displacement economies approach is an argument discussed in detail by Hammar (2014). She defines displacement as *enforced changes in interweaving spatial, social and symbolic conditions and relations"*. This definition acknowledges the use of 'force' whether directly or indirectly to change the spatial, social and symbolic conditions and relations of people. This displacement economies approach:

"...considers the complex and shifting political economies underpinning or sustaining displacement, which might include the interests of central states, municipalities, military, rebel movements, private companies or development agencies, either alone or in alliance with one another. Additionally, the approach takes into account those benefiting directly or indirectly from displacement and how they affect both informal and formal economies. This may include political parties, state agents, new and old entrepreneurs and investors, new and old gatekeepers or brokers, as well as those among the displaced who might, in fact, find ways to benefit differentially from the

condition of displacement...it (the approach) is interested in locating the interests and effects of those 'managing' the displaced, such as state agencies, donor agencies, non-governmental organizations, church organizations, border agencies and so on" (Hammar 2014:08).

This paper studies those Zimbabweans 'forced' by the situation to move-spatial' displacement from Zimbabwe to South Africa as undocumented migrants and their fate along the way and even upon arrival in Johannesburg. It also considers the migrant smugglers who themselves benefit from the process of displacement. It stresses that migrants are not passive recipients of a displacement economy, they exercise agency by moving. Hammar (2014:16) reiterates that "it is clear that even when subjected to and diminished by dislocating force, 'one moves in not on space' but as an *active agent*, occupying and remaking space through the best use of available if highly circumscribed resources, networks and capacities".

Zimbabwean migration to South Africa (particularly the crossing of the border) has been facilitated by both state and non-state actors. State actors include the border control officers, the police and home affairs officials and soldiers. Non-state actors include the activities of bus operators, long distance taxi operators (commonly known as malayitsha), *impisi* (agents of the malayitsha) and magumaguma (commonly referred to as the human scavengers). They also rely on networks based on family, religious and other forms of affiliations. For the malayitsha migration is big business and a source of livelihood that they jealously protect and promote (Nyoni 2012). Undocumented migration is particularly attractive to the malayitsha because of the high transportation fares charged although it is at the same time quite risky to the same malayitsha who must design strategies to deal with government officials and the magumaguma who threaten the business of smuggling undocumented migrants.

Who Are the Maguma Guma?

Arai and Monson (undated) argue that the magumaguma are a variety of non-state actors who are responsible for various forms of abuse, exploitation and extortion along the border. For some, *magumaguma* are unscrupulous smugglers who turn on their clients and rob, beat or abandon them during the border crossing (this might even include the *malayitsha* and *impisi*). For others, *magumaguma* are independent gangsters, viewed as human scavengers that roam the border area, preying on human smugglers (the malayitsha and impisi) and their clients alike. Maphosa (2010) seems to conflate the two definitions of magumaguma when he states that the *magumaguma* mainly operate in two ways: (a) offering assistance to potential migrants in crossing the border unofficially and later robbing the same individuals or (b) waylaying the potential migrants in-order to steal, rape or kill them. Rutherford (2008) further states that magumaguma are malicious groups of young men operating on the Zimbabwean side along the Zimbabwean South African border. Because their presence has been known and suspected over a long period of time Rutherford (2008) wonders why there seems to be no official action taken to deal with such unscrupulous individuals. This inaction by government officials might almost give the impression of state acquiescence to such lawless activities.

Still others believe that the magumaguma are a fiction, a ploy by cunning smugglers to boost the market for their services by creating the impression that the assistance of a smuggler is crucial to safe passage. Jinga's (2012:10) work takes the imagination of the magumaguma to another level comparing them to pirates at sea: "the magumaguma are to the Zimbabwe-South Africa border area what pirates are at sea. The only difference is that the former rape, kill and maim faster than pirates can demand ransom money".

Methods and Setting

This paper is based on a qualitative research that attempted to discover the survival strategies of Zimbabwean migrants in Johannesburg. The research was conducted in 2012. The study involved fifty-eight (58) migrants; both documented and undocumented, who had been in South Africa for more than six months on a continuous basis. There were 33 males and 25 females who participated in the study. The migrants studied specifically lived in Kempton Park and Tembisa, areas that are approximately 25km north-east of Johannesburg central. This particular paper focuses on 29 migrants whose first entry into South Africa was as an undocumented/illegal migrant. Research methods used were mainly semi structured and in-depth life history interviews based on a sample that was purposively selected. These were supplemented by moments of participant observation by the researcher who stayed in Tembisa for duration of the study. The research is mainly based on life history interviews/narratives. Life history interviews are geared towards understanding the migrants' whole life course (Van Nieuwenhuyze 2009). The use of the word narratives here is to emphasise the focus on how migrants create 'their stories' in explaining their life courses. In-order to observe good ethical conduct, the research maintained participants' anonymity at all times. The purposes of the research were well known to the migrants. Pseudonyms are used to refer to different participants in the study.

Presentation of Findings and Discussion

Both men and women braved the perilous journeys as undocumented migrants. In terms of ethnicity there are more Ndebele (19) than Shona (10) who used undocumented migration. There were marked differences between Shona and Ndebele women where more Ndebele women crossed the border as undocumented migrants using dabulapu compared to Shona women most of whom crossed the border legally. While the number of Shona men (8) who used dabulapu was almost the same as that of Ndebele men (9), most Shona men (12) crossed the border as documented migrants than Ndebele men (4). In terms of level of education, those with the least education engaged in dabulapu than those with diplomas and degrees.

Migrants who used *dabulapu* expressed fear of *magumaguma* and wild animals. For female migrants, rape by *magumaguma* was their greatest fear. Male migrants commonly joked about not wanting to marry female migrants who came via *dabulapu* because some of them would have been violated by *magumaguma.* Some migrants recalled harrowing stories of how they crossed the Limpopo River. One particular lady (Tatenda) who crossed the border in 2008 recounted how they spent 2 weeks in the forests after being duped by the *malayitsha* that had ferried them:

"I had R600 at the border and one malayitsha tricked us saying he could help us cross the border directly without going through the forests. I gave him R300 and hid the other R300. We stayed in the forest for two weeks. The man provided food but he was stingy because we only ate pap (thick porridge) and cabbages while other groups of people being smuggled by other malayitsha ate pap and meat. There were groups of people belonging to different malayitsha who were already there. In our group there were 14 of us and we were told to wait until we were twenty because the malayitsha's car needed to carry a full load of twenty. I discovered five more groups belonging to other malayitsha".

Another migrant, Mary, also broke into tears narrating how they stayed for two weeks in the forest after her first attempt to cross was foiled by the police at Musina in 2008. She discovered that there were more than seventy (70) people in the forests belonging to different *malayitsha*. She was even more perturbed to discover some individuals who had been in the forests for two months waiting for their *malayitsha*'s cars to have the needed full load.

Crossing the Limpopo River

There are many cases of potential migrants who have lost their lives while trying to cross the flooded Limpopo River. Others have succumbed to the crocodiles in the same river. There are many myths associated with crossing the Limpopo River. In some cases, migrants stated that there were medicine men that would jump into the water to chase crocodiles. In all the cases, men and women were made to cross the river stark naked. Rituals of crossing the river involved: crossing the river in the early hours of the day, for example at 2am; killing, beating or leaving behind small children who cried at the river; removing all the clothes and holding hands while crossing. A vivid description of how the river was crossed came from Scott who crossed the river in January 2012:

"We crossed the river at a certain place (name withheld on ethical grounds) which is near a soldiers' camp. The water in the river was just above the waist of a tall adult male. Women cried. Some had children. I grew up in rural areas, so I knew how to swim. I was not really afraid. What I was afraid of was the fact that they said we should hold hands with women and cross the river in a single file. We were arranged in a single file. No one was harmed by crocodiles because there were men who were hired to help us cross the river. These men jumped into the water to test it and then told us it was ok for us to cross. Those women who had crying babies were beaten up and made to stop their children from crying. The malayitsha are very harsh and hard hearted. They were hurling insults and vulgar language. We crossed the river at around 3am".

This particular migrant did not differentiate between a malayitsha and a hyena/impisi. It was important to choose the timing of migration from June to October which were dry months. However, some crossed in January when the river was almost full. Desperation tended to be the major factor.

Analysis

Zimbabwean migration posts the introduction of the United States dollar (which was meant to stabilise the economy and help reduce the rate of inflation etc) shows that the United States dollar has not solved Zimbabwe's problems. Now with the current shortage of the same US dollar and the introduction of Zimbabwean bond notes, more migrations can be expected. Unfortunately, some of those Zimbabweans in South Africa face grim chances of surviving comfortably. Research indicates that they face food insecurities, unemployment and economic pressure (Crush and Tawodzera 2016). The factors that have led to the spatial displacement of these Zimbabweans continue to work in Zimbabwe and keep them in South Africa as they still perceive that the economic environment in South Africa is far much better than that of Zimbabwe.

The problem of unemployment in Zimbabwe has worsened. In fact there were several company closures between 2010 and 2016. These were necessitated by various factors including the landmark Supreme Court ruling on the *Nyamande and Donga vs. Zuva Petroleum* case which clarified that employers could terminate employee contracts on notice making it easy for companies to fire even long serving workers. The unemployment rate is currently around 90% although the official rate is 11%. The ZIMSTAT (2015) however acknowledges that the majority (over 80%) of the individuals recorded as 'employed' in the country are working in the informal sector while those in formal employed constitute 11%. Only 8% of the Zimbabwean population had access to health insurance. Such a statistic reveals the vulnerability of the population in terms of health. Using the Multiple Indicator Cluster Survey of 2014 the level of food insecurity in the country is high while child nutrition is in some cases low. More than a quarter of children (27.6 percent) were moderately stunted or too short for their age and 3.3 percent were moderately wasted or too thin for their height. Stunting and wasting reflect chronic malnutrition as a result of failure to receive adequate nutrition over a long period and recurrent or chronic illness, (ZIMSTAT 2015).

Female migrants are more vulnerable to rape and sexual assault than men. While statistics are lacking on how often women migrants are raped during crossing, organisations working with migrants' report that it is not uncommon. One NGO worker interviewed in a different study argued; "it is difficult to say how many rapes happen, because there are many hidden cases. If you talk to the men, they will tell you that most women are raped while crossing" (Shaeffer 2009). Writing about the migration of undocumented Mexican to the United States of America, Rhoad (2012:215) states that in the remote parts of the deserts are rape trees where women's underwear has been strewn across braches, reportedly by perpetrators marking the site of sexual assaults. Women are not only vulnerable to rape or sexual assault by the magumaguma and the malayitsha but also from the soldiers, police or other men who may pretend to be helping them.

Conclusion

This paper addresses an area that has not received much attention in the study of Zimbabwean- South African migration – the area of human smuggling. This is an interesting area where the formal and informal sometimes collide and meet. The role of the malayitsha, *impisi* and magumaguma has been explained in the illegal crossing of the Limpopo River. The presence of the Limpopo River has not deterred aspirations to migrate to South Africa; if anything, migrants have always calculated the costs of entering South Africa via *dabulapu* across the Limpopo. Some migrants have paid the highest cost of migrating – by their own lives lost in the Limpopo or along the dense bushes of South Africa. The paper recommends that the government of Zimbabwe must begin to take seriously the magumaguma and act against them lest the state be accused of acquiescence. The research provides an analytical framework for understanding the typical journey to South Africa and for those that make it to Joburg, the life after the journey. Following Hammar's (2014) conceptualisation of displacement economies, I argue that Zimbabwean migration was and continues to be an involuntary but realistic a response to political economic processes of displacement which have winners and losers. The *malayitsha* may themselves have engaged in their business in response to displacement but have over time benefited by exploiting the more vulnerable undocumented migrants who seek better existences in South Africa.

The Undocumented Migrant's Journey and Experiences

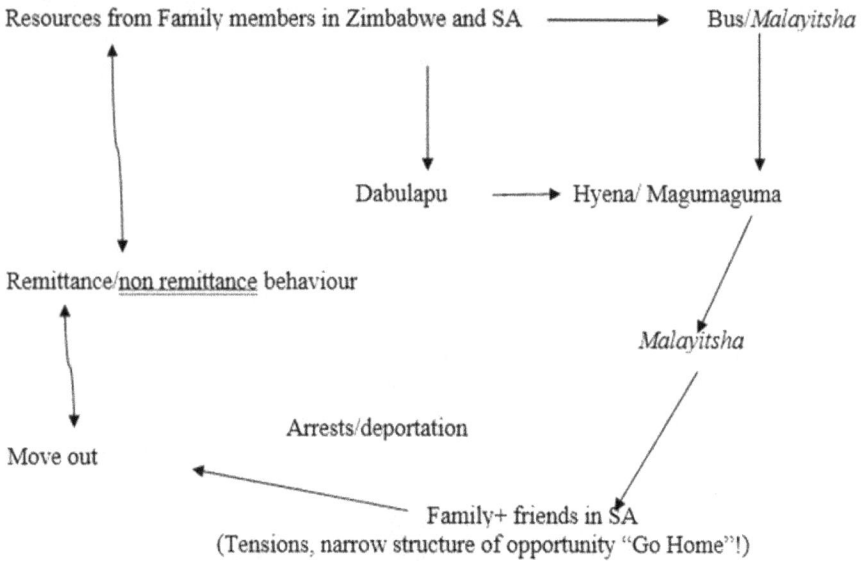

Resources from Family members in Zimbabwe and SA ⟶ Bus/*Malayitsha*

Dabulapu ⟶ Hyena/ Magumaguma

Remittance/non remittance behaviour

Malayitsha

Move out

Arrests/deportation

Family+ friends in SA
(Tensions, narrow structure of opportunity "Go Home"!)

References

Araia, T. & Monson, T. (undated) *South Africa's Smuggler's borderland* (No city of publication: No publisher).

Bolt, M. 2015. *Zimbabwe's migrants and South Africa' border farms: the roots of impermanence.* Cambridge: Cambridge University Press.

Castles, S. 2002. Migration and community formation under conditions of globalisation. *International Migration Review* 36 (4) Winter 2002: 1143-1168.

Castles, S & Miller, MJ. (2009). *The age of migration: international population movements in the modern world* 4th edition. Hampshire: Palgrave MacMillan.

Crush, J. & Tawodzera, G. 2016. *The food insecurities of Zimbabwean migrants in urban South Africa.* Urban Food Security Series Number 23, Cape Town: AFSUN.

Crush, J & Tevera, D. 2010. Exiting Zimbabwe, in *Zimbabwe's Exodus: Crisis, Migration and Survival,* edited by J Crush & D Tevera. Ottawa: SAMP in cooperation with IDRC: 1-51.

Hammar, A (ed). 2014. *Displacement economies, paradoxes of crisis and creativity.* London: Zed books.

Human Rights Watch. 2006. *Unprotected migrants: Zimbabweans in South Africa's Limpopo Province.* July 2006: 18 (6) Washington: HRW.

Jinga, T. 2012. *One foreigner's ordeal.* No city of publication: Author House.

Maphosa, F. 2010. Transnationalism and undocumented migration between rural Zimbabwe and South Africa, in *Zimbabwe's Exodus: Crisis, Migration and Survival,* edited by J Crush & D Tevera. Ottawa: SAMP in cooperation with IDRC: 345-362. .

Miles, MB & Huberman, AM. 1994. *Qualitative data analysis,* 2nd edition. Thousand Oaks, CA: Sage.

Nyoni, P. 2012. New insights on trust, honour and networking in the informal entrepreneurship: Zimbabwean malayishas as informal remittance couriers", *Anthropology Southern Africa,* 35 (1&2):1-11.

Rhoad, M. 2012. Violence against immigrant women in the United State, in Minky Worden (ed) *The unfinished revolution*, pp 209-220, The Policy Press: Bristol.

Rutherford, B. 2008. An unsettled belonging: Zimbabwean farm workers in Limpopo Province, South Africa. *Journal of Contemporary Africa Studies*, 26 (4): 401-415.

Shaffer, R. 2009. *No healing here: violence, discrimination and barriers to health for migrants in South Africa.* Washington: Human Rights Watch.

Standing, G. 2011. *The precariat.* London: Bloomsbury.

Tevera, D. & Zinyama, L. 2002. *Zimbabweans who move: Perspectives on International migration in Zimbabwe.* Cape Town: *SAMP* Migration Policy Series Number 25.

Van Nieuwenhuyze, I. 2009. *Getting by in Europe's urban labour markets: Senegambian migrants' strategies for survival, documentation and mobility.* Amsterdam: Amsterdam University Press.

Zimbabwe National Statistics Agency (ZIMSTAT), 2015. *Zimbabwe Multiple Indicator Cluster Survey 2014, Final Report.* Harare, Zimbabwe.

Zimbabwe National statistics Agency (ZIMSTAT), 2015. *Labour force Survey 2014*, Harare, Available at www.zimstat.co.zw.

Chapter 33. Gender Identity and Performance of Filipino Female Student Migrants in Korea

Cathe Ryne Denice Basco Sarmiento*

Abstract

Korea is one of the countries in the Asia-Pacific region with the highest student net migration. An increasing number of international students, specifically from neighbouring Asian countries, have been moving to the country to pursue higher education. As one of such countries, the Philippines has a greater number of female students engaging in Korean study abroad programmes compared to their male counterparts. Recognizing the differences in educational principles and socio-cultural relations between the two countries, this research aims to explore the academic experiences and examine the gender identity and performance of Filipino female student migrants in Korea. This qualitative study was carried out by conducting in-depth interviews of five (5) Filipino female students enrolled in a graduate school programme in Korea at the time of study. As high-skilled women from a developing country, Filipino female students construct an understanding of the society they are in based on observations and experiences from both home and host cultures. In some cases, they choose to reconstruct their gender identity and performance to align them with Korean gender norms. The results of this study provide supplementary insights on educational migration and how this process affects gender relations.

Keywords: educational migration, gender identity and performance, the Philippines, South Korea, study abroad

Introduction

The Human Capital Theory underscores that education is a key element of human capital, since it is perceived as the primary means of developing knowledge and skills (Acemoglu & Autor, 2012; Ehrenberg & Smith, 2011; Organisation for Economic Co-operation and Development [OECD], 2011). It is recognized to contribute to greater economic growth, healthier populations, and more stable societies (United Nations Children's Fund, 2013). Globalisation has induced the expansion of the educational process; hence, students find themselves physically leaving their home country to study abroad. Studying abroad in migration discourse is otherwise referred as educational migration, and international students pursuing post-tertiary education have been considered as high-skilled migrants (Hawthorne, 2008; She & Wotherspoon, 2013).

The number of mobile students continue to surge over the years. The Republic of Korea (Korea, henceforth) has become one of the strongest centres for student migration. It does not only send student migrants to other countries, but it also serves as a prospective home for international students. There has been a steady number of Filipino students who engage in educational sojourn in Korea; most of which are women. Despite being Asian countries, the cultures of Korea and the Philippines are different in ostensible ways. Socio-

---

* Korea University Graduate School of International Studies, Seongbuk-gu, 145, Anam-ro, Seongbuk-gu, Seoul, Republic of Korea 02841. E-mail: crdbsarmiento@korea.ac.kr.

cultural factors, such as social expectations, values, and beliefs towards college education, compose some of these differences (Turingan & Yang, 2009). The increasing arrival of Filipino female students in Korea consequently leads to observations of their personal educational sojourn in a foreign country.

Using in-depth interviews of Filipino female graduate students, this research aims (1) to explore the experiences of Filipino females as student migrants in Korea and (2) to examine the gender identity and performance of Filipino female student migrants. This paper addresses how Filipino female students situate themselves and perform within multiple hierarchies of power. This research posits that Filipino female students, as high-skilled women from a developing country pursuing further education in a patriarchal society, construct an understanding of the society they are in and act based on these assumptions. It also postulates that female students adjust their gender performance in consideration of the similarities, but most especially the differences, in culture and gender relations between the Philippines and Korea.

Literature on international students in Korea is mostly centred on Chinese youths (Lee & Fang, 2013; Lin & Kim, 2011). Previous studies that explore Filipino student migration and its effects are of students that are studying in the United States (Myers-Walls, Frias, Kwon, Ko, & Lu, 2011; Park, 1997). The lack of literature that examines the educational experiences and gender perceptions of Filipino female students in Korea is one of the motivations of this research. This paper may also contribute to the growing number of research that focuses on educational migration, specifically on South to North movement, and how this process is gendered.

Literature Review and Theoretical Base

Student Migration and International Students

The rise in educational migration is reflected with statistics collected in 2013, in which over 4.3 million youths were actively engaged in this type of migration process as compared to 1.3 million in 1990 (United Nations Educational, Scientific and Cultural Organization [UNESCO], 2013). Fifty-one percent of these international students moved from South to North due to higher quality, prestige and reputation, and greater availability of part-time jobs. Female students are more likely to engage in educational migration than male students. In the United States, there is a 65–35 percent split between women and men respectively, and this has held steady for more than a decade (Institute of International Education, 2015). The disparity is attributed to gender-based differences in how students are influenced by personal circumstances, academic environments, and social interactions. The intent to study abroad among women is affected by influential authority figures and educational contexts, while men's intention is shaped by emerging personal values, experiences, and peer influence (Schmidt, 2009).

Based on figures released by the Korea Immigration Service of the Ministry of Justice (2016), the number of long term foreign migrants[1] in Korea increased from 1.8 million in 2014 to 1.9 million in 2015. A total of 66,334 foreign migrants had a D-2 visa status[2] in 2015, a slight increase of 8.29% from the previous year. Approximately 77.46% of the total number of D-2 visa holders were women. Most foreign students in Korea come from China (61.43%)[3], Vietnam (7.73%), Mongolia (5.03%), Japan (2.30%), and Uzbekistan (1.50%). They are mainly enrolled in a degree programme or a language course (OECD, 2015).

The Philippines is one of the countries with the highest net migration – an average of 60,000 people move out of the country every year for employment purposes (International Organization on Migration [IOM], 2013). It is still a minor player as consumer and provider in the international student market. Statistics from 2008 show that the number of outbound students was 8,443, with less than two percent sponsored by official development assistance and government programmes (UNESCO, 2013). The destination countries of Filipino outbound students are the United States, United Kingdom, Australia, Japan, New Zealand, and Korea. Interestingly, these countries are also the top destinations of the country's Overseas Filipino Workers (OFW) or top remittance sources of OFW earnings.

Studying abroad has been encouraged for its positive effects, from personal development and character growth (Park, 2007), improved cultural and pragmatic competency (Reynolds-Case, 2013) to enriched professional interests (Twombly, Salisbury, Tumanut, & Klute, 2012) and increased likelihood on subsequent employment (Di Pietro, 2015). Earlier literature on experiences of international students have recognized that the well-being of these students is profoundly affected during their educational sojourn (Du & Wei, 2015; Wang, Wei, & Chen, 2015). Apart from the expected strain and anxiety brought by academic workload, they also have to face the challenges of acculturation and cross-cultural socialization (Nasirudeen, Koh, Lau, Lim, & How, 2014; Sullivan & Kashubeck-West, 2015). Such setting is a

---

1 Long term migrants are foreigners residing in Korea for more than 90 days.

2The D-2 visa is accorded to foreigners who "intend to receive education in a standard course (Bachelors, Masters, and Ph. D), or research specialist fields in junior colleges, universities, graduate schools established based on the Korean Education Law, or academic research institutions established under the provisions of a special law of a status as least as high as a junior college" (Korea Immigration Service, 2008).

3This category includes Chinese and Korean-Chinese students.

prerequisite for stress and produces greater possibilities of unsatisfactory experiences.

There is a divide among scholars on the impact of educational migration between the sexes. A few studies found that female international students fared better in educational sojourns than their male counterparts (Lee, Park, & Kim, 2009). Others established that there are no gender differences on well-being among international students (Nasir, 2012; Nasirudeen et al., 2014). However, a vast number of academic literature reported that female international students have more difficulty adapting to the social and academic demands of a new environment and have experienced higher levels of stress than male international students (Bhandari, 2012; Manese, Sedlacek, & Leong, 1988; Neto & Barros, 2007; Scheyvens, Wild, & Overton, 2003).

Gender Identity and Educational Migration

Gender refers to the social roles, responsibilities, and behaviours believed to belong to men and women, such as "men as income earners" and "women as child caregivers" (International Labour Organization, 2007). The framework of multiple dimensions of identity conceptualized by Jones and McEwen (2000) reflects the diverse experiences and backgrounds through which identity is formed. In this multi-dimensional identity model, there exists a core sense of self or one's personal identity. Intersecting circles adjoining the core identity represent significant identity dimensions, (i.e., gender, race, culture, and religion), and contextual influences (i.e., family background, socio-cultural conditions, and current experiences). Hence, gender identity is the outcome of the circumstances in which men and women live, which includes cultural, economic, historical, ideological, and religious factors.

This identity model supports in illustrating how educational migration influences the formation of gender identity. Living and studying abroad may unlock identity assumptions with which students were raised, encouraging them to be more cognizant of their externally defined dimensions of identity as they explore and create meanings of alternative understandings in a new cultural context (Jessup-Anger, 2008). Even though migration is a gender-neutral process, it is related to gender because men and women are mobilized for varying reasons, utilize different channels, and have distinctive experiences (IOM, 2004). The social context in which the migration process takes place is therefore strongly influenced by one's gender. Gender relations strongly affect migration behaviour and experiences that men and women go through. Furthermore, the migration process is not shaped by gender alone but is also a product of other significant factors, such as race, class, and religion.

In the study of gender observations among Caucasian students who participated in a study abroad programme in New Zealand and Australia,

Jessup-Anger (2008) discussed that students used experiences in their home country as a focal point. Without an ostensible juxtaposition in home and host cultures, gender roles were not observed by these students and were assumed to be similar as in their home culture. Not examining these embedded assumptions, however, risks students in developing a false understanding of a new culture – one that is loaded with their own sociocultural perspective instead of the context of the host culture. In an earlier study of female international students by Twombly (1995), experiences within the host culture were different enough from the home culture to cause them significant distress and bring about a new and painful gender identity awareness.

Pessar and Mahler (2001, 2003, 2006) created a framework that can be used to examine gender across transnational spaces. *Gendered geographies of power* is a framework that analyses "people's social agency – corporal and cognitive – given their own initiative as well as their positioning within multiple hierarchies of power operative within and across many terrains" (Pessar & Mahler, 2001, p. 447). In line with this framework, gender operates simultaneously on multiple spatial and social scales, such as the body, the family, and the state. Multiple dimensions of identity shape, discipline, and position people and the ways they think and act. People are born into a social location that confers on them certain advantages and disadvantages; thus, irrespective of their own efforts, they are situated in hierarchies they have not constructed. Nevertheless, individuals possess a certain type and degree of agency affected by individual characteristics and cognitive processes. This study therefore builds on this rhetoric by showing that Filipino women, through their social location as privileged and educated residents in the Philippines, initiate and take advantage of mobility opportunities available to them. Their arrival in Korea thus involves a complex shift in their social location and an adjustment of their power geometry. How Filipino female students understand their current location and how such dynamics influence their actions are the underlying objectives of this research.

Research Method and Materials

This study is a qualitative research, as it aims to explicate the experiences of Filipino female graduate students as well as observations and performances of their gender identity. It modestly seeks to examine gender relations of Filipino women within the academic context. Data for this study were gathered by collecting open-ended and voice-recorded in-depth interviews. Interview questions explored the Filipino female students' perceptions of gender, academic motivations and experiences, interactions with professors, school staff, and classmates, experiences of gender equality/discrimination, insights about studying and living in Korea, and plans after finishing their educational sojourn. This study intends to examine how their observations and meaning-making structures have illustrated and informed their understanding of their own gender identity. Considering that Filipino female students in Korea are situated in multiple hierarchies of power, it is thus interesting to identify how they construct meanings of gender identities of themselves based on their experiences and observations in the school setting.

The number of Filipino students in Korea since 2010 ranges from 400 to 600 per annum (KIS, 2016). Overall, it was observed that there are more female students than male students. As of 2015, a total of 390 Filipino students are taking graduate programmes[4], occupying more than half of the Filipino student population in the country. Like the overall trend, the number of female students taking graduate programmes exceeds that of men. The respondents were narrowed to Filipino female students who are at least on their second semester as a graduate student regardless of university and area of study. By limiting students in such fashion, they have been residing in Korea for more than six months during the research period. This length of time is sufficient for them to construct perspectives of being an international student. Due to limited resources, the research locale encompasses graduate schools in Seoul, the country's largest and most urbanized city. A total of five respondents have been invited for this study in November 2015 and were gathered through the network of Filipino students in Korea named *Pinoy Iskolars sa Korea* (Filipino Scholars in Korea). Data analysis commenced by thoroughly listening to the voice transcripts, coding them based on emergent themes related to gender observations as well as academic and social experiences, and scanning for patterns among the participants. Selected vignettes from the respondents' interviews were included to illustrate the research findings. The respondents are addressed throughout the paper using pseudonyms.

Findings and Discussion

Academic Life of Student Migrants

The remarkable quality of education was the respondents' primary motivation in pursuing graduate education in Korea. All five respondents received a scholarship for their education, and this was the major deciding factor for them. Family members, friends, or colleagues, informed them about the opportunity and encouraged them to apply. They chose to study in Korea due to existing ideas and assumptions about its culture and society based from watching Korean television shows or from previous travels in the country. Four of the respondents were already working as professionals in the Philippines prior to studying abroad. Despite having stable careers, they desired to acquire further education.

---

4 In this study, students taking graduate programmes are composed of those enrolled in a masters (D-2-3), doctoral (D-2-4), or research (D-2-5) programmes.

Filipino women's decision to study in Korea is influenced by better educational prospects and the probability of earning higher wages after completing their education. They acknowledge that Korea's quality of education is better than that of the Philippines. If there are opportunities, the respondents mentioned that they are willing to work in Korea, since they can earn higher wages than if they intend to work in the Philippines. They take advantage of the opportunities for mobility. For these Filipino women, becoming student migrants is used to achieve upward mobility, both geographically and economically. Parallel to low-skilled Filipino migrant workers, Filipino students have the same motivations in their decision to be student migrants.

When the respondents were asked to compare the education system and academic life between Korea and the Philippines, it was more difficult for them to identify similarities. The differences between the two countries are starker and more evident. In general, the educational pedagogy is almost analogous for both countries. For their class programmes, the small class size and advanced use of educational technology in Korean graduate schools allowed them to have easier facilitation of discussions. Moreover, the students observed that studying in Korea has motivated them to work harder. All of them highlighted the necessity to maintain their scholarship and to earn money for their living expenses. In the Philippines, their parents and other relatives shouldered their school and miscellaneous fees when they were still undergraduate students. Since studying in a graduate school abroad is their independent decision and tuition fees in Korea are higher than in the Philippines[5], they must give attention to their education while committing to part-time jobs. Maintaining a scholarship and earning money by working part-time entitled them the feeling of independence from family burdens.

Filipino female students use migration to achieve greater freedom and opportunity. In the Filipino culture, daughters are expected to take care of their parents and to delay their education to help their family with living expenses (Liwag, Dela Cruz, & Macapagal, 1999). As students who are working part-time in Korea, they are independent in making everyday decisions. Meanwhile, the case of Angelina helping her family by working in a Korean guesthouse and sending a portion of her salary to her family in the Philippines may be comprehended as adherence to traditional Filipino norms, but it can also be a way of showing her capability of helping the family while receiving education.

---

5 As of 2017, the tuition fee for a graduate school programme in Korea per semester ranges from 6–7 million KRW (6,000–7,000 USD); meanwhile, studying the same programme in the Philippines costs approximately 150,000–200,000 PHP per semester (3,100–5,300 USD).

Experiences of Gender Equality and Discrimination

The respondents recognize that being a female student in a Korean graduate school is a gratifying experience. They relate this achievement in both Philippine and Korean contexts. In the Philippines, taking a graduate programme is considered a form of "luxury" and is not easily achieved unless a person has adequate financial resources. In the context of the Korean culture, studying in a graduate school as a Filipino woman would mean that she is "breaking the barrier or stereotype" and such achievement is viewed as a source of self-confidence.

The Filipino female students, prior to their arrival in Korea, had expectations of being discriminated for their nationality as a Filipino than for their gender. As they share their experiences of equality or discrimination in the academic setting, they frequently interlinked such interactions based on their gender and nationality. For Filipino female students, these two identifications are inseparable when explaining their experiences of discrimination in Korea. This condition is a prime example of how individuals occupy varying kinds of social location.

Despite the absence of discrimination in the academic setting, it is not the same for their life outside school. The respondents have individual experiences of discrimination. Particularly striking is Queenie's recurring experience of being mistaken as a *mail-order bride* by both Koreans and Filipinos when she was still learning the Korean language in Daegu province. Despite that, she has learned to accept the differences between the Korean and Filipino cultures. Instead of restricting herself to only one culture, she expanded her perspective and tried to be more understanding and respectful of other beliefs and perspectives.

All respondents believe that the degree of immersion into the Korean society is associated to the extent of discrimination an individual will experience. The higher the engagement of foreigners into the culture, there is a higher possibility that they will observe incidents of discrimination. Regardless of nil personal experiences of gender discrimination within the school setting, they have personal observations of how women are discriminated generally. In classroom activities, it is usually male students who take active roles while women take passive roles. Both Queenie and Angelina mentioned that male students are likely to take the role of leaders. Meanwhile, Arianne presumed that the professors of her department expect male students to excel and perform better academically.

What is common about the experiences of gender equality and discrimination is the influence of the person with the highest position and biggest authority. The professors – the actor holding the highest power in the classroom – have the biggest influence of reinforcing or bending gender norms. According to Queenie, the time she feels most aware of the differences between men and women in school is when the professor is an old Korean man. She explained that, "There is always an inclination for old, male Korean professors to pick male students in class." Such experiences affect how these Filipino female students perceive their own gender identity, gender performance, and their gender group in school. The observation of such behaviours has triggered the Filipino female respondents to examine their embedded assumptions of the Korean culture and to reconstitute their gender performance.

Gender Identity and Performance in Korea

The Filipino female students in this study frequently use the Filipino culture as basis of comparison when analysing personal experiences and observations of other people's gender behaviours. The respondents have embedded assumptions of what it means to be a male or a female in the Korean society. When asked about how they perceive themselves as a woman, they initially explained it in the context of their experiences in the Philippines, most particularly with interactions with their families. The principal foundation of the respondents' gender identity is composed of their early and present interactions with their family, experiences in school and proximate environment, as well observations of other people.

All respondents concur that being a woman is an important aspect of their life; however, none of them contemplate their identification as a woman in decision-making whether in the Philippines and in Korea. Since being a woman has never been a constraint for them in the past, it never hindered them from living a comfortable life presently. Nonetheless, the respondents consider that gender equality in the Philippines is more evident than in Korea. The respondents believe that women are more empowered in making life decisions in the Philippines. This assumption is based on how Filipino women and Korean women are regarded by their respective societies and how the culture itself emphasizes and tolerates such behaviours. Three respondents connote the gender roles the Korean society has from the huge influence of Confucianism. Despite these gender and cultural differences and their perceptions of gender inequality in Korea, they are in the process of adapting to how women are treated in the country. When they come across circumstances they would usually not experience in the Philippines, the respondents would either question their own identities or the Korean culture itself.

There were a few cases when the Filipino female students reconstruct their gender performance based on their experiences of gender equality and discrimination and their observations of gender roles in Korea to avoid adverse reactions from the Korean society. This is consistent with the earlier study of how examining the host culture and making gender more salient create avenues in the formation or reformation of identity (Jessup-Anger, 2008). The Filipino female students question their identity and, in selected cases, restructure their gender performance; nevertheless, they eventually remain firm with it. Remaining firm with their stance implies that the respondents do not completely reconstitute their gender identity to match the host culture and the traditional gender norms of the society.

Conclusion

As theorized in gendered geographies of power, the case of Filipino female student migrants in Korea presents that migration indeed occurs within different hierarchies of power. The experiences related to educational migration as a Filipino and as a woman are difficult to isolate. In such geographic scales, whether within the context of the school or the larger society, gender ideologies and relations are both reaffirmed and reconfigured. The students themselves practice varying degrees and types of agency as they acculturate to the Korean society. This study particularly found that they have embedded assumptions about the host culture based on their own experiences and observations. They frequently position their experiences and observations in comparison with their home culture. As they evaluate the gender roles they have observed, they may either question their own identity or question the host culture and society. In the process, they may prefer to reconstitute their gender identity and performance and align them with the host society's gender norms.

Earlier research on Filipino migration has mostly concentrated on domestic workers and marriage migrants. This study intended to fill the gap in literature by providing additional perspectives on one of the types of modern mobility, which is educational migration. This study specifically looked at the educational experiences of Filipino students in Korea and how such experiences shape their gender identity and performance. Acknowledging that migration is a gendered process, this study can serve as a supplementary literature that looks at the impact of this type of migration to gender relations.

The findings of this study provide some propositions for practice and policy. Filipino female students are in a precarious position, as they perceive themselves to be subjected to both gender and racial marginalization in Korea. The students themselves may create efforts to surpass these challenges. As foreign students have higher difficulty in adjusting to the Korean culture during the first six months, this is the period where they should develop more diverse networks. Such measures can help students acculturate easily.

Respective educational institutions should regularly establish adjustment programmes to address cultural transition among international students. As Filipino female students spend most of their time in the academic environment, they should be assisted in acclimating to the academic norms and expectations of Korean educational institutions. These can be carried out through department and class orientations, counselling and mentoring services, and academic assessments. Since the classroom is one of the primary venues where gender and racial expectations are reflected, there should be available opportunities that will prepare Filipino female students. The university faculty should facilitate this process by making classroom and academic expectations clear and by creating a learning environment that accepts and embraces cultural diversity and respects gender differences.

Lastly, the findings of this study show how important the support of both sending and receiving countries is throughout the educational migration process. Prior to departure, there should be sufficient resources accessible to Filipino students to acquaint themselves with the academic culture of the receiving country. With the growing number of Filipinos who aspires to participate or is currently engaging in study abroad programmes, the Philippines should pursue an educational strategy that can equip prospective student migrants of necessary skills during their sojourn. The Philippine embassy in the receiving country should particularly maintain communication with Filipino students and assist them in culture assimilation. Such endeavours should be carried out in conjunction with pertinent Korean government agencies. The cooperation between the Philippine and Korean governments is indispensable, as it concerns the integration of two important facets of development and poverty reduction, which are education and migration.

References

Acemoglu, D., & Autor, D. (2012). *Lectures in labor economics* [PDF document]. Retrieved from http://economics.mit.edu/files/4689

Bhandari, P. (2012). Stress and health related quality of life of Nepalese students studying in South Korea: A cross sectional study. *Health and Quality of Life Outcomes, 10*(26), 1-9. doi: 10.1186/1477-7525-10-2

Di Pietro, G. (2015). Do study abroad programs enhance the employability of graduates? *Education Finance and Policy, 10*(2), 223-243. doi: 10.1162/EDFP_a_00159

Du, Y., & Wei, M. (2015). Acculturation, enculturation, social connectedness, and subjective well-being among Chinese international students. *The Counseling Psychologist, 43*(2), 299-325. doi: 10.1177/0011000014565712

Ehrenberg, R. G., & Smith, R. S. (2011). *Modern labor economics: Theory and public policy.* New Jersey: Prentice Hall.

Hawthorne, L. (2008). *The growing global demand for students as skilled migrants.* Washington, DC: Migration Policy Institute.

Institute of International Education. (2015). *Open Doors 2015: International students in the U.S. up ten percent to nearly one million; study abroad by American students picks up momentum* [Press Release]. Retrieved from http://www.iie.org/Who-We-Are/News-and-Events/Press-Center/Press-Releases/2015/2015-11-16-Open-Doors-Data

International Labour Organization. (2007). *ABC of women workers' rights and gender equality.* Retrieved from http://www.ilo.org/wcmsp5/groups/public/---dgreports/---gender/documents/publication/wcms_087314.pdf

International Organization on Migration (IOM). (2004). Migration and gender. In *Essentials of migration management: A guide for policy makers and practitioners* (Vol. 2). Retrieved from http://www.rcmvs.org/documentos/IOM_EMM/v2/V2S10_CM.pdf

__. (2013). *Country migration report: The Philippines 2013*. Retrieved from https://www.iom.int/files/live/sites/iom/files/Country/docs/CMReport-Philipines-2013.pdf

Jessup-Anger, J. E. (2008). Gender observations and study abroad: How students reconcile cross-cultural differences related to gender. *Journal of College Student Development, 49*(4), 360-373. doi: 10.1353/csd.0.0015

Jones, S. R., & McEwen, M. K. (2000). A conceptual model of multiple dimensions of identity. *Journal of College Student Development, 41*(4), 405-414. doi: 10.1.1.458.8533

Korea Immigration Service. (2016). *Korea immigration statistics 2015*. Retrieved from http://immigration.go.kr/HP/COM/bbs_01/Download.do?FileDir=/attach/imm/f2016/&UserFileName=1.pdf&SystemFileName=20160615257980_1_1.pdf

Lee, C. S., & Fang, W. (2013). Mediating Effects of Hope between Leisure Satisfaction and University Life Adjustments of Chinese Students in Korea. *International Journal of Digital Content Technology and its Applications, 7*(11), 407-415. Retrieved from http://www.academia.edu/6945176/Mediating_Effects_of_Hope_between_Leisure_Satisfaction_and_University_Life_Adjustments_of_Chinese_Students_in_Korea

Lee, S. A., Park, H. S., & Kim, W. (2009). Gender differences in international students' adjustment. *College Student Journal, 43*(4), 1217-1227. Retrieved from http://eric.ed.gov/?id=EJ872337

Lin, Q. L., & Kim, H. K. (2011). A prediction model on adaptation to university life among Chinese international students in Korea. *The Journal of Korean Academic Society of Nursing Education, 12*, 501-513. doi: 10.5977/JKASNE.2011.17.3.501

Liwag, M. A. C., Dela Cruz, A., & Macapagal, M. E. (1999). *A UNICEF and Ateneo study – How we raise our daughters and sons: Child-rearing and gender socialization in the Philippines*. Quezon City: UN Children's Fund and Ateneo Wellness Center.

Manese, J. E., Sedlacek, W., & Leong, F. T. (1988). Needs and perceptions of female and male international undergraduate students. *Journal of Multicultural Counseling and Development, 16*, 24-29. doi: 10.1002/j.2161-1912.1988.tb00398.x

Myers-Walls, J. A., Frias, L. V., Kwon, K., Ko, M. M., & Lu, T. (2011). Living life in two worlds: Acculturative stress among Asian international graduate student parents and spouses. *Journal of Comparative Family Studies, 42*(4), 455-478. doi: 10.2307/41604463

Nasirudeen, A. M. A., Koh, W. N. J., Lau, L. C. A., Lim, L. S., & How, A. L. (2014). Acculturative stress among Asian international students in Singapore. *Journal of International Students, 4*(4), 363-373. Retrieved from https://jistudents.files.wordpress.com/2014/04/2014-4-4-6-acculturative-stress-among-asian.pdf

Neto, F., & Barros, J. (2007). Satisfaction with life among adolescents from Portuguese immigrant families in Switzerland. *Swiss Journal of Psychology, 66*, 215–223. doi: 10.1024/1421-0185.66.4.215

Organisation for Economic Co-operation and Development (OECD). (2011). *Report on the gender initiative: Gender equality in education, employment, and entrepreneurship*. Retrieved from http://www.oecd.org/education/48111145.pdf

__. (2015). *International migration outlook 2015*. Retrieved from http://ifuturo.org/documentacion/InternationalMigrationOutlook.pdf

Park, C. (1997). Learning style preferences of Asian American (Chinese, Filipino, Korean, and Vietnamese) Students in Secondary Schools. *Equity & Excellence in Education, 30*(2), 68-77. doi: 10.1080/1066568970300208

Park, E. (2007). A qualitative analysis of Korean university students' perceptions about the effects of studying abroad. *English Language Teaching, 19*(4), 51-74. Retrieved from http://www.pketa.org/tt/board/ttboard.cgi?act=download&db=conf&aidx=424&fidx=1

Pessar, P. R., & Mahler, S. J. (2001). Gendered geographies of power: Analyzing gender across transnational spaces. *Identities, 7*(4), 441-459. doi: 10.1080/1070289X.2001.9962675

__. (2003). Transnational migration: Bringing gender in. *The International Migration Review, 37*(3), 812-846. doi: 10.1111/j.1747-7379. 2003.tb00159.x

__. (2006). Gender matters: Ethnographers bring gender from the periphery toward the core of migration studies. *The International Migration Review, 40*(1), 27-63. doi: 10.1111/j.1747-7379.2006. 00002.x

Reynolds-Case, A. (2013). The value of short-term study abroad: An increase in students' cultural and pragmatic competency. *Foreign Language Annals, 46*(2), 311-322. doi: 10.1111/flan.12034

Scheyvens, R., Wild, K., & Overton, J. (2003). International students pursuing postgraduate study in geography: Impediments to their learning experiences. *Journal of Geography in Higher Education, 27*(3), 309–323. doi: 10.1080/0309826032000145070

Schmidt, P. (2009, November 6). Men and women differ in how they decide to study abroad, study finds. *The Chronicle of Higher Education.* Retrieved from http://chronicle.com/article/MenWomen-Differ-in-How/49085/

She, Q., & Wotherspoon, T. (2013). International student mobility and highly skilled migration: A comparative study of Canada, the United States, and the United Kingdom. *SpringerPlus, 2*(132), 1-14. doi: 10.1186/2193-1801-2-132.

Sullivan, C., & Kashubeck-West, S. (2015). The interplay of international students' acculturative stress, social support, and acculturation modes. *Journal of International Students, 5*(1), 1-11. Retrieved from http://files.eric.ed.gov/fulltext/EJ1052843.pdf

Turingan, J. P., & Yang, Y. (2009). A cross-cultural comparison of self-regulated learning skills between Korean and Filipino college students. *Asian Social Science, 5*(12), 3-10. Retrieved from http://ccsenet.org/journal/index.php/ass/article/view/4542

Twombly, S. B. (1995). Piropos and friendships: Gender and culture clash in study abroad. *Frontiers: The Interdisciplinary Journal of Study Abroad, 1*, 1-27. Retrieved from http://files.eric.ed.gov/fulltext/EJ608162.pdf

Twombly, S. B., Salisbury, M. H., Tumanut, S. D., & Klute, P. (2012). *Study abroad in a new global century: Renewing the promise, refining the purpose* (ASHE Higher Education Report Volume 38 Number 4). San Francisco: Jossey-Bass.

United Nations Children's Fund. (2013). *A post-2015 world fit for children: Sustainable development starts and ends with safe, healthy, and well-educated children.* Retrieved from http://www.unicef.org/publicpartnerships/files/SD_children_FINAL(1).pdf

United Nations Educational, Scientific and Cultural Organization (UNESCO). (2013). *The international mobility of students in Asia and the Pacific.* Retrieved from http://unesdoc.unesco.org/images/0022/002262/226219E.pdf

Wang, K. T., Wei, M., & Chen H. (2015). Social factors in cross-national adjustment: Subjective well-being trajectories among Chinese international students. *The Counseling Psychologist, 43*(2): 272-298. doi: 10.1177/0011000014566470

Chapter 34. Stakeholder's Concerns into the Federal Registration and Procedure Centres in Switzerland[1]

Marwan Alkhouli[2], Rémi Baudoui[3]

Abstract:

This paper aims to explore the administrative and accommodation process of asylum seekers in Registration and Procedure Centres (CEP) of Swiss Confederation, which are managed by the State Secretary for Migrations (SEM). It is the result of an unprecedented survey we have conducted in two federal Centres. By interviewing the three main field actors, we highlight the interactions between SEM administrative staff, management and accommodation employees and asylum seekers who are received in the CEPs for a temporary period at the beginning of the asylum procedure. We will be confronted with the hypothesis that despite the integrated reception process in these centres, the implementation of the Sectoral Asylum Plan and the acceleration of asylum procedures, as well as the varied concerns and priorities of the main actors impact the development of future federal centres (CFA) and cannot satisfy all the requirements of asylum process stakeholders.

Keywords: Accommodation, Asylum Seekers, Reception and Procedure Centres, SEM, CEP, CFA.

Introduction

If one of the defining global issues of the early 21st century was the asylum seekers, Switzerland is a particularly interesting case for studying state asylum process and stakeholders' concerns for refugees. In the first part of 2017, Switzerland received 4731 asylum applications. The Swiss average of 3.4 asylum applications per 1000 inhabitants far exceeds the European average of 2.5 asylum applications per 1000 inhabitants (SEM, 2017a). In March 2016, the Balkan route was largely shut off. As a result, the number of asylum applications from persons reaching Europe along this route quickly dropped. This development is also reflected in the significant decline of asylum applications filed in Switzerland by asylum seekers (**Table 1**).

[1] This paper is part of a research work financed by an excellence scholarship from Swiss Confederation. It explores the accommodation politic of asylum seekers in Switzerland. We would like to thank the Swiss Confederation for the funding of this research, as well as the State Secretary of Migration, ORS Service Society and Asylum Organisation Zürich for their close cooperation and the data provided for this purpose.
[2] Dr. Marwan ALKHOULI is a post-doc fellow and a lecturer in Geneva University, department of Political Sciences and International Relations. UniMail, Office 4257, Boulevard du Pont d'Arve 40, 1205 Geneva, Switzerland. E-Mail: marwan.alkhouli@unige.ch

[3] Dr. Rémi BAUDOUI is a Professor of Political and Environmental Sciences in Geneva University, department of Political Sciences and International Relations. UniMail, Office 4252, Boulevard du Pont d'Arve 40, 1205 Geneva, Switzerland. E-Mail: remi.baudoui@unige.ch

Table 1. Main Origin Countries for asylum seekers in Switzerl

Source: SEM (2017a)

The mathematically calculated duration of asylum applications handled in the first

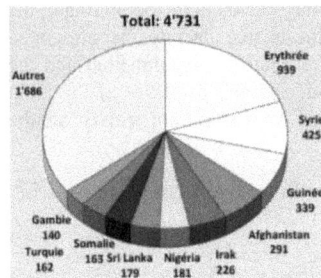

Nationalité	Demandes d'asile 1er trimestre 2017	En % du total	Compar. avec trim. préc. (abs.)	Compar. avec trim. préc. (%)	Demandes d'asile janv. à mars 2017	En % du total	Compar. avec an-née préc (absolu)	Compar. avec an-née préc. (%)
1 Erythrée	939	19.8	-457	-32.7	939	19.8	298	46.5
2 Syrie	425	9.0	-74	-14.8	425	9.0	-448	-51.3
3 Guinée	339	7.2	-22	-6.1	339	7.2	218	180.2
4 Afghanistan	291	6.2	-48	-14.2	291	6.2	-1750	-85.7
5 Irak	226	4.8	-4	-1.7	226	4.8	-505	-69.1
6 Nigéria	181	3.8	30	19.9	181	3.8	-120	-39.9
7 Sri Lanka	179	3.8	-94	-34.4	179	3.8	-284	-61.3
8 Somalie	163	3.4	-55	-25.2	163	3.4	-197	-54.7
9 Turquie	162	3.4	5	3.2	162	3.4	27	20.0
10 Gambie	140	3.0	12	9.4	140	3.0	-222	-61.3
Autres	1'686	35.6	-387	-18.7	1'686	35.6	-601	-26.3
Total	4'731	100.0	-1'094	-18.8	4'731	100.0	-3'584	-43.1

instance in 2016 stood at 249 days. This figure varies sharply, depending on the volume of incoming asylum applications and SEM's handling strategy. The handling strategy is broken down into three categories of asylum applications: Dublin cases, which accounted for 35% of the asylum applications received in 2016, with an average duration of around two months (72 days); Priority 1 asylum applications, which accounted for 6% of the incoming asylum applications, with an average duration of around six months (182 days); and Priority 2 asylum applications, which accounted for 59% of the cases, with an average duration of about a year (SEM, 2017a).

Problematic & hypothesis

Asylum seekers arriving in Switzerland are initially received at six Registration and Procedure Centres (CEPs)[4] run by the State Secretary for Migration (SEM, 2016). The reception includes registration of their personal details, taking of passport photos, fingerprints as well as a medical examination at the border. We consider that the implementation of the Sectoral Asylum Plan[5] (SEM, 2017b), approved by a popular vote the 5 June 2016 and the acceleration of asylum procedures (**Figure 1**) have considerably impacted

---

4 These CEPs are situated actually in Basel, Vallorbe, Kreuzlingen, Altstätten, Chiasso, Bern as well as the pilot centre of Zurich.

5 It distinguishes three types of future federal infrastructure: federal centres for asylum seekers (CFAs, actually CEPs), specific centres and special infrastructure to control fluctuations.

the stakeholders' collaboration and the progress of asylum process in these centres while ensuring its conformity with the principles of the asylum rules.

Actually, first-instance decisions on asylum as well as enforcement of removal orders are reached at the CEPs. 60% of the asylum procedures reach a binding decision within a maximum stay at an accommodation and provisioning centre is 140 days, instead of 90 days before (SEM, 2015). Asylum seekers whose application cannot be decided at the Registration and Procedure Centres will be assigned to a canton for the entire duration of processing of their application. They are assigned according to a distribution ratio calculated on the basis of population size.

Figure 1. Difference in the processing of asylum applications after the accelerated procedure

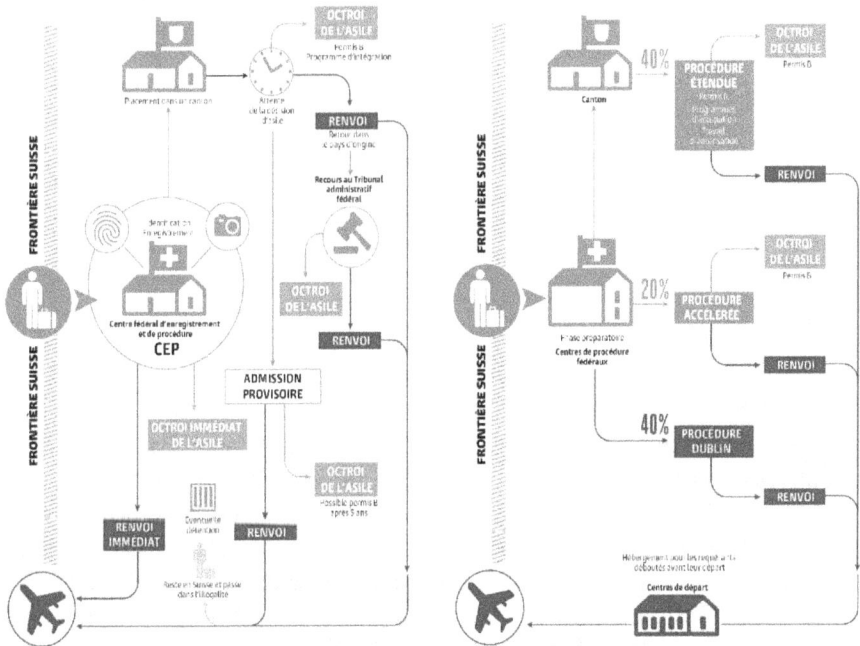

Source: ERARD, P. (2016)

For an annual volume of some 24,000 asylum applications, approximately 5,000 places[6] will be needed in the future federal centres (CFA) for asylum seekers (SEM, 2017b) in order to implement the Sectoral Asylum Plan (**Figure 2**). In their current form, existing Registration and Procedure Centres (CEP) don't all lend themselves to the new procedures. Some of them don't reach the critical size necessary to effectively implement the new procedures. Other

---

6 This figure already includes a 20% reserve to control fluctuations and handle up to 29,000 applications per year.

centres require more workstations and beds on site. Consequently, the Swiss Confederation must considerably develop its asylum infrastructures and its monitoring management of accommodation centres.

Figure 2. The asylum infrastructure of the Swiss Confederation.

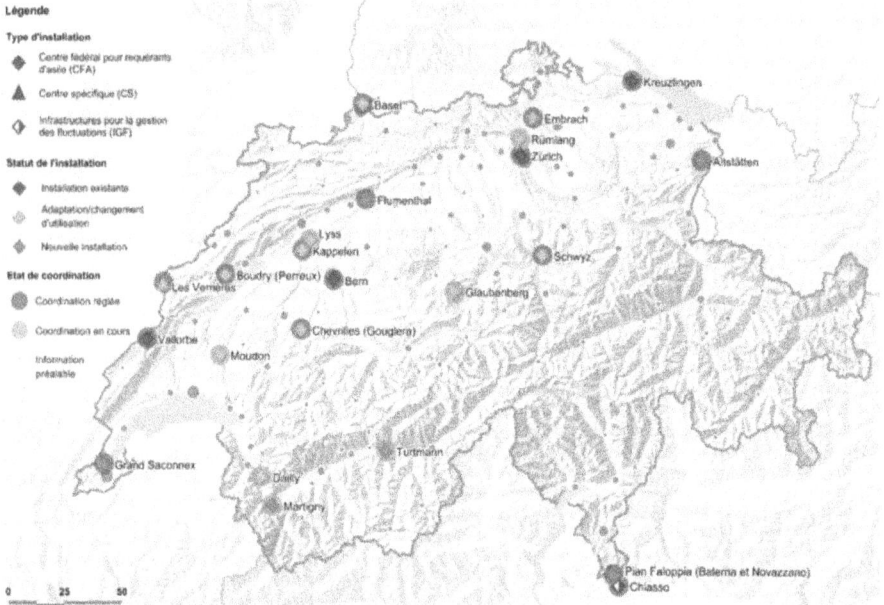

Source: SEM (April, 2017)

Method

To explore our hypothesis and see if the future federal centres as planned by the State Secretary for Migration respond to the administrative staff and the asylum seekers' needs, we rely on the reception and accommodation process in two actual Registration and Procedure Centres: Vallorbe and Zurich. Based on formal operational documents and recent photos, we interviewed the administrative staff of State Secretary for Migration (SEM), the coaching and accommodation services (ORS & AOZ) as well as asylum seekers between November 2016 and March 2017. This exploratory work with the three main actors in actual CEPs will illustrate the difficulties, internal problems to resolve and the real needs to satisfy in the future Swiss federal centres (CFA).

The Asylum Federal Centre of Vallorbe

Open since November 2000, this centre is located on the French border and provides also personnel to deal with the asylum procedure at Geneva airport. To maintain the objective of treating most of the asylum procedure in the centre, all the stakeholders involved in the asylum process work closely together in the centre of Vallorbe, which include the State Secretary of

Migration (SEM staff), the interpreters, the management and accommodation staff (ORS Service), the security service (Sécuritas), the fingerprint service (Sitasys) and other service providers responsible for meals, cleaning, laundry and maintenance (**Figure 3**).

Figure 3. Organizational chart of stakeholders in the CEP of Vallorbe.

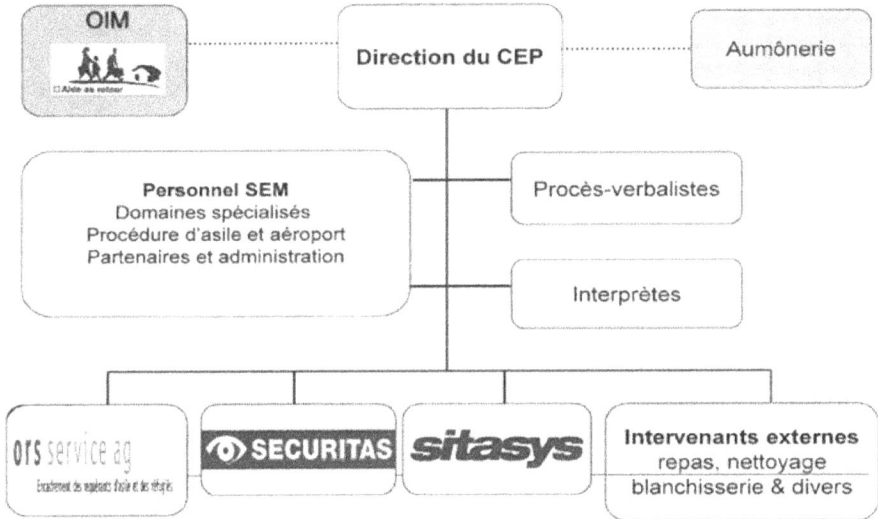

Source: Alkhouli, M. (2017)

During our on-site investigation, SEM and ORS staff expressed the urgent need for space in order to meet the administrative and activities needs of the asylum seekers (**Figure 4**).

However, the State Secretary for Migration considers that no enlargement will be necessary in Vallorbe as part of its restructuring project. The SEM considers that it meets the criteria of a federal centre for the waiting and departure functions and will become a CFA from 2019 until a location of a third CFA for the same functions will be decided and realized. Workplaces for administrative staff will be reduced and reallocated (**Figure 5**); Workplaces for management and security personnel will be maintained. As regards the asylum-seekers' needs in the centre, they complained mainly about the condensation of the dormitories, while there were other unoccupied spaces. It seems that this measure increases the already existing tensions between asylum seekers issued from very different socio-cultural backgrounds. They express also the sensation of confinement and movements' restrictions, as well as the confiscation of mobile phones (**Figure 6**). When interviewed the head of the centre, it appears that unallocated dormitories are used to manage potential fluctuations.

Figure 4. Illustrations of exterior and interior spaces in Vallorbe centre

Source: Alkhouli, M. (2017)

Figure 5. First hearing of an asylum seeker in an administrative workplace

Figure 6. An asylum seeker who complains about overcrowded dormitories and confinement sensation

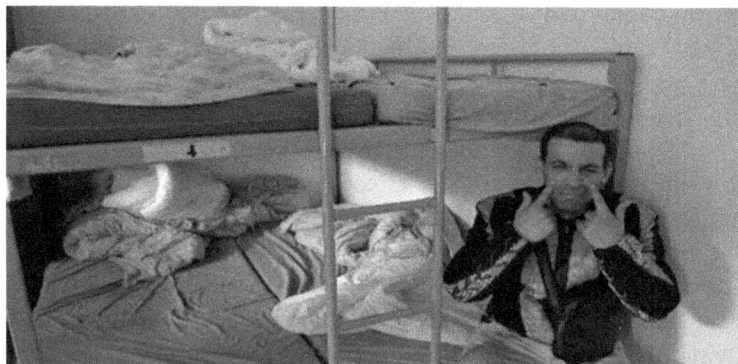

Source: Alkhouli, M. (2017)

The Asylum Federal Centre of Zurich:

The Juch Centre in Zurich was chosen by the Swiss Confederation to test the new accelerated asylum procedure. During the test period between 1 January 2014 and 31 August 2015, the length of proceedings was reduced by 39% and the appeal rate dropped by one third to just 17.1%. In addition, voluntary returns increased to 6% (Restructuration Group, 2014). The quality of the different stages of the asylum process, transparency and a better understanding of decisions by the applicants were guaranteed in this pilot centre. The fact that all important actors were brought together on the same floor of the building contributed greatly to the overall success of the experiment.

Figure 7. The actual Juch-Areal Centre for asylum seeker in Zurich - Altstätten

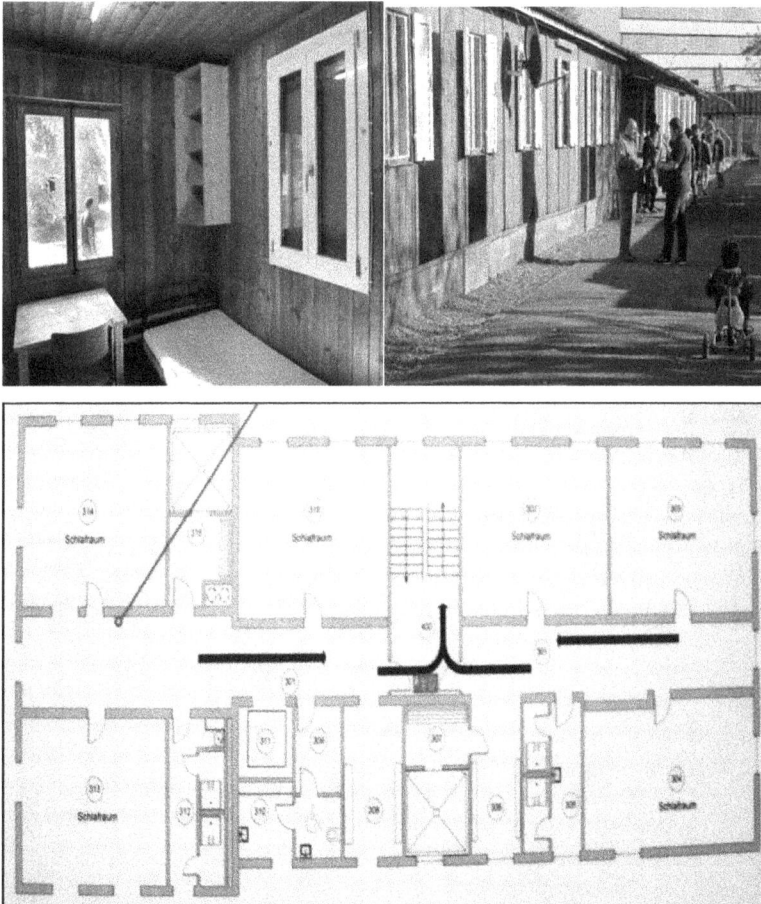

Source: Alkhouli, M. (2017)

Unlike the Vallorbe centre, where a private company (ORS) manages the accommodation of asylum seekers, a public-law company from the Zurich City Department of Social Affairs carries out this task at the Juch centre in Zurich. The Asylum Organisation Zürich (AOZ) manage 300 asylum seekers in the centre since January 2014. It negotiated with the State Secretary for Migration to obtain different conditions of accommodation for asylum seekers: extending the hours of accessibility, managing itself the security of spaces without resorting to Securitas, and the facilitation of access to representatives of the civil society. For women, families, unaccompanied minors and vulnerable persons, there are separate dwellings. Consequently, the asylum seekers that we met express their satisfaction about space management and the presence of legal representatives during the procedure. In addition, AOZ has taken the lead in finding solutions for sustainable housing. It has built a centre with containers and recyclable materials that offers good accommodation quality (**Figure 7**).

Unlike other asylum federal centres in Switzerland, the SEM offices are located at a different location than the accommodation places in Juch centre. The future federal centre in Duttweiler areal will replace the Juch structure around 2020 and will be operated for an initial period of 15 years. One of the objectives is to regroup the administrative offices of the SEM and AOZ with the reception and accommodation places for asylum seekers (**Figure 8**).

Figure 8. The plan of the future federal centre in Zurich - Duttweiler areal

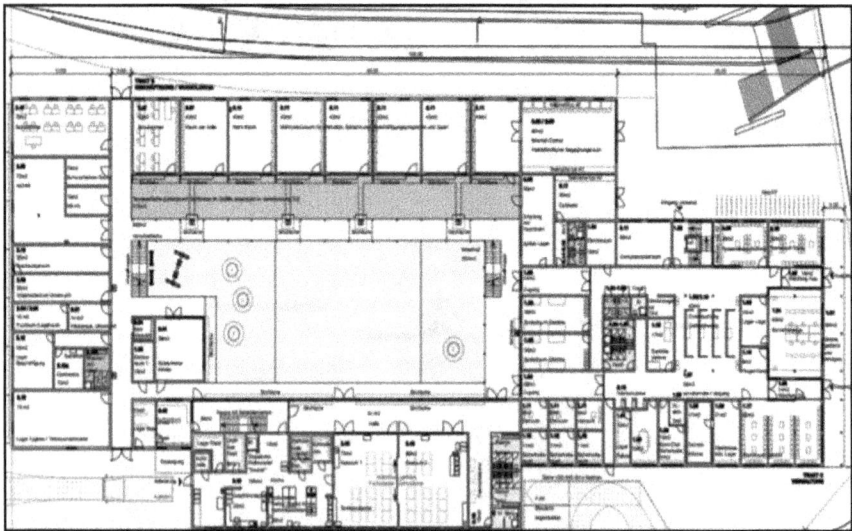

Source: SEM

Conclusion:

Following the exploration of the two previous federal centres, we can see that the needs of the three main field actors are not always satisfied by the State Secretary for Migration. The actual strategic priority is to assume the sectoral asylum plan which provides a better distribution of the applicants on six Swiss regions according to their number of inhabitants.

For Vallorbe, the demographic and geographical situation of Vaud canton where the centre is situated makes it more receptive of asylum seekers from other centres on the Italian border (Chiasso) and German border (Kreuzlingen). Regular asylum seekers' transfers to Vallorbe during the last years led to the SEM reflection to transform it into a waiting and departure centre. This new transitional situation doesn't reassure the inhabitants of the village who fear the re-emergence of tensions and the flight of rejected asylum-seekers. On the other hand, it doesn't allow administrative staff to carry out integration activities and principal education programs under better conditions.

For Zurich centre, despite the provision of free legal assistance, the Swiss Democratic Lawyers association (JDS) considered that the appointment by the SEM of persons providing legal representation for asylum seekers is incompatible with the requirements of the independence of consultation and legal representation. The JDS accuses also the restriction of exit possibilities and the relatively limited time for appeal under the accelerated procedure (Caroni M. & Scheiber N., 2015). The main critic of the future federal centre lies on its location in the heart of a dense residential area.

References:

Alkhouli, M. (2017). Quelle politique d'hébergement des requérants d'asile en Suisse? [Which accommodation politic for asylum seekers in Switzerland]. Post-doc report, Department of Political Sciences and International Relations, Geneva University (in French).

Caroni, M. & Scheiber, N. (2015). Rechtliche Fragestellungen im Zusammenhang mit der Neustrukturierung im Asylbereich und der Beschleunigung im Asylverfahren [Legal issues related to the restructuring and the acceleration of the asylum procedure]. Lucern University. 80 p (in German).

Erard, P. (2016). Asile, ce qui changera avec la nouvelle loi [Asylum, what will change with the new law]. Le Temps Journal. Published online the 30 May (in French). Received from: https://www.letemps.ch/suisse/2016/05/30/asile-changera-nouvelle-loi Accessed: 20.05.2017.

Restructuring Group (2014). Planification générale de la restructuration du domaine de l'asile [General Planification of the Asylum Restructuring]. Final Report. State Secretary for Migration, Swiss Confederation. 100 p (in French). Received from: https://www.sem.admin.ch/dam/data/sem/aktuell/news/2014/2014-03-28/ber-agna-f.pdf Accessed: 20.05.2017.

SEM (2017a). Statistique en matière d'asile, 1er trimestre 2017 [Asylum Statistics, First Semester 2017]. State Secretary for Migration, Swiss Confederation (in French). Received from: https://www.sem.admin.ch/dam/data/sem/publiservice/statistik/asylstatistik/2017/stat-q1-2017-kommentar-f.pdf. Accessed: 20.05.2017.

SEM (2017b). Plan sectoriel Asile: Partie conceptuelle et partie relative aux objets [Sectorial Asylum Plan: Conceptual Part and a Part relative to subjects]. Project for Consultation and Participation, Art. 19 OAT. State Secretary for Migration, Swiss Confederation. Received from: https://www.sem.admin.ch/dam/data/sem/asyl/beschleunigung/sachplanasyl/konzeptteil-entw-f.pdf. Accessed: 20.05.2017.

SEM (2016). Overview of the reception and procedure centres. State Secretary for Migration, Swiss Confederation. Received from: https://www.sem.admin.ch/sem/en/home/asyl/asylverfahren/empfang/uebersicht_evz.html. Accessed: 20.05.2017.

SEM (2015). Evaluation de la phase de test: Résumé des résultats [Evaluation of Test Phase: Summary of Results]. State Secretary for Migration, Swiss Confederation (in French). Received from: https://www.sem.admin.ch/dam/data/sem/asyl/beschleunigung/testbetrieb/ber-sem-ergebnisse-eval-testbetrieb-f.pdf. Accessed: 20.05.2017.

Chapter 35. Asylum Under Pressure: international Deterrence and access to asylum

Vasiliki Kakosimou[1]

Abstract

In order to respond to the refugee crisis or control the migration flows, States may take certain measures to keep migrants out of reach of their borders. These measures involve push-backs, interception at high seas, erecting fences, bilateral agreements for off-shore processing etc., under national security reasons or for mainting public order. All these measures are referred to as deterrence strategies, they do not conform with States' obligations under International Human Rights Law and they result in preventing refugees from having access to asylum. Through treaties, customary law and case law, the principle of non-refoulement has an extra-territorial application. States are bound by the principle of non-refoulement by the moment States agents exercise effective control upon migrants -potential refugees. Unless States cooperate with each other, share the burden, build -up their capacity for fair asylum procedures and comply with International human rights law obligations, refugees cannot have access to international protection and enjoy their fundamental rights.

Keywords: Deterrence, extra-territorial application, non-refoulement.

Introduction

As a result of mass refugee influxes, few states have the willingness and capacity to assess each entrance individually. Faced with many challenges, receiving States have responded to the increase in the number of migrants by increasing border surveillance and reinforcing migration controls. The measures taken include visa restrictions, push-backs by building fortresses, financing third states for capacity building or bilateral agreements to patrol their borders. All these measures are aimed at preventing refugees and other migrants from entering a state's territory by controlling or managing migration flows or maintaining internal security -even though these deterrence policies imply breaching obligations of states under national and international law. The deterrence policies do not comply with the non-derogable principle of non-refoulement and violate the right to have access to protection from persecution, torture, degrading or other inhuman treatment

Non -Refoulement

International refugee law and international human rights law are complementary and mutually reinforcing legal regimes. It follows that Article 33(1), which embodies the humanitarian essence of the 1951 Convention and safeguards fundamental rights of refugees, must be interpreted in a manner which is consistent with developments in international human rights law.

---

[1] Vasiliki Kakosimou is Head of the Regional Asylum Office of the Greek Asylum Service in Piraeus, Nav. Notara 106, Piraeus, 18535, Greece, e-mail: v.kakosimou@asylo.gov.gr

Non-refoulement is a concept which prohibits states from returning a person to any territory where there is a risk that his or her life or freedom would be threatened on account of race, religion, nationality, membership of a particular social group or political opinion. The principle of non-refoulement reflects customary international law and is most prominently reflected in the Geneva Convention relating to the Status of Refugees and its 1967 Protocol. Article 33(1) of the Convention provides that:

"No Contracting State shall expel or return ('refouler') a refugee in any manner whatsoever to the frontiers of territories where his life or freedom would be threatened on account of his race, religion, nationality, membership of a particular social group or political opinion."

The prohibition of refoulement must be respected in any type of forcible removal, including deportation, expulsion, extradition, informal transfer or 'renditions' and return of refugees to countries of origin or unsafe third countries. The principle of non-refoulement requires not only that refugees or asylum seekers shall not be returned to a country where their life or freedom is threatened, but also implies that they cannot be prevented from requesting protection, even if they enter unlawfully, or if they are at the border. It encompasses non-admission of stowaway asylum seekers, fences, border closures and push-backs of boat arrivals or interdictions on the high seas and in general the non-rejection at the frontier, if rejection would result in an individual being forcibly returned to a country of persecution.

Application of Non-Refoulement at Borders

States have a right under international law to control the entry of non-nationals into their territory. However, states that turn asylum seekers away at their border or erect walls and fences to avoid giving asylum seekers the opportunity to have their status determined, can breach the prohibition of refoulement. In Amuur v. France (ECtHR, Amuur v. France, No 19776/92, 25 June 1996, paras. 43 and 5) the ECtHR clarified that people in international transit zones of airports are protected by the ECHR. Thus, borders should not be closed or impenetrable to prevent the entry of refugees, as this may violate the state's non-refoulement obligations.

Extra-Territorial Application of Non-Refoulement

The obligation set out in Art. 33(1) of the 1951 Convention is subject to a geographical restriction only with regard to the country where a refugee may not be sent to, not the place where he/she is sent from. The extra-territorial applicability of the non-refoulement obligation under Art. 33(1) is clear from the text of the provision itself. The principle of non-refoulement in a human rights context is a fundamental component of the prohibition of torture, cruel, inhuman or degrading treatment or punishment. UNHCR has stressed that the principle of non-refoulement applies equally on a state's territory, at a state's borders, and on the high seas. States are bound by their obligations not to return any person over whom they exercise jurisdiction to a risk of irreparable harm. In determining whether a State's human rights obligations with respect to a particular person are engaged, the decisive criterion is not whether that person is on the State's national territory, or within a territory which is de jure under the sovereign control of the State, but rather whether or not he or she is subject to that State's effective authority and control.

Under human rights law, a state's obligations are engaged as soon as the State can be said to be exercising effective control. The ECtHR in Hirsi Jamaa v. Italy (ECtHR, Hirsi Jamaa and Others v. Italy, No 27765/09, 23 February 2012) and the UN Committee Against Torture in Marine I (UN, CAT, J.H.A. v. Spain, CAT/C/41/D/323/2007, 21 November 2008) both held that states are bound by the prohibition of refoulement from the moment a person comes within the jurisdiction of a state, even if this person is outside the state's physical territory. This ruling was reinforced by the UN Special Rapporteur on Torture who explained that "the obligations enshrined in the Torture Convention also apply to state vessels patrolling or conducting border control operations on the high seas and states' pushbacks of migrants under their jurisdiction can breach the prohibition of torture and ill-treatment and non-refoulement obligations (UN General Assembly, "Interim report of the Special Rapporteur on torture and other cruel, inhuman or degrading treatment or punishment" UN Doc A/70/303, 7 August 2015, para 42)". The decisive criterion for extraterritorial human rights obligations is thus a state's acts, which must create a qualified relationship with the victim of the violation. De facto control creates de jure responsibilities. De facto control over persons requires a certain level of physical constraint (UN, Human Rights Committee (2004), para 10). In addition, an internationally wrongful act can consist of either an action or an omission; if the third country's authorities violate human rights and the EU Member State's authorities fail to fulfill their legal obligation to stop these violations, they become co-responsible.

Hirsi – a landmark case: In Hirsi Jamaa and Others v Italy the ECtHR, issued a landmark judgment regarding the interpretation of Article 4 of Protocol No 4 of the ECHR. The case concerned Italy's push back practices of Somali and Eritrean migrants travelling from Libya who had been intercepted by the Italian authorities at sea, way out of Italian territorial waters by the Italian authorities and sent back to Libya[2]. The ECtHR noted that the personnel on

---

2 Within the territorial waters of the Member States, the EU asylum acquis applies, including all substantial and procedural guarantees for applicants. In contrast, the EU asylum acquis does not extend to persons who seek asylum while they are rescued or intercepted at high seas, including within a Member States' search and rescue zone, or in the territorial sea of third countries

the military ships which returned the migrants to Libya were neither trained to conduct personal interviews nor assisted by interpreters or legal advisers. It concluded that the absence of such guarantees made it impossible to examine the individual circumstances of each person affected by the return measures. As to the question of territoriality and where the used definition mentions 'to leave the country', the ECtHR clarified that whenever state agents exercise control and authority over an individual, then that state is obliged to respect the principle of non-refoulement, even if the state is operating outside its own territory. Furthermore, the prohibition of collective expulsions also applies to measures taken at high seas, the effect of which is to prevent migrants from reaching the borders of the state or even to push them back to another state (Hirsi Jamaa and Others v Italy, Application No 27765/09, Council of Europe: European Court of Human Rights, 23 February 2012, paragraphs 74-75, 180-181 and 183-186, available at: http://www.refworld.org/docid/4f4507942.html).

Deterrence Strategies

States have pursued a series of measures to prevent refugees and other migrants from entering their territory. These have included imposing restrictive visa regimes and air carrier sanctions, erecting physical barriers at borders, the summary rejection of asylum-seekers at borders or points of entry, creating international zones, creating buffer zones or designating safe areas as well as the maritime interception of asylum seekers and other migrants.

Pushbacks, interception on the High Seas, off-shore processing arrangements, financial assistance and other policies of extra-territorial deterrence are pursued, sometimes under the guise that a receiving country is a safe third country.

US (geographic limitation of non-refoulement): By preventing people from landing in the US and not being able to make a claim for refugee status, these persons cannot avail themselves of the principle of non-refoulement.

Australia: They are processing refugee claims offshore. However, refugee claimants are living in remote refugee camps for protracted periods of time, which constitutes harsh and unusual treatment.

EU- Turkey: According to the EU-Turkey deal (agreement) of the 18th March 2016, asylum-seekers are being held in refugee settlement centers and then sent back to Turkey; they are not allowed to travel to any EU States to claim asylum.

Some EU Member States have similarly sought to limit the extraterritorial nature of the prohibition of torture and ill-treatment to minimize its impact on expulsion cases. In Saadi (Saadi v. Italy (Grand Chamber), Appl no 37201/06, 28 February 2008), the Grand Chamber of the European Court of Human Rights made clear that Human rights law allows for no derogations; the absolute prohibition of torture allows for no balancing of the risk of torture against national security risks and is not subject to any exception whatsoever. Since protection against the treatment prohibited by Article 3 is absolute, that provision imposes an obligation not to extradite any person who would run the real risk of being subjected to such treatment. The conduct of the person concerned, however undesirable or dangerous, cannot be taken into account.

When people in distress are found at the sea, the States involved in such a case have certain responsibilities to rescue these people and bring them to safety. Their responsibilities derive from various international human rights instruments (see 1982 UN Convention on the law of the Sea) and States are bound by these obligations from the moment effective power or control is exercised upon these people by State agents including actions or omissions.

Apart from depriving refugees from their right not to be refouled to a territory where his/her life or freedom would be at risk, these people cannot ask for international protection, get involved into the asylum procedure or enjoy the rights of the recognised beneficiaries of international protection.

Also, preventing people from entering a State's territory may expose them to risk of torture, inhuman or degrading treatment, another fundamental and non-derogable human right.

Conclusion

Deterrence strategies breach the States' responsibilities under human rights law, expose refugees to persecution, torture or other inhuman treatment and violate the right to fair asylum procedure. The States' responsibilities and the migrants' right not to be refouled and also not to be exposed to risk of torture or inhuman treatment overcome the States' right to control the entry of migrants and to safeguard national security, security of the community or public order

Burden sharing is a vital ingredient for responses to mass influxes; however it can only work if states find ways to work collaboratively beyond what they perceive to be their own national interests and accept that a part of burden sharing is accepting resettlement. Fair systems are therefore crucial to ensuring that refugees are recognised, and that no-one who has been tortured or ill-treated, or faces a risk of such treatment, will have to experience any treatment akin to this while looking for safety and protection. A State is bound by its obligation under Article 33(1) of the 1951 Convention not to return refugees to a risk of persecution wherever it exercises effective jurisdiction. As with non-refoulement obligations under international human rights law, the decisive criterion is not whether such persons are on the State's territory, but rather, whether they come within the effective control and authority of that State.

References/ Sources

Amnesty International, Amnesty International Report 2016/17 - Bulgaria, 22 February 2017, available at: http://www.refworld.org/docid/58b0341613.html

Amnesty International, EU-Turkey deal: Greek decision highlights fundamental flaws, 20 May 2016, available at: http://www.refworld.org/docid/5742b63b4.html

Cambridge University Press, The Scope and Content of the Principle of Non-Refoulement: Opinion, June 2003, available at: http://www.refworld.org/docid/470a33af0.html

Council of Europe: Committee of Ministers, Declaration on Territorial Asylum, 18 November 1977, available at: http://www.refworld.org/docid/3ae6b3611c.html

Council of Europe: Committee of Ministers, Resolution (67) 14 : Asylum to Persons in Danger of Persecution, 29 June 1967, 14 (1967), available at: http://www.refworld.org/docid/3ae6b38168.html

Council of Europe: Parliamentary Assembly, Monitoring the return of irregular migrants and failed asylum seekers by land, sea and air, 7 November 2013, Doc. 13351, available at: http://www.refworld.org/docid/52f49c9f4.html

European Commission, Return Handbook (annex to Commission Recommendation of 1.10.2015 establishing a common 'Return Handbook' to be used by Member States' competent authorities when carrying out return related tasks), available at http://ec.europa.eu/dgs/home-affairs/what-we-do/policies/european-agenda-migration/proposal-implementation-package/docs/return_handbook_en.pdf

European Court of Human Rights (ECtHR), case of Saadi v Italy, 2008, available at: http://hudoc.echr.coe.int/eng?i=001-85276#{"itemid":["001-85276"]}

European Court of Human Rights (ECtHR), factsheet 'Collective expulsions of aliens', September 2015, available at: http://www.echr.coe.int/Documents/FS_Collective_expulsions_ENG.pdf

European Court of Human Rights (ECtHR), factsheet 'Dublin Cases', July 2015, available at: http://www.echr.coe.int/Documents/FS_Dublin_ENG.pdf

European Court of Human Rights (ECtHR), factsheet 'Expulsions and extraditions', July 2013, available at: http://www.echr.coe.int/Documents/FS_Expulsions_Extraditions_ENG.pdf

European Union: European Agency for Fundamental Rights, Scope of the principle of non-refoulement in contemporary border management: evolving areas of law, December 2016, available at: http://www.refworld.org/docid/5857b3bb4.html

European Union: European Agency for Fundamental Rights, Guidance on how to reduce the risk of refoulement in external border management when working in or together with third countries, December 2016, available at: http://www.refworld.org/docid/5857b2b94.html

European Union: European Agency for Fundamental Rights, Fundamental Rights Report 2016, May 2016, available at: http://www.refworld.org/docid/574fce384.html

European Union: European Agency for Fundamental Rights, Opinion of the European Union Agency for Fundamental Rights concerning an EU common list of safe countries of origin, 23 March 2016, available at: http://www.refworld.org/docid/576d48a94.html

Fundamental Rights Agency (FRA), Fundamental rights at Europe's southern sea borders, available at https://fra.europa.eu/sites/default/files/fundamental-rights-europes-southern-sea-borders-jul-13_en.pdf

Fundamental Rights Agency (FRA), Handbook on European law relating to asylum, borders and immigration, available at: http://fra.europa.eu/sites/default/files/handbook-law-asylum-migration-borders-2nded_en.pdf

Hungarian Helsinki Committee, Pushed Back at the Door: Denial of Access to Asylum in Eastern EU Member States, 2017, available at: http://www.refworld.org/docid/5888b5234.html

International Association of Refugee Law Judges, Extraterritorial Effect of Non-Refoulement, 9 September 2011, available at: http://www.refworld.org/docid/557030f64.html

International Commission of Jurists (ICJ), Procedural rights in the proposed Dublin IV Regulation" - Comments of the International Commission of Jurists on specific procedural measures in the Recast of the Dublin Regulation, 27 September 2016, available at: http://www.refworld.org/docid/57ee6de04.html

Office of the United Nations High Commissioner for Refugees (UNHCR), UNHCR Manual on Refugee Protection and the ECHR Part 4.1 Selected Case Law on Article 3, available at http://www.refworld.org/pdfid/3f4cd5c74.pdf

Office of the United Nations High Commissioner for Refugees (UNHCR), UNHCR Manual on Refugee Protection and the ECHR Part 2.1 – Fact Sheet on Article 3, available at: http://www.unhcr.org/3ead2d262.pdf

Office of the United Nations High Commissioner for Refugees (UNHCR), Rescue at Sea. A Guide to Principles and Practice as Applied to Refugees and Migrants, January 2015, available at: http://www.refworld.org/docid/54b365554.htm

Overseas Development Institute (ODI), Closing borders: the ripple effects of Australian and European refugee policy. Case studies from Indonesia, Kenya and Jordan, September 2016, available at: http://www.refworld.org/docid/57dbed964.html

Sir Elihu Lauterpacht and Daniel Bethlehem, The scope and content of the principle of non-refoulement: Opinion, available at: http://www.unhcr.org/419c75ce4.pdf

UN General Assembly, Declaration on Territorial Asylum, 14 December 1967, A/RES/2312(XXII), available at: http://www.refworld.org/docid/3b00f05a2c.html

UN High Commissioner for Refugees (UNHCR), La protection des refugies en droit international, 2008, available at: http://www.refworld.org/docid/5177ffda4.html

UN High Commissioner for Refugees (UNHCR), UNHCR Note on the Principle of Non-Refoulement, November 1997, available at: http://www.refworld.org/docid/438c6d972.html

UN High Commissioner for Refugees (UNHCR), Advisory Opinion on the Extraterritorial Application of Non-Refoulement Obligations under the 1951 Convention relating to the Status of Refugees and its 1967 Protocol, 26 January 2007, available at: http://www.refworld.org/docid/45f17a1a4.html

UN High Commissioner for Refugees (UNHCR), Note on Non-Refoulement (Submitted by the High Commissioner), 23 August 1977, EC/SCP/2, available at: http://www.refworld.org/docid/3ae68ccd10.html

UN High Commissioner for Refugees (UNHCR), Regional Refugee and Migrant Response Plan for Europe - Eastern Mediterranean and Western Balkans Route, January-December 2016, January 2016, available at: http://www.refworld.org/docid/56a9e5134.html

UN News Service, UN rights chief concerned over 'collective expulsion' of migrants after EU-Turkey deal, 24 March 2016, available at: http://www.refworld.org/docid/56fa200840d.html

United States Department of State, Office of the Historian, The League of Nations, 1920 https://history.state.gov/milestones/1914-1920/league

Univ.-Prof. MMag. Dr. August Reinisch, LL.M /Mag. Melanie Fink, University of Vienna, Non-Refoulement and Extraterritorial Immigration Control – The 15. Case of Immigration Liaison Officers', available at

https://intlaw.univie.ac.at/fileadmin/user_upload/int_beziehungen/Internetpubl/Baxewa
nosl.pdf

Chapter 36. Migration: A Triangle of Aspiration, Opportunity or Exploitation? A Migrant's Perspective

Shweta Sinha Deshpande[1], Aashna Banerjee[2]

Abstract

The number of international migrants worldwide has continued to grow rapidly over the past decade. Nevertheless, migration leads to controversial conversations within multiple spheres. Therefore, there is a need to explore a perspective on migration—of migrants themselves. This paper aims to situate 25 case studies on migration within interlinked realities of exploitation in the habitus, migrant aspirations, and opportunities provided by the experience of migration; against the backdrop of migrant agency. Analysis of the data collected indicated that migration offers opportunities to avoid and escape socio-economic traps, achieve aspirations and a higher level of well-being; the interactions between entities in the process of migration can be positively exploitative; and that negative lived experiences of the present are overlooked by migrants due to their aspiration of a better future. Most importantly, the authors emphasize that migration is a tool and a strategy which can be used to overcome structural inequalities and build capabilities.

Keywords: aspirations, lived experience, positive exploitation

Introduction

Migration is an expression of the human aspiration for dignity, safety and a better future. It is part of the social fabric, part of our very make-up as a human family (Ban Ki-Moon, October 3rd, 2013).

The act of migration or the "roving instinct" is said to be intrinsic to human nature (King, 2012, p. 4). For centuries, the phenomenon of migration has illustrated the human capacity for survival and determination to overcome adversity in the hope of achieving a better life (Sen, 2001). Currently—with changing political, economic, and cultural systems; and ideologies for equitable growth and development as is reflected in the Sustainable Development Goals—migration appears to be taking the center stage as a tool or strategy for overcoming structural inadequacies for capacity building (United Nations Office for Disaster Risk Reduction, 2017).

The number of international migrants worldwide has continued to grow rapidly over the past fifteen years reaching 244 million in 2015, which is an increase from 2.8 percent in 2000 to 3.3 per cent in 2015 (United Nations, 2015). Nevertheless, the phenomenon of migration leads to controversial conversations within economic, political, and socio-cultural spheres. Hence, there is a need to relook at migration—through the eyes of the migrant.

---

[1] Shweta Sinha Deshpande, PhD, is a professor of Anthropology and Migration Studies at the Symbiosis School of Liberal Arts in Pune, India. E-mail: deputydirector@ssla.edu.in.
[2] Aashna Banerjee is a student at the Symbiosis School for Liberal Arts in Pune, India. E-mail: aashnabanerjee95@gmail.com

This paper aims to situate 25 case studies on migration within interlinked realities of exploitation in the habitus, migrant aspirations, and opportunities provided by the experience of migration, in order to explore a perspective on migration by migrants themselves. This exploration of migrant narratives aims to understand increasing migration—both legal and illegal—in the face of economic, social, and cultural inequalities faced within host spaces.

Review of Literature

Migration research and theory has been a part of academic and public debate since the late 1800's and was viewed primarily as an economic phenomenon. Past research and writing have outlined two broad theoretical frameworks: functionalist theories, which view migration as a positive phenomenon that serves the interests of most people, and contributes to greater equality within and between societies; and historical-structural theories that reinforce structural inequalities through exploitation of cheap labor that migration provides in the world (Castles, de Haas & Miller, 2014, p. 27-28). Other theoretical conceptualizations of the phenomenon of migration lay emphasis on concepts of agency (Lieten & Nieuwenhuys, 1989); human capital of the migrant (Massey, Arango, Hugo, Kouaouci, Pellegrino & Taylor, 1993; Stark, 1980); and capabilities and capacity building (Carling, 2002; Castles et al., 2014, p. 50). Further, recent work has identified and approached migration studies through the micro, meso, and macro levels which guide human agency and consequently, the process of migration (Castles et al. 2014, p. 31; King, 2012; Zolberg, Suhrke, & Aguayo, 1989; Lee, 1966). This approach asserts that lived experience is subjective to the individual and households.

The role of the migrant is further emphasized in the conceptualization of migration as a "self-selected process" (Czaika & Vothknecht, 2014, p. 20). Migration can be understood as a function of the capabilities and aspirations to move within the structural constraints for capacity building and achieving a higher level of wellbeing (Sen, 2001). Bonfanti (2014) argued that migration as a process can enhance migrants' well-being both through its "intrinsic" value which is the experience of freedom, and its "instrumental" value which is the effect of mobility based on the capability set of the migrant themselves. This approach views "migration as a fundamental capability" (Bonfanti, 2014, p. 4) which enhances ability and possibly overcomes past "hopelessness, despair, and acute loss" through conversion factors. Notably, the "migrant's peculiarities" (Bonfanti, 2014), or the migrant's "human capital" (Sjaastad, 1962, p. 87) play an important role in enhancing the human agency and achievement of optimal wellbeing in migration. Pine (2014, p. 96) perceives migration as "both a symbol and an enactment of hope and of faith in the future.

On one hand, migration as a process is understood as a key opportunity to achieve aspirations of progress and is identified as a tool for development. Alternatively, exploitation is a structural and systemic problem with regards to migration and migrants, which is a reality and is emphasized within the historical-structural theories of migration (Amnesty International, 2013; Castles, 2014). Though there is no dearth of literature on migration as a phenomenon itself, the perspectives of migrants appear to be lacking as a basis for theoretical conceptualization. Previous works have not been able to situate the aspiring migrants within the reality of structural deprivation, the experience of *exploitation* in the host space; along with guiding aspirations and opportunity granted by the act of migration. Thus, migration needs to be re-evaluated and contextualized as a subjective experience for migrants and their families offering *opportunities*—real or perceived—to fulfill personal and familial *aspirations* (Carling, 2014) in the contemporary globalized space.

This paper documents the situated and lived experiences of twenty-five migrants within the three dimensions of time--past, present and the future--within the *triangle of aspiration, opportunity and exploitation* to understand how the migrant perceive these interlinked realities. The past, including the immediate lived past represents real or perceived lack of well-being or *exploitative experiences* due to multiple socio-culture realities. The present or the migrant's lived reality represents *aspiration and hope* for a better life and *opportunity for capacity building* in the future, beyond both the past and the present for self, family and future generations. The migrant narratives help understand increasing migration, both legal and illegal in the face of economic, social and cultural inequalities faced within host spaces.

Methodology

The primary objective of the current research was to evaluate the phenomenon of migration through an understanding of the experiences of migrants themselves. Hence, the multiple case study method was employed for data collection, which allowed the researchers to explore, describe and record the migration processes of the sample population (Baxter & Jack, 2008; Zainal, 2007). The case study research method can be defined as "an empirical inquiry that investigates a contemporary phenomenon within its real-life context; when the boundaries between phenomenon and context are not clearly evident; and in which multiple sources of evidence are used" (Yin, 1984: 23). The multiple case study research design (Zainal, 2007; Baxter and Jack, 2008) was optimal for this study because it allowed the researchers to explore, describe and record the migration processes of the sample population. This study combined aspects of intrinsic and instrumental case studies because while the researchers desired a better understanding of migration processes from the migrants' perspective, the study also aimed to provide an insight into the phenomenon of migration as a positive process (Stake, 2003). The research design enabled the researchers to capture the complexities of the lives of their participants, which may not be as holistically understood and analyzed using quantitative research methods.

A heterogeneous sample of twenty-five case studies was collected between January 2015 and May 2017. The sample population is diverse in gender, caste, class, and socio-economic backgrounds with international (n=10) and internal migrants (n=15).

Case Studies

This research paper aims to look at migrant experiences, in order to determine their perspectives on the experience of migration. The heterogeneous sample of migrant experiences are diverse from villages to metropolitan cities; international migrations into and out of India including the reality of the myth of return; and mobility across cities for education, employment and marriage. Notably, this paper does not mitigate realities or problems that the migrants faced in their experience of migration, Further, it takes into account the skills and capabilities migrants acquired as resources during the process of mobility, which were used as tools to achieve a higher level of well-being.

This section contains excerpts of case studies which were conducted by the researchers.[3]

Soham Ghosh from Bardaman in West Bengal, who dropped out of school and currently is employed as a bartender in a restaurant in Pune. He is able to send money back home to his widowed mother, which makes him happy.

Karan and Vishwakarma both moved out of Nepal from small villages currently work as household help in Pune earning up to Rs. 40,000 a month. Today, Karan wants to go back to his village and complete his education which he gave up at the age of 14 when he moved out.

Bapu, (a second-generation migrant) son of a scheduled caste landless labourer, is contemplating migrating to a Middle Eastern country in search of better job opportunities because as he feels his caste identity is a hindrance to further progress though he feels that he has received an education because his father migrated to a city, thereby surpassing restrictions of the village community.

Pushpa and her husband (who currently works as a wage laborer on construction sites) moved to Pune with the youngest of their three children. They left behind a son and a daughter with their extended family in their village. They want to save money to help their family and marry their daughter.

---

3 All names have been changed to protect the anonymity of our subjects,

Though both of them face difficult and dangerous working conditions, problems of language, and cramped living conditions, they are happy to invest this time and effort for their future.

Vanmala and Maya live in a slum and work as household help. Vanmala left behind a well settled household in a village in Ahmednagar 15 years ago as her family believed that migration to a city and an English education will open up opportunities of social and economic mobility. Her sons today are earning well and one of them is a gym instructor. Further, over the last year she has managed to build a two-floored cement structure because all family members earn and contribute to the family's well-being. She says she puts in long hours of work much more than she used to when she was in the village, but she and her family are happy because they see themselves better placed today than 15 years ago.

Maya grew up in the city and was educated till 8th grade. She was married into a family in the village who had their own house, land which they cultivated, and a joint family that took care of her and her children. However, she moved to a slum in the city and lives in a single room. Yet, she is happy because she can send her children to an English medium school and she earns well. She feels that though she had a better social status in the village, she has more opportunities in the city.

Ram works as a driver and today owns a home that he has built over the last 30 years in Pune. His family in the village is very well placed with agricultural land and a large home. One of his brothers is the village headman (sarpanch, an elected position). Ram enjoys entertaining his fellow villagers in his city home because he feels that his work in the city gives his ancestral family greater respect and social capital.

Bhushan Singh and his extended family from the village have migrated to Pune and set up plant nurseries. Their business has been flourishing for multiple years. Though they miss the cultural space of their home, they are treated as aliens, do not have many local friends, and often feel lost during festivals that they have never celebrated; they are happy that their children go to English medium schools which will be an asset for the future. They send back money home and hope to return to their village sometime in the future.

Rahul is a farmer from a small village in Uttar Pradesh. He works as a gardener in many households and housing societies and takes pride in his knowledge and skills. Living in Pune for the last 20 years, he is completely bilingual and speaks the local language with ease and fluency. He is happy in Pune as the city allowed him to raise his physically disabled child with dignity.

Amla migrated to USA in the early 1980s due to the lack of educational opportunities in India. She wanted to pursue a degree in biotechnology and

THE MIGRATION CONFERENCE 2017 PROCEEDINGS

work in the field. A decade later, working and raising a family in USA was not the ideal emotional choice—but the host space allowed the family to lead a good life and follow their aspirations. Today they are back in India but still have a home in the US.

Yash is a young twenty-five-year-old electronic chip design architect at his dream company—Intel computers in USA. All his friends are Indian and they meet to celebrate Indian festivals. He misses home but intends to continue living in USA to pursue his career opportunities, which may not be the same in India.

Rakesh moved to Dubai from Kerala like many of his friends; Bina and her husband moved to Singapore; Amit and his wife moved to New Zealand; and Manu has traveled the continents and is currently pursuing his ultimate dream to own and set up his own vineyard in Italy. All of them in their conversations speak of family and friends that they have left behind and problems they face as expatriate communities in foreign lands. Nevertheless, they emphasize the opportunities that they had access to because of their migration that they feel would not have been possible in their home country.

Gloria moved from Goa to Portugal to set up a new home as a Portuguese citizen (Goa was a Portuguese colony). She is unhappy about her identity as a second-class citizen of a non-European stock, but she is happy about the social and financial gains they have achieved. Her family struggled with language and discrimination, but they presently own a large property. They know they will never have the same life as the white Portuguese population, but she hopes it will change with the family living there for the next few generations.

Lastly, even though the general perception in migration speaks of a south-north mobility, there are three case studies which speak of north-south migration—two who migrated to work and one that moved back in seek of family and social support. Nelson Sigurd from Norway enjoys the life of an expatriate in Pune. Though he misses his life including the weather and family, he is already planning his next move to Malaysia. His children study in an international school, and he has some acquaintances that he can call friends. The financial gains for him are tremendous and the losses few in comparison. He is well connected to his homeland as he manages to travel at least thrice a year to spend the festive season at home. Hans Arm, a young German IT professional is exploring the Indian social scenario to put to use his software application to help prevent rape. He misses home and the life he has left behind, but for him, this time is an investment for the future he intends to create back at home.

The Triangle of Aspiration, Opportunity and Exploitation

On analysis of the data collected, three concepts emerged prominently in the narratives of migratory experiences—aspiration, opportunity, and exploitation. Notably, these three concepts are interlinked and highly dependent on migrant agency.

Aspiration

The concept of *aspiration* stems from the inherent need of humankind to be optimistic (Jones, 2015) and consequently, achievement oriented (Bohme, 2012). Its understanding in academic literature is varied; Bohme (2012, p. 2) broadly defined aspiration as the desire to attain a certain objective in an ideal world without constraints; Gutman and Akerman (2008, p. 3) defined aspiration as "an individual's ability to identify and set goals for the future", with the need to act in order for their aspirations to be realized. Notably, aspirations can be long and short-term influences (Salikutluk, 2013, p. 11) or idealistic and realistic (Haller, 1968).

Migration as understood by Carling (2014) is guided by aspiration. In other words, migration is neither an ultimate aspiration nor the final goal, but a path to close aspiration gaps (Czaika & Vothknecht, 2012; Ray, 2003) and aspiration windows (Czaika & Vothknecht, 2012; Carling 2014; Gutman & Akerman, 2008; Hannan 1969; Mullet & Neto, 1991). Further, individuals are agents (or subjects of action) whose agency results in their capability to act, which leads to them exploring migration as a tool to realize their aspirations (King, 2012 & Castles, et al. 2014).

This paper defines aspiration as "the desire to achieve socio-cultural-economic progress and a higher level of well-being, which provides motivation to work for a better future. It is culturally determined, created in the knowledge of limitations in the social structure and leads individuals to display agency, operate on their habitus and seize opportunities in order to attain progress."

Opportunity

Opportunity is explained in the Oxford dictionary as "a time or set of circumstances that makes it possible to do something" while Merriam Webster explains it as "an amount of time or a situation in which something can be done". It appears to be a favourable juncture of circumstances which provides a good chance for advancement or progress or attainment of a goal. The need to attain goals (which can be related to the individual, family, or community); or a sense of achievement or accomplishment; or a move forward or development within the current state of existence/affairs; or the flexibility of choice and freedom to individuals to take their own paths is key to the conceptualization of opportunity.

The Capability Approach emphasizes on the freedom of choice or opportunity that individuals have—to practice and participate in activities for monetary or non-monetary growth (Sen, 2001) and individual human dignity (Nussbaum, 2011). It emphasizes on diversity in human ability "to achieve outcomes that they value and have reason to value" (Sen, 2001: 291) and thus allows individuals to identify their meaning of well-being and quality of life.

This paper defines opportunity as "encompassing a range of circumstances which open doors to socio-economic mobility and human progress, that allows an individual, family or community to move beyond the existing structural and cultural discrimination and the ensuing inequalities." As opportunity provides avenues to change circumstances and conditions—which is the determining factor of aspiration—migration as a process is understood as a key opportunity to achieve aspirations of progress, not necessarily for under-privileged but for all individuals who aspire for social mobility or a higher level of well-being.

Exploitation

A report by the Global Migration Group (2013, p. 6) defined exploitation as "the act of taking advantage of something or someone, in particular the act of taking unjust advantage of another for one's own benefit". However, the experience and perception of exploitation is subjective. While exploitation can be harmful and unfair, it can also be mutually beneficial (Powell & Zwolinski, 2012; Wertheimer 1996, 2011; Zwolinski 2009). To clarify, exploitation is said to be mutually beneficial when both interacting groups or parties gain benefits and can be described as being better off than before the interaction or exchange (Wood, 1995). Therefore, in order to determine if the experience of exploitation is positive or negative, the experiential reality of the interacting entities need to be re-examined.

This paper defines exploitation as "a series of subjective interactions between two (or more) entities where one of the entities is treated unfairly by the second entity and experiences a lack of agency at the hands of the latter. This lack of agency results in mitigated abilities to acquire capabilities and achieve a higher level of well-being."

The Triangle

The *triangle of aspiration, opportunity, and exploitation* refers to migrants experiencing a reality where these concepts are interlinked. It aims to understand how migrants perceive their realities in relation to these predominant concepts faced as a result of their migratory processes. Notably, their perception is fueled by migrant agency and is situated within three dimensions of time—past, present and future. To clarify, the past includes the immediate lived past that represents real or perceived lack of well-being or *exploitative experiences* due to multiple socio-culture realities; the present or the migrant's lived reality represents *aspiration and hope* for a better life and *opportunity for capacity building* in the future, beyond both the past and the present for self, family and future generations.

Analysis

The researchers draw conclusions from the data collected based on multiple premises stemming from the review of literature—first, aspirations are guided by individual and household agency which aim to overcome existent social structures that hinder the optimal well-being (Jones, 2015; Carling, 2014). Second, the crucial identifying element of exploitation is the absence of agency (presence of domination) within unequal social structures (Vrousalis, 2013). Third, opportunities provide avenues to change circumstances and are a determining factor of aspirations (Czaika, & Vothknecht, 2014). Lastly, individuals perceive migration to open opportunities for future well-being (Bonfanti, 2014) though the degree of perception will vary with the habitus and the five scapes as outlined by Appadurai (1990). Having stated the premises of their data analysis, the researchers have drawn the following conclusions from 25 case studies on migration.

First, migration offers opportunities to avoid and escape socio-economic traps and achieve aspirations (Czaika & Vothknecht, 2014). However, migratory decisions are highly dependent on the social structures, because aspirations are a result of the social structure in which an individual has been encultured. Aspirations are multidimensional and are realized by individuals becoming agents of change in their habitus (Gutman & Akerman, 2008; Natahn, 2005).

Second, the link between aspiration and migration is non-linear. Aspirations of migrants are constantly changing due to the experiences and environment of the migrant which are directly related to the migratory experience of the former (Carling, 2014; Gutman & Akerman, 2008). Therefore, aspirational windows and aspiration gaps of the migrant do not automatically close with migration. Rather, aspiration windows may enlarge as a result of migration if the achieved well-being is lower than expected, or if the migration has resulted in knowledge of greater opportunities which lead to higher aspirations. In other words, aspirations are a precondition, but can be a consequence of migration as well. Czaika and Vothknecht (2012) call this phenomenon the hedonic treadmill.

Third, the authors recognize that most interactions between entities (entities are interacting bodies involved in the process of migration) are set within unequal structures.. Therefore, these interactions may be viewed negatively and as exploitative in nature. Nevertheless, interaction between the entities may help migrants overcome structural inequality and existing lack of opportunity in their lives (Wood, 1995). This leads to an increase in their present capabilities which will benefit their future. This increase in capabilities for both entities over time may not have occurred in the absence of the migratory process (Bonfanti, 2014; Carling 2014). Therefore, these interactions may be viewed as positively exploitative in nature.

Fourth, migrants are often exploited and experience discrimination, low wages, and social and cultural marginality in the host space. These experiences are frequently accompanied by emotional trauma, loneliness, bleak residential spaces, and unfulfilled desires. Nevertheless, these lived experiences of the present are overlooked by migrants due to their aspiration of a better future. The labor performed by migrants is perceived as opportunities to move beyond the limitations, presented by the current socio-cultural-economic environment. In other words, the opportunities available due to the process of migration surpass the exploitation experienced by migrants.

In conclusion, structural deprivation is exploitative because it mitigates the capability and agency of the individuals and households to achieve aspired levels of wellbeing (Global Migration Group, 2013). Individuals and households with subjective *aspirations* of social, structural, and cultural mobility and optimal wellbeing seek and pursue migration as an *opportunity* to achieve aspirations. Alternatively put, migrants are important social actors who implement their agency by challenging the existent system to seek opportunity for themselves at the meso and micro level of development in the home and host space. The migratory process implants the migrant beyond the home space where they engage in labor to enhance capacity and capabilities to achieve their aspirations.

Conclusion

The interplay of agency, aspiration, and ability (capability as put forth by De Haas, 2010) of the individual within the habitus ultimately leads to either the phenomena of migration or the immobility paradox. For the former, the ability to migrate becomes an opportunity to achieve aspirations and migration consequently can increase the capacity of individuals, or their capability to achieving a higher level of well-being. The case studies do not deny the limitations and problems faced, but all the subjects emphasized that migration allowed them opportunities to build capabilities which benefitted their future. As stated by Pine (2014, p. 96), migration is "a symbol and an enactment of hope and of faith in the future". This shift in understanding can potentially help explain the constant increase in migrant mobility despite the increasing rhetoric against mobility.

This paper thus helps develop a framework to explore the experiential triangle of aspiration, opportunity and exploitation of the migrants. Their narratives aid an understanding of the subjective causes, actions undertaken, and outcomes experienced during the course of migration to objectively arrive at this triangular phenomenon which is potentially typical of migratory processes. Hence, this study adds to the real experiences of the agencies of migration; and aims to shift the narrative of migration from macro, political, and economic theorization, to the individual and community experiences. Further the research displays that fueled by their agency and aspiration for a higher level of well-being, migrants primarily view their experience of migration as opportunistic and not exploitative. Second, for migrants, migration is an opportunity to achieve aspirations which are related to attaining higher levels of subjective well-being. Lastly, and most importantly, migration is a tool and a strategy which can be used to overcome structural inequalities and build capabilities. Alternately put, the lived experiences of migrants in the context of "aspiration", "opportunity", and "exploitation" demonstrate the importance of migration as a tool for development and progress at all levels of human society.

References

Appadurai, A. (1990). Disjuncture and difference in the global cultural economy public culture spring. *Public Culture, 2*(2), 1-24.

Baxter, P., & Jack, S. (2008). Qualitative case study methodology: Study design and implementation for novice researchers. *The Qualitative Report, 13*(4), 544-559.

Bohme, M. (2012). Migration and educational aspirations: Another channel of brain gain? Germany: Kiel Institute for the World Economy. Retrieved from https://www.econstor.eu/bitstream/10419/67348/1/731585712.pdf

Bonfanti, S. (2014). Towards a migrant-centered perspective on international migration: The contribution of Amartya Sen's capability approach. *Social Work & Society, 12*(2). Retrieved from http://www.socwork.net/sws/article/view/411

Carling, J. (2014). The role of aspirations in migration. *Determinants of International Migration,* International Migration Institute, University of Oxford, Oxford, 23-25.

Carling, J. (2002). Migration in the age of involuntary immobility: Theoretical reflections and Cape Verdean experiences. *Journal of Ethnic and Migration Studies, 28*(1), 5-42.

Castles, S., Haas, H, & Miller, M. J. (2015). *The age of migration: International population movements in the modern world.* Johanneshov: MTM.

Czaika, M., & Vothknecht, M. (2012). Migration as cause and consequence of aspirations. Oxford: International Migration Institute.

Czaika, M., & Vothknecht, M. (2014). Migration and aspirations – are migrants trapped on a hedonic treadmill? *IZA Journal of Migration, 3*(1). doi:10.1186/2193-9039-3-1

De Haas, H. (2010) Migration and development: A theoretical perspective. *International Migration Review, 44*(1), 227-64.

Global Migration Group. (2013). *Exploitation and abuse of international migrants, particularly those in an irregular situation: A human rights approach.* Retrieved from http://www.globalmigrationgroup.org/system/files/uploads/news/GMG-Thematic-Paper-20131224-updated.pdf

Gutman, L., & Akerman, R. (2008). *Determinants of aspirations [wider benefits of learning research report no. 27].* Centre for Research on the Wider Benefits of Learning, Institute of Education, University of London.

Haller, A. O. (1968). On the concept of aspiration. *Rural Sociology, 33*(4), 484-487.

Hannan, D. F. (1969). Migration motives and migration differentials among Irish rural youth. *Sociologia Ruralis, 9*(3), 195–220.

Jones, O. (2015). Enabling Aspiration. In: Tyler, I. and Bennett B (2015) *What is aspiration?* London: Centre for Labour and Social Studies. pp. 4-5.

Ki-Moon, B. (2013). Secretary-general's remarks to high-level dialogue on international migration and development. Retrieved from https://www.un.org/sg/en/content/sg/ statement/2013-10-03/secretary-generals-remarks-high-level-dialogue-international

King, R. 2012. *Theories and typologies of migration: An overview and a primer* in Willy Brandt Series of Working Papers in International Migration and Ethnic Relations, Malmö: Malmö University, Malmö Institute for Studies of Immigration, Diversity and Welfare (MIM) retrieved from https://www.mah.se/upload/Forskningscentrum/ MIM/WB/WB%203.12.pdf on 30th August 2016

Lee, E.S. (1966). A theory of migration. *Demography*, *3*(1), 47-57.

Lieten, G. K. & Nieuwenhuys, O. (1989). Introduction: Survival and Emancipation. In *Women, Migrants and Tribals: Survival Strategies in Asia*. Ed. G. K. Lieten, O. Nieuwenhuys and L. Schenk-Sandbergen. New Delhi: Manohar,

Massey, D. S., Arango, J., Hugo, G., Kouaouci, A., Pellegrino, A., & Taylor, J. E. (1993). Theories of international migration: A review and appraisal. *Population and Development Review*, 431-466.

Mullet, E. & Neto, F. (1991). Intention to migrate, job opportunities and aspiration for better pay: An information integration approach. *International Journal of Psychology*, *26*(1), 95–113.

Nussbaum, M. (2011). *Creating Capabilities*. Cambridge, MA: Harvard University Press.

Pine, F. (2014). Migration as hope: Space, time, and imagining the future. *Current Anthropology*, 55(9), 95-104.

Powell, B., & Zwolinski, M. (2012). The ethical and economic case against sweatshop labor: A critical assessment. *Journal of Business Ethics*, *107*(4), 449-472.

Ray, D. (2006). Aspirations, poverty, and economic change. *Understanding Poverty*, *409421*.

Salikitluk, Z. (2013). Theoretical Explanations and Determinants of the aspiration Gap between Native and Immigrant Students, University of Mannheim working paper 150. Retrieved from http://edoc.vifapol.de/opus/volltexte/2014/5093/pdf/wp_150.pdf

Sen, A. (2001). *Development as freedom*. New York: Knopf.

Sen, A. (1993). Capability and well-being. *The Quality of Life*, 30-53.

Sjaastad, L. A. (1962). The costs and returns of human migration. *Journal of Political Economy*, *70*(5, Part 2), 80–93.

Stark, O. (1980). On the role of urban-to-rural remittances in rural development. *Journal of Development Studies*, *16*(3), 369–374.

United Nations Office for Disaster Risk Reduction. (2017). Terminology on disaster risk reduction. Retrieved from https://www.unisdr.org/we/inform/terminology

United Nations Department of Economic and Social Affairs. (2016). *International Migration Report 2015: Highlights.* Retrieved from http://www.un.org/en/development/ desa/ population/migration/publications/migrationreport/docs/MigrationReport2015_Highligh ts.pdf

Vrousalis, N. (2013). Exploitation, Vulnerability, and Social Domination. *Philosophy and Public Affairs*, *41*(2). 131–157.

Wertheimer, A. (1996). *Exploitation*. Princeton: Princeton University Press.

Wertheimer, A. (2011). *Rethinking the ethics of clinical research: Widening the lens*. Oxford: Oxford University Press

Wood, A. (1995). Exploitation. *Social Philosophy and Policy*. 12(2), 136–58.

Zainal, Z. (2007). Case study as a research method. *Jurnal Kemanusiaan, 9*, 1-6.

Zolberg, A. R., Suhrke, A., & Aguayo, S. (1989). *Escape from violence: Conflict and the refugee crisis in the developing world*. New York: Oxford University Press.

Chapter 37. Engaging Albanian Communities Abroad: One on One Mentoring

Joniada Barjaba[1] and Arben Malaj[2]

Abstract

The objective of this paper is the engagement of Albanian communities abroad (ACA) with the purpose of increasing the quality of social capital in Albania. Studying Albanian migrants abroad and their potential capacity to contribute to the development of the country is important due to the characteristics of the Albanian migration. ACA possess valuable skills, experiences, and contacts that they can transfer to individuals in Albania. Based on Albania's context, we suggest that knowledge transfer through mentoring and counseling is an important approach that should receive more attention. Besides improving the skills of colleagues in the homeland, communities abroad can offer career guidance and study abroad counseling. Hence, Albanian communities abroad can enhance country's development through the outflow of knowledge and skills. We conclude that different actors such as government, universities and entrepreneurs should build mechanisms to improve the ties between Albania and Albanian communities abroad, specifically with groups of individuals belonging to academic and business environments.

Key words: Albania, development, diaspora, mentoring.

Introduction

Currently, the Western Balkans is facing the challenge of reinforcing peace and prosperity. While peace establishment is taking place, prosperity remains a challenge. One way to achieve prosperity is through integration and economic cooperation. Also, peace establishment through prosperity is an important task, taking into account that the EU integration process has not been at its full potential. Some examples that we are referring to are: lower acceptance of EU membership, increasing migration flows, and higher geopolitical uncertainty.

Successful development of economic integration requires sustained economic growth. More specifically, Fukuyama (1995) states that good social capital is a potential determinant that contributes to economic growth in the region. In addition, many other factors such as technology, human capital, and the market have an impact of the economic performance of a country. However, according to Fukuyama, social capital has a strong impact on economic growth. Social capital resources are diverse, but in this paper we only focus on diaspora's potential role. We focus on Albania's diaspora because of several unique factors such as high migration flows, highly educated professionals, and effective cooperation with diaspora.

---

[1] Joniada Barjaba is a PhD Candidate at the University of Sussex, UK.
E-mail: J.Barjaba@sussex.ac.uk.
[2] Prof. Dr Arben Malaj is the Rector of Luarasi University in Albania.
E-mail: arben.malaj@gmail.com.

This paper is organized into five sections. Section 1 (Introduction) presents the problem and the importance of exploring this topic. Section 2 (Literature review) gives an overview of the migration and development nexus. Section 3 (Methods of data collection) discusses the methodological approach of this study. Section 4 (Engaging the Albanian communities abroad) analyzes the involvement and engagement of Albanian communities abroad in the development of the country. The final section outlines some of the recommendations in support of synergy between emigration and development and increased diaspora engagement in Albania's development.

Literature Revie

There is an agreement that migration and development are linked. However, the impact of migration on development in the origin countries continues to be an open debate. Scholars are divided between migration optimists and migration pessimists. The optimists see migration as a positive phenomenon, having a beneficial impact on the development of sending and receiving countries (Lewis, 1954; Todaro, 1969; Barjaba, 2003; Faist, 2008). Faist (2008) further explains that the positive role attributed to migrants is related to the claim that remittances, defined as the flows of money, knowledge, and universal ideas, have a positive impact on the development of the migrant sending countries. Therefore, diaspora has an important impact on the country's development. On the other hand, pessimists consider migration as a negative phenomenon undermining the sustained development of migrant sending countries (Frank, 1969; Wallerstein, 1974; Papademetriou, 1985).

In this paper, we examine the argument that Albanian communities abroad have the potential to assist in the development of Albania. One way for communities abroad to contribute is through promoting research and development and innovation. Studies show that these areas are important for the country's development (Falk, 2007; Afza & Nazir, 2007; Khan, 2015). Hence, Albania, as a developing country should focus on the advancement of scientific research and innovation through diaspora's engagement.

Methods of Data Collection

For this paper both qualitative and quantitative data were used. For gathering qualitative data, we used document review and analysis that involved examination of a variety of policies and literature in order to develop the theoretical framework of the research. Although our research was mainly based on qualitative approach, quantitative data were also collected. With the quantitative data, we were able to identify Albanian populations abroad and get country-specific information. The data mainly come from census and immigration sources available online. It is important to highlight that data and statistics on the presence and contribution of Albanian migrants abroad are limited and most of them rely on sources of the host countries. This limitation gives rise to the need for Albanian institutions to be more actively involved in collecting migration data and making this information available to researchers and policymakers.

Engaging the Albanian Communities Abroad

In 2016, the Albanian government organized the Diaspora Summit, an initiative for developing a road map for engaging the Albanian communities abroad (ACA) in national development. The summit is an important step to establish a bridge of communication and sustainable cooperation between the country and ACA. At the summit, ambitious commitments were made that will put us on the fast track toward our goal. And more importantly, Albania has the political momentum to do this. But, what are the next steps that should follow the summit?

This paper focuses on engaging the Albanian communities abroad (ACA) in the development of the country and having a clear approach to diaspora engagement. The term "Albanian communities abroad" refers to Albanian citizens abroad and any other individual that has ancestral or affinity based linkages with Albania. According to the United Nations, by the end of 2015, there were about 1.5 million Albanians residing abroad. The large-scale migratory flows have created Albanian communities in different countries around the world. The majority of them are located in Italy, Greece, and Germany. There are also growing communities in Canada, the USA, and UK.

With the growing number of Albanians around the world, there is a growing interest for them to retain their sense of identity and connection to home. They maintain ties with their homeland mainly through sending remittances. Data show that Albania's economy has benefited significantly from remittances. In 2013, remittances accounted for nearly US $1.1 billion (World Bank, 2015). Also, in 2015, remittances represented about 9.2 percent of the country's GDP (World Bank, 2016). Albania's economy has benefited significantly from remittance, yet there is a need to find new ways for ACA to contribute to Albania.

Studies show that Albanian communities abroad are becoming increasingly important for Albania's social and economic development (see, for example, Volunteer and King, 2011; King et al., 2013). While some scholars see Albanians abroad as a loss, the engagement of ACA can also be an asset for Albania. Brain drain can become brain gain and brain exchange (Stark et al., 1997; Ite, 2002). More specifically, diaspora can contribute to increasing the skills and qualifications of individuals, but also to building the capacity and performance of Albanian institutions and agencies. The Global Talent Competitiveness Index (2015–16) ranks Albania 85 out of 109 countries.

Various dimensions of the Index such as attracting people from abroad and retaining talented people show that Albania is in need for talented people. Albania needs a sustainable platform for cultivating and attracting talented Albanians from abroad.

Diaspora engagement policies consist of various initiatives such as extending rights to the diaspora members, addressing institutional capacity building, and contributing to socio-economic development. Many countries have established institutions and programs that reach out to their populations abroad. Based on Albania's context, we suggest that knowledge transfer through diaspora is an important approach that should receive more attention. Albanian communities abroad can enhance development through the outflow of knowledge and skills. Kosmo and Nedelkoska (2015) confirm that Albanian-American communities have a qualification advantage when compared to non-Albanian counterparts. Also, data shows that the most popular approaches of engaging communities abroad in the country's development are education (81%) and professional exchange (76%). Thus, Albanian communities abroad and professionals in the country should find areas of collaboration and common interest.

Scholars confirm that the majority of Albanians abroad are well educated and overqualified (Barjaba, 2015). ACA possess valuable skills, experiences, and contacts that they can transfer to individuals in Albania through mentoring and coaching. Besides improving the skills of colleagues in the homeland, ACA can offer career guidance and study abroad counseling. Albania has an increasing number of students leaving to study abroad every year. From unofficial sources, around 5,000 students go abroad to study each year.

Scholars believe that mentoring is an effective and powerful way to help different individuals progress in their lives and careers (Kuznetsov dhe Sabel, 2006). Many skilled professionals from ACA can share their knowledge and expertise with the individuals living in Albania through temporary return in the country. However, a mentoring web platform can also be built, which does not require diaspora members to be physically present in Albania. Nowadays, the technological advances can empower and increase diaspora knowledge transfer.

For increasing diasporas' engagement with their countries of origin, we can also use the experiences of other countries with high migration flows. Some of the countries that have implemented successful models in diaspora engagement are Ireland, Israel, India, and China. For example, Ireland is one of the countries offering a series of initiatives designed to engage the diaspora at the national, local, and community levels. One of Ireland's successful initiatives is the creation of the WildGeese Network, founded in 2011, with the aim of linking Irish scientists living abroad.

Similar experiences are also found in other neighboring countries such as Macedonia. "Macedonia 2025" is a highly productive model of diaspora engagement in the development of the country of origin. The model is based on the following actors: the scientific and university diaspora, the prestigious American and European universities, and the private sector of the country. This cooperation is being implemented as an initiative of the Macedonian private sector with prominent representatives of the Macedonian Diaspora in the Western countries as well as with prestigious business and management schools in the US and EU countries. These universities have established specific programs for the qualification of young managers and entrepreneurs from Macedonia, with the financial support of the Macedonian Diaspora in these countries. The initiative is organized annually by Macedonia2025, which promotes Diaspora's contribution to improving the qualifications of young leaders and managers, as well as to creating a favorable entrepreneurship environment in the country.

Based on the above discussion, we suggest that Albanian researchers residing abroad should serve as a counseling and mentoring tutor for researchers living and working in Albania. For instance, they can assist researchers in Albania in selecting a research topic that enables a better connection of scientific research with the market in the country and advice on the standards and practices of research conduct of international standards. Mentoring will help in having more well prepared academic and research staff in Albania and give the country a new standard of human and social capital.

Conclusions and Policy Recommendations

Albania needs to have an environment that encourages and supports engagement of Albanian communities abroad. We need to have a better understanding of how to facilitate cooperation among ACA and Albania. Also, the Albanian government and other related actors must have a plan that features a clear approach to diaspora engagement.

Statistical profiling of Albanian communities abroad is limited and remains a key task to be completed before trying to engage these communities. The government should consider building and implementing mechanisms to strengthen the country's ties with Albanians abroad, specifically Albanians coming from academia and business communities. Albanian universities and enterprises should lead this process.

Moreover, establishing professional networks that would connect Albanians abroad with professionals in the homeland is an important step. Networks provide information regarding job positions, facilitate mentoring, and highlight the scientific and professional achievements of overseas fellows. Lastly, policy makers should ensure that Albania is a promising country with favorable conditions for the individuals who want to engage in the development of innovation, research and entrepreneurship promotion in Albania. One way could be through initiatives and projects related to academic and entrepreneurial activities.

References

AFZA, T. & NAZIR, M. S. (2007). Economic competitiveness and human resource development: An FDI perspective. Political Economy and Social Review. 45 (2), 167-180.

BARJABA, K. (2003). Shqiptarët. Këta ikës të mëdhenj. Tiranë: Korbi.

BARJABA, K. (2015). Migrimi i Varfërisë. Akademia e Shkencave e Shqipërisë, Tirana.

FALK, M. (2007). R&D spending in the high-tech sector and economic growth. Research in Economics. 61 (3), 140–147.

FAIST, T. (2008). Migrants as transnational development agents: an inquiry into the newest round of the migration–development nexus. Population, space and place. 14 (1), p. 21-42.

FRANK, A. G. (1969). Capitalism and Underdevelopment in Latin America. New York: Monthly Review Press.

FUKUYAMA F. (1995). Trust: The social virtues and the creation of prosperity. New York: Free Press.

INSEAD (2015). The Global Talent Competitiveness Index 2015-2016. [Online] Available from: http://global-indices.insead.edu/gtci/documents/INSEAD_2015-16_Full_Book _Ebook.pdf [Accessed: 23 January 2017].

ITE, U. E. (2002). Turning brain drain into brain gain: Personal reflections on using the diaspora option. African issues. 30 (01), 76-80.

KING, R., MATA CODESAL, D., & VULLNETARI, J. (2013). Migration, development, gender and the "black box" of remittances: comparative findings from Albania and Ecuador. Comparative Migration Studies. 1 (1), p. 69-96.

KOSMO, M. & NEDELKOSKA, L. (2015). Albanian-American Diaspora Survey Report. [Online]   Available   from: http://albania.growthlab.cid.harvard.edu/files/albaniagrowthlab/files/diaspora_survey_re sults_report_v5.pdf [Accessed: 23 January 2017].

KUZNETSOV, Y. & SABEL, C. (2006). International migration of talent, diaspora networks, and development: Overview of main issues. Diaspora networks and the international migration of skills, 3-20.

KHAN, J. (2015). The Role of Research and Development in Economic Growth: A Review. Journal of Economics Bibliography. 3 (2).

LEWIS, W. A. (1954). Economic development with unlimited supplies of labour. Manchester School of Economic and Social Studies. 22 (2), p. 139-191.

PAPADEMETRIOU, D. G. (1985). Illusions and reality in international migration: Migration and development in post-World War II Greece. International Migration. 23 (2), p. 211-223.

STARK, O., HELMENSTEIN, C., & PRSKAWETZ, A. (1997). A brain gain with a brain drain. Economics letters. 55 (2), 227-234.

TODARO, M. (1969). A model of labor migration and urban unemployment in less developed countries. The American Economic Review. 59 (1), p. 138-148.

UNITED NATIONS (2015). Trends in International Migrant Stock: Migrants by Destination and Origin [Online] Available from: http://www.un.org/en/development/ desa/population/migration/data/estimates2/estimatesorigin.shtml [Accessed: 23 January 2017].

VULLNETARI, J. & KING, R. (2011). *Remittances, gender and development: Albania's society and economy in transition.* I.B.Tauris & Co Ltd, London.

WALLERSTEIN, I. (1974) The Modern World System I, Capitalist Agriculture and the Origins of the European World Economy in the Sixteenth Century. Academic Press, New York.

WORLD BANK, World Development Indicators (2015). [Online] Available from: http://databank.worldbank.org/data/reports.aspx?source=2&type=metadata&series=BX. TRF.PWKR.CD.DT [Accessed: 23 January 2017].

Chapter 38. Mobile People - Mobile Ethnographer: Thinking about Cultural Mobilities

Maria Panteleou[1]

Abstract

This presentation, starting from the field research reflections and seeking a theoretical framework for continuous mobile immigrants, suggests the approach of cultural mobilities as an analytical lens for understanding modern and multiple forms of movement. It argues that all movements are culturally constructed and should be considered within the particular social, economic and political contexts that unfold. The emergence of subjective migration experiences about mobilities (from below), in conjunction with an examination of the policies adopted by the states for these (from above) can help us to understand better how different types of movement are being promoted or are limited by states and how these overlaps are interpreted by the people themselves. It also proposes multi-sited ethnography as a methodological tool for understanding how people's cultural concepts and practices are transformed or reproduced when they move. Finally, it concludes that mobilities are simply the means to illuminate the particular aspects of each culture and the way they are expressed, interpreted and renegotiated in the contemporary, diverse spatial and temporal contexts.

Keywords: migration studies, cultural mobilities, multi-sited ethnography

In 2015, when I began studying about Albanian immigrants working seasonally in Corinth, a city near Athens (Greece), I came across two facts. Firstly, these people often visited their homeland to see their relatives, to settle family and other issues either for long or short periods of time. And secondly, although these people live in villages and in the city of the wider region of Corinth and work there seasonally, they often move to neighboring villages, even in Athens for other possible job opportunities. Looking for conceptual tools that could frame the multiple movements of my informants; I realized that the term *circular migration* attributed to them by many scholars was inaccurate (Triandafyllidou 2011, 2013; Maroukis & Gemi, 2011). We cannot refer to circular life when the point of departure and the point of arrival are not identical. When they say: "Neither here nor there, we are on both sides", we need to treat "here" and "there" as a continuous term and the researcher looking only at one side of the coin is doomed to the partiality? These questions will remain rhetorical; I have only point out the meaning of, the beginning of the journey and how to get to know the cultural mobilities that are the focus of my presentation.

The current global economic and humanitarian - refugee crisis experienced by most states proves in the most eloquent way that the world is complexly linked

---

[1] PhD Candidate, Department of Social Anthropology and History, University of the Aegean, Greece. Email: pantmaria@hotmail.com,The doctoral thesis is funded by the State Scholarships Foundation, the Act "Scholarships program for postgraduate studies of the second cycle of studies" with resources of the OP "Human Resources Development, Education and Lifelong Learning", 2014-2020 with the co-financing by the European Social Fund (ESF) and the Greek State.

and interdependent. Many people choose to migrate in search of better living conditions, desiring to escape from these new precarious transformations experienced locally in their homelands, but the processes, that allow them to move around and global interconnections also promote their immobility and exclusion (Salazar & Smart, 2011, p. iv). The perception that the movement equals freedom and conceptually as a priori positive experience ignores the fact that the same set of global power relations and rules mobilizes some people while immobilizes others (Hackl, Schwarz, Gutekunst, & Leoncini, 2016, p. 24, 27).

Looking carefully at the way in which national states participate in the formation and legalization of mobility regimes at a global level, we observe that they use national identities and nationalist ideologies as tools to justify the exclusion or inclusion of people crossing the borders of a country (Glick Schiller & Salazar, 2013, p. 195). Transnational borders are constantly being reconstructed to encourage various "desirable" types of mobility, such as entrepreneurs, tourists, migrant workers and students, and to discourage other "unwanted" types, such as irregular migrants and refugees. The nation states, in turn, following national interests, also define the basic categories of these people, imparting either the positively charged sign of the "legal" migrant, if are desired, or the negatively charged sign of the "illegal", if they are unwanted, images that eventually reflect and affect how people's mobility and immobility are understood (Salazar & Smart, 2011, p. iii).

Anthropological studies claim that the movement of people in modern globalized world is an ongoing, continuous and complex process in which migrants establish relations, create networks and connect many places beyond local and national boundaries (Withaeckx, Schrooten, & Geldof, 2015, p. 23-24). The possible routes of immigrants are often involuntary, unpredictable and affect their status (Schrooten, Salazar, & Dias, 2016, p. 1199). Some of them, like the Brazilians living in Belgium and the United Kingdom today, "living in mobility" to improve their living conditions in their home country. Hence leaving someone's home is a temporary strategy to stay in it. This practice challenges the perception that immigration leads, on the one hand, to building a new life abroad and, on the other, to integration. Their ability to remain mobile ensures and maintains their quality of life in the country of origin and highlights that the dynamics of human mobility depend to a large extent on their status in space and time and on the policies adopted by the states (legal or illegal regime) (Schrooten et al., 2016, p. 1210-1212). In order to be able to capture the experiences of migrants, we must therefore study the international context of their lives, which is constantly changing but also influenced by historical and structural factors, as well as by the perceptions prevailing in both the country of origin and the host country (Glick Schiller, Basch, & Blanc-Szanton, 1992, p. 8).

THE MIGRATION CONFERENCE 2017 PROCEEDINGS

The image of migration as a one way movement, according to which migrants "are being uprooted from their homeland and face the painful process of integration into a different society and culture" is no longer accepted by modern immigration scholars (Withaeckx et al., 2005, p. 24), because it fails to capture the experiences and strategies of people such as the Brazilians mentioned above, who either intentionally or unintentionally choose a more mobile lifestyle that is not limited to a stable ground but is part of multiple spatial networks and ephemeral interconnections (Glick Schiller & Salazar, 2013, p. 185-186).

The aim of this presentation is to propose the approach of cultural mobilities as an analytical lens for the understanding of these modern forms of movement. By placing particular emphasis on subjective immigration experiences, it is recognized that certain cultural factors shape the mobility of people (for example, who moves, how moves and for how long it moves), which in turn affects their own culture and society (Salazar, 2010a, p. 55). Understanding this interrelationship leads us to the conclusion that mobilities are a culturally constructed ideology that should be interpreted within the concrete social, economic and political structures that unfold. The establishment of a unified approach to mobility, which will examine the general category of movement or travel in their full range becomes problematic, because all forms and types of mobility are deeply penetrated by the cultural meanings of each society and therefore "mean different things, to different people, to different social contexts" (Salazar & Smart, 2011, p. ii).

The instability and fluidity that characterize the cultural mobilities of immigrants' routes lead us develop new methodological tools, far removed from the traditional fieldwork that predominantly performed in stable environments. Already in 1995, George Marcus has argued that the multi-sited ethnography can better capture the cultural phenomena, practices and meanings that people attach to them at various spatial and temporal contexts. Multi-sited ethnography, which is one solution to address these modern challenges, does not attempt to deconstruct long-term field research but to enrich it by analytically overcoming obsolete distinction between local and global (Marcus, 1995). Salazar aptly states that it is more accurate to use a relational perception of globalization and local rather than territorial. Globalization is always taking place in a particular locality, while local is reproduced and eventually transformed into global product circulation, discussions, imaginations and movements. In other words, the local do not oppose the global, but it constitutes the global and vice versa (Salazar, 2010b, p. 189).

In the era of globalization where technology, people, ideas and products circulate penetrating the borders, the multi-sited ethnography can easily follow the movement of these cultural meanings and their transformations into various spatial and temporal contexts (Marcus, 1995). The fieldwork among the mobile groups is a practice that unfolds, according to Kurotani, into scenes and spaces and not in sites or places, which exist only through active participation and presence of the informants (Kurotani, 2004, p. 210). The ethnographer is asked to follow their temporary lives and to put himself within the global system where the multiple aspects of their experiences reveal and to understand their experiences living with them and not looking at them and interpreting them "from above" (Marcus, 1995). Wulff emphasizes the importance of the ethnographer's presence in the different locations where informant's social life and practices develop, saying that if she was not able to follow the Irish dancers who studied on their trips to Japan and Washington, she would be the only one that would be left behind in the field. Think of a field researcher without field (Wulff, 2002, p. 119). Concerns on particularism of knowledge in multi-sited research which results in this context should be sidelined because even if we succeed we are constantly present in the movements of our informants, paraphrasing Geertz, we will always hear a discussion that has started before we have arrived to the field and which will continue after we have gone (Kurotani, 2004, p. 211).

Adopting the approach of cultural mobilities in migration studies, we are also wove away from the trap of methodological nationalism, the tendency to look at national states and borders as natural and given units (Wimmer & Glick Schiller, 2003, p. 576) and to define and understand as movers only those who are moving to or settling in another state (Hackl et al., 2016, p. 22). The ethnography of Duany about the mobile practices of Puerto Ricans between their island and the United States proves in practical terms that our exclusive focus on examining movements that are crossing national borders limits the way in which modern forms of movement are understood. The Puerto Ricans are not required to have travel documents (visa) during their trips, because Puerto Rico is a territory of the United States. Their movements are not transnational, but they believe that they are moving to another country, although their crossing took place not along national borders, but along cultural borders as defined by the different language, ethnicity, and gendered ideologies etc. (Duany, 2002, p. 358).

Karagiannis has aptly argued that sociology and ethnology have no room for appropriating the problems of national states. On the contrary, they need to distance themselves from their political-normative discourse of states (Karagiannis, 2006, p. 29). Examination of mobilities "from below" attempts to highlight the subjective migratory experiences, practices and strategies adopted by people during their movement, combined with the study of policies "from above" which are planning by national states to prevent, restrict or even allow the movement of people. The marriage of these two perspectives enables us to understand how different types of movement under certain conditions are bounded, promoted or constrained, and how these overlaps are experienced and interpreted by the people themselves (Hackl et al., 2016, p. 26).

In conclusion, recognizing the culturally constructed aspect of all mobilities, and following the transient lives of our informants, we can unravel from the concept of culture as rooted on a stable ground and look at it as a place of both residence and movement. The cultures themselves are the products of a widespread human movement and exchange of cultural concepts, practices and perceptions along the borders that are evaluated and interpreted differently in space and time (Salazar, 2010a, p. 55). Mobilities is simply a means of enlightening the particular aspects of each culture and of understanding how they are expressed, interpreted and renegotiated in modern, diverse spatial and temporal contexts.

References

Duany, J. (2002). Mobile Livelihoods: The sociocultural practices of circular migrants between Puerto Rico and the United States. *International Migration Review*, 36(2): 355-388.

Glick Schiller, N., Basch L., & Blanc-Szanton, C. (1992). Transnationalism: A New Analytic Framework for Understanding Migration. In N. Glick Schiller, L. Basch, & C. Blanc-Szanton (Eds.), *Towards a transnational perspective on migration: Race, class, ethnicity and nationalism reconsider* (pp. 1-24). New York: New York Academy of Sciences.

Glick Schiller, N., & Salazar, N. B. (2013). Regimes of Mobility across the Globe. *Journal of Ethnic and Migration Studies*, 39(2): 183-200.

Hackl, A., Schwarz J., Gutekunst S. M., & Leoncini S. (2016). Bounded mobilities: An introduction. In M. Gutekunst, A. Hackl, S. Leoncini, J. S. Schwarz., & I. Götz (Eds.), *Bounded mobilities: Ethnographies perspectives on social hierarchies and global inequalities* (pp. 19-34). Bielefeld: transcript Verlag.

Karagiannis, V. (2006). Migration- transnationality- mobility: Observations on transnational migration research. *Modern issues,* 92, 23-30. (in Greek).

Kurotani, S. (2004). Multi-sited Transnational Ethnography and the Shifting Construction of Fieldwork. In L. Hume & J. Mulcock (Eds.), *Anthropologists in the field: Case in participant observation* (pp. 201-215). New York: Columbia University Press.

Marcus, G. (1995). Ethnography in/of the world System: The emergence of multi-sited ethnography. *Annual Review of Anthropology,* 24, 95-117.

Maroukis, T., & Gemi, E. (2011). *Circular migration between Albania and Greece: A case study.* Metoikos Project. Europe European University Institute: Robert Schuman Centre for Advanced Studies. Retrieved from https://www.eui.eu/Projects/METOIKOS/Documents/CaseStudies/METOIKOSCaseStudyGreeceAlbania.pdf

Salazar, N. B. (2010a). Towards an anthropology of cultural mobilities. *Crossings: Journal of Migration and Culture,* 1, 53-68.

Salazar, N. B. (2010b). From local to global (and back): Towards glocal ethnographies of cultural tourism. In: G. Richards & W. Munsters (Eds.), *Cultural tourism research methods* (pp. 188-198). Wallingford, Oxfordshire, UK: CABI.

Salazar, N. B., & Smart, A. (2011). Anthropological Takes on (Im)mobility. *Identities: Global Studies in Culture and Power,* 18, i–ix.

Schrooten, M., Salazar N. B., & Dias, G. (2016). Living in mobility: trajectories of Brazilians in Belgium and the UK. *Journal of Ethnic and Migration Studies*, 42(7): 1199-1215.

Triandafyllidou, A. (2011). *Circular migration and integration - A short guide to policy makers*. Metoikos Project. European University Institute: Robert Schuman Centre for Advanced Studies. Retrieved from https://www.eui.eu/Projects/METOIKOS/Documents/GuidePolicyMakers/METOIKOS GuideforPolicyMakersGREEK.pdf (in Greek)

Triandafyllidou, A. (2013). Circular migration at the periphery of Europe: choice, opportunity or necessity? In A. Triandafyllidou (Eds.), *Circular migration between Europe and its neighborhood: Choice or necessity?* (pp. 212-236). Oxford: Oxford University Press.

Withaeckx, S., Schrooten M., & Geldof, D. (2015). Living across borders: The everyday experiences of Moroccan and Brazilian transmigrants in Belgium. *Crossings: Journal of Migration and Culture,* 6(1): 23–40.

Wimmer, A., & Glick Schiller N. (2003). Methodological Nationalism, the Social Sciences, and the Study of Migration: An Essay in Historical Epistemology. *International Migration Review,* 37(3): 576-610.

Wulff, H. (2002). Yo-Yo fieldwork: Mobility and time in a multi-local study of dance in Ireland. *Anthropological Journal on European Cultures, Shifting Grounds: Experiments in Doing Ethnography,* 11, 117-136.

Chapter 39. Breaking the Myth of Universality in National Health Care Systems: Undocumented Immigrants and Asylum Seekers' Health Care Access in Spain and Sweden, 2011-2015

Daniela Cepeda Cuadrado[1], Camila Rodrigues Vieira[2]

Abstract

Between 2011 and 2015, the Spanish and Swedish national health care systems did not grant comprehensive health care access to asylum seekers and undocumented immigrants. In these systems, regional health authorities were liable for the management and provision of health care, as they were better prepared to respond to the health needs of local communities. However, decentralization did not foment universal access. In Spain and Sweden, regions responded differently to the provision of health care access for these immigrant groups. Whereas Madrid and Västra Götaland followed the restrictive national guidelines on health care access for these targeted groups, Catalonia and Stockholm made efforts, although insufficient, to provide better assistance to their health care needs. Thus, Spain and Sweden failed to fulfill international and European legal obligations on health for immigrants. To guarantee health care access for asylum seekers and undocumented immigrants, better coordination between national and regional health authorities is essential. The application of Human Rights Based Approach (HRBA) tools can serve this purpose.

Keywords: asylum seekers, health care access, integration, migrant health policies, undocumented immigrants

Introduction

Part of the challenge brought on by recent immigration patterns has been the need for European countries to fulfill international and regional obligations related to securing the health of all their citizens and foreign residents. Based on the Spanish and Swedish health care policies between 2011 and 2015, this paper responds to the question: *to what extent have decentralized universal health care systems fostered asylum seekers and undocumented immigrants' access to health care?* This study follows a method of agreement to compare the Spanish and Swedish National Health care Systems (NHSs). In addition, it conducts within-case studies at the regional level, analyzing the Spanish autonomous communities (CCAAs – Spanish acronym) Madrid and Barcelona as well as the Swedish counties Stockholm and Västra Götaland. With this analysis, the paper connects two theoretical strands: the nexus between immigration and health care access, and the effects of decentralization on health care access.

---

[1] Daniela Cepeda Cuadrado is a Master of Public Policy Graduate from the Hertie School of Governance and Associate Research Fellow at the United Nations System Staff College – Knowledge Centre for Sustainable Development, Martin-Luther-King-Strasse 8, 53175 Bonn. E-mail: d.cepeda@unssc.org

[2] Camila Rodrigues Vieira is a Master of Public Policy Graduate from the Hertie School of Governance and Project Manager in Social Finance, Friedrichstrasse 180, 11017 Berlin. E-mail: c.rodrigues-vieira@mpp.hertie-school.org

This paper firstly explains the relevance of conducting this research project. Secondly, it provides literature reviews on the nexus between immigration and health care access, as well as on the decentralization of health care systems. Thirdly, it outlines this paper's research design. Fourthly, it summarizes the study's findings in Spain and Sweden, both at the national and regional levels. Finally, it concludes with the authors' recommendations.

Relevance

Studies on asylum seekers and undocumented immigrants' health care access cane be useful to assess whether countries fulfill their human rights obligations on health. Internationally, Spain and Sweden have recognized the right to the highest attainable health through numerous instruments, including ratification of the International Covenant on Economic, Social and Cultural Rights (ESCR) (1966), the 1951 Convention relating to the Status of Refugees and the 1967 Protocol; as well as the endorsement of the World Health Organization's constitution (WHO, 1946). In 2007, the WHO's (2005) International Health Regulations (IHR) came into force to respond to acute public health risks that have the potential to cross borders and threaten people worldwide. At the European level, Spain and Sweden are bounded by the European Committee of Social Rights, which establishes that everyone should enjoy health care access (Pace, 2011, p. 60). Spain and Sweden are also part of the 2007 Bratislava Declaration on Health, Human Rights and Migration, which recognizes that further work was needed "towards eliminating the practical obstacles and barriers to the enjoyment of any access to appropriate protection of health of all people on the move, including those in an irregular situation as far as emergency health care is concerned". Moreover, they have endorsed both the Lisbon Treaty, which allows the EU to share competence with Member States in the areas of common public health safety concerns, and the Treaty on European Union, which states that the European Commission proposals should be changed if they have adverse effects on the health of its populations (Pace, 2011, p. 62)

Moreover, this study's findings can inform the Spanish and Swedish governments about their policy gaps with regard to the protection and endorsement of undocumented immigrants and asylum seekers' health care rights. Healthy immigrants are more likely to undertake education and employment opportunities and as such be more empowered to integrate and contribute in their host countries (Norredam, 2008). Otherwise limited access to health care may increase the probability of countries facing a higher burden of untreated communicable and non-communicable diseases (WHO, 2008). This study's policy recommendations can help Spain and Sweden avoid the economic and social burdens created by non-access.

Theoretical Approach

Health care is one of the core fields of social policy (Beckfield, Olafsdottir, & Sosnaud, 2013; Cuadra, 2012), yet there is very little public health research on how different population groups fare in different health care systems (Bambra, 2007; Kawiorska, 2015). Moreover, a review of the most relevant literature shows that, to this date, there is not a comprehensive academic study focused on how the decentralization of health care systems can have an impact on different immigrant groups' access to health care.

Literature on Immigrants' Access to Health Care

Many scholars have analyzed government policy approaches regarding immigrants' entitlement and access to health care systems (Cuadra, 2012; European Migration Network, 2014; Mladovsky, 2009; Norredam & Krasnik, 2011; Norredam, 2008). Their focus has primarily been on barriers shaping access and utilization of health care services by immigrants. In terms of formal barriers, studies have referred to legal frameworks and financial factors. With regard to informal barriers, scholars have concentrated on language constraints, health care personnel attitudes towards migrants, cultural differences, trauma and newness (Norredam & Krasnik, 2011; Norredam, 2008). While these studies have generally focused on explaining the barriers, they have provided little insight on what causes those barriers in the first place.

To expand on this literature, this paper takes the decentralization of universal health care systems as the mediating factor shaping the causal relationship between formal/informal barriers and immigrant groups' access to health care.

Literature on the Nexus between Decentralization and Equal Access to Health Care

A common concern in the health policy literature is the effects of decentralization on equitable access to health services. Those who support decentralized health care systems argue that "local decision makers have greater knowledge of the health needs of their populations and of local conditions that affect the production of health care than national policymakers" (Jiménez-Rubio & Smith, 2005, p. 11).

Contrastingly, opponents of decentralization consider that the devolution of power may increase the power of local lobbies, who might in turn push their agenda in service delivery at the expense of other groups' access (Antón, Fernández-Macías, Muños de Bustillo, & Rivera, 2014). Furthermore, decentralization can hinder the development of the welfare state, in this case health care services, by including more veto points to the decision-making process (Obinger, Leibfried, & Castles, 2005).

To this date, there is no sufficient empirical evidence that strongly supports one view over the other – that is, whether that decentralization actually hinders or facilitates health care access (Galiani & Schargrodsky, 2002; p. 275). However, what is also lacking from this scholarly literature is a consideration of how decentralization can influence different population groups' access to public services. This paper seeks to contribute to this gap by conducting research on asylum seekers and undocumented immigrants' access to health care in NHSs.

Research design

This paper follows a method of agreement (Hancké, 2009; Heijden, 2014) to compare the Spanish and Swedish NHSs between 2011 and 2015. To make cross-country comparisons, this paper identifies policies and programs, and assesses whether they weaken or strengthen formal and informal barriers faced by asylum seekers and undocumented immigrants when trying to access health care services. It also conducts the same level of analysis at the regional level, carrying out within-case studies of the most-populated immigrant regions: Madrid, Barcelona, Stockholm and Västra Götaland (Instituto Nacional de Estadistica, n.d.). The purpose is to identify any discrepancy between the regional and national approaches.

Spain and Sweden have been selected for having universal and decentralized health systems. They fall under the OECD's category of NHS, which includes countries with health care systems characterized by universal coverage, funding out of general taxation, and public ownership/control of health care delivery (Burau, Blank, & Pavolini, 2015). Spain and Sweden also follow a decentralized governance approach, on the basis that this may help ensure everybody's health care access (Burau et al., 2015; Anell, Glenngård & Merkur, 2012; Ley 16/2003).

Beyond this, these countries differ in many important aspects related to immigrants. To begin with, Spain and Sweden are characterized by different histories of immigration. In Spain, the socio-demographic reality started to change in the early 2000s (Gea-Sánchez et al., 2017). Contrastingly, Sweden's demographic profile started changing from the second half of the last century (Fredlund-Blomst, 2014; Westin, 2006).

The composition of immigration is also different in these two countries. Spain has dealt with large numbers of undocumented immigrants, estimated to be between 400,000 to 1.3 million (Gea-Sánchez et al., 2017), whereas the number of asylum seeker applications in Spain has remained one of the lowest in Europe (Eurostat, 2017a). In contrast, Swedish' undocumented immigration is quite low (Kraler & Reichel, 2009) while asylum seeker applications are high, increasing from 29,650 in 2011 to 162,350 in 2015 (Eurostat, 2017a).

Furthermore, these countries also express different levels of acceptance to the recent flow of asylum seekers. Based on Eurostat data, the proportion of asylum seekers who were granted a positive decision to stay (either refugee status, subsidiary protection status, authorization to stay for humanitarian reasons or temporary protection) was much larger in Sweden than Spain between 2011 and 2015 (See Figure 1). With regard to undocumented immigrants, the Swedish and Spanish' approaches have also been at opposite spectrums. Sweden has had only one regularization program in 2005 (Cuadra, 2010). Spain by comparison has engaged in six regularization initiatives in 1985, 1991, 1996, 2000, 2001 and 2005 (Finotelli & Arango, 2011, p. 503).

Figure 1. Proportion of positive decisions based on the total number of asylum applications in EU-28, 2011-2015

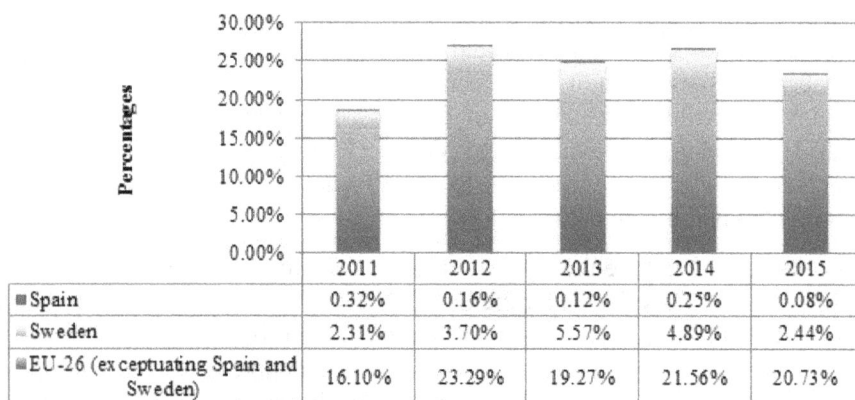

	2011	2012	2013	2014	2015
▪ Spain	0.32%	0.16%	0.12%	0.25%	0.08%
▪ Sweden	2.31%	3.70%	5.57%	4.89%	2.44%
▪ EU-26 (exceptuating Spain and Sweden)	16.10%	23.29%	19.27%	21.56%	20.73%

Source: Eurostat (2017a, 2017b), own estimates.

Findings

Between 2011 and 2015, the Spanish and Swedish national governments provided limited health care access for asylum seekers and undocumented immigrants, thus not complying with their international and EU obligations. Their national policies set a minimum threshold for health protection of asylum seekers and undocumented immigrants at the regional level. Out of all the four regions studies, only CCAA Catalonia deviated from national legal standards and made efforts to extend undocumented immigrants' rights to health care. Regarding informal barriers, different national and regional efforts were identified. While at the national level Madrid had a much more comprehensive approach to informal barriers through its national integration plan, at the regional level Swedish counties had more programs in place to address information gaps, language constraints and trainings for health care professionals. Nevertheless, those efforts remained insufficient.

National Similarities

Spain and Sweden provided asylum seekers and undocumented immigrants with access to care only in emergency scenarios. In Spain, the Law 12/2009 determined that asylum seekers had access to health care "only when in need" (Ley 12/2009); while undocumented immigrants could only access emergency care since the enactment of the Royal Decree-law 16/2012 (Real Decreto-ley 16/2012). Likewise, the Health Care Acts of 2008 and 2013 in Sweden established that asylum seekers and undocumented immigrants could only access emergency care (Anell, Glenngård & Merkur, 2012).

Additionally, Spain and Sweden did not fulfill all international and EU obligations on health, such as the ESCR (1966), CERD (1965), the 1951 Convention relating to the Status of Refugees and the 1967 Protocol, the WHO's constitution (1946), and the premises established by the European Committee of Social Rights.

Instead, they focused their attention on public health security obligations, as stipulated by the Bratislava Declaration (Council of Europe, 2007) and the IHR (2005). In Spain, the government was allowed by law to refuse any asylum application on the grounds of health risk and national security (Ley 12/2009). In Sweden, the Health Care Acts of 2008 and 2013 as well as their attached regulations emphasized the use of health assessments to detect communicable diseases that could pose public health risks (Anell, Glenngård & Merkur, 2012). Their focus on public health risks suggests that Spain and Sweden have neglected their obligation to provide access to specialized care for asylum seekers and undocumented immigrants.

National Differences

At the national level, Spain and Sweden differ in their strategies to address informal barriers to health care cassess. Spain enacted a national integration plan called PECI, which tackled informational and language barriers, as well as set up training programs for health care professionals working in diversity-based contexts (Abascal, 2011). Contrastingly, the Swedish national government's integration plans only focused on employment opportunities (Engkvist et al., 2014) and did not address informal barriers to health care access. Sweden only addressed language and informational barriers through health assessments as prescribed by the 2008 and the 2013 Health Care Acts (Lagen SFS 2008:344; 2013:412).

Regional Similarities

In Spain, CCAA Catalonia, and to a lower extent Madrid, shared a concern for the information-related challenges affecting asylum seekers and undocumented immigrants. CCAA Catalonia allocated funding to the development of a telephone service to improve the health assistance and created informational booklets with the contact details of the health organizations in the region (Generalitat de Catalunya, n.d.), while CCAA Madrid provided information on the functioning of the NHS at local reception centers (Área de Gobierno de Familia y Servicios Sociales, 2009).

In Sweden, Stockholm and Västra Götaland offered the same health care entitlements stipulated by national laws – i.e. emergency care, maternity-related care, and one free health assessment (Ahlberg et al., 2015). Additionally, both counties addressed informal barriers related to information, language, and training for health care professionals working in diversity-based contexts (1177.se, n.d.). However, Stockholm offered more comprehensive information to asylum seekers and undocumented immigrants, as well as trainings for health care professionals in both health promotion and disease prevention.

Regional Differences

The Spanish CCAAs and the Swedish counties mainly differed on their approaches to the national legal frameworks. In Spain, while CCAA Madrid followed the changes brought by the Royal Decree-law 16/2012, which abolished undocumented immigrants' access to the NHS, CCAA Catalonia circumvented that national policy by ensuring that undocumented immigrants were still entitled to primary and specialized care in the region (AMIC, 2012: CatSalut Instrucció 10/2012; Oficina Municipal de Información y Orientación para la integración de Inmigrantes, n.d.).

In Sweden, the Health Care Acts of 2008 and 2013 vaguely described the benchmarks to be used for granting asylum seekers and undocumented immigrants with health care access. In those policies, entitlements were defined as "care that cannot wait" (Asylum Information Database, 2015). Thus, regional governments had room to make different interpretations of the law. In Stockholm, "care that cannot wait" meant access to specialized services on chronic diseases and mental health care (Stockholm County Hospital, n.d.-a); whereas in Västra Götaland, it only included rehabilitation (Västra Götalandsregionen, n.d.-a; n.d-b).

Overall, Spain and Sweden provided the bare minimum health rights protection to asylum seekers and undocumented immigrants at national and regional levels between 2011 and 2015 (see Table 1 in Appendix). National frameworks limited health care access to emergency scenarios. These legal restrictions were also sustained by regional authorities, except by Catalonia. In Sweden, legal restrictions acquired distinct nuances in each region due to vague national benchmarks for health care entitlement. Regarding informal barriers, distinct regional efforts were identified. Nevertheless, those efforts remained insufficient. For instance, regions provided information on health care organizations, but did not necessarily inform asylum seekers and undocumented immigrants on their health care rights.

Together, the minimum national standards and the insufficient regional responses to the health care access for asylum seekers and undocumented immigrants point to the incoherent functioning of the Spanish and Swedish NHSs. While decentralization did not lead to these countries' compliance to human rights obligations, the authors argue that a human rights-based approach (HRBA) to health policies can improve and help their decentralized NHSs to ensure universal access.

Policy recommendations

The implementation of HRBA tools represents a real opportunity for Spain and Sweden to proactively engage in translating human-rights principles into practice. This research identified three main reasons for the application of this approach.

Firstly, HRBA can assist Spain and Sweden in ensuring an optimal and cohesive NHS structure, while also guaranteeing the fulfillment of international and EU obligations in health. Moreover, HRBA enable better risk management and guarantee the legitimacy of their universal NHSs (Victorian Equal Opportunity & Human Rights Commission, 2008).

Secondly, HRBA is relevant where local lobbies and political parties follow their own agendas and do not consider the needs of minority communities (International Council on Human Rights Policy, 2002). Authorities might have ignored asylum seekers and undocumented immigrants' needs because they are not part of their electoral constituency (Ahokas, 2010, p. 18). For example, in Spain the extent to which the Royal Decree Law 16/2012 was implemented partly depended on the political party in power at the CCAA level (Moreno Fuentes & de Figueiredo Ferreira, 2013). Thus, HRBA would help integrate the interests of minority communities who usually have limited participation in the decision-making processes that directly affect them.

Thirdly, HRBA might strengthen participation of vulnerable communities. The participation of asylum seekers and undocumented immigrants in the enactment of health care policies could contribute to the attainment of health goals at the regional level (International Council on Human Rights Policy, 2002). Additionally, HRBA provides a list of expected duties to be realized by authorities. Through those universal benchmarks, policies and practices can be measured more effectively (Victorian Equal Opportunity & Human Rights Commission, 2008). Finally, HRBA reinforces participation by sustaining the principle of non-discrimination as well as advocating tolerance of difference (International Council on Human Rights Policy, 2002).

HRBA has a role to play in fostering asylum seekers and undocumented immigrants' health care access in the Spanish and Swedish NHSs. This paper proposes that the inter-territorial bodies in charge of coordinating national and regional policies – that is, the Spanish the Inter-Territorial Council of the National Health System (CISNS - Spanish acronym) and the Swedish Association of Local Authorities and Regions (SALAR) implement HRBA tools with a focus on migrant health.

In Spain, the CISNS brings together representatives from the Ministry of Health and regional health authorities (Ministerio de Sanidad, Servicios Sociales e Igualdad, n.d.). To fulfill its coordinating role, the CISNS utilizes a Plenary, a Delegated Commission, Technical Commissions and Working Groups. The Plenary congregates the highest-raking government representatives of the NHS; the Delegated Commission is integrated by representatives of the General Secretary of Health, the CCAAs and cities with autonomous statuses, as well as the Ministry of Health; and the Technical Commission and Working Groups develop their own agendas according to the specific tasks given by the CISNS (Ministerio-de-Sanidad-Servicios-Sociales-e-Igualdad, n.d.). Additionally, the CISNS is linked to the Consultative Committee, which formulates proposals for the well-functioning of the NHS. With representatives of business organizations and labor unions joining representatives of the national, CCAA and local administrations, the Consultative Committee ensures that the CISNS considers views from non-governmental stakeholders (Ministerio de Sanidad, Servicios Sociales e Igualdad, n.d.). Nevertheless, the absence of NGOs advocating for human rights and/or immigrant rights is indicative of the CISNS's limited consideration of non-citizens' health care rights.

In Sweden, SALAR represents the interests of governments, providers, and professionals. It brings together regional authorities, health care providers and professionals, to set collective agreements with the parliament, the central government, the NBHW, and other executive agencies on health issues. To fulfill its coordinating role, the SALAR operates with a Congress, a Board, Delegations on Health Care and on Negotiations, and a Committee on Primary Care (Sveriges Kommuner och Landsting, n.d.). The Congress formulates the guidelines for SALAR' operations; the Board is responsible for SALAR's political work; the Delegation on Health Care is focused on specialized care; the Delegation on Negotiations sets agreements between health employers and employees; and the Committee on Primary Care promotes the dialogue between actors to stimulate cooperation and disease prevention. Additionally, SALAR's Steering Committee promotes multi-stakeholder dialogues involving government as well non-government actors (Sveriges Kommuner och Landsting, n.d.). However, it is not specified how integrated the work of the Steering Committee, the Delegation on Health Care and the Committee of

Primary Care is, and whether those bodies have embraced the concerns of NGOs advocating for human rights and immigrants' rights in national policies. Moreover, it is unclear how SALAR and NBHW together have seriously considered immigrants' health care rights.

CISNS and SALAR's structures fail to consider immigrant groups' health care rights and address their health care needs. In view of this, this paper proposes the following HRBA tools:

1. Ensure participation from multiple stakeholders

It is essential to create synergies across all government sectors related to immigrants' health policies. In the case of Spain, CISNS does not include the Ministry of Interior, which is responsible for managing the health conditions of immigrants in detention centers (Real Decreto 162/2014), and the Secretary of Immigration and Emigration under the Ministry of Employment, which is tasked to develop the PECI (Zuppiroli, 2014). Additionally, the consultative body should include NGOs advocating for immigrants' rights (Ministerio de Sanidad, Servicios Sociales e Igualdad, n.d.).

In Sweden, SALAR could simultaneously cooperate with the representatives of NBHW, Parliament, and NGOs advocating for immigrant's health care rights. This could ensure the consideration of human rights standards in all health policy decisions. SALAR could also promote synergies between those bodies and the Ministry of Employment, which is responsible for enacting integration plans (Engkvist et al. 2014).

2. Create a working group focused on immigrants' health care access

This working group should act as a platform for actors to share knowledge on how every member is approaching asylum seekers and undocumented immigrants' health care rights, and have a monitoring and reviewing function to ensure actors' compliance with human rights. The working group could develop indicators and define outcomes by assessing regional approaches, obtaining information from reports made by pro-immigrant health-rights NGOs and government bodies. This working group should involve national and regional health government authorities, as well as representatives of health professional associations, NGOs pro-immigrant rights, and other governmental bodies connected to the issue of migration, such as the Ministry of Interior in Spain, and the Ministries of Employment in Spain and Sweden.

While the CISNS and SALAR would have no power to issue codes of conduct, they do have a role in highlighting a more rigorous attention to the fulfillment of human rights in health. They could adopt assessment criteria, such as selecting questions for discussions in meetings occurring at least twice a year. Working groups could use the policy assessment' questions elaborated by the UNFPA/ Harvard School of Public Health, which focus on human rights principles of participation, non-discrimination, rule of law, and accountability (United Nations Population Fund & Harvard School of Public Health, 2010). The compilation of the results of those assessments and monitoring exercises, as well as their further disclosure of findings to the wider society could guarantee the transparency of the policy-making processes and foster cohesion in the decentralized NHSs' structures.

1. Provide training on HRBA

These trainings should be focused on asylum seekers and undocumented immigrations' health care access, and target members of the working group. The expectation is that the lessons learned by participants are passed on the entire NHSs' structures.

For example, a two-day training could start with an introduction to human rights and a presentation on the key aspects of HRBA – e.g. non-discrimination and accountability. On the second day, a discussion on cross-cultural issues in access of asylum seekers and undocumented immigrants to health care services could be promoted. In the medium and long run, these cross-cultural trainings could contribute to the removal of legal barriers affecting the enjoyment of health care rights, as well as the informal barriers affecting asylum seekers and undocumented immigrants' health care access.

In Spain and Sweden, the decentralized governance of NHSs did not foster asylum seekers and undocumented immigrants' access to health care between 2011 and 2015. The reason is that decentralization could not guarantee a cohesive health system structure. However, it is through their decentralized structures that a commitment to human rights obligation can be enabled. Therefore, the adoption of HRBA tools by bodies responsible for coordinating national and regional efforts can foster the protection of asylum seekers and undocumented immigrants' health care rights. This paper proposes the use of three HRBA tools: broader multi-stakeholder participation; creation of working groups focused on immigrants' health care access, and HRBA trainings.

References

Abascal, J. (2011). *Plan estrategico ciudadania e integracion 2011-2014*. Madrid, Spain: Ministerio de Trabajo e Inmigración.

Ahlberg, B. M., Ahlm, C., Hurtig, A. K., Nkulu Kalengayi, F. K. & Nordstrand, A (2015). Perspectives and experiences of new migrants on health screening in Sweden. *BMC Health Services Research, 16*, 14. doi:10.1186/s12913-015-1218-0

Ahokas, L. (2010). Promoting immigrants' democratic participation and integration. Tampere, Finland: EPACE Project.

Anell, A., Glenngård, A. H., & Merkur, S. (2012). Sweden: Health system review. *Health Systems in Transition, 14*(5), 1-159. Retrieved from http://www.euro.who.int/__data/assets/pdf_file/0008/164096/e96455.pdf

Antón, J. I., Fernández Macías, E., Muños de Bustillo, R., & Rivera, J. (2014). Effects of health care decentralization in Spain from a citizens' perspective. *European Journal of Health Economics*, *15*(4), 411–431. doi:10.1007/s10198-013-0485-0

Área de Gobierno de Familia y Servicios Sociales (2009). II Plan Madrid de Convivencia Social e Intercultural. Madrid, Spain: Author.

Associació d'Ajuda Mútua d'Immigrants a Catalunya [AMIC]. (2012). *Acceso a la asistencia sanitaria en Cataluña para los extranjeros empadronados [Access to health care for registered foreigners in Catalonia]* [Brochure]. (n.p.): Author.

Asylum Information Database (2015). *Country report: Sweden*. Retrieved from http://www.ecre.org/wp-content/uploads/2016/06/aida_se_update.iii_.pdf

Bambra, C. (2007). Going beyond the three worlds of welfare capitalism: Regime theory and public health research. *Journal of Epidemiology and Community Health*, *61*(12), 1098–1102. doi:10.1136/jech.2007.064295

Beckfield, J., Olafsdottir, S., & Sosnaud, B. (2013). Health care systems in comparative perspective: Classification, convergence, institutions, inequalities, and five missed turns. *Annual Review of Sociology*, *39*, 127–146. doi:10.1146/annurev-soc-071312-145609

Burau, V., Blank, R. H., & Pavolini, E. (2015). Typologies of healthcare systems and policies. In E. Kuhlmann, R. H. Blank, I. L. Bourgeault, & C. Wendt (Eds.), *The palgrave international handbook of healthcare policy and governance* (101–115). Basingstoke, United Kingdom: Palgrave Macmillan.

Burström, L, Engström, M. L., Thulesius, H. & Starrin, B. (2013). Waiting management at the emergency department – a grounded theory study. *BMC Health Services Research, 13*(1), 95. doi:10.1186/1472-6963-13-95

CatSalut. Instrucció 10/2012, 30 d'agost, Accés a l'assistència sanitària de cobertura pública del CatSalut als ciutadans estrangers empadronats a Catalunya que no tenen la condició d'assegurats o beneficiaris del Sistema Nacional de Salut, 2012.

Convention Relating to the Status of Refugees, 28 July 1951, 189 UNTS 137 (entered into force 22 April 1954).

Council of Europe (2007). Bratislava declaration on health, human rights and migration. Retrieved from: http://www.coe.int/t/dc/files/ministerial_conferences/2007_health/20071123_declaratio n_en.asp

Cuadra, C. B. (2010). *Policies on health care for undocumented migrants in EU27. Country report - Sweden*. Malmö, Sweden: NowHereland.

Cuadra, C. B. (2012). Right of access to health care for undocumented migrants in EU: A comparative study of national policies. *European Journal of Public Health*, *22*(2), 267 271. doi:10.1093/eurpub/ckr049

Engkvist, R., Karlsson, S., Johansson, M., Moberg, U. & Rauhut, D. (2014). *Baseline study on diversity and urban policies in Stockholm County*. Retrieved from https://icecproject.files.wordpress.com/2014/09/icec_sto_baseline_study_22092014.pdf

European Migration Network. (2014). *Migrant access to social security and healthcare: policies and practices*. (n.p.): European Commission.

Eurostat (2017a). Asylum and first time asylum applicants by citizenship, age and sex Annual aggregated data (rounded). Retrieved from http://appsso.eurostat.ec.europa.eu/nui/submitViewTableAction.do Date extraction 7 March 2017 13:37:15.

Eurostat (2017b). First instance decisions on applications by citizenship, age and sex Annual aggregated data (rounded). Retrieved from http://appsso.eurostat.ec.europa.eu/nui/show.do?dataset=migr_asydcfsta&lang=en Date extraction 8 March 2017 13:10:20.

Finotelli, C., & Arango, J. (2011). Regularisation of unauthorised immigrants in Italy and Spain: determinants and effects. *Documents d'Anàlisi Geogràfica*, *57*(3), 495–515.

Fredlund-Blomst, S. (2014). Assessing immigrant integration in Sweden after the May 2013 riots. Retrieved from: http://www.migrationpolicy.org/article/assessing-immigrant-integration-sweden-after-may-2013-riots

Galiani, S., & Schargrodsky, E. (2002). Evaluating the impact of school decentralization on educational quality. *Economia*, *2*(2), 275–314. doi:10.1353/eco.2002.0004

Gea-Sánchez, M., Alconada-Romero, Á., Briones-Vozmediano, E., Pastells, R., Gastaldo, D., & Molina, F. (2017). Undocumented immigrant women in Spain: A scoping review on access to and utilization of health and social services. *Journal of Immigrant Minority Health*, *19*, 109–204. doi:10.1007/s10903-016-0356-8

Generalitat de Catalunya. (n.d.). Serveis específics [Specific Services]. Retrieved from http://canalsalut.gencat.cat/ca/salut-a-z/i/immigracio-i-salut/immigracio-i-salut/recursos-per-a-professionals/serveis-especifics/

Hancké, B. (2009). *Intelligent research design: A guide for beginning researchers in the social sciences*. Oxford, United Kingdom: Oxford University Press.

Heijden, J. Van Der. (2014). Selecting cases and unferential types in comparative public policy research. In I. Engeli & C. R. Allison (Eds.), *Comparative Policy Srudies* (35–56). Basingstoke, United Kingdom: Palgrave Macmillan.

Instituto Nacional de Estadística (n.d.). Flujo de inmigración procedente del extranjero por comunidad autónoma, año, sexo y edad [Flow of immigration from abroad by autonomous community, year, sex and age]. Retrieved from http://www.ine.es/jaxi/Tabla.htm?path=/t20/p277/prov/e01/l0/&file=02001.px&L=0 Date extraction 14 January 2017 14:25:10.

International Council on Human Rights Policy (2002). Local rule: Decentralization and human rights. Versoix, Switzerland: Author.

International Covenant of Economic, Social and Cultural Rights, 16 December 1966, 993 UNTS 3 (entered into force 3 January 1976) [*ICESCR*].

Jiménez-Rubio, D., & Smith, P. (2005). *Decentralisation of health care and its impact on health outcomes*. York, United Kingdom: University of York.

Kawiorska, D. (2015). *Healthcare in the light of the concept of welfare state regimes - comparative analysis of EU MS* (*Institute of Economic Research Working Papers* - No. 58). Toruń, Poland: Institute of Economic Research and Polish Economic Society Branch.

Kraler, A., & Reichel, D. (2009). Sweden. In M. Baldwin-Edwards & A. Kraler (Eds.), *REGINE - Regularizations in Europe* (138-141). Amsterdam, Netherlands: Amsterdam University Press.

Lagen SFS 2008: 344 om hälso- och sjukvård åt asylsökande m.fl. (Svenk författningssamling [SFS] 2008:344) (Swed.).

Lagen SFS 2013: 412 om hälso- och sjukvård till vissa utlänningar som vistas i Sverige utan nödvändiga tillstånd m.fl. (Svenk författningssamling [SFS] 2013: 412) (Swed.).

Ley 16/2003, de 28 de mayo, de cohesión y calidad del Sistema Nacional de Salud, B.O.E. 2003, No. 128.

Ley 12/2009, de 30 de octubre, reguladora del derecho de asilo y de la protección subsidiaria, B.O.E. 2009, No. 263.

Marín, C. (2015). Alonso enmienda a Mato: los inmigrantes irregulares volverán a a tener atención sanitaria [Alonso amends Mato's mistakes: irregular immigrants will again have health care]. Retrieved from http://www.elmundo.es/salud/ 2015/03/31/ 551a50f522601d677c8b4574.html

Ministerio de Sanidad, Servicios Sociales e Igualdad (n.d.). El consejo interterritorial. https://www.msssi.gob.es/organizacion/consejoInterterri/home.htm

Mladovsky, P. (2009). A framework for analysing migrant health policies in Europe. *Health Policy*, *93*(1), 55–63. doi:10.1016/j.healthpol.2009.05.015

Moreno Fuentes, F. J., & de Figueiredo Ferreira, S. (2013). Inmigración, sanidad, crisis económica y politización de la inmigración en España [Immigration, health, economic crisis and the politicization of immigration in Spain]. *Revista Interdisciplinar Da Mobilidade Humana*, *21*(40), 27–47. doi:10.1590/S1980-85852013000100003

Norredam, M. L. (2008). *Migrants' access to healthcare* (PhD thesis). University of Copenhaguen, Copenhaguen, Denmark.

Norredam, M., & Krasnik, A. (2011). Migrants' access to health services. In B. Rechel, P. Mladovsky, W. Devillé, B. Rijks, R. Petrova-Benedict, & M. McKee (Eds.), *Migration and health in the European Union* (67–80). Berkshire, United Kingdom: Open University Press.

Obinger, H., Leibfried, S., & Castles, F. G. (2005). *Federalism and the welfare state: New world and European experiences*. Cambridge, United Kingdom: Cambridge University Press.

Oficina Municipal de Información y Orientación para la integración de Inmigrantes. (n.d.). *Manual de integración en la ciudad de Madrid [Integration Guide in the City of Madrid]* [Manual]. Madrid, Spain: Área de Gobierno de Equidad, Derechos Sociales y Empleo.

1177.se. (n.d.). Västra Götalandregionen: New in Sweden. Retrieved from https://www.1177.se/Vastra-Gotaland/Other-languages/New-in-Sweden---healthcare/English--Engelska/

Pace, P. (2011). The right to health of migrants in Europe. In B. Rechel, P. Mladovsky, W. Devillé, B. Rijks, R. Petrova-Benedict, & M. McKee (Eds.), *Migration and health in the European Union.* (55–66). Berkshire, United Kingdom: Open University Press.

Protocol Relating to the Status of Refugees, 31 January 1967, 606 UNTS 267 (entered into force 4 October 1967).

Real Decreto 162/2014, de 14 de marzo, por el que se aprueba el reglamento de funcionamiento y régimen interior de los centros de internamiento de extranjeros, B.O.E. 2014, No. 64.

Real Decreto-ley 16/2012, de 20 de abril, de medidas urgentes para garantizar la sostenibilidad del Sistema Nacional de Salud y mejorar la calidad y seguridad de sus prestaciones, B.O.E. 2012, No. 98.

Stockholm County Hospital (n.d.-a). Mottagning för asylsökande [Reception for asylum seekers]. Retrieved from http://fittjavardcentral.se/vi-erbjuder/halsoundersokning-for-asylsokande/

Sveriges Kommuner och Landsting. (n.d.). Om SKL [About the Swedish Association of Local Authorities and Regions]. Retrived from https://skl.se/tjanster/omskl.409.html

United Nations Population Fund & Harvard School of Public Health. (2010). *A human rights–based approach to programming: Practical implementation manual and training materials.* Retrieved from http://www.unfpa.org/resources/human-rights-based-approach-programming

Västra Götalandsregionen. (n.d.-a). Enheten Asyl-och flyktingfrågor i hälso- och sjukvården [Unit for asylum and refugee issues in health care]. Retrieved from http://www.vgregion.se/sv/Vastra-Gotalandsregionen/startsida/Vard-och-halsa/Sa-styrs-varden/Halso--och-sjukvardsavdelningen/Enheten-for-asyl--och-flyktingfragor/

Västra Götalandsregionen. (n.d.-b). Hälsoundersökning av asylsökande med flera [Health investigation of asylum seekers and others]. Retrieved from http://www.vgregion.se/sv/Vastra-Gotalandsregionen/startsida/Vard-och-halsa/Sa-styrs-varden/Halso--och-sjukvardsavdelningen/Enheten-for-asyl--och-flyktingfragor/Halsoundersokning/

Victorian Equal Opportunity & Human Rights Commission. (2008). *From principle to pratice: Implementing the human rights-based approach in community organizations.* Retrieved from http://www.humanrightscommission.vic.gov.au/our-resources-and-publications/toolkits/item/303-from-principle-to-practice-implementing-the-human-rights-based-approach-in-community-organisations-sept-2008

Westin, C. (2006, 1 July). Sweden: Restrictive immigration policy and multiculturalism. Retrieved from: http://www.migrationpolicy.org/article/sweden-restrictive-immigration-policy-and-multiculturalism

World Health Organization. (1948). *Constitution of the World Health Organization*. Geneva: Author.

World Health Organization. (2005). *International Health Regulations*. Geneva: Author.

World Health Organization. (2010). Health of migrants, the way forward: Report of a global consultation. Madrid: Author.

Zuppiroli, J. (2014). *Informe de revisión sobre los mecanismos de seguimiento existentes para la integración de migrantes en España [Report on existing monitoring mechanisms for the integration of migrants in Spain]*. (n.p.): Accem.

Appendix

Table 1. Summary of the findings on the national and regional approaches to barriers to asylum seekers and undocumented immigrants' health care access.

TYPES OF BARRIERS		SPAIN	CCAA MADRID	CCAA CATALONIA	SWEDEN	STOCKHOLM COUNTY	VÄSTRA GÖTALAND COUNTY
FORMAL	Existence of legal restrictions to health care ENTITLEMENTS	☑	☑		☑	☑	☑
	Existence of HEALTH ASSESSMENTS	☑ (only in detention centers)			☑	☑	☑
INFORMAL	Programs tackling LANGUAGE barriers	☑		☑	☑ (only provided during health assessments)	☑	☑
	Programs tackling INFORMATIONAL barriers	☑	☑ (only to a limited extent)	☑	☑ (only provided during health assessments)	☑	☑ (only on disease prevention)
	Programs providing TRAINING TO HEALTH PROFESSIONALS working in diversity-based contexts	☑		☑			☑ (only on health assessments)

Source: Authors' own compilation based on this research's findings.

Chapter 40. Status and Stigma - Careers of Self-employed of Turkish Origin in Salzburg

Heiko Berner [1]

Abstract

The paper focuses on self-employed of Turkish origin in the province of Salzburg/Austria. The research questions concern educational processes on the way to self-employment and changes of living conditions of the self-employed. Educational processes here are understood as transformations of self-relations and of the relationship to the world. They are influenced by turning points or crises in ones live. The results show that the reasons for getting self-employed very often correspond to structural disadvantages of persons of Turkish origin in Salzburg, for example unemployment, economic uncertainty or dequalification. They are accompanied by intrinsic motivation and by support of role models or family. Discrimination as a motif for quitting a former employment is not mentioned very often. But experiences of discrimination in other spheres of live are an important issue. At the same time, new forms of discrimination arise due to self-employment itself. Two kinds of status coexist for the entrepreneurs interviewed here. (1.) Status as increasing prestige. It rises gradually through social upward mobility. (2.) They perceive their membership to a status group of entrepreneurs. Yet, the majority of autochthonous categorically denies them this membership: The self-employed are not recognized as business people of a higher social position. Finally, they therefore develop a higher degree of sensitivity against stigmatization and discrimination.

Introduction

The number of migrant enterprises in Austria rises continuously and there is extensive research on this subject. Research often focuses on the economic relevance of migrant businesses or on their effects on society. Contrary to this, less is known about the perspective of the entrepreneurs themselves and about the changes in their lives.

This paper [2] intends to show the motifs for becoming self-employed and the consequences on the lives of successful entrepreneurs of Turkish origin in the province of Salzburg/Austria. Motifs are considered as being part of a wider context of educational processes. A crucial hypothesis is that the way to self-employment is accompanied by educational processes. These are understood here as transformations of self-relations and of the relationship to the world (Koller 2012). The research questions concern educational processes that entrepreneurs of Turkish origin realized on their ways to self-employment and changes of living conditions of the then self-employed. Educational processes are influenced by turning points or crises in one's life. Education in this sense is situated in daily life and does not exclusively take

---

[1] Fachhochschule Salzburg - University of Applied Sciences, Salzburg, Austria.
[2] The paper is based on a doctoral thesis that was submitted to the Pedagogic Faculty of the University of Innsbruck in Austria in May 2017. Twelve semi-structured interviews were conducted with self-employed persons of Turkish origin. The analysis followed a mixed design consisting of a content analysis of the whole interview corpus (Mayring 2010) and a more interpretative textual analysis of single cases (Koller 2012).

place in institutional contexts. The theoretical frameworks that inform this paper are the educational theory of John Dewey (2008, orig. 1916) and different understandings of affiliation to social groups.

In the following chapter ("Educational processes"), the theoretical approaches will be presented briefly. Then, the reasons for choosing the term "Turkish origin" will be explained and statistical data will outline the starting position of persons born in Turkey who want to get self-employed in Salzburg ("The group is not a group, pros and cons"). After the socioeconomic situation, personal motifs will be discussed, mentioned by entrepreneurs in twelve interviews ("Reasons for starting a business"). Finally, consequences on their actual situations will be shown ("Status and stigma").

Educational processes

Educational processes – as understood here – are not targeted. A person does not intend to reach a certain goal by means of an educational process. This would rather be "learning"[3]. Instead, educational processes result from changing external conditions which require new forms of action (Oevermann 1991). In many cases, these changing conditions are crises, and routine-driven actions do not seem to fit to a new situation any longer. Then, a process of experiential learning starts (Dewey 2008), which can be understood as a trial and error process in which new actions are realized and evaluated at the same time. Oevermann explains this co-occurrence of (re)acting and evaluating with George Herbert Mead's comprehension of the self (ibid., p. 298): it consists of the "I" and the "me". The "I" is the spontaneous part of one's self that allows everybody to act immediately, the "me" is responsible for the following rational judgment, according to common social norms. These two parts coincide within the process of an experience. In this sense, experience is not so much a passive encounter but an action that is reflected to a certain degree. Under these conditions the personality of a person changes. When two persons interact, the transformation of the relationship to the world becomes possible (Stojanov 2006). In the ideal case, they start negotiating their perspectives – and a new understanding of the world can result from this. This does not mean, however, that they come to a common understanding of the world. It is also possible that they maintain their former perceptions but become a bit more tolerant in respect of the point of view of the opponent. Then, a higher degree

---

[3] "Learning "(in German "Lernen") can be contrasted with "Bildung". "Learning/Lernen" means the pure acquirement of knowledge while "education/Bildung" refers to personal development (Koller 2012). The English term "educational process" as applied here follows the German term "Bildungsprozess".

of tolerance forms the new relationship to the world, which came up with the educational process.

The group is not a group, pros and cons

Until now, we have talked about "self-employed of Turkish origin" without defining "Turkish" or "Turkish origin". For this, we chose two different definitions.

(1.) First, it is either the citizenship or the place of birth that determines one's group affiliation. In this case, nation is the benchmark of membership to a group. These categories become relevant when looking at statistical data. The goal of an analysis of statistics is to find out if there exist structural particularities for people with the relevant characteristics. However, both characteristics – citizenship and place of birth – do not consider that people with the same attribute – here: a Turkish nationality – can be totally different in terms of other characteristics, such as sex, age, educational qualifications or personal experiences. The concentration on the national context as a crucial group characteristic overemphasizes this issue in relation to the others. For example, sex or age may lead to disadvantages too, or the combination of various characteristics can cause multiple discrimination (Bielefeldt 2010).

Yet, the simplifying definition cannot be avoided because structural particularities or disadvantages can be realized only by its means. With regard to people who live in Salzburg and were born in Turkey, statistics show a clear difference between them and people born in Austria (see also Berner 2016). About 80% of the Turkish migrants living in Salzburg are workers[4] while the rate of workers amongst the population born in Austria is at around 30%. Furthermore, there are considerably less employees and self-employed amongst migrants from Turkey as compared to the autochthonous (employees: 11.8 vs. 50.3%; and self-employed: 7.4 vs. 13.5%). The unemployment rate with over 18% in the year 2015 is more than four times higher than the unemployment rate of people born in Austria.

(2.) In contrast, "Turkish" can be considered as a weaker attribute, not focusing on socio-demographic characteristics but on common experiences. In addition to the direct migration experiences, experiences made at the actual place of residence are relevant. These may range from experiences of exclusion to manifest forms of discrimination (Scherr 2015). But also the involuntary allocation to a pretended group of "Turks" or "foreigners" is a well-known phenomenon (Terkessidis 2004). It can be explained by labeling processes (Bukow, Llarayora 1988).

---

[4] Statistical data: Statistik Austria, Abgestimmte Erwerbsstatistik 2015.

The sample of the survey being discussed here consists of twelve interviewees. They were chosen according to the weak definition, which means that a Turkish second name was the basic characteristic when contacting the business people. The second name can be considered as a label (Bukow, Llaryora 1988) that – in the case of racism and discrimination – leads to stigmatization (Goffman 1975). Moreover, all the other characteristics were to be as heterogeneous as possible: the eldest self-employed came to Austria as a "Gastarbeiter". Most of the interviewees immigrated to Austria in the 1980s and 90s as children of "guest-workers". The youngest ones were born in Salzburg. They all work in different branches as the table below shows.

Table 1: Overview, Interviewed Self-employed

IP	Sex	Age	Branche	Self-employed since
Mr Aydın	M	34	Tailor	2008
Mr Bilge, sen.	M	61	Butcher, sen.	2013
Mr Bilge, jun.	M	35	Butcher, jun.	(employed in the family's shop)
Mr Çoban	M	51	Jeweller	2004
Mr Deniz	M	43	Tailor	2012
Mr Ercan	M	32	Distributor of Catering Equipment and Food	2015
Mr Güçlü	M	55	Glazier	2000
Mr Kaya	M	42	Painter	2009
Mr Memiş	M	41	Garage Owner	2009
Mrs Sarı	f	34	Restaurant	2012
Mrs Şen	f	41	Hijab-Fashion Boutique	2012
Mrs Yeşilçay	f	27	Men's Fashion Boutique	2015

Reasons for starting a business

A crucial question when investigating educational processes relates to decisive turning points (often: crises) that make it impossible for an individual to continue acting as usual. A person is forced to find new ways of acting, appropriate to the new situation. In terms of vocational development from employment to self-employment, such crises can be unemployment, dequalification or job insecurity, for example. At the same time, these motifs correspond to the structural disadvantages for Turkish migrants, as shown above. The common motifs being discussed in the literature (Bergmann 2013, Schütt 2015) were confirmed by the survey and completed by some other reasons:

Changes in the family (mostly: newborns)

Unemployment

Health

(low) Contribution

Dequalification

Economic uncertainty

Legal uncertainty

Discrimination

In nearly all cases, combinations of more than one motif were decisive. An example may illustrate this. The owner of a car garage, Mr Memiş, reported a dialogue with his brother while being unemployed:

"And we [my brother and me] went to dinner and I say: Yes, no job, what shall I do? Where do I begin? And in my former job I earned quite well. And if I start a job somewhere, I get, let's say about 1,200, 1,300 euros, how shall I live with that? Then, what do people do in such a situation? Where do they go? Some make the taxi license. Some do construction work. But physically I'm not fine. Stomach problems, back problems. I formerly worked at railroad construction. For two years. Now I said: I don't go back to construction works. But in other jobs I can't earn money. And my brother said: Okay, there are these car conditioners." (Mr Memiş)

In this case, unemployment, health problems and low contribution occurred together and formed the reason for the decision to start the business. Also, dequalification matters, because Mr Memiş had finalized an apprenticeship as mechanic before, and all his former jobs were not adequate to this vocational qualification. Later, Mr Memiş opened a car garage.

In the literature, two main motifs for starting a business are distinguished:

"Economy of Misery "(in German: "Ökonomie der Not", Schmid et al. 2006) and

"Economy of Self-fulfillment" ("Ökonomie der Selbstverwirklichung", ibid.).

"Research into the reasons for the take-up of self-employed suggests that the deterioration of employment opportunities of migrant workers resident in Austria became a motivating force to start up a business" (Biffl 2016, p. 116). It seems to be evident that an economically disadvantaged group is the first to suffer from risks resulting from a neoliberal system. But a common motif discussed in the literature is also represented in a kind of born entrepreneur who intends self-fulfillment by starting a business: "People with relatively good job and income opportunities and who feel attracted to self-employment and activities that are not bound by instructions often follow a rationality of self-fulfillment" (Schmid et al 2006, p. 78). These motifs are considered as two opponent possibilities: either one suffers from a misery or he/she aims for self-fulfillment. This differentiation is not stable because misery is situated on a structural level while the aim for self-fulfillment refers to personal development. In an indirect way, the two categories come close to each other since personal development can be interpreted as an impact of a social situation as well. Thus, it is more plausible to regard the two types of motifs on different levels: the first ones are extrinsic reasons, the latter intrinsic. It is important to say that intrinsic reasons can result from born talents, but it rather is socialization that creates it in the form of an incorporated habitus (Bourdieu 1987). Empirical research approves this point of view. Both motifs – intrinsic and extrinsic – could be shown in many cases at the same time, enhancing the decision to open up a business.

So Mr Çoban, a jeweller, tells about his decision to start his business:

"He [my uncle] sold everything and rented a small shop, gold-branch. In the third generation they still continue. Well, my knowledge about the branch is from school times, as a holiday job." (Mr Çoban)

He knew a "jeweller's habitus" combined with an "entrepreneur's habitus" when he was young, working in the jewellery of his uncle. On the other hand, these reasons alone were not decisive. The intrinsic motivation was extended by family changes and health problems causing unemployment:

"'94 was the reason, in my family, my son came to school and, at the same time, my daughter was born. And I had a surgery on the vocal chords. For six months I was ill, then one and a half years a therapy."(Mr Çoban)

Another interviewee, Mr Kaya, explained that a reason for becoming a painter was his father's profession:

"Yes, painter was not my desired profession. My father back then worked in the enterprise in which I later made the apprenticeship. And automatically I came there too." (Mr Kaya)

Again, socialization was responsible for the subsequent choice of branch. But also, extrinsic motifs played a role. In this case, it was the social circumstances during the financial crisis in 2008:

"Economic crisis, back then, that was it. That was the push. I always had thought about getting self-employed, but that accelerated the decision, the crisis in 2007, '08." (Mr Kaya)

In only one case discrimination was mentioned as a reason to quit a former employment. This seems to be astonishing because discrimination of migrants in vocational contexts is a well-known phenomenon (Riesenfelder et al 2011; Schmidt 2015; Krause et al. 2010; Schneider, Weinmann 2015). It is possible that the interview partners did not talk about these experiences because they managed to handle them: they successfully took action and started their businesses. On the other hand, they often perceive racist experiences or discrimination in their actual jobs, for example, if the Salzburg authorities deny a good place for opening up a kebab kiosk (Mr Bilge). But they emerge not only within vocational contexts but also in daily life, for example when an Austrian woman talks to a woman wearing a hijab as if she did not speak German (Mrs Şen) or when a student is not allowed to change to a higher secondary school although his grades are well enough (Mr Kaya).

Status and stigma

Leading an enterprise means having reached a higher social status. Two kinds of status coexist for the entrepreneurs interviewed here:

Gradually risen: status as increasing prestige.

Categorically risen: membership to a higher status group.

Status rises gradually. The interviewees in most cases now have more money than in the past or they feel more secure than in their former employment situation. This is important because it allows the entrepreneurs to feel like a more recognized person in general terms:

"And then, when for a social activity some voluntary commitment is needed, just like recently in our town, the community organized such a refugees welcome event. Then I said 'Okay, tea and coffee from me!' And my wife baked some cakes and so on. Now, if you start calculating, it's like a few hundred euros. And you can pay this without thinking about it." (Mr Güçlü)

The business people perceived not only a higher prestige but also membership to a status group of entrepreneurs. In the interviews, they expressed this membership through common values that are typical for entrepreneurs, such as discipline, diligence or endurance. But the quotation of Mr Güçlü above also shows a strong identification with the group of entrepreneurs. A remark of Mrs Sarı also shows this affiliation to a status group:

"I'm a person, I have always been working. But I just wanted to say: 'This is mine. I'm fighting for mine'. That means I'm fighting not just for any enterprise but for myself, for my family. For us, we have a business we're fighting for." (Mrs Sarı)

At the same time, discrimination gets a new assessment because the entrepreneurs – now in a higher status group – are more aware of it than before. The majority of the autochthonous categorically denies them the membership to the higher status group: The self-employed are not feeling recognized as business people of a higher social position. Finally, they therefore develop a higher degree of sensitivity to stigmatization and discrimination on grounds of their Turkish origin.

Being aware of the stigma rises with a higher social appreciation (more money, more job security) and with the feeling of being part of a reputable status group: as a result of learning processes in the course of self-employment, discrimination is now felt more clearly. Even new experiences of discrimination appear as a result of self-employment. The following graph summarizes these findings:

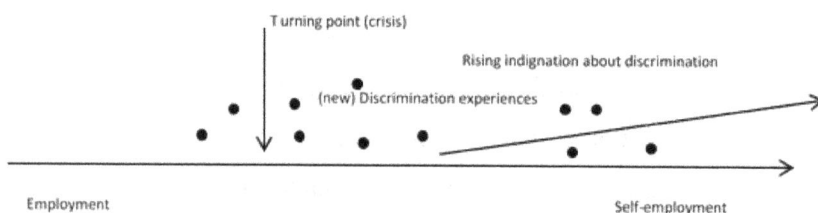

In addition to the rising consciousness of the stigma it is obvious that also indignation about social exclusion becomes relevant. A story of Mr Güçlü about the relation to the members of his sports club may illustrate this:

"The other members, for example when they… Well normally, when they are sober, they talk quite nice and normal, but when they are getting drunk: 'Hey Ali, how about Islam?' Yes, then they start and try to ridicule you, your religion, your origins. And why should I be the 'Watschenmann'?" (Mr Güçlü)

With higher prestige and being part of a more reputable status group, awareness of discrimination and stigmatization as well as indignation about it turn out more clearly.

References

Berner, Heiko (2016): Are Ethnic Entrepreneurs Social Innovators? Turkish Migrant Entrepreneurs in Salzburg. Border Crossing. December 2016 Volume: 6, No: 2, pp. 363–371.

Bourdieu, Pierre (1987): Die feinen Unterschiede. Kritik der gesellschaftlichen Urteilskraft. Frankfurt a. M.: Suhrkamp Verlag.

Bukow, Wolf-Dietrich; Llaryora, Roberto (1988): Mitbürger aus der Fremde. Soziogenese ethnischer Minoritäten. Opladen: Westdeutscher Verlag.

Dewey, John (2008): Democracy and Education. An Educational Classic. Radford: Wilder Publications.

Goffman, Erving (1975): Stigma. Über Techniken der Bewältigung beschädigter Identität. Frankfurt a. M.: Suhrkamp Verlag.

Koller, Hans-Christoph (2012): Bildung anders denken. Einführung in die Theorie transformatorischer Bildungsprozesse. Stuttgart: Kohlhammer.

Krause, A., Rinne, U. & Zimmermann, K. F. (2010): Anonymisierte Bewerbungsverfahren. IZA Research Report, 27. http://legacy.iza.org/en/webcontent/publications/reports/report_pdfs/iza_report_27.pdf [06.03.2017].

Müller-Doohm, Stefan (ed.) (1991): Jenseits der Utopie. Frankfurt a. M.: Suhrkamp Verlag.

Oevermann, Ulrich (1991): Genetischer Strukturalismus und das sozialwissenschaftliche Problem der Entstehung des Neuen. In: Müller-Doohm, Stefan (ed.): Jenseits der Utopie. Frankfurt a. M.: Suhrkamp Verlag, pp. 267–336.

Riesenfelder, Andreas; Schelepa, Susanne; Wetzel, Petra (2011): Beschäftigungssituation von Personen mit Migrationshintergrund in Wien. Wien: L&R SOZIALFORSCHUNG. http://media.arbeiterkammer.at/wien/PDF/studien/Kurzbericht_MigrantInnen_2012.pdf [06.03.2017].

Scherr, Albert (ed.) (2015): Diskriminierung migrantischer Jugendlicher in der beruflichen Bildung. Stand der Forschung, Kontroversen, Forschungsbedarf. Weinheim, Basel: Beltz Juventa

Schmid et al. (2006): Entrepreneurship von Personen mit Migrationshintergrund. Endbericht. Wien: Arbeitsmarktservice Österreich.

Schmidt, W. (2015). Diskriminierung und Kollegialität im Betrieb. In: Scherr, Albert (ed.): Diskriminierung migrantischer Jugendlicher in der beruflichen Bildung. Stand der Forschung, Kontroversen, Forschungsbedarf. Weinheim, Basel: Beltz Juventa, pp. 259–281.

Schneider, J. & Weinmann, M. (2015). Diskriminierung türkeistämmiger Jugendlicher in der Bewerbungsphase. Ein Korrespondenztest am deutschen Arbeitsmarkt. In: Scherr, Albert (ed.): Diskriminierung migrantischer Jugendlicher in der beruflichen Bildung. Stand der Forschung, Kontroversen, Forschungsbedarf. Weinheim, Basel: Beltz Juventa, pp. 115–142.

Stojanov, Krassimir (2006): Bildung und Anerkennung. Soziale Voraussetzungen von Selbst-Entwicklung und Welt-Erschließung. Wiesbaden: VS-Verlag.

Terkessidis, Marc (2004): Banalität des Rassismus. Migranten zweiter Generation entwickeln eine neue Perspektive. Bielefeld: Transcript Verlag.

Chapter 41. Labor Market Effects of Migration: An extension of the Ricardian Model[1]

Karen Jacqueline Contreras Lisperguer[2]

Abstract

One important discussion today is the possible negative effects that immigrants have on the wages of natives. In accordance with the theory of labor demand and supply, people believe that new immigrants could take the jobs of the existing workers. Many researchers have showed that there is little impact of immigration on wages and employment of existing workers as for example for the U.S. and the UK[3]. The model fails to explain job polarization and wage inequality between natives and immigrants. Is it possible to model the effects of migration on wages in a different way that has the potential to be more tractable? Many of the shortcomings of the model can be addressed by using a task-based approach to the effects of migration in the labor market. This paper presents such extension following the Ricardian Skill Model[4] (Autor, Levy, & Murnane, 2003). An analysis, without solving for the equilibrium and keeping capital and technology constants in the short run, gives us the following results: In the presence of migration, there will be a re-assignation of tasks. The wages of local workers will not be necessarily affected, but wage inequality within the labor market should increase.

Keywords: Migration, economics, labor market effects, short-run, proceedings, template, short paper.

Introduction

A model to look at the labor market effects of migration is developed in this paper. It is based in the Ricardian Skill Model, a task-based static model where there is a clear distinction between tasks and skills. It is static because it looks at the very short run. It is inspired on the work of David Autor, Daron Acemoglu and others[5]. A migration shock of low-educated workers takes place, keeping capital and technology constants. The paper presents the model and its phases, and a discussion on the mechanism at work. The ensuing section will introduce environment in which such shock takes place.

---

[1] Acknowledgements to the supervisor in my master's thesis professor Halvor Mehlum, since this model was developed within that work and to professor Emeritus Olav Bjerkholt for unconditional support.

[2] Karen Contreras Lisperguer is a master's student at the Department of Social Science at the University of Agder in Norway. She holds also Master's degree in Economics from the University of Oslo, Norway. Address: Benneches gate 5b 0169 Oslo, Norway. E-mail: karenc16@uia.no.

[3] Examples are Ruhs & Vargas-Silva, 2015; Peri, 2014; and Longhi & Poot, 2005.

[4] The Ricardian model of the labor market as presented by David Autor (Autor, Levy, & Murnane, 2003) (Acemoglu & Autor, 2011).

[5] I follow the intuition from the model developed and explained at Acemoglu & Restrepo, 2015; Massachusetts Institute of Technology, 2012; and Massachusetts Institute of Technology , 2014.

Environment

It is an imperfect labor market where firms have monopsony power, and there are positive possibilities of discrimination. Discrimination was not practiced before migration because "everybody knows each other"; I imagine a small receiving country in terms "labor stock" and firm's reputation between local workers matters for hiring the best workers. Migration makes possible discrimination because it is assumed that the elasticity of their labor supply curve is less elastic than the one of natives[6]. The main reason behind this assumption is the higher cost of migration, especially in terms of opportunity costs, and the lack of supportive networks in the receiving country. I am also assuming a Labor supply curve derived from the Labor-Leisure choice model. The analysis goes from a scenario without migration, to a new scenario with migration, assuming the immigrants are low educated. Local and foreign labor, n_L and n_F, are endowed with a set of skills. Skills are a worker's stock of capabilities for performing various tasks, and workers apply their skills to tasks in exchange for wages (Acemoglu & Autor, 2011, p. 1118). There are **3 types of skills**: general skill type **1** for low education, general skill type **2**, and country-specific skill, **h**. The notation is: **1, 2** and **h**.[7] For simplicity, I assume that all local workers have equal endowment of **h**.

The aggregate output, **Y**, is giving by all the tasks (*i*) been performed in the economy. There are two types of tasks been performed, tasks that requires human country-specific skill (**h**) and tasks that do not. The production of one task *i* is defined as $y(i)$. We can define the aggregate output as:

$$Y = \left(\int_{N-1}^{N} y(i)^{\frac{\sigma-1}{\sigma}} di \right)^{\frac{\sigma}{\sigma-1}}$$ The elasticity of substitution $\sigma \in (0, \infty)$.

A *task*, **i,** one unit, that produces output. The assignment of factors to tasks is determined by comparative advantages. In the production of each task, in the very short run, capital $(\overline{K})$ and technology $(\overline{A})$ are kept constant. In order to avoid any distortion related to capital and technology capital is not included in the analysis $k = 0$, and let $\overline{A} = 1$.

The model

---

[6] There is empirical evidence on immigrants' labor supply been less elastic than the one for local workers, at Dahle-Olsen, Røed and Schøne 2014 (for Norway), Hisch and Jahn 2015 (for Germany) and Naidu, Nyarko and Wang 2015 (for the United Arab Emirates).

[7] For graphical reasons 1, 2 and h are measured in years. 1 is 12 or less years of education, 2 are more than 12 years of education. h is also in years, but years living in the receiving country, scoring higher h for those persons who had been born in the receiving country. In order words, second generations of immigrants have equal h than locals.

In this model, the economy contains a unique final good, **Y.** It is produced with a continuum of tasks **y(i),** on the unit interval $[N - 1, N]$:

$$Y = \left(\int_{N-1}^{N} y(i)^{\frac{\sigma-1}{\sigma}} di \right)^{\frac{\sigma}{\sigma-1}}$$ The elasticity of substitution $\sigma \in (0, \infty)$. **(1)**

In the very short run capital and technology are kept constant, so there are no new tasks been created due to technology advance. Capital, k, is ignored in the production of tasks. This implies that there are no machines that can substitute for labor in the production of specific tasks.

Assumption 1: There is specialization. Workers that are assigned fewer tasks are more productive because it implies task specialization. Variety is costly in the Smithian sense in that forgoes the gains from specialization.

Before migration

Before migration takes place, skills 1 and 2 are the only important skills in the assignation of tasks to a worker given that all workers have the same endowment of skill **h.** We can say that the task assignation is in equilibrium. When migration takes place, firms will assign tasks to the foreign workers if, and only if, they can increase profits by using the new available input, and the task assignation equilibrium will change. The higher indexed tasks in the economy need skills **h** to be performed, and its production is increasing with skill **2.**

Assumption 2: For any set of skills in the production of tasks, each skill-set will have a unique productivity. With this in mind, a task productivity schedule for each type of worker, with a specific set of skills, is represented by the parameter, γ_{skills} . For simplicity, I will use **s** when I refer to a set of skills, so notation is γ_s.

As an example, we can say that, $\gamma_1(i)$ is the productivity of a low-educated worker with only skill 1, a foreign worker, in the production of a task *i,* and that $\gamma_{2,h}(i)$ is the productivity of a high-educated local worker in the production of a task *i.*

Before migration, there was some task threshold, **T,** such that tasks $i \leq \mathbf{T}$ were performed by low-educated local workers and $i > \mathbf{T}$ were performed by high-educated workers. The production of tasks *i,* for $i \leq \mathbf{T},$ before migration was given:

$$y(i) = \left[(1 - \tau) \left(\gamma_1 n_L^1(i) + \gamma_h n_L^h(i) \right)^{\frac{\varsigma-1}{\varsigma}} + \tau \left(\gamma_{1,h} n_L^{1,h}(i) \right)^{\frac{\varsigma-1}{\varsigma}} \right]^{\frac{\varsigma}{\varsigma-1}}$$ **(2)**

$\tau \in [0,1]$ and $\varsigma \in (0,\infty)$. ς is the elasticity of substitution between types of tasks. The assumption is that they are gross complements, so $\varsigma < 1$, but we could also be in the special case of $\varsigma \to 0$, when the substitution is Leontief. Why? It is because tasks are not competing with each other.

The first argument tells us that some of the tasks $(1 - \tau)$, can be performed either by workers that have skill **1 or h**, they are substitutes of each other performing this type of tasks. The second argument tells us that some of the tasks τ, need workers with both skills **1 and h** in order to be performed. This is irrelevant for the assignation of tasks before migration, given that all low-educated local workers had **h**, but it will be relevant with migration.

The production of tasks i, for $i > \mathbf{T,}$ before migration is given by:

$$y(i) = \left[(1 - \tau)\left(\gamma_2 n_L^2(i) + \gamma_h n_L^h(i)\right)^{\frac{\varsigma-1}{\varsigma}} + \tau \left(\gamma_{2,h} n_L^2(i)\right)^{\frac{\varsigma-1}{\varsigma}} \right]^{\frac{\varsigma}{\varsigma-1}} \quad (3)$$

The first argument tells us that some of the tasks $(1 - \tau)$, can be performed either by workers that have skill **2 or h**, they are substitutes in the production of this type of tasks. The second argument tells us that some of the tasks τ, need workers with both **2 and h** in order to be performed. This is irrelevant for the assignation of tasks before migration, given that all high-educated local workers have **h**, but it will be relevant with migration when task may be reassigned.

After migration

In the presence of migration, tasks that do not require skill h will be assigned to foreign workers, as long as it minimize costs. By doing this, firms will assign fewer tasks per worker, increasing their productivity. For example, in a coffee shop, owners will assign tasks to foreign workers, as cleaning tables and making coffee, while local workers will sell the coffee to the customers; or in the kitchen of a restaurant, the head chef will assign to the foreign workers to cut vegetables, to clean or to make dishes from their home-countries.

I assume that the immigrants that arrives to this society are low educated and at working age. It is reasonable to think that there are high costs of migration[8], and we can assume that:

$$n_L^{1,h} > n_F^1$$

Now tasks can be reassigned between local and foreign workers according to new threshold as follow, for workers with skill 1 according to a threshold $T^{1,h}$, so for $i \leq T^{1,h}$ **we have that:**

$$y(i) = \left[\left(\gamma_1 n_F^1(i) + \gamma_{1,h} n_L^{1,h}(i) \right)^{\frac{\varsigma-1}{\varsigma}} \right]^{\frac{\varsigma}{\varsigma-1}} \quad (4)$$

In the production of these tasks, low-educated foreign workers are perfect substitutes of low educated native workers, and firms will hire them if they can minimize their costs.

For tasks $T^{1,h} < i \leq T^{2,h}$, we will have the following production function:

$$y(i) = \left[(1 - \tau) \left(\gamma_{1,h} n_L^{1,h}(i) \right)^{\frac{\varsigma-1}{\varsigma}} + \tau \left(\gamma_2 n_L^2(i) + \gamma_h n_L^h(i) \right)^{\frac{\varsigma-1}{\varsigma}} \right]^{\frac{\varsigma}{\varsigma-1}} \quad (5)$$

$\tau \in [0,1]$ *and* $\varsigma \in (0, \infty)$. ς is the elasticity of substitution between types of tasks? The assumption is that they are gross complements, so $\varsigma < 1$, but we could also be in the special case of $\varsigma \rightarrow 0$, when the substitution is Leontief.

The first argument tells us that some of the tasks τ, need workers with both **2 and h** in order to be performed. The second argument tell us that some of the tasks $(1 - \tau)$, can be performed either by workers that have skill **2 or h**, they are substitutes. It means that if we have local workers with skills set **(1, h)** and its cost in producing i is less than the costs of local workers with skills **(2,h)** they will be reassigned those tasks.

For $i > T^{2,h}$, we will have the following production function:

$$y(i) = \left[\gamma_{2,h} n_L^{2,h}(i)^{\frac{\varsigma-1}{\varsigma}} \right]^{\frac{\varsigma}{\varsigma-1}} \quad (6)$$

Assumption 3: Local and foreign workers with different skills set can perform tasks, but the comparative advantage of skills groups differ across tasks. This is captured by the term γ_s. Following the idea that higher indexed tasks require **h** in order to be performed, we impose the following assumption on the structure of comparative advantage:

For tasks:

$\gamma_{1,h}/\gamma_{2,h}$ *and* $\gamma_1/\gamma_{1,h}$ are continuously differentiable and strictly decreasing.

It means that higher-educated local workers are better than lower-educated local workers and both high and low educated foreign workers in performing higher indexed tasks. Given that skills groups differ in efficiency at each task, and respectively bundles of tasks, it is possible to state that before migration the factor clearing required for bundles of tasks was:

$$\int_{N-1}^{T} n_L^{(2,h)}(i)di \ \leq N_L^{(2,h)} \text{ and } \int_{T}^{N} n_L^{(1,h)}(i)di \ \leq N_L^{(1,h)}$$

In a perfect equilibrium model with migration, the new factor market clearing will also require:

$$\int_{N-1}^{T1,h} n_F^1(i)di \ \leq N_F^1, \int_{T1,h}^{T2,h} n_L^{(1,h)}(i)di \ \leq N_L^{(1,h)}, \text{and} \qquad \int_{T2,h}^{N} n_L^{(2,h)}(i)di \ \leq N_L^{(2,h)}$$

Allocation of skills to tasks

I have mentioned that tasks are assigned according to a (some) threshold(s), T. Now I will formalize that assumption.

Lemma 1: For any equilibrium, there is a (some) threshold (T) that acts as a rule to the allocation of tasks. Before migration, we have an equilibrium such that, $T \in [N-1, N]$, and for any $i < T$, $n_L^{(2,h)} = 0$, and for any $i > T$, $n_L^{(1,h)} = 0$.

Migration changes the threshold for the assignation of tasks. Two new thresholds are established as follow: There exists $T_{2,h}$ and $T_{1,h}$ such that tasks are assigned to workers, and for any $i < T_{1,h}$, $n_L^{(1,h)} = n_L^{(2,h)} = 0$, for any $i \in (T_{1,h}, T_{2,h})$, $n_F^1 = n_L^{(2,h)} = 0$, and for any $i > T_{2,h}$, $n_F^1 = n_L^{(1,h)} = 0$.

This lemma is similar to the one in Autor & Acemoglu, 2011, in an environment where there are two types of workers and three different skills sets.

Figure 1: "The task space" before migration.

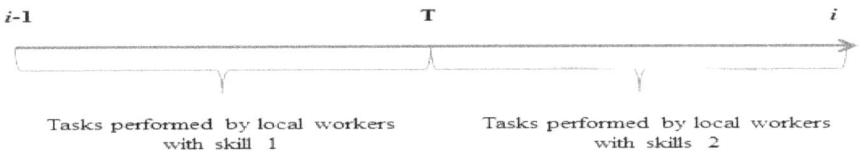

Tasks performed by local workers with skill 1   Tasks performed by local workers with skills 2

Figure 1 shows us the "the task space": how tasks are being assigned in this space to workers according to the threshold T before migration takes place. The firms assign tasks to the workers according to the principle of comparative advantages, and lower educated have a comparative advantage in the production of tasks that requires skill 1. Figure 2 represents "the task space after migration": Tasks are being re-assigned among foreign and local workers according to the principle of comparative advantages; tasks that do not require h to be performed are assigned to foreign workers. Local workers with skills (1, h) will be performed more advanced tasks, they are assigned tasks that were performed earlier by higher educated workers.

Figure 2: "The task space" after migration

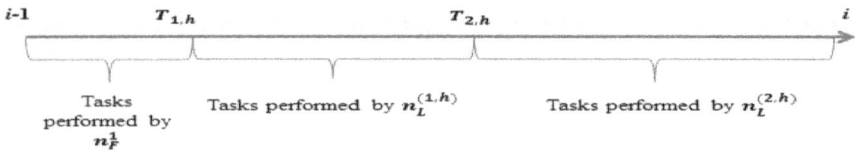

No arbitrage across skills

The threshold tasks, $T_{1,h}$ and $T_{2,h}$, decides the equilibrium in the model. The assumption of no arbitrage across skills is essential to secure equilibrium in the Ricardian Skill model, and it applies to this model. This assumption states that a type of "no arbitrage" condition, equalizing the cost of producing these threshold's tasks using different skills, will determine the thresholds.

The threshold task $T_{1,h}$, must be such that it can be profitably produced using either foreign workers with skill type **1** or local workers with skill set **(1, *h*)**, and the threshold task $T_{2,h}$, must be such that it can be profitably produced using either low-educated local workers or high-educated local workers.

The wages and inequality

Once the threshold tasks, $T_{1,h}$ and $T_{2,h}$, are determined, wages and earnings differences across skill groups can be found in a very straightforward manner. Firms in this labor market have market power, given that foreign workers will accept lower wages than local workers. The wages are set as the value of the marginal products of different types of skills, but in the case of foreign workers firms will discriminate if they can do so. There is a wage setting equation for a worker *i* with a skill set **s** that can be written as follow:

$$W_s^i = \mathrm{p}\,(i)\,\gamma_s - \omega_i(\varphi_i, \mu)\ (7)$$

I assume local worker are not been discriminated, as in the basic model, $\omega_L(\varphi_L, \mu) = 0$. Now we can write the wage setting function for workers of each skill-set as:

$$w_1^F = \mathrm{p}(i)\,\gamma_1 - \omega_F(\varphi_F, \mu)\ (8) \qquad w_{1,h}^L = \mathrm{p}(i)\,\gamma_{1,h}\ (9) \qquad w_{2,h}^L = \mathrm{p}(i)\,\gamma_{2,h}\ (10)$$

This is a simplification, because it could be the case that some groups of local workers are been discriminated[9]. As long as firms can discriminate, they will offer a lower wage to foreigners than the one they should have offered in equilibrium.

---

[9] Examples are aborigines' groups in the Americas, and descendants of Africans in countries like the U.S. and the Dominican Republic. This have been well documented in the literature in the Social Sciences, many studies have evidence of these groups been discriminated.

Productivity is increasing in **h** and **2**, and wages are different between workers with different skill sets, and it is therefore it is possible to say that:

$$w_{2,h}^L > w_{1,h}^L > w_F$$

Discrimination of foreign workers reinforces the inequality between the wages of foreign and local workers. The wage ratios are more important than the levels because they inform us about the wage structure and inequality. An example is the following:

$$\frac{w_{2,h}^L}{w_{1,h}^L} = \frac{p(i)\,\gamma_{2,h}}{p(i)\,\gamma_{1,h}} \text{ (11)}$$

Equation **(b.11)** let us evaluate the wages of high-educated local workers respect to the wages of the low educated local workers. By using equation **(8)**, **(9)** and **(10)** and given the principle of specialization, it is possible to compare the wages of local workers before and after migration in order to see if they have changed, and we assume that as fewer tasks are assigned to local workers they will become more specialized, hence more productive.

Conclusion

The intuition is clear in the model. There will be a re-assignment of tasks among workers, low indexed tasks, if possible, will be assigned to low-educated foreign workers. Given that foreign workers lack of country-specific skills firms can increase productivity by assigning to them low-indexed tasks that do not require **h** to be performed, and paying lower wages to them. At the same time, given that their supply curve is less elastic than the one of natives; firms will see an opportunity to minimize costs, offering a lower wage than the equilibrium wage. What happen with the low educated native workers? They will specialize, as much as it is possible, on task that requires **h,** been more productive and by doing so, kceping their wages at the same level.

A key factor is to consider that the country specific skills (**h**) has a role to play for increasing the local workers productivity. The firms following their desire to maximize profits will do as much as they can to re-allocate tasks between workers fast. Within this model framework we can able to justify why local workers' wages are little affected by migration. The model left us also with the bitter conclusion that wages inequality within an economy will increase with migration, but a discussion about if it is a desirable or not desirable affect are beyond this paper.

References

Acemoglu, D., & Autor, D. (2011). Chapter 12: Skills, Tasks and Technologies:Implications for Employment and Earnings. In D. Card, & O. Ashenfelter, *Handbook of Labor Economics, Volume 4b* (pp. 1043-1171). North Holland: Elsevier.

Acemoglu, D., & Restrepo, P. (2015, December). The race between man and machine: Implications of technology for growth, factor shares and employment. *Working paper*.

Autor, D., Levy, F., & Murnane, R. (2003). The skill content of recent technological change:an empirical exploration. *Quarterly Journal of Economics 118(4)*, 1279-1333.

Longhi, N., & Poot, J. (2005). A meta-analytic assessment of the effects of immigration on wages. *Journal of Economic Surveys*, 451-477.

Massachusetts Institute of Technology . (2014, Autumn). *Courses Daron Acemoglu.* Retrieved from Labor Economics I: http://economics.mit.edu/faculty/acemoglu/courses

Massachusetts Institute of Technology. (2012, Spring). *Classes David Autor*. Retrieved from Labor Economics II David Autor and Daron Acemoglu: http://economics.mit.edu/faculty/dautor/courses

Peri, G. (2014). Do immigrant workers depress the wages of native workers? *IZA World of Labor - Evidence-based policy making*.

Ruhs, M., & Vargas-Silva, C. (2015). *Briefing. The Labour Market Effects of Immigration.* Oxford: The Migration Observatory at the University of Oxford.

Chapter 42. Leaving or Staying?[1] Migration Motifs of People of Turkish Origin with German Graduation[2]

Cemal SARI[3]

Abstract

The aim of this research project is to examine why highly skilled Turks propose to migrate from Germany to Turkey and whether there are gender-related disparities in migration intentions. The rising migration of highly skilled Turks of the second and third generation has recently paid attention in both, Germany as in Turkey in research, politics, and economy as well as in the media. These highly skilled academics were born and grew up in Germany, enjoyed the education here and leave the country towards Turkey, to reach their career goals there. Fourteen qualitative interviews with highly skilled individuals of Turkish origin of the second and third generation in the Ruhr area (Bochum, Duisburg, Essen and Dortmund) were the foundation of a qualitative study to examine their motives to leave Germany towards Turkey. The results of this research project show that for the majority of the interviewees principally exists an openness to imagine a future life in Turkey. While women predominantly intend to leave Germany for family and partnership reasons, men would primarily migrate to Turkey for professional reasons and for their career. The study comes to the result that not a particular motif, but only the compound of numerous reasons, leads to a motivation for a migration from Germany to Turkey.

Keywords: Turkish-German migration, Highly skilled Turks, Migration motivations.

Introduction

The migration of highly skilled Turkish academics from Germany to their parents' native country has become a stronger focus for the integration debate in recent years. The problem appears particularly through the fact that structurally well integrated Turkish migrants of the second and third generation, who are intercultural and multilingual focused, leave Germany willingly and thus their work capacity is consequently lost in Germany (Sari, & Alkan, 2016). As motifs for migration, unfavorable chances of success in career are often mentioned, which are associated with a disadvantage and discrimination in employment and furthermore are accompanied by social exclusion mechanisms (Griese, & Sievers, 2010, Sezer, & Dağlar, 2009). Many of them do not feel being completely accepted in Germany and therefore they want to leave the country in order to move to Turkey, where they can expeditiously become successful in career using their in Germany acquired professional qualifications (Alkan, 2011). The migration can thus be interpreted as an averting from the German society as well as an evidence of a lack of integration and a failed integration policy, because despite the fact that

---

[1] I like to thank the participants in my survey, who have willingly shared their precious time during the process of interviewing.

[2] The survey was made before the coup attempt of the 15th and 16th July 2016.

[3] Ph.D. Cemal Sari, Ruhr-University of Bochum, Faculty of Social Science, Department of Sociology/ Organization, Migration, Universitätsstraße 150, 44780 Bochum, Germany. E-mail: cemal.sari@rub.de.

these individuals were born and grew up in Germany and went through the German education system, they desire to leave the country (Aydın, 2012).

However, it cannot be assumed exactly who leaves Germany and why, because there is a lack of studies and data. Therefore, this paper investigates the question of why highly skilled Turks are motivated to migrate from Germany to Turkey and whether there is a difference between genders regarding the migration purposes (Sari, 2016). This paper likewise presents results of a qualitative study on German-Turkish highly skilled university graduates from the second and third generation in Germany. By the use of an empirical survey the process of a problem-focused interview is applied, which combines different question techniques and methods. Thereby, an impartial collection of the migration-motivated inhabitants' experiences, actions and perceptions of social reality is registered (Sari, & Alkan, 2016).

Migration Motivation of Turkish Academics

For a long time the migration research attracts attention to the return intentions of migrants of Turkish origin. As the annual expert report "Migrationsland 2011" of the Expert Council of German Foundations on Integration and Migration emphasizes, Germany has at the present time in terms of Turkish origin citizens not an immigration but instead, an emigration problem. Since 2008, more individuals of Turkish origin leave the country than they move into - and predominantly the highly skilled academics leave. Quite a number of the so-called German-Turks validate this development as well: For instance, in 2008, a quantity of 28,741 Turks immigrated to Germany, while 38,889 Turks returned from Germany to Turkey in the same year (BAMF, 2012). In accordance with a quantitative online survey study, 36 percent of the questioned Turkish university graduates and students stated a motivation to leave Germany towards Turkey for a short, medium or long-term (Sezer, & Dağlar, 2009). According to Sezer and Dağlar's study a "lack of feeling home in Germany", "professional disadvantages" and "economic aspects" are the central motifs to turn one's back on Germany.

The "representative study on the integration behavior of Turks in Germany" by telephone from March 2011 achieved further results regarding a potential migration. A total of 1,003 people (including 674 without and 329 with the German citizenship) have been interviewed. Due to the question "Are you planning or intending to return to Turkey?" four percent of the people of Turkish origin answered with "Yes, in the next two years", 12 percent said "Yes, in the next decade", and 30 percent declared "Yes, but later". Thus, 48 percent of the interviewees without the German nationality plan to move or return to Turkey. In the group of people with German citizenship however, only 39 percent think of leaving Germany (Liljeberg, 2011). The studies of the OECD (Organization for Economic Cooperation and Development) from

2007/2010 come to the conclusion that graduates from migrant families in Germany are more often affected by unemployment than graduates without a migrant background. These results are being justified by referring for example to the ethnic discrimination in the job market. Candidates with a Turkish name, regardless of their German nationality and German language native speaker likeness, have inferior chances for an invitation to a job interview than those with a German name (Kaas, & Manger, 2010). Appropriate to the state of research the question about the motifs for leaving Germany and the alternative of Turkey as a migration destination therefore raises.

Research Methods

For the study conducted with university graduates of Turkish origin from the second and third generation who are willing to leave Germany towards Turkey, the choice of methodology fell to a qualitative interview. That includes fourteen handbook-supported expert interviews conducted in the Ruhr area (Ruhrgebiet) and realized in German. The empirical study was based on the method of problem-focused interviews, combining different methods and question techniques (Witzel, 2000). The analysis of the empirical material was based on the documentary interpretation. For the compilation of the study group of highly skilled Turks, initially, a combination of the snowball principle and the arbitrary sampling was used (Frankfort Nachmias, & Nachmias, 1995). It was about a neutral registration of the actions, motifs and perceptions of the interviewees and their awareness of the social reality. All of the fourteen examinees had completed the entire school and university education in Germany, came from the Ruhr area and were aged between 20 and 55. Four of them hold the Turkish citizenship and the others own the German. All respondents hold contacts to Turkey - some had very intense, even job-related contacts, while others had exclusively contact to their relatives.

To the implementation of the research project, the respondents were asked to answer, in addition to the biographical information, 19 questions in order to analyze exactly the reasons and motifs of females and males for the migration intentions from Germany to Turkey. The survey was conducted using different multipliers (in the Ruhr area - Duisburg, Bochum, Essen, Dortmund - and Participants of the German-Turkish year of research, education and innovation in 2014 at the Ruhr-University of Bochum) from 27 October 2014 to August 2016 in Germany. The focus on the Ruhr area arises from the fact that the Ruhr area is strongly marked by immigration (Pries, 2011). It is important to mention that due to the small study group and its composition (seven females, seven males) the range of generalization of the results is highly limited. Nevertheless, this study can be called an exploratory study in order to gain first insights and findings in a yet nearly unexplored area (Przyborski, & Wohlrab-Sahr, 2008).

Migration Reasons

Attention will be drawn here especially to the survey results of the qualitative interviews. The reasons and personal migration intentions, which were expressed or indicated by the migration-motivated highly skilled Turks or emerge from their stories, are summarized in this paper into four categories.

Bad career prospective

The majority of the surveyed Turkish academics mentioned in the interview primarily the aspect of "unfavorable career prospects in Germany" as a main reason for a migration to Turkey, so Sercan Zengin. He was born in 1980 in Germany and lives in Essen where he obtains his doctorate contemporaneously. In the recent years he has observed that people with a doctorate, could live in Turkey, especially in large cities like İstanbul and İzmir, at least as good as in Germany:

Unfortunately, I have not the same chance like a German, although I finish my doctorate in the nearest future. In İstanbul I´ll be definitely getting a better job than in Germany.

This hope he keeps for himself, but whether his desires come true, "the future" will decide on that. He could imagine to "try" how life is all about in Turkey and then he wants to "look further", he confesses in the interview. By "hearsay" he knows that graduates being fully competent in three languages are mostly preferred in Turkey:

I've heard that applicants with at least three languages like German, English and Turkish at a very advanced level, is highly welcome to the job market in İstanbul, where I would also feel emotionally more satisfied.

Sercan hopes to achieve a leading position in a German company in Turkey in which he would like to support the German-Turkish industrial relations. However, he realizes that he does not want to work permanently in Turkey, but only temporarily, he stressed then. The fact that professional reasons are often essential for a migration to Turkey suggests that for highly skilled Turks primarily the professional career and the social advancement is important. The willingness to migrate from Germany to Turkey then seems an option if the career advancement and upward social mobility in Germany appears to be no (more) feasible or if Turkey promises better prospects (Sari, & Alkan, 2016).

Discrimination Experiences

The given fact that the majority of highly qualified individuals of Turkish origin considered their own professional perspective as "unfavorable" in Germany, can be literary lead back to the discrimination restrictions on the German job market and the structural disadvantages in many areas of society.

A majority of interviewees have already experienced discrimination in everyday life and in the daily working life. Individuals with a Turkish sounding name are already discriminated in the first application phase. For that reason, someone with a German name must write five applications to receive an invitation to a job interview, whereas a competitor with a Turkish name has to write seven (OECD, 2007/2010). The same marks, similar strengths - but different names (Bürgin, & Erzene-Bürgin, 2013). The straight out graduate educational academic Gülay Öztürk for instance, who is currently looking for a suitable job, manifested herself in this regard by saying:

I don`t want to complain about my childhood in the Ruhr area. I just grew up with both the German culture as well as with the Turkish culture. It was a quite nice time. I had been lucky enough to where I lived, because there were not that many Turks. But nevertheless, I was never fully recognized as one of them. At least, I never felt hundred percent accepted by my German fellows. For them, I`ll always keep being a Turkish women in between them, although I grew up here and spent my whole life time here in Germany.

Without being directly asked about discrimination, also Deniz Aslan, a social scientist reported from his experiences of discrimination. Already at school he had been confronted with all kinds of discrimination. This motivated him rather to "fight" than to think of migrating from Germany to Turkey. He had to make a discrimination experience already in the housing market: When he came to an inspection date and the landlord has seen that he is of Turkish origin and having three children, the landlord looked for excuses in order to not let him rent the house. However, this negative experience could not be a migration intention for Deniz. Nowadays, he can imagine migrating with his family from Germany to Istanbul - but for other reasons than being discriminated or disadvantaged.

Missing *Homeward Bound*

Many of the results of this study confirm that a majority of surveyed academics think of a migration towards Turkey because of a "lack" of identification or because they feel the antagonism being between these two cultures and countries. Due to the question: "What are the reasons for you to intend to move to Turkey?" For instance Leyla Açıkgöz, who was born in Turkey but lives with her parents in Germany since the age of 3, answers:

It is difficult to explain it for me. I'm not sure if I'm German or Turkish. I`m actually both, German and Turkish. In Turkey I am Alamancı and in Germany I`m always somehow a Turkish woman. When I am in Turkey for a longer time, I miss my German friends and my neighborhood. But when I don't visit for a long time, I really miss it hardly. I´m caught between chairs but might actually feel in both cultures very well.

At the end of the interview, she calls herself a Turkish-German woman. She thus explains that she has two homes. Since two or three years Leyla thinks of working and living in Turkey. But whether she actually takes that step, she does not know yet. The other interviewees also take both Turkey and Germany as their home country:

For me it makes no difference emotionally. I feel like being a German, but at the same time I would never forget my Turkish roots. I feel assigned to both countries, to two citizenships. I can now make no distinction as to whether I'm a German or a Turk, I guess. I'm standing right in the middle and have a bit of both. I feel at home in both countries. When I go to Turkey and there I get a steady job, that doesn't mean to me that I go back, it means that I go for a certain period to my other home.

On the one hand, the interviewees feel emotionally and ancestry moderately rooted in Turkey: "The Turkish outweighs maybe", but on the other hand they feel "a hyphenated identity, as a Turkish-German" and would not work in a long term period in Turkey but only time limited. They consider Germany and Turkey as their home countries and would not describe their future stay in Turkey as a "return".

The meaning of socio-cultural networks

Among the possible reasons of a migration we find also socio-cultural networks including friendships and family ties. It should be noted that mostly women, particularly at a young age, feel more being in the obligation to return with their parents to Turkey than men (Zirkeci, & Zeyneloğlu, 2014). A majority of the interviewees has familial and professional ties and contacts to Turkey and has been for both, job-related and personal reasons more often there. These individuals watch Turkish TV, read Turkish newspapers and therefore pursue regular information about the country. Some interviewed academics indicated to travel to Turkey several times to accept lectureships at Turkish universities, to attend conferences or to visit their relatives. In addition to academic purposes and friendship networks, partnerships belong to the most important factors which influence the decision and the complementation of a possible migration (Sari, & Alkan, 2016).

Migration intentions based on a partnership play also a key role in the migration projects of Aylin Kaya. While studying in Bochum she met her future husband who had come as an exchange student to Germany. Since her fiancée has currently spent his schooling and most of his studies in Turkey, it was difficult for him to "foothold" in Germany. It therefore seems as the most appropriate solution to them to move to Turkey. Süleyman Karadeniz, who does not want to migrate for professional reasons to Turkey, the existing social network in Istanbul embodies an important migration intention for him. The young economist, who is increasingly traveling to Istanbul due to his doctoral degree, commented:

For my doctorial studies I often travel to İstanbul for attending conferences and work for German-Turkish projects over there and here. Therefore I could really imagine working in İstanbul for a longer period of time.

This statement shows his openness towards a job-related living in Turkey which is facilitated by the given fact that he has already a pre-existing social connection to his destination country.

Results and Discussion

Which conclusions can be drawn from this study regarding the migration willingness of highly skilled Turks? The object of this survey was to investigate the migration behavior of highly skilled Turkish academics from Germany to Turkey and to conclude whether there are gender typical reasons and motifs for migration intentions. This empirical work has on the one hand shown that for all of those, in principle, exist an openness to imagine a future and working life in Turkey temporarily. Among the reasons why they would leave Germany, mainly economic motifs or the prospect of a better job or faster advancement opportunities in the destination country, where they can use their particular language and intercultural skills (as in international companies or institutions, but also in the university sector), are mentioned. A few respondents could imagine that they would, after a few years of residence in Turkey, return back to Germany if they would professionally fully being recognized here.

On the other hand, it has emerged that females and males have different motifs to leave Germany. Especially for women, partnerships and family reasons play a central role to the migration decision. Men instead, would mainly migrate for work reasons. The study furthermore suggests that Turkish highly skilled academics who live in Germany and have grown up here and participate in the social life, at the same time maintain intense relations with the home country of their parents, because hey likewise feel emotionally attached to Turkey. They regularly communicate with relatives and friends, consume the Turkish media and thereby follow the happenings in Turkey. There are reasons like disadvantages and discrimination that might induce highly qualified academics to migrate. But however, it is rather to be interpreted as an (un-) satisfaction factor or disruptive factor for their personal situation in Germany.

Besides, a majority of participants could decide neither for Germany, nor for Turkey. They felt not adequately addressed by an "either-or" classification and rely on a dual affiliation, which designates a "as well as" belonging. The results of this analysis show that the reasons can under no circumstances be contemplated separately but must clearly be considered as a variety of motifs.

Not single motifs, but only the confluence of different reasons leads to the migration willingness.

References

Alkan, M. N. (2011). Transmigranten auf dem Weg in die Heimat? [Transmigrants on Their Way Back Home?]. Konrad Adenauer Stiftung, Ankara (in German).

Aydın, Y. (2012). Emigration of Highly Qualified Turks: A Critical Review of the Societal Discourses and Social Scientific Research. *Paçacı, E. and S. Straubhaar, T. (eds.) Turkey, Migration and the EU: Potentials, Challenges and Opportunities. Hamburg: University Press. pp. 199-227.*

BAMF (2012). *Migrationsbericht 2012.* Bundesamt für Migration und Flüchtlinge. Nürnberg.

Baysan, A. (2013). Heute Studium, morgen Abwanderung? Deutsch-türkische AustauschstudenInnen in Istanbul [Studying Today, Migrating Tomorrow. German-Turkish Exchange Students in Istanbul]. *Pusch, B. (ed.) Transnationale Migration am Bespiel Deutschland und Türkei, Wiesbaden: Springer Fachmedien. pp. 267-278* (in German).

Bürgin, A. Erzene-Bürgin, D. (2013). Abwanderungsmotive türkeistämmiger Personen mit deutschem Schulabschluss: Ergebnisse einer Online-Umfrage. *Pusch, B. (ed.) Transnationale Migration am Bespiel Deutschland und Türkei, Wiesbaden: Springer Fachmedien. pp. 339-358.*

Frankfort-Nachmias, Nachmias, C., & Nachmias, D. (1995). *Research Methods in the Social Science.* New York: Worth Publishers.

Griese, H. M., & Sievers, I. (2010). Bildungs- und Berufsbiographien erfolgreicher Transmigranten. *Aus Politik und Zeitgeschichte (APuZ)*, (Magazine 46-47), 22-28.

İçduygu, A., & Biehl, K. (2009). *Managing International Urban Migration. Türkiye-Italia-España.* Istanbul: Koç University.

Kaas, L., & Manger, C. (2010). Ethnic Discrimination in Germany's Labour Market: A Field Experiment [Special issue]. *IZA Discussion Paper*, 4741.

Liljeberg Research International/Unabhängiges Meinungsforschungsinstitut INFO (2011). Repräsentative Studie zum Integrationsverhalten von Türken in Deutschland. Ergebnisse einer telefonischen Repräsentativbefragung. Received from: <http://www.liljeberg.info/aktuell/DTR-Bus-01-2011-Charts-PK.pdf> available on: 02.02.2016.

Pries, L. (2011). Transnationale Migration als Innovationspotenzial [Transnational Migration as Innovation Potential]. *Engel, K. Großmann, J. and Hombach, B. (eds.) Phönix flieg! Das Ruhrgebiet entdeckt sich neu. Essen: Klartext Verlag. pp. 213-231* (in German).

Przyborski, A., & Wohlrab-Sahr, M. (2008). *Qualitative Sozialforschung. Ein Arbeitsbuch.* München: Oldenburg Verlag.

Pusch, B. (2012). Bordering the EU: Istanbul as Hotspot for Transnational Migration. *Paçacı, E. S. Straubhaar, T. (eds.) Turkey, Migration and the EU: Potentials, Challenges and Opportunities. Hamburg: University Press. pp. 167-197.*

Sari, C. & Alkan, M. N., (2016). Goodbye Germany, Migration Intentions of Highly Qualified Turks, *Deniz Eroglu, Jeffrey H. Cohen, Ibrahim Sirkeci, Turkish Migration 2016 Selected Papers. pp. 231-237.*

Sari, C. (2016). Türkiye Kökenli Akademisyenlerin Almanya'dan Türkiye'ye Göçü ve Göç Eğilimleri, *VIII. Ulusal Sosyoloji Kongresi, Farklılıklar, Çatışmalar ve Eylemlilikler Çağında Sosyoloji,* Middle East Technical University, Ankara.

Sezer, K., & Dağlar, N. (2009). *Die Identifikation der TASD mit Deutschland.* Krefeld/Dortmund: Futureorg-Institut.

Witzel, A. (2000). Das problemzentrierte Interview, Forum: Qualitative Forschung [Special issue]. 1 (22).

Compiled by F. Tilbe, E. Iskender, I. Sirkeci

Sirkeci, I., & Zeyneloğlu, S. (2014). Abwanderung aus Deutschland in die Türkei: Eine Trendwende im Migrationsgeschehen? *Alscher, S. and Kreienbrink, A. (eds.) Abwanderung von Türkeistämmigen, Wer verlässt Deutschland und warum? Beiträge zur Migration und Integration, Bundesamt für Migration und Flüchtlinge, (6). pp. 30-85.*

Chapter 43. Refugee Status Determination Policy and Practice: The Australian Experience

Petra Playfair[1], Adriana Mercado [2]

Abstract

"Migration is an expression of the human aspiration for dignity, safety and a better future. It is part of the social fabric, part of our very make up as a human family." (Ban Ki-moon)

Forced migration is the coerced movement of people from their country of nationality or habitual residence. The phenomenon presents challenges which affect the individual, their receiving communities, and then become a highly-politicized issue which transcends borders. Although Australia has historically been built on migration flows, its island-nature underpins a national psyche of rigorous border control, clearly contrasting the European situation where flows of people have been a constant theme throughout history. We explore Australia's approach to dealing with those forced migrants who have arrived by boat without a valid visa (thus, "unauthorized maritime arrivals"), detailing a) the impact of policies and law, b) the practical disorder following certain policy application, c) the financial and human cost, d) the juxtaposition of Australia's current policy, which acts to deter "unauthorized maritime arrivals" while simultaneously increasing the number of authorized refugee arrivals in response to acknowledged human crises. Finally, we explore the repercussions that arise when a human issue becomes a political tool.

Keywords: Australia-migration, boat people policy, border control, detention, forced migration, refugees.

Introduction

Australia is a country that has been built on waves of migration flow throughout its history and has developed law and policy as a mechanism for maintaining border control. Being an island, the determination to control the border has become part of the national psyche. This paper explores Australia's policy and practise in response to asylum seekers, particularly those reaching Australia's border as boat people[3]. As major policy shifts have been triggered by changing political leadership and ideological differences, this paper will divide the policy changes and their practical implications into periods defined by government change. We will then present a comparison study of these policies in relation to the costs involved. Finally, we conclude with best policy recommendations that permit a long term, cost effective and humane approach.

---

[1] Petra Playfair, CEO, Playfair Visa and Migration, L5, 37 Bligh St, Syd, NSW, Aust. E: petra@playfair.com.au

[2] Adriana Mercado, Lawyer for Playfair Visa and Migration, L5, 37 Bligh St, Syd, NSW, Aust. E: adriana@playfair.com.au

[3] Wars and other national disasters, force people to leave their country under harsh circumstances if visa application procedures are not available; people rely on smuggler's illegal underground networks to migrate unofficially, sometime by boat, hence called "boat people."

History of Australian Refugee Policy for Boat People

Period: 1975-1983, Trigger: end of Vietnam War, Prime Minister (PM): Fraser (Liberal Party: DEC '75)

Prior to 1976, Australia had not utilised a regulated visa assessment process for determining which Asylum Seekers[4] were to be accepted for settlement as Refugees[5]. The small number of people who sought asylum in Australia were dealt with on an individual basis by the Immigration Minister, utilising their discretion to grant entry permits under International Covenants, within the *Migration Act* 1958 (Cth). Between 1976 and 1981, 56 boats arrived, carrying more than 2,000 Indochinese boatpeople. This was "historically important", representing, for the first-time, large number of refugees, family reunion entrants and humanitarian[6] migrants were being accepted from Asia (Viviani, 1980) and the first large-scale intake of settlers whose language and culture were markedly different from previous waves of European refugees.[7] As policy intended to better manage the arrival of boatpeople, the Department established the first immigration processing centre near Sydney in 1976[8] and introduced major programs to deter asylum seekers from traveling by boat to Australia.

Practical result: A bipartisan policy welcomed over 150,000 Indochinese refugees at an average rate of 25,000 per year, who had departed Indochina by boat (Higley, Nieuwenhuysen & Neerup, 2011, p.8). Under Liberal Government leadership, Australia welcomed its largest intake of Refugee entrants to date, prompting the introduction of RSD mechanism and procedures in accord with international obligations.

Period: 1983-96, Trigger: Indochinese Wars, PM: Hawke (Labour Party: MAR '83) & Keating (Labour Party: DEC '91)

A focus on bipartisanship government in the 1980s underpinned the creation and implementation of multicultural policies to better settle and integrate boat

---

[4] Displaced people, in fear of being persecuted if forced to return home (to the country of habitual residence) may seek legal protection from a country's government, which has signed the Refugee Convention. Become asylum seekers upon request.

[5] Governments who are signatures to 1951 Refugee Convention and 1967 protocol are obligated to provide safe refuge to asylum seekers undertaking a legal assessment called Refugee Status Determination (RSD). Recognition as Refugees prevents people from being returned home (refoulement.)

[6] If refused refugee status, displaced people voluntarily returned or deported home, unless owed humanitarian protection under other international conventions or treaties. Non-refoulement is a universally recognized safety net and is a principle of customary international law prohibiting the forced return of displaced people to their state of origin or another state where their life or freedom could be threatened for discriminatory reasons.

[7] Published in Cultural Diversity and the Family (Ashfield: Ethnic Affairs Commission of NSW, 1997), Volume 3,

[8] DIEA (1977) p.22. cited in https://www.border.gov.au/CorporateInformation/Documents/immigration-history.pdf

arrivals. The success of these multicultural programs resulted in Australia being distinguished as a world leader in the implementation of multiculturalism. In parallel, growing resentment by Anglo Australian society against the rise of multiculturalism, led to the gradual dismantling of political bipartisanship. In 1988, the newly elected opposition leader John Howard argued for a return to "one Australia" through a reduction in Asian immigration, effectively linking it to the increasing push for anti-multicultural policies (Lobo, 2011, p.24). In 1989, new immigration policy created a legal basis for detention, by categorising all the asylum seekers who had arrived since November 1989 as "designated persons". Practical disorder soon followed when some of the Cambodian asylum seekers who arrived near Broome were not offered refuge, but prolonged detention.

In 1989, Australia joined the Comprehensive Plan of Action (CPA), a multinational organisation created to attain a coordinated international response to recurring outflows of refugees from Indochina and reducing the growing numbers languishing in camps across South East Asia. Under UNHCR leadership the CPA set the global standard, successfully operating for 7 years, obtaining the cooperation of enough third countries to maintain resettlement opportunities and inspiring some countries involved to establish formal, quota-based refugee resettlement programs.

Practical result: Overall the application of RSD policy and law up to 1996 may be considered successful. Australian refugee policy was bipartisan (all political parties agreed), resulting in stable effective management, an acceptance of diversity in Australian culture and the development of multiculturalism, within a socially cohesive framework. Australia co-operated under the UN, which managed the exodus of 3 million people, resettling over 2 million and repatriating 0.5 million. The UN's application of policy stopped the boats by allowing for family re-unification and a durable resettlement solution.

Period: 1996-2007, Trigger: Influx of approximately 9,500 boat arrivals (predominantly from Middle East), PM: Howard (Liberal Party: MAR '96)

The next influx of boat people commenced arriving in 1999. Predominantly Middle Eastern, their arrival prompted the Liberal Government to introduce a draconian Temporary Protection Visa (TPV) policy, under which refugees' claims required reassessment every 3 years and removed the opportunity for family reunification. This reflects a recent shift in Australian immigration and multicultural policy, with policy around boat arrivals increasingly focused on deterrence and border security for political gain and electioneering. In August 2001, the Government refused entry into Australian waters of a Norwegian cargo ship, the *Tampa*, which was carrying 483 rescued Afghan asylum-seekers. Soon followed the establishment of offshore processing centres in Nauru and Papua New Guinea (PNG) and a boat 'turnbacks' policy which mobilised the Australian Navy to prevent asylum-seeker boats reaching Australia. As a further safety measure, the Australian territories of Christmas Island and Ashmore Reef were 'excised' from the application of Australia's *Migration Act*. This "Pacific Solution" was widely criticized as being contrary to international refugee law, unjustifiably expensive to implement, and psychologically damaging for detainees.

Practical result: Almost 7 years after the institution of the Pacific Solution, virtually no asylum seeker boats had reached Australia, representing a policy success for the Liberal Government. However, stopping the boats and minimizing deaths at sea came at a substantial human cost and the UNHCR denounced the program as inhumane.

Period: 2007-13, Trigger: Labour Party Change, PM: Rudd (NOV '07), Gilliard (AUG '10)
In 2008, in an effort to align with UN policy, the newly elected Rudd Labour Government championed a more humane approach to boat arrivals. This significant policy shift prompted the termination of The Pacific Solution, the closure of Nauru's offshore processing centre, and the replacement of TPVs with Permanent Residence Visas (PRVs).

Following this change in Government policy, boat arrivals increased, hence deaths at sea increased, (noting no deaths at sea had been registered from Dec 2002 until Jan 2009[9]). Although the policy intention was legally correct, by dismantling the *Pacific Solution* to honour Australia's obligations to provide refugees with the right to permanent resettlement and the right to family reunion, practical disorder followed. The politicians who did not foresee the consequences of policy change, did not adequately plan to manage the increased numbers of boatpeople and, hence, a substantial unintended human and financial cost ensued, culminating in PM Rudd (Labour) losing the leadership in August 2010. The new Labour PM announced a change of direction to toughen government refugee policy by initiating an arrangement with the Malaysian government to take asylum seekers held in detention in Australia. In August 2011, it was successfully challenged in Australia's High Court and abandoned. As detention centres were overflowing, increasing pressures and financial costs, in December 2011, the Government abandoned their policy of extended mandatory detention for boat arrivals. Asylum seekers were progressively released from detention following identity, health and security checking. In March 2012, the Government introduced a

---

[9] Phillips. J (2014). Boat arrivals in Australia: a quick guide to the statistics, Parliament of Australia, Retrieved from http://www.aph.gov.au/About_Parliament/Parliamentary_ Departments/Parliamentary_Library/pubs/rp/rp1314/QG/BoatArrivals

streamlined RSD process, which contributed to a surge in boats arrivals and subsequent deaths at sea (see Graph 1 and 2).

Graph 1. Number of Unauthorised Maritime Arrivals (1989-2017)

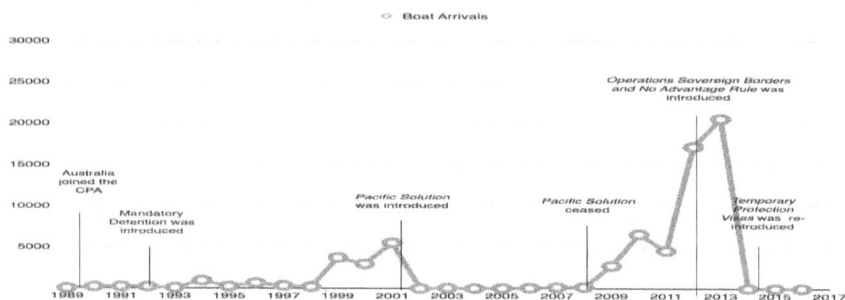

Source: Courtesy of the authors

Graph 2. Deaths of Boatpeople at sea (1989-2017)

Source: Courtesy of the authors

In response, the government introduced a number of deterrence mechanisms including the re-opening of the PNG and Nauru offshore processing centres in September 2012. In November 2012, "the no advantage rule" was introduced, to stop people who had arrived by boat after 13 August 2012 from being processed for RSD any faster than their counterparts who applied for RSD with the UNHCR in Indonesia. In 2013, the Australian mainland was excised from Australia's "migration zone", resulting in all UAM arrivals being unable to legally lodge a refugee claim in Australia and the introduction of a policy that would see all boat arrivals sent offshore to Nauru and Manus Island (PNG) for RSD processing and if successful, resettlement (Phillips, 2017).

Practical result: The impact of these policy changes was disorder and substantial human and financial cost. Due to increased numbers and RSD being under resourced, timeframes for primary and review decisions slowed dramatically. Between March and April 2011, a number of riots and demonstrations were across Australian in onshore detention centres, with unrest being attributed to overcrowding and RSD process delays, contributing to a further sense of hopelessness. Successful challenges in Australia's High and lower courts, due to poorly trained assessors and rushed and/or poorly designed government policy created costly delays.[10].

The policy of sending all asylum seekers offshore for processing failed, as both the Nauru and Manus' centres reached capacity before the majority of boat arrivals were transferred. A loss of confidence in the Labour Government ensued as their many policy changes failed to stop the increasing number of boat arrivals and deaths at sea, resulting in major political damage, which cumulated in an election loss in September 2013. This period is considered a failure by the majority of the voting population, synonymous with instability and fickle refugee policy centred on short-term political influence not proven policy precedent. This was intensified by a lack of political bipartisanship which resulted in increasingly divisive media coverage and brought about by political islamophobia, promoting border security to a key election issue for the Australian population.

Period: 2013-present, Trigger: Change of Government to Liberal, Prime Minister: Abbot (SEP '13), Turnbull (SEP '15)
As part of their core election promise, the Liberal Government introduced their "boat turn-back" policy under Operation Sovereign Borders (OSB)[11], a military-led border security operation aimed at combating maritime people smuggling. Boat arrivals were turned back to the country of departure and a "code of silence" policy was introduced, preventing media from accessing offshore processing centres or reporting boat turn backs. Legal aid funding was removed all RSD processing of onshore applicants halted until legislation making it more difficult to obtain refugee status was introduced. This cumulated in December 2014 with the introduction of legislative changes to **Replace:** Permanent Residence Visas (PRV), with Temporary Protection Visas (TPV), thus prohibiting family re-union, **Redefine:** Australia's international obligations in the Migration Act, remove references to the Refugee Convention in the legislation replacing it with a more restricted interpretation, and **Restrict:** the right to independent review.

---

[10] For example, in March 2013 the court found that the Government had applied the incorrect test under Convention Against Torture and International Covenant on Civil and Political Rights of UN.

[11] Australian Government: DIBP (2017). Operation Sovereign Borders, Retrieved from http://www.osb.border.gov.au/en/Operation-Sovereign-Borders

These policies were juxtaposed with the Government announcement in September 2015 that it would make an extra 12,000 humanitarian places available to Syrian and Iraqi refugees, in addition to the 13,750 places under its Humanitarian Programme.[12] In November 2016, the Australian Government announced that UMAs, in Nauru or PNG, would be considered for refugee resettlement in the United States, upon referral by UNHCR.

RSD processing offshore resulted in a high percentage of positive RSD outcomes, but with few successful applicants waiting to remain in Nauru or PNG. Nauru has only been prepared to grant 20-year visas to recognised refugees, whilst the PNG Government's position is to grant refugee visas that require annual renewal over 8 years, after which applicants will be eligible for citizenship. This policy has been further complicated by the April 2016 PNG Supreme Court ruling that detention was unconstitutional and ordering the end of 'illegal' detention. In Australia, High Court challenges to the legitimacy of offshore processing failed.

30,000 asylum seekers intended to be sent offshore remained in Australia and have been permitted to lodge RSD applications. Furthermore, since June 2015, only 3 of the 7 refugees who volunteered to settle in Cambodia remain, despite Australia covering all settlement costs for the initial 12 months in addition to the AUD 40 million of development assistance provided to Cambodia in exchange for cooperation.

Practical result: The period from 2013 onwards is considered by most Australian voters to be a success because "OSB" reduced the boat arrivals to almost zero. Although this policy was viewed as successful by voting Australians, it is considered an abdication of Australia's international obligations; employing the "Deterrence Model" principle, by not allowing any recognised refugee from the offshore processing centres to be resettled in Australia.

How Much Does Australia's Asylum Policy Cost?
The National Commission of Audit reported[13] that in 2010 the **annual expenditure** on the detention and processing of UMAs was **$118.4 million**, in contrast to the **$3.3 billion** spent in 2014. The per year cost of processing asylum seeker offshore is $450,000, compared to $239,000 for onshore processes, $100,000 for community detention processing, and $40,000 for those processed on community-based bridging visas. Australia's 2017–18 Federal Budget includes $713,641 million of funding for offshore processing

---

[12] Australian Government: DIBP (2017). Australia's response to the Syrian humanitarian crisis, Retrieved from https://www.border.gov.au/Trav/Refu/response-syrian-humanitarian-crisis

[13] The Kaldor Centre. (2017). The cost of Australia's asylum policy, Retrieved from http://www.kaldorcentre.unsw.edu.au/publication/cost-australias-asylum-policy

and settlement arrangements, down from more than $1 billion in 2016–17. This trend is projected to continue with the cost of offshore processing predicted to decrease to $430 million p.a. between 2018–21.

A Juxstaposed Policy Stance
A disconnect exists between Australia's crimogenic border policing and it's supposed commitment to a new humanitarian refugee resettlement policy. During the Leaders' Summit on Refugees the Australian PM, Malcom Turnbull stated that Australia would; i) provide an extra $130 million over 3 years to increase support for refugee communities in key countries of first asylum[14] and recently announced a $220 million Syrian humanitarian assistance package; ii) maintain the Humanitarian Program at 18,750 places from 2018-19 onwards; iii) assign a minimum number of places to those displaced from protracted refugee situations; iv) create new pathways for resettlement through the establishment of 1,000 places under a Community Support Program, v) support better settlement outcomes; and vi) participate in a US-led multilateral program to resettle refugees from Central America.

The period from 2013 onwards is considered a success given a combination of government policies to "stop the boats" succeeded. Although successful with the voting populous, it came with a substantial human cost due to Australia failing to meet international obligations. This cost was due to deterrence model principles banning recognised refugees at offshore processing centres from being resettled in Australia and saw the re-introduction of *TPVs*, compelling the UNHCR to voice "deep concerns" at the "worrying departure from international norms" reflected in the current resettlement policy developed by Australia and its Pacific partners. A lack of resources resulted in major delays, self-harm, suicide, children growing up in offshore detention in marginalised conditions causing mental breakdown and large-scale depression. Although Australia appears progressive in relation to the refugee context, ranking 3rd for resettling refugees through the UNHCR, the UNHCR however only resettled 107,000 refugees in 2016, a small proportion of displaced people around the world ($65.3 million) of whom only $16.1 million are assisted by the UNCHR.

Finally, studies have shown that refugees can bring material, cultural and demographic benefits to the communities in which they settle. We propose that in all future cost evaluations we should take these benefits into account.

Conclusion

After spending $9.6 billion the Australian government has *stopped the boats*, winning popular electoral support. However, whilst we acknowledge the need to *stop the boats* this has been at the expense of asylum-seekers and refugee rights. With 50% of our population born overseas or of foreign descent,

---

[14] Examples include: Jordan, Lebanon and Pakistan.

Australia is one of the world's most multicultural countries, which now faces challenges of balancing the long-term effect of increasing diversity, whilst preserving social cohesion. Only by finding this balance can Australia engender in its leadership the political-will needed to remove the issue of boatpeople from party politics and create practical solutions to manage refugee resettlement, repatriation and migration policies. In the world of increasing mobility, a globally adopted policy offering a legal pathway to refugees should incorporate; i) the identification of refugees through the provision of a robust RSD, ii) the inclusion of the right to family reunion; iii) a focus on minimising those financial and emotional costs resulting from leaving people to languish without an immigration outcome and iv) engendering the political will and regional cooperation across UN member states and countries of first reception to enable a durable solution for refugees. We believe these policy tweaks will help facilitate a more future-focused, cost effective and humane approach to forced migration.

References

Higley, J., Nieuwenhuysen, J.P. & Neerup, S. (Eds.) (2011). Immigration and the Financial Crisis: The United States and Australia Compared, *Monash Studies in Global Movements Series,* pp.8.

Lobo, M. (2011). Migration, Citizenship and Intercultural Relations: Looking Through the Lens of Social Inclusion, *Ashgate Publishing,* pp 24.

Phillips, J. (2017). Boat arrivals and boat 'turnbacks' in Australia since 1976: a quick guide to the statistics, *Parliament of Australia.* Retrieved from http://www.aph.gov.au/About_Parliament/Parliamentary_Departments/Parliamentary_L ibrary/pubs/rp/rp1617/Quick_Guides/BoatTurnbacks

Viviani, N. (1980). The Vietnamese in Australia: New Problems in Old Forms, *Griffiths University Research Lecture No 11, pp2. Published in Cultural Diversity and the Family (Ashfield: Ethnic Affairs Commission of NSW, 1997), Volume 3.*

Chapter 44. Building or Burning the Bridges? The Determinants of Return Migration Intentions of German-Turk Generations

Tolga Tezcan[1]

Abstract

What drives German-Turks to return to Turkey? This study attempts to answer this question by investigating the determinants of return migration intention among German-Turks. While German-Turks, invited to work in the booming post-war economy, have always been defined as "guest workers" and expected to return to Turkey eventually, they have preferred to stay in Germany, enjoy increased wealth by earning high wages, and benefits from the German welfare system. But things have changed since 2006, and the net migration number of Turks has now fallen to below zero for the first time. This study aims to identify the factors that influence the multifaceted issue of return migration intentions. I use the most recent "Migration Sample (M1)" of the German Socio-Economic Panel (SOEP), which includes 463 respondents who have a Turkish background, to estimate logistic regressions models for return intentions. This study focuses on testing the effects of four domains: (1) economic integration, (2) social and economic ties with Turkey, (3) discrimination, xenophobia, and multiple identities, and (4) generational status. The results indicate that all these domains make a contribution to return decisions.

Keywords: Germany, guest workers, return migration intentions, Turkey.

Introduction

Germany is arguably the most important country to examine Turkish immigrants within an international migration context. Germany is the largest Turkish community outside of Turkey and German-Turks are the largest ethnic minority group, with a population of approximately 2.9 million (The Statistisches Bundesamt, 2016). Beyond question, today's Germany cannot be understood without the presence of its German-Turkish population (Kaya, 2007). Regardless of contemporary debates, whether they constitute the "melting pot" or resist assimilation, the fact is that they are part of Germany, at least statistically. Nonetheless this fact has begun to evolve. Not only Germany, but also other developed countries have been facing the same demographic change: *return migration.*

According to The Migration Report (Statistisches Bundesamt, 2016), while 22,058 Turks immigrated to Germany, 25,520 Turks returned to Turkey in 2014. As of 2013, the number of new Turkish immigrants and returnees were 23,230 and 27,896, respectively. This trend has been consistently witnessed after 2005, and net migration of Turks has been negatived since then. Turks have immigrated to Germany for mainly family unification purposes, not as a labor force since that time. This trend has raised a minor alarm about the population dynamics of both Germany and Turkey, but its impact may be larger in the near future. The inevitable question is why do German-Turks

[1] Tolga Tezcan is a PhD candidate in the Department of Sociology at University of Florida, Department of Sociology, University of Florida, Gainesville, Florida, US. E-mail: ttezcan@ufl.edu.

initiate this remigration flow? To address these questions, in this paper through the critical evaluation of the relevant literature, I examine why, in what ways, and based on which factors German-Turks intend to return to Turkey. Bu utilizing the data of "Migration Sample (M1)" of the German Socio-Economic Panel (2014), this study aims to answer the following research questions: (I) How well do indicators of economic integration explain the increased patterns of return migration intention, and which economic approach is applicable to German-Turks' return migration intentions? (II) Do German-Turks maintain transnational activities to negotiate conflicts in the host in order to find ways to stay or is "staying connected" with home a strategy to prepare them for the possibility of returning? (III) To what extent do perceived collective discrimination and xenophobia shape the magnitude of return migration intentions? (IV) In what ways do self-identification, (feeling Turkish or feeling German) determine return migration intentions? Specifically, do multiple identities take place together or do identities become dichotomous in shaping return intentions? (V) What are the main differences among German-Turk generations in terms of adopting different return intention trajectories?

Theoretical Background and Hypotheses

The neoclassical model explains return migration on the basis of a cost-benefit decision, or in other words, unfulfilled income expectations (Todaro, 1969). Generally, migrants move to another place to maximize net lifetime earnings, however, they may return if the income differential gap between home and host decreases. With this theory, return is considered a "failure" caused by a miscalculation of the migrants and their inability to benefit from the migration. Their human capital no longer corresponds to the market needs or as they initially expected it would (Constant & Massey, 2002; Cassarino, 2004). This interpretation of return migration is based on conceiving migration as a "one-way process" in which migrants attempt to achieve a permanent settlement and family unification. Subsequently, there is no rationale to return since life conditions in the host country are assumed to be satisfactory.

Yet, under the new economics of labor migration model (Stark, 1991), migration is seen as a livelihood strategy by the household instead of an individual decision because often the best suited members of the household are sent to another area in order to maximize the household income (de Haas et al. 2014). For this model, fulfillment of the role as a migrant is equalized to the degree of contribution to the household income, which requires either remitting earnings or saving up for future investments at the home country. Within the context of the above economic models, and the "guest worker" characteristics of German-Turks, *I expect to find evidence for neoclassical economics model in that German-Turks who have economic challenges will be more prone to form a return intention (H1).*

The two previous models focus on the "success / failure" paradigm within the context of economic motives. Alternatively, new debates have been initiated in efforts to reveal the existing social and economic ties with both the home and host countries. Migration studies have since adopted a new term, "transnationalism", introduced by Schiller and colleagues (1992) in the early 1990s. This perspective pays extensive attention to the back-and-forth movement of migrants, who attempt to construct physical connections and identities towards home and host countries simultaneously. Due to technological advances and reduced costs in transportation and communication, transnational connections and practices have steadily strengthened (Vertovec, 2008). Migrants create "fluid and multiple identities grounded in both their society of origin and in the host societies" (Schiller et al. 1992, p.11), and the return is no longer interpreted as the end of the migration cycle (Cassarino, 2004). Although return is seen as part of an ongoing-process, within the German-Turk case, it could be argued that having "feet in two societies" eases and enables the return. Taking into consideration the transnational approach, *I hypothesize that transnational activities would be positively correlated with greater return intentions (H2).*

After more than fifty years of Turkish migration flows to Germany, there is still the presence of collective discrimination. Collective discrimination, as a semantic knowledge acquired with socialization, precipitates ethnic identification, even if migrants have never witnessed it, which then leads to cutting ties with the outgroup and may lead to migrants considering their return to the home country (Holtz et al. 2013). New generations cannot escape from the cumulative disadvantages transferred from their migrant ancestors. Because the first Turkish migration waves were composed of only uneducated and unqualified masses, and they were engaged in only 3-D (dirty, dangerous, and difficult) jobs, the type of occupations younger generations' parents performed becomes a source of irritation and anger, and corresponds to a stigmatized identity in the collective memory of German-Turks, especially for younger generations. This is especially the case once migrants are blamed for taking resources in the era of economic difficulties (White, 1997) which increases the xenophobia. To shed light on the link among collective discrimination, xenophobia, and return intentions, *I expect that German-Turks who perceive collective discrimination against their ingroup and have concerns of xenophobia tend to have a stronger intention for return (H3).*

It is well documented that migrants actively manipulate their identities to accommodate to multiple social localities and resist subordination (Schiller et al. 1992), to live transnationally (de Haas, 2010), to prepare better for return (Farrell et al. 2012), and to revive the image of "home" as "a mythic place of desire in the diasporic imagination" (Brah 2005, p.188). However, the factors that lead to adopting different levels of multiple identities has received less attention. Portes (1999) suggests that the level of discrimination and perceived hostility faced by migrants are key to comprehend their attachments to mainstream identity. Once they face such discriminatory attitudes, they steadily begin to identify themselves with their origin roots which separate them from the host society both symbolically and physically. In the case of German-Turks, it is especially the younger generation that tends to form stronger (re-)ethnisation when they perceive that they or other German-Turks are discriminated against (Skrobanek, 2009). Taking into consideration self-identification through (re-)ethnisation, I hypothesize that *the degree of feeling both Turkish and German have positive and negative effects on return migration intention, respectively, which means that how German-Turks identify themselves determines their return plans (H4).*

Generational status is a missing component within return intention debates, yet, there are some studies that integrate generation in trying to understand return intentions. In a qualitative study focusing on British Pakistanis, Bolognani (2007) argued that 1st generations' idea of returning is mainly shaped by socio-economic issues, whereas the subsequent generations' return intentions are motivated by political tensions and Islamophobia. Kunuroglu (2015) suggests that 2nd generation German Turks have two motives to return: either (1) they do not envision a future similar to the life of the 1st generation in Germany, or (2) they do not want to raise their children in a social and economic environment in which they are still struggling. In these regards, it is highly likely that *migrants who belong to different generational status will adopt different return intention trajectories, along with having distinct motivations for doing so. Specifically, I expect that younger generations are more likely to form return migration intentions than 1st generation (H5).*

Data and Methods

I use the most recent "Migration Sample (M1)" of the German Socio-Economic Panel (SOEP). SOEP, launched in 1984, provides longitudinal data on residents of Germany. Due to the dynamic structure of populations with migration, background regarding underrepresentation of new immigration waves in the last decade necessitated a different type of research that includes a representative sample size focusing on immigrant households. In accordance with this purpose, the first wave of this research was initiated in 2013. For this study, I focused on the most recent data set from 2014, which included 463 respondents who have a Turkish background. The fact that respondents of this sub-research are also the respondents of the main SOEP research in 2014 allowed me to examine the extensive information about the households and their members. To accomplish this, I generated a dataset including background information on immigrant households and their members by combining the migration survey, the household survey, the individual survey, and generated variables which are consolidated from different datasets. Using Migration Sample (M1) of the SOEP, I estimated logistic regressions to predict German-Turks' return migration intentions. Given that some of the variables are measured at the household level, the models adjusted the standard errors by taking into account the cluster effect *(vce(cluster))* in Stata.

Findings

As predicted by the neoclassical economics model, except the unemployment subsidy II, all the economic integration predictors - being employed, receiving payment for more than one child, satisfied with household income, and owning a house in Germany – are associated with return intentions in Model 2 and Model 3. Economic integration via labor market participation significantly influenced return decisions in that being employed decreased the likelihood to develop return intentions. However, receiving unemployment benefit II as a household had no impact on the decision-making process. Even though these benefits are distributed to prevent people from falling into poverty, it does not influence stay intentions like being employed. Additionally, German Turks who receive child benefits for more than one child are more likely to stay; however, receiving a benefit for only one child is not an enough economic motive to stay, and at this point parental concerns may also influence return intentions, particularly the concern of "raising a child in a foreign land" may result in increasing return intentions. Based on the data available, those migrants who have bought a house in Germany are 3 to 4 times more likely to stay in all three models. This could be due to the house in the host country turning into a barrier to move to another area, alternatively the investment in a house is the manifestation of staying intention by itself. Finally, satisfaction with household income had a negative effect on return intention. That is, the higher the household income; the less likely migrants are to consider returning to Turkey. These results confirmed the expected negative effect of economic integration on return migration intentions in accordance with the neoclassical economics model (H1).

As predicted by the transnational perspective, social and economic ties with Turkey enhanced German-Turks' intention to return. Respondents who mostly use Turkish media, have very good Turkish language skills, contact with friends and relatives in Turkey, send remittances abroad, and visited Turkey more than once in the last 2 years, are more likely to have higher return intentions. Models showed that intentions to return are most prevalent among German-Turks with strong transnational ties (H2). Return intention was strongly influenced by visiting Turkey more than once in the last 2 years. This influence on return intention, through attachment to Turkey, depends on the frequency of the visits. Those migrants that visited Turkey only once in the last 2 years did not initiate return intention. The migrants that only visited

Turkey once could be categorized as those that never visited Turkey either because they have no ties, or all their relatives are living in Germany. The migrants that visited Turkey more than once, showed a strong commitment to the homeland because of various agendas. These trips may be made to set up a business, to buy a house or land, to familiarize the children to the homeland, to fulfill longing, or for just a "training" for their possible future.

Media also played an important role in return intention. The use of Turkish media fosters links with the homeland, which is a determinant of return intention. Those that follow Turkish media have a 2.24 times higher chance of considering return. Turkish media often imposes cultural comparisons that emphasize a superiority of Turkish culture. The persistence of using Turkish media has been described as "some kind of internal ghettoization." (Ögelman 2003, p.180) However, Turkish media is mainly implemented as a strategy used by parents to remind children of their "cultural heritage". Except for limited in-house dialogues, Turkish channels appear as a vital source of learning Turkish for the children who are exposed to only German in the schools.

Estimates in model 3 show the contribution of discrimination and identities as predictors of return intention. Perceived collective discrimination (odds ratio: 2.38) and being concerned by xenophobia (odds ratio: 2.78) are positively and strongly associated with return intention (H3). German-Turks cannot escape from their stigmatized identity, and a general hate of foreigners in Germany increases the likelihood of German-Turks forming return intentions. In German-Turks case, hostility and discrimination catalyzes the entrenched national-origin identification (Ögelman, 2003). It is evident that the results confirm hypothesis 4: how migrants identify themselves also determined their return plans. For a one-unit increase in the level of feeling Turkish there was an increase in the odds of return intention of 3.26 times when they did not feel German ("not at all"). Despite the fact that feeling German was not significant predictor, a negative interaction effect (odds ratio: 0.80) was present. When the level of feeling Turkish increased, the effect of feeling German decreased, and vice versa. This outcome controverts the approach that "multiple identities" take place together posed by transnationalism. However, these two self-identifications become dichotomous on the impacts on return intention. Not to mention, it could be claimed that the degree of feeling Turkish has a positive, and the degree of feeling German has a negative effect on return migration intention (H4).

Models 1 and 2 showed that 1.5 generation and 2nd generation German-Turks are more likely to consider return as compared to 1st generation. In model 2, the 2nd generation had the highest probability of forming return intentions (odds ratio of 4.23), however when discrimination and identities are controlled for in model 3, the 1.5 generation gained the highest probability (odds ratio of 4.00) of return intention. This outcome supports H5.

Table 1. Binary logistic regression analysis for return migration intention to Turkey

	(1) Economic Integration	(2) + Social and Economic Ties with Turkey	(3) + Discrimination and Identities
Economic Integration (NE and NELM)			
Employed	**0.60*** (0.2)	**0.50*** (0.1)	**0.43*** (0.1)
Households receive unemployment subsidy	0.60 (0.2)	0.72 (0.3)	0.66 (0.3)
Number of children eligible for child benefit (ref. more than one)			
One	1.59 (0.6)	1.79 (0.7)	**2.46*** (1.1)
No child, not eligible, or in somewhere	1.07 (0.4)	1.51 (0.6)	1.49 (0.6)
Satisfied with household income	**0.61*** (0.2)	**0.45**** (0.1)	**0.42**** (0.2)
Owner of a house in Germany	**0.36**** (0.1)	**0.33**** (0.1)	**0.23***** (0.1)
Social and Economic Ties with Turkey (Transnationalism)			
Mostly Turkish media		**2.93**** (1.1)	**2.20*** (0.9)
Turkish oral proficiency		**2.48*** (0.9)	**2.09*** (0.9)
Contact to friends and relatives in Turkey		**4.73***** (2.2)	**4.59**** (2.3)
Remittances		**2.22*** (0.9)	**2.13*** (0.9)
Visits to Turkey last 2 years (ref. never)			
Once		1.42 (0.5)	1.31 (0.5)
More than once		**2.95*** (1.5)	**2.49*** (1.3)
Discrimination and Identities			
Perceived collective discrimination			**2.38**** (0.8)
Concerned by xenophobia			**2.78**** (0.9)
Feel Turkish			**3.26**** (1.4)
Feel German			2.01 (1.1)
Feel Turkish × Feel German			**0.80*** (0.1)
Control variables			
Generations (ref. 1st generation)			
1.5 generation	1.39 (0.6)	**3.63**** (1.7)	**4.00**** (2.1)
2nd generation	1.62 (0.5)	**4.23***** (1.9)	**3.56**** (1.8)
Female	0.89 (0.2)	0.67 (0.2)	**0.52*** (0.2)
More than basic education	1.56 (0.4)	1.36 (0.4)	1.68 (0.6)
Age (ref. 46+)			
Under 29	1.96 (1.0)	2.46 (1.4)	**3.90*** (2.4)
30-45	**2.35*** (1.1)	**2.45*** (1.2)	**2.70*** (1.4)
N	463	463	463
Pseudo R^2	0.07	0.18	0.27
Wald Chi-Square	26.18	58.51	85.33
Log-pseudo likelihood	-191.7	-168.4	-148.5

Exponentiated coefficients; Standard errors in parentheses * $p < 0.05$, ** $p < 0.01$, *** $p < 0.001$

Discussion and Concluding Remarks

This study examined the determinants of return migration intention among German-Turks. While German-Turks, invited to work in the booming post-war economy, have been always coded as "guest worker" and expected to return eventually, they have preferred to stay, enjoy instant wealth by earning high wages, and benefit from German welfare system. But things have changed after 2006, and the net migration number of Turks has now fallen to under zero for the first time.

This study is focused on testing the effects of four domains: (1) economic integration, (2) social and economic ties with home country, (3) discrimination, xenophobia, and multiple identities, and (4) generational status. First, the neoclassical economics model, which assumes migrants are more likely to return once they face economic difficulties, is seen as more applicable to the German-Turks case, instead of the new economic labor model, which asserts the argument that migrants are essentially "target earners" who are expected to return when they reach their goals. It is also noteworthy that, in line with neoclassical economics model, having more than two children receiving child benefits decreases the return intention, but unemployment benefit II has no impact. Many feel "Europe has come to an end", and Europe cannot fulfill what it promised anymore.

Second, the domain of social and economic ties with Turkey triggers return considerations. Examining social and economic practices across borders with a transnational lens is quite helpful to understand return migration, however, not in the direction of what transnationalism argues at its core. While this theoretical framework predicts that "staying connected" triggers attachments to both home and host, and serves as grounds to negotiate with both cultures, in the German-Turks' case these ties rule out the possibility of staying intention in Germany. In light of the evidence shown by this study, transnational ties are the growing mechanisms thanks to the technological advances and the reduced costs in transportation and communication. German-Turks are increasingly preparing for their future in Turkey.

Third, perceived collective discrimination and concerns on xenophobia were found to be catalysts of returning. German-Turks are the targets of collective discrimination based on their stigmatized identity, hate of foreigners, and xenophobia, in Germany. German-Turks raise concerns that they may have the same destiny as Jews who had been exterminated in the concentration camps. This study also found an evidence that how migrants identify themselves also influenced their return plans: The degree of feeling Turkish has a positive, and the degree of feeling German has a negative effect on return migration intention.

Fourth, and finally, this study sheds new light on generational status. The 1.5 and 2nd generation German-Turks are more likely to develop return migration intentions than the 1st generation. Two decades ago, the common interpretation of the 1st generation's return intention was built as follows: 1st generation German-Turks always dream about returning after retirement, but as their family expanded in Germany they wanted to be close with their children and grandchildren, the 2nd and 3rd generation, who have limited exposure to Turkey, who are not fully integrated into either German or Turkish culture, and have less inclination to return to a place with which they are unfamiliar. At the same time, as the 1st generation aged the high-quality medical care in Germany delays their return (White, 1997). In brief, for the 1st generation the decision of staying or in other words delayed returning was determined by the existence of their children and grandchildren, and their reluctance of returning. Of the moment, the wind is now blowing backwards. With or without required social and economic capital, younger generations precipitate the return arrangements.

References

Brah, A. (2005). Cartographies of diaspora: Contesting identities. London: Taylor & Francis.

Cassarino, J. P. (2004). Theorising return migration: A revisited conceptual approach to return migrants." International Journal on Multicultural Societies, 6, 253–279.

Constant, A., & Douglas S. M. (2002). Return migration by German guestworkers: Neoclassical versus new economic theories. International Migration 40(4), 5–38.

de Haas, H., Fokkema, T., & Fihri, M. (2014). Return migration as failure or success? Journal of International Migration and Integration, 16(2):415–429.

de Haas, H. 2010. Migration and development: A theoretical perspective. International Migration Review, 44(1):227–264.

Farrell, M., Mahon, M., & McDonagh, J. (2012). The rural as a return migration destination. European Countryside 4(1):31–44.

Holtz, P., Dahinden, J., & Wagner, W. (2013). "German Muslims and the 'integration debate': Negotiating identities in the face of discrimination. Integrative Psychological and Behavioral Science, 47(2):231–248.

Kaya, A. (2007). German-Turkish transnational a separate space of their own space: A Separate space of their own. German Studies Review, 30(3):483–502.

Kunuroglu, F. (2015). Turkish return migration from Western Europe: Going home from home. Unpublished doctoral dissertation, Tilburg University.

Ögelman, N. (2003). Documenting and explaining the persistence of homeland politics among Germany's Turks. International Migration Review, 37(1):163–193.

Portes, A. (1999). Conclusion: Towards a new world - the origins and effects of transnational activities. Ethnic and Racial Studies, 22(2):463–477.

Schiller, N. G., Basch, L., & Blanc-Szanton, C. (1992). Transnationalism: A new analytic framework for understanding migration. Annals New York Academy of Sciences, 645:1–24.

Skrobanek, J. (2009). Perceived discrimination, ethnic identity and the (re-)ethnicisation of youth with a Turkish ethnic background in Germany. Journal of Ethnic and Migration Studies, 35(4):535–554.

Stark, O. (1991). The migration of labour. Oxford: Blackwell.

Statistisches Bundesamt. (2016). Migrationsbericht des bundesamtes für migration und flüchtlinge im auftrag der bundesregierung (Migrationsbericht 2014). Received from http://www.bamf.de/SharedDocs/Anlagen/DE/Publikationen/Migrationsberichte/migrati onsbericht-2014.pdf. Accessed: 23.05.2017.

Todaro, M. P. (1969(. A model of labor migration and urban unemployment in less developed countries. The American Economic Review, 59(1):138–148.

Vertovec, S. (2008). Circular migration: The way forward in global policy? Canadian Diversity, 6(3): 36–40.

White, J. B. (1997). Turks in the new Germany. American Anthropologist, 99(4):754–769.

Chapter 45. Crimmigration in Brazil and the Netherlands: How the Phenomenon of Securitization can be a Fuel to These Processes?

Laís Azeredo Alves[*]

Abstract

The purpose of this paper is to verify the extent to which Brazilian Migration Policy has been influenced by the US War on Drugs and how, justified through a security discourse, it employs practices that violate human rights. A key objective is to determine if the combined effects of drug securitization and historical racism are resulting in the start of a "crimmigration" process. The fact that the federal police, the agency in charge of policing drug trafficking, is also the one that manages immigration, is a major factor in this assessment. This paper further analyses the immigration policy of the Netherlands, for two key reasons. Because a Crimmigration process is also apparent in the Netherlands comparison with the Brazilian context provides for an assessment of the relative degrees of Crimmigration. Secondly, because Dutch drugs policy is fundamentally different to Brazil's, it provides scope for valuable insights into how differing causal factors lead to the same results, such as the fact both countries treat migration policy with a security bias. The methodology applied in this research is based on bibliographic materials and governmental documents related to the immigration process in Brazil and in the Netherlands.

Keywords: Brazil, Crimmigration, Netherlands

Introduction

The purpose of this paper is to verify to which extent the Brazilian Migration Policy has been influenced by the US War on Drugs and how, justified through a security discourse, it employs practices that violate human rights. A key objective is to determine if the combined effects of drug securitization and historical racism are resulting in the start of a "crimmigration" process. The fact that the federal police, the agency in charge of policing drug trafficking, is also the one that manages immigration, is a major factor in this assessment. This paper further analyses the immigration policy of the Netherlands, for two key reasons. Because a Crimmigration process is also apparent in the Netherlands (Leun; Barker; Woude, 2017), comparison with the Brazilian context provides for an assessment of the relative degrees of Crimmigration. Secondly, because Dutch drugs policy is fundamentally different to Brazil's, it provides scope for valuable insights into how differing causal factors lead to the same results, such as the fact both countries treat migration policy with a security bias.

The research sets out to develop the proposition that Migration Policy is influenced by exogenous and endogenous factors. Amongst the exogenous factors, it is necessary to consider the influence of the US on Brazilian policies since the XIX Century (Monroe Doctrine). Due to the Globalization process, the International System values have also proven important influencers of

---

[*] Institute of Geography and Spatial Planning - University of Lisbon.
E-mail: laasaleh@gmail.com

governing policies, this is clearly evident in the prevalence of a security approach towards two phenomenon: drug trafficking and irregular migration. Among the key endogenous factors to consider for Brazil, is racism towards afrodescendents and the prevalent perception of this ethnic group as crimminals, linked to ethnic profiling practices. Similarities can be drawn with the Netherlands in this respect; there are indications according to Leun and van der Woude (2011), that some ethnic groups, notably people from Antillean or Moroccan background are subject to greater police suspicion and investigation compared to the rest of the population.

Differently from the Dutch historical welcome policy for immigrants from distinct origins during periods of high economic demand, Brazilian migration policy has historically selected desired immigrants in a racial basis. The situation in Netherlands changed over the past decades, prevailing a security bias towards some immigrant groups, characterizing what could be called a "culture of control" (Leun, Woude, 2011). In Brazil, migration law dates from the military dictatorship (1980) and, though not strictly racist in its official content, identifies migration as a security risk. This needs to be borne in mind when recent practices by the government and its agencies need to be observed considering these aspects.

The Crimmigration Process: why?

The "crimmigration" theory emerged in the United States and was created by Juliet Stumpf (2006) as a way of understanding the process that had taken place in the country since the 1980s. The core of this theory was related to the consonance between the migratory and criminal policies, which resulted in the loss of rights by immigrants in the United States. This was due to the hardening of the criminal law for irregular immigrants and the insertion of violations of the immigration law as infractions of criminal law. Therefore, even detention takes place through accelerated procedures that do not respect the due legal process (Hernandez, 2014).

The intersection point between criminal and migration law is easily understandable through the inclusion and exclusion characters present in the two policies. Being an immigrant in an irregular situation makes the punishment harder, which implies a differentiation of treatment and access to rights between nationals and non-nationals (Stumpf, 2006). It is not only about criminal law, but also about social practices that strengthen the crimmigration process. The perceptions that are built about some immigrants groups that they are in not only an irregular situation and are undesirable, but that they represent a danger to the society are being prevalent. (Guild, 2008).

An irregular immigrant is the focal point of the criminalization process. This occurs without a problematization about the situation of irregularity and the deconstruction of the idea that it is not about an option of the immigrant, but a real imposition of the State. A perception of certain groups of immigrants as "enemies" is built and this corroborates the policies that make it difficult to regularize their migration status from undocumented to documented. This situation generates a cycle that favors the process of criminalization of these groups, since it is difficult to regularize and the main factors of attraction and repulsion are not solved, people continue to migrate in an illegal way. As the States are not able to control theses flows, especially the ones through irregular ways, the decision for the criminalization is a possible response, trying to prevent more immigrants to come. In this way, irregular immigration introduced as a crime is presented as a challenge to national security, which must be combated with the use of military means, such as policing and border closure (Guia; Pedroso 2015).

The consonance between immigration and criminal policies can be very problematic and result in violation and loss of rights on the part of the immigrants and also to collaborate in the insertion of the migratory issue in the scope of the security. Criminalization can occur in a number of ways, such as from the hardening of the criminal law for immigrants, to the insertion of violations of the migratory law as violations of criminal law, so that even detention occurs through accelerated procedures that do not respect the due to legal process (Hernandez, 2014). In addition, other aspects such as deportation serving as an addendum to penalization in cases of immigrants, even those in a regular situation, thus occurring the application of migratory law in the service of criminal law. The reverse is also possible, when criminal law is used in what should be the jurisdiction of migratory law, increasing penalties (Moraes, 2015). In this way, there is clearly a differentiation between nationals and non-nationals in the treatment of criminal matters, so that being a foreigner means being more vulnerable to more punishments and, therefore, access to rights between these two groups is different. A neuralgic similarity between the two policies is observable, both of which are responsible for distinguishing the "included" and the "excluded" (Sumpf, 2006).

Geographical, cultural, economical and historical terms are important aspects that must be taken into consideration when analyzing who is more plausible to be in or out the citizenship agreement. In this way, to highlight the criteria that defines the desired and unwanted individuals in a society is important, so that it is possible to question and problematize the permanence of racist criteria, derived from historical processes. Determining who is a criminal is also part of a historical and social process, what is considered as crime changes depending on the country. Who you are, where you are from, your religion, your level of education and your culture are aspects analyzed when the State is deciding whether you are welcome or undesired. There is also the possibility of being the perfect type of irregular immigrant who will be allowed to stay in the country as long as you keep yourself productive and silent (MIGIANO, 2009), without requiring any rights or public assistance.

Determining exclusion does not mean inserting someone or something into the security sphere. However, in the last three decades, exclusion has been increasingly securitized, as a form of social control, to enable the state to manage more effectively its control over civil bodies (Foucault, 2000). The fluidity of flows and borders and the inability of the State to deal with these issues in an imperative manner may be one of the explanations for securitization of the excluded. In addition to the aforementioned aspects, the creation of an external enemy is a rhetoric widely used in situations in which the State is inefficient in the exercise of its functions and blames another factor for the problems of its interference. After the end of the bipolar conflict it became necessary to justify the continuity of investments in security and defense since there was no more the imminence of a war between the then superpowers. From this, social issues like immigration and drugs became security matters, treated as threats that needed to be controlled and banned.

In the 1970's, at the European level, with the oil crisis of 1970, which weakened economies worldwide, intolerance against immigrants increased. Currently, the irregular stay in ten member states started to be punishable by arrest and / or fine. This allowed to the isolation and exclusion of these groups, who feared being discovered and deported (Miggiano, 2009 2006). This security approach has reached other countries, such as the Netherlands (Leun, Woude, 2011). The irregular immigrant is inserted in a criminal status similar to transnational crimminals like drug dealers, human traffickers and terrorists. In the next topic we will understand how the crimmigration process occurred in the Netherlands, what possibly had created the grounds to make it happen.

Crimmigration in the Netherlands

In the European context, the Netherlands has emerged as a case study for the phenomenon of crime due to its role in adopting restrictive policies on immigration. In the last two decades countless actions have been implemented to stop entry, to exclude (from social benefits and public assistance) and to expel irregular immigrants. (Leun, 2006). The Dutch government has made the threshold of legal residence for foreigners more vulnerable, with an increase in the number of crimes committed by immigrants in the criminal sector. As a result, these individuals, not only undocumented, became subject to more severe punishments. The fact that the crime was commited by an immigrant makes the offense potentialized. Understanding this starts from the idea of the immigrant as someone who is wrong in itself to be present in a land that is not his or her home. In this way, all of their sins are doubled and aggravated by the sin of immigration (Molfetta, 2017).

In the last decades, the Netherlands has developed a culture of control in which criminals and immigrants are seen in an associated way. In the midst of the emergence of a control culture, there has been a justice system based on prevention and in this expansion of preventive means, the search for possible risks has become a routine policy (Woude, Leun, 2011). The so-called actuarial justice is accompanied by discretionary powers of those who exercise the law. The problem is that such discretion can be permeated by racial, ethnic, religious, and national generalizations rather than more objective behavioral evidence. For some scholars, there is a process of ethnic profiling in the Netherlands - the use of criteria based on race, ethnicity, skin color, nationality, language and religion in law enforcement at operational and organizational levels without objective justification, which determines action (Amnesty, 2017; Woude, Leun, 2011).

In the case of the Netherlands, the country has long been recognized as a space of tolerance, without obsession with issues of crime. Fear and crime have now become the core of Dutch government policy. Despite the drop in crime rates since 2002, high incarceration rates, political discourse, and the construction of the other as a threat have become prevalent (Woude, Leun, Nijland, 2014).

September 11 contributed to this situation, but the fertile terrain of this kind of perspective had been watered for some time. Criticism of the multicultural model adopted by the Netherlands coupled with the high representativeness of non-Western minority ethnicities in crime registries, coupled with integration problems generated domestic discussions about possible ways forward. The association between ethnicity and social problems, especially crime, gained political relevance and the population began to support stricter measures, such as deportation to immigrants who had committed crimes - mostly of Moroccan origin - and the use of Measures such as searches and seizures for young people targeted to Antillean nationals (Woude, Leun, Nijland, 2014).

This social construction legitimized a greater rigidity in the approach of public security agents. The target audience for these interventions had specific ethnic characteristics, where offspring or immigrants from African countries were standing on the streets with recurrence and Poles, for example, were more likely to be stopped by the police to check their blood alcohol level. A series of measures were taken to deal specifically with groups of Moroccan and Antillean immigrants, which fit the spectrum of the symbolic suspect. It is possible to observe the recurrence of these practices in the European Union, although it is not allowed by the International Law, because besides contributing to racist policies and practices, it also leads to stigmatization and social polarization (Woude, Leun, Nijland, 2014).

Inumerous political and social issues have made this connection between immigration, ethnic minorities and security possible. These issues influenced policy work and the use of "proactive" security control policies that allowed police officers to approach suspected persons, meant actions focused on specific groups, showing signs of discrimination (Mutsaers, Siebers & de Ruijter, 2015).

There is substantial evidence of ethnic profiling by the Dutch police and the Royal Netherlands Marechaussee in the context of traffic control, identity and immigration stops, and preventative searches. Studies show that ethnic profiling is a structural problem caused by broad and vaguely articulated police powers, weak accountability mechanisms for police stop-and-search operations (International Amnesty, 2017, p.10). This process of building certain ethnic groups from a negative perspective has become quite present in Dutch society. Even more when treated also under an economic bias, in which immigrants find themselves in more vulnerable conditions, due to processes that are recurrently associated with their cultural specificities, in the condition of another. In this sense, political factors are ignored in the process of social and economic integration of these individuals (Mutsaers, Siebers & de Ruijter, 2015). (Woude, Leun, Nijland, 2014).

In the next topic, we will discuss the situation in Brazil, if it can be said that some level of crimmigration might be happening there based on some institutional and legal aspects, bearing in mind the dutch case.

Crimmigration in Brazil: is it happening?

The situation in Brazil is full of nuances and complex issues, this part of the research only intends to explore which aspects might be considered to understand if there is a prevalence of a security perspective in the Brazilian Migration Policy. The general hypothesis is that there a historical racism in Brazil that has always determined who are the desired and who are the ones not welcome in the territory. This can be seen, considering some historical moments in the Brazilian Migration Policy. Besides this, there is the historical influence of the USA in the Brazilian policy basis.

The image of a welcoming country has accompanied Brazil since the colonial period, because it was the territory of several peoples, especially from Europe, but also from Africa, who were brought here forcibly. The receptivity of the natives, however, had as answer the imposition of values and rules by the settlers, who understood to be in a "civilizatory mission". This image of a large immigrant receiving country was strengthened at the turn of the 19th and 20th centuries, with the national project of reception and integration of immigrants, which were directed to work in coffee growing. In the period, it was also sought the construction of the ideology of Brazilian nation, which should consist of a population with a white majority, with European culture and customs prevailing over those of the native population of Indians and enslaved

Africans (Oliveira, 2014). The model of "sanitation" was based on racial criteria, in which the majority of the population - represented by Indians and mestizos - represented a supposed bankruptcy of the nation (Oliveira, 2014, p.4). The encouragement of population whitening represented the perpetuation of the understanding of blacks and mestizos as inferior, which was corroborated by pseudoscientific theories that preached the superiority of certain races over other (Moraes, 2016, p.307).

In the last decades of the XIX century, the State imposed restrictions to the entry of "indigenous people from Asia or Africa". These people could enter the country only under authorization of the National Congress. As for other nationalities, it was enough to be "fit for work" and "not subject to the criminal action of their country" in accordance with Decree 528 of 1890. In addition, the decree foresaw that the commanders of the vessels that brought these people would be subject to fines, and in case of recidivism, would be subject to the loss of privileges. (Chamber of Deputies, 2017). The Penal Code of 1890 corroborated this restrictive immigration of a racist nature, so that it legalized ways to reduce the number of blacks and mestizos in society by predicting "the expulsion of strangers or capoeira foreigners" (Moraes, 2016).

In 1930, the government enacted acts that limited the entry of foreigners in Brazil (Demartine, 2011). The labor supply was reduced and with the establishment and in 1934 quotas were established that established the maximum of 2% of immigrants from each nationality who had arrived in the country in the last 50 years (Constituição Federal, 1934). According to Moraes (2015, p.309), the quotas, limited on the basis of national characteristics and the physical working conditions of the immigrants, served to indirectly curb the immigration of Asians considered as "unassimilable".

Between 1930 and 1945, expulsion and deportation practices recurred, on the grounds that foreigners represented an ideological and economic danger to the state, as Moraes (2015) explains. This control of immigration in Brazil, not only by the police, but also by the Executive, under the justification of protection for the Brazilian worker and for the economic and moral development of the country (Moraes, 2015) consolidated the construction of a racist migration policy and security. This type of political approach to migratory flows was reiterated during the military dictatorship from the 1960s.

At that moment, the Cold War separated the world into two big blocks, capitalist and socialist. Brazil, because it was in the US sphere of influence, was strongly influenced by its policy. The American power to exercise dominion over the rest of the continent is due initially to the Monroe Doctrine in the nineteenth century, which envisaged an American dominated America. The permanence of this type of influence, with the consolidation of the US as a power, reached the migratory control in the period of the Cold War. The criteria that began to be used in Brazil for the restriction of migration began to present ideological contours against those who were understood as communists. Moreover, during this period, the perspective of national security was very strong and was associated with a national development policy (Moraes, 2015). At the moment, however, there was no significant influx of immigrants in Brazil, the exit of Brazilians was what led the migratory balance pending for emigration. In the 1980s, however, a new immigration law was created that corroborated the previous perspective.

The Foreigner Statute, created in 1988, had the prerogative of the immigrant's understanding as a threat if he did not serve as an investor. The purely utilitarian and securitarian perspective characterized the then regiment of migratory flows in Brazil. Among the planned practices were expulsion and deportation, which represent state violence against the immigrant (Domenech, 2015). The expulsion occurs due to the understanding by the public agents that the immigrant has attacked national security, public order, morality or the national economy; the deportation consists of the return of the foreigner who has entered or remained in the country in an irregular manner (Milesi, 201?). The Alien Statute survived for decades, although anachronistic and incompatible with the Federal Constitution of 1988 (especially with Article 5) and with several international human rights treaties ratified by Brazil as the International Covenant on Civil and Political Rights (1966), which guarantees non-discrimination, independent of nationality (Article 2). (Ventura, Illes, 2010).

This understanding of immigration as a threat corroborates the perception built at this time of the Cold War in the process of identity and national crisis, when it takes place a process which prioritizes and strengthens the national interest to produce "selection and exclusion, emphasizing and reiterating 'external threats'" (Campbell, 1996, p.169 apud Lacerda; Gama, 2016). In Brazil, in turn, the search for affirmation of a national identity is established from the recurring process of differentiation, where the construction of the self occurs from the definition of who is other. This phenomenon that "opposes alleged 'Brazilian values' to the presence of immigrants, especially Haitians" (Gama, Lacerda, 2016, p.70), but also includes immigrants from African countries such as Nigeria, Democratic Republic Of Congo, Angola; neighbors such as Bolivia, Paraguay and also those from the Middle East, as is the case in Syria. This may spur an already consolidated process in the US and Europe, labeled by Campbell as "evangelism of fear." This process of "evangelization of fear", which allows the transformation of social phenomena into themes of security, is what helps in the process of securitization.

One of the main issues related to this possible crimmigration approach in Brazil is that the same agency that is responsible for the immigration issues is also the one responsible for federal crimes: the Federal Police. As the immigration flows in Brazil until 2010 were happening in less intense way, the theme was not part of a social debate. But since the arrival the 800% increase in the number of asylum requests between 2010 and 2014, the immigration is receiving again more attention (Ministerio da Justiça, 2014). By having the same agency dealing with criminal and immigration issues, it might stimulate the possibility of association among these subjects. Most recently, what is happening in Brazil is that justifying a control in drug trafficking and the perpetuation of the US policy of "War on Drugs," the agency responsible for managing migrations in Brazil, the Federal Police, has taken an approach based on rigid measures that associate certain groups of immigrants to criminal activities, and thus violates international refugee law and human rights guidelines by adopting measures of retention and expulsion of foreigners. It could be presumed that Brazil, not only in law, but in practice, inserts migratory issues in the area of security.

The detention for migratory reasons are practices involving the cessation of the right to personal liberty of those who enter, transit or remain undocumented or unauthorized in a State. This kind of punishment is something that should be used only under the highest exceptionality, due to its high punitive character. Thus, there should be the assurance that the deprivation of liberty comes within a legality framework, not arbitrariness (Holzhacker, Tavares, 2016). Moreover, the Brazilian Refugee Law states that any foreigner who arrives at National territory has the right to request refuge, and under no circumstances shall he be deported to a territory where his life or freedom is endangered. No matter, how the foreigner entered in the country, the right to ask for asylum is even for irregular immigrants. Furthermore, under the Brazilian law of refuge, the argument for protection of national security and public order can only be used to justify the expulsion procedure, or the determination of the termination of refugee status, but never to prevent the foreigner from seeking refuge To the Brazilian authorities. (Holzhacker, Tavares, 2016)

However, what is happening in one of the largest points of access to the Brazilian territory, the international airport in São Paulo, is that people are being deported without the chance to ask for asylum, and some of them are in need of international protection, but they have to face the absence of a specific procedure for the identification of persons in need of international protection, what ends up leading to violations of many of human rights principles. In 2013 about 960 people were inadmissible, having to return to their countries of origin and this keeps happening. (Holzhacker, Tavares, 2016).

Besides, having to turn to the Federal Police to deal with documentation issues often greatly inhibits and intimidates migrants to seek help, especially those in an irregular situation who fear retaliation and deportation. In addition, the agency already has numerous other tasks and is not prepared to deal with the increasing demand (Marcolini, 2015). Moreover, most PF staff are outsourced servers that are not trained to deal with the vulnerabilities and specificities of the migration issue. In addition, the federal police perspective has a narrower approach to opening borders for immigrants, because of this, many immigrants are afraid to seek help from this institution (Sequeira, 2011). It is noted that the absence of an immigration service, a political body that could deal with the issue fully and effectively, based on the nuances of human rights, is a serious flaw in Brazil and prevents a less secure and more integrative regulatory logic (Ventura, Illes, 2012).

References

DEMARTINI, Zeila de Brito Fabri. Imigrantes: entre políticas, conflitos e preconceitos. Cadernos CERU, [S.l.], v. 21, n. 2, p. 49-75, dec. 2010. ISSN 1413-4519. Disponível em: <http://www.revistas.usp.br/ceru/article/view/11917>. Acesso em: 02 july 2017.

DOMENECH, Eduardo. O controle da imigração "indesejável": expulsão e expulsabilidade na América do Sul. Cienc. Cult., São Paulo, v. 67, n. 2, p. 25-29, June 2015. Available from <http://cienciaecultura.bvs.br/scielo.php?script=sci_arttext&pid=S0009-67252015000200010&lng=en&nrm=iso>. Access on 02 July 2017. http://dx.doi.org/10.21800/2317-66602015000200010

INTERNATIONAL AMNESTY. The Netherlands: Excessive Immigration Detention, Ethnic Profiling and Counter-terrorism Measures: Amnesty International Submission for the UN Universal Periodic Review – 27th Session of the UPR Working Group, May 2017 Disponível em: <http://www.refworld.org/category,COI,AMNESTY,,NLD,5878f4124,0.html>. Acesso em: 15 ago. 2017

GUIA, Maria J.; PEDROSO, J. A Insustentável Resposta da "Crimigração" Face À Irregularidade Dos Migrantes: Uma Perspetiva Da União Europeia. REMHU- Rev. Interdiscip. Mobil. Hum., Brasília, Ano XXIII, n. 45, p. 129-144, jul. /dez. 2015 2015. Disponível em: <http://www.scielo.br/pdf/remhu/v23n45/1980-8585-REMHU-23-45-129.pdf>. Acesso em: 15 ago. 2017

GUILD, Elspeth. The Migration Security Nexus in the XXI century. Routledge, 2009.

HOLZHACKER, V.; TAVARES, A. Detenção por Razões Migratórias a Proteção dos Direitos Humanos no Brasil. In: Direitos Humanos e Vulnerabilidade em Juízo. Unisantos, Liliana Lyra Jubilut, Rachel de Oliveira Lopes (Organizadoras). Santos (SP); Editora Universitária Leopoldianum, 2015. 284 p. Disponível em: <http://www.unisantos.br/wp-content/uploads/2016/05/Direitos-Humanos-e-Vulnerabilidades-em-Ju%C3%ADzo.pdf>. Acesso em 02 ago. 2017

LACERDA, Ana Luiza; GAMA, Carlos Frederico P. S. O SOLICITANTE DE REFÚGIO E A SOBERANIA MODERNA: A IDENTIDADE NA DIFERENÇA. Lua Nova, São Paulo, n. 97, p. 53-80, abr. 2016. Disponível em <http://www.scielo.br/scielo.php?script=sci_arttext&pid=S0102-64452016000100053&lng=pt&nrm=iso>. Acesso em: 27 maio 2016.

Leun J.P. van der & Woude M.A.H. van der (2011), Ethnic profiling in the Netherlands? A reflection on expanding preventive powers, ethnic profiling and a changing social and political context, Policing and Society 21(4): 444-455.

MARCOLINI, Adriana. Especialistas defendem criação de agência de imigração no Brasil. Estadão. Disponível em: <http://politica.estadao.com.br/noticias/geral,especialistas-defendem-criacao-de-agencia-de-imigracao-no-brasil,875080>. Acesso em: 13 ago. 2015

MIGGIANO, Luca. States of exception: securitisation and irregular migration in the Mediterranean. Disponível em: <http://www.unhcr.org/research/working/4b167a5a9/states-exception-securitisation-irregular-migration-mediterranean-luca.html>. Acesso em 15 ago. 2017

MINISTÉRIO DA JUSTIÇA. Solicitações de refúgio no Brasil cresceram 800% nos últimos quatro anos, 15/05/2014, disponível em:<http://www.justica.gov.br/noticias/solicitacoes-de-refugio-no-brasil-cresce-ram-800-nos-ultimos-quatro-anos>. Acesso em: 11 nov. 2014

MOLFETTO, Eleonora di. Rethinking Research Approach in sentencing decicion-making process for immigrants with a vulnerable legal status. CrimEUR. Disponível em: <http://www.crimeur.nl/rethinking-research-approach-in-sentencing-decision-making-processes-for-immigrants-with-a-vulnerable-legal-status/>. Acesso em: 07 ago. 2017

MORAES, Ana Luisa Zago. Crimigração: a relação entre política migratória e política criminal no Brasil.Tese apresentada como requisito para a obtenção do grau de Doutor pelo Programa de Pós-Graduação em Ciências Criminais da Faculdade de Direito da Pontifícia Universidade Católica do Rio Grande do Sul.

_____. A Criminologia da mobilidade humana e a atuação da Defensoria Pública da União da defesa do "crimigrante". Jornal da Escola Superior da Defensoria Pública da União. 4º tri, ed. 3, n.1, 2015.

OLIVEIRA, Adriana Capuano de. Um ideal transnacional: a participação política dos emigrantes brasileiros e o sonho do 28º estado da República Federativa do Brasil. IX ENCONTRO DA ABCP, Brasília 4-7 ago. 2014. Disponível em: <http://www.encontroabcp2014.cienciapolitica.org.br/resources/anais/14/1403742871_ARQUIVO_TrabalhocompletoAdrianaCapuanodeOIiveiraIXEncontrodaABCP2014.pdf >. Acesso em: 17 maio 2016

SEQUEIRA, Claudio Dantas. Polícia Federal S/A. Istoé. Brasil. 20 maio 2011. Disponível em: <http://istoe.com.br/138194_POLICIA+FEDERAL+S+A/>. Acesso em: 07 fev. 2017

STUMPF, Juliet. The Crimmigration Crisis: Immigrants, Crime, and Sovereign Power." American University Law Review 56, no. 2 (December 2006): 367-419. Disponível em: <http://digitalcommons.wcl.american.edu/cgi/viewcontent.cgi?article=1274&context=a ulr>. Acesso em: 15 ago. 2017

VENTURA. D.; ILLES, P. Qual a política migratória do Brasil? Le Monde Diplomatique. 2012. Disponível em: <http://www.diplomatique.org.br/artigo.php?id=1121>. Acesso em 14 jul. 2015

WOUDE, Maartje A. H. van der; LEUN, Joanne P. van der; NIJLAND, Joanne A. Crimmigration in the Netherlands. Law & Social Inquiry, v., Issue aug. 2014. Disponível em: <https://www.researchgate.net/publication/263858963_Crimmigration_in_the_Netherla nds?enrichId=rgreq-d778876421398df4723e9586cac2c4b6-XXX&enrichSource=Y292ZXJQYWdlOzI2Mzg1ODk2MztBUzozMTY2NjUyNjUzNj A4OTlAMTQ1MjUxMDI5MTA5MQ%3D%3D&el=1_x_2&_esc=publicationCoverPdf >. Acesso em: 08 jun. 2017

Chapter 46.   The Immigrant-Native Wage Gap in Malaysia: The Preliminary Results

Borhan Sareya Abdullah, Alexandros Zangelidis, Ioannis Theodossiou[*]

Abstract

This paper focuses on the wage gap between native and immigrant workers in Malaysian labour market. This paper uses the Productivity and Investment Climate Survey (PICS) 2 for 2007 to explore the components of the immigrant-native wage gap. The Oaxaca decomposition analysis and quantile regression decomposition were applied in this study. By exploiting the PICS data, the result of this study shows that the immigrant has a lower human capital return on earnings compared to native. Another significant finding is that the wage gap between native and immigrant is mostly explained by the difference in the characteristics of the workers, while, the remaining were explained by the discriminatory effects.

1.   Introduction

Recently, immigrations have sparked intense debate in Malaysia because of the mass migration of people from the close neighbouring countries such as Indonesia, Philippines and Myanmar. The number of immigrant workers has increased, and it contributes 15 percent of the total workforce in 2004 (Statistical Department of Malaysia, 2004). The immigrant workers are needed to fill the gap of the labour supply in the Malaysian labour market.

The majority of empirical studies indicates that immigrant and native are paid differently in the labour market, although they do the same job or/and have the same abilities. Therefore, the purpose of this study is to explore the wage gap between native and immigrant in the labour market. Besides, the increasing interest in immigrant-native wage gap in the United States (U.S) and European countries has heightened the need for investigating this issue in Malaysian labour market. To the author's best knowledge, this is the first study that focuses on the immigrant-native wage gap in Malaysia. Most of the labour market studies in Malaysia have only focussed on the gender wage gap (Schafgans, 2000; Ismail, 2011; Jajri & Ismail, 2012).

Most of the previous studies found that immigrants earn significantly less than natives. One of the main reasons is the human capital such as education, skills and experience acquired abroad are not relevant in the host country due to the difference in the economic development between the host and the home country. However, there is still a lack of evidence from previous studies for labour migration across developing countries.

Wages should be paid based on the productivity of the workers. In the labour market, human capital is an indicator to measure the productivity to determine worker's wages (Becker, 1964). Wage is also determined by the inherited traits or the personal identity of the workers such as gender, nationality, or race.

[*] Borhan Abdullah, University of Aberdeen, UK. E-mail: r03ba15@abdn.ac.uk

According to Becker (1957), discrimination by the employer is not because of the employer is prejudice on gender, nationality or certain races, but some employers are being ignorance. The employer might underestimate the productivity of a particular group of workers. Thus, the employers might pay lower salary to the group, compared to other groups of workers.

There are two areas of the empirical studies that would be useful in order to identify the wage determinants and investigate the immigrant-native wage gap; (1) the difference in individual human capital; and (2) the discrimination in the labour market. First, the difference in the human capital of workers will cause a wage gap (Brenzel & Reichelt, 2015). In human capital theory, a wage is directly related to the worker's productivity. Thus, workers who acquire human capital, i.e., education, experience, or language ability will be able to increase their wages (Becker, 1964). This theory is one of the theories that explained the wage gap between workers and also the most prominent theory in explaining the difference in wages between immigrants and natives (Brenzel & Reichelt, 2015).

Most of the empirical studies on the immigration claim that immigrant might earn low wages in the destination country as compared to native, although they have the same level of education, skills or experience in the labour market. One of the reasons is the imperfect transferability of human capital acquired abroad (Rodriquez-Planas, 2012) due to the lack of proficiency of the dominant language in the destination country. The proficiency of the dominant language is very important in determining the immigrant's wages, and it has a positive relationship with wage (Chiswick, 1978; Adsera and Chiswick, 2007; Chiswick and Miller, 2009). Language is not directly related to the productivity. However, the lack of proficiency of the dominant language will cause an obstacle for an immigrant to adapt to the labour market in the destination country.

According to Chiswick and Miller (2009), the immigrant will receive lower pay if the human capital acquired abroad cannot be transferred to the destination country. Among other results, they found that over-education is more common on the recent immigrant. It shows that most of the immigrants are not able to use their education, skills, or experience that acquired in their home country. The immigrant has a poor job matched due to the less-than-perfect international transferability.

The existence of the wage gap is also due to the immigrant's human capital from the countries of origin is not relevant in the destination country (Chiswick & Miller, 2009). For example, an immigrant from the developing country has difficulties to use their knowledge or skills in a developed country (Barth, Bratsberg, & Raaum, 2012). However, if the immigrants migrate to a country that has the same level of economic development with their country of origin, they might get the same wage as natives.

On the other hand, the Segmented Labour Market (SLM) theory explains that the assimilation of an immigrant in the labour market and the equalisation of the wage differential between native and immigrant would not exist. In the SLM theory, it believes that labour markets are never perfectly competitive and workers are not able to choose jobs based on their own preferences or abilities which contradict with the neoclassical theory (Leontaridi, 1998). If the segmentation of workers in the labour market exists, the assimilation of the immigrants will be hardly taking place. Therefore, if there is a segmentation based on nationality in the labour market the rewards of human capital would differ for immigrant and native. Thus, another factor of existing immigrant-native wage gap is due to discrimination in the labour market. The discrimination could happen because of the imperfect information about the individual productivity in the labour market (Arrow, 1971). According to Arrow (1971), the employers are not able to observe the productivity of each of the workers. Therefore, wages are paid based on the general observation or based on the group productivity.

In a nutshell, there are two main factors of the immigrant-native wage gap occurs in the labour market. First, is due to the differences in term of human capital and second, because of the discrimination in the labour market.

The structure of the remainder of this paper is as follows; section 2 will describe the data that were used and followed by the methods that were applied in section 3. Section 4 will present the empirical result of the immigrant-native wage gap in the Malaysian labour market, while, the Section 5 which is the last part will be the conclusion of this study.

2. Data

This study used the cross section data that obtained from Productivity and Investment Climate Survey (PICS) 2 for 2007 that were collected by the Economic Planning Unit and Department of Statistics Malaysia in collaboration with the World Bank. The PICS includes 1200 firms in the manufacturing sector, about 32.1 percent out of the population and 300 out of 2502 establishments for the service sector. The PICS contains random samples of 13,533 workers in the various sizes of firms that consist of immigrant and native workers. The selection of the industries is based on the employment threshold, the employment threshold for the manufacturing sector is more than ten employees. For the service sector, the employment threshold for information technology, telecommunications, advertising and marketing firms is more than ten employees, whereas, business logistics and accounting and the related professional services threshold are more than 20 employees.

3.　　Method

In studying the immigrant-native wage gap in Malaysia, there are three analyses need to be conducted. First is multiple regression analysis, followed by Oaxaca decomposition and the third analysis will be the quantile regression decomposition.

The analysis begins with the estimation of the relationship between earnings and the explanatory variables by applying a single equation approach. In this equation, a dummy variable 'immigrant' is included to distinguish the nationality of the workers either they are Malaysian or non-Malaysian;

$$\ln\_hwage_i=\beta_0+\delta_0 immigrant+\beta_1 HC_i+\beta_2 DC_i+\beta_3 EC_i+\mu_i \qquad (1)$$

where, the dependent variable is the hourly wage rate includes bonuses, allowances and other sources of income of an individual, i. The 'immigrant' is a dummy variable that refers to the nationality of the workers (1 for immigrant and 0 for native workers). The HC refers to the human capital that consists of education that can be measured by the level of education of the workers, training, workers' potential experience and its square, and tenure and its square. DC is demographic characteristics such as gender, marital status, citizenship and year of immigration. While, EC is the employment characteristics that consist of the type of work such as management, professional, skilled or unskilled workers, and the membership of a trade union. β_i is the vector of coefficient and μ is the error terms or the individual unobserved characteristics which expected to be zero?

The analysis followed by the separate equation for both native and immigrant estimation equations. Consider the equations as follows;

$$\ln\_hwage_{ni}=\beta_{n0}+\beta_{n1}HC_{ni}+\beta_{n2}DC_{ni}+\beta_{n3}EC_{ni}+\mu_n \qquad (2)$$

$$\ln\_hwage_{mi}=\beta_{m0}+\beta_{m1}HC_{mi}+\beta_{m2}DC_{mi}+\beta_{m3}EC_{mi}+\mu_m \qquad (3)$$

where, in equation (2) and (3) the dependent variables are the individual log hourly wage rate, for native, n, and immigrant, m.

Next, the Oaxaca (1973) decomposition will be applied to explore the wage gap between native and immigrant. Following the Oaxaca (1973) the formula can then be shown as follows;

$$G=\frac{\bar{W}_n-\bar{W}_m}{\bar{W}_m} \qquad (4)$$

where, G is the native-immigrant wage gap, $\overline{W}_n$ and $\overline{W}_m$ are the average hourly wages of native and immigrant. In logarithm expression, it can be written as;

$$\ln(G+1)= \ln(\overline{W}_n)- \ln(\overline{W}_m) \tag{5}$$

The wage differential can be written in the Ordinary Least Square (OLS) estimation of the logarithmic wage is as follows;

$$\ln(G+1)=\overline{X}_n\hat{\beta}_n-\overline{X}_m\hat{\beta}_m \tag{6}$$

where,

$$\Delta\overline{X}=\overline{X}_n-\overline{X}_m$$
$$\Delta\hat{\beta}=\hat{\beta}_m-\hat{\beta}_n$$

thus,

$$\ln(G+1)=(\overline{X}_n-\overline{X}_m)\hat{\beta}_m-(\hat{\beta}_m-\hat{\beta}_n)\overline{X}_n \tag{7}$$

As shown in equation (7), the $(\overline{X}_n-\overline{X}_m)\hat{\beta}_m$ is the component of the wage differential between two groups; native and immigrant, due to the difference in their characteristics. The second term, $(\hat{\beta}_m-\hat{\beta}_n)\overline{X}_n$ is representing the effect of discrimination on the wage differential. Thus, based on Oaxaca decomposition the wage differential between native and immigrant can be divided into two components, the effect of coefficient and the effect of the difference in characteristics of workers.

However, Oaxaca and Ransom (1994) claim that the discrimination in the labour market is not only affecting the minority group (immigrant) but also will influence the wage of the majority group (native). The advantage of the majority group known as 'overpayment' and disadvantage of the minority group due to discrimination is known as the 'underpayment' (Oaxaca & Ransom, 1994). To know if the workers are 'overpayment' or 'underpayment' the non-discriminatory wage structure should be identified. Consider the equation as follows;

$$\ln(G+1)= \ln(D+1)+ \ln(P+1) \tag{8}$$

where, DD is the market discrimination coefficient and PP is the productivity of individuals. Thus,

$$\ln(G+1)= \ln \left(\frac{W_n}{W_m}\right) - \ln \left(\frac{W_n^o}{W_m^o}\right) + \ln(P+1) \qquad (9)$$

$$\ln(G+1)= \ln \left(\frac{W_n}{W_n^o}\right) + \ln \left(\frac{W_m^o}{W_m}\right) + \ln(P+1) \qquad (10)$$

$$\ln(G+1)= \ln(\delta_{no}+1) + \ln(\delta_{mo}+1) + \ln(P+1) \qquad (11)$$

In equation (9) and (10), W^o is the hourly wage in the absence of discrimination. In equation (11), the overpayment, δ_{no}, is the difference between the current wage of native and the wage of native in the absence of discrimination. The underpayment, δ_{mo}, is the difference between the current wage of immigrant and their wage in the absence of discrimination. Equation (11) can be written in the OLS form as shown in equation (12) (Oaxaca & Ransom, 1994).

$$\ln(G+1)=\bar{X}_n(\hat{\beta}_n\text{-}\hat{\beta})+\bar{X}_m(\hat{\beta}\text{-}\hat{\beta}_m)+(\bar{X}_n\text{-}\bar{X}_m)\hat{\beta} \qquad (12)$$

where, $\hat{\beta}$ is the weighted average of the hourly wage or also known as the non-discriminatory wage structure of the coefficient vector β_n and β_m. The non-discriminatory wage structure must lie between the wage structure of majority (overpayment) and minority (underpayment). According to Oaxaca and Ransom (1994) the representation of the non-discriminatory wage structure can be written as follows;

$$\hat{\beta}=\Omega\beta_m+(I\text{-}\Omega)\beta_n \qquad (13)$$

where, Ω is the weighting matrix and I is the identity matrix[1]. In Oaxaca (1973), it employed male wage structure as the non-discriminatory wage structure. Oaxaca (1973) also stated that the wages of female or male could be used as the non-discriminatory wage structure in decomposition analysis. In the study, he proposed that Ω be equal to I; for the current male wage structure

---

1 Based on Oaxaca and Ransom (1994) the relationship between discrimination and productivity with estimated wage structure and weighting matrix is shown as follows;

The overpayment, $\tilde{\delta}_{no} = \exp[\bar{X}'_n(\hat{\beta}_n - \hat{\beta})] - 1 = \exp[\bar{X}'_n(I - \Omega)(\hat{\beta}_n - \hat{\beta}_m)] - 1$

The underpayment, $\tilde{\delta}_{om} = \exp[\bar{X}'_m(\hat{\beta} - \hat{\beta}_m)] - 1 = \exp[\bar{X}'_m\Omega(\hat{\beta}_n - \hat{\beta}_m)] - 1$

Workers productivity, $\tilde{P}_{nm} = \exp[(\bar{X}_n - \bar{X}_b)'\hat{\beta}] - 1 = \exp\{(\bar{X}_n - \bar{X}_b)'[\Omega\hat{\beta}_n - (I - \Omega)\hat{\beta}_b]\} - 1$

or Ω equal to 0; for the female wage structure if it uses as the weighted wage (Oaxaca & Ransom, 1994). However, according to Fortin (2008), when female is selected to be the weighting wage or the non-discriminatory wage structure, it will yield a different result as male does.

Newmark (1988) proposes the pooled wage regression for the majority and minority groups. The estimated coefficient from the pooled sample will define the non-discriminatory wage structure for both majority and minority groups (Rodgers, 2006). Oaxaca and Ransom (1994) proposed an alternative to estimate the non-discriminatory wage structure as the extension of Neumark (1988) approach to study the discrimination among White and non-White in the US labour market. Oaxaca and Ransom (1994) proposed the value of Ω to be;

$$\Omega = \left(X'X\right)^{-1}(X'_n X_n) \tag{14}$$

where, X is the observation matrix of the pooled sample[2] and X_n is the observation matrix for the native. Thus, the non-discriminatory wage structure estimate can be written as follows;

$$\beta = \left(X'X\right)^{-1}(X'_n X_n)\beta_m + (I - \left(X'X\right)^{-1}(X'_n X_n))\beta_n \tag{15}$$

Therefore, it can be seen that Neumark (1988) and Oaxca and Ransom (1994) prevail the estimation of a pooled model to derive the counterfactual coefficient of vector $\hat{\beta}$. Thus, under the zero-mean assumption, $(E(\varepsilon_{im}) = E(\varepsilon_{in}) = 0)$, the expression of decomposition with a pooled wage structure under Oaxaca and Ransom (1994) can be written as follows[3] (Fortin, 2008);

$$\overline{\ln W_n} - \overline{\ln W_m} = (\bar{X}_n - \bar{X}_m)\hat{\beta}_p + \left[\bar{X}_n\left(\hat{\beta}_n - \hat{\beta}_p\right) + (\hat{\beta}_{0n} - \hat{\beta}_{0p})\right] - \left[\bar{X}_m\left(\hat{\beta}_m - \hat{\beta}_p\right) + \left(\hat{\beta}_{0m} - \hat{\beta}_{0p}\right)\right] \tag{16}$$

where, $\hat{\beta}_{0n}$, $\hat{\beta}_{0m}$ and $\hat{\beta}_{0p}$ are the intercepts for native, immigrant and pooled estimation. However, Fortin (2008) argues that pooled model will be overstating the effect of variables with a large difference between two groups. Pooled coefficient capture part of the "between" overpaid and underpaid effect. Thus, if the advantage (overpayment) and disadvantage

---

2 Where the $X'X = X'_n X_n + X'_m X_m$ (Oaxaca & Ransom, 1994).

3 The estimation of decomposition in Oaxaca (1973) can be written as follows when choosing native or immigrant wage as the non-discriminatory wage structure;

$$\overline{\ln W_n} - \overline{\ln W_m} = (\bar{X}_n - \bar{X}_m)\hat{\beta}_n + \bar{X}_m(\hat{\beta}_n - \hat{\beta}_m) + (\hat{\beta}_{0n} - \hat{\beta}_{0m}) = (\bar{X}_n - \bar{X}_m)\hat{\beta}_m - \bar{X}_n(\hat{\beta}_n - \hat{\beta}_m) - (\hat{\beta}_{0n} - \hat{\beta}_{0m})$$

(underpayment) effect is not equal, the value of the non-discriminatory wage structure is not plausible.

To overcome this issue, as proposed by Fortin (2008) this study will include the citizenship intercept shifts and identification restriction in the regression of native and immigrant pooled together. Consider the equation of native and immigrant as follows (Fortin, 2008);

$$\overline{\ln W_n} = \hat{\gamma}_0 + \hat{\gamma}_{0n} + \overline{X}_n\hat{\gamma} + E(v_i|M_i=0) \tag{16}$$

$$\overline{\ln W_m} = \hat{\gamma}_0 + \hat{\gamma}_{0m} + \overline{X}_m\hat{\gamma} + E(v_i|M_i=1) \tag{17}$$

Then,

$$\overline{\ln W_n} - \overline{\ln W_m} = (\overline{X}_n - \overline{X}_m)\hat{\gamma} + (\hat{\gamma}_{0n} - \hat{\gamma}_{0m}) + [E(v_i|M_i=0) - E(v_i|M_i=1)] \tag{18}$$

In equation (18), under zero mean assumption, $((E(v_i|M_i=0)-E(v_i|M_i=1)=0)$, $(\overline{X}_n-\overline{X}_m)\hat{\gamma}$ is the wage differential due to the difference in the characteristics of the workers. The $(\hat{\gamma}_{0n}-\hat{\gamma}_{0m})$ is the wage differential due to the coefficient effect, where, $\hat{\gamma}_{0n}$ denotes as the advantage of the majority group (native workers) and $\hat{\gamma}_{0m}$ is the disadvantage of the minority group (immigrant workers) in the labour market. Thus, the value of the immigrant coefficient, $\hat{\gamma}_{0m}$, will be negative. In this study, the wage gap decomposition analysis that was introduced by Oaxaca and Ransom (1994) by pooling the data will be applied. The approach will be implemented together with the approach that proposed by Fortin (2008).

To explore the immigrant-native wage gap across distribution, the quantile regression decomposition analysis need to be conducted. Suppose the regression equation as follows;

$$y_i = \beta_n x_i + \mu_i \tag{19}$$

where the dependent variable, y, refer to the log hourly wage, x is the explanatory variables, β is the coefficient and μ is the error term which expected to be zero. The i is the sample of the population and $n=1....n$. Thus, following Chiswick, Le, and Miller (2008) a simple quantile regression for this equation can be written as follows;

$$Q_\theta(y_i|x_i) = x_i\beta_\theta + Q_\theta(\mu_{\theta_i}|x_i) \tag{20}$$

In equation (20) the $Q_\theta(y_i|x_i)$ is the conditional quantile process, where, $0 \le \theta \le 1$ and by assuming that $Q_\theta(\mu_{\theta_i}|x_i) = 0$, while, β_θ is the vector of quantile regression coefficient. In this study, the quantile regression is estimated with 99 quantile regressions on a grid of quantiles $\theta = [0.01, 0.02, \dots, 0.98, 0.99]$.

The quantile regression decomposition cannot be made directly because quantiles do not generate an exact result for wage decomposition. Based on the decomposition analysis as in the previous chapter, the wage decomposition proposed by Fortin (2008) is applied. It can be written as;

$$\overline{\ln W_n} - \overline{\ln W_m} = (\bar{X}_n - \bar{X}_m)\hat{\gamma} + (\hat{\gamma}_{0n} - \hat{\gamma}_{0m}) + [E(v_i|M_i=0) - E(v_i|M_i=1)] \quad (21)$$

Canal-Dominguez and Rodriquez-Gutierrez (2008) pointed out that the wage equation estimation subject to the log wage being equal to its unconditional quantile of order θ, $\ln W_i = \ln \omega_\theta$, because the previous outcome cannot be obtained in quantile regression due to the wage decomposition (Machado & Mata, 2005). Thus, the quantile regression decomposition can be written as follows;

$$\overline{\ln W_n} - \overline{\ln W_m} = \begin{bmatrix} (\bar{X}_n | \ln W_i = \ln \omega_\theta) \\ -(\bar{X}_m | \ln W_i = \ln \omega_\theta) \end{bmatrix} \hat{\gamma} + (\hat{\gamma}_{0n}^\theta - \hat{\gamma}_{0m}^\theta)$$

$$+ [E(v_n^\theta | \ln W_i = \ln \omega_\theta) - E(v_m^\theta | \ln W_i = \ln \omega_\theta)] \quad (22)$$

where, the $[E(v_n^\theta | \ln W_i = \ln \omega_\theta) - E(v_m^\theta | \ln W_i = \ln \omega_\theta)]$ is a part that cannot be explained by quantile regression.

4. Results

Table 1 presents the result obtained from the regression analysis with robust standard errors for equation (1), (2) and (3). The third column in Table 1 confirms that all independent variables of native wage estimation are statistically significant at 1 percent, except for the seniority and skilled production work, whereas, the immigrant wage estimation in the second column shows that there are five variables statistically significant.

Based on the immigrant and native estimations, it can be concluded that the return of education level is greater for native compared to immigrant. On the other hand, the return of professional job is higher for immigrant than native. Interestingly, the membership in a trade union has an adverse effect on earnings of native with the magnitude of 0.9 percent. The possible explanation of this is that native become a member of a trade union if they earn low wages. Thus, being a member of a trade union seems to be negatively affecting wage.

Compiled by F. Tilbe, E. Iskender, I. Sirkeci

Table 1: Estimated regression coefficient

Log hourly wage	Immigrant	Native	All samples (ᵉ)
Degree	0.534***	0.988***	0.956***
	(0.123)	(0.027)	(0.027)
Diploma	0.478***	0.667***	0.648***
	(0.142)	(0.023)	(0.023)
Upper secondary	0.053	0.244***	0.228***
	(0.053)	(0.017)	(0.016)
Training	-0.001	0.003***	0.003***
	(0.002)	(0.001)	(0.001)
Potential experience	0.012	0.033***	0.031***
	(0.010)	(0.002)	(0.002)
Potential experience squared	0.000	-0.001***	-0.001***
	(0.000)	(0.000)	(0.000)
Tenure	0.015	0.022	0.022
	(0.009)	(0.003)	(0.003)
Tenure squared	0.000	0.000***	0.000***
	(0.000)	(0.000)	(0.000)
Male	0.160**	0.190***	0.191***
	(0.052)	(0.013)	(0.013)
Married	0.091**	0.090***	0.088***
	(0.045)	(0.016)	(0.015)
Management	1.103	0.341***	0.354***
	(0.237)	(0.023)	(0.023)
Professional	0.502**	0.344***	0.354***
	(0.162)	(0.025)	(0.025)
Skilled	-0.042	-0.002	-0.008
	(0.098)	(0.019)	(0.018)
Unskilled	-0.128	-0.247***	-0.232***
	(0.092)	(0.021)	(0.020)
Union	0.009	-0.009***	-0.008***
	(0.008)	(0.002)	(0.002)
Immigrant			-0.143***
			(0.012)
Native			0.143***
			(0.012)
Constant	1.074***	1.042***	0.931***
	(0.130)	(0.027)	(0.028)

Notes: (1) Numbers in parentheses are standard errors.

(2) Reference groups are low education and non-production/apprentice

*(3) * Statistically significant at p<0.1*

*(4) ** Statistically significant at p<0.05*

*(5) *** Statistically significant at p<0.01*

(ᵉ) Applied Fortin (2008) estimation

In column four, the analysis exploits the whole sample that consists of 13,310 observations, for both native and immigrant workers in manufacturing and service sectors. All the variables included in the estimation have the expected sign as in the previous studies, and it is in line with the theories. Besides, all variables are statistically significant at 1 percent, except for the tenure and

509

skilled production job. The regression analysis proves that workers with a degree education level earn 95.6 percent more than those low educated workers. Other levels of education such as diploma and upper secondary level also show a positive relationship with hourly wages. The result implies that education and hourly wage have a positive relationship. Besides, it indicates that the hourly wage increases with the level of education (Ilkkaracan & Selim, 2003).

The effect of training on the wage is subtle. The result proves that a month of training will increase the hourly wage by 0.3 percent. On the other hand, the coefficient of potential experience shows that an increase in one year of experience will give a positive change in the hourly wages by 3.1 percent. However, since the experience has a non-linear relationship with wage, the following calculation should be conducted;

$$\frac{\partial \log \text{hourly wage}}{\partial \text{ potential experience}} = 0.031 + 2(-0.001) \text{ potential experience}$$

Thus, the maximum return of education is when a worker has about 15.5 years of experience by assuming that other variables are constant. Another significant finding is that being married could increase the hourly wage rate. Besides, male workers statistically earn 19.1 percent more compared to female. Whereas, the membership in a trade union reduces wage by 0.8 percent. This effect is due to the effect of union on native workers as discussed earlier.

In terms of the type of work, the management and professional works have a positive effect on wages relative to the non-production/ apprentice work. On the other hand, working in Skilled or Unskilled work has a negative effect on wage relative to the reference group. Last but not least, being immigrant reduces wage about 14.3 percent, which is below the non-discriminatory wage, while, native workers earn 14.3 percent above the non-discriminatory wage. Therefore, in the next analysis, it will explore further the wage gap between native and immigrant.

Pooled Oaxaca decomposition can divide the effect of discrimination into a part that is an advantaged group which refer to the majority group (native) with higher wages and a disadvantaged group which refer to the minority group (immigrant) who earn wages below the non-discriminatory wage structure. Table 2 shows that when the Unexplained component divided into two, the wage differential due to the contribution of the advantage of native on the wage gap is 15.4 percent and portion of the disadvantage of immigrant is 13.3 percent. This result reveals that immigrants are paid lower than the non-discriminatory wage structure. However, at the same time native have the advantage effect due to discrimination and it has increased their wage above the non-discriminatory wage structure.

Furthermore, as presented in Table 2, 59.2 percent of the difference of the raw log wage gap between native and immigrant is explained by the difference of the characteristics. The wage differential due to the discrimination contributes 40.8 percent of the native-immigrant wage gap.

Table 2: Regression-Compatible Decomposition on the Immigrant-Native Wage Gap

	Coefficient	*Exp (β)*
Native	2.079***	7.996***
	(0.008)	(0.062)
Immigrant	1.378***	3.966***
	(0.021)	(0.082)
Raw log wage gap	0.701***	2.016***
	(0.022)	(0.045)
Difference in characteristics/ Explained $(\Delta \bar{X}' \hat{\gamma})$	0.415***	1.515***
	(0.015)	(0.022)
as percentage of raw gap	59.20%	
Discrimination/ Unexplained $(\gamma_{0n} - \gamma_{0m})$	0.286***	1.331***
	(0.023)	(0.031)
as percentage of raw gap	40.80%	
Advantage of native (γ_{0n})	0.143***	1.154
	(-0.012)	
Disadvantage of immigrant (γ_{0m})	-0.143***	0.867
	(-0.012)	

*Notes: (1) * Statistically significant at p<0.1 (2) ** Statistically significant at p<0.05 (3) *** Statistically significant at p<0.01*

In the next analysis, the quantile regression is applied to calculate the decomposition of differences along the income distribution. It decomposed the differences in the wage gap into two components; Characteristics and Coefficient. As discussed in Oaxaca-Blinder decomposition analysis, the Characteristics component explains the wage gap that occurs due to the difference endowments between immigrant and a native, while, the Coefficient effects are the wage gap due to unobserved factors. Thus, the discrimination should result in the unobserved factors. The result of the quantile regression decomposition is shown in Table 3.

Table 3: Quantile regression decomposition of the wage gap between native and immigrant

Components	Quantile									
	OLS	0.1	0.2	0.3	0.4	0.5	0.6	0.7	0.8	0.9
Wage differential	0.701	0.579	0.663	0.735	0.779	0.797	0.770	0.784	0.762	0.543
Characteristics	0.415	0.381	0.397	0.407	0.402	0.414	0.417	0.424	0.426	0.468
Coefficient	0.286	0.198	0.266	0.328	0.377	0.383	0.353	0.360	0.336	0.075
% of discrimination	40.80	34.19	40.08	44.61	48.38	48.02	45.84	45.97	44.06	13.75

Notes: Quantile regression decomposition, using Fortin (2008) estimator.

On Table 3, the positive sign presents the discriminatory differential, $\left(\hat{\gamma}_{0n}^{\theta} - \hat{\gamma}_{0m}^{\theta}\right)$. The interesting features are presented in row 2 and 4. Row 2 shows the Wage differential between native and immigrant. At the 10th percentile, the wage differential is 0.579 and it increases along the income distribution. However, the wage differential decreases at the 90th percentile to 0.543. The Coefficient effect in row 4 has the same trend as the Wage differential. By comparing the Characteristics and Coefficient effects, most of the differential in the hourly wage rate of native and immigrant is explained by the differences in the Characteristics. However, the Coefficient effect is still an important factor because it contributes nearly half of the wage differential.

In Table 3, it also presents the percentage of discrimination on the wage gap of native and immigrant. The amount of discriminatory component varies along the distribution. The discrimination is relatively low at the 10th percentile. This is because the immigrants are 'overqualified' for the low-paid job (Lehmer & Ludsteck, 2011). It shows that immigrants are less likely being discriminated or treated unfairly when they have more human capital, and/or more productive than native (Canal-Dominguez & Rodriquez-Gutierrez, 2008). The discriminatory component is larger between the 20th to 80th percentile because most of the immigrants have the same level of education as native.

The result of the decomposition of differences in distribution is shown in Figure 1. In this analysis, the lowest quantile is 10th percentile and the highest is 90th percentile. Based on the figure, the Total differential and Coefficient effect curves have the same movement along the distributions. The highest wage differential is at 50th percentiles. This result is likely to be similar to Table 3. In this figure, it also presents that the Characteristic effects dominate over the Coefficient effect. This result is in line with Lehmer and Ludsteck (2011). In their study, they concluded that the immigrant-native wage gap is mainly explained by poor Characteristics of the workers.

Figure 1: The decomposition of differences in distribution

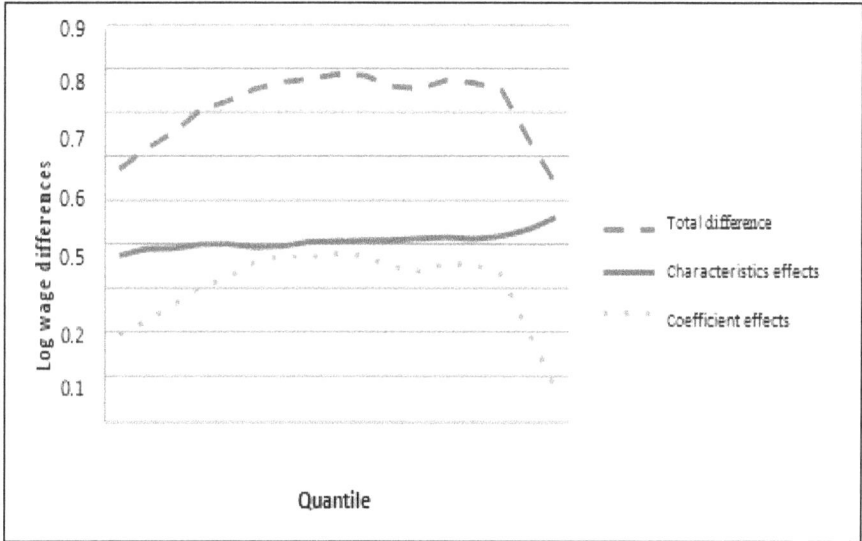

Besides, as referred to Figure 1, it clearly shows that the wage gap in lower earnings is smaller compared to top earnings. This result is also similar to a study by Nicodemo and Ramos (2011) where there is a small discriminatory effect on lower earnings than at the top of the wage distribution. There are many possible explanations of this situation. First, the wages of workers who are doing basic jobs are hard to justify because all of them are doing the same task (Melly, 2005). Second, the lower earning is less being discriminated because most of the workers are immigrants (Melly, 2005) (Joona, 2009). Third, it might be that the immigrant in the lower decile has a higher education level than native (Joona, 2009). Thus, the immigrants are hard to be discriminated (Canal-Dominguez & Rodriquez-Gutierrez, 2008). Fourth, the small immigrant-native wage gap also could be due to the compressive effect exerted by labour market institutions such as the minimum wage (Joona, 2009) and collective agreements (Anton, Bustillo, & Carrera, 2010). On the other hand, there is an enormous immigrant-native wage gap in the middle of wage distributions. The huge gap could be due to the level of human capital or specifically the education level of native and immigrant are the same. Thus, the immigrants were easier being discriminated. Besides, it also due to the reservation wage of immigrant is lower than native, and the immigrant has lack of alternatives or job option (Joona, 2009). Summing up, the wage discrimination is more intense in the middle wage distributions than in the lower and higher distributions.

5.   Conclusion

This study is an empirical study of the case of migration across developing countries which focussing on the Malaysian labour market. Most of the findings are significant and as expected. This research helps to identify the discrimination in Malaysian labour market between native and immigrant since there has been very little research on the nationality discrimination in the country. From this study, it proves that most of the immigrant-native wage gap is explained by the difference in endowments which in line with other previous studies. However, the wage gap due to discrimination should be accentuated since the discriminatory effect explained almost half of the wage gap. The different return on the endowments could be due to the imperfect transferability of human capital.

In quantile regression decomposition, it clearly shows that the immigrant-native wage gap varies across wage distribution. The Characteristics effect is fairly constant, and it is mostly explained the immigrant-native wage gap along the distribution. The Coefficient effect lies below the Characteristics effect line. When comparing the trend of the total wage differential and the coefficient effect, it can be concluded that the coefficient effect drives the changes in the total wage gap across the wage distribution.

This study also found that there is a small immigrant-native wage gap at the lower decile. The small wage gap at the lower decile can be explained by the education, type of job and also the trade union. Besides, the small immigrant-native wage gap at the lower decile is because the immigrants have higher education compared to native workers. Thus, the immigrant workers are hard to be discriminated. Furthermore, immigrant and native workers are doing the same task at the lower decile, therefore, the employer has to pay the same salary to the workers regardless their nationality.

The interesting result from this study is that there is a large wage gap between native and immigrant in the middle income compared to lower and higher income distribution. In order to understand better what is causing the difference in coefficient between native and immigrant, especially at the middle-income distribution, a further analysis should be conducted by focussing on the skill mismatch and over-education among the immigrant workers. Besides, it is also important to explore the difference in labour market integration between immigrant who acquire education from the host and home country.

References

Adsera, A., & Chiswick, B. R. (2007). Are there gender and country of origin differences in immigrant labor market outcomes across European destinations? Journal of Population Economics, 495-526.

Anton, J. I., Bustillo, R. M., & Carrera, M. (2010). Labor market performance of Latin American and Caribbean Immigrants in Spain. Journal of Applied Economics, 233-261.

Arrow, K. (1971). The theory of discrimination. Discrimination in labour market. United States: Industrial Relation Section Princeton University.

Barth, E., Bratsberg, B., & Raaum, O. (2012). Immigrant wage profiles within and between establishments. Labour Economics, 541-556.

Becker, G. S. (1957). The economics of discrimination. London: Cambridge University Press.

Becker, G. S. (1964). Human capital. Chicago: The University of Chicago Press.

Brenzel, H., & Reichelt, M. (2015). Job mobility as a new explanation for the immigrant-native wage gap. IAB Discussion paper, 2-25.

Canal-Dominguez, J. F., & Rodriquez-Gutierrez, C. (2008). Analysis of wage differences between native and immigrant workers in Spain. Spanish Economic Review, 10, 109-134. doi:10.1007/s10108-007-9033-3

Chiswick, B. R. (1978). The effect of Americanization on the earnings of foreign-born men. Journal of Political Economy, 897-921.

Chiswick, B. R., & Miller, P. W. (2009). The international transferability of immigrants' human capital. Economics of Education Review, 162-169.

Chiswick, B. R., Le, A. T., & Miller, P. W. (2008). How immigrants fare across the earnings distribution in Australia and the United States. Industrial and Labor Relations Review, 353-373.

Cotton, J. (1988). On the decomposition of wage differentials. The Review of Economics and Statistics, 236-243.

Fortin, N. M. (2008, September 18). The gender wage gap among young adults in the United States. The Journal of Human Resource, 884-918. Retrieved from http://econ.arts.ubc.ca/nfortin/Fortinat8.pdf

Ismail, R. (2011). Gender wage differentials in the Malaysian services sector. African Journal of Business Management, 7781-7789.

Jajri, I., & Ismail, R. (2012). An analysis of relationship between human capital and economic growth. Life Science Journal, 3735-3742.

Joona, P. A. (2009). The native-immigrant income gap among the self-employed in sweden. International Migration, 118-143.

Lehmer, F., & Ludsteck, J. (2011). The immigrant wage gap in Germany: Are east Europeans worse off? International Migration Review, 872-906.

Leontaridi, M. R. (1998). Segmented labour markets: Theory and evidence. Journal of Economic Surveys, 63-39.

Machado, J. A., & Mata, J. (2005). Counterfactual decomposition of changes in wage distributions using quantile regression. Journal of Applied Econometrics, 445-465.

Melly, B. (2005). Decomposition of differences in distribution using quantile regression. Labour Economics, 577-590.

Neumark, D. (1988). Employers' discriminatory behavior and the estimation of wage discrimination. The Journal of Human Resources, 279-295.

Nicodemo, C., & Ramos, R. (2011). Wage differentials between native and immigrant women in Spain: Accounting for deferences in the supports. IDEAS Working Paper Series from RePEc.

Oaxaca, R. (1973). Male-Female Wage Differentials in Urban Labor Markets. International Economic Review, 693-709.

Oaxaca, R. L., & Ransom, M. R. (1994). On Discrimination and the Decomposition of Wage Differentials. Journal of Economics, 5-21.

Reimers, C. W. (1983). Labor market discrimination against Hispanic and Black Men. The review of Economics and Statistics, 570-579.

Rodgers, W. M. (2006). Handbook on the Economics of Discrimination. Cheltenham, UK: Edward Elger Publishing Limited.

Rodriquez-Planas, N. (2012). Wage and occupational assimilation by skill level: migration policy lessons from Spain. IZA Journal of European Labor Studies.

Schafgans, M. M. (2000). Gender wage differences in Malaysia: parametric and semiparametric estimation. Journal of Development Economics, 351-378.

Chapter 47. Mapping Shipwrecks of Refugees and Immigrants in the Mediterranean Sea Since 2015

Artemis Tsiopa[1]

Abstract

In the recent years, the continuous political tensions and the multiple civil wars in many countries have caused a dramatic increase of people emigrating. Most of these people are trying to reach a European country. Since 2015, the number of immigrants and refugees is so high that this is considered a migration crisis. Most immigrants enter the EU by sea. They use boats to reach the shores of Greece, Italy and Spain. These boats very often sink due to a great variety of reasons, such as the dangerous weather conditions. These shipwrecks cause the death of thousands of immigrants and refugees. This paper aims to record and present the shipwrecks that have occurred during the period 2015-2017 in the Mediterranean Sea, as well as, the number of the dead and the missing persons from each shipwreck. For this purpose, data from the International Organization for Migration (IOM) are being used. From the produced maps it is evident that the majority of the shipwrecks occur in the Central Mediterranean Sea, as well as the majority of the dead and the missing. In the same context, the missing from the recorded shipwrecks appear to be more than the dead.

Keywords: Immigrants, Mediterranean, refugees, sea routes, shipwrecks.

Introduction

Migration is a global phenomenon that affects significantly the enactment and the amendment of each country's policies. Migration can be caused by a variety of reasons, mainly financial, and it involves a conscious decision in order to improve one's living conditions. Nevertheless, there are people that are forced to leave their place of origin. This is often caused by conflicts, wars and persecutions due to ethnicity, race, religion or political views.

Since 2015, the European Union (EU) has been forced to face one of the most challenging and controversial migration and refugee crises. The ongoing conflicts and civil wars in the Middle East and Africa (and particularly Syria) have generated an increasing number of people leaving their homes and moving to different countries. The main destinations during this displacement have been the member-states of the EU. In order to reach their desired county, the immigrants and the refugees often cross the Mediterranean Sea. The most popular sea route is the Eastern Mediterranean route which leads to Greece. Another popular routes lead to Italy, Malta and Spain.

The danger of these sea routes is evident due to the significantly high number of shipwrecks that occur. These shipwrecks are the reason why hundreds of people lose their lives, including minors. There is a variety of factors that induce the shipwrecks, such as the dangerous weather conditions. The main aim of this paper is to explore these factors, as well as to present the position

[1] Department of Geography, Harokopio University, Athens, Greece.
Email: artemistsiopa@gmail.com

of the shipwrecks, by using data acquired from the International Organization for Migration (IOM). It is, also, intended to analyze the number of the dead and the missing persons from these shipwrecks.

Data

The data used in the present paper come from various sources. The number of people that have crossed each sea route were obtained both from Frontex (2017) and from the UN Refugee Agency (UNHCR, 2017). The exact coordinates of the recorded shipwrecks and the number of the dead and the missing persons from each one of them were retrieved from the International Organization for Migration (IOM, 2017). It is essential to be noted that the shipwrecks that are presented are not all the shipwrecks that have occurred, but the ones whose exact geographical coordinates are known.

Migration Crisis

The political tension in the Middle East and in some African countries has been the main reason for the ongoing migration and refugee crisis that the EU has to face. People decide to flee these countries and move to a member-state of the EU, in order to avoid persecutions. The Mediterranean Sea is the main passage from these countries to the European countries. It should be noted that the Mediterranean Sea has been a popular passage from Africa and Asia to Europe, since the 1980s (Guild et al., 2015). This passage contains several specific routes. The selection of a specific route depends mainly on the country of departure and its proximity to one of the routes. According to the European Border and Coast Guard Agency (Frontex) the primary migratory routes to Europe through the Mediterranean are the Eastern Mediterranean route, the Western Mediterranean route, the Central Mediterranean route and the Apulia and Calabria route, which has been combined with the Central Mediterranean route since 2014.

Since the beginning of the current crisis, the most popular route has been the Eastern Mediterranean route, which leads to the Greek islands of the Eastern Aegean Sea. This route is chosen mainly by Syrian refugees, due to its proximity to Turkey that shares borders with Syria. It should be noted that Greece is not the immigrants and refugees' main destination, but only a passage in order to reach northern member-states of the EU (especially Germany and Sweden) through the Western Balkan route (Dimitriadi, 2015; Heisbourg, 2015; Park, 2015). In 2015, more than 885,000 people crossed the Mediterranean Sea using this route (UNHCR, 2016). The following year, the phenomenon seemed to decrease, mainly because of the closed border policies that have been enforced, which have "trapped" the immigrants and the refugees inside the Greek borders. As a result, in 2016 more than 180,000 people followed this route (Frontex, 2016). The same policies have caused an even bigger decrease of arrivals through the Eastern Mediterranean route in 2017. Specifically, by August 6th, 2017 about 12,000 people had followed this route (UNHCR, 2017).

The second most popular route has been the Central Mediterranean route, which is chosen mainly by immigrants of African origin (Tunisia, Nigeria, Somalia and Eritrea). This route (that leads to Italy) had been the most popular before the current crisis began. In 2014 more than 170,000 people chose it, while in 2015 this number decreased by 20,000 people (Frontex, 2016). The following year, due to the closed border policies that reduced the arrivals from the Eastern Mediterranean route, the number of people choosing the Central route increased again. As a result, in 2016, more than 180,000 people crossed this route (Frontex, 2016). In 2017, it is evident that this route has become again the most popular one since more than 96,000 people (by August 8th) chose it in order to reach the European shores (UNHCR, 2017).

The Western Mediterranean route has, traditionally, been chosen by a significantly low number of immigrants and refugees. It leads people mainly from Morocco, Algeria, Senegal, Mauritania, Nigeria, Côte d'Ivoire and Benin to the Spanish shores. In 2015, it was chosen by 7,164 people. This number increased in 2016, reaching 10,231 people (Frontex, 2016). In 2017, by the end of July more than 12,000 people had chosen this route (UNHCR, 2017).

Figure 1. Refugees and immigrants crossing each Mediterranean Sea route (2014-2017)

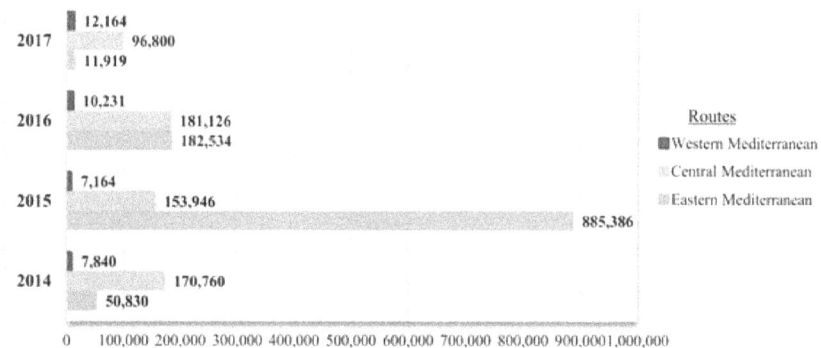

Data Source: Frontex (2017) and UNHCR (2017)

Shipwrecks

In order to cross each one of the migratory sea routes that were mentioned above, the immigrants and the refugees have to use boats. One of the most important aspects of the crisis is the capsizing of these boats, which leads to the death of hundreds of people. The sinking of these boats is caused by a variety of reasons. One of the main reasons, is the overcrowding of the boats. Traffickers seek to increase their profit and thereby they transfer more people in each journey. The increase of their profit is the reason why they also tend to use unfit boats (not certified under the International Convention for Safety of Life at Sea) with low quality equipment. The lifejackets that are usually being used are not made to international standards and are not able to turn the people wearing them in a safe position (Tzafalias, 2016). The third reason that causes shipwrecks is the dangerous weather conditions. Most of the transports take place during the winter months, when the cost of the travel is significantly lower (Achilli, 2016). Finally, some of the shipwrecks that occur mostly in the Eastern Mediterranean route can be intentional. The International Law requires that castaways or people in need should be protected and given assistance without regard to whether they entered the country's waters with or without permission (Kirchner et al., 2015; Achilli, 2016). Consequently, in cases that the Coast Guards detect sinking boats or people in need at sea, they are obliged to save them and transfer them to the shores. There they are given shelter and medical assistance and they have the right to apply for asylum.

Figure 2. Shipwrecks of refugees and immigrants in the Mediterranean Sea (1.1.2015-11.8.2017)

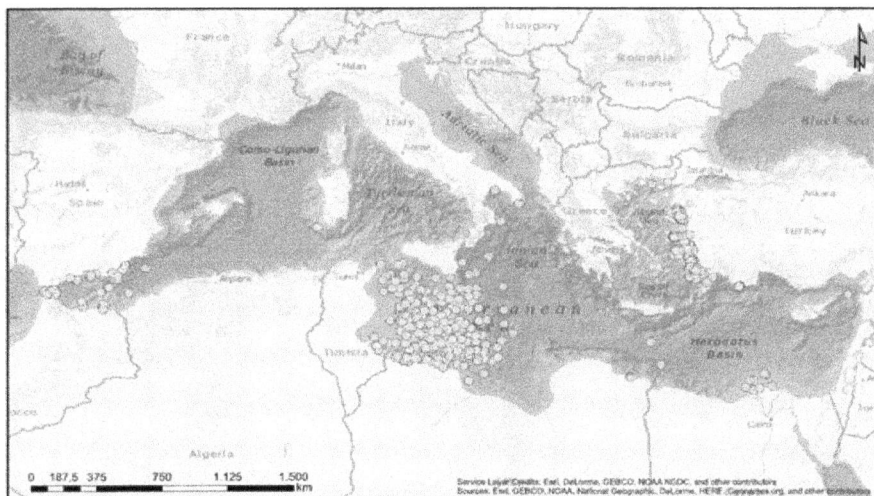

Data Source: IOM (2017)

When an attempt is made to map all of the shipwrecks that have occurred, complications arise. For the majority of the shipwrecks, it is quite difficult to ascertain their exact geographical coordinates, owing to the fact that most of the boats are not being detected while sinking. Some are found in different locations due to sea currents, while others are found on the shores. According to data from the IOM, during the period January 1st 2015 to August 11th 2017, more than 471 shipwrecks had occurred. The majority of these shipwrecks had taken place in the Central Mediterranean route (253 shipwrecks). Many shipwrecks, also, had taken place across the Eastern Mediterranean route (160 shipwrecks), while, only, 58 shipwrecks had occurred across the Western Mediterranean route. These numbers are extremely significant, since they present a highly larger number of shipwrecks in the second most popular sea route, which was chosen, during the examined period, by notably less immigrants and refugees.

Figure 3. Number of dead refugees and immigrants from each recorded shipwreck in the Mediterranean Sea (1.1.2015-11.8.2017)

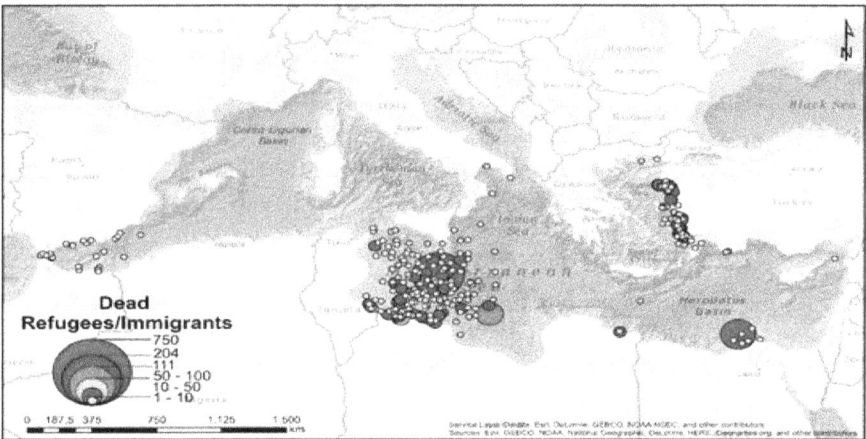

Data Source: IOM (2017)

Figure 4. Number of missing refugees and immigrants from each recorded shipwreck in the Mediterranean Sea (1.1.2015-11.8.2017)

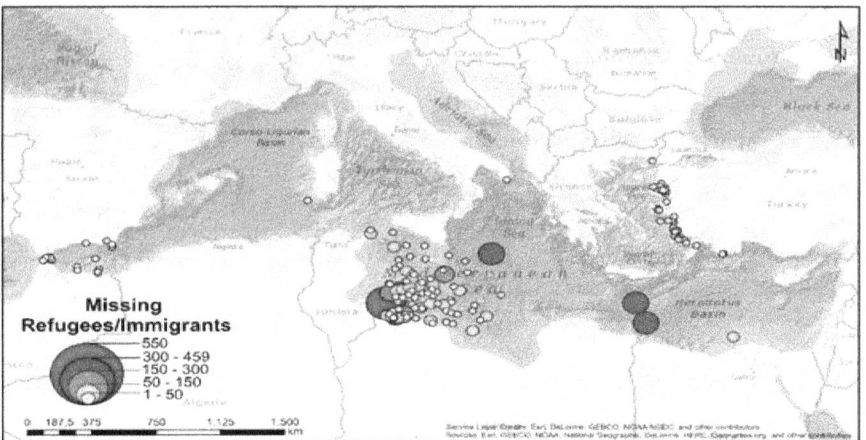

Data Source: IOM (2017)

The same pattern can, also, be noticed in the number of the dead and the missing persons from each one of the recorded shipwrecks. In total, 399 of the recorded 471 shipwrecks caused the death of at least one person and 169 left at least one person missing. The shipwreck with the highest number of dead took place on April 18th 2015, in the Central Mediterranean Sea and caused the death of 750 people. In the same area, also, occurred the shipwreck with the highest number of the missing. This shipwreck occurred on May 25th 2016 and left 550 immigrants and refugees missing. In total 3,608 people died from all the presented shipwrecks and 6,809 people went missing from them.

Implications and Conclusion

In conclusion, the refugee and migration crisis, which began in 2015, is a major issue for Europe, as it is the main destination for the people fleeing their countries. The most popular routes to Europe are the Central and the Eastern Mediterranean routes. In order to cross these routes the immigrants and the refugees use boats that due to a variety of reasons, often, sink. Even though, the Eastern Mediterranean route has been chosen by a significantly higher number of people during the last years, the majority of the shipwrecks have occurred in the Central Mediterranean route. Moreover, the shipwrecks that have occurred in this route have caused the majority of the dead and the missing. To that end, the Central Mediterranean route has been described as the most dangerous sea route (Fargues, 2015).

The shipwrecks and the crisis, in general, have a major impact on hosting societies (such as Greece and Italy), as well. These societies are requested to provide shelter, food and medical care to all the people who reach their shores. In order to do that they have to provide significant funds. They, also, have to reinforce their migration and asylum services due to the notably higher number of people that need them. All these provisions, cause, in some cases, political tension. This is because of the fact that the main hosting societies (Greece and Italy) are facing a financial and humanitarian crisis as well. In certain cases, it is, also, noticed that the crisis can have a negative impact on local tourism.

References

Achilli, L. (2016). Displacement trends of Syrian Asylum Seekers to the EU, European University Institute.

Dimitriadi, A. (2015). "Greece is like a door, you go through it to get to Europe": Understanding Afghan migration to Greece, Hellenic Foundation for European and Foreign Policy (ELIAMEP).

Fargues, P. (2015). 2015: The year we mistook refugees for invaders, European University Institute.

Frontex (2016). Trends and Routes. Retrieved from http://frontex.europa.eu/.

Guild, E., Costello, C., Garlick, M., Moreno-Lax, V. (2015). The 2015 Refugee crisis in the European Union, Centre for European Policy Studies.

Heisbourg, F. (2015). "The strategic implications of the Syrian refugee crisis", Survival: Global Politics and Strategy, 57(6), 7-20.

International Organization for Migration (IOM) (2017). Missing Migrants Project. Retrieved from https://missingmigrants.iom.int/.

Kirchner, S., Geler-Noch, K., Frese, V. (2015). "Coastal State Obligations in the Context of Refugees at Sea Under the European Convention on Human Rights", Ocean and Coastal Law Journal, 20(1), 57-82.

Park, J. (2015). Europe's Migration Crisis, Council on Foreign Relations.

The UN Refugee Agency (UNHCR) (2017). Operational Portal: Refugee Situations. Retrieved from http://data2.unhcr.org/en/.

Tzafalias, M. (2016). "Fake Lifejackets Play a Role in Drowning of Refugees", Bulletin of the World Health Organization, 94(6), 411-412.

Chapter 48. Rethinking Refugee Activism within and beyond the State: The Trajectory of Refugee Activism

Birce Altıok Karşıyaka [1]

Abstract

This paper aims to build a spatial model on refugees' political struggle for human rights with connection to activism and social movement theories in relation to sovereign control spaces. The research undertakes an interdependent theoretical approach to Critical Citizenship Studies (CCS) and Autonomy of Migrants (AoM) perspectives through categorizing forms of activism under *the hierarchical model of migrants' access to rights* by decomposing *variance* in refugee activism cases. Through such classification, it aims to find a middle ground for the discussions between refugee/migrant struggle within the AoM and CCS by integrating the limits of right-based actions that are shaped by the sovereign state policies and practices using empirical evidences collected from Greece and Turkey for the period between 2011-2016.

Keywords: Activism, autonomy, control, citizenship, refugee, space.

Introduction

International refugee regime has been in crisis for a very long time in all over the world. The main aim of this theoretical research is to establish interrelated link between the effects of state policies and practices on the emergence of migrant and pro-migrant activism, and in sequence, how that trigger different positioning of migrants seeking access to their rights contra the state. This paper offers a theoretical inquiry to the 'impossible activism' against the paradox of sovereign control (Nyers, 2003, p. 1080), and how their activism diversifies as a result.

Through constructing a spatial model on refugees' political struggle for human rights with connection to activism and social movement theories in relation to sovereign control spaces, this research undertakes an interdependent theoretical approach to Critical Citizenship Studies (CCS) and Autonomy of Migrants (AoM) perspectives through categorizing forms of activism under *the hierarchical model of migrants' access to rights* by decomposing *variance* in refugee activism cases. Through such classification, it aims to find a middle ground for the discussions between refugee/migrant struggle within AoM and CCS by integrating the limits of right-based actions that are shaped by the sovereign state policies and practices using empirical evidences collected from Greece and Turkey for the period between 2011-2016. A dataset with regards to social protests of refugees are collected to see divergence and variance followed by a qualitative interpretative approach to decompose underlying meanings and policies attached to refugee movements. The outline, first,

[1] Birce Altıok Karşıyaka is PhD Candidate in Political Science and International Relations, Koc University, Rumelifeneri Yolu, Sariyer, Istanbul, 34450 TURKEY. E-mail: baltiok@ku.edu.tr

presents the current debate between AoM and CCS, and then, present the theoretical spatial model supported with evidences using the dataset.

Literature Review – Citizenship and beyond

The literature on refugee and migrant activism conduct theoretical discussions *within and beyond* the realms of *citizenship* (Turner, 2016, p.151). The former, referred as the *critical citizenship studies* (CCS), challenges the traditional understanding of citizenship and broaden the meanings attached to it through analysing the struggles of migrants exposing "new spaces of citizenship that potentially enable both new ways of being political and new visions for the type of politics" (Nyers and Rygiel, 2012, p.9; see Ataç, Rygiel and Stierl, 2016). It is through the political acts that of migrant subjects' challenge and transform citizenships. Whereas, the latter, the *autonomy of migration* (AoM) perspective takes a critical stand on the widening definition of citizenship which incorporates migrant struggles into the framing of citizenship that reinforces control and governance role attributed to the sovereign and fails to embrace autonomous actions by the migrant agency (Papadopoulos and Tsianos, 2013). As "citizenship cannot be thought outside of sovereignty and control" (Tyler, 2010, p.83), according to AoM, citizenship framework presents a 'wall' against migrant practices by asserting limits of the sovereign (Papadopoulos and Tsianos, 2013, p.179). In other words, CCS constricts study of migrant movements in access to *rights* and *representation* that are already determined by the sovereign power ('double-R' calls Papadopoulos and Tsianos, 2013). Therefore, citizenship framework fails to include 'what lies after citizenship' (Ibid. p.179). This is where the autonomy debate directs the attention towards migrant agency's own logic, motivation, practices, tactics and trajectories that escape sovereign control, that is to say, in direction of what is left beyond the control spectrum of the state (Ibid. p.184-5). The *organization* ontology behind AoM, Papadopoulos and Tsianos (2013) argue, is that new forms of life are produced in which the autonomous actions create alternative forms of existence and new forms of life beyond the control of the sovereign (also see Papadopoulos, 2011, 2012).

Another crucial effort trying to fit citizenship perspective into AoM approach was adopted by Peter Nyers by proposing a different category: migrant citizenship, in which "people constitute themselves as political subjects, citizens, prior to being legally or discursively recognized as such by state authorities... acts of citizenship emphasize the contingencies, ambiguities, and contestations of citizenship, as opposed to the certainties, assuredness, and formalities of legal approaches to citizenship" (Ibid., p.23,33). The reason it is called critical citizenship actually due to the fact that it challenges the sovereign definition of traditional citizenship. To put in reverse phrasing, CCS also tries to eradicate the 'wall' of citizenship in which the AoM accuses CCS of. Against AoM's critique of CCS taking citizenship as a fixed entity determined by the sovereign control, CCS affirms that the acts of citizenship actually challenges the firm political definitions of the citizenship regime. Whereas AoM is critical of such reductionist views of migrants' experience staying within the idiom of the institution of citizenship, on the contrary, they argue that there exists a migrant experience that actually goes beyond the boundaries determined by the institution of citizenship.

A middle ground effort is adopted by looking at migrant mobility through an independent subjectivity: noncitizenship (Johnson, 2016; Tonkiss and Bloom, 2016). Noncitizenship (different than non-citizenship to differentiate the dichotomous approach against citizenship) does not mean lack of citizenship status, rather, as a political agency, it asserts a "powerful and transgressive subjectivity in its own right" (Johnson, 2016). "[N]oncitizenship is far more than the binary opposite of citizenship but rather itself is a relationship between a noncitizen and a State in its own right, and highlights the complex, overlapping and fragmented nature of memberships in contemporary societies" (Tonkiss and Bloom, 2016, p.848). Johnson argues "the protesters are exhibiting a noncitizenship that is a political subjectivity in its own right, and that opens up possibilities for rethinking and reimagining political action. It asserts noncitizenship as autonomous and independent rather than simply a status marking an absence of citizenship. The politics of noncitizenship are more than a demand for inclusion in citizenship frameworks, and instead represent a powerful political agency that calls upon new and dynamic political relations across multiple lines" (2016, p.963). Again, it is more like a continuation of the CCS version of citizenship but trying to settle down the debate without framing it under 'citizenship'.

Such middle ground efforts face the problem of what Giovanni Sartori (1970, 1984) describes as conceptual traveling (applying the concept to new cases) and stretching (the adopted concept does not fit the new cases). As studies trying go beyond the traditional and legal definitions, practices and aims affiliated with citizenship trying to analyze migrants' social movements, the scientific focus attempts to assign meanings to them, but struggles within the existing boundaries of already defined concepts. On the one hand, the critical analysis of citizenship applied to migrant activities is a valid one, as migrants situate themselves against 'the exclusionary technologies of citizenship' (Tyler and Marciniak, 2013) and adopts 'acts of citizenship' (Isin and Nielson, 2008) portraying similar mobilizations as of citizens; on the other hand, the ontological definition of who a migrant is also distances itself from the definition of citizenship as they detach from claiming citizen-based demands. AoM is actually trying to fulfill this gap, yet, by focusing its energy against the citizenship as the main dichotomy against its scientific focus; it misses the opportunity to achieve how autonomy emerges and being practiced. Instead, other research fields, such as the social movements literature, are highly rich in focusing on the forms of activism and social movements by providing an ample source on how agents create new forms of resistances and distance themselves from the radar of state control (see Ataç, Rygiel and Stierl, 2016). The similar effort has recently started to be conducted for CCS in analyzing contentious social movements of migrants (see Ibid.). It is empirically as well as theoretically necessary to fulfill the gap between the two perspectives. In doing so, social movements studies can be used as guidance. This paper tries to contribute on to such efforts by integrating an empirical analysis on refugee movements without generalizing, instead, by decomposing refugee movement's elements in relation to sovereign control by categorizing under spatial modeling. For that reason, this necessitates a closer empirical focus on further expansion of autonomy and migrant citizenship literature. Chimienti and Solomos (2011) are critical of the transformative power of citizenship perspective assigned to non-citizens social movement due to some migration cases being ignored in claim-making, government response being limited and the existing social movements contributing to the reproduction of existing repertoires and structures of the status-quo. They conclude that to grasp the impact and emergence of irregular migrants' mobilizations, it is necessary to expand and look in detail at the types of mobilizations and conditions underneath (p.356).

The Issue of Politics of Migration under Spatial Theorizing

The concept of citizenship is subject to transformation and the limits cannot be reduced to state sovereignty (Nyers, 2015). In other words, it would be inaccurate to take citizenship as fully autonomous contra the state, or associate it completely with the sovereign. Rather, the autonomy and sovereign state perspectives are connected to the spaces of migrants' political action and to the control spaces of the state. Hence, migrant activities respond differently to sovereign control spaces, therefore, just like *yin yang*, they pull and push each other towards a more complementary form of survival, affecting the emergence of different types of practices by the migrants and their way of claiming rights. Since the history of men is the history of struggle against the powerful, whether there emerges a global citizenship (Isin and Nyers, 2014) or 'acts of citizenship' (Isin and Nielson, 2008), the fight for *equaliberty* (Gündoğdu, 2015, p.23) and the acts *to right the wrong* manifest itself in the form of varying voices that needs a much more detailed look.

The trajectory perspective, therefore, aims to decompose refugee claims for rights from the initial act of refugee flight. I argue that activism is inherent in different dimensions of refugee acts. The initial act of flight is a political act in the sense of contesting against the real/perceived threat of persecution (Nyers and Rygiel, 2012, p.8). It is an 'act of resistance' to counter intolerable conditions (Lewis, 2006) or 'for many, [it is] simultaneously a strategy of resistance and an attempt to better one's life conditions through mobility' (Isin and Rygiel, 2007, p.187). The act of refuge, whether internally or internationally, becomes a compulsory act, but it is not necessarily explicit.

Accordingly, the initial act of flight is categorized under the *inexplicit form of activism*. It is *inexplicit* due to forced and involuntary nature of the act completely different than the contentious politics or activism adopted as the flight continues and knocks on other countries doors, and the political act takes different forms with varying characteristics. It is the main focus of this theoretical paper to stress on the continuance and difference in acts of resistances by the refugee migrants followed by the act of 'taking a refuge.'

Since "mobility has the power, because of the movement of people itself" (Martignoni and Papadopoulos 2014, p.39), the *inexplicit* transforms itself to *explicit forms* through change from *involuntary* to *voluntary* activism as the flight takes new forms. The *hierarchical model* presented below, therefore, disintegrates rights claiming of refugees through the prism of control spaces and takes into account 'acts of citizenship' and the autonomy of migrants as interdependent and interconnected. For instance, in a nutshell, an open-door policy of a state fulfilling the *non-refoulement* principle opens up new debates for state refugee policies to realize followed by executive steps, for better or worse, and in return, refugees' levels of expectations and satisfactions in accordance with these policies in different control spaces such as camps, urban or border space, highlight the agenda of politicization and create varying contentious political actions to emerge in connection to migrants' own interpretation and selective engagement in an explicit form.

Hierarchical model, therefore, aims to decompose the boundaries that both CCS and AoM accuse each other of doing: for AoM it is the 'wall' argument against CCS for limiting activities to the framework of citizenship, and for CCS, it is the rejection of the claim that citizenship framework only includes actions of migrants against the sovereign control. In fact, every protest, activism and/or individual journey has a unique characteristic on its own since they involve actions of particular individuals and their lives, supporting the thesis of what is left below-the-radar argument of AoM; but also, these acts continue to maintain struggles against control and governance mechanisms determined by the state and its apparatuses, in other words, as Foucault argues, "there are no relations of power without resistance" (1980). Whether these struggles emerge on individual or collective level, the issue of politics of migration reveals itself in varying forms of resistance everywhere around the globe (see Lewis, 2006) and instead of theorizing 'space as contentious politics' in the social movement literature (in Ataç, Rygiel and Stierl, 2016; Tilly 2000; Sewell, 2011; Martin and Miller, 2003; Leitner, Sheppard, and

Sziarto, 2008; Monforte 2016), here, the departure point is the thematic realm of refugees' social movements in connection to control spaces by the state.

High-level Control Space

The figures below (Figure 1, 2 and 3) present the prism-shaped hierarchical space model in profiling state control, agency and social movements of refugees. In Figure 1, the upper wide base represents the highest level of state control and maximization of power spaces in which direct control, state apparatuses and power dynamics are highly vivid and efficiently adopted. Refugee camps, detention centers and borders can be given as examples to such spaces. Going towards the lower levels of the pyramid, the control mechanisms start to diminish but as opposed to AoM perspective, even at individual level decision-making, this thesis argue that power factor never disappears but weakens as anonymity, autonomy and individualism increase, and collective visibility and explicit participation decrease towards lower spaces of control, such as in the urban space, and even more weakened in the private sphere.

Figure 1. State Control, Power and Efficiency

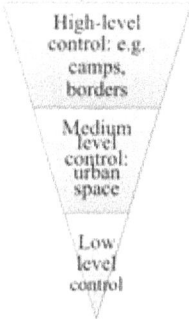

Figure 2. Agency

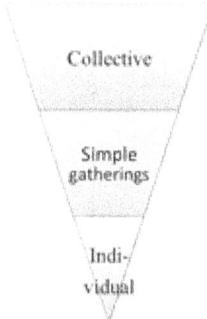

Figure 3. Social Movements and Activism

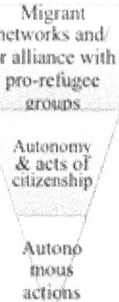

High-level control: e.g. camps, borders	Collective	Assembled: Social movements	Migrant networks and/ or alliance with pro-refugee groups
Medium level control: urban space	Simple gatherings	Dispersed: Protests and activism	Autonomy & acts of citizenship
Low level control	Indi-vidual	Every day activities	Autonomous actions

The opposite thesis is also valid for the maximum level control space, though, how strict the control mechanisms are, there still exist fractures within the control spaces in which migrants can manipulate, and this is against Agamben's 'spaces of exception' thesis in which the political life is suspended and refugees turn into complete disempowered individuals and reduced to 'bare life' (2005). On the contrary, camp-based protests portray struggles against control. While migrants target the policies within the control space via protesting against camp-conditions, in addition, everyday life also continues to materialize practices and informal autonomous action escaping the regime of control (see Ramadan, 2013). Here, the questionable aspect is when approaching camps, for acts against the 'exclusionary technologies of citizenship', are protestors "compelled to make their demands in the idiom of the regime of citizenship they are contesting" (Tyler and Marciniak, 2013, p.146)? By categorizing political constitution of refugees under the citizenship framework as part of a marginalized space (Turner, 2016), we routinely put refugee activities of claiming rights under binary categorization of exclusionary practices of citizenship, and fail to grasp noncitizen and other practices outside of citizenship framing. Johnson prefers to grasp actions and practices of refugees within the camps under noncitizenship thesis arguing, "it is not a claim to citizenship as 'the' territorially relevant identity, but to bypass citizenship and to claim political agency on the basis of being located, present and here" (Johnson, 2016, p.960). While noncitizenship brings forth a new approach while categorizing it not under traditional definition of citizenship, it seems that their approach continues to extend the meanings attached to what citizenship is and is not, whereas, it is necessary to divert our attention to what really goes on with the practices of refugees under such control spaces and how that affect variance across cases, their mobilization efforts and social movements in return.

According to the protest data collected between the years 2011-2015 in Greece and Turkey, the main connection of control spaces in understanding divergence in migrant activities and practices under maximum control mechanisms, firstly, the citizenship framework does not explain diversity of protests, such as protests against forced evictions of refugees from the camps, as happened at Idomeni in 2016, or the unaccompanied children's protest in the same year. Secondly, the camp-protest data portrays different protest directions against different control spaces such as protesting of the UNHCR sites and policies, state asylum applications or the conditions within the camps, and the inter-ethnic conflicts (e.g. Algerians and Syrians in Souda refugee camp, among Syrian and Afghanis in Vial, both in Chios in 2016), therefore, each protest's relation to targeting of the control space differs. To explain this in empirical terms, for instance, among 49 cases, 15 cases are camp based protests in which 13 of them adopted violent measures by the refugees meaning actions such as destruction of property, setting tents on fire as a form of contentious claims, and in return, security forces intervened to 12 of them using tear gas, and 5 of the cases (2 in Turkey, 3 in Greece) were ended up in instances of deportations. This highlights camp-based protests where the refugees are collectively located emerge in more violent forms different than in spaces with lesser control. Considering the thematic aspect in each protests, the protests challenging the boundaries of camp-space in demanding access to better living conditions encounter more repression in both Turkey and Greece cases, and deportations are widely adopted for the case of Turkey, and to a lesser extent for the protests against asylum procedures as stepping outside of the control space of camps, whereas, if the protests within the camps staged a protest issue outside of the control space such as protests related to home country of Syrians in the town of Yayladağı in Turkey in slogans of 'people want freedom,' no counter challenge was adopted. So, as collectivity in refugee camps push the limits of the control space both via the contentious forms and the agenda of the protest, the protest culture turns out to be adopting violent forms and in return facing more repression. In addition to visible activities of refugees under the spatial category of control and agency, third point is about how everyday activities within the camps are materialized (see Ramadan's geography research for Palestinian camps in Lebanon, 2013). The point important to stress here is that these actions by the refugees should be categorized differently considering their relation to both control space and issue connection, in addition to framing such activities under critical citizenship framework.

Medium-level Control Space

The medium-level state control includes spaces and actions mainly in the urban space, including execution of laws and regulations, governance at municipality level, local neighborhoods, in which refugees find the opportunity to act more freely and in similar fashion demanding rights as of citizens also expanding the meanings attached to citizenship. While this category represents 'acts of citizenship' framework to become realized, categorizing actions of refugees under medium-level control also answers the dilemma of challenging the boundaries of citizenship while refugees aiming to acquire legal definitions entitled to citizens. Mainly, as migrants demand access to papers or as they mobilize politically aiming legal framework, they take state as the direct interlocutor while forcing the boundaries and the discourse shaping the traditional citizenship but not necessarily against the 'exclusionary technologies of citizenship' (Tyler and Marciniak, 2013) but within the realm of citizen's space. They find the opportunity to establish alliances with the pro-refugee groups, or freely organize their own refugee networks, and expand their right claiming as the control space loosens. For instance, in 2011, 300 Migrant Hunger Strikers demanded access to legal status in 2011 in Athens and Thessaloniki, and asked the legalization of all migrant men and women and equal political and social rights and obligations with Greek workers (see Topak, 2017). Therefore, this is why the protests include the elements 'illegality' and "call for legalization simultaneously reinforc[ing] the authority of citizenship as the foremost measure of belonging" (McNevin, 2007, p.670; see Nyers, 2015).

Within the same medium-level category, beyond the radar of the state control, everyday practices of migrant movements also take place because the same hierarchical space with loosened control also empowers the autonomous action realm by the refugees due to anonymity and invisibility the urban space provides. The dispersed category (under Figure 3) enables protests and activism, and hosts elements of CCS and AoM. The space is open to refugees challenging boundaries of existing control and mechanisms by simple gatherings and protests, but also provide them the opportunity to in-and-out choice while continue to shape their lives as they escape the control space. That is the main problem in CCS and AoM perspectives face because the boundaries separating migrant actions are not clear and can be highly intermixed. As an example, the Greek anarchist community in Exarcheia district presents a high level of solidarity with refugee groups and support the activism and social movements of refugees. The occupation of buildings, volunteer run-schools, collective movements in solidarity with refugees are example to that interconnected nature of autonomous and critical acts of citizenship.

Low-level Control Space

Whereas, towards the lower bottoms of the prism, autonomous actions by the refugees gain more power and has ability to escape state control, yet, escape does not mean full independence, but on the contrary, the ability to act autonomously is continued to be shaped by the power dynamics, even affecting the decision-making of individuals. To refer everyday activities, Bayat calls 'social non-movements' (2010); Papadopoulos and Tsianos call 'non-politics' (2013); Moulin and Thomaz call 'small politics' of everyday life (2016). Still, these actions can be referred under the realm of political space, though small or invisible, they continue to shape migrants' actions and decision-making in their everyday struggle. For instance, the leftist community space in Turkey is more distant in including transnational elements with regards to defending refugee rights compared to those in Greece, and under more repressive control by the state due to their radical activities, and historical struggle with the state. As these leftist spaces are characterized by lack of transnational elements and face state control, refugees in Turkey mostly prefer more conservative neighborhood spaces linked to their religious and ethnic identities, and shape their everyday activities within such conservative community spaces.

Perhaps, the critics are valid in saying that we are "not trained to perceive them as 'proper' politics" (Papadopoulos and Tsianos, 2013, p.188) but the feminist studies have the background to analyze the private realm of activism, yet, for refugees Ataç et al.'s study is an important one in which they argue "diverse forms of migrant struggles exist that take place in less publicly visible spaces in the micro-political spectrum of everyday life and the private sphere" (2015, p.17). If we categorize migrants' activities from extensive to less effective spaces of control, the struggle among different research frameworks will be disclosed more vividly to observe varying politicizations having different effects on the emergence of migrant activism and this might also contribute to explain variation across cases.

Conclusion

This theoretical inquiry into migrant agency's actions against state control and demanding access to rights tried to lay down a general perspective on the variances of refugee activisms across different control spaces in a hierarchical approach. The debate among sovereign control versus the autonomy of migration requires a much more detailed inquiry into the actions of migrants within different control spaces instead of arguing what is included and what is not.

References

Agamben G. (2005). *State of exception.* Chicago IL: University of Chicago Press.

Ataç, I., Rygiel, K., & Stierl, M. (2016). Introduction: The Contentious Politics of Refugee and Migrant Protest and Solidarity Movements: Remaking Citizenship from the Margins. *Citizenship Studies*, *20*(5), 527-544.

Ataç, I., S. Kron, S. Schilliger, H. Schwiertz, and M. Stierl. (2015). Struggles of Migration as In-/visible Politics. *Movements. Journal für kritische Migrations- und Grenzregimeforschung*, 1(2), 1-18.

Bayat, A., 2010. *Life as politics. How ordinary people change the Middle East.* Amsterdam: Amsterdam University Press.

Chimienti, M., & Solomos, J. (2011). Social movements of irregular migrants, recognition, and citizenship. *Globalizations*, 8(3), 343-360.

Gündoğdu, A. (2008). *Rightlessness in an Age of Rights: Hannah Arendt and the Contemporary Predicament*. New York: Oxford University Press.

Isin, E. F., & Nielsen, G. M. (2008). *Acts of Citizenship*. London: Zed Books.

Isin, E. F., & Nyers, P. (2014). Introduction: Globalizing Citizenship Studies. In: Isin, E. F., & Nyers, P. (eds) *Routledge Handbook of Global Citizenship Studies*, New York: Routledge. pp. 1–11.

Isin, E. F., & Rygiel, K. (2007). Abject spaces: Frontiers, zones, camps. In: Dauphinee, E., & Masters, C. (eds.) *The Logics of Biopower and the War on Terror.* New York, NY: Palgrave Macmillan. pp. 181-203.

Johnson, H. L. (2015). These fine lines: locating noncitizenship in political protest in Europe, *Citizenship Studies*, 19(8), 951-965.

Leitner, H., E. Sheppard, and K. M. Sziarto. (2008). The Spatialities of Contentious Politics. *Transactions of the Institute of British Geographers*, 33, 157-172.

Lewis, M. (2006). 'Nothing Left to Lose? An Examination of the Dynamics and Recent History of Refugee Resistance and Protest', Paper presented at the 4th Annual Forced Migration Post-Graduate Student Conference University of East London, London, UK, 18-19 March. Received from http://schools.aucegypt.edu/GAPP/cmrs/reports/Documents/Lewis.pdf Accessed: 20.02.2017

Martin, D., & B. Miller. (2003). Space as Contentious Politics. *Mobilization: An International Journal*, 8(2), 135-156.

McNevin, A. (2007). Irregular Migrants, Neoliberal Geographies and Spatial Frontiers of 'the political.' *Review of International Studies*, 33(4), 655-674.

Monforte, P. (2016). The Border as a Space of Contention: The Spatial Strategies of Protest Against Border Controls in Europe. *Citizenship Studies*, 20(3–4), 411-426.

Moulin, C., & Thomaz, D. (2016). The tactical politics of 'humanitarian'immigration: negotiating stasis, enacting mobility. *Citizenship studies*, 20(5), 595-609.

Nyers, P. (2003). Abject cosmopolitanism: the politics of protection in the anti-deportation movement. *Third World Quarterly*, 24(6), 1069-1093.

Nyers, P. (2015). Migrant Citizenships and Autonomous Mobilities. *Migration, Mobility and Displacement,* 1(1), 23–39.

Nyers, P., & Rygiel, K. (Eds.) (2012). *Citizenship, migrant activism and the politics of movement.* London, UK: Routledge.

Papadopoulos, D. (2011). Alter-ontologies: towards a constituent politics in technoscience. *Social Studies of Science*, 41(2), 177-201.

Papadopoulos, D. (2012). Worlding justice/commoning matter. *Occasion: Interdisciplinary Studies in the Humanities*, 3.

Papadopoulos, D., & Tsianos, V. S. (2013). After citizenship: autonomy of migration, organisational ontology and mobile commons. *Citizenship studies,* 17(2), 178-196.

Martignoni, M. & Papadopoulos, D. (2014). Genealogies of autonomous mobility. In: Isin, E. F., & Nyers, P.(eds) *Routledge Handbook of Global Citizenship Studies*, New York: Routledge. pp. 38-48.

Ramadan, A. (2013). Spatialising the Refugee Camp. *Transactions of the Institute of British Geographers*, 38, 65-77.

Sartori, G. (1970). Concept Misformation in Comparative Politics. *American Political Science Review,* 64, 1033-53.

Sartori, G. (1984). Guidelines for Concept Analysis. In: Sartori, G. (ed.) *Social Science Concepts: A Systematic Analysis*, Beverly Hills: Sage.

Sewell, W. (2001). Space in Contentious Politics. In: R. R. Aminzade, J.A. Goldstone, D. McAdam, E.J. Perry, W. H. Sewell, Jr., S. Tarrow, and C. Tilly (eds) *Silence and Voice in the Study of Contentious Politics*, Cambridge, UK: Cambridge. pp. 51-89.

Tilly, C. (2000). Spaces of Contention. *Mobilization: An International Journal,* 5(2), 135-159.

Tonkiss, K. and T. Bloom. (2015). Theorising noncitizenship: concepts, debates and challenges, *Citizenship Studies*, 19(8), 837-852.

Topak, Ö. E. (2017) Migrant protest in times of crisis: politics, ethics and the sacred from below. *Citizenship Studies*, 21(1), 1-21.

Turner, J. (2016). (En)gendering the political: Citizenship from marginal spaces. *Citizenship Studies*, 20(2), 141-155.

Tyler, I. (2010). Designed to Fail: A Biopolitics of British Citizenship. *Citizenship Studies*, 14(1), 61-74.

Tyler, I. and K. Marciniak. (2013). Immigrant Protest: An Introduction. *Citizenship Studies.* 17(2), 143-156.

Chapter 49. "The Application of the Analytical Hierarchy Process Model in the Process of Conflict Management"

LL.M. Nena Nenovska Gjorgjievska [1]

Abstract

The incitement and the occurrence of the conflicts, their escalation, ceasefire and de-escalation are processes which are continually appearing, lasting and resolving. Consequently, the conflicts usually pull migratory flows. Migration is an issue which nowadays is very present, and it needs to be resolved. The migration usually starts where conflicts arise. Having that in mind, the main concept in the paper is focused on the conflicts and the emergence of the migration flows. It also gives a suggestion how the conflicts can be resolved in the Middle East countries. The purpose of this research is to find out real reasons for appearance of migrations and most rational solutions for their solving. For doing that the Analytical Hierarchy Process (AHP) method is applied. A short overview will be given of the main elements of the AHP method and how it is applied in the conflict resolution. AHP method is enforceable and leads to concrete recommendations for further conflict resolution. The results of the research will show that resolving the conflicts may contribute in suppression of the migration and it can also protect countries for further armed conflicts and unwanted migration flows.

Key words: Analytical hierarchy process, conflicts, migration, resolution

Introduction

Conflict resolution is a process which governments, states and international organizations face daily. As a field of study, conflict resolution is a process that occurred at the height of the Cold war, when the development of nuclear weapons and conflicts between major powers represented a great danger to the nations (Ramsbotham, Mail and Woodhouse, 2006). Since then, the governments as actors try to find appropriate ways to resolve conflicts. Many theorists and practitioners offer their ideas, methods and ways of dealing with conflicts but have not yet found the appropriate method for handling that would be applicable to any kind of conflict. They rather point out that conflict is determined by several factors which influence its resolution. Therefore, the method of Analytical Hierarchy Process (AHP) will be analyzed for the purposes of this paper. This is a method that has proven successful in resolving specific conflicts. The same method, AHP, will continue to serve as a reference for examing the current refugee processes of the countries of the Middle East (Syria, Iraq, Afghanistan) to the Balkan countries (Turkey, Greece, Macedonia), in that its application will serve to measure elements of the conflicts arising in these countries from the Middle East in order to obtain qualitative and quantitative indicators at the beginning and continuation of these conflicts, and consequently measurement of refugee processes of those conflicts.

---

[1] PhD student in international relations and conflict management – Faculty of philosophy, University St. Cyril and Methodius, Blvd. 3-ta Makedonska Brigada, No. 43/4-16, Skopje. E-mail: nnenovska@hotmail.com

Defining the Concept of "Conflict Resolution"

The term "conflict resolution" is a term that contains conflict transformation, de-escalation of conflict, conflict management etc. In this context, "conflict resolution" is a generic term that covers all stages of de-escalation of the conflict until its finalization. Conflict resolution refers to peaceful end of the conflict or at least a significant de-escalation of the conflict. The principles of resolving any type of conflict are the same: defining the conflict, creation of a cordial atmosphere for exploring the conflict, clarification of the relevant issues and misconceptions, negotiation, agreement and reconciliation. (Bryce, 2001, p. 57-58) Hence "Conflict Resolution" means a situation where the conflicting parties enter into an agreement that solves their central incompatibilities, accept each other's continued existence as parties and cease all violent action against each other (Walensteen, 2007). This of course means that by this situation "conflict resolution" comes after the already existing conflict. So what exactly would constitute a "conflict"? According to Galtung, conflict is a dynamic process in which structures, attitudes and behavior are constantly changing and they influence to each other. As evolving dynamics, it is manifested in the form of conflict, from where the interests of the conflicting parties become unbearable. Then, the conflicting parties are organized around the structure to meet their interests. They form opinions and violent conflict behavior. Thus, the formation of the conflict begins to grow and intensify. This elaboration of conflict by Galtung, is one of the starting and most influential definitions of conflict. It forms the basis for further strengthening and developing the definition of conflicts by other schools.

According to the definition of Walensteen, on what constitutes "conflict resolution", there are several elements to be analyzed. *Signing a contract* means a formal document that is signed under certain conditions. *Acceptance of common existence of conflicting parties* is the withdrawal of troops and weapons from areas where the conflict took place, by opposing parties and thereby accepting the terms outlined in the formal agreement on ceasefire.

Following the Galtung's hourglass model, later adapted from Ramsbotham, conflicts and their resolution is conducted in two phases. The first phase refers to the occurrence or escalation of conflict as well as narrowing of the political space, and the second phase is characterized by a de-escalation of the conflict, including the expansion of the political space. The process of narrowing and expansion is explained by the different types and stages of conflict resolution. They are: contrast, contradiction, polarization, violence, war, a ceasefire agreement, the normalization of the situation and reconciliation. These stages are divided into two parts. The first part covers the first five stages that consist of an incentive, animosity between the parties to the conflict and the process of escalation, to the culmination of the war. Following Braithwaite and Lemke

(Vol.28 (2), 2011, p. 111-123) there are several measures of escalation that lead to conflict. The first measure of escalation refers to whether the conflict is "reciprocal", and to achieve the purpose of the conflict will be necessary to use a fire activity. The second measure of escalation is associated to the "use of force" in the conflict. The third measure of escalation combines the first two, or whether there is a "Shared use of force." The last measure refers to whether a conflict involves more than 1,000 victims. If included, the result is an interstate war. War is the culmination of a conflict. The second part of the de-escalation of the conflict, according to Galtung, comprise the steps leading to defuse the conflict situation through various forms of their transformation (de-escalation). The steps to de-escalation start primarily with the ceasefire, then by signing a contract, which in turn leads to a stage of normalization of the situation. The final phase of de-escalation includes reconciliation between conflicting parties. Various techniques for conflict resolution are specific for Galtung's model, and they refer to: limitation of the war, peacekeeping, peacebuilding, structural peace building and cultural peace building. (Ramsbotham at all; 2005; 2011)

Foregoing indicates the structure of the conflict, the manner of their occurrence and the various forms and stages of conflict resolution. What is significant about this work is the use of a specific method for resolving certain conflicts, which is about an alternative process for conflict resolution. The application of the Analytical hierarchy process method is different from the previous ways of negotiating the conflict resolution. It represents an econometric method that includes mathematical formulas. Considering the mathematical exactness as a science, this kind of conflict resolution will lead to the correct parameters of how a conflict can be resolved, certainly if the conflicting parties are satisfied with the outcome and if they declare themselves in favor of accepting the results of applying this method. The final result of this process is added as a value dimension of the negotiations, and resolution of the conflicts. (Saaty, Zoffer, 2012) The analysis of the Analytical hierarchy process (AHP) method will indicate applicability to particular conflict situations and simultaneously on its success in specific cases.

Analysis of the Analytical Hierarchy Process (Ahp) Method

Analytical hierarchy process (AHP) is a basic approach to decision-making, based on Multifactor analysis. According to Cvetkoska (2013), this method allows solving real problems according to multifactorial decisions which by their nature are complex, so they are decomposed to its constituent components: purpose, criteria (sub-criteria) and alternatives that are represented hierarchically, and then the decision maker should compare the elements of each hierarchy level in pairs and express their preferences for using the fundamental scale of Saaty, and therefore the adequate mathematical model is used to calculate priorities (weights) of elements. In this process, the entity which decides makes priority ranking of the alternatives. The hierarchical decomposition of a complex system is emerging as a primary tool which should handle with different elements. (Saaty, 2012) Once you set the whole structure by which the criteria and alternatives will be determined, the goal will be achieved.

The decision-making process can be presented through the following six steps (Saaty, 2006, p. 209):

1. Structuring the specific problem with a model that will show its key elements and their relations.

2. Then, the assessments which reflect knowledge, feelings or emotions, should be extracted.

3. The assessments should be presented with an explanatory number.

4. These numbers are to be used in calculating the priorities of the elements of the hierarchical model.

5. The results should be synthesized to determine an overall score.

6. A sensitive analysis should be conducted.

Application of the Method on Concrete Cases

This method was used in the analysis of the resolution of several conflicts, which occur often in the Middle East. Saaty and Zaffran (2012) explain the application of the AHP method in analyzing the Israeli-Palestinian conflict. In order to obtain prioritization of the deviations of the conflicting parties, they performed an analysis by measuring the gains and losses with deviations on each side. Namely, there have been eight hierarchical forms set, involving benefits and costs, out of which four hierarchical forms were set for Israel, and four for Palestine. Each of these hierarchical forms had set a target and a set of criteria and sub-criteria that were relevant for achieving the main objective. All possible deviations from conflicting parties were evaluated separately with each of the criteria. These criteria were set by an equal number of representatives from both conflicting parties, while the prioritization of deviations was made by each party separately without the knowledge of the other party.

The results obtained highlight the differences between Israel and Palestine. They emphasize the value of deviations of Israel that are measured from Palestine, compared with the deviations of Palestine measured from Israel. Considering the inequality of the parties, it is possible one of the parties to take a leadership role in the process of resolving the conflict. Saaty, Vargas and Zoffer (2015) suggest that the AHP method structures the problem much more efficiently than traditional "face to face" negotiations. In the past 6 decades a number of negotiators (presidents, foreign ministers, international organizations, alliances) are trying to establish peace in Israel and Palestine. The basic premise of these negotiations was that if you sit at the same place and start negotiations, a decision will be brought. But this proved ineffective for a solution to the conflict. Unlike negotiating skills, the AHP method could at least offer an option for resolving the conflict. AHP as a mathematical method can offer exactly where to place the boundaries of Israel and Palestine, it will identify which neighborhoods to stay in Israel and which in Palestine, East Jerusalem can be recognized as the capital of Palestine, the "status quo" position of the holy places in Jerusalem will be kept, etc.

The aforementioned example confirms that the analysis of specific conflicts by applying the AHP method is enforceable and leads to concrete recommendations for further conflict resolution. Thus, the AHP method proved constructive enough and has the potential to contribute to a better understanding of conflict resolution.

Conclusion

Considering the definitions of Walensteen and Galtung on what constitutes a conflict and how it could be resolved, it can be concluded that it is a complex problem that is composed of several elements. The analysis of these elements suggests various ways of resolving conflict. In an effort to find appropriate ways to resolve conflicts, the states, international organizations and a number of scholars offer a number of methods to deal with conflicts through their attitudes and policies. In fact, conflicts are adverse effects arising from human factors, therefore requiring a human factor in their dismissal. To that end, Thomas L. Saaty developed the Analytical hierarchy process method in the early seventies of the last century (Saaty, 1977, Saaty 1980, Begićević, 2008). This method allows structuring the problem of decision making and it simulates the decision-making process starting with defining the purpose, criteria (sub-criteria, if any) and alternatives, then comparing criteria (sub-criteria) and alternatives in pairs and getting the overall priority for every particular alternative. The advantage of the AHP method is based on its diversity or inclusion of a number of factors in order to reach a certain goal. This method proved to be an appropriate way in the analysis of conflict resolution, in several cases in some Middle East countries. Therefore, this Analytical hierarchy process will be the leading method in the research on the influence of the armed conflicts in the Middle East countries (Syria, Iraq and Afghanistan) and on the refugee crisis towards the Balkan countries (Turkey, Greece and Macedonia).

References

Braithwaite, Alex, Douglas Lemke. Conflict management and peace science. Unpacking escalation. Vol 28(2):111-123. SAGE, 2011

Bryce, Cyralene. Conflict Interventions. In insight into the Concept of Stress. Washington, 2001

Cvetkoska, Violeta. Methods and models of Multifactor decision making in management: an empirical study to evaluate the efficacy of certain units in the Republic of Macedonia (doctoral dissertation). Skopje, 2013

Ramsbotham, Oliver, Hugh Miall, Tom Woodhouse. Contemporary Conflict Resolution. Cambrige, UK, Massachusetts, USA. Polity, Apr 11, 2011

Saaty, Thomas L., Luis G. Vargas. Models, Methods, Concepts & Applications of the Analytic Hierarchy Process. Springer Science & Business Media, Dec 6, 2012

Saaty, Thomas L., H. J. Zoffer. A New Approach to the Middle East Conflict: The Analytic Hierarchy Process. Journal of multi-criteria decision analysis 19: 201–225 (2012)

Saaty, Thomas L., Luis G. Vargas and H. J. Zoffer. A structured scientific solution to the Israeli–Palestinian conflict: the analytic hierarchy process approach. SPRINGER, (2015) 2:7

Wallensteen, Peter. Understanding Conflict Resolution. SAGE, Apr 9, 2015

Chapter 50. Deciding to Stay: Bissau-Guinean Labour Migrants in Cabo Verde, West Africa1

Brandon D. Lundy[2], Kezia Lartey[3]

Abstract

Cabo Verde, once serving as a migration transit country into Europe and the Unites States, is becoming a final destination for some West African labour migrants, especially those from Cabo Verde's sister republic, Guinea-Bissau. Many enter Cabo Verde under the Economic Community of West African States' open borders agreement, eventually overstaying. The aim of this research was to discover why and how Cabo Verde is becoming a choke point for irregular labour migrants from Guinea-Bissau, and the effects these changes are having on immigrant/host community relations. As an illustrative case study on the effects of increased structural barriers to mobility from underdeveloped to developed countries, this study asks, how do marooned Bissau-Guineans integrate into host communities in Cabo Verde, especially when tensions rise alongside migrant populations and resource pressures? What is convincing them to stay? This study is based off of data collected from structured and semi-structured interviews and focus group discussions in twelve communities on two islands. We found that a majority of immigrants had stable, fulltime work, began families, and joined community organizations. Additionally, what friction was observed stemmed from displaced and disenfranchised domestic youth mainly from the capital city of Praia competing over employment with more highly-skilled or experienced migrants. We also found that conflict seems to have lessened with the adoption of the 2012 National Immigration Strategy, the first of its kind in Cabo Verde, although we also argue that more can still be done to improve integration and community relations. This study has implications for realizing successful economic and community integration of irregular labour migrants, especially at choke points in the developing world resulting from structural changes intensifying the role of host in buffer countries within the Global South.

Keywords: Cabo Verde, Guinea-Bissau, buffer countries, choke points, community integration, labour migrants, migration motives, south-south migration.

Introduction

Europe received more than one million Mediterranean Sea arrivals between January 2015 and March 2016 (UNHCR, 2016). People travelling from Africa are part of this 'migrant crisis' making their way across the Mediterranean from Morocco into Spain, and Libya into Italy and Greece (BBC, 2016).

The Western African route between Senegal, Mauritania, Morocco, Cabo Verde, and the Spanish Canary Islands 'was once the busiest irregular entry

[1] Funding for this study was provided by the 2015 Office of the Vice President for Research Pilot Grant to Attract External Funding award from Kennesaw State University. We thank our translators especially Artur Rocha and everyone who gave us their time by participating in this study.

[2] Brandon D. Lundy is Associate Professor of Anthropology and Associate Director in the School of Conflict Management, Peacebuilding and Development at Kennesaw State University, 365 Cobb Avenue NW, Kennesaw, GA 30144, USA. E-mail: blundy@kennesaw.edu.

[3] Kezia Lartey is a Ph.D. Candidate in the International Conflict Management program at Kennesaw State University, 365 Cobb Avenue NW, Kennesaw, GA 30144, USA. E-mail: klartey@kennesaw.edu.

point for the whole of Europe, peaking at 32,000 migrants arriving in 2006. The numbers dropped by 60 per cent in 2007 following bilateral agreements between Spain and Senegal and Mauritania' (Frontex, 2016).

Signed on January 14, 2011, the agreement between Frontex and the National Police of Cabo Verde aimed 'to enhance cooperation ... to counter illegal/irregular migration and related cross- border crime ...to strengthen border security'. The agreement worked. By January through April of 2016, only 164 persons traversed the West African migration route (Frontex, 2016). Travelers were forced to find alternative entry points into Europe, return home, or stay in developing 'buffer' countries such as Cabo Verde (Marcelino, 2016). In the current study, Bissau-Guinean migrants residing in Cabo Verde are used as a case to unpack decisions by migrants to stay in communities and countries now serving as barriers to entry into developed countries and regions. We ask, how irregular labour migrants are integrating (or not) into host communities in the face of resource pressures, and what (if anything) is convincing them to stay? In essence, we examine the effects on labour migrants, hosts, and host communities when transit routes from underdeveloped to developed countries are blocked causing migrant choke points in developing countries.

Bissau-Guinean migrants in Cabo Verde were selected as an illustrative case that highlights the localized effects of tightening structural barriers on mobility from developing to developed countries as demonstrated by the effective closure of the West African migration route. As representative of this choke point phenomena, we focus on the influx of Bissau-Guinean migrants as a case because the majority of labour migrants residing in Cabo Verde are from this sister republic (Table 1). Other migrant groups such as the wave of Senegalese in Cabo Verde have been treated elsewhere (Jung, 2015). While Guinea-Bissau and Cabo Verde share an interesting and well-documented history (Lundy, 2010, 2012) including a shared independence struggle from Portugal, Bissau-Guineans in Cabo Verde are still considered 'low status' migrants (Alba and Foner, 2014, p. 5264). Low status immigrant groups often have low levels of education, low paying jobs, and are often stigmatized in the host community because of this background (Alba and Foner, 2014). It is feasible, therefore, to use Bissau-Guinean migrants to probe the nuances of host-migrant relationships that may not be as obvious because of their shared heritage. The novelty of choosing Bissau-Guineans in Cabo Verde also exists in the fact that 'Cape Verde is widely known for emigration and not for immigration', which is a relatively 'new and until now barely researched phenomenon' (Jung, 2015, pp. 79, 84).

Another point to consider is intergroup tensions between Bissau-Guineans and Cabo Verdeans, which began to escalate after the 2007 border restrictions. Case in point, a headline about an incident on a Cabo Verdean island read:

'Boavista get [sic] to the streets for peace after a brutal murder: The murder of a Guinean citizen provokes a revolt of the community of this country in Cabo Verde that will have an effect in the granting of visas' (Valdigem, 2010). According to the report, 'Boavista has witnessed the biggest demonstration in its history... Nearly 3,500 people joined the march organized in just two days by the Commission for Peace, Security and Integration...The march began in the heart of the slums. Thousands of people in white shirts wanted to alert authorities about cases of hate, racism and intolerance that... are growing in the multicultural Boavista' (Valdigem 2010, italics ours).

We argue that improved human security and the meeting of basic needs for both hosts and migrants should decrease incidents of discrimination and conflict (Lartey & Lundy, 2017). Therefore, this study examines the direct and localized effects of the choke point phenomena in Cabo Verde as an illustrative case that should inform other similar cases where irregular migrant populations are marooned in developing countries awaiting the opportunity to move on or are forced to return home. The case under consideration here is both typical of increased mobility barriers internationally including the population and resource pressures that result, and atypical due to historical ties between the host and migrant nations, regional considerations such as ECOWAS's 90-day mobility concessions, and Cabo Verde's recent shift from a sending to a receiving nation. This paper both addresses the typicality and atypicality of this case.

Background

Since the United Nations (UN) created the least developed country (LDC) category based on three criteria – poverty, human resource weakness, and economic vulnerability – only three countries have graduated from LDC to 'developing country' status, one of which was Cabo Verde in 2007. That same year a 'Joint Declaration on a Mobility Partnership between the European Union and the Republic of Cape Verde' was approved to 'facilitate the movement of persons between their territories ... and preventing and combating illegal immigration' (Council of the European Union 2008; Gorjão & Seabra 2010). As a result, Cabo Verde agreed to strengthen their coast guard and radar system (Baker, 2009; Carling, 2007; Marcelino, 2011). This artificial border and the country's recent economic development are making the islands more appealing for upwardly-mobile Africans (Jung, 2015; Lundy, 2010; Marcelino, 2011).

Furthermore, Cabo Verde validated the Economic Community of West African States (ECOWAS) Protocol of Free Movement of Persons and the Right of Residence and Establishment, although by 2008 they had backtracked by enacting a new Labour Code that 'only foreigners in legal status have the right to work' (Varela & Barbosa, 2014, p. 459). West African immigrants in

Cabo Verde who overstay now become irregular migrants or 'denizens' left unprotected (Marcelino, 2016).

When considered together, these developments introduce a new transnational migration pattern in which 'buffer' countries like Cabo Verde are now becoming final destinations for many economic migrants (Jung, 2015). The added burden on limited resources has the potential to create societal tension and conflict between host populations and the growing immigrant population (Gagnon & Khoudour-Castéras, 2012).

Available data on residence permits (1976-2008) for Cabo Verde show that the main country of origin of applicants was Guinea-Bissau (19.8%) (Carvalho, 2010, p.32). The National Institute of Statistics of Cabo Verde's (INECV) census data from 2013 listed the number of Bissau-Guinean foreign nationals living in Cabo Verde at 3,961. By 2015, the UN Population Division in the Department of Economic and Social Affairs counted 5,015 people of Bissau-Guinean origins residing in Cabo Verde which was 33.6% of the total number of migrants in the country (UN, 2015). This was the largest immigrant group by nationality living on the islands (Table 1).

Table 1. Migrants Residing in Cabo Verde by Origin, 2015

Country of Origin	# of Migrants	% of Total
Guinea-Bissau	5,015	33.60
São Tomé and Príncipe	1,712	11.47
Senegal	1,478	9.90
Portugal	1,159	7.77
Russian Federation	698	4.68
Other	4,862	32.58
TOTAL	**14,924**	**100**

Source: UN (2015).

Unemployment rates have remained high in Cabo Verde in spite of the overall national trend of economic improvement. For example, between 2010 and 2014, overall unemployment rates increased from 10.7% to 15.8% while youth unemployment jumped from 21.3% in 2000 to 35.8% by 2014 (INECV, http://www.ine.cv/). High unemployment suggests real labour-related stressors within society, especially among the youth. All of these indicators suggest continued conflict within communities competing over these scarce resources. The friction between nationals and foreigners seems potentially explosive unless these groups can find common ground. According to Sherif et al. (1961), it is the 'integration stage' where tensions can be reduced through intergroup cooperation.

Mere perception of resource scarcity is enough to lead to increased tension and conflict between groups (Esses et al., 1998). If the community feels that immigrants are responsible for higher crime and unemployment rates, then this would be enough to derail successful community integration and intensify competition, discrimination, and conflict (Sireci & Cohen, 2016).

Theoretical Framing

The specific aim of this research was to study Bissau-Guinean immigrants in Cabo Verde as a representative case of a little understood south-south migration phenomenon, what we refer to as the 'choke point' phenomenon (Nawlyn, 2016; Rath & Shaw, 2007).The study assesses immigrant integration through an examination of security, livelihood, and conflict potential within host communities most affected by increasing numbers of foreign guests. Three theories were selected to help explain community integration patterns of foreign guests: (1) realistic conflict theory (RCT) used to measure things like 'hate, racism and intolerance' as indicators of conflict potential; (2) human security to assess migrants' levels of vulnerabilities; and (3) human needs theory to gauge whether or not basic human needs are being met.

RCT helps to explain incidents of intergroup hostility arising from competition over limited resources as well as the associated feelings of prejudice and discrimination (Brief et al., 2005; Sidanius & Pratto, 1999). Sherif et al. (1961) modelled RCT into three phases associated with the processes outlined above: (1) ingroup formation, (2) friction phase, and (3) integration stage. For the mitigation of ethnocentric attitudes and the institutionalization of the integration phase to be successful, the shared initiatives must be embodied as crucial, such as toward meeting human needs and human security including economic, food, health, environmental, personal, community, and political security (Lundy & Adebayo, 2016).

We use this theory to analyse community integration patterns of the Bissau-Guineans by focusing on data related to expressions and manifestations of prejudice, discrimination, resource allocation, and violence as well as community integration initiatives at the formal and informal levels aimed at managing conflict. An expectation of this research is that a real or perceived shortage of resources can lead to an increase in discrimination and violence which can be then be managed through the advancement of community development and human security initiatives. We shed light on this as something that happens in many world migration contexts. What becomes interesting in this case, is how the intensification of conflict between 2007 and 2012 becomes clearly and effectively mitigated by the successful implementation of the 2012 National Immigration Strategy, the first of its kind in the country, which we treat elsewhere (Lartey & Lundy, 2017).

In this study, integration is looked at from two perspectives. First, integration that occurs as a result of maintaining independence as a group, and second, how well this group has integrated into the community. Integration occurs when host communities and immigrant groups maintain a degree of cultural integrity while seeking to participate in a larger social project together (Berry, 1997). According to Alba and Foner (2014), integration generally refers to the levels of similarities that immigrants have in relation to members of the host community as well as recognition as being part of the receiving society. More specifically, Bissau-Guineans are assessed based on their levels of labour and community integration. Patterns of employment, unemployment, and underemployment are considered. We also evaluate the levels of community 'friction' between the various groups identified, and assess the levels of integration of Bissau-Guinean immigrants based on their self-reported feelings about their and their communities' needs and security.

Methodology

Cabo Verde was selected for this research project based on its transition to a receiving country experiencing community-level tension due to the influx of economic migrants. Two of the largest immigrant labourer populations in Cabo Verde on the islands of Santiago and Boa Vista were purposefully selected. Santiago has the capital city of Praia and Boa Vista has been tapped by developers as the next major site of tourism expansion (Jung, 2015, p. 84). The study sample was selected purposefully from among community leaders, community activists, and other relevant persons involved in immigrant relations. The research team – the principle investigator, a graduate research assistant, and three local translators – over one-month in the summer of 2015 (May-June) conducted 57 structured interviews, 6 semi-structured interviews, and 2 focus groups in twelve communities on two islands. While we recognize that our data is two years old, we feel that the findings presented here still reflect the broader effects of the choke point phenomena being felt and intensifying in many countries around the world. Findings are based on descriptive statistics as well as thematic and content data analysis. All standard ethical procedures for conducting research with human subjects including the collection of written informed consent were followed.

Findings

The aim of this research was to discover why and how Cabo Verde is becoming a destination point for labour migrants from Guinea-Bissau and the effects these changes are having on immigrant and host relations. The emergent thematic findings from the qualitative data are presented in five sections: (1) Cabo Verdean context; (2) migration motives and livelihood; (3) conflict and human security; (4) community integration; and (5) deciding to stay.

Cabo Verdean Context

Aggregate data from INECV (2013) shows that the capital of Praia, Santiago (40.8%), Sal (11.2%), and Boa Vista (10.9%) are the three counties with the most immigrants. Some Bissau-Guineans are now viewing Cabo Verde as a 'land of opportunity' where they can find work and remit money home (Lundy, 2012). According to the census data, immigrants are finding permanent, fulltime work (88.2%) primarily in service (28.9%), skilled construction (18.9%), and manual labour (18.4%) (INECV, 2013).

The President of the Guinean Association in Boa Vista stated, 'Guineans first started arriving in Cabo Verde because both countries were colonized by Portugal. ... When Cabo Verde and Guineans fought for their independence together... some Guineans came to Cabo Verde for political reasons' [in fact, from independence until the coup in 1980, these countries were unified] (May 30, 2015).

Guineans often have a good reputation on the islands as trustworthy, hard workers, sharing history, language, and culture with Cabo Verdeans (Lundy, 2010, 2012). This affords Bissau-Guineans the opportunity and the flexibility to seek opportunities on the islands with some impunity. As one respondent put it: 'I have been working on a big public works project called 'Casa para Tudu' (Housing for All), but now the government has a problem financing the project…There are always ups-and-downs in Cabo Verde's economy … When another island is better [for work], people go to the other island [for example, most recently from Sal to Boa Vista]' (May 16, 2015).

With increased global migration barriers, economic migrants look for opportunities where they can. The Head of the National Immigration Platform in Cabo Verde noted, 'Now there are more migration controls put in place. You cannot go to the U.S., you cannot go to Europe. The European Union is imposing its will on Cabo Verde' (May 29, 2015).

Respondents appreciated Cabo Verde for its peace and good governance in comparison to their home country of Guinea-Bissau where narcotics trafficking and political instability have taken center stage (Chabal & Green, 2016; UN News Centre, 2016; Vigh, 2012). One respondent described why he liked Cabo Verde: 'The tranquility, the quietness of the place. Although life is sometimes harsh, people are quite calm' (May 23, 2015). The peace experienced by respondents in Cabo Verde is an indicator of how receptive a place is towards newcomers. If immigrants find the place welcoming, they are more likely to stay (Harden et al., 2015).

As a side note, more Cabo Verdeans are returning from abroad, potentially further increasing population and resource pressures. Cabo Verdean returnees represent another reason for concern regarding the Bissau-Guinean population, although further investigation is necessary (Batalha & Carling, 2008; Carling, 2004).

Migration Motives and Livelihood

Of the 57 survey respondents, 49 indicated that they emigrated for a better life. Respondents' $3,422.28 average annual salary allowed them to remit on average $1,007.45 back to family in Guinea-Bissau. The average Bissau-Guinean's per capita gross national income in that same year was less than half at $1,450.00 (World Bank, 2016).

The periods of the most migrant activity based on the year of immigration for the survey respondents was 2002-03 (15) and 2008-09 (14). The average age at the time of migration was 25.6 years old, while the average age at the time of the survey was 34, suggesting an average of more than 8 years of residency in Cabo Verde.

Guinean Association of Boa Vista members explained what they felt were the motives of Bissau-Guinean migration to Cabo Verde: 'Most Guineans came here as a result of the instability in Guinea looking for a better life. .... It's easier for us to communicate ... Especially after 2000 when the political situation in Guinea got really bad, a lot of Guineans came to look for opportunities' (May 24, 2015).

When asked directly why they decided to migrate, study participants cited better work opportunities, greater political stability, a stronger currency, and potential opportunities to increase their chances to migrate elsewhere. One survey responded said, 'The conditions for families in Guinea-Bissau are miserable. ... I prefer to stay here [in Cabo *Verde]* ... I always have the possibility of finding a job and trying to improve my life' (May 18, 2015).

Conflict and Human Security

The researchers were often informed about youth gangs robbing victims using the expression 'kaçubodi?' which taken from English literally translates as 'cash or body?' The victim was given a choice to either give up their valuables or suffer a beating (Pardue, 2016). These (perceived) increased crime rates are cause for concern and likely affect the successful integration of foreigners into society.

There were many instances when Bissau-Guineans narrated acts of violence and discrimination against them or their community. Ten (10) of the 57 respondents mentioned being called 'manjako' as a discriminatory label used against anyone from the mainland. One survey respondent explained, 'One sign of bigotry that is quite common is when the locals call us Manjako. The first arrival of Bissau-Guineans in Cabo Verde belonged to the Manjack ethnic group. After that, everyone else who comes from the West African mainland is referred to as Manjako in the pejorative sense' (May 17, 2015).

Sometimes, these instances of discrimination escalate to violence. Interestingly, much of the disrespect and violence was not attributed to Boa Vista 'locals,' but were instead explained as problems of youth and idleness coming from the capital city of Praia. One person recounted: 'The fact that I live in a stigmatized community within the city is clear based on its geographical division. Most people who live in the neighbourhood of Barraca [baraka means 'hut' in Capeverdean creole] are people from West African countries and people from Praia, who are a lot of young males that are troublemakers' (May 17, 2015).

According to the police chief of Boa Vista, 'The statistics on crime rates on the island are very low and have decreased significantly between 2012 and 2014... But something bad will happen and the whole perception of safety will go down...The most recent incident of note was when a member of the Guinean immigrant community was assaulted by a youth from Praia. Thousands of immigrants gathered in front of the suspected perpetrator's house... I believe this event went down without incident because I had established rapport with the community' (May 25, 2015).

Discrimination and prejudice occasionally flare up and exacerbate intergroup conflict into violent outbursts. Often, the discrimination and violence take place around a shortage of opportunities for youth, suggesting a lack of resources as a serious driver of conflict at Cabo Verde choke points with high immigrant populations.

Community Integration

President of the National Immigration Platform in Cabo Verde suggested, 'Integration is a long process. People have to know that they are in a foreign country and that they have to respect it' (May 29, 2015). An immigrant in Boa Vista participating in a Day of Africa radio program advised her listeners, 'always try to contribute to the development of your own country and to the country where you are now' (May 25, 2016). This belief fit our argument that shared goals of livelihood and economic development provide the community an opportunity to work together for the common good. In this sense, we argue for a win-win mentality when it comes to intergroup cooperation. Many of these improvements are taking place at the institutional level.

For example, the City Hall of Boa Vista's Immigration Office representative explained that her office was created in 2012 to 'build a bridge between the authorities and the communities' (May 25, 2015). One way they did this was through an amnesty program to start the process of legalization for all Africans residing in Cabo Verde. As documented elsewhere, however, this program needs strengthening as it has not been entirely successful in accomplishing its goals (Lartey & Lundy, 2017). For example, many Bissau-Guineans were unable to process their residency requests during the amnesty period due to difficulties getting proper documentation from their home government. This has left many Guineans as 'denizens' or irregular migrants excluded from formal employment opportunities as a result of the Labour Code (Marcelino, 2016).

Family and intermarriage were other factors promoting rapid community integration. Thirty (30) of 57 survey respondents were currently residing with family members in Cabo Verde. One respondent explained a particular form of living arrangement; 'People live together and have children without getting officially married. We call it "djuntadu." ...when I first got here, I had kids so I thought it was my moral obligation to stay here and raise them. I am committed to my family' (May 16, 2015).

Bissau-Guineans participated actively in community life, raised families, worked, and voted in Cabo Verde, which helped them better integrate. Bissau-Guinean immigrants maintain a level of cultural integrity through the founding of and participation in various community associations, but at the same time they look to integrate within the larger Cabo Verdean society through partnerships and campaigns to raise awareness about healthcare, community development, sanitation, and harmony (Berry, 1997). As they integrate, they become biculturally adapted (Hofstede & Hofstede, 2001) allowing them to have options as to whether to stay, return to Guinea-Bissau, or move on (Brettell, 2003).

Deciding to Stay

Bissau-Guinean immigrants have many reasons to stay in Cabo Verde such as employment opportunities, good governance, and education. When asked directly if they intended to stay in Cabo Verde, the typical response was that if an opportunity presented itself to migrate somewhere with better livelihood prospects, they would go. Furthermore, if/when Guinea-Bissau stabilized politically and developed economically, most respondents expressed an interest to return with their new skills and capital to apply them to the betterment of their families and home country. In the meantime, many respondents have begun families, held down fulltime employment, purchased homes (24/56), and remained for more than 10 years (24/56). They seem to genuinely like life on the islands. In reference to long term investment in the country, one person said, 'I hope to one day build one or two more floors onto my house. That way when the children are grown they have a place to live and I could rent the ground floor in order to have some income' (May 17, 2015).

While residing in Cabo Verde, most study participants intended to establish themselves and integrate within their host communities by being good citizens, working hard, actively participating in the social life and development of the community, and resolving disputes effectively. These findings are consistent with study expectations that integration into a community is the result of having basic needs fulfilled (i.e., freedom from wants), feeling secure (i.e., freedom from fears), and being accepted by the community, indicated by working toward intergroup goals of community and economic development. In the area of labour and community integration, Bissau-Guineans under investigation can be said to have successfully integrated at the time of the study.

Conclusion

After the analysis of the data, the major themes of the Cabo Verdean context, migration motives, livelihood, conflict indicators, integration, future plans and permanence indicators all suggest varying ways of measuring the complex relationships between host and immigrant communities. The take-away from this research is that looking at integration from an individual's perspective is not enough (i.e., the acculturation approach). Community analysis examining group integration reflects a complex undertaking in which success means having the needs of the community met and working together to achieve a secure environment. RCT predicted that incompatibility between groups would be expressed through outward discrimination, which could eventually escalate into violence. This is indeed what was observed in some communities in Cabo Verde as the host communities and growing immigrant communities competed over scarce resources such as employment. At the same time, community leaders, immigrant associations, and government institutions began to improve relations through discourse, practice, policies, and capacity-building aimed at integration and economic improvements in the lives of the citizenry. This was achieved through the improvement of human security at all levels, both actual and perceived. Based on this study, these communities seem to be heading in the right direction in part thanks to national level initiatives and support (Lartey & Lundy, 2017). Similar approaches could be undertaken at other labour migrant choke points forming throughout the developing world as opportunities for labour migration into the developed world continue to constrict, especially in the era of expanding populism.

References

Alba, R., & Foner, N. (2014). Comparing Immigrant Integration in North America and Western Europe: How much do the grand narratives tell us? International Migration Review, 48(s1), S263-S291.
Baker, B. (2009). Cape Verde: Marketing Good Governance. Africa Spectrum, 44(2), 135-147.

BBC. (2016, March 4). Migrant Crisis: Migration to Europe Explained in Seven Charts. BBC World News, http://www.bbc.com/news/world-europe-34131911.

Berry, J.W. (1997). Immigration, Acculturation, and Adaptation. Applied Psychology, 46(1), 5-34.

Brettell, C.B. (2003). Anthropology of Migration. Hoboken, NJ: Blackwell Publishing.

Brief, A.P., Umphress, E.E., Dietz, J., Butz, R., Burrows, J., & Schoelten, L. (2005). Community Matters: Realistic Group Conflict Theory and the Impact of Diversity. Academy of Management Journal, 48(5), 830–844.

Carling, J. (2004). Emigration, Return and Development in Cape Verde: The Impact of Closing Borders. Population, Space and Place, 10, 113-132.

Carling, J. (2007). Migration Control and Migrant Fatalities at the Spanish-African Borders. International Migration Review, 41(2), 316-343.

Batalha, L. & Carling, J. (Eds.). (2008). Transnational Archipelago: Perspectives on Cape Verdean Migration and Diaspora. Amsterdam University Press.

Carvalho, F.A. (2010). Migração em Cabo Verde: Perfil Nacional 2009 [Migration in Cape Verde: National Profile 2009]. Geneva, Switzerland: International Organization for Migration (IOM) (in Portuguese).

Chabal, P., & Green, T. (Eds.). (2016). Guinea-Bissau: Micro-State to 'Narco-State'. London: Hurst.

Council of the European Union. (2008, May 21). Joint Declaration on a Mobility Partnership between the European Union and the Republic of Cape Verde. 9460/o8 ADD 2. Brussels.

Esses, V.M., Jackson, L.M., & Armstrong, T.L. (1998). Intergroup Competition and Attitudes toward Immigrants and Immigration: An Instrumental Model of Group Conflict. Journal of Social Issues, 54(4), 699-724.

Frontex. (2011, January 14). Working Arrangement establishing operational cooperation between the European Agency for the Management of Operational Cooperation at the External Borders of the Member States of the European Union (Frontex) and the Policia Nacional de Cabo Verde. Partners: Third Countries, http://frontex.europa.eu/assets/Partners/Third_countries/WA_with_Cape_Verde.pdf.

Frontex. (2016, June 20). Trends and Routes: Migratory Routes Map. FRAN and JORA data as of 3 June 2016, http://frontex.europa.eu/trends-and-routes/migratory-routes-map/.

Gagnon, J., & Khoudour-Castéras, D. (2012). South-South Migration in West Africa: Addressing the Challenge of Immigrant Integration. No. 312. OECD Publishing.

Gorjão, P., & Seabra, P. (2010). Cape Verde's role as a bridge builder: Is there political substance beyond the rhetoric? IPRIS Lusophone Countries Bulletin, June.

Harden, S.B., McDaniel, P.N., Smith, H.A., Zimmern, E., & Brown, K.E. (2015). Speaking of Change in Charlotte, North Carolina: How Museums Can Shape Immigrant Receptivity in a Community Navigating Rapid Cultural Change. Museums and Social Issues, 10(2), 117-133.

Hofstede, G.H., & Hofstede, G. (2001). Culture's consequences: comparing values, behaviors, institutions and organizations across nations. Thousand Oaks, CA: Sage.

Jung, P. (2015). Migration, Remittances and Development: A case study of Senegalese labour migrants on the island of Boa Vista, Cape Verde. Cadernos de Estudos Africanos, 29, 77-101.

Lartey, K., Lundy, B.D. (2017). Policy Considerations regarding the Integration of Lusophone West Africa Immigrant Populations. Border Crossing, 7(1), 108-121.

Lundy, B.D. (2010). Transnational Ties that Bind? The Divergence of Cape Verde and Guinea-Bissau. Third Conference of the Research Group 'Integration and Conflict along the Upper Guinea Coast:' The Upper Guinea Coast in Transnational Perspective. December 9-11. Halle/Saale, Germany: Max Planck Institute for Social Anthropology.

Lundy, B.D. (2012). The Involution of Democracy in Lusophone West Africa. In: Adebayo, A.G. (ed.) Managing Conflicts in Africa's Democratic Transitions. Lanham, MD: Lexington Books. pp. 119-140, 191.

Lundy, B., D. & Adebayo, A., G. (Eds.). (2016). Special Issue: Sustainable Livelihoods, Conflicts and Transformation. Journal of Global Initiatives: Policy, Pedagogy, Perspective, 10(2), 1-168.

Marcelino, P.F. (2011). The New Migration Paradigm of Transitional African Spaces: Inclusion, Exclusion, Liminality and Economic Competition in Transit Countries: A Case Study on the Cape Verde Islands. Saarbrücken, Germany: Lambert Academic Publishing.

Marcelino, P.F. (2016). The African 'Other' in the Cape Verde Islands: Interaction, Integration and the Forging of an Immigration Policy. In: Knörr, J., & Kohl, C. (eds.) The Upper Guinea Coast in Global Perspective. New York: Berghahn Books. pp. 116-134.

Pardue, D. (2016). 'Cash or Body': Lessons on Space and Language from Cape Verdean Rappers and Their Beefs. Popular Music and Society, 39(3), 332-345. doi: 10.1080/03007766.2016.1141522

Sherif, M., Harvey, O.J., White, B.J., Hood, W., & Sherif, C.W. (1961). Intergroup Conflict and Cooperation: The Robbers Cave Experiment. Volume 10. Norman, OK: The University Book Exchange.

Sidanius, J., & Pratto, F. (1999). Social Dominance: An Intergroup Theory of Social Hierarchy and Oppression. New York: Cambridge University Press.

Sirkeci, I., & Cohen, J.H. (2016). Cultures of Migration and Conflict in Contemporary Human Mobility in Turkey. European Review, 24(3), 381-396.

UN News Centre. (2007, June 14). UN advocate salutes Cape Verde's graduation from category of poorest States. UN News Service, http://www.un.org/apps/news/story.asp?NewsID=22918andCr=capeand Cr1=verde.

UN News Centre. (2016, June 14). Prolonged political crisis could erode Guinea Bissau's development gains, UN envoy warns. UN News Service, http://www.un.org/apps/news/story.asp?NewsID=54224#.V4Y66PkrJpg .

UN (United Nations, Department of Economic and Social Affairs). (2015). Trends in International Migrant Stock: Migrants by Destination and Origin. United Nations database, POP/DB/MIG/Stock/Rev.2015.

UNHCR (United Nations High Commissioner for Refugees). (2016). UNHCR: The UN Refugee Agency, http://www.unhcr.org/en-us/.

Valdigem, A. (2010). Boavista get to the streets for peace after a brutal murder. GuinGuinBali: All About Africa, http://www.guinguinbali.com/index.php?lang=enandmod=newsandtask =view_newsandcat=2andid=363, October 5.

Vigh, H. (2012). Critical States and Cocaine Connections. In: Utas, M. (ed.) African Conflicts and Informal Power: Big Men and Networks. New York: Zed Books. pp. 137-157.

World Bank. (2016, July 1). Gross national income per capita 2015, Atlas method and PPP, http://databank.worldbank.org/data/download/GNIPC.pdf.

Chapter 51. Nature and Consequences of Migration to Gulf Countries: A Study of Selected Rural Areas of Allahabad District in India

Mohammed Taukeer[1]

Abstract

The study of migration in the selected rural areas of Allahabad district of State Uttar Pradesh in India showed that migration is not economic matters but also social and cultural phenomena. Labourers are migrating from origin to transit destination and finally abroad through a well recognised pathway of migration. Social networks system determined to pathways of migration as well as system of economic and non-economic support for migration. Inflow of both individual and collective remittances giving contributed in the socio-economic development of villages as well as migrant households. The impact of migration created to migration based society which led to culture of migration from village to Saudi Arabia via internal migration to city of Mumbai.

Key words: Migration, remittances, development

Introduction

"Migration refers to the relocation of individuals to a new geographical area. These change an individual's place of residence from country to country, state to state, or town to town are all considered forms of migration" (Magill, 1997: 978). Migration may be dividing into internal and cross-border migration both. Internal migrants move within their country of origin while cross-border migration is process of movement of person across international border of their origin country (International Organisation of Migration, 2015:196-198). Process of International migration is being facilitated by the modern and cheaper transportation system in the globalised world and obsolete to barriers of migration between countries of origin, transit and destination. Poverty, inequality, lacks employments and conflict force to people for leave their home regarding search of better future (United Nation, Department of Economic and Social Affairs, 2015:2-5).

India received total $68,910 million remittances from across the globe in 2015. Out of these total remittances, total $ 38,910 million remittances were received from countries of Gulf Cooperation Council (GCC) and it accounted 55.8 per cent of the total inflow of remittances in India (World Bank, 2016). There is long history of labour migration from India included indentured labour migration, kangani/maisry migration and free migration during colonial period. British India government passed the "Indian Emigration Act 1922" regarding the control and manage for fair recruitment of unskilled labour migration from India to abroad (Shirras, 1931:599). Oil companies of Gulf

---

[1] Mohammed Taukeer is doctoral student in Govind Ballabh Pant Social Science Institute, Jhusi, Allahabad 211019. State- Uttar Pradesh. India. E-mail:tauk2216@rediffmail.com

countries opened formal recruitment offices in Bombay (Mumbai) for recruitment of Indian labourers under the regulations of Indian Emigration Act 1922. These oil companies recruited to labourers through series of concessional agreements with British India government (Seccombe & Lawless, 1986:558-562). Indian labourers migrated to Gulf countries via Bombay (Mumbai) through formal and informal channel both in the colonial period. They used to work as unskilled labourers in oil companies, construction sector and housemaids (Kumar, 2016: 84-85). At present, labour migration from India to Gulf countries are managed and controlled by regulations of Indian "Emigration Act 1983" which provided guarantee of safe and secure labour migration as well as safe working-cum-living conditions to Indian migrant labourers at their destinations (The Emigration Act 1983, Government of India). Labour migration from India to Gulf countries was begun by discovery of oil in the Gulf regions in 1930s but mass labour migration from India to Gulf countries was started by increasing demand of labourers following the beginning of lavish development projects due to the reason of oil boom in the oil producing countries of Gulf Cooperation council in 1973 (Khadria, 2008:91). India had enormous surplus labourers that could fill the demand in Gulf countries; hence India government had taken as opportunities regard to supply the unskilled, semi-skilled and skilled labourers to Gulf countries (Naidu, 1991:349). Out of the total stock of 7.2 million Indian migrant labourers in the Gulf countries, about 2,070,854 Indian migrant labourers belonged to Southern Indian state namely Kerala (Zachariah and Rajan, 2015: 6 &46). There was a cordial relation between social networks and migration to Gulf countries from Kerala to Gulf countries. Labourers migrated in other cities of India for search of jobs due to poverty and unemployment but later they migrated to Gulf countries through help of their relatives and friends who already worked in the Gulf countries (Prakash, 1978:1107-1111).Early 1970s, Kerala was characterized by internal migration because labourers used work in India urban centre namely -Mumbai, Delhi and Chennai before migration to Gulf countries (Skeldon, 2006: 21). In the initial phase of labour migration from India to Gulf was led by mainly from state namely Kerala. At recently northern states namely Uttar Pradesh and Bihar have been emerged as leading states in labour migration to Gulf countries (Ministry of Overseas Indian Affairs, Govt.of India 2014-15:4). Approximately 785,291 labourers migrated to Gulf countries from India in 2013. Among them highest nearly 27.3 per cent of the labourers migrated from state of Uttar Pradesh followed by 12.0 per cent Bihar and 10.8 per cent from Kerala (Overseas Employment Division, Ministry of External Affairs; Government of India). In Uttar Pradesh, approximately total 1632 labourers migrated to countries of Gulf Cooperation Council (GCC) from selected district Allahabad in 2013. Among them, highest 85.0 per cent (total 1386) of the labourers migrated to Saudi

Arabia and rest to other GCC countries (Overseas Employment Division, Ministry of External Affairs; Government of India).

Study Zone and Methodology

The present study explored the nature, causes and consequences about labour migration from selected rural areas of Allahabad, district of state Uttar Pradesh in India. We conducted a pilot visit between October 2015 and November 2015 in the rural areas of selected district for recognize to international migration prone zone. Finally, we selected cluster of villages namely –*Inayat Patti, Dhorhan, Saidhan, Mahrupur, Utraon, Basgit, Damgarah, Pursotammpur, Kahara,* and *Punch Purva* villages for understand the process and consequences of Gulf migration. We gathered qualitative information about migration in the selected villages based on the informal conversation with local aged person, relatives of the migrant individuals, retired migrant labourers; return migrant labourers and local agents of village. It was found that youth were attracting to Gulf countries due to the reasons of glamour of jobs and swift earning in the Gulf countries. Muslims were found in majority in these selected villages. They were homogenous with social, cultural and economic practices and also interconnected to each other. All these villages showed similar pattern of labour migration to Gulf countries because labourers were migrating to Gulf countries mainly in Saudi Arabia via Mumbai.

The history of migration from these villages went back to 1950s when the underprivileged labourers used to migrate to work in the coal fields of Bihar including Jharkhand and West Bengal states in India. The coal-field region around the city of Dhanbad in Jharkhand was preferred by migrant labourers. Social networks between migrants and non-migrants helped in the migration to coal-belt fields of Dhanbad. Migartion to Mumbai city was turning point for these villages. Migartion to city of Mumbai that started around the 1960s, when labourers used to migrate to Mumbai for work in mainly in cotton textile industry and partly working in the port areas. The migration to Mumbai opened to the gate for migration to Gulf countries among Muslims. Inflow and utilisation of remittances created culture of migration to Gulf countries among Muslims. The impact of Gulf migration was showed in their life styles at root. These determined their decision for migration to Saudi Arabia. They used combined term of words "Mumbai-Saudi" for their livelihood. They preferred to Mumbai and Saudi Arabia because their family members, relatives and friends were working in these destinations. Labourers migrated to Mumbai where they worked one to two years before migration Saudi Arabia.

Among the cluster of these villages, namely *-Inayat Patti* village was unique for study of migration because migration to both Mumbai and Saudi Arabia occurred very first in this village and at present this village is working as centre for among the cluster of villages.

The following qualities founds were Inayat Patti village:

o It was named *Siddan Ahamad,* who had very first person migrated from Inayat Patti village to Saudi Arabia in 1985 with help his relatives those already worked in Saudi Arabia.

o There were three "Western Union" branches during pilot visit which provided services for transfer of remittances to migrant labourers from Mumbai and Saudi Arabia.

o There was one branch of India's largest bank namely "State Bank of India" (SBI) in village during pilot visit, which also provided services for receiving of remittances to migrant households of these villages.

o There were three travel agent offices in village during pilot visit. Those were working for providing services about migration to Saudi Arabia for employment and *Haj* Pilgrimage.

o Three young migrant labourers namely Wasim, Jeeshan and Mursheed of this village have been died in a road accident during to their duties in Saudi Arabia but this type of cases did not occur in rest of villages.

Above, all these made unique to this village among cluster of villages. Therefore, we selected Inayat Patti village for broadly emphasize to understand about process and consequences of migration with qualitative and quantitative information from migrant households and return migrant households.

There were total 348 households with total population of 2425 and literacy rate was 74.9 in selected village (Census 2011, Govt.of India). In this study, migrant households considered as where at least one member was working in the Gulf countries. Out of the total households, about 95 households identified as migrant households to using stratified random sampling. Quantitative information was collected from return migrant households for understanding of migration. Return migrant households were referred where at least one member in migrant households had been returned to root from Gulf countries after completed minimum two years contract. Out of the total migrant households, we selected 25 return migrant households which accounted 26.3 per cent of migrant households.

Process of Migartion

The situation oriented explains the nature and causes of migration through push and pull factors. The push and pull are important economic and non-economic factors associated with process of migration. Push factors are the negative factors in the place of origin while the pull factors are the positive factors the destination place. Apart, intervening factors and personal factors of migrants influences the processes of migration from roots to destinations (Lee, 1966:49-50). The decisions of migration are not taken by individual migrants but also strategies of households drive the process of migration (Stark & Bloom, 1985:173-178). Network of migration played as pull factors in migration because it minimises the risk of migration and also decline the cost of migration (Massey et al, 1993:448-449). Migrant labourers provide information about availability of the jobs, wage rates as well as economic and psychological support to potential migrants for migration. The process of international migration is high cost and risky, but it gives high economic return relative to internal migration (Taylor, 2006:4-5). Migartion itself create a set of networks of friend and relatives with valuable experienced migrants. It brings to "cumulative causation "of migration which creates the more migration from origin to destination (Massey, 1990:17). When migration to be started from origin it gives the space to private institutions and voluntary organizations for facilitating the labour migration from root to destination in the exchange of financial cost of migration from labourers(Massey et al., 1993:450).

The oil boom of 1973 created a dual labour market in the Gulf countries with national labourer engaged in public sector with high wage rate and luxurious working conditions while foreign migrant labourer engaged in private sector with dirty and dangerous jobs and low wage rate than local native labourers (Winckler, 2010:9-10). The *Kafala* (sponsorship) system ensures the supply of cheap contract labourers in the bottom segmentation of labour market in the Gulf countries (Roper and Barria, 2014:36). *Kafeel* (sponsor/employer) retain passport of contract labourers and exploited them physically and mentally (Rajan and Prakash, 2012). These migrant labourers to work in very poor conditions and they have to face deprivation from basic human rights and labour-right in Gulf countries (Rahman, 2010:17-18).

The entire processes of migration from village to Gulf countries were functioned by social networks. The social network centred on the homogeneity in social-cultural and economic practices among the cluster of villages where the family members, friends, relatives and familiars were interconnected to each other. Support of family members, relatives, friends and local agents of villages with homogeneity of localities determined the social networks. All these villages were dominated by Muslims and showed similar pattern of cultural practices as well as migration to Gulf countries. The family of migrant labourers preferred to marriage of their sons and daughters in migrant households of cluster of these villages which also provided to economic and social support for entire process of migration from root to destinations. This type of marriage system was deep rooted among Muslims which interconnecting social ties among Muslims. There was pattern of dual step migration from these villages. Among, most of the migrants first moved to the city of Mumbai with an aspiration for migration to Saudi Arabia. Migrants know that they would to get socio-economic and cultural support from their familiars of these villages who already working in the city of Mumbai. Those households already migrated to city of Mumbai, provided socio-economic support to new migrants of their familiar. These migrants were learnt skills by doing works like drivers of cars, welders, plumbers and manual jobs in city of Mumbai. They lived in groups in small rooms in the slum settlements of city of Mumbai. Around eight to ten labourers used to live by rotation in small room based on works by shifting by day and night. These labourers used to take food in mess which was ran by the wives of migrant labourers who migrated with their family. Therefore, these socio-economic conditions were creating social networks among migrants in the city of Mumbai. There was cordial links between Mumbai and Saudi Arabia because Mumbai was a hopper's stop for migration to Saudi Arabia and stable platform for the return migrants in the case of loss of jobs in the Saudi Arabia as well as end of normal end of contract of jobs Saudi Arabia.

Labourers were migrating to Saudi Arabia following the reason of higher wages as well as attraction of jobs. They preferred to Saudi Arabia because their family members, relatives and friends were working in Saudi therefore, they easily obtained to information about working and living conditions to them. Therefore, they migrated with help of their family members, relatives and friends those working in Saudi Arabia. Processes of international migration were more complex and expensive rather than internal migration because migrants had to arrange to Passport-Visa, medical clearance certificate and flight ticket for migration to Saudi Arabia. The family members and relatives provided them initial financial support for this and some migrants arranged cost of migration through self-saving. They expected that they would earn many times what they spent on the process of migration as well as earned in the labour market of Mumbai. Most of the migrant gained Passport from local agents those were working as travel agents in cluster of these villages at root. They gained visa with help their familiars those working in Saudi Arabia. Most of the labourers were working as drivers, plumbers, welders, electric technicians and manual labourers in Saudi Arabia where they earned three to four times than Mumbai and their villages. They worked under their *Kafeel* (sponsor) in Saudi Arabia. They told that just after arrival in Saudi Arabia; *Kafeel* retained their Passport-visa forcefully. The orders of *Kafeel* determined their working-cum-living conditions. *Kafeel* issued *iqama* (identity card) after retained their Passport and Visa. *Kafeel* had to right to cancel to their work permit visa hence; they had to work as tied labourers. They were abused and physically exploited by their *Kafeel,* but these labourers did not protest these incidents because they migrated for matters of money and better life of their family members at root, therefore did not protest these incidents. These labourers had to be honest, punctual and silent on behalf of their *Kafeel*. Apart, *Kafeel* forced them to work beyond 12 hours that was against the rules of contract and they had not to right of take advance wage and leave. These labourers lived with labourers from rest of India and other south Asian countries in labour camp which was provided by their *Kafeel*. They told that labour camp was better than rooms of Mumbai. These labourers were kept distances from Arab citizens by different socio-cultural practices. Some of the migrant labourers who migrated from the cluster of these villages worked under same *Kafeel* lived together in same room of labour camp. On the occasion of public holiday on each Friday within a week, they used to meet and pray together in Mosque. Once a year they got chance to meet their family members, neighbours, relatives who migrated to Saudi Arabia on the occasion of Haj pilgrimage.

In Inayat Patti village, out of the total 25 return migrant labourers, 22 return migrant labourers told that they worked in Mumbai before migration to Gulf and rest straight migrated to Gulf countries. Mostly labourers worked as unskilled and semi-skilled labourers in both Mumbai and Saudi Arabia.

The earned income was varied according to skills of migrant labourers. The annual income was varied between Rs.72, 001 and Rs. 120,000 annually for 68.8 per cent of the migrant labourers. If the exception of one migrant is left out, no migrant labourers earned less than Rs.48, 000 annually in the Mumbai (Table).

Table 6: Annual Income of Migrant Labourers in Mumbai

Annual Income	Number	Per cent
24,000-48,000	01	4.6
48,001-72,000	05	22.7
72,001-96,000	08	36.3
96,001-1,20,000	07	31.8
1,20,001-1,40,000	01	4.6

Source: Field Survey, 2015

They migrated to Mumbai and Saudi Arabia through help of their family members, relative and friends those worked these destinations. They migrated to Mumbai with aspiration of migration to Saudi Arabia and they worked 2-3 years before migration to Saudi Arabia. They migrated to Saudi Arabia followed by higher wages as well as attraction jobs. They earned three to four times in Saudi Arabia compared to Mumbai and root (Box).

Compiled by F. Tilbe, E. Iskender, I. Sirkeci

Box: Comparative Profile of Migrant Labourers between Internal and International Migartion

Facts	Internal Migration	International Migration
Destination	Mumbai (n=22)	Saudi Arabia(n=22), UAE(n=2) and Qatar(n=1)
Category of Migrant Labourers according to Skills	82.0 per cent were **semi-skilled labourer** (drivers, welders, A.C. technician) and rest of 18.0 per cent were **unskilled labourer** (manual labour)	12.0 per cent **skilled labourer** (technical supervisor, managerial work in business),72.0 per cent **semi-skilled labourer** (drivers, welders, A.C. technician & washer men) and 16.0 per cent **unskilled labourer** (manual labour in construction & domestic Servant)
Time of Stay(Average)	2.5Years	3 years
Average Annual Income per Migrant Labour(Rupee)	94,080	431,040
Average Annual Income of Unskilled Labourers(Rupees)	90,000	279,000
Average Annual Income of Semi-Skilled Labourers(Rupees)	95,004	399,996
Average Annual Income of Skilled Labourers(Rupees)	Not any migrant labourers worked as skilled labourers in Mumbai.	819,996

Source: Based on the interviewed from labourers in *Inayat Patti* village in 2015

Impact of migration

Indian Diaspora community contributes in development of their community and households through private remittances and collective remittances (Upadhaya & Ruttern, 2012:54-62). In India, Punjabi Diaspora contributed in the development of their community as well as households at root. They sent the foreign remittances from Middle Eastern countries, United States, Canada, Europe and Australia. Migrant households used to vast majority of the remittances in items of consumption, branded gadgets and social ceremonies (Singh &Singh, 2017:63). Patel Diaspora also contributed in development of their root namely Javalpur village in Mehsana district of Gujarat in India through Diaspora Philanthropy. This village know as the name of *Dollariya gaon* (Dollar village) because inflow of the remittances from Untied States

561

positively changed the socio-economic scenario of village as well as migrant households (Basu, 2016:56-61). Gulf migration positively improved the socio-economic development of migrant households in rural areas of Bihar. Migrant households invested remittances into unproductive consumer durables which created demonstration culture among Muslims (Rahman, 2001:120-121). The impact of Gulf migration created culture of migration among Muslims in Hyderabad city in India. It determined the economic decision of migrants for migration (Ali, 2007:54).

Collective remittances

The impact of Gulf migration positively affected the socio-economic life of Muslims as well as their households in cluster of these villages. Migrant labourers of these villages those working in Mumbai and Saudi Arabia sent individual remittances their households as well as collective remittances for development of their communities at root. Muslim migrant labourers remitted to development of their communities which led to cordial relation among them. The operators of "Western Union" branches those working in the Inayat Patti village reported that migrant labourers of cluster of these villages sent individual remittances to their households and community of their villages both. These migrants gave *Zakat (religious tax)* as 2.5 per cent of total individual annual income to poor people of their villages because it was necessary religious duty of every prosperous Muslims. Apart, they remitted collectively from Saudi Arabia for constriction and reconstruction of Mosques, religious schools in their villages. Youth told that religious education was more important than modern education for them. They wanted to know about *Islam and Muslims* because they would go to holy land of Saudi Arabia for livelihoods. Migrants also remitted for organise to religious and social activities in their villages. On the occasion of *Eid-Milad-e-Nabi (*Birth day of Prophet Muhammad), they especially remitted for organising to religious programme to describe about ideas of Prophet Muhammad. They also organised religious programme before migration to Gulf countries as well as after returned to root. They told that it was bless of Prophet Muhammad that they were swift earning in Saudi Arabia. Apart, migrants gave financial support to poor households for marriages of their daughters and gift to their family members, friends, relatives and familiars. These social-cultural and economic activities created a social networks system among Muslims.

Inayat Patti village was got beneficiary of collective and individual remittances both which positively affecting the socio-economic development of community of village as well as migrant households. It was observed that there were three beautiful mosques with around 200 feet steeples which showed Islamic identities of this village. Apart, there were two religious schools where children of this village used to get religious education. Both mosques and religious schools were constructed by collective remittances of migrant labourers those working in Saudi Arabia and other Gulf countries. People of this village organised religious programmes before beginning of every ceremony like marriage, inaugural of shops and business and migration to Saudi Arabia. Migrant labourers gifted financial support for marriages of daughters in poor households their village and neighbouring village. It was reported by the migrant labourers that they also collected *Zakat* (religious tax) from rich *Sheikh* (Local people of Saudi Arabia) for development of their community at root. This village was known as name of *Saudi-village* because Gulf migration positively changed the socio-economic environment of village. Impact of Gulf migration showed in their life style as well as social and economic activities. They developed separate social-cultural and economic identities through their migration to Gulf countries. Muslims had splendid houses, luxury vehicles which showed their physical culture. Migrant labourers used words of *Arabi* language with their native *Hindi* tongue. They were to be dressed in western and Islamic styles both. They prayed per day after return to Saudi Arabia as well used luxurious consumer durables also. Gulf migration created a jobs market for such persons those working as travel agents for facilitating the migration to Saudi Arabia. Retired migrant labourers contributed through giving their skills and experiences for development of skills among new migrant labourers those were preparing for migration to Mumbai and Saudi Arabia. It is also observed that retired migrant labourers started their own business in this village and neighbouring village which led to development at root. It created job market of local Muslims who could not migrate to Mumbai and Saudi Arabia due to the individuals and other reasons.

Muslim community purchased agricultural lands for cultivation where poor Hindus labourers worked as agricultural labourer. Muslims also gave their agricultural land on lease to Hindus peasants. It was interviewed that Muslims were migrating to Gulf countries for sustain their present socio-economic identities following the positive influences of migration to Gulf countries. It was also found that demonstration effect of Gulf migration developed a culture of migration among youth. They expressed that they did not like to engage in other work instead of migration to Saudi Arabia because it had been deep rooted in their veins. It worked as pull factor for migration to Gulf countries.

Inflow of Remittances and its Utilisation in Return Migrant Households in Inayat Patti village

Out of the total return migrant labourers, 96.0 per cent of the labourers earned up to Rs. 750,000 per annum or Rs.62,500 per month while one labourers earned above than Rs. 750,001 per annum(Table)

Table: Income per annum of Return Migrant Labourers in Gulf Countries

Income (Rupees)	Numbers	Per cent
Less than 5,00,000	16	64.0
5,00,001-7,50,000	08	32.0
7,50,001- 1,200,000	01	4.0
Total Labourers	25	100.00

Source: Field Survey, 2015

Out of the total return migrant labourers, 52.0 per cent of the labourers remitted between Rs. 180,000 and 360,000 followed by 36.0 per cent remitted to between Rs.360,001 and Rs.420,000 per annum(Table).

Table: Annual Remittances by Return Migrant Labourers to Village

Remittances (Rupees)	Number	Per cent
1,80,000 – 3,60,000	13	52.0
3,60,001- 4,20,000	09	36.0
4,20,001-540,000	02	8.0
5,40,001-840,000	01	4.0
Total Labourers	25	100.00

Source: Field Survey, 2015

Migrant labourers remitted through both Banks and Western Union. Based on the obtained quantitative information from return migrant labourers in Inayat Patti village, it was found that unskilled labourers remitted 80.6 per cent of their annual income in Gulf countries followed by semi-skilled labourers remitted 76.3 per cent and skilled labourers remitted 70.7 per cent. Overall, migrant labourers remitted 75.5 per cent of their total income in Gulf countries (Table)

Table: Average Annual Income, Expenditure and Remittances to Root (in Indian Rupee)

Migrant Labourers	Income	Expenditure	Remittances(Rs)
Migrant Labourers	4,31,040	1,06,000 (24.5%)	3,25,440 (75.5%)
Skilled- Labourers	8,19,996	2,40,000 (29.3%)	5,79,996 (70.7%)
Semi-skilled Labourers	3,99,996	94,788 (23.7%)	3,05,208 (76.3%)
Unskilled Labourers	2,79,000	54,000(19.4%)	2,25,000 (80.6%)

Source: Field Survey, 2015

The migrant households spent remittances on lump-sum expenditures on items like house, vehicle, and agricultural land. The other major item was expenditure on marriage that was demonstration of expenditure in the locality. Expenditure on education was an exception by number of households (Table)

Table: Remittances Spent on Items by Return Migrant Households (in Indian Rupee)

Items	Households		Remittances Spent per Households(Rs.)
	Number	Per cent	
Construction/repair of House	22	88	4,00,000
Purchase of Vehicles	11	44	3,61,818
Marriage	5	20	4,30,000
Purchase Agricultural land	2	08	5,00,000
Education	1	04	90,000

Source: Field Survey, 2015

Concluding Remarks

The study showed that there was pattern of dual-step migration where internal migration led to international migration. Network of migration between villages and destinations determined the distance of migration within specific geographical and social regions. The economic decisions of migrants were determined by their social and cultural perception about origin and destinations. Therefore, labourers used to follow to social pathways of migration from their villages to Saudi Arabia via internal migration to city of Mumbai. Labourers migrated individually but entire process of migration was functioned by strategies of households and other organisation which were directly and indirectly influencing to these processes. These migrants maintained their social networks with homogeneity in social, cultural and economic practices in the entire cycle of the migration which showed into their working –cum-living conditions in both origin and destinations. The impact of Gulf migration positively affected the socio-economic development of the communities of migrants as well their households in origin. These phenomena created to migration based communities in these villages which developed to separate socio-economic identities of Muslims in these villages. Remittances were not only economic matter but also social and psychological matters which influenced the behaviour of migrants, their family members and ultimately their communities. They invested to collective remittances into the social and cultural activities of their communities. Migrant households used remittances on the items of consumer durables which created a demonstration culture among them. We recommend that Government of India should be motivated to migrant households for productive utilization of remittances.

References

Ali, S. (2007). Go West Young Man: The Culture of Migration among Muslims in Hyderabad City India. *Journal of Ethnic and Migration Studies, Vol. 33 No-1* , 37-58.

Annual Report 2014-15 .Ministry of Overseas Affairs Government of India (at Presnt merged by Minsitry of External Affairs Govt.of India). (2015). Retrieved 2015, from http//:www.moia.gov.in

Basu, S. (2016). Diasporas Transforming Homelands.Nuancing Collective RemittancePractices in Rural Gujarat . *Economic and Political Weekly* , 54-62.

bilateralremittancematrix2015_Oct2016 (1). (n.d.). Retrieved 2017, from http://www.data.org.world.bank

District,State/Country wise number of Emigrants going to emigration check required countries(ECR). (2013). Retrieved from https://emigrate.gov.in/ext/preViewPdfGenRptAction.action

International Migration Report. (2015). Retrieved 2016, from http://www.un.org/en/development/.../migration/.../migrationreport/.../MigrationReport2015

Khadria, B. (2008). India: Skilled Migration to Developed Countries,Labour Migration to the Gulf. In S. Castless, & R. D. Wise, *Migration and Development :Perspective from the South* (pp. 79-112). Geneva,Switzerland: International Organization for Migration.

Kumar, K. (2016). Indian labour in the Gulf: issues of migration and the British Empire. In P. C. Jain, & G. Z. Oomen, *South Asian Migration to Gulf Countries* (pp. 71-92). New York: Routledge.

Lee, E. S. (Vol-3,No-1(1966)). A Theory of Migration. *Demography* , 47-57.

Magill, F. (1997). *International Encyclopeadia of Economics. Volume Two.* London: FD,Publication.

Massey, D. S. (1990). Social Structure, Household Strategies, and the Cumulative Causation of Migration. *Population Index,Vol. 56, No. 1 (Spring)* , 3-26.

Massey, D. S., Arango, J., Hugo, G., Kouaouci, A., Pellegrino, A., & Taylor, J. E. (1993). Theories of International Migration: A Review and Appraisal. *Population and Development Review. Vol. 19, No. 3* , 431-466.

Naidu, K. (1991). Indian Labour Migartion to Gulf Countries. *Economic Political Weekly* , 349-354.

Popuation Enumeration Data of District Allahabad.DDW_PCA0944_2011_MDS with UI xlsx-Microsoft Excel . (2011). Retrieved 2012, from http://www.census.gov.in

Prakash, B. (1978). Impact of Foreign Remittances: A Case Study of Chavakkad Village. *Economic & Political Weekly* , 1107-1111.

Rahman, A. (2001). *Indian Labour Migration to Gulf*. New Delhi: Rajat Publication.

Rahman, A. (2010). Migration and Human Rights in the Gulf. *Middle East View Points: Migration and Gulf* , 16-18.

Rajan, S., & Prakash, B. (2013). Migration and Development Linkages Re-examined in the Context of Global Economic Crisis. In S. Rajan, *Indian Migration Report 2012:Global Financial Crisis, Migration and Remittances.* Delhi,India: Routledge Taylor & Francis Group.

Roper, S. D., & Barria, L. A. (2014). Understanding Variation in Gulf Migration and Labour Practices. *Middle East Law and Governance* , 32-52.

Seccombe, I. J., & Lawless, R. (1986). Foreign Workers Dependnece in the Gulf and the International Oil Companies 1910-50. *International Migration Review.Vol.20 No.3(Autumn)* , 548-574.

Singh, N., & Kulwinder, S. (2017). International Migartion, Remittances and Development in Rural Punjab. *Journal of Regional Development and Planning. Vol.6,No.1* , 45-65.

Skeldon, R. (2006). Interlinakges Between Internal and International Migration and Developement in the Asian Region. *POPULATION, SPACE AND PLACE* , 15-30.

Stark, O., & Bloom, D. E. (1985). The New Economics of Labor Migration. *The American Economic Review, Vol. 75, No. 2* , 173-178.

State-wise/ Country- wise number of Emigrants going to emigration check required(ECR) countries through recruitment agency(RA)and Direct Recruitment by foreign employer (FE)(2015). (2015). Retrieved 2017, from https://emigrate.gov.in/ext/pre ViewPdfGenRptAction.action

Taylor, J. E. (2006). *INTERNATIONAL MIGRATION AND ECONOMIC DEVELOPMENT.* Retrieved from http://www.un.org/esa/population/migration/turin/Symposium.../ P09_SYMP_Taylor.pdf

The Emigartion Act 1983.Govt.of India . (n.d.). Retrieved 2016, from https://emigrate.gov.in/ext/static/emig-act.pdf

Upadhya, C., & Rutten, M. (2012). Migration, Transnational Flows and Development In India. A Regional Perspective. *Economic and Political Weekly.Vol.27.Issue no.19* , 54-62.

Winckler, O. (2010). Labor Migration to the GCC States: Patterns, Scale, and Policies. *Migration and the Gulf. Middle East Institute Viewpoints* , 9-12.

World Migration Report 2015: Migrants and Cities: New Partnerships to Manage Mobility. (2015). Retrieved 2016 , from publications.iom.int/system/files/wmr2015_en.pdf

Zachariah, K., & Rajan, I. (2015). *Dynamics of Emigration and Remittances in Kerala:Results from the Kerala Migartion Survey 2014.* Retrieved 2016, from www.cds.edu/wp-content/uploads/2015/10/WP463.pdf

Chapter 52. Economic Behavior of Albanian Immigrants during the Economic Crisis in Greece[1]

Dorina Kalemi[2]

Abstract

This paper develops an empirical model to investigate the main determinants of economic behavior of Albanian immigrants in Greece. The aim of this study is to investigate Albanian immigrants' rate of monthly individual income and their savings in the economic crisis. In addition, the results analyze the remittances that the Albanian immigrants sent to their home country from 2008 to 2011. Also, the results show the expected income of immigrants. The study is based on 371 survey responses from the area of Attica, Greece and they are analysed econometrically using regression techniques. In particular, the empirical results, based on the estimation of regression analysis suggest that economic and consumer variables are significant factors for making them return to their home country. Finally, the empirical analysis showed that the factors affecting the possibility of return to their home country because of the economic crisis, are the participants who believe that they are still paid less than the natives, the participants who have said that their income in the host country is being reduced and the participants who own assets in their home country.

Keywords: Albanian immigrants in Greece, economic behavior, economic crisis, survey, regression models.

Introduction

The reasons for migration might be economic, political and cultural. According to these factors, developed countries in Europe, particularly those in the north, such as Germany, Netherlands, France, Britain, Belgium, have acquired migrant minorities. Three decades ago, Greece was a country which sent its citizens abroad, but in 1990s it began to be a country of destination for migrants (Lianos and Cavounidis, 2010, Papadopoulos et al., 2013).

Greece is the only country of the European Union that the rate of immigrants who come from one nationality exceeds 65% among all foreigners of the country (Ministry of Interior, 2004). Specifically, in 1990, Albania's immigrants, according to the Ministry of Public Order and Citizen Protection, reached just 440 people, including both legal and illegal residents. As the time passed by, the growth of Albanian immigrants increased rapidly. As a result, the current number of regular immigrants registered with the Ministry of Interior are 577.359 of which 401.402 are Albanians (Ministry of Interior, 2016).

[1] **Acknowledgements**: This survey was conducted in Harokopio University, MSc Sustainable Development-Consumer Behavior with a three-member committee G. Hondroyiannis, A. Saiti and E. Sardianou. Also, Thanks are due to Apostolos G. Papadopoulos for valuable comments for this paper.
[2] Dorina Kalemi, Department of Home Economic and Ecology, Harokopio University, 76 El. Venizelou Str.,17676 Athens, Greece. E-mail: dkalemi@hua.gr, kalemidorina@gmail.com.

According to the Ministry of Public Order and the Hellenic Statistical Authority, Table 1 shows that the registration of Albanian immigrants has been increasing over the years. In particular, it appears to be a large population gap between 1998 and 2004, due to the change of legislation, where all immigrants, both legal and illegal were eligible to apply for permanent residence.

Table 1. Albanian population through years

Years	1990	1991	1992	1993	1994	1995	1996	1997	1998
Albanians	440	1169	3215	3731	4188	4565	4833	4550	6125

Years	...	2004	2005		2006	2007
Albanians	...	434810	448152		481663	577504

Source: Ministry of Public Order (1999), Hellenic Statistical Authority (2007)

Empirical Model and Methodology

In order to conduct the research, a questionnaire was set up to identify the consuming behavior of immigrants from Albania. The research emphasized on demographic characteristics, consuming habits, investments made by immigrants, migrant grounds, remittances to their country of origin, the way they send the remittances, where are the remittances addressed to, and finally whether the reason they are returning back to their country is the economic crisis.

There were distributed 460 questionnaires to households in the Prefecture of Attica, of which 371 were fully completed and returned. The survey began on April 18, 2011 and it was completed on December 20, 2011. The samples were chosen randomly. The questionnaire was distributed to people being in city squares, in places where immigrants tend to gather, such as Foreigners Directorate in various areas of Attica, Police Departments addressing homogeneous people from Albania, the Foreigners Employment Directorate, the Albanian School (Porta), the Embassy of Albania and Various Albanian clubs. Only one questionnaire was distributed to each household, including any active member aged 18 or older.

The sampling survey questionnaire consists of five modules. The first module includes demographic questions, in order to investigate the profile of respondents. This section also includes questions about how long they live in Greece, where can their family members be found at the moment, and whether the respondent or their family members have the Greek citizenship. It also includes what kind of residence they have in Greece, whether they have assets in their country of origin and what was the reason for immigrating to Greece.

The second module contains questions about financial status, such as whether they send money to their relatives in their country of origin, how is money sent, when and where remittances are sent. The third section includes questions about how much money they spend on their consuming needs in the country of residence, Greece. The fourth module includes questions about their investment activities in Greece and the fifth one includes questions about consuming habits of Albanians in Greece.

In the sample that was examined in this study, most participants were men (62.8%) and 37.2% were women. The age was between 18 to 78 years old, of which 66.8% were married. Also, the survey was conducted in Attica, where most of the residents lived in Downtown Athens (45%). Initially the data of questionnaires were analyzed statistically through the use of SPSS 16.0.

Empirical Model and Methodology

Below there is an analysis of the results of the assessment of regressions for the determinants of immigrants in a period of economic crisis. Estimates are made by accounting and multiple regression. More specifically, the results of the assessment of regression models for the determinants are presented below

(i) the amount of individual monthly income; (ii) the savings rate of the respondents; (iii) the determining factors for making them return to their country

of origin due to the economic crisis in the host country. There were various model checks made and the following examples are found:

i) the amount of individual monthly income

The estimated results of the multiple regression model for the determinants that affect the amount of their income, where the linear regression (OLS) method is applied. The regression equation is defined as follows:

$lnincome = b_0 + b_1 \, gender_i + b_2 \, age_i + b_3 \, age_i^2 + b_4 \, lnfun_i + b_5 \, business_i + b_6 \, GrSq_i + \varepsilon_i$ **(1)**

where the dependent variable "lnincome" is a quantitative variable and expresses the amount of their monthly individual income in euros. Independent variables, such as (gender) is a false one and it gets the value 1, when the respondent is a male and the value 0 when the respondent is a female; (age) is a quantitative variable that expresses the respondent's age; (Age2) the square of the respondent's age; (lnfun) is a quantitative variable that expresses the amount spent in euros on entertainment and entertainment per month; (business) is a false variable and receives the value 1, when the respondent owns his/her own business in the host country and the value 0 elsewhere; (GrSq) is a quantitative variable expressing the square meters of the residence; (εi) are the regression estimation errors. The statistic F (F-statistic) expresses the overall explanation of the regression with the following hypothesis H0: b1=b2 =b3=...=bk = 0 versus H1: let one of the above estimated coefficient be different from Zero.

The specific independent variables were chosen according to previous research, which took place in European countries and the U.S (Durand et al., 1996; Barrett and McCarthy, 2007; Theodoropoulou and Kosmas, 2007; Bettin et al., 2009; Ulku, 2010; Karamba et al., 2011).

Table 2. Determining factors that affect the amount of individual income

Independent variables	OLS
C	3.802***
	(9.07)
Gender	0,178**
	(2.53)
Age	0.075***
	(4,50)
age2	-0.001***
	(-4,70)
Lnfun	0.108**
	(2.42)
Lnfood	0.128**
	(2.01)
Business	0.416***
	(4.58)
Grsq	0.002*
	(1.68)
Independent variables	
R² adj	0.244
F-statistic	13.698***

Notes: The signs (***), (**) and (*) represent the 1%, 5% and 10% level of significance respectively; numbers in parenthesis are the t-ratios.

The results of this model show that men have higher income than women. Karamba et al (2011) and Barrett and McCarthy (2007) came up with similar results in the surveys that were conducted for Ghana and Ireland, respectively. According to the (age) variable, as the age of migrants increases, their individual monthly income increases, too. Also, in the (age2) variable we see that the increase in income by age is valid for individuals up to 38 years old, which results from the following equation:

$$\frac{\Theta\,(b_1\,\text{"age"} + b_2\,\text{"age}^2\text{"})}{0} = b_1 + 2b_2\,\text{"age"} = 0{,}075 + 2*(0{,}001)*\text{"age"} =$$

$$\Theta\,\text{"age"}$$

Immigrants who spend more money on entertainment seem to have higher individual income. In addition, immigrants who spend more money on food each month in the host country have higher individual incomes. The research of Theodoropoulou and Kosmas (2009) on migrants residing in Greece showed similar results, as well as Ulku (2010)'s survey for migrants residing in Germany.

We conclude that men and older people have higher individual incomes. Specifically, by increasing the age variable into square (age 2,) we observe that the increase in income by age is valid up to 38 years old, where this effect takes place at a decreasing rate because the sign of the estimated coefficient is negative. Also, respondents who have their own business in their host country, big houses (in square meters), spend more money on entertainment and food consumption tend to have higher individual income.

ii) the savings rate of the respondents

The aim of this regression assessment is to determine the effect of certain parameters such as age, gender, educational level, personal income, assets in their country of origin, years of residence in the host country, nationality, the income percentage given for rent, the income percentage given for food, the Income Percentage given to Mortgage payment and also Albanians who give more money for clothing and entertainment. The specific independent variables are consistent with previous investigation, which have taken place in different countries from Merkle and Zimmermann (1992), Durand et al. (1996), Yang (2004), Osili (2007), Massey and Basem (2007). The conclusion of all these researchers are that migrants save more than the locals. In order to assess the determinants, the method of multi-linear regression is applied (OLS). The regression equation is defined as follows:

Ratesave = $b_0 + b_1\,aei_i + b_2\,lnincome_i + b_3\,yearsgr_i + b_4\,origin_i + b_5\,ratehome_i + b_6\,ratefood_i + b_6\,rateloans_i + b_7\,ratecf_i + b_8\,ratefun + \varepsilon_i$ **(2),**

where the dependent variable "Ratesave" is a quantitative variable and expresses the percentage that immigrants save per month in their host country. Independent variables, such as (aei) is a false one and it gets the value 1, when the respondent is a University graduate and the value 0, for other; (lnincome) is a quantitative variable and expresses the amount of their monthly individual income in euros; (yearsgr) is a quantitative variable and expresses the number of years residing in host country; (origin) is false variable and receives the value 1, when the respondent is Albanian and the value 0, when the respondent is Albanian of Greek descent; (ratehome) is a quantitative variable and expresses the income percentage given for rent; (ratefood) is a quantitative variable and expresses the income percentage given for food; (rateloans) is a quantitative variable and expresses the income percentage given to mortgage payment; (ratecf) is a quantitative variable and expresses the income percentage given for clothing; (ratefun) is a quantitative variable and expresses the income percentage given for pleasure or entertainment; (εi) are the regression estimation errors. The statistic F (F-statistic) expresses the overall explanation of the regression with the following hypothesis H0: b1=b2 =b3=...=bk = 0 versus H1: let one of the above estimated coefficient be different from Zero.

Table 3. Determining factors that affect the savings rate of the respondents in host country.

Independent variables	OLS
C	16.358***
	(2.60)
Aei	1.871*
	(1.66)
Lnincome	4.095***
	(5.08)
Yearsgr	-0.252*
	(-1.76)
Origin	3.368***
	(2.87)
Ratehome	-0.457***
	(-10.10)
Ratefood	-0.562***
	(-10.48)
rateloans	-0.527***
	(-9.71)
ratecf	-0,240***
	(-2,81)
ratefun	-0,227***
	(-3,58)
diagnostic tests	
R^2 adj	0,432
F-statistic	31,978***

Notes: The signs (***), (**) and (*) represent the 1%, 5% and 10% level of significance respectively; numbers in parenthesis are the t-ratios.

iii) The determining factors for making them return to their country of origin due to the economic crisis in the host country

The results of this model show that the respondents who have higher education, monthly individual income and Albanians in relation to Albanians of Greek descent save more money of the income per month in the host country. In particular, there are studies that provide empirical support of Merkle (1992) who have compared the locals with immigrants in Germany. On the other hand, determining factors that affect the percentage of income negatively are the number of years residing in Greece, the income percentage given for rent, the income percentage given for food, the Income Percentage given to Mortgage payment and also Albanians who give more money for clothing and entertainment or pleasure save less money of income per month in the host country. Similar results are consistent of Durand et al (1996) from Mexican immigrants from the United States and Bettin et al (2009) for migrants in Australia.

The methodology of logistic regression was applied (Binary Logistic Regression) in the dependent variable "origincrisic", which is a false variable and receives the value 1, when the respondents are thinking to return to the country of origin, due to the economic crisis and the value 0 elsewhere. The estimation of the logistic regression is made by taking into account the ratio of probabilities and the estimation of the bi parameters is done by the method of maximum likelihood method.

The regression equation is defined as follows: $Origincrisic_i = b0 + b1\ man_i + b2\ lnincome_i + b3\ ownhomeGr_i + b3\ upaidless_i + b4\ redincome_i + b5\ origin_i + b6\ moneyan_i + b7\ eatout_i + b8\ yearsGr_i + b9\ assetsA_i + \varepsilon_i$ (3)

Independent variables, such as (man) is a false one and it gets the value 1, when the head of the family is a man and the value 0 elsewhere; (lnincome) is a quantitative variable and expresses the amount of their monthly individual income in euros; (ownhomeGr) is a false variable and receives the value 1, when the respondent owns his/her own home in the host country and the value 0 elsewhere; (upaidless)) is a false variable and receives the value 1 when the respondents continue to get paid less than the locals and the value 0, when he/she does not agree; (redincome) is a false variable and receives the value 1, when the respondent agrees that there is a decrease in his/her income due to economic crisis in the host country and the value 0 elsewhere; (origin) is a false variable and receives the value 1, when the respondent is Albanian and the value 0 when the respondent is Albanian of Greek Descent; (moneyan) is a false variable and receives the value 1, when the respondent sent money to the origin country and the value 0 elsewhere; (eatout) is a false variable and receives the value 1, when the respondent is eating out less than once a month and the value 0 elsewhere; (yearsGr) is a quantitative variable expressing the number of Years Residing in the host country; (assetsA) is a false variable and receives the value 1, when the respondent have assets in their home country and the value 0 elsewhere; (εi) are the regression estimation errors. All of the independent variables are studies that provide empirical support of previous investigation (Gedeshi, 2002; Houle and Schellenberg, 2008; Ulku, 2010).

Table 4. Determining factors of the possibility of returning to country of origin

Independent variables	BLR
C	*2,432*
	(2,29)
man	*-0,610***
	(4,85)
lnincome	*-0,647****
	(9,18)
ownhomeGr	*-1,069****
	(10,41)
upaidless	*0,802****
	(8,91)
redincome	*1,899****
	(24,79)
origin	*0,580***
	(4,00)
moneyAn	*0,621***
	(4,21)
eatout	*0,548**
	(3,49)
yearsGr	*-0,081***
	(4,53)
assetsA	*0,594**
	(2,80)
diagnostic tests	
R² Nagelkerke	*0,395*
2 Log likelihoods	*365,658*

Notes: The signs (***), (**) and (*) represent the 1%, 5% and 10% level of significance respectively; numbers in parenthesis are the statistic Wald.

It is clear from this regression that the factors that affect negatively the decision of respondents to return to the country of origin due to the economic crisis are the head of the family who is a male, the high individual income, their own home in the host country and the years of residence in Greece. On the other hand, the factors that influence positively the decision of thinking to return to their country of origin due to the economic crisis are respondents who consider that they continue to get paid less than the locals, respondents who have stated that their income has been reduced in the host country due to economic crisis, Albanians in relation to Albanians of Greek Descent, respondents who send money to their country of origin, respondents who eat out less than once a month and finally, respondents who have assets in their home country. Ulku (2010) came up with similar results in the surveys with immigrants in Germany, specifically with the conclusion that the respondents who intend to return to their origin country in the future send more remittances.

Conclusion

The aim of this article is to state the economic and consuming behavior of Albanianonomic immigrants who reside in Attica, Greece, during economic crisis. The emphasis of our empirical investigation is the three important issues that arise, such as the amount of individual monthly income, the savings rate of the Albanians and the possibility of returning to their country of origin because of the economic crisis in Greece.

As can be seen from the statistical analysis carried out on a sample of 371 people, the average monthly consumer personal income is 974.66 euros. Consequently, the income of migrants is estimated to be related to demographics, such as gender, age, size of residence, as well as characteristics related to the economic behavior of respondents, such as fun and entertainment, food consumption, respondents who have their own their business. (Durand et al., 1996; Barrett and McCarthy, 2007; Theodoropoulou and Kosmas, 2007; Bettin et al., 2009; Ulku, 2010; Karamba et al., 2011). We conclude that men and older people have higher individual incomes. Also, we observe that the increase in income by age is valid up to 38 years old. (Karamba et al, 2011; Barrett and McCarthy, 2007).

Albanians save 212.99 euros per month. We conclude that the Albanians who have higher education, monthly individual income and Albanians in relation to Albanians of Greek descent save more money of the income per month in Greece. This may be due to the fact that the Albanians have acquired Greek citizenship or have deposited the papers to obtain it, so they feel more secure (Merkle, 1992). On the other hand, determining factors that affect the percentage of income negatively are the number of years residing in Greece, the income percentage given for rent, the income percentage given for food, the income percentage given tomortgage payment and also Albanians who give more money for clothing and entertainment or pleasure. They tend to save less money of income per month in the host country (Durand et al, 1996; Bettin et al, 2009).

Lastly, we examined the determining factors for making them return to their country of Albania due to the economic crisis in Greece. Of the 371 Albanian respondents, 60.4% said they would return back, while 39.6% did not think to return. It is clear from this regression that the factors that affect negatively the decision of Albanians to return to the country of origin due to the economic crisis are the head of the family who is a male, the high individual income, their own home in Greece and the years of residence in Greece. On the other hand, the factors that positively influence the decision and they are thinking to return to their country of origin due to the economic crisis are Albanians who consider that they continue to get paid less than the locals, Albanians who have stated that their income has been reduced in the host country due to economic crisis, Albanians in relation to Albanians of Greek Descent, Albanians who send money to their country of origin and finally, Albanians who have assets in their home country (Ulku, 2010).

The economic crisis hits immigrants more than the locals. As a result, the unemployment rate increases. Albanian immigrants who come from the neighbour country will come back and forth. Their decision to stay in Greece or not depends on how the crisis will affect their employment and income, as well.

References

Barrett, A., & McCarthy, Y. (2007). The Earnings of Immigrants in Ireland: Results from the 2005 EU Survey of Income and Living Conditions. Economic and Social Research Institute (ESRI), Working Paper 206.

Bettin, G., Lucchetti, R., & Zazzaro, A. (2009). Income, Consumption and Remittances: Evidence from immigrants to Australia. MO.FI.R, Money and Finance Research Group, Worker Paper 34, Univ. Politecnica Marche - Dept. Economics.

Durand, J., Kandel, W., Parrado, E.A., & Massey D.S (1996). International Migration and Development in Mexican Communities. Demography J-STOR, 33(2), 249- 264, May.

Gedeshi, I. (2002). Role of Remittances from Albanian Emigrants and their Influence in the Country's Economy. Eastern European Economics, 48(5),49-72, September- October.

Hellenic Republic, Ministry of Interior (2016). Received from www.ypes.gr/en/Elections

Hellenic Statistical Authority (2007). Received from http://www.statistics.gr/en/home/

Houle, R., & Schellenberg G. (2008). Remittances by recent immigrants. Statistics Canada, 75(1), 5- 16.

Lianos, T. P., & Cavounidis, J. (2010). Immigrant remittances, stability of employment and relative deprivation. International Migration, 48(5), 118-140.

Massey, D.S., & Basem L. (2007). Determinants of savings, Remittances, and Spending Patterns among U.S. Migrants in Four Mexican Communities. Sociological Inquiry, Wiley Online Library, 62(2), January.

Merkle, L., & Zimmermann K.F. (1992). Savings, remittances and return migration. Economics Letters, 38(1), 77-81, January.

Osili, U. O. (2007), Remittances and savings from international migration: Theory and evidence using a matched sample. July, Journal of Development Economics, Indiana University, Purdue University Indianapolis N. 83(2), 446-465.

Papadopoulos, A. G., Chalkias, C., & Fratsea L.M. (2013). Challenges to immigrant associations and NGOs in contemporary Greece. Transnational Press London Ltd, 10(3), 342.

Theodoropoulou, H.. & Kosmas P. (2007). The Socio-Economic Characteristics, Consumer behavior and Social Integration of Economics Immigrants in Athens, Greece. Consumer Citizenship, 3, 81-94.

Ulku, H. (2010). Remitting Behaviour of Turkish Migrants: Evidence from Household Data in Germany. Social Science Research Network, Brooks World Poverty Institute (ISBN), Manchester, The University of Manchester, BWPI Working Paper No. 115.

Ulku, H., & Arun T. (2010). Determinants of remittances: The case of the South Asian community in Manchester. Development Economic and Public Policy, Working Paper.

Chapter 53. In Searching Law on The Indonesian Diaspora: Lessons Learnt from South Korea and India Experiences[1]

Susi Dwi Harijanti[2], Bilal Dewansyah[3], Ali Abdurahman[4], Wicaksana Dramanda[5]

Abstract

The existence and movement of diaspora across the world, challenge the existing legal norms on citizenship and migration. The responses from the law-makers from origin countries vary. Most of European, Latin America and African countries adopt dual citizenship law to their diaspora for the different reasons: immigrant integration, maintenance of loyalty to ex-citizen or because the closeness ethnic relation. However, most of countries in Asia-Pacific region - which gain the independence through decolonization process - do not favor dual citizenship towards their diaspora, including Indonesia, mostly because of the ideological perception of citizenship. In this sense, many countries grant the special status or scheme to their diaspora (neither citizens nor residents of the country) as an external quasi-citizenship based on ethnic descent as coined by Bauböck as "ethnizenship." In Indonesia case, while the rejection of dual citizenship proposal is unavoidable, it leads idea to adopt a kind of ethnizenship status as an alternative regulatory model for Indonesia diaspora. In order to search the suitable and realistic regulatory scheme for Indonesian diaspora, this paper compare experiences from India and South-Korea which adopt a quasi-citizenship for their descendants overseas. The result from this comparison will be considered as a benchmark to develop regulatory model for Indonesian diaspora.

Keywords: Indonesia, law, diaspora, ethnizenship, South-Korea, India.

Introduction

The existence and movement of diaspora across the world have challenged the existing legal norms on citizenship and migration. The responses from the law-makers from origin countries vary. Most of European, Latin America and African countries adopt dual citizenship law to their diaspora for the different reasons: immigrant integration, maintenance of loyalty to ex-citizen or because the closeness ethnic relation (Dewansyah, 2016). However, most of countries in Asia-Pacific region - which gain the independence through decolonization process - do not favor dual citizenship towards their diaspora, including Indonesia, mostly because of the ideological perception of

---

[1] This paper based on the on-going socio-legal research titled "Model Pengaturan Diaspora Dalam Rezim Hukum Kewarganegaraan dan Keimigrasian Indonesia" (The Regulatory Model of Indonesian Diaspora in Citizenship and Immigration Law Regimes) funded by Universitas Padjadjaran (UNPAD).
[2] Associate Professor in Constitutional Law, Faculty of Law, Universitas Padjadjaran (UNPAD), susi.dwi.harijanti@unpad.ac.id
[3] Lecturer on Constitutional Law, Faculty of Law, Universitas Padjadjaran (UNPAD), b.dewansyah@unpad.ac.id
[4] Senior Lecturer on Constitutional Law, Faculty of Law, Universitas Padjadjaran (UNPAD), b.dewansyah@unpad.ac.id
[5] Reasercher of Pusat Studi Kebijakan Negara (PSKN)/ Study Center of State Policies, Faculty of Law, Universitas Padjadjaran (UNPAD), wicaksanadramanda@live.com.

citizenship (Hassall, 1999, p.49). In this sense, many countries grant the special status or scheme to their diaspora (neither citizens nor residents of the country) as an external quasi-citizenship based on ethnic descent as coined by Bauböck as "ethnizenship." (Baubock, 2007, p.2396).

In Indonesia case, while the rejection of dual citizenship proposal is unavoidable (Harijanti, 2016), it leads to the idea of adoption of ethnizenship status as an alternative regulatory model for Indonesia diaspora. For instance, former President of Indonesia Diaspora Network (IDN), a global network of Indonesian diaspora), Al Arief refers such regulatory alternative to Indian diaspora status which is formally not dual citizenship (Dewansyah, 2016, p.7). Similarly, Iman Santoso, Indonesian immigration law professor, also suggest giving a Person of Indonesia Descendant's Card (*Kartu Keturunan Orang Indonesia*) for ex- Indonesia's citizens and their descendents that will be used to have an exemption for visa requirement and they are entitled to have some legal rights, except political rights (Santoso, 2014, p.118). However, the discourse is not merely academic because it has political relevance in the context of Citizenship Law amendment plan as stated in National Legislation Plan 2014 – 2015.

In order to search the suitable and realistic regulatory scheme for Indonesian diaspora, this paper - which based on the ongoing research - will compare experience from other countries which adopt a quasi-citizenship for their descendants overseas, that is India and South Korea. India creates the Person of Indian Origin (PIO) card scheme since 1998 and Overseas Citizens of India (OCI) card scheme in 2003 (Naujoks, 2015, pp.21-24). These two schemes merged in 2015 into Overseas Citizens of India Card Holder (OCC) scheme through Citizenship (Amendment) Act 2015 (Section 7A). The new scheme gives benefit to Indian diaspora not only in the form of visa exemption to visit and stay in India, but also it guarantees some legal rights with exception in political and participation rights (Xavier, 2011, p.46). While India adopts regulatory model of diaspora through citizenship law regime, South Korean's experience shows the different path toward their diaspora. The Korean government refuses the demand of Korean diaspora in North America for dual citizenship, and consequently it creates a semi-citizenship called 'Overseas Korean' status through the immigration law regime as regulated in the Act on the Immigration and Legal Status of Overseas Koreans (the Overseas Koreans Act/OKA) in 1999 with F-4 visa scheme with its amendment in 2004 which include Korean-Chinese diaspora (Lee, 2012a, pp.93-94). This law gives benefit for the Korean diaspora in the form of important rights such as freedom in employment and economic activity, and national treatment with regard to real property rights and transactions, foreign exchange transactions, and health insurance and pensions (Lee, 2003, p.109).

Both India and South Korea have chosen as comparison not only because they have the law that recognize and regulate diaspora status, but they have also been considered as two countries which have a similar stage of development with Indonesia as post-colonial Asian states that gain independence in nearly period. This paper will use the result from this comparison as a benchmark to develop regulatory model for Indonesian diaspora.

Diaspora Setting Models in India and South Korea: A Comparison

In general, the presence of Indian and South Korean diaspora is based on a phenomenon of immigrant workers (Sahai, 2013, p.51). The magnitude of diaspora communities from both countries result in a need for a formal policy governing the diaspora in each country that aim to develop and to build relationships with diaspora communities. The Indian diaspora policy is made by changing the citizenship law in which the government of India allowed dual citizenship (Xavier, 2011, p.45). Sadly, the fully-dual citizenship proposal was failed because of three main obstacles: constitutional provision that ban dual citizenship; legislative trend that hardening such acquisition; and security consideration (Xavier, 2011, p. 43, p.45).

This Indian policy is different with that of South Korea which regulates its diaspora policies through immigration laws. One of the reasons why India government makes the use of citizenship laws is the perception that immigration laws are merely instruments to provide protection in the context of the outflows and entering the territory of the state. Moreover, the diaspora policy does not merely deal with immigration protection, but rather it is about "management" of the diaspora "(Sahai, 2013, p.52). In the case of South Korea, the development of diaspora policy under the immigration laws is based on ethnizenship concept which is broader than the concept of citizenship. Thus, through the concept of ethnizenship, the Korean Government needs to maintain relationships with ethnic Koreans who have obtained citizenship status from other countries before the Republic of Korea established that cannot be resolved by modern citizenship approach (Lee, 2012a, p. 86). In addition, the South Korean government has opinion that by using the immigration law regime, it will have less effect on diplomatic relations between South Korea and the country where the Korean diaspora are now settled, such as China (Yoon, 2007, p.95).

The regulation of diaspora in India was first made through the amendment of citizenship law in 1999 under the scheme of Person of Indian Origin (PIO) which regulated three categories of Indian diaspora: 1) former Indian citizens; 2) Descendants of Indian Citizen to third generation; and 3) spouses of those belonging to categories 1 and 2. This PIO Card was valid for 15 years and could be extended. Nevertheless, former Indian citizens who were Pakistani, Bangladesh, Afghanistan, China, Iran, Bhutan, Sri Lanka, and Nepal citizen were excluded as Indian diaspora. In the same year, South Korea also issued a diaspora regulation through the Act on the Immigration and Legal Status of Overseas Koreans, known as the Overseas Koreans Act (Lee, 2012a, p.93). Based on the Overseas Korean Act, those who could be categorized as diaspora were former citizens of Korea and their descendants to second generation. The meaning of "former citizens of Korea" means that those who are recognized as Korean diaspora are the ones who have formally held the status of a Korean citizen, namely ethnic Korean who migrated before the government of the Republic of Korea established in 1948 were not recognized as diaspora (Lee, 2012a, p.93). Therefore, ethnic Korean residing in the territory of China and some former Soviet Union countries are not recognized as diaspora because they migrated before Republic of Korea was established (Lee, 2012a, p.93).

Based on the above categorization, both India and South Korea perceive diaspora as an ex-citizen, including its descendants to some extent. From these limitations, it appears that India has a looser restriction in which diaspora status can be granted until the third generation. The difference to these restrictions happen to occur because the diaspora phenomenon in India is older than the diaspora phenomenon in South Korea. Based on the history, the phenomenon of the spreading or migration of Indian society began a century and a half ago and has reached 5 to 6 generations (Kumar, 2015, p.1), so India forms a looser policy so that more descendants of former Indian citizens that can get status as a diaspora. The conditions differ from those of South Korea where the South Korean community's dispersion or migration only began in 1860 (Yoon, 2007, p. viii). In addition to differences in the diaspora category, the diaspora policy in South Korea does not include "spouse" of its former citizens in the diaspora category.

The diaspora policy in India and South Korea has changed over time. In India, diaspora policy changes occurred in the period 2003-2015. In 2003 and 2005, the Government of India issued another diaspora policy model in addition to the PIO model, a policy model called Overseas Citizen of India (OCI). The OCI scheme clarifies the diaspora categories that can accept OCI cards as follows: 1) Who is a citizen of India at the time of, or at any time after the commencement of the Constitution i.e. 26.01.1950; 2) who was eligible to become a citizen of India on 26.01.1950; 3) who belonged to a territory that became part of India after 15.08.1947; 4) who is a child or a grandchild or a great grandchild of such a citizen; 5) who is a minor child of a person mentioned above; 6) who is a minor child and who is both a citizen of India is one of the citizens of India; 7) spouse of foreign origin of an overseas Citizen of India Cardholder registered under section 7A of the Citizenship Act, 1955 and whose marriage has been registered and subsisted for a continuous period of not less than two years Immediately preceding the presentation of the application. The latest amendment took place in 2015 resulting a new diaspora policy under the Overseas Citizen of India Cardholder (OCC) scheme that merged the PIO with OCI. Under this policy the Diaspora Indian who has held the PIO card, deemed as OCC (Section 7A para. (2) the Citizenship (Amendment) Act 2015).

Meanwhile, the diaspora policy change in South Korea resulted from a constitutional complaint filed by Korean Chinese (ethnic Korean whose Chinese citizen) who are not categorized as diaspora under the Overseas Korean Act. In 2001, the South Korean Constitutional Court granted the complaint and forced the South Korean Government to amend the Overseas Korean Act in 2004. The amendment includes ethnic Koreans originally excluded under the Overseas Korean Act of 1999 as diaspora (Lee, 2012a, p .5).

The granting of diaspora status is always followed by the granting of certain rights. For example, those registered as Indian diaspora in the OCC scheme may freely exit and enter India (multiple entry life-long visa). OCC holders are also granted other rights in the form of financial, educational, and economic rights, except in matters relating to the acquisition of agricultural/plantation properties, and some political rights in the form of the right to occupy public positions. Meanwhile, granting certain rights to diaspora in South Korea is done in a more complex way. Because South Korea's diaspora policy is built within immigration law regimes, the granting of certain rights to diaspora is based on the type of visa that can be obtained by diaspora.

The types of visas that can be obtained by South Korean diaspora are F-4 visa and H-2 visa. Both types of visas are basically a special visa to get a job in South Korea without going through the employment permit system as foreigners of non-Korean origin who are to be employed in South Korea. Diaspora holding an F-4 visa has the rights attached to it in the form of the right to stay, the right to work, the right to freedom of financial transactions, the right to land and property ownership, and the right to health insurance (Lee, 2012b, p.5). The F-4 visa is valid for 3 years and can be continually renewed. The F-4 visa is intended for diaspora who wish to work in a field of work requiring certain expertise. Thus, low-skilled job sectors are prohibited for holders of this type of visa. The impact is that ethnic Korean originating from China and ex-Soviet Union countries that are generally low-skilled workers cannot obtain this type of visa. Therefore, South Korean diaspora with low expertise can obtain H-2 visas that are intended for low-skilled job sectors. Although the work sector is differentiated, holders of H-2 visas still get the same rights as F-4 visa holders (Lee, 2012b, p.5). The H-2 visa cannot last for five years or more.

Based on the diaspora regulatory model in India and South Korea, it appears that the context of the South Korean diaspora's need to return to its home country is a factor in South Korea's diaspora economic needs for better livelihoods in South Korea as the South Korean economy improves. In contrast, the Indian diaspora policy context intended to capture the contribution of Indian diaspora to the interests of Indian development, for example through remittance. World Bank data show that remittances received by India in 1991 reached $ 2.1 billion and continued to increase to $ 27 billion in 2007 (Dubey, 2013, p.77).

Lesson Learnt from India and South Korea: Potential Regulatory Model for Indonesian Diaspora

From regulatory model optic, the initial idea of incorporation of Indonesia's diaspora status has similarity with India's model that is to accommodate the status of dual citizenship for Indonesian citizens or former Indonesian citizens and their descendants. In Indonesia, this proposal becomes the major substance advocated in the on-process amendment plan of Law No. 12/2006 on Citizenship. Interestingly this amendment planning stated clearly in *Prolegnas* 2015 - 2019, a national legislative planning as initiated by House of Representative.

From legal aspect point of view, Indonesia does not have a constitutional issue to apply dual citizenship, compared with that of India. In the case of India, constitutional amendment took place in order to allow full dual citizenship. In addition to the constitutional problem, the main barriers to adopt dual citizenship in Indonesia mainly because the amendment of Act no. 12/2006 includes to the issue of legislative trends and non-legal aspects. From the aspect of citizenship law development, the principle of single citizenship has been institutionalized in Indonesian citizenship legislation since the beginning of independence (Act No. 3/1946) to the present legislation. So, the principle of single citizenship is inseparable from the understanding of Indonesian nationalism as a postcolonial country, similar with that of India and South Korea. In addition, Indonesia experienced problems in the past related to dual citizenship with the People's Republic of China (PRC) which applies the dual principles of citizenship to Chinese descendants in Indonesia. In that case, the Indonesian government perceive dual citizenship to be ended primarily for reasons of loyalty and allegiance (Harijanti, 2017, p.7). In the current context, although the dual citizenship application is fully supported by IDN, and some NGOs, the Government and several members of the House of Representatives are reluctant to accomodate the idea, and more favour to 'softer' approach in the sense that full dual nationality is not the only solution to accommodate the Indonesian diaspora (Harijanti, 2017, p.18) based on nationalism reasons (Dewansyah, 2016, p.10). This reflects that Indonesian citizenship is still seen as "ideological construction of politics and history" (Harijanti, 2017, p.19).

In terms of substance, the current policy of the Government of Indonesia which began introducing the Diaspora Card (Budiari, 2017), appears to be influenced by OCI / OCC practices in India, although it has no legal implications yet. But, apparently the development of diaspora card program to be more regulatory based diaspora status, will be done in a way beyond the citizenship law amendment. In addition, the incorporation of diaspora status and rights in India through the amendment of citizenship law is also criticized, because the OCI (or OCC currently) although it is intended to recognize dual citizenship, but that the result is reverse, not citizenship (Xavier, 2011, p.45). It means that amending citizenship law becomes an ambiguous way if it is to be regulated not a citizenship status or recognition of dual citizenship, but a special status for an Indonesian diaspora not a citizenship.

In addition, the political setting in Indian when adopting OCI was different from Indonesia's current political design. In India, the idea of dual citizenship comes from the Government to draw the diaspora's economic potential to India, but the Parliament did not agree upon the amendment to citizenship laws, primarily referred to national security (Naujoks, 2015, p.27, p.29). Meanwhile, in Indonesia, the idea of dual citizenship has emerged from the aspirations of the people, especially to the Indonesian diaspora. Sadly, serious efforts from the Government and the House of Representative have not yet been clear until now. In the near future, it is very likely that the adoption of full dual nationality through the amendment of the existing citizenship law would be rejected.

The Indonesian government is likely to adopt the pragmatic way dealing with Indonesian diaspora. It seems that the regulatory model to be pursued by the Government of Indonesia is more like the way South Korea organizes overseas Korean through the immigration law regime as reflected by the Diaspora Card program and the extension of multiple entry visit visa only for the Indonesian citizen and his / her family based on Government Regulation (GR) 26/2016 (amendment of GR No. 31/2013 regarding Implementing Regulation of Law No. 6/2011 regarding Immigration). However, in contrast to the Overseas Korean Act which also recognizes a number of Korean diaspora legal rights, the current policy of the Indonesian Government is still limited to providing limited immigration privileges for diaspora, minus special legal rights. However, in relation to the rights of the Korean diaspora, Lee (2017) criticized the South Korean Government's policy that in his opinion is "too much concern to diaspora", for example affirming the right to health insurance that can be obtained by anyone. This means that the fundamental needs of the Indonesian diaspora should be a major consideration, while still providing a comprehensive consideration for certain sensitive legal rights. For example, although diaspora ownership of land and property in South Korea is not a problem, the idea of granting land rights to Indonesian diasporas should be considered carefully or even excluded.

Reflecting on the experience of South Korea, setting the status and rights of diaspora in immigration law regime, not enough in executive regulation, but with act of legislature (Overseas Korean Act). However, South Korea's choice to form a separate law for the diaspora is not a substantive issue, as it is the legislation tradition in South Korea when faced with new needs (Lee, 2017). Meanwhile, for Indonesia whose politics of immigration law since 1992 is intended to unify various immigration legislation, the arrangement of Indonesian diaspora should be done by amending Law No. 6/2011 on Immigration.

Moreover, based on the experiences of India and South Korea, Indonesia needs to redefine the category of diaspora that will be legally regulated. During this time, the diaspora category is mainly based on the opinion of Dino Patti Djalal – one of IDN founder - too broad, because it covers not only the Indonesian citizen and his descendants, but also Indonesian citizens abroad and foreigners who "love" Indonesia (Dewansyah, 2017, p.8). It is difficult to develop criteria according to the Djalal's category (Santoso, 2014, p.118). In addition, India and South Korea also distinguish the non-resident or overseas citizens from the diaspora category because their principalities are still citizenship status on their hand. Indonesia also has no special needs to grant certain status to Indonesian citizens abroad. GR No. 26/2016 which recognizes three diaspora categories: the former Indonesian citizen, spouse (wife / husband) and they children can be the starting point for redefining who diaspora Indonesia in the future.

Conclusion

The Indian and South Korean experimentation of diaspora arrangements reflects a politically sensitive character of citizenship. The failure of the full dual citizenship adoption in India can be an important lesson for Indonesia which also places citizenship as an ideologically sensitive concept. Although the proposal for dual citizenship in South Korea has never surfaced, the effort to develop a diaspora legal regime through immigration schemes also reflects that dual citizenship is not possible in South Korea because it will trigger conflict with other countries, especially China. For Indonesia, other schemes beyond dual citizenship should be developed as early as possible, given the current political tendency of seemingly unable to accept fundamental change on citizenship legal policy. It is important to start discussing the legal categorization of Indonesian diaspora and the threshold rights that needed by diaspora community and realistically will be accepted by government and legislature.

References

Baubock, R. (2007). Stakeholder Citizenship And Transnational Political Participation: A Normative Evaluation Of External Voting. *Fordham Law Review, 75*(5), 2396-2447.

Budiari, I. (2017, August 19). Diaspora to get state recognition from new card. *The Jakarta Post.*

Dewansyah, B. (2016). Indonesian Diaspora Movement and Citizenship Law Reform: Towards "Semi Dual Citizenship" for Overseas Indonesian Descendants. paper presented in The Asian Law & Society Association (ALSA) Inaugural Conference, Faculty of Law National University of Singapore, 22 & 23 September 2016.

Dubey, M. (2013). Changing Salience of the Relationship Between the Indian Diaspora and India. *Diaspora Studies 1*(3), 73-84.

Hassall, G. (1999). Citizenship in the Asia-Pacific: a Survey of Contemporary Issues. In Alastair Davidson and Kathleen Weekle (eds.) *Globalization and Citizenship in the Asia-Pacific*. London-New York: Macmillan Press Ltd & St. Martin's Press Inc. pp.49-70.

Harijanti, S.D. (2016). Dwi Kewarganegaraan dan Politik Hukum Kewarganegaraan Indonesia [Dual Citizenship and Indonesia Legal Policy on Citizenship]. paper presented in Workshop of "Dual Citizenship and Urgency of Amendment of Law Number 12/2006 on Citizenship" held by Badan Keahlian DPR RI (Expert Council of Indonesian House of Representative), Jakarta, 1 September 2016. (in Bahasa Indonesia).

_____. (2017). Report on Citizenship Law: Indonesia. *Country Report 2017/04.*

Lee, C. (2012a). How can you say you're Korean? Law, governmentality and national membership in South Korea. *Citizenship Studies 16*(1), 85 – 102.

_____.(2012b). The Transnationalization of National Membership in the Era of Globalization: Ethnizenship and Beyond. Public Lecture in University of Washington Law School.

_____. (2003). 'Us' and 'them' in Korean law: the creation, accommodation and exclusion of outsiders in South Korea. In Arthur Rosett, Lucie Cheng and Margaret Y.K.Woo (eds), *East Asian Law— Universal Norms And Local Cultures.* London: Routledge Curzon. pp. 105 – 134.

_____. (2017). Interview by second and fourth authors, tape recording, Yonsei University, Seoul – South Korea, May 10.

Naujoks, D. (2015). The Securitization of Dual Citizenship. National Security Concerns and The Making of The Overseas Citizenship of India. *Diaspora Studies 8*(1), 18 – 36.

Sahai, P. S. (2013). India's Engagement with Diaspora: Government Communication, Platform, and Structure. *Diaspora Studies 6*(1), 50 – 60.

Santoso, M. I. (2014). *Diaspora, Globalisme, Keamanan dan Keimigrasian [Diaspora, Globalism, Security and Immigration].* Bandung: Pustaka Reka Cipta. (in Bahasa Indonesia).

Xavier, C. (2011). Experimenting with Diasporic Incorporation: The Overseas Citizenship of India. *Nationalism and Ethnic Politics 17*(1), 34 – 53.

Yoon, I. (2007a). A Comparison of the South and North Korean Policy of Overseas Koreans, in "Korean Diaspora and Strategies of Global Networking. *Korean and Korean American Studies Bulletin, 16* (1), 80-99.

_____. (2007b). Introduction, in "Korean Diaspora and Strategies of Global Networking. *Korean and Korean American Studies Bulletin, 16* (1), vii-x.

Kumar, P. (2015). Introduction: Socio Religious and Cultural World of the Indian Diaspora. In Kumar, P. (ed). *Indian Diaspora: Socio-Cultural and Religious World.* Leiden: Brill. Pp. 1 – 18.

Chapter 54. Importing a Labor Force for Catalonian Agriculture. A Case of Human Rights Deprivation in Spain. Sustainability and Successes.

Olga Achón Rodríguez [1]

Abstract

This paper aims to disclose the consequences that the system designed by the Catalonian agricultural union "Unió de Pagesos" to recruit, import and distribute foreign labor produces, a subject deprived of its liberties and fundamental rights. Once the model of family farming was substituted by an industrial agricultural system of production, the agricultural union, with the consent of the State, reinvented itself as a provider of services related with the acquisition of manpower through this system –as we designate the set of practices that materialize the recruitment of foreign workers abroad and their concentration is lodgments controlled by the Union. The State's migration polity is responsible of the emergence of such a system, and we can trace its origin in the symbiotic relation between the State and the union, whose interests-the social control of the foreign worker and the just in time delivery of labor- are harmonized in it.

Keywords: Immigration Laws, Social Control, Total Institutions, Circular Migration, Agricultural Labor.

Introduction

This paper aims to disclose the results of the investigation that backs the doctoral thesis "Contratación en Origen e Institución Total. Estudio sobre el sistema de alojamientos de trabajadores agrícolas extranjeros en el Segrià (Lleida)". Its main objective is to show the consequences that the system designed by the Catalonian agricultural union "Unió de Pagesos" to recruit, import and distribute foreign labor produces, a subject deprived of its liberties and fundamental rights.

Once the model of family farming was substituted by an industrial agricultural system of production based on hired labor, the agricultural union, with the consent of the State, reinvented itself as a provider of services related with the acquisition of manpower through this system –as we designate the set of practices that materialize the recruitment of foreign workers abroad and their concentration is lodgments controlled by the Union. The State's migration polity is responsible of the emergence of such a system, and we can trace its origin in the symbiotic relation between the State and the union, whose interests- the social control of the foreign worker and the just in time delivery of labor, respectively- are harmonized in it. In the lodgment -infrastructure of the system- a transformation is intended through different devices –lodgment regulations, the presence of personnel in charge of the facilities, a visit regime and exit permissions, among others- close to other institutions, as labor camps, where the tame of the individuality is aimed through its subordination

---

[1] Universitat de Barcelona, GRECS (Grup de Recerca sobre Exclusió i Control Socials), Facultat de Geografia i Història, Departament d'Antropologia Social i d'Història d'Amèrica i Àfrica, C. Montalegre, 6 08001 Barcelona, Spain. Email: olga_achon@yahoo.es

to a dominating power in order to create a new subject, whose value is exteriorized in its obedience to the will of those who administrate the institutions.

The text that follows approaches, in its first title, the construction of the working hypothesis of the investigation. Its second title focuses on the terminological aspect of the investigation, while the third is dedicated to a synthetic exposition of the research and its conclusions.

Methodological Frame

Formulating A Hypothesis

In the history of the development of production systems, labor fixation strategies constitute a solution to the basic problem of men's freedom, which is an omen of a possible desertion of work.

These have been established in many different ways: by assigning specific places in the social ladder to the individuals that integrate the work force; creating bondages that tie men to some economic activity –whether to a specific geographical area or to a concrete productive activity-; establishing an obligation to work and, therefore, legal control to vagrancy or simply reifying individuals and putting them under the control of someone that can dispose of them. Such systems usually imply the creation of different legal status that legitimize them and, in some cases, even institutions that prevent the leakage of the productive forces through their escape.

It seems that societies which are built over closed social divisions, as caste systems or feudal estates, are in a less degree dependant of such institutions, for they, as a whole, are configured as prisons where the individual has no freedom to alter his position in the social ladder. On the contrary, societies which allow certain porosity in the social frontiers and where individuals that compose them are free to initiate mobility processes, structural or topographical, usually require the presence of institutions to confine manpower, for its autonomy implies a problem for the development, consolidation or survival of some specific economic activities. The existence of places for the storage of labor created under the rule of law is a paradox for these societies, or, following Foucault, it is a consequence of the establishment of the formal universal freedom that defines them (Foucault, 2000:234).

The lodgment for foreign workers recruited in their homeland of the agricultural union Unió de Pagesos is not an exception to this rule. It was built following similar principles that those which favored the emergence of the Roman ergastulum, the English workhouse or the French hospital, it constitutes a manpower reserve aimed to help an economic area from where those who have higher levels of freedom have deserted, given their bigger social power. Its form, which also resembles, in a way, to jails and military barracks, helps to deliver, fixated and distribute men spatially, to classify them in order to obtain the maximum of their time and power, to educate their body and codify their behavior, to keep them visible to the power that submits them, not only by architectonically configuring a space suitable for it, but by trapping them in a web of registers and annotations that holds a knowledge that it is been accumulated and centralized. The lodgment is the place to observe the specific product of the system of recruitment of labor in foreign countries which it is the object of this study. Our hypothesis is that such system of recruitment, importation, concentration and supply of labor implemented by Unió de Pagesos prevents the exercise of personal freedoms that the political order considers basic, producing a subject deprived of fundamental rights, mainly freedom of work and, consequently, of circulation and residence.

Notes on the Fieldwork.

Our first approach to the context of the investigation happens while the author was hired as personnel in charge of one of the lodgments in Montblanc during the grape harvest in 2003. During those two months we had a privileged to appreciate what was developing there. Inside the lodgment we noticed a subtle domination that worked its way over men and, therefore, we observed how the relations of power developed between the Union and the workers. From this first experience had a need to understand the reasons and mechanisms that contributed to such domination. The spatial characteristics of the lodgment, that led to the performance of everyday activities in communion with the rest of the workers hosted there, holding them in a regulated common way of life, together with our presence as personnel in charge of the facilities, with the faculty to penalize behaviors unwanted by the Union, led us to interpret the lodgment as something related to what Goffman had defined as *total institutions*. Considering it from this perspective, for its closeness to such institutions –some of which, following Goffman, are erected to protect the community from those who are considered to be dangerous to it, while other are instruments to control labor (Goffman, 2007:18) - we had to assimilate it, in a certain degree, to other institutions, as prisons and labor camps, that are also means to deprive of specific freedoms.

During the fruit harvest in Lleida, from June to September, we started that same year our fieldwork, which developed every year until 2008, when we made our last field trips. It was easy to make contact with the Union's personnel, especially with those of the Servei de Contractació de Treballadors (Hire Labor Service) and of the foundation Pagesos Solidaris (Solidarity Farmers), for the author had taken contact with them when she worked in the lodgments. Thanks to their collaboration, she obtained valuable documental information from inside the service and came into contact and interviewed personnel in charge of the lodgments. While visiting different lodgments in the district of the Segrià, interviews were made to workers hosted there. Nevertheless, during the agricultural campaign of 2006, the collaboration of the Union decreased in intensity, maybe because of some reluctance of the Union towards this investigation. This perception was confirmed when we found some resistance from the Union to carry on this investigation on the hiring system and the lodgments. This lead us to carry on our field work until 2008 without the collaboration of the Union. From then onwards, we had to approach the system from outside. We had to meet and interview the workers in the bars and cafeterias of the small towns where they worked and go around the lodgments where they lived. This way, a chain of informants was configured once some workers asked others, usually lodgment fellows, to offer their testimony in interviews.

From this moment, the information we could obtain through our fieldwork varied substantially from the one we had access to while we worked as personnel in charge of the lodgments, The knowledge of the internal dynamics, the supply protocols and the disciplinary tactics which we observed from the inside, was enriched by this external work, specially thanks to the testimonies given by the workers and the personnel in charge. This way, beyond the experience of the harvest of 2003, we were able to corroborate that what happened inside that particular lodgment was also predicable of the rest of the collective lodgments administrated by the Union.

Our study was focused on the so called "collective" lodgments, different to those which the Union categorizes as "particular" –which do not have personnel in charge and host a small number of works- for a special dynamic develops inside of them. Its main characteristic is the permanents control and supervision of the workers, which is fundamental for their transformation into subjects ready to deliver. That is why our fieldwork is exclusively involved with collective lodgments, whether they belong to agribusiness companies or to local administration, usually to town hall, who gives its administration to Unió de Pagesos for the benefit of local farmers. Most of the collective lodgments are concentrated in the district of the Segrià, followed by l'Urgell and the Plà d'Urgell, so our fieldwork was primarily done in these locations. This methodological option is backed by the higher density of collective lodgments found in the district of Segrià. In this district we visited Alcarràs, Alcoletge, Soses, Torres de Segre, Artesa de Lleida, Puigverd de Lleida, Corbins, Aitona and Serós, where we visited a total of 12 collective lodgments, both of public or private ownership, which constitute a 29% of the total of a district that holds a 45% of the total lodgments subsidized by the Catalonian government. In the Plà de Urgell we visited six lodgments allocated in Bell.lloc, Bellvís, Mollerusa and Miralcamp, which constitute a 55% of the total of a district that holds a 12% of the officially subsidized Catalonian lodgments. In the case of l'Urgell, we visited three lodgments in Bellpuig, La Fuliola and Verdú, which constitute a 60% of the total of collective lodgments in a district that holds a 5% of the subsidized lodgments in Catalonia. Additionally, we also visited the lodgments in Montblanc, Les Pobles and Batea, which belong to different districts with a lower presence of lodgments than the ones where we focused our fieldwork.

These lodgments were the ground on which we made the necessary incursions to create a typology of lodgments. In them, we had the chance to get in contact with the personnel in charge and the workers that would become the nerve of our group of informants, who we interviewed both inside and outside of the lodgment. Nevertheless, some of the information that helped us in its interpretation and analysis –regarding what was happening inside the lodgments, or about what its implantation meant to the agricultural entrepreneurs or concerning its impact in the town- came from many casual circumstances. Farmers, who hired the labor supply service of Unió de Pagesos or who did not and rather used irregular immigrants as a work force, neighbors from the district that occasionally became involved with the lodgment network for they rented houses to city hall to provide shelter to the workers, immigrants searching for work, they all gave us information through informal conversations in sceneries so colorful as land clearing, a pear field, a bakery, a small town square or the stairs of a church. When these meetings took place, our field diary became essential. In it, we wrote our impressions on every event, our intuitions on what was happening and also some thoughts that would, eventually, transform while the investigation developed. The descriptions of the lodgments would be also written in this notebook, which became the binnacle of this expedition.

Analyzing the System.

The pages that compose this work aim to expose a system and demonstrate that is produces a subject whose rights and liberties –that should be protected not only as workers, but as human beings- are under severe limitations.

The observation of the workers attitudes inside the lodgments, interacting mainly with the personnel in charge of their management, gave signs of a decrease in their capacity to untie themselves from the labor obligations they had acquired and, even more, of a limitation of their faculties to develop their lives in the way they believed more suitable. Attitudes that revealed unequal powers, a contractual obligation to necessarily live in the lodgments fulfilling pre-established behavior norms which conduct to the normativization of their everyday life and the limitation of some of their basic individual freedoms, as the freedom of movement, were signs of a deeper problem. Neither the lodgment regulations nor the prohibitions imposed by contract seemed enough to explain the results of the agreement subscribed by the workers, the deprivation of their own liberties.

A larger agreement than the one subscribed by the workers seemed to be the nerve of the problem. That pact, which took form in the "Collaboration Agreement for the Management of Migration" (Convenio Marco de Colaboración para la Ordenación de las Migraciones) revealed itself as the key element of the contractual operation through which the labor recruitment, importation and supply is implemented. A triangular system of relations between workers, union and agricultural entrepreneurs took place, reflection of the pact on which it is based and which provides the mechanisms to implement it. The corporate legal representation of agricultural entrepreneurs given to the union by the State to recruit labor for all of them as a group and a public function delegated to the union in order to confer to it faculties to execute part of the State's migration policy are the mechanism provided to implement the system. They tend to order the migration flux and to provide labor permanently available to the agricultural entrepreneurs that demand manpower to the union. The agricultural entrepreneur, although formally subscribes a labor contract with the worker, has not a real employer-employee relation with him, for the system implies a triangular relation, for which the rights which usually concern the employer lay on the union, while the worker is deprived from a significant part of his basic rights, as for instance the right to quit the job.

The system implies a break in the classical bilateral conception of contracts, and specifically of employment contracts (Chacártegui Jávega, 2000: 55). The lack of a real contractual relation between labor and entrepreneur takes the system far from modern Labor law and close to other types of relations between entrepreneurs and manpower, such as the slave lease in ancient Rome, which was especially common in the last two centuries of the Republic (Pérez Guerrero and Rodríguez-Piñero Royo, 2005: 189; De Martino, 1985: 113). In the Unio de Pagesos' system the agricultural entrepreneur behaves as a consumer of labor, the worker as a commodity in a market and the union as its supplier. In fact, the legal figure of the employment contract seems unable to describe the system, as there is not a labor market, but a market of workers.

The grounds lay on the genetic relation of the system, designed to harmonize the interests both of the State and the union, that is to say, the control of the migration flux through work, on one hand, and the creation of a monopolistic position for the union as a labor supplier which provides it enough political influence to keep their leadership as the most representative business organization of the Catalonian agricultural sector. Nevertheless, the symbiotic relation between State and union is not the only ground that stimulated the creation of the system. The workers interest to find a job in Spain, even in the offered conditions, as also the convenience for the agricultural entrepreneurs to dispose of a labor force in serfdom were determinant elements in its instauration. To have manpower which through recruitment comes under *status subjectionis*, as the serf bound to the land by a vassalage agreement (Bazán Cabrera, 1982: 40), helps the agricultural entrepreneurs to ensure their presence in the economical structure and to avoid its reconversion.

The legal framework that configures the system lays in the Immigration law and in the policy of job quotas applied to migration. By its exam a new working hypothesis can be formulated: that through this regulatory policy the State aims to replace the illegal immigrant by those recruited in their homeland, at least in economic sectors as agriculture, affected by a lack of competitiveness in the international markets. Although the irregular immigrants are certainly a cheaper labor, they are also more volatile and their presence generates public uneasiness, for they represent an intrusion in public space and welfare, where they would allegedly practice spoliation and abuse. The recruited foreign worker, on the other hand, represents the tame of the insolent barbarian; a domestication that avoids the typical mobility of the free men, even when subject to persecution and harassment after been categorized as an illegal. The survival of the Catalonian agricultural structure is the target of this substitution, favoring the agricultural entrepreneur's subtraction from the labor market, thanks to a system that imports manpower without the possibility to freely participate in it and generating a service market where union and entrepreneurs trade manpower. In it, the worker is simply a commodity, while the entrepreneur is a consumer of a service offered by the union. By reifying workers, controlling their mobility and fixating them as work force, it emerges the possibility to compare this subject to an inhabitant of the nomad cities, once imagined by soviet anti-urbanism (Fourquet and Murard, 1978: 67), or even with the zek[2], settlers of the gulags (Soljenitsin, 1976: 426-427).

The regulatory policy that permits the emergence of such a system, revels a legal framework designed for the social control of the nomad (Gaudemar, 1981: 29), that is to say, the irregular immigrant. Analogously as to the creation of the first vagrancy laws in England during the first half of the XIV century (Chambliss, 1964: 69; Foote, 1956: 615) or in Castilla, after the arrival of the Black Death[3] and with similar aims, the immigration law, as a legal framework of the job quotas policy fulfills the purpose of subjecting labor in order to make an intensive use of it. The mandatory settlement was a measure taken to ensure the provision of manpower, so dispositions provided to fixate residence, as Settlement Certificates (Foote, 1956: 615, Polanyi, 1989: 151;

---

2 We refer to the prisoners of the soviet concentration camps, administered by the General Direction of Labor Camps, whose acronym make the word GULAG.
3 Novísima Recopilación de las Leyes de España, p. 429, T. V, Madrid, 1804

Hammond & Hammond, 1987: 91) become parallel to the system's workers duty to reside in the lodgments.

A new status for workers emerges as a solution to the problem of the need of available labor. Without the power to freely wander, choose a place of residence, a job or to negotiate its conditions, this new subject is able to contest the irregular migrant's presence in Catalonian agriculture. The social benefits this new category implies are the eradication of the settlement of poor foreign migrants in the country and to keep the viability of a productive model based in the recruit of workers deprived of some of their liberties and rights. Capitalism without a labor market (Polanyi, 1989: 206) threats a democracy, outworn by economic crisis that still requires servile labor. Analogously as it occurred with the implantation of the Prussian system of recruitment of polish laborers, thanks to the decree that allowed the partial reopening of the eastern borders (Weber, 1990: 240; Mezzadra, 2005: 74), the union's system aims to neutralize the effects of market. The impossible permanent availability of the worker's body in a Liberal state (Bazán Cabrera, 1982: 54-55) has excited the union's imagination to create a system, within the legal framework, which resembles closely the one implemented the Prussian junkers. They formed the Prussian Fieldworkers Central (Preuische Feldarbeiter Zentrale) to recruit workers in the polish border that could neither rescind their labor contracts nor participate in the labor market (Mezzadra, 2005: 75).

What is accomplished through the network of lodgments is the intensive provision of labor force under the "just in time" formula. The hiring of one specific worker by an entrepreneur has no practical relevance, for the pressing need of labor force in harvest time and the demand of a "quality service" compels to the permanent provision of this same worker to other entrepreneurs. The condition of the worker as a subject of commercial transactions is stressed by the labor provision system. The union amortizes the costs of its recruitment and importation and obtains benefits by increasing its circulation among the entrepreneurs. The union considers the workers as commodity capital (Marx, 1972: 11-12). While in the lodgments they are in state of reserve, in disposition to be mobilized intensively every time there is an imbalance between the demand of workers and the offer provided by the union, increasing by the circulation its exchange value (Marx, 1972: 705). The estimate of the possible circulations of the worker, favored by the network of lodgments, enables its constant revalorization by eliminating the possibility of unproductive immobilization (Coriat, 1982: 50) giving a Fordian character to the administration of men's movements.

As in an assembly line, the leisure of materials is minimized (Allan Nevins cit. Coriat, 1982: 49). Its concentration appears as an essential element of the system, for it allows, on one hand, the storage of men in disposition to be supplied –which constitutes the union's interest in the system-, while, on the other, it enables their seclusion, avoiding their presence in the public space – which is the State's ideal of the way to handle this kind of foreigner, poor and without qualification, while he remains in the country. Through a communitarian utopia -center of fascist and socialist machinations to make the workers a mean for the greater good of the nation (Soljenitsin, 1976: 426)- the exploitation of the worker is intended. As a leftover of agriculture's productive gear, his presence can only be justified as an apple picker or as a nectarine packer. His existence is marked by the footprint of the total institution and the discipline as a mean to correct his conduct (Foucault, 2000:175 and Weber, 2008:883).

Migration law is functional to the fulfillment of this objective, for it intimidates the worker by menacing its statue as a legal worker –mainly in the cases of attempt of strike, quitclaim or refusal to accept a job (all of these rights are affected for their exercise is considered abandonment of work and, therefore, it is constitutes a breach of contract which's ultimate consequence is the devolution of the subject to his homeland)- and therefore represses any attempt to contest authority that could affect the power of the union.

To prevent any impediment to the proper supply of labor becomes fundamental. Discipline must be imposed as a condition for the implementation of the calculated movement of the docilized worker's (Weber, 2008: 882). Its exercise revels the union's longing to submit the worker under its power. An arsenal of images concerning the dreamt worker (Sierra Álvarez, 1990: 83) illustrates the union's conception of labor, which can be perceived in the lodgment regulations and in the behavior of the personnel in charge of the facilities. The historical need of the capital to transform labor (Sierra Álvarez, 1990: 244) into docilized beings drove the industrials and entrepreneurs to examine his nature. As a consequence, a whole series of representations of the worker nourished a discourse functional to the social control of the poor, favoring its forced incorporation to labor and the maximum exaction of surplus value (Chambliss, 1964: 69; Foote, 1956: 615; Gaudemar, 1981: 28; Polanyi, 1989: 138-151). The private sphere of the individual became subject of surveillance and the reconstitution phase of his life was transformed in the scope for paternalistic measures directed to his domination.

The worker's housing raised as a strategy for the panoptic supervision of individuals through inspection and regulation of everyday life. In it, the power of the old industrial extended –as the union's does now- with the aim to docilize men who are called to collaborate in the accumulation of capital. In these kind of spaces the power intents to reproduce the domination that already exists in the working places. The lodgment is one of those and therefore it appears proper to assimilate the lodgment regulations to factory regulations

(Marx, 1972: 444-445; Engels, 1976: 232), as the personnel in charge of them to foremen, both been essential mechanisms for the maintenance of an order convenient to the reproduction of power. The union reproduces the image that represents the worker as an undisciplined, dirty, trouble maker. It reconstructs the old prejudice on the need to discipline the poor (Sierra Álvarez, 1990: 4). By prohibiting some behaviors and commanding others, it secures a smooth cadence in the supply. Drunkenness and disputes, understood as a manifest declaration of disobedience must be suppressed, for they suspend temporarily the domination and unveil the true autonomy of men. They short-circuit power and put it into crisis, manifesting the sterile nature of the lodgment regulations and the personnel in charge for the production of tamed individuals.

The preconception the union holds of the workers is visible in the behavior of the personnel in charge, as also in the way the workers handle themselves, as an answer to that behavior. In the base of their conduct, as the element that sets in motion the relation, the racist prejudice of the personnel in charge can be found. They develop a conduct pattern that both, infantilizes and criminalizes the subject, evidencing the danger that he allegedly implies. The behavior of the personnel develops between welfarism and repression of the conducts that are considered harmful. What would appear as a contradiction, protect to submit, is a consequence of the paternalist logic that aims, through graceful handouts, to ensure the obedience of those who are under the union's protection. Their work is in line with the notion of the foreigner both helpless and menacing. The handle of a job becomes a gift by which the union reinforces its power and secures obedience. Acting as a social legitimizing strategy of the system, the foundation "Pageses Solidaris" (Solidarity Farmers) can be found. Through it, the union intends to order and discipline the workers free time resembling a nineteenth century worker's circle (Revuelta González, 1984: 565-56; Babiano Mora, 1998: 166-169) as also to administrate some co-development projects to reward the most loyal workers and to self consolidate as a recipient of subsidies.

The moralization of the worker does not seem to be the main objective of the union, for his honesty and integrity are not relevant for the success of the labor supply service. On the other hand, his disobedience and defiance can shake the system and interrupt the supply. The abandonment of the institution is the most dangerous conduct in which the worker can fall, the greatest of all possible subversions. The runaway, as the union calls a worker who abandons the lodgment, stands out in his desertion from the rest of the workers who remain in the lodgment as an individual who becomes a free man to practice nomadism (Gaudemar, 1981: 29; Mezzadra, 2005: 80). By conquering the frontiers of the lodgment, breaking the law of the union, he mutates into a deserter who will carry the stigma of the "sans papiers", the paperless migrant. His existence points out the penitentiary character of the space destined to the concentration of men. This character is configured by a set of regulations that prohibits the worker's exodus and even constrains their capacity to return to their homeland. The worker, who is even subject to a visit regime, acquires the appearance of a convict whose only act of self-determination is his self-subtraction from the power of the union through the escape. Through it, the liminal nature of the lodgment becomes evident, manifesting itself as a space where segregation takes place, whose political dimension obstructs the full incorporation of the individuals into society. The lodgment is the spatial representation of the deprivation of rights and liberties that the workers suffer, a kind of frontier that can only be exceeded by escaping from the institution. In this sense, the escape is the most important political act that the workers can do. Its result is no other than the legitimate assertion of their freedom.

Through the escape it is also possible to interpret the lodgment as a mechanism of reproduction of the social reality that the migrant has to endure, constructed by rejection and discrimination, which is activated every time the worker is unwilling to submit himself to the power of the union and abjures of his commitment to be subject of exploitation. It is a power device, whose shape refers to different kinds of collective equipments with similar aims, the production of subjects, as the military barracks, hospitals, prisons or convents. The principle of closure manifests in all of them as necessary to the fulfillment of their purpose, that is to say, the transformation of those who inhabit them into perfect soldiers, patients, convicts or monks. The strict separation by sex and nationality, the existence of bunk beds and common service areas, like bathrooms, kitchens or dinners, announce the exclusion of family life from the institution and make both analogous.

The interchangeability of the subjects, a requirement of the system, is manifest in the configuration of the institutions that have been visited. Every time a worker replaces another the reification of the subject can be discovered, which is also manifest in the infrastructure provided for their concentration. A system to fixate labor is subject of this investigation, which has led to a doctoral thesis that has tried to give some light to a reality that silently develops in the Catalonian agriculture.

Conclusions

The effective deprivation of rights and the consequent limitation of liberties of the workers recruited by the system of importation and supply of labor designed by "Unió de Pagesos" is the main conclusion of this investigation.

We came to this conclusion through the observation and analysis of what happens inside the lodgments disposed for the concentration and storage of this captive manpower. Is from the delegation of a public function –which is manifest in the fact that the union has an authority to control the space and discipline the workers' lives- that this system raises. It is implemented by a contractual mechanism, whose main effect is the contractual waiver of the worker's freedom to work and move. From such an abdication a new subject is produced, whose status is similar to the serf for the submission that he experiences.

The *status subiectionis*, in the words of Bazán Cabrera (1982), is the concept that best suits the position of the workers regarding the authority of the union, for they have renounced such important liberties that they find themselves at its mercy. This is especially relevant because the organization wields a power delegated by the State similar to the one that the organs of the State hold, that is to say, those who are in charge of achieving the common welfare. The superior interest of the nation, proposed as a constitutional principle of society over individual interest, seems to be its content, whose achievement only concerns to those who have a strong position in society.

In Spain citizens and foreign posses their own statue defined by the Constitution and law so that their rights and liberties are clearly determined in order to give, at least in theory, legal certainty to its exercise. Nevertheless, the introduction of a system such as the one described distorts the legal framework, for it produces a subject whose legal status is configured factually, beyond legality, by the power if the union. One should consider what made possible that an organization without political legitimacy finally determines the rights and duties that configure the liberties of the workers recruited by it. The exam of the faculties and obligations determined by the union through regulations of lodgment and working conditions leads us to conclude that the worker recruited in the system has a different legal status from both the regular migrant -whose rights, which enable him to enjoy of freedoms, at least in theory, are not restricted- and from the one that experiences the irregular migrant -directly deprived of certain rights and whose liberty is merely factual. The status of the system's worker is defined by the power of the union and he is deprived of the real exercise of his liberties in a deeper way than the irregular migrant, for at least this last has a factual autonomy.

As they are condemned to satisfy the needs of an economic sector which struggles to escape its reconversion, their existence goes by in an undetermined legal framework, so that any institution interested in profiting from their vulnerable position is able to do so, as "Unió de Pagesos" does. A consequence for the labor market is that the system allows the agricultural economic sector to obtain manpower avoiding the market.

An even more fundamental risk for labor market is the possibility that the system expands to other areas, also incapable to provide competitive working conditions. It would mean to progressively subtract larger areas to the labor market and to formally establish a dual labor market, which would be constituted, on one side, by free workers legally protected and, on the other, by a reserve army of imported proletarians, deprived of rights and prepared to work in serfdom. Anytime an economic area would not be able to improve labor conditions for whatever reasons, the employers could adduce that, not having an autochthonous labor force available for their productive aims, they would have to appeal to a similar system for the provision of imported manpower. The struggle to improve labor conditions would reveal useless before the expansion possibilities of the system to other economic sectors, depressing labor market to a point where the conditions offered to the protected autochthonous labor would deteriorate until they become equivalent to those endured by the captive imported workers.

These economic sectors whose existence is threatened, like agriculture, have tried to overcome their lack of productivity by appealing to the informal labor market hiring irregular migrants since the beginnings of the eighties, thanks to the effects of immigration laws that produce a worker with a weaker legal position in the market. Nevertheless, the persecutory aim of the State has led to the eradication from the public space of this character, created to solve the competitiveness problems of such economic sectors. Therefore, a replacement strategy seems cogent with such objective. The substitution of the irregular migrant -which was once useful for the stability of these productive structures and anonymously collaborated to its subsistence suffering the contempt of those who hire him and of the rest of the population who benefits from the wealth they create- for the worker recruited in the homeland.

Systems of analogous nature are rising, as a first step in the future transformation of the status of the irregular migrant into forced labor. One can get a glimpse through the analysis of the inform on the proposal of the Directive on Return elaborated by the Committee of Civil Liberties, Justice and Home Affairs of the European Parliament (COM(2005)0391-C6-0266/2005-2005/0167(COD)). A first attempt to transform the detention centers for migrants into storehouses of captive manpower. In the amendment 11 to the recital 11a (new) it was established the duty to give "a useful occupation to a third-country national who is in temporary custody"[4], which would have led to a forced labor regime. If it had been approved, the European Parliament would had opened the possibility to convert the detention centers

---

[4] Amendment 11 Recital 11 a (new): (11a) All possibilities for giving prospects or a useful occupation to a third-country national who is in temporary custody should be considered.

Justification:

It is considered in the best interest of the returnee to have the possibility to use the time in temporary custody for education, useful occupation or any other kind of activity. This provision is also important in order to decrease the level of aggression and to enhance the chance of a successful return.

for migrants into places where labor would be concentrated and used in economic sectors that lack competitiveness, before sending it back to their homelands. A national system of manpower supply, captured among the nomad foreigners could be created, uncovering the weakness of the Spanish Democratic and Social State. The extension of the model beyond, to a forced labor system in all the European Union, would mean decadence at a continental level of the principles that promote the exercise of individual freedom, where individual rights would lose their effectiveness to become mere privileges. Modern democracy, founded on freedom and equality, would become a fiction.

References

Babiano Mora, José (1998). Paternalismo industrial y disciplina fabril en España (1938-1958). Madrid: Consejo Económico y Social.

Bazán Cabrera, José (1982). Contrato de Trabajo y Ordenamiento Jurídico. Madrid: Akal.

Chacártegui Jávega, Consuelo (2000). Empresas de trabajo temporal y contrato de trabajo. Valencia: Tirant Lo Blanch.

Chambliss, William J. (1964). A Sociological Analysis of the Law of Vagrancy. In Social Problems, 12-1, pp. 67 y ss.

Coriat, Benjamín (1982). El taller y el cronómetro. Ensayo sobre el taylorismo, el fordismo y la producción en masa. Madrid: Siglo XXI.

De Martino, Francesco (1985). Historia económica de la Roma antigua. Madrid: Akal.

Engels, Friedrich (1976). La situación de la clase obrera en Inglaterra. Madrid: Akal Editor.

Foote, Caleb (1956). Vagrancy Type Law and Its Administration. In University of Pennsylvania Law Review, 104-5, 603-650.

Foucault, Michel (2000). Vigilar y castigar. Madrid: Siglo XXI de España Editores, S.A.

Fourquet, François and Murard, Lion (1978). Los equipamientos del poder. Ciudades, territorios y equipamientos colectivos. Barcelona: Editorial Gustavo Gili, S.A.

Gaudemar, Jean Paul de (1981). La movilización general. Madrid: La Piqueta.

Hammond, J. L. and Hammond, B. (1987). El trabajador del campo. Madrid: Ministerio de Trabajo y Seguridad Social. Centro de Publicaciones.

Marx, Karl (1972). El Capital. Madrid: Edaf.

Mezzadra, Sandro (2005). Derecho de fuga. Migraciones, ciudadanía y globalización. Madrid: Traficantes de sueños.

Pérez Guerrero, María Luisa y Rodríguez-Piñero Royo, Miguel (2005). El artículo 43 del Estatuto de los Trabajadores: Empresas de Trabajo Temporal y cesión de trabajadores. In Revista del Ministerio de Trabajo y Asuntos Sociales, 58, 185-219.

Polanyi, Karl (1989). La gran transformación. Crítica del liberalismo económico. Madrid: Las ediciones de La Piqueta.

Revuelta González, Manuel (1984). La compañía de Jesús en la España Contemporánea: Supresión y reinstalación (1868-1883). Madrid: Universidad Pontificia Comillas, Sal Terrae y Ediciones Mensajero.

Sierra Álvarez, José (1990). El obrero soñado. Ensayo sobre el paternalismo industrial (Asturias, 1860-1917). Madrid: Siglo XXI de España Editores, S.A.

Soljenitsin, Alexandr (1976). Archipiélago GULAG 1918-1956. Ensayo de investigación literaria (Vols. 3-4). Barcelona: Plaza & Janes, S.A., Editores.

Weber, Max (1990). La situación de los trabajadores agrícolas en la Alemania del Este del Elba. Visión general (1892). In Revista Española de Investigaciones Sociológicas, 49, 233-255.

Weber, Max (2008). Economía y sociedad. México: Fondo de Cultura Económica.

Chapter 55. From *"Haponesa"* to *"Issei"*: Ethnicized Identities of Okinawan War Brides in Post-War Philippines

Johanna Orgiles Zulueta[*]

Abstract

This paper looks at these so-called "war brides" (Sensou hanayome) in the post-war Philippines, and their experiences upon migration to the Philippines in the 1950s to the 1960s. More specifically, I examine how ethnicity has become stigmatized in Philippine society of that time due mainly to wartime experiences. I also explore their how they lived their lives in varied degrees of discrimination, inclusion and exclusion. I particularly use the ascribed ethnic marker "Haponesa" or Japanese woman, in the Filipino vernacular, to illustrate how ethnicity has been stigmatized. I utilize life stories of those women who lived decades of their lives in the Philippines. While several of them choose to go back to Okinawa, many of them made the Philippines their home. Semi-structured interviews were done in 2009 and 2012, both in Okinawa and in the Philippines. I also use data I gathered in late 2011 to 2013, when I was doing on-and-off fieldwork in Okinawa.

Introduction

Post-war Okinawa has been administered by the American forces upon the defeat of Japan in the Second World War in 1945 up until 1972 when the prefecture was reverted to Japan. In the immediate post-war years, Filipinos, mostly male, were hired to work for the construction of U.S. military facilities in the prefecture as well as to staff these bases. There was also a significant migration of Philippine soldiers, i.e. Philippine Scouts, who served as auxiliary units to the U.S. forces, in the earlier years of the American Occupation (Yu-Jose, 2002). These Filipino men married (and in some cases, co-habited with) Okinawan women who they met while working in and around the bases, where these women also worked as maids, waitresses, clerks, and laundrywomen. Upon the termination of the Filipinos' contracts, they returned to the Philippines with their Okinawan wives.

This paper looks at these so-called "war brides" (Sensou hanayome) (Ohno, 1990) in the post-war Philippines, and their experiences upon migration to the Philippines in the 1950s to the 1960s. More specifically, I examine how ethnicity has become stigmatized in Philippine society due mainly to wartime experiences and how they lived in the Southeast Asian country in varied degrees of discrimination, inclusion and exclusion. I particularly use the ascribed ethnic marker "Haponesa" or Japanese woman in the Filipino vernacular to illustrate how ethnicity has been stigmatized. I also look at how these women began to veer away from an ethnic stigma to identifying themselves as first generation migrants, as well as their role/s as cultural transmitters through their migration experiences. For this study, I utilize life stories of those women who lived decades of their lives in the Philippines.

[*] Soka University Faculty of International Liberal Arts, Japan. Email: zulueta@soka.ac.jp

While several of them chose to go back to Okinawa, many of them made the Philippines their home. Semi-structured interviews were done in 2009 and 2012, both in Okinawa and in the Philippines. I also use data I gathered in late 2011 to 2013, when I was doing on-and off fieldwork in Okinawa. Much of this data is in the form of conversations with these women while I was doing participant observation at a Catholic Church in Okinawa for a related study. I conducted most of the interviews in Japanese, with some interspersed Tagalog words and expressions. However, for one interview done in the Philippines, I had to request someone to interpret for me from Bisaya (the vernacular in Davao, a city in Mindanao, southern Philippines) to Tagalog as my informant has forgotten much of her Japanese (and Okinawan).

First, I look at these Okinawan women's lives upon their migration to the Philippines. Starting with a discussion on how these women lived their lives as "Haponesa" (Japanese woman) in the Philippines and with their varied experiences of discrimination, inclusion and exclusion in Philippine society during the immediate post-war years, I also explain the use of the term Issei (first generation migrants) – the term they use to call themselves – to identify these women, rather than calling them "war brides (sensou hanayome)" (Ohno, 1991) or Okinawan Woman (Okinawa Uuman) (Hosoda, 2010) as mentioned in the scant literature written on this particular group. I also argue that Issei, as an identity marker, has indicated these women's significant role as transmitters of culture through their migrant experience/s.

"Haponesa": Ethnicized Identity as Stigma

During the immediate post-war years, Filipinos' memories of the War were still ripe and heightened sentiments against Japanese atrocities greatly affected the Japanese (and Okinawans) as well as their descendants living in the country at that time. Marriages between Filipinos and Japanese, as well as those between Filipinos and Okinawans were not very much accepted ("amari yurusanakatta") in society then, much like in Okinawa, where marriages to Filipinos were frowned upon since Filipinos were associated with the Americans, who were seen as the "enemies" at that time (Maehara, 2001; Zulueta, 2011).

In the immediate post-war years, these women moved to the Philippines with their husbands for a variety of reasons, but mainly expecting a "new beginning" and a life "different" from the war-torn and poverty-stricken Okinawa (Maehara, 2011). However, the land of settlement was also war-ravaged, and the locals' animosity towards the Japanese was intense. These women were called "Haponesa" (Japanese woman), a term deemed derogatory at that time. "Hapon", and its feminine form, "Haponesa" are Filipino (Tagalog) terms referring to Japanese (male) and Japanese female, respectively.[1] While seemingly harmless identity markers in themselves, Hapon and Haponesa became racialized and ethnicized, and became identified with the wartime enemy – the Japanese. The "Haponesa" can be seen as the "woman-as-other" (Ang-Lygate, 1996: 152) during this time, where "other" does not only point to her foreignness and her gender, but also the "other-as-enemy". In post-war Philippines, there was no distinction given to Okinawans and Japanese and they were seen as one and the same. Hence, Okinawans were also seen as Japanese. For this reason, Okinawan women who migrated with their husbands to the Philippines during this time were called "Haponesa" and were identified with the wartime enemy. Not a few of these women experienced discrimination, and what would have been a seemingly neutral and harmless identity marker, Haponesa became imbued with prejudice and contempt. Of course, not all of these women experienced grave discrimination as opposed to the descendants of pre-war Japanese and Okinawan migrants, as these women migrated along with their Filipino husbands and at times, their husbands' social standing in the community also earned them respect.

Inheriting the Stigma: Children of the "Haponesa"

It was not only the Okinawan women who experienced discrimination from the locals. Their children also experienced discrimination and bullying in local schools, and were called "anak ng Haponesa (child of a Japanese woman)". One Okinawan woman, Katsuko, laughingly recalled how her children were called "anak ng Haponesa" in those times. She also said that even the teachers were calling their children "Hapon (Japanese)", which in those times were deemed derogatory remarks (Zulueta, 2011: 146). While these women did not explicitly tell me what their feelings about being called "Haponesa" during that time were, it can be surmised that many Okinawan women suffered as a consequence of Filipinos' prejudices then. Being mothers, they too were affected by the discrimination that their children faced – whether "anak ng Haponesa" was a mere friendly banter or a more serious case of discrimination.

In my interviews and conversations with these women's children, there were those who encountered bullying in school in the Philippines. Raphael, currently a retired base worker, spoke of having had to transfer to a different high school every year as he used to get into fights, "I was always getting into fights because of my identity," he said. Meanwhile, Eric, who I talked to back in 2003, and is based in Manila, mentioned that he had unpleasant experiences when he was growing up in Manila (he was born in Okinawa and lived there until he was 10 years old): "They threw stones at me, they spat on me, they challenged me to a fight, and every day I had to fight... when I went to

---

[1] "Hapon" mainly refers to Japan, the country, and the Japanese (both male and female) are often referred to as "Hapones" or "Hapon" in the vernacular (i.e. Filipino).

school... minumura ako sa daan, binabato ako... (they hurled curses at me, they threw stones at me...)"

Another Okinawan woman, Chieko, told me that because of the war-time atrocities committed by the Japanese military in her husband's province, many, but not all Filipinos in the area had anti-Japanese sentiments that her husband advised her not to go outside their house. Katsuko also said that there were Filipino families who disowned their sons who married an Okinawan woman. This was echoed by some of their children who spoke of how their grandparents on their fathers' side did not like their Okinawan mothers, with some of them even angry at their fathers for marrying an Okinawan. Some of these women have been ostracized in the place of settlement, and what made matters worse for some of these women was the fact that their ties with their families back in Okinawa were cut off upon marriage to their Filipino husbands. Fortunately for some of these Okinawan women migrants, they managed to receive support from friends in Okinawa and this helped them overcome difficulties adjusting to their new way of life in a different land.

"Conscious Assimilation"

For many of these "Haponesa", the experience of being identified with the wartime enemy in a foreign land led them to hide their ethnic identities, and culturally and socially integrate into Philippine society, with most of them raising their children in a "Filipino" way. This "conscious assimilation" may have also been a strategy on their part for them not to be seen as Japanese/Okinawan, but rather as one of the locals, thereby working as a means for them to mask the painful memories of the War they have experienced while growing up in Okinawa, and the difficulties they experienced in migrating and settling in a foreign land. These women emphasized their Okinawan identity by telling people that they are Okinawans and not Japanese, thus dissociating themselves from the perceived "enemy" and identifying themselves also as victims of the War, as the Filipinos themselves were. Katsuko mentioned that even her husband kept on telling their neighbours that she is not Japanese, but rather a Ryukyuan.[2] Nevertheless, in later years (i.e. in the 1970s, onwards), their identity as "Haponesa" paved the way for them to be associated with an economic superpower, i.e. japan. Likewise, the shift in the Filipinos' perceptions towards Japan as the erstwhile enemy nation to that of a significant economic partner,

---

[2] The Okinawan archipelago used to an independent kingdom, the Kingdom of the Ryukyus, before it was made into a prefecture by the Meiji government of Japan in 1897. Under U.S. Occupation, the Americans, wanting to separate the Okinawans from the mainland Japanese, referred to the locals as Ryukyuans, referring to how Okinawa used to be called.

as well as a country to look up to (economically), also led to a decreased hostility towards the Japanese (and Okinawans) in the country.

"We are Issei": Reclaiming an Identity

While "Haponesa" is an ascribed identity-maker constructed to identify these women, Issei or first generation is being used by these Okinawan women to identify themselves. This self-ascribed identity marker can be argued to be a way for these women to see themselves as actively constructing their own identities and resisting "definitions of their 'Otherness' by others", as well as insist on "defining difference from their own perspectives", which Trinh calls "inappropriate/d others" (Ang-Lygate citing Trinh (1991), 1996: 154).

As Issei or first generation migrants, these women put forth a claim to their migration process and experiences as women who decided to move (thus pointing to their agency) and start a new life in a place that was unfamiliar to them. While being war brides point to the fact that women move because of marriage to a military personnel and that the decision to migrate to their husbands' countries was out of their own will, these women's identification as Issei can be said to challenge this particular image of women who moved in the post-war era. Being first generation, these women transmitted various aspects of their own Okinawan culture through child rearing as well as interactions with the locals. It can also be said that because of the negative image that the term "war bride" – they were equated with being prostitutes and base girls – had in Japan and Okinawa (Yasutomi, 2009: 160), these women refrained from identifying themselves as such.

References

Ang-Lygate, M. (1996). "Women who Move: Experiences of Diaspora." In Maynard, M. and J. Purvis, (Eds.), New Frontiers in Women's Studies: Knowledge, Identity, and Nationalism (pp. 151-163). London: Taylor and Francis, Ltd.

Hosoda, A. (2010). "Okinawa Sengo Joseishi no Shougen to Hakkutsu: Firipin ni Ikiru Okinawa Uuman no Imin Haikei." In Nagasaki Kokusai Daigaku Ronsou, 10, pp. 83-93.

Maehara, Y. (2001). Negotiating Multiple Ethnic Identities: The Case of Okinawan Women in the Philippines. Unpublished M.A. Thesis, University of the Philippines, Quezon City.

Ohno, S. (1991). Hapon: Firipin Nikkeijin no Nagai Sengo. Tokyo: Daisan Shokan.

Yasutomi, S. (2009). "Amerika no Sensou Hanayome e no Manazashi: Soushutsusareru Hyoushou wo Megutte." In Shimada, N. (Ed.), Shashin Hanayome, Sensou Hanayome no Tadotta Michi: Josei Iminshi no Hakkutsu (pp. 151-183). Tokyo: Akashi Shoten.

Yu-Jose, L. (2002). *Filipinos in Japan and Okinawa (1880s-1972)*. Tokyo: Research Institute for the Languages and Cultures of Asia and Africa, Tokyo University of Foreign Studies.

Zulueta, J.O. (2011). *A Place of Intersecting Movements: A Look at "Return" Migration and "Home" in the Context of the "Occupation" of Okinawa*. Unpublished Ph.D. Dissertation, Hitotsubashi University, Tokyo.

www.ingramcontent.com/pod-product-compliance
Lightning Source LLC
Chambersburg PA
CBHW050327270326
41926CB00016B/3343